The IT Measurement Compendium

Manfred Bundschuh • Carol Dekkers

The IT Measurement Compendium

Estimating and Benchmarking Success with Functional Size Measurement

Manfred Bundschuh
Sander Höhe 5
51465 Bergisch Gladbach
Germany
manfred.bundschuh@netcologne.de

Carol Dekkers
8430 Egret Lane
Seminole, FL 33776
USA
dekkers@qualityplustech.com

ISBN 978-3-642-08786-8   e-ISBN 978-3-540-68188-5

ACM Computing Classification (1998): D.2.8, D.2.9, K.6.3, K.6.1

Cover design: KünkelLopka GmbH, Heidelberg

Printed on acid-free paper

9 8 7 6 5 4 3 2 1

springer.com

Preface

"As projects get more complicated, managers stop learning from their experience. It is important to understand how that happens and how to change it….Fallible estimates: In software development, initial estimates for a project shape the trajectory of decisions that a manager makes over its life. For example, estimates of the productivity of the team members influence decisions about the size of the team, which in turn affect the team's actual output. The trouble is that initial estimates usually turn out to be wrong." (Sengupta, 2008)

This book aims directly to increase the awareness among managers and practitioners that estimation is as important as the work to be done in software and systems development. You can manage what you can measure!

Readers will find in this book a collection of lessons learned from the worldwide "metrics community," which we have documented and enhanced with our own experiences in the field of software measurement and estimating. Our goal is to support our readers to harvest the benefits of estimating and improve their software development processes. We present the 5 ISO/IEC-acknowledged Functional Sizing Methods with variants, experiences, counting rules, and case studies – and most importantly, illustrate through practical examples how to use functional size measurement to produce realistic estimates. *The book is written in a practical manner, especially for the busy practitioner community. It is aimed to be used as a manual and an assistant for everyday work.*

Estimation can be a win–lose job: it has to be done professionally to enable transparency, efficiency, and control of IT projects.

Software project estimation is the first step to determine how successful projects, processes, and product goals will develop and also how they will be measured and how their goals will be reached.

The thesis presented in this book is that software project estimation can be done in a highly professional manner and that it can be done accurately. *The authors also point out that the process of estimation and the required time for it must be planned "a priori"!*

The first step for the success of a software project is to ensure that it is started in a professional manner. This requires a planning period supported by a highly professional estimation process to ensure a solid foundation for project planning. Accurate estimates require quantitative measurements, ideally tool-based, to reduce measurement variations. *Furthermore, estimating does not gain the respect it deserves when it is done using only paper and pencil support – when the software engineers who provide the input data work professionally with the newest technologies.*

The application of an estimation method as well as the use of estimation tools and benchmarking data are nowadays "sine qua non" conditions for best practices in software engineering. In the unanimous opinion of estimation experts, this is the worldwide "state of the art."

Software project managers must also monitor and actualize their estimates during the project. *Estimates and project measures provide key risk indicators* and hence are excellent for the tracking of the progress of a software project and the monitoring of its success – that is, *they can provide valuable early warning signals if set up properly!* Fire fighting can be exciting, but does not help in fire prevention nor in the avoidance of significant costs and delays. A proper estimation process presents an opportunity for people tired of fire fighting to correctly plan and manage their software projects.

Estimation is an activity of the right brain: (the right brain being known for emotions and imagination, and ideas about the future and the unknown). *Estimation can also be performed with the left brain* (where logic and experience, and ideas about the past and known reside).

History of This Book

This book has a history as long as it took to implement a software measurement and metrics program in the IT department of an international insurance company in Germany. The initial text was published as the diploma thesis of Axel Fabry, when he was a student of Manfred Bundeschuh, working in a practicum project to plan and initiate the estimation program for the IT department. Fabry's thesis reported lessons learned about the trip wires involved with the implementation of estimating and laid the foundation for the first edition of this book. Regrettably, Mr. Fabry could not support the second edition, and its actualizations were done by Manfred Bundschuh.

The translation of the second edition into English was triggered by the German publisher Springer, who asked for an English translation and update, which has become the version you now possess. This led to the involvement and beneficial improvement, enhancement and actualization of the book done by the American author Carol Dekkers.

Why did Springer ask for an English translation and further updating of the successful German book on software estimation?

Initially, the demand emanated from colleagues at the European metrics organizations in Spain and Italy, and later from others who heard about the benefits gained by introducing metrics in Germany over the past years.

Secondly, the ISBSG collection of figures published as *The Benchmark* and other products are featured prominently in this book. These form a treasure trove of data that are of interest in the whole of the English-speaking metrics community.

Thirdly, this book presents an orderly overview of software -estimation, -metrics, -measurement, -measurement standards, and -benchmarking, with all related facets, augmented by many practical experiences of both of the authors. The book is aimed for beginners as well as experienced colleagues working with software -estimation, -measurement, and -metrics.

Last but not least, themes like productivity measurement, estimation tools, software reuse and redevelopment, and estimation in the maintenance process as well as in Object-Oriented-, Data Warehouse-, or Web- environments are dealt with in this book.

The Books' Content

This book delivers a framework for novices who are getting started in software project estimation, and also offers to the practitioner practical information for transfer into the profession. The text is derived from years of experience by the authors in software development and project management, and supported by a national and international networking in European and worldwide metrics- and standards- organizations.

Chapter 1 provides an entrance portal into the theme and introduces the first concepts. Chapter 2 lays the fundamental concepts, and together with Chapter 3 presents an overview for the reader desiring quick access to the information. The remaining chapters present topics on estimation in more detail, progressing in several steps:

- Estimation prerequisites and implementation, together with methods of estimation
- Estimation of maintenance effort
- Software measurement and metrics fundamentals, and product and process metrics
- Measurement communities and resources for measurement and benchmarking
- The IFPUG Function Point Method and the other four ISO/IEC-acknowledged Functional Size Measurement Methods
- Function point related measurement variants, experiences, counting rules, and case studies

- Measurement and metrics in object-oriented environments and data warehouse environments, and in software reuse and redevelopment
- A chapter about tools and their methods
- An appendix with examples and checklists.

Each chapter ends with a management summary for the reader who wants a quick synopsis or a list of important internet addresses for further reading.

Acknowledgements

An ambitious book translation and actualization project like this one (about 700 pages), which was performed as a hobby besides family, profession, lectureship of the German author at the University of Applied Sciences and his commitments in the German metrics organization DASMA over a 10-year timeframe and the commitments of the American author to her consulting business, international speaking engagements, and ongoing leadership endeavors, undoubtedly produces some loss by friction. The more important are the positive direct and indirect contributors each author would like to acknowledge and thank:

- Manfred's family in Germany (who had to live some time with his conscious absence and the partial occupation of the living room as author)
- Carol's two grown children, Corinne and Alex, who continue to be a source of inspiration and support in her international business
- *Good* managers who backed Manfred during the introduction of the metrics program at the international insurance corporation
- Ambitious colleagues at the same organization who were willing to widen their horizon and did not fear the additional effort to embrace estimation with Manfred during the management of their projects; colleagues who maintain an active network in professional and metrics organizations and who generously shared their own experiences. These include especially Luigi Buglione (GUFPI-ISMA), Ton Dekkers (NESMA), Peter Fagg (UKSMA), Peter Hill (ISBSG), Capers Jones, Roberto Meli (GUFPI-ISMA), Jolijn Onvlee (NESMA), Tony Rollo (UKSMA), Luca Santillo (GUFPI-ISMA), Charles Symons (UKSMA), Frank Vogelezang (NESMA), as well as Professors Alain Abran, Reiner Dumke, and Eberhard Rudolph. A special thanks also to Pekka Forselius, president of ISBSG and senior advisor to the Finnish Software Measurement Association (FiSMA), who provided essential contributions including the FiSMA Functional Size Measurement Method, experiences with ISBSG, and expertise about the practical implementation of estimating and software measurement
- Numerous students who committed their practical term and thesis to the introduction of a metrics program in their organizations. These students managed great effort and complex investigations of large amounts of data, some of them being rewarded with a DASMA students thesis award

- Note that the experiences herein are provided from the personal experiences of both authors. Our belief in the importance of professional estimating and benchmarking is passionate and results in opinions that are sometimes articulated in a very pronounced manner to foster an awareness that proven methods should be professionally used
- One final note: during the writing of this book we have used information and communications technology (ICT), information technology (IT), software intensive systems, and similar terms in an approachable and some-times interchangeable manner. For readers desiring a more formal treatise on the use of these and other industry terms, the reader is referred to the foreword and appendix of the American author's April 2008 book: Program Management Toolkit for software and systems development, co-authored with Pekka Forselius et al. by Talentum (ISBN: 978-952-14-1338-4).

Manfred Bundschuh
Carol Dekkers
Bergisch Gladbach and Tampa
Spring 2008

Contents

List of Figures

List of Tables

1 The Estimation Challenges

Estimation has to do with **uncertainty**

For estimation you need **Information about the *object* of estimation**

Dangerously often **estimation is mistaken for negotiation**

Fig. 1.1. The estimation challenges

The statements depicted in Fig. 1.1 hint at a few of the innate problems associated with estimating. Beyond these realities, we also issue a semi-serious warning for the reader:

Engaging in estimating increases the risk of becoming addicted to the practice. Many people dealing professionally with estimation will be fascinated by the clever application of estimation methods and tools and can quickly get drawn into an addiction with the whole estimation subculture.

Every IT project should commence with an estime of effort, cost, schedule dates and duration, as a *basis of project planning* as well as for the *measurement of project success* at the end of the project. Early *estimates before project initiation* are not only challenging, but rely on the collective corporate knowledge of similar past projects. To produce sound estimates, estimating professionals need knowledge garnered from market trends and trend interruptions, as well as from vendors touting the latest in technological developments. In addition, estimators must rely on historical experiences and scenarios from their own project portfolios. Unfortunately, until recently, there existed little published data to support such early estimation.

The output of the estimating process is typically a *line in the sand* estimate of cost and/or effort hours to develop or enhance a piece of software. As such, the progress of the project can be gauged, and corrective action can be taken when identified that the project deviates from the plan. Control and tracking against the plan (estimates) is an important component of successful project management. This enables controlling of project size (also called *project scope*) as well as the measurement of success. *Paradoxically, project leaders do not measure adequately either at the beginning or during their projects, yet it is precisely the measurement activity and resultant numbers that create a project conscience. The lack of quantification of project progress hinders the ability of even the best project managers to react and recover because often they will not detect in time an out-of-control project.* Measures such as effort expended versus effort budgeted, size delivered versus size estimated, project scope creep (planned versus actual), and earned value management measures can easily be collected during a project and provide project managers with a project *dashboard* on which to gauge the direction and speed of the project underway.

Even with tools available to perform accurate project estimation, the resultant estimates are far too often overridden or ignored by project management in favor of artificially determined delivery dates set by their customers or promised by their management. As the software industry frequently emboldens the term *software engineering* when describing the increased rigor associated with software development processes, it is astounding that the psychology of conflict avoidance and unrealistic optimism pervades software estimating. Date-driven estimating is one of the most prevalent estimating techniques employed in the software development professions today (McConnell, 2004) whereby a preset date governs the delivery of an often undetermined product. Software engineers routinely balk at overly optimistic delivery dates, yet succumb to management and customer pressure to meet such dates – even when they are set sometimes even before the project is named. "Engineers can wait until the end of design to perform production estimates, yet software engineers routinely must estimate software delivery before the end of the requirements phase" (Card, 1998). Can you imagine a construction manager announcing that a building will be set for occupancy within 6 months when not only the type of building, but also the location, floor plans, and intended usage are not yet known? To do so prior to a meeting with the owners and contractors would be obviously foolish, yet it is fairly common for software development management to commit their teams to such proposals simply as a matter of course.

This book does not purport that solid estimating principles will change the overoptimistic nature of development managers or customers, nor alter the course of history currently being written. It is our fervent hope, however, that if even one software project disaster is averted by the words or practices outlined here, then our work is a success. Software projects are simply too expensive and too wrought with human interaction to leave the science of estimating to date-driven proponents. There is a better way, and this book aims to shed light on the many techniques and methods for fact-based estimating of software projects.

Why do software professionals and managers reject solid software-estimating techniques? Reasons vary, but include the following:

- Everyone is doing the best job he/she can today – given his/her training, experience, and job demands. There simply is not a lot of time to read up on the best practices for software estimating
- There is no one size that fits all approach to software estimating, and it is difficult to figure out which method would be better than the *expert* or guru model we use today, whereby our developers each give their best guess to the work they think has to be done. Besides, according to some developers, the customers will never agree to our estimates no matter how they are derived
- Software development is still viewed as an artistic venture by many companies, and therefore standardized methods are often ignored
- Project teams are often rewarded based on their adherence to current processes no matter how arbitrary. An example of this is the practice of can be illustrated as: *if you can get the project done by this <artificially set> date within the <artificially set> budget, then you will be promoted*
- Project success is often gauged based on artificially set and managed to dates, regardless of how impossible the resultant schedule may be
- There is an inherent misunderstanding and mistrust of software developers. In fact, in some organizations, it is assumed that software developers inflate their estimates so that they can do less productive work. In such cases, whatever estimate the project experts submit for a project, it is routinely cut by 50% thinking that it will motivate project teams to become *more productive*
- Engineers and computer scientists are experts at technical work, and less so in the area of communication. While it is human nature to avoid conflict, it is even more so in the technical professions where communication is not a strong competency. The is exacerbated when the software project manager must tell the customer that the cost and schedule are inadequate to deliver a quality software product
- The attitude that nothing ever changes. Project professionals over the past 15 years are change-weary – that is they have been subject to so many changes in process, technology, methodologies, and programming languages that it seems futile to fight management and customers about the need to adopt "new" practices for creating solid estimates

- Users and customers do not understand their own role in software projects, and therefore do not realize the impact of their non-participation, changes, or rework demands on project estimates
- The gap between software developers and customers, despite years of lip service to business analysis and user-focused approaches, is simply not closing in many organizations. There is still the *customer is always right* mentality held by some of those who acquire software
- The lack of clear communication, solid requirements, and a *line in the sand* upon which to base a firm estimate compounds the whole notion of software estimating. Without jelled software requirements that are mutually agreed upon by both the customers and the software developers, it is virtually impossible to arrive at a reliable or semiaccurate estimate
- The duration estimates that come out of even sophisticated software estimating tools often seem so elongated or unrealistic that we are prone to cut down the estimate based on our own gut feel.

It is likely that you have encountered many other reasons why software estimating seems to remain more of an art than a science. By such (mis)behavior, chances for project success are often carelessly reduced even before the project starts. According to *the 2003 Standish Group's CHAOS Report* more than 2/3 (66%) of all projects are declared as failures/unsuccessful. With the current climate of continuing threats of outsourcing, layoffs, and continued fiscal restraint, it would seem no better time for project leaders to see themselves critically and aim to improve the success rates of their projects through good estimating practices, among others. Attributes of a good problem solver and project leader are needed more than ever today. The following capabilities of a professional problem solver are also unrestrictedly valid for professional project leaders:

A talented project leader

- Handles himself and the actual project progress critically. He has the ability of self-reflection without undue hardship to his self-esteem
- Can step back from the everyday details of the project to view it from an objective and whole perspective
- Can manage the project with the bare minimum of given information since he is an expert himself and has access to qualified experts on his project team who augment any weak areas of his experience
- Can separate the project wheat from the chaff – in other words, filter the essential and necessary information from that which is peripheral or distracting from the project. He has the ability to view complex matters in a condensed form
- Can formulate objectives precisely to attain the highest level of success given the project attributes. He has communicative talents allowing him to express the objectives in a manner understandable to other project stake-holders

- Is able to proceed in a structured manner and to decide consequently. He has the capacity to think logically and the capability to recognize connections and evaluate their importance to the project
- Is able to progressively elaborate problems to a workable and attainable solution. He is able to also incorporate lessons learned from the past in new situations.

While it might appear that the ideal project leader almost has to walk on water, there are also other prerequisites that must be in place for solid estimating processes to be successful. These are outlined in the paragraphs that follow:

1. Availability of historical project data
2. Organizational acceptance of best practices
3. Availability of appropriate supporting software tools.

Availability of historical data: an important prerequisite for the professional application of estimating techniques. Not only must there be availability of historical project data, but also it must be *relevant and applicable* historical project data.

This leads to an estimation paradox: estimates are most relevant and demanded at a point in time when there is a minimal of measurable information (at project initiation), and when one is able to perform the estimation with absolute exactness (at project postmortem) it is no longer required.

IT estimation is done for an object of estimation that is, per definition, unique. For this reason, it can be a burden for IT professionals to collect and evaluate empirical data during the progress of IT project, even though such data is easiest and most accurate to collect at that time. Far too often, data collection tasks *during* the project create additional effort that is seen to be of minimal value and *overhead* – an effort that is most likely to be avoided. But the value of such data collection to future project estimates can be enormous because data captured at the source and in the heat of a project can be more precise and reflect true project circumstances than to collect data after the project has closed. The issue becomes: *how to incorporate effortless and transparent project data collection during a project – especially on a project that was underestimated and challenged with unrealistic schedules?* This is where a few industry best practices are useful. It is well known that data are most accurate when they are still *fresh*.

Organizational acceptance of best practices: Before management will embrace a new way of doing business, even proven industry best practices, there must be a formidable likelihood that the new practice will aid the organization to move forward. Formalized estimating processes often fail to gain acceptance, in practice, due to the following situations or experiences:

Even the best method(s) without tool support have only scanty chances for survival.

This means that the implementation of an estimating method in and of itself is often insufficient to gain the buy-in and trust of an organization – it must be supported by adequate tools, and if the organization is lacking in historical project data, also a prepopulated database of relevant industry project data. Hence, most of *the following practical experiences* and examples are often based on the application of tools for estimation or for support of single methods.

Note: While there are many commercially available estimating tools available to the software professional today, we have restricted our treatise to those with which the authors have had direct and successful experiences. This is not to say that these are the only and best tools available at the time of this printing and thereafter; only that we have experience with particular estimating approaches which work(ed) successful in our own practices. The reader is urged to be aware that there will always be newer and more promising estimating tools on the market; however, the ones we have included by means of example herein are those whose manufacturers and authors we know personally, and who stand faithfully behind their products. There is no slight intended to any software vendor whose toolset has not been included in our select list of successful experiences. One can never be complete and all inclusive with such lists.

The software estimating support tools we will profile and mention here include the following:

- Function Point Workbench (FPW) by Charismatek Software, based in Melbourne, Australia (www.charismatek.com). This award-winning functional-size measurement repository software stores the details of the functions included in the functional size of a software project. FPW does not support project estimating; however, it provides support for scoping and sizing the software project to be estimated.
- KnowledgePLAN® (and its predecessor: Checkpoint for Windows) by Software Productivity Research of Cambridge, MA, USA (www.spr.com). This software package relies on a database of historical projects that number over 8,000 together with user input of functional size (function points) or other sizing mechanisms, plus project attributes to arrive at an estimate of project effort. The KnowledgePLAN database is augmented by the data from the International Software Benchmarking Standards Group (ISBSG) repository of completed project data.
- Experience® Pro by 4SUM Partners (www.4sumpartners.com). This robust tool for functional sizing, software estimating, and scope management provides development life cycle support for sizing, estimating, and tracking of a project's functionality, and is based on a validated database of completed software projects. The Experience® repository is also augmented by the data from the ISBSG repository of completed project data.

- SLIM suite of tools by QSM (www.qsm.com/database.html), where project data is collected (250–500 per year) and added to the SLIM database. SLIM measurement and estimating products are based on QSMs own research and estimating algorithms, and the QSM database is maintained at QSM.

The present experiences in this book can be easily transferred to other estimation tools without any problem. Thus, the mentioning of this or other tools should not be taken as an endorsement or advice to buy any of the aforementioned tools. In the upcoming chapter "Tools for Estimation," more tools are presented with their URL addresses so that the reader can make his/her own informed choice.

Availability of appropriate supporting software tools: The software functionality (i.e., the number of appropriate and supporting tools) available to the project team members to allow them to work efficiently and effectively is the third prerequisite to software estimating (besides time and money). Automated support for project estimating is a critical time saver that can be a critical prerequisite to overcome the resistance and skepticism about embracing the new processes. Manual estimating techniques, while useful for small projects, become an arduous and untenable set of tasks, which quickly lose momentum and support as soon as projects get underway. Without adequate tool support, historical data becomes difficult to track and associate with the original estimates. In addition, project estimates can quickly become lost, misplaced, and untraceable – rendering the process more work than it is worth. Such situations often result in a failed estimating initiative – even with sound and proven estimating methods – because the data are not integrated and available for sub-sequent project estimates. In these situations, it becomes even more difficult to try to implement software-estimating techniques at a future point – even when there may be tool support available to the project team. It is similar to the saying *Fool me once, shame on you – fool me twice, shame on me*. It is difficult enough to get an organization to embrace best practices the first time – it is almost impossible to do so after a botched first attempt.

Further to the three prerequisites, it is the authors' experiences that software estimating and metrics initiatives succeed more often when there is the support of a *Competence Center*. Such a group of specialists delivers, besides others, services and benefits for the project leaders by doing the following:

- Securing uniform procedures for estimation
- Creating consistency
- Providing a central and homogeneous collection and evaluation of project experience data
- Delivering estimating know-how – in other words, the Competence Center is the central repository of knowledge for the estimating methods.

The advantages and disadvantages of a Competence Center for estimation and Information Technology (IT) metrics will be discussed in the chapter "The Implementation of Estimation – Frequently Asked Questions (FAQs)."

The most important concepts of software estimation

✓ Knowing what is the Object of estimation
✓ The right point(s) in time for estimation
✓ The precision of estimates
✓ Estimation errors
✓ The effort to perform estimation processes
✓ The right estimating method for the purpose
✓ Tracking estimates
✓ Estimation tools
✓ Estimation parameters (input variables)
✓ Realistic (honest) estimates
✓ Estimation experience and historical data
✓ Introduction of formalized estimation
✓ Culture supportive to estimation

Fig. 1.2. The most important concepts of software estimation

Figure 1.2 depicts the most important concepts of software estimation at a glance. It is integral to the whole of software estimating that there be information available about the Object of estimation (what the software product will do) and defined milestones for performing project estimates (and revising those estimates) during the project. Estimating precision is also a central theme, as well as the concept of estimation error (underestimation, overestimation). The effort to perform project estimates must also be taken into account. Where and when estimates are to be performed, tracked, and reestimated during the project (as a matter of course or when scope changes arise) must also be defined and planned accordingly. This makes the availability of appropriate supporting software estimation tools even more critical, as essential estimation parameters have to be documented along the way. Those persons performing project estimates have to do so consistently and honestly in order to gain worthwhile estimation experience. Each of these concepts is an important consideration if a successful estimation culture is to be established.

The remainder of this chapter deals with the basic principles and regulations for performing software estimation.

1.1 The Basics of Software Estimation

There are a number of different approaches and methods in use today to estimate the cost, effort, and duration of IT projects (see chapter "Estimation

Methods"). However, only a handful of these have gained any significant market share. Our starting point, therefore, is the practical experiences of the authors, particularly those that include functional size measurement (FSM) – also known colloquially as the Function Point Methods (FPM). It should be noted that our experiences can easily be transferred to apply to any other functional measure.

Here we explain only the general principles of the most commonly used techniques (for further detail, see also the chapter "Estimation Fundamentals") and address the important concepts of software estimating: precision of estimates, the object of estimation, sizing the estimation object, and measurement, documentation, and the problem of applicable and relevant historical data.

During the estimating processes, one must use care to distinguish between the two essential estimating activities as follows:

1. *Measurement*
   Determination of the functional size of the object of estimation (e.g., size of the software application in place, or the size of the software to be developed or enhanced in a project); and the impact of the non-functional (quality and performance) requirements.
   But: What is that?
2. *Estimation of the following*:
   (a) Effort
   (b) Duration
   (c) Resources
   (d) Cost
   But: On what basis?

1.1.1 Measurement

It is generally understood that the size of the object of estimation (i.e., the size of the software application or the size of the software construction "area" developed or enhanced in a project as applicable) is one of the most important correlation factors that drive project effort and productivity! Hence, the measurement of software size is a major core discipline of IT project planning! Another important driver is the impact of non-functional requirements (similar to a "building code" for the software which can according to Barry Boehm, originator of the COCOMO II cost estimation model and Watts Humphrey of Capability Maturity Model (CMMI(SM)) fame – double the effort estimate for the development or enhancement of a piece of software.

It is impossible to estimate any project in any industry if one does not know the size of the object or product being developed. For example, in manufacturing, one cannot estimate the cost to manufacture an new item unless the particulars of the said item are known. It is similar in building construction – if the size of a construction or building renovation is unknown (or furthermore if it is not known whether it is a renovation or a construction project), it is impossible to perform an estimate worth the paper on which it is written. IT projects are no different.

IT projects cannot be estimated without an assessment of the software or systems to be built. One of the oldest methods to evaluate software size involves estimating the number of (non-comment) Source Lines of Code (SLOC) or 1,000 SLOC (known as KLOC or KSLOC). In recent years, the source lines of code approach to software sizing has come under fire, most notably due to the fact that SLOC is difficult to estimate at the beginning of a project, particularly when multiple technologies or programming languages are involved. Additionally, SLOC-based software sizing suffers from the inverse productivity dilemma – the more lines of code that are produced to implement a certain set of software functions, the more productive the team appears to be – when, in fact, the number of lines of code may be programmed and stylistically dependent on the programmer's way of coding. Software estimating industry guru, Capers Jones, has been often quoted for his hardline stance on this issue whereby he states that any manager who bases their performance measures (e.g., delivery rates, productivity or quality) on source-lines-of-code can be considered to be guilty of management malpractice. While the authors tend to agree with Capers' position, we have also seen evidence in some homogeneous software development environments where lines-of-code measures were of value to the customer and supplier relationships.

Another emerging standardized approach to evaluate software size is called Functional Size Measurement or FSM, which is independent of the programming language because it is based on an assessment of the functional user requirements to be implemented in the software. Further details on FSM and how to derive software's functional size can be found in the following chapters about Function Points.

Hence, in this book, estimation is always understood to be based on a measurable size of the object of estimation, augmented by an assessment of the non-functional and technical requirements for the software. The widespread *expert estimation technique* (also called the guru method in some publications) is to the authors' convictions better than no estimation (that is, if it is well documented and therefore, transparent and traceable), but it is not considered to be state of the art in the professions of project management or software engineering. This book focuses on the best practices for software estimation and illustrates the advantages of using formal, structured methods as we have experienced through our projects, as well as those collected by leading software metrics organizations and practitioners.

Expert Estimation Techniques

The *expert estimation* techniques employed by software development organizations worldwide range from none to ad hoc to formally documented. While we understand that some organizations enjoy the luxurious market position whereby they have a monopoly and do not see the value of doing any project estimation, this book does not address those companies. Ad hoc approaches may be standardized in the head of the expert estimator, but are rarely written down or shared among experts. Formally documented techniques are becoming more common especially with the advent of the Capability Maturity Models (CMMs) and software process improvement (SPI) movements (see the chapter about Measurement Communities and Resources). Expert estimation in these cases usually involves a variation of the following steps (if done professionally):

- Specification that the estimating following steps are to be performed independently by at least two estimation experts before any comparison of results is done
- Subdivision of the work to be performed into discrete software applications or functional projects (i.e., if there are multiple pieces of software to be developed and/or renovated, each one would comprise a separate subproject or separate piece of software to be estimated) Note: The Program Management Toolkit for software and systems developers (2008) by Forselius, Dekkers et al., outlines a structured approach to divide of IT programs into (sub)projects. See the bibliography for further details.
- Definition of the project type, structure and identification of the work tasks (also called Work Breakdown Structure or WBS) to be performed
- Determination of the situational constraints and environmental factors involved in the project(s) to be estimated (also called the non-functional and technical requirements)
- Performance of an independent effort estimate for each work task identified for the project(s)
- Roll-up (summation) of the total effort for all the tasks and all of the subprojects involved in the project (as applicable)
- Comparison of estimation results and building consensus between all estimation experts involved
- Addition of add-on tasks to accommodate uncertainty (e.g., instability of requirements, novelty of software or subject matter), as well as for known risks, and requirements/scope creep (Note: scope creep is also addressed separately in subsequent sections due to its potential impact on estimates throughout the project)
- Agreement on the precision probability (confidence level) and range of the estimates for total effort. The precision probability or confidence level for an estimate will increase as more information is known about the project as the project progresses. In addition, the range surrounding the estimated effort will

narrow as more information becomes known during the project. (A graphic showing the increasing accuracy of estimates as the software development life cycle progresses is also called the cone of uncertainty as depicted in Fig. 1.7. It begins at early requirements where the uncertainty of estimates is typically no more precise than ±100% (and sometimes up to +/– 400% depending on how "early" are the early requirements) and narrows to ±10% by the end of the project. Attributions in published literature credit this cone of uncertainty variously to Barry Boehm of the University of Southern California and COCOMO II fame, William Perry, CEO of the Quality Assurance Institute, or Capers Jones, Scientist Emeritus of Software Productivity Research).

Expert estimating techniques often deliver lower effort and cost estimates than estimates based on historical data. There are two primary reasons for this:

1. With expert estimation, there is often an overconfidence in the team productivity that will be achieved. This overconfidence can lead to a lower than realistic estimate of work effort.
2. High estimates trigger resistance and mistrust from managers, customers, and the promotional sales force, many of whom do not understand the estimating process or how uncertainty can increase an estimate. (This may be true from the viewpoint of other stakeholders too).

Functional Size Measurement

The second approach to software estimating identified earlier in this chapter involves the FSM of the software application or of the software to be developed or enhanced in the IT project. As an analogy, the functional size of software can be compared with the measurement of the distance for a trip, or the size of a building to be constructed. Following the first analogy – the distance to be taken on a trip – requires firstly that such distance be estimated based on the choice of the route and the particular mode of travel (airline or passenger vehicle etc.) This choice accordingly delivers the necessary information for the planning of time, duration, effort, costs, and quality of the journey. In a similar manner, the size of a piece of software becomes a fundamental component (the size of the object of estimation) along with the constraints (non-functional quality requirements), and how the software will be built, when estimating the time, duration, effort, costs, and quality for the IT project. Functional size measurement is akin to measuring the size of a floor plan (or in the case of enhancement – the size of a renovation to a floor plan), and the non-functional (quality) requirements are similar to the building code constraints required by the customer.

The SWEBOK (The Software Engineering Body of Knowledge) of the IEEE Computer Society (currently undergoing ISO/IEC JTC1 SC7 standardization) describes software measurement as an incorporated core element within the field of software engineering because it is essential to the development criteria of the SWEBOK and is persistent throughout (Buglione et al.). Nine of the ten knowledge areas of the current SWEBOK refer to software measurement processes. Software measurement and analysis is also identified as a Process Area (PA) for level 2 of the Capability Maturity Model Integration (CMMI®) Standard, and measurement plays an important role also in various standards of the ISO/IEC standard suite 15504 Software Process Improvement Capability dEtermination (SPICE), and is the focus of the ISO/IEC 15939 Software Measurement Process Framework standard.

Figure 1.3 depicts a simplified model of the basic ingredients of software estimation: Determining the functional size of the object of estimation is the first step. The second step involves identifying and defining the values of the relevant project parameters, which are then combined with the project size from step 1, and the effort is estimated. This effort then becomes the basis for cost and duration (time to market) calculations. *This overall estimating model depends on the existence of reliable empirical historical project data that are collected.*

As mentioned earlier, the size measurement of the object of estimation (e.g., an application or IT project piece of software) can be determined with different techniques and result in different sizing units, for example:

- Non-commented SLOC:
  Lines of code (KSLOC = Kilo SLOC). Note: this method is discouraged for the aforementioned reasons, however, there are organizations that profess success in estimating with these and other non-FSM methods
- Functional size measurement units including the following:
  - IFPUG Function Points (IFPUG = International Function Point Users Group, see chapter "The IFPUG Function Point Counting Method")
  - COSMIC Function Points (Cfp, COSMIC = Common Software Measurement International Consortium; see chapter "Functional Size Measurement Methods")
  - FiSMA Function points (Ffp, FiSMA = Finnish Software Measurement Association; see chapter "Functional Size Measurement Methods")
  - Mark II Function Points (see chapter "Functional Size Measurement Methods")
  - NESMA Function Points (NESMA = Netherlands Software Measurement Association)
  - Data Points, Object Points, and other variants of software sizing (see chapter "Variants of Functional Size Measurement").

Because of its popularity in the USA and its current dominance in the ISBSG data repository, Functional size measurement using IFPUG Function Points is described in the chapters "The IFPUG Function Point Counting Method" and "IFPUG Function Point Counting Rules." Four other FSM methods are currently standardized by the International Organization for Standardization (ISO) and

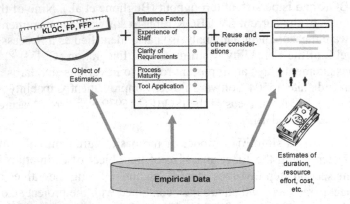

Fig. 1.3. The basic ingredients for software estimation

the International Electrotechnical Commission (IEC) joint technical committee on information engineering ISO/IEC JTC1, and are the focus of the chapter "Functional Size Measurement Methods."

1.1.2 Estimation

Once the size of the software application or enhancement to a piece of software is estimated, the other relevant software estimating input factors are also assessed, and then the estimation is performed for project planning purposes. Estimates of project size are usually estimated first, because it is the project size that is one of the most dominant input variables to an estimating model that determines the resources (number of people), duration (how long the project will take), and costs (based on how many people for how long). Since the size of the estimation object (e.g., the software size) is not the only parameter for estimation, all relevant factors for estimation are evaluated before an estimate can be calculated. Examples of these influential estimating input factors include the following:

- Clarity and stability of requirements
- Experience of the development team with the technology and subject matter
- Business sector
- Project goals and constraints (e.g., maximum quality with minimum duration will double an estimate)
- Maturity of the organization with respect to formalized development processes (CMMI® level)
- Maturity of the technology to be used
- Hardware platform(s)
- Programming language(s)

- Degree of user involvement
- Quality requirements (maintainability, portability, reliability, and other quality constraints as outlined in ISO/IEC 9126 or the emerging ISO/IEC 25000 SQUARE series of software quality standards).

Our experience bears out that one of the primary drivers that can impact the effort and duration of application development is the introduction of a second or subsequent hardware platform to what was formerly estimated as a single-tier architecture. The ISBSG (see chapter "Measurement Communities and Resources") as well as the FiSMA have reported that the choice of the development platform and of the programming language are two of the strongest drivers of the development effort aside from the software's functional size. As previously mentioned, the effort for an IT project is not only dependent on the size of the software to be developed/enhanced, but also on many different influencing factors (see Fig. 1.4).

Thus, functional size measurement and estimation (determining the influencing factors and performing the estimate) are two consecutive, but clearly dependent tasks involved in effort estimation.

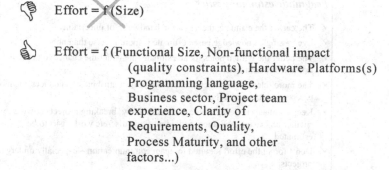

Effort = f (Size)

Effort = f (Functional Size, Non-functional impact
(quality constraints), Hardware Platforms(s)
Programming language,
Business sector, Project team
experience, Clarity of
Requirements, Quality,
Process Maturity, and other
factors...)

Fig. 1.4. Effort estimation depends on software size *plus* many other influencing factors

For both activities the existence of empirical data, – data from historical IT projects – is the basis for accurate estimating and as such is a necessary prerequisite (see Fig. 1.3).

It will come as no surprise that the estimation process must be trustworthy from a business perspective, and the results from each step of the estimating process must clearly document the input values and assumptions made because important investment and project budget decisions will be based on them. The whole estimation process must be auditable! The strength of a project estimate is only as reliable as that of the weakest partial process involved.

To perform a size-based estimate, there are six prerequisites:

1. A basic understanding of the functional requirements for the software
2. The ability to measure the size of the product in a precise manner

3. The ability to evaluate the complexity of the product
4. The knowledge about the capability of the organization to manage projects and deliver products
5. The knowledge about how the product will be delivered (including reuse requirements)
6. The existence of relevant historical data in order to calculate productivity (that can be used to estimate work effort).

A practical experience of experts when estimating software project effort bears out that if there are too many unknowns when attempting to measure the software size, then at least the functional requirements lack precision and clarity. Even this knowledge can force those professionals and customers who articulate the software requirements to improve the quality of their processes.

Pragmatic rules that help to foster an estimating consciousness are summarized in Fig. 1.5.

One of the most frequent questions asked when deciding whether to embrace size-based project estimation is a question about the precision of estimating.

Pragmatic estimating rules

✓ The earlier the estimate, the larger the bandwidth of uncertainty.
✓ Even a single knowledge based estimate is more precise than none.
✓ The better the written notes for an estimate, the better the chance to improve the estimate the next time.
✓ The more relevent (and accurate) are the project attributes you collect, the more precise an estimate can be.
✓ Keep estimates understandable and traceable by: breaking projects down into smaller objects of estimation; and, identifying discrete work tasks to be estimated.
✓ Don't forget the effort required for team communication – especially on large projects.
✓ The more that effective team communication is planned into the project, the less rework occurs.
✓ Remember that estimating is not a 1:1 formula of size to effort.
✓ Project estimating should never be an exercise in self-esteem – it should reflect only the realistic team capability to deliver.

Fig. 1.5. Pragmatic estimating rules

1.1.3 Estimation Precision

A literature search regarding completed software projects attests to the fact that (mostly larger) software projects typically exceed their effort and schedule estimates by 300–1,500%. Our experience and those of others presented at US and European measurement conferences is tighter – but a deviation of 10–20% of the actual effort (even using Function Point Analysis as the functional sizing method), or even 30–100% is accepted in industry as very good early estimates. Such deviations can sometimes be attributed to Parkinson's Law:

Work tends to consume all available time.

So it can be difficult to gauge whether an estimate was really too high or too low when the entire allocated schedule is taken up (by Parkinson's Law) or exceeded (sometimes through unmanaged change). Note: that mismanaged requirements – even in the most mature of organizations – can lead to estimating inaccuracies. This is part of why we advocate functional size measurement – so that there is a basis on which estimates are based, even if they turn out to be incorrect. At least on the basis of documented functional size, estimates can be improved from a theoretical model (and often unrealistic set of assumptions) going forward.

As discussed previously in this chapter, the effort for the IT project delivery depends on the software size *plus* many other parameters. This is an important concept worth repeating: While the size of the software to be developed or enhanced in a project is a major determinant for the project effort, it is far from being the only one! Size matters, but only from a relative point of view. To use a building construction analogy: the larger the building the more effort to build. On IT projects, the larger the software, the more the effort to deliver. But, in the same way that the type of building, type of project (new vs. renovated), building code, location, intended usage, and constraints (e.g., marble floors) change the effort, cost, and schedule, so too with IT projects. A 1,000 FP project will take various amounts of delivery effort depending on whether the software involves complex scientific data manipulation (complexity), simple reporting, or if the delivery will be custom-coded or installed using a commercial off-the-shelf (COTS) package.

The exact values for the majority of these other non-functional, situational, environmental, and technical delivery parameters are typically unknown at the project onset and do not become precisely known until project (post) delivery. Additional parts of these parameters include, for example: qualifications of the development team and clarity and stability of user requirements.

Regarding the precision of estimation, we have compiled a list of pragmatic rules as presented in Fig. 1.6.

Estimating precision depends in large part on the complexity of the object of estimation (the software), on the software development life cycle (where in the project the estimate is made), the quality of available historical data, as well as the quality of actual effort measurement data. It is critical to the understanding of the actual team effort to know on what basis the measures were taken. For example, there can be a high degree of variance in reported team effort. Consistency and comparability of work effort across projects depend on a clear and consistent

Precision of estimation

✓ An estimate should never be presented alone as an absolute figure, but rather accompanied by an interval or range.

✓ The bandwidth of this interval depends on how much information is available about the object of estimation.

✓ Estimating uncertainty decreases as the project progresses.

✓ In general, it is good practice to document your error margins and communicate them with project stakeholders.

✓ Always present integer rounded figures (because significant figures perpetuate the illusion of non-existent precision).

✓ Alway perform multiple estimates (e.g. Function Point based estimation plus expert estimation).

✓ To increase reliability, always involve more than one estimator.

Fig. 1.6. Precision of estimation

definition of what constitutes project work effort. The definition must address at least the following items in order to minimize variances in reported efforts:

- Overtime work effort: whether or not overtime hours are compensated. The overtime hours *must be* recorded if any reliable figures are to be captured for future estimating. Overtime work hours can increase a project's recorded work effort remarkably – often in the range of up to 30% of the overall work effort. This is not a factor to be overlooked or taken lightly. It is important to note that recording of overtime is independent of payroll and financial accounting considerations.
- Project start and end points: The points in time where the software development life cycle (and thus, the work effort measurement) begins and ends can vary widely across projects unless it is clearly and objectively defined. If one project records its starting point at the project initiation stage and stops on the day of software release or installation, and another records its start as the first day of requirements articulation and stops 30 days after delivery, we clearly have an "apples to oranges" (i.e., inconsistent measurement) comparison. It is critical to the development of a historical project database to ensure that there is a consistent and recorded definition for the project (i.e., project start and stop point).
- Who is included as part of the team work effort: again this must be consistent – are data base administrators, project clerks, project managers, technical writers, contractors and others included in the definition of team work effort? This is an important consideration, and who is included or not included can have a huge impact on the number of effort hours reported for a project.
- Software development or enhancement: the type of project, minimally development or enhancement, is also a critical driver of the effort. One would

not want to base a new development project estimate on the historical values for enhancement projects.

- Software development methodology and included work breakdown structure (WBS) tasks: this must be clearly defined and recorded for the project being measured. One would obviously anticipate a higher work effort number of hours for a project that included formal user training than one where users trained themselves. As well, any project where package selection is part of the WBS approach will necessarily vary in effort to one where custom code development, testing, and implementation are part of the project.

These factors are essential to understand, standardize, and record on every project for which work effort is collected. Without knowing the basis for team effort, it becomes impossible to perform any sort of precise future – even if more knowledge about the object of estimation and other factors is known.

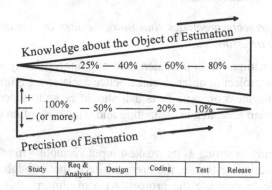

Fig. 1.7. Precision of estimates as a project progresses

To make sense of historical project data, one MUST know the context from which it came.

The relationship between the precision of estimation and the amount of knowledge about the object of estimation is depicted in Fig. 1.7.

The problems associated with the precision of estimation imply that with formal (serious) estimation:

- General error margins should accompany the estimate (±confidence).
- Estimates are generally rounded up or down ((in) significant decimal places simply discredit non-existent precision).
  Note that while an estimate *can* be rounded down, it is generally more dangerous because seldom does an IT project take *less time than anticipated!* In actual practice, it is more realistic so many project to provide a range based on the estimated figures +50% rather than +/–50%.

- Good estimators rely on more than one way to do estimates (e.g., Function Point as well as expert estimation).
- To increase reliability of estimates, several estimators (expert opinions) are usually involved.

A survey by Chris Kemerer of MIT (Massachusetts Institute of Technology) in the 1990s stated that trained Function Point counters generally could achieve function point values for a project that consistently came within ±10% of each other.

Do not forget that another influencing factor for estimating precision is knowledge about the object to be estimated.

1.1.4 The Object of Estimation

Estimation of IT projects precludes that more or less information is known about the object to be estimated.

The purpose of estimation is to understand and appropriately apply known effort drivers to our project in order to make better decisions. Figure 1.8 helps to sharpen our consciousness of some facts that should be self-evident, but which unfortunately are often forgotten in estimating and which are often unfortunately neglected.

An estimate is only as strong as its weakest input variable – in other words, in order to derive a realistic estimate, the prerequisite is that enough usable information is available to evaluate the project. At a minimum, this includes the software requirements as documented in the following ways

---

Object of Estimation

✓ Estimates for IT projects demand as a prerequisite more or less known information about the object of estimation.

✓ You cannot control what you cannot or do not measure.

✓ The more informations about an estimation object you have, the more precise the estimation can be.

✓ The more clear is the definition of the goals of the IT project, the less requirements creep can be expected (calculated).

Fig. 1.8. Object of estimation

- Overview of the necessary data requirements from the user perspective (e.g., object catalogue or relational data model from a data dictionary or knowledgeable users)
- Preliminary mock-up or layout of screens and reports
- Interfaces (number and size)
- Procedures from the user view, dialogue steps, e.g., process flow models with their composite activities, use cases, etc.

If estimates are required before the requirements are set and before this information is available, then assumptions for these parameters must be made and documented. When such estimates are performed with assumed data, they are called more applicably *guesstimates*. The certainty with which this assumption will become reality later influences the result of the estimate considerably. The following are commonly held truths about estimation:

- The more there is information available for an estimate the more precise the estimate can be.
- The software on when estimating effort, consider the project parts and tasks to be done. Therefore, estimation is one method for the discovery of information about both the project (detailed requirements) and its risks (uncertainty in the estimate and the requirements). In fact, the process of deriving the functional size may increase the completeness of overall requirements because in order to count or estimate the FP, one must have at least rudimentary information about which to capture data.
- When we estimate, we often do not know the object of estimation (i.e., the piece of software) accurately. Thus, the first task is to identify the software boundary that depicts what is within and external to the software under consideration. This affords some time and discussions with the customer that extraordinarily contributes to the success of the project. In the following, more time is necessary to determine the user requirements. From this, project risks can be deduced that can influence effort and duration. Only on this basis is a profound project plan possible. But, planning is the lust of reason, whereas *improvisation is the joy of fantasy*, and reality has a lot of surprises ready.
- A commonly known but often overlooked effect is the requirements scope creep as further detailed below.

1.1.5 Requirements (Scope) Creep

During project estimation, the requirements change as well as the knowledge about the object of estimation. Thus, another effect exists, mostly known by all project leaders and appropriately coined *requirements creep* (sometimes also called *scope creep*).

Quoting Capers Jones: "Problems are excessive time pressure as well as a high rate of requirements creep that can exceed two percent per month of project *duration* (for information systems the rate is 1.5%, military and system software is 2%, and commercial software is 3.5%) during project progress".

Requirements creep negatively correlates to a clear definition of objectives. Hence, *the clearer are the objectives of an IT project, the less requirements creep will typically occur.*

Continuous tracking of the project's objectives and project size gives the project leader control, i.e., the chance to get a grip on requirements creep. This implies that measurements of the size of the object of estimation must be repeated or at least updated several times during project progress. Sidenote: the American author is involved in an initiative with the European Certificates Association (ECA) to create a common body of knowledge and certification for a Certified Scope Manager (CSM) based on the Finnish Software Measurement Association's (FiSMA) northernSCOPE(TM) concept. For further information refer to the FiSMA website (http://www.fisma.fi/in-english/scope-management/).

The Software Engineering Laboratory (SEL) of the NASA reminds its project leaders, by way of its Manager's Manual, that the originally planned effort typically increases by about 40% during a project.

The IT group of an international insurance company in Germany measured an average requirements creep of 1.27% per month of project duration based on Function Point counts of 38 software development projects. This figure is cited as an example of average scope creep at a real organization; however, we also recall that for one large project the values were much larger. On that project, requirements creep was 2.4% per month as indicated by the 12-month size increase from 2,659 to 3,774 Function Points.

When the object of estimation is defined clearly, its functional size can be measured quantitatively. Often this is done using FSM, an approach whereby the functional size of a piece of software is calculated by counting and measuring *functional units*, similar to sizing the number and size of rooms on a building floor plan. The resultant functional size is typically expressed in function points or some variation thereof.

1.1.6 Measurement and Estimation

The two main activities in the framework of operative estimation, measurement, and estimation are not singular, discrete activities, but must continually be performed throughout the software development project. As such, measurement values are not static but dynamic and evolve in time. Only by continuous tracking of counts, estimates, and changes can meaningful target values for project planning be achieved.

Generally, the phrase (popularized by Tom DeMarco) holds:

"What you cannot measure, you cannot control."

Measurement does not guarantee organizations that a can produce software with acceptable quality within time, cost, and effort constraints – however, measurement is the catalyst that can make that achievement possible. To be truly effective, measurement must facilitate improved estimation and provide management with the means to gauge and improve the productivity of the software process and the quality of the product. Without measurement, it is difficult to detect and uncover problems early enough – before the project becomes out of control.

Figure 1.9 demonstrates that unreliable or late information have an effect on the accuracy of estimation and hence on the project team's ability to control subsequent estimate variations. Generally said: "Measurement fosters knowledge since the better we can express something with figures, the better we understand it."

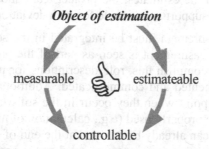

Fig. 1.9. Connection between measurement, estimation, and control

To gain the most benefit from the measurement of effort the following rules should be followed:

- Document the actual and the remaining effort of each project task at least once a week (even better is daily recording).
- Support the planning process by significant and relevant graphics.
- Update project plans by comparing the planned and actual values (akin to Earned Value Management practices).
- Time accounting practices must be clearly defined and communicated (e.g., is overtime reported?).
- Foster a measurement culture early so that the team understands the significance of reporting all worked hours for the project.
- Planning must be as detailed as necessary, but as aggregated as possible.

- Coordinate project planning, estimating, and measurement practices so that rework is avoided as much as possible (i.e., it is much more efficient to conduct project planning, estimating, and coordinating of measurement practices from a single set of applicable historical data at the same time to minimize inaccurate comparisons, as well as minimize spending double time doing the same historical information retrievals).
- To be able to use actual effort as a basis for future estimates, project effort must be measured in a consistent manner using consistent definitions. For example, it is important to know what tasks were included in the effort, whose effort was included, and whether overtime was included.
- Measurement participants must understand the context and purpose for reporting in order to facilitate correct measurement (i.e., developers need to know how their reported effort is used so that they can report it correctly and accurately).
- When deviations occur between estimated and actual effort, it is important to let the project team know before the project runs out of budget and time, or it is necessary to cut functionality or quality in order to finish on time. Additionally, if the measurements are taken after the project is completed and the actuals exceed the estimates, the project team should be given the opportunity to provide supporting rationale for such deviation.

The activities for measurement must be integrated in the software development life cycle so that measurement is seen as part of the process and not as tiresome overhead. To accomplish this, role descriptions for measurement and reporting must be documented and communicated. Additionally, data should only be measured at the point when they occur in the software life cycle and only measured if they are properly used (e.g., calculation of metrics). As such, because Function Points can already be counted at the end of the requirements phase, they can readily be reused as necessary as changes occur (change management) as well as part of test case determination, etc.

It has to be clearly distinguished between project FSM of the software to be developed and the estimation of effort to develop it. This is one of the first lessons to be learned when implementing an estimation process in an organization. The counting of Function Points or KSLOCs or other parameters for software size measurement delivers a prerequisite and necessary basis, which can be used for a following estimation. It may help to consider an analogy – the square foot size of a building to be constructed is not the same as the effort it will take to build it. The size is one of the influencing factors of such effort, but it is not the same as the effort itself. The same goes with functional size – it is the size of the software and an input to the effort estimation – but it is not the same as work effort. In practical work, this is expressed humorously by: "So you've got Function Points (KSLOCs. ...) – what now?"

The difference can be shown with the following practical example:

The Function Points of about 15 applications – the majority of which were host-based Management Information Systems (MIS) applications – in an organization were counted. The 16th application to be counted delivered five times as many Function Points as the largest of the other 15. *Reaction of the Management*: *"You must have counted something wrong!"*

Not at all, it just was not a *normal* MIS as the others but a central text administration system used by all other 70 applications of the organization, with thousands of different outputs. Much the same, another application delivered almost no inputs and outputs. Further investigations led to the result that it was compared to another dissimilar application – the other MIS was only the pure query system, thus delivering mostly Function Points for External Inquiries. Such discoveries (or measured affirmations) in one's own application portfolio are often found with the first inventory taken when estimation is formally implemented in an organization.

For this reason, the documentation of estimating experiences for an IT project is a prerequisite to experiential learning from historical experiences for the planning of the future and improvement of estimation in software development (this is called feed forward).

A serious and well-founded project estimate for software development delivers metrics, which make the software development process transparent, measurable, comparable, and controllable. A prerequisite to effective project management is that the estimates are formally documented and controlled. Additionally the measurement of spent effort is required for the improvement of the estimation accuracy used in future estimations.

1.1.7 Measurement of Effort

The measurement of actual effort for the different phases of an IT project is a mighty tool for learning, understanding, and communication of the project status. Hence, it is a decision aid par excellence for project management.

A working group of the DASMA (German software metrics organization) constructed the following basic scaffolding for the measurement of actual data as indispensable:

Time	Effort/Costs	Quality
Size (e.g., Function Points, KSLOCs)		

In this process, the effort should be measurable by following phases and activities:

Measurement of the effort by phases:

- Elaboration of the feasibility study (note that this is extra to the 5 phases of software development and enhancement per the definition of project effort outlined by the International Software Benchmarking Standards Group (ISBSG) which includes User requirements articulation, design, coding/programming, testing, and preparing for full implementation as the 5 phases)
- Determination of the user requirements
- IT Design
- Programming
- Test
- Implementation (note that this does NOT include full software rollout – simply the first implementation/installation).

Measurement of the effort by activities:

- End user (note that the end user effort is often not included in the project work effort per ISBSG and other benchmarking databases)
- IT developer
- System programming
- Quality assurance
- Project management
- Data modeling
- Database management
- Methods and systems
- Network
- Testing department
- Production/computing center.

Table 1.1 connects both views. Note: it is important to know which of these categories of effort are to be included in your project BEFORE an estimate is performed using an historical database!

Measurement and estimation are closely connected – but are not interchangeable terms! Organizations with a history of measuring IT projects should have solid empirical data available.Organizations not measuring must accept subjective estimates or must rely on the support of estimation tools. However, when using estimation tools, the results nevertheless have to be calibrated with actual measured data to ensure estimating accuracy. This is why measurement is a valuable and a necessary prerequisite to avoid estimation problems.

Table 1.1. Basic scaffolding for measurement of actual data

Categories for work effort reporting based on DASMA definition	Feasibility study	User require- ments	IT design	Program- ming	Test	Imple- mentation
End user						
IT developers						
System programming						
Quality assurance						
Project management						
Data modeling						
Database management						
Methods and systems						
Network						
Testing department						
Computing center						

1.1.8 Documentation

Good documentation of counting and estimation data is a treasure for metrics programs. Practical experience shows that valuable metrics can be gained from the collected data. A documented estimation process and documented estimates are required to reach level 3 of the CMMI® (Capability Maturity Model Integration of the SEI: Software Engineering Institute). Typically, documentation is neglected in operative and strategic project management. The additional effort caused by documentation in the progress of an IT project is often used as an excuse for not doing it.

The consequent and especially authentic documentation of project experiences is a necessity to ensure that project management know-how gained in this project is captured and goes beyond the expertise of a single project team member. Moreover, an efficient knowledge-based, learning organization should ensure that the right information is available to the right people at the right time so that they can appropriately plan future IT projects. Non-existent documentation of the development environment and estimating assumptions can hinder learning and improvement of estimation a priori. This can be clearly seen by the problem of historic data as outlined in the following section.

1.1.9 The problem of Historic Data

Practical experience shows that sound estimates often predict higher effort than reported in the past for an organization. However, Capers Jones does not blame these higher estimates as being faulty, *but rather doubts whether the historic data were reported and documented correctly.* It is often found that the documented historic data does not comprise even 30% and sometimes even up to 70% of the actual work effort. Thus, for example, unpaid overtime work or other effort was regularly not reported.

When talking with project leaders, they often narrate about effort figures without any information to depict the context of what is included in these figures. To simplify the effort for an IT project in a large organization, keep note that it comprises the following components:

- Effort for project management, risk management, and quality assurance (mostly disliked by the project leaders as unnecessary overhead – a gross negligent and unprofessional attitude – and sometimes uttered as *who estimates is a coward*)
- Effort for specialists (system architects and administrators, network support etc.) – sometimes called development team support
- Effort of the developer (analysis, design, programming, test) – also known as the IT core effort
- Effort of end users
- Effort for implementation and support.

Usually not included or calculated (wrongly) is the postproject effort for maintenance and enhancement necessary during the rest of the software life cycle. We know large applications operating successfully for more than 15 years – with increasing annual effort to support their survival. Not measuring this effort causes *the problem of the legacy systems.*

A typical cause of estimates done by project leaders being considerably lower than estimates done by a Competence Center is the fact that project leaders typically only estimate the project management and developer effort, whereas the Competence Center can involve full life-cycle components (such as those from the earlier list). Generally, it holds: "Estimation without infor-mation about what is included in the estimate is worthless".

If there is no documentation available or if a legacy system cannot be counted completely, the functionality can be at least approximated by back-firing. In this case, the code size and code complexity of an existing application are used to deduce its functionality in Function Points.

From the aforementioned problems of estimation, we have created a short list of rules for estimation.

1.2 Rules for Estimation

It has always been a challenge to sell the benefit of measurement. One often-used argument for the boycott of metrics initiatives (and one that often kills them) is that one lived successfully in IT without measurement in the past. Thus, in this chapter some advice about basic *to do's* and *don'ts* is documented: common estimation errors, estimation conferences, honesty and culture of estimation as well as training for estimation.

1.2.1 Basic Principles

Estimation should be as follows:

- *Repeatable* (*at various points in the project*)
  The repetition of an estimation allows subsequent estimates to be done with better information more accurately. Furthermore, the comparison with the previous estimates delivers experiences for future estimations. A *continual tracking of the estimations* constitutes an *early warning system for deviations* and gives transparency and enables an overview of changes. Only repeated estimations can help to gain experiences with requirements creep.
- *Performed using different methods*
  The use of several estimation methods allows comparative estimations from different viewpoints and reduces the estimation imprecision and gives you more safety for estimations.
- *Documented with sufficient detail*
  In principle, the parameters of estimation must be revealed since they strongly influence the estimation result a priori. For example:
  - Developments in client/server environment with 4GL languages must be distinct from estimates for conventional Mainframe COBOL development.
  - Large organizations in one business area must be distinct from estimates in small organizations in another business area.
  - The basis for size measurement (e.g., using SLOC methods (SLOC = source lines of code) and counting comments or not or when using program generators and counting or not counting the generated statements must be documented.
  - SLOCs are more easily counted in COBOL programs and not so good when programming was done with Powerbuilder or VBA (Visual Basic for Applications).

- Additionally estimates with SLOC occur later in the project, and thus have only marginal benefit for estimation and planning as well as tracking of project progress.
- There must be general standards for how many working hours a person day, person month, and person year has (time accounting).

- *Controllable*
  Only controllable estimates deliver the chance for comparisons and thus enable a *feed forward* (learning from past estimations for future estimations).
- *Documented*
  The main problem of estimation is non-existent or unavailable documentation. This means that we are estimating without the benefit of comparable and relevant historical information. The better and the more estimations are documented the better they can be estimated and estimation experience gained.

Besides these basic principles, some other estimating aspects must also be considered to avoid failures when estimating.

1.2.2 Do's and Don'ts When Estimating

How are estimations being performed? To get a standardized measurement platform on project level, the estimation must be done by the project leader. Only in this way, it can be guaranteed that the scale, for e.g., *Complexity*, is used in all projects in the same manner.

The process of estimation is no substitute for the determination of the effort parameters, which has to be done by the person responsible for planning. It simply delivers the chance to orient subjective estimates using a standardized method. The project environment factors can be determined with support of a tool (or manually) after counting the Function Points.

Parallel projects should not be compared. This leads easily to manipulation of the method to be better (on the paper) as compared with another project.

Two common opinions extremely hinder continous estimates:

1. *Estimation is regarded as a separate task.* This leads to prioritizing estimations as less important when the project deliverables, milestones, or the entire project is delayed.
2. *Estimation is seen as a task not belonging to the own responsibility.* This leads to neglecting of estimation when the responsible person is not present (a Competence Center off-site – far away from daily work).

Some organizations may justify their lack of a formal estimating process due to the fact that they do not have a database of reliable historical data. This is not an optimum attitude and fosters an ignorance of the benefits of organizational learning. As such, the organization is prone to repeat mistakes of the past, and will continue to do the following:

- *Lack know-how of how to do things better*
  Lacking know-how about principles, methods, and better estimations of effort.
- *Missed opportunities and chances for learning*
  Learning cannot occur since opportunities for learning were not taken.
- *Suffer from a crisis*
  The chance to run into a crisis by bad (or none) estimates increases enormously. As already told in the preface, firefighting can be exciting, but also leads to burnout. Estimation is a chance for people who are tired of firefighting to gain early success on projects.
- *Lost opportunities for process improvement*
  Sometimes regret costs more than learning and performing professional estimates would have cost. Only one abandoned project is sufficient to prove this, since the costs for one failed project are more than the costs for the implementation of an estimation process. Moreover, estimating processes deliver a better basis to control IT projects and reduce the risk of failures.
- *Maintain the status quo and not move forward.*

1.2.3 Estimation Errors

The most common estimation errors pertain to the following topics:

- *Prerequisites of estimation*
  - The assumptions and decisions made during the estimation process are not documented or not completely documented.
  - Estimates are not updated when situational or scope factors change.
  - The deliverables are not clearly defined.
- *Planning of estimation*
  - The effort for estimation is not planned.
  - The effort for quality assurance and project management is not planned.
  - Early estimates use non-transparent and often arbitrary surcharges for uncertainty and risks and requirements creep, if at all.
- *Actuality and tracking of estimation*
  - Estimates are not repeated as the project progresses or when change is introduced (feedback of actual data and new estimates).
  - Estimates are not regularly checked.
- *Quality of estimation*
  - The estimate is not formally reviewed for completeness and accuracy by a third party.

  - The resultant estimate is not validated by other estimates (second esti-
    mation).
  - The communication factor in the project is not adequately addressed.
- Especially for *external contracting*, the estimates of the contractor must be
  reviewed by the client in order to avoid unpleasant surprises or contractual
  dispute.
- *Political estimations*
  This can be a top risk as outlined in the next section.

1.2.4 Political Estimates

A major obstacle for the implementation of an estimation culture is *political
estimates*. There may be many reasons for this, especially in large organizations,
e.g., lust for power, human vanity, and others. The following list presents some
associated problems.

- Estimation is often mistaken for bargaining. Missing historical data often
  results in the dictation of unrealistic deadlines.
- The size of the project is often obviously/consciously wrongly estimated
  (trimmed estimations).
- When cutbacks of the IT project occur (e.g., budgets or deadlines), the estimation is often erroneously trimmed according to the cutbacks instead of by
  reducing the other primary goals (quality, functionality, costs, time).
- Voluntary unpaid overtime work will be planned into the project but not
  considered in the estimates.
- Goal conflicts often arise from *vanity*. The desire for success and acknowledgement often leads to *turf wars* in the IT project environment, for pres-
  tige projects to the end that project leaders must consider *power politics* in
  the environment of their IT project. The initiators of such projects collaborate
  with political promoters who are less interested in the functionality but more
  in the *memorial monument effect*.
- There is a widespread prejudice that application cost in terms of software
  and hardware are higher in the host environment than in client/server (C/S)
  applications when both software or hardware are considered. This leads
  to increased negotiation/more bargaining in the client/server environment
  instead of realistic estimates.
- The phase of nicely calculated figures leads at the end to a political approval of the project. Disillusionment and the search for realistic risk carriers
  typically follow soon afterward.
- A main cause for underestimation is the fact that political estimation is done
  more often instead of a realistic estimate. In reality, the effort of an IT project
  is typically underestimated to gain approval for the initiation and performance of this IT project. What a crazy world! Here, we have the decision makers

who are not guided by estimates, but rather by the effort. The practical result is that the effort is not estimated but is determined by bargaining.

Management and staff should thus avoid all these obstacles in order to foster a good estimation culture.

1.2.5 Underestimation and Overestimation

Besides the parameters shown in Fig. 1.10, others are often under- or overestimated.

In a survey performed by Lederer and Prasad in 1993 of 112 software managers, 63% reported about considerable overestimating and 14% about consi-derable underestimations of effort. Heemstra in 1992 reported much the same regarding cost estimations in The Netherlands: 80% of the projects underestimated budget and duration about 50% in the average; 35% of the organizations did not perform formal estimations. Since underestimation especially has serious effects, these parameters are discussed in the following and enhanced by others.

Overestimation

✓ Qualification of staff
✓ Productivity of staff
✓ Consequences of adding more people
✓ Productivity of new tools and methods

Underestimation

✓ Effort for training
✓ Effort for documentation
✓ Effort for error correction and quality assurance
✓ Communication problems

Fig. 1.10. Under- and overestimation factors

Underestimation of the following factors:

• Training effort (learning curve), especially concerning the training concepts and necessary know-how acquisition of staff when external staff is hired.

- Documentation effort – this is the first one to be reduced for cost savings – leading unavoidably to follow-up cost overruns as well as lack of quality. Thus, also head monopolies are promoted (knowledge is power).
- Effort for defect correction and quality assurance: especially C/S projects have an enlarged awareness for quality.
- Communication effort or communication problems especially in projects with special *management attention* (agreements, reporting) as well as with external consultants or customers.
- Costs and duration (as follow-up from the other underestimated parameters).
- Costs for hardware: if less than necessary hardware is purchased this leads to larger project duration and effort, since working conditions are more troublesome, defect rate increases, and motivation decreases.
- Costs for software and licenses as well as maintenance contracts.
- Costs for project management (approval process, team building, hiring of rooms and staff, contract negotiations, time- and status-reports, estimation, project planning, quality assurance, controlling, reporting).
- Especially surplus effort in C/S projects for new software releases occurring more often as in host environment.
- Effort for test preparation, test performance, and after-test documentation and reordering, especially for the integration test.
- Effort for preparation and performance of new releases of software including (organizational and technical) interfaces. Sometimes old functionality can be lost in new releases and sometimes this leads to substantially more effort.
- Effort for interfaces with other organizational units or projects.
- Necessary new staff in computing center by creeping demand for more people due to large projects for supporting them during project duration as well as for the follow-up maintenance of the produced applications.

Overestimation

It is commonplace for at least two factors to be overestimated in practice: i) quality of the team and ii) influence of tools. An IT project with a team size of 20 instead of 10 persons will not necessarily be finished in half the time. The causes are the non-linear relationship of people to work effort, and the different qualifications of the people and unavoidable communication and frictional losses within a larger number of people. These effects are known since long but are often underestimated in estimations. An additional effect is that *software developers are often optimistic about their own efficiency.* At the end, these overestimations lead unavoidably to underestimation of the effort for defect removal and quality assurance measures.

Much the same grandiose optimism is shown when new development tools and methods are implemented in an organization. Then, the estimators often forget that the development productivity merely increases by short-term usage of new tools. On the contrary, a programmer with 20-years experience in COBOL is surely not more productive in the beginning by using object-oriented analysis and design methods and a new programming environment, for e.g., SmallTalk. The effort for training and the necessary time for the integration of the new methods and tools in his skills are often underestimated, and the learning curve is ignored.

We can summarize that an overestimation of effort-relevant factors results in the underestimation of IT projects.

Weltz and Ortmann found in a survey about the causes for immense underestimations of costs and time for software development projects, which are presented in the following core statements:

- The misestimations affect organizations with few experiences in software engineering as well as organizations with long-time excellent and IT experience.
- A minority of organizations use formalized systematic methods. An example for this would be the FPM combined with estimations by an expert system and the integration of this in the formalized software engineering life cycle.
- Most of the organizations estimate with the *PI Times Thumb Method* (see chapter "Estimation Methods, Heuristic Methods, The PI Times Thumb Method"). Usually this method estimates the average of a worst-case estimation and a best-case estimation. Bases for these estimations are normally the individual experiences of – mostly only one – the estimating person. When this person leaves the organization, the estimation know-how leaves too (head monopoly).
- In organizations with long-time excellent and IT experience as well as in organizations with less systematic estimations occur extreme discrepancies between estimation and actual effort. But the differences are less in the first-named organizations.
- Organizations using formalized methods often do this not consequently. Sometimes at the start of the project the size was estimated (e.g., with the FPM), but it was neglected during project progression that the size can vary considerably due to the requirements creep. A continual and periodic estimation throughout the project life cycle was nearly never found.

David Locke reports in an investigation of the Compass benchmarking database that almost all IT projects were underestimated. They consumed in average about 30% more effort. This effort in excess could not even be explained with a requirements creep of 5%.

As a single improvement, it can be recommended to start with the elaboration of checklists and collection of costs according to the items in the checklists, e.g.,

- Cost of investments
- Cost of depreciation
- Cost of staff

- Cost of integration of standard software (customization of Enterprise Resource Planning (ERP) Systems)
- Other important items mentioned in this chapter.

Another critical success factor for estimating success is the estimation conference.

1.2.6 The Estimation Conference

Estimations can be done by different individuals and the average of their estimate can be used. But there exists a proven alternative: an estimation conference. Several persons from the project team (e.g., leaders of parts of the project) discuss together on how to estimate the estimation object in view of the total IT project. *This leads to an estimate that is accepted by all involved persons*, which is more objective than the aforementioned average, and hence can be better defended against other opinions. The results may not differ widely, as we found in some cases.

Another benefit of the estimation conference is that the involved estimators gain awareness of the uncertainties and possible risks of the IT project. Furthermore, everyone involved gets the same information. *An estimation conference is a team-building experience and fosters risk awareness!*

Accomplishing this estimation conference together with the end users motivates them to cooperate and become more engaged, and thus helps to improve the user satisfaction. This is an important project success factor!

An estimation conference also promotes the estimation culture in an organization, since it helps to solve acceptance problems by finding a consensus through discussions in a team. *These benefits can often be gained in a 2-hour estimation conference!*

1.2.7 Estimation Honesty

Estimation is a process that is closely bound up with resistance: not wanting to estimate, not wanting to commit oneself, and, last but not least, not wanting to be measurable. To overcome these acceptance problems, estimations should never and by no means be used in relation to people but only in relation to processes or products. This is the cause of the question of estimation honesty: one estimation for the steering committee, one for the boss, and one that the project team can live with (and meet).

Project managers often do not like to estimate because they like to map the progress of their project. This desire can only be overcome by education and repeated information about the benefits of estimation. It is evident for project mangers that their acceptance of an estimate is their commitment and that their success will be measured by achieving this goal. A possible motivation in this case is a financial bonus for success.

On the other hand, organizations must clearly express their opinion about the sense of manipulated estimations or lies on time sheets or unrealistic Gantt charts or time schedules.

1.2.8 Estimation Culture

A lasting estimation culture can only be fostered if the estimation process is clearly defined and transparently performed and thus estimation honesty is promoted. The development of an estimation culture evolves in following phases:

1. *Problem*: Estimation is not viewed positively.
2. *Awareness:* Management and staff become increasingly aware of the estimation theme yet do not start to handle it systematically.
3. *Transition*: Transition from viewing estimation as management task to viewing it as a team task.
4. *Anticipation*: Transition from subjective estimation to measuring and use of metrics and tools.
5. *Chances*: Positive vision of estimation; everybody is responsible for it.

A good estimation culture can prevent management and project leaders from playing political games with estimation and promotes motivated and effective project teams. A good estimation culture is also a positive vision of estimation, which is the responsibility of every team member. Its foundation can be built by sound training.

Introduction of Estimation - Fostering Estimation Culture

✓ Concrete consciousness for the problems of estimation
✓ Plan and control the project through the introduction of estimation processes
✓ Appropriate consideration of the required level of accuracy and precision
✓ Promote motivation and acceptance
✓ Foster estimation honesty and an estimation culture
✓ Training, information and participation of all involved persons
✓ Organize know how transfer and exchange of experiences

Fig. 1.11. Estimation culture

Figure 1.11 comprises the most important tasks for the installation of esti-mation as well of the fostering of an estimation culture.

1.2.9 Training for Estimation

Training for estimation occurs primarily through the exchange of experiences and lectures, workshops at congresses of IT metrics associations. Consultants and trainers are often members of metrics associations and offer training for all aspects of estimation. Many organizations arrange courses for their staff from these consultants or training institutes.

Estimation is often (only) a part of project management training (sometimes not even this). The same holds for (the passive training medium) books. An intermediate approach is interactive learning programs.

The International Function Point User Group (IFPUG), as well as the COSMIC consortium, and the Dutch NESMA, (IT metrics organizations), each offer certi-fications for various methods (the IFPUG Function Point Method, COSMIC Method, and the NESMA Function Point Method, respectively). The FiSMA (Finnish Software Measurement Association) has published solid guidelines for its FiSMA 1.1 FSM method and finds that the consistency of counting is high enough without needing practitioners to be certified.

1.3 A Checklist for Estimating

Figure 1.12 comprises the most important steps to be taken during estimations.

Professional Estimation principles

- ✓ First measure the components (input variables), then estimate (define object of estimation)
- ✓ Revise estimates as conditions change (as more information is known or when scope changes)
- ✓ Multiple estimates should be done in different ways (micro and macro estimating) to mitigate risks of using wrong assumptions
- ✓ Document estimates and the process in a transparent manner
- ✓ Avoid common estimation errors: especially over/under estimation
- ✓ Calculate the effect of historical requirements (scope) creep
- ✓ Control the project according to the estimate

Fig. 1.12. Professional estimation

Figure 1.13 shows what has to be regarded for the efficient organization of estimations.

In summary, the estimation problem can be characterized by the theses of Fig. 1.14.

Efficient Organization of Estimations

✓ Plan effort and resources to conduct the estimating
✓ Collect effort data (prerequisite data base, problem of missing historical data)
✓ Use estimation methods (comparability, standardization)
✓ Use tool support
✓ Perform estimation reviews (fosters team building and consensus)
✓ Collect experiences and results, and document and investigate them
✓ Learn from experiences and results (benchmarking)

Fig. 1.13. Efficient organization of estimation

Formal software estimation - a win-win proposition

✓ Estimation must be performed professionally!
✓ Software projects can be estimated accurately!
✓ The estimation and the necessary time for it must be planned from very beginning!
✓ Firefighting can be amazing, but the practice leads to burnout and doesn't help to prevent future fires, nor does it help to significantly save costs or reduce time to market!
✓ Formal estimating techniques provide an alternative for people who are tired of firefighting and who want to plan and effectively manage their software projects!

Fig. 1.14. The estimation challenge

1.4 Internet Links for Software Measurement Associations and Estimation

The following information resources on the Internet – given in Table 1.2 – are recommended for further reading:

Table 1.2. Further information resources in internet

Source	WWW link
DASMA e.V. Deutschsprachige *A*nwendergruppe für *S*oftware-*M*etrik und *A*ufwandschätzung e.V. – German metrics organization	http://www.dasma.org
ESI The *E*uropean *S*oftware *I*nstitute, Spanish	http://www.esi.es
FiSMA, Finnish Software Measurement Association	http://www.fisma.fi
Fraunhofer Institute (IESE) in Karlsruhe, Germany (Prof. Dieter Rombach, Chairman)	http://www.iese.fhg.de
GI-Fachgruppe 2.1.10 Software-Messung und -Bewertung Research Laboratory of Prof. Dumke and the German GI metrics group	http://ivs.cs.uni-magdeburg.de/sw-eng/us/
IFPUG *I*nternational *F*unction *P*oint *U*sers *G*roup	http://www.ifpug.org
MAIN – Metrics Association's International Network Network of European metrics organizations	http://www.mai-net.org
NESMA Metrics organization of The Netherlands	http://www.nesma.nl/ http://www.nesma.org
SEI – Software Engineering Institute, Carnegie Mellon University, Pittsburgh, PA, USA	http://sei.cmu.edu
UKSMA- United Kingdom Software Metrics Association	http://www.uksma.co.uk/
UQAM Research Laboratory of the University of Quebec, Montreal, PQ, Canada	http://saturne.info.uqam.ca/recherche/index.html
University of Southern California, – Sunset Center (COCOMO II)	http://sunset.usc.edu/research/COCOMOII/

1.5 Management Summary

Every IT project should commence with an estimation of effort, cost, schedule dates, and duration, as a basis of project planning, as well as for the measurement of project success during the project postmortem.

Paradoxically, project leaders do not measure adequately either at the beginning or during their projects, yet it is precisely the measurement activity and resultant numbers that create a project conscience.

The lack of quantification of project progress hinders the ability of even the best project manager to react and recover because often they will not detect in time an out-of-control project.

Estimates are most relevant and demanded at a point in time when there is a minimal of measurable information (at project initiation), and when one is able to perform the estimation with absolute exactness (at project postmortem) it is no longer required.

Even the best method(s), without tool support, have only scanty chances for survival.

Automated support for project estimating is a critical time-saver that can overcome the resistance and skepticism to embrace the processes.

Further to the three prerequisites, it is the authors' experiences that software estimating and metrics initiatives succeed more often when there is the support of a Competence Center.

It is generally understood that the size of the object of estimation (i.e., the size of the software application or the size of the construction project as applicable) is one of the most important correlation factors that drive project effort and productivity! Hence, the measurement of such size is a major core discipline of IT project planning!

Hence, in this book estimation is always understood to be based on a measurable size of the object of estimation.

The choices of the development platform and the programming language are two of the strongest drivers of the development effort.

Size measurement and estimation are two consecutive, but clearly dependent tasks to be performed during effort estimation.

It will come as no surprise that the estimation process must be trustworthy from a business perspective, and the results from each step of the estimating process must clearly document the input values and assumptions made, because important investment and project budget decisions will be based on them.

The whole estimation process must be auditable!

Auditability and traceability are also valid to document for each of the partial processes.

The strength of a project estimate is only as reliable as that of the weakest partial process involved.

Work tends to consume all available time.

To make sense of historical project data, one MUST know the context from which it came.

Estimates are generally rounded up or down (significant value simply non-existent precision).

Note that while an estimate can be rounded down, it is generally more dangerous because seldom does an IT project take less time than anticipated!

Estimation of IT projects precludes that more or less information is known about the object to be estimated.

The purpose of estimation is to understand and appropriately apply known effort drivers to our project in order to make better decisions.

The more there is information available for an estimate the more precise the estimate can be.

Requirements creep negatively correlates to a clear definition of objectives. Hence, the clearer are the objectives of an IT project, the fewer requirements creep will occur.

Only by continuous tracking of counts, estimates, and changes can meaningful target values for project planning be achieved.

Without measurement, it is difficult to detect and uncover problems early enough – before the project becomes out of control.

Measurement fosters knowledge, since the better we can express something with figures, the better we understand it.

A prerequisite to effective project management is that the estimates are formally documented and controlled.

Measurement is a valuable and a necessary prerequisite to avoid estimation problems.

Non-existent documentation of the development environment and estimating assumptions can hinder learning and improvement of estimation a priori.

Estimation without information about what is included in the estimate is worthless.

Only repeated estimations can help to gain experiences with requirements creep.

Only controllable estimates deliver the chance for comparisons and thus enable a feed forward (learning from past estimations for future estimations).

The process of estimation is no substitute for the determination of the effort parameters, which have to be done by the person responsible for planning.

Parallel projects should not be compared. This leads easily to manipulation of the method to be better (on the paper) as compared with another project.

Sometimes regret costs more than learning and performing professional estimates would have cost. Only one abandoned project is sufficient to prove this, since the costs for one failed project are more than the costs for the implementation of an estimation process. Moreover, estimating processes deliver a better basis to control IT projects and reduce the risk of failures.

Goal conflicts often arise from vanity.

It is commonplace for at least two factors to be overestimated in practice: these influences include quality of the team and influence of tools.

An estimation conference is a team-building experience and fosters risk awareness!

To overcome these acceptance problems, estimations should never and by no means be used in relation to people but only in relation to processes or products.

A lasting estimation culture can only be fostered if the estimation process is clearly defined and transparently performed and thus estimation honesty is promoted.

A good estimation culture can prevent management and project leaders from playing political games with estimation and promotes motivated and effective project teams.

Hopefully you are already embracing the fact that changes in your estimating processes can be good, and that better software estimates and project management are possible given industry-proven techniques and approaches to software estimation.

2 Estimation Fundamentals

This chapter introduces an estimation framework to enable the reader to position estimation in project management, project control, and quality assurance. The reader will also become acquainted with the characteristic parameters of estimation.

Objectives of organizations to survive in the market today can all be derived from quality, productivity, and predictability. Quality pertains to the effectiveness of the processes (doing the right processes) and the product (building the right product). Productivity and predictability both pertain to the efficiency of the processes used to develop the product. *Hence, estimation will be an essential part of project management* and must be regarded in the complete context mentioned earlier. *Project management without estimation (often justified because it seems to be too time consuming) is like driving a car without planning to refuel along the way.* Typically, project management falls into two main types:

1. Strategic project management
2. Operative project management.

Strategic project management organizes the overall life cycle development of all IT projects of an organization. Synonymously it is called program management or project portfolio management. Conversely, operative project management concentrates on a single project level. The major components of both kinds of project management include the following from the Project Management Institute Project Management Body of Knowledge (PMBOK®) Guide):

1. *Project Initiation.*
2. *Project planning (including Project Estimation) provides the basis for the main tools of project control.* As a project progresses, it tends to deviate from plans. To avoid this entropy and to stay on a goal-oriented direction it is necessary to have a detailed plan.
3. *Project execution.*
4. *Project Control.*
5. *Project Closing provides the basis on which project actual hours and other project lessons should be recorded for historical purposes and use on future*

projects. Note that the PMBOK does not explicitly prescribe the data collection at the end of a project, rather it specifies that the project have a formal end (the closing). The authors advocate the northernSCOPE(TM) concepts (www.fisma.fi/in-english/scopemanagement) that organizational learning (via the collection of project actuals at the close of the project) is an important corporate best practice.

Estimation is the foundation of viability assessment of IT projects. The tools of estimation include e.g., cost benefit analysis, Functional Size Measurement, assessment of non-functional requirements (quality requirements), and a myriad of diverse estimation methods.

The distinction between operative and strategic project management must also be made for its subtasks. Hence, there exists *operative and strategic project control* as well as *operative and strategic estimation*.

2.1 Estimation in a Project Controlling Environment

The traditional tasks associated with project control are as follows:

1. Planning (determination of metrics)
2. Information gathering
3. Control
4. Steering.

Exactly these are the core functions of operative project control within operative project management.

Its task is to deliver to the project management the necessary information about project progress:

- At the right time
- Condensed (in summary form)
- Problems and how they can be adequately addressed.

Hence, it has to perform the following tasks:

1. Definition of the effort targets for IT project subtasks based on sound and professional estimating (planning task)
2. Continuous measurement of actual effort for the subtasks of the IT project (information gathering)
3. Continuous comparison of actual effort versus planned effort during project progress (control)
4. Analysis of causes for eventual deviations and recommendations for the actualization of the project plans (steering).

These tasks belong in the context of the cybernetic control circuit (see also "The Cybernetic Estimation Control Circuit" part of this chapter) of project management. Estimation gets its strategic or long-term character through the capability to provide experiences of the past for the improvement of future estimations. This is part of organizational development whereby lessons of the past are used to master the future (*feed forward*). In strategic estimation, this is accomplished by documentation of the estimate and analysis of this documentation for the development of IT metrics and benchmarking. Estimation is the sound foundation of planning and thus also the foundation of project control.

In reference to the many surveys that showed evidence that only a marginal number of IT projects that were started were actually finished on time and within budget one has to conclude: "*Anyone who does not perform the project management task of estimation could be considered as acting grossly negligent!* "

The same premise holds for the project management task of *documentation* (see also the chapter "The Estimation Challenges, Documentation").

In particular, the measurement of project size as a basis for estimation additionally delivers the benefit of providing an objective requirements review for the IT project.

Documentation (also of estimates) is important to be able to quantify and understand the system to be developed. Only with this prerequisite is it possible to extract basic experiences that can be integrated into the project management manual. This is an important prerequisite for organizational learning. If the functional size measurement fails because documentation is not available (i.e., either not existing, not actual, or indecipherable) or there is a lack of know-how on the IT project, then it can be concluded that the requirements analysis is not yet complete. *Alternatively, it is an important early warning sign that shows that the IT project has lost its bearing so early in its lifecycle.*

2.1.1 Adjusting the Estimate to Take into Account Project Environment Factors

A number of factors from the environment of IT projects have an enormous influence on the actual effort and hence must be considered by the project leader as input to the estimate. These factors must be taken into account at the level of project tasks where they can be used to adjust and enable the development of sound estimates. Some of these factors are as follows:

- The development environment and platform such as PC, mainframe, Client/ Server, Expert System,...)
- The development language (Assembler, Cobol, C++, Program Generator, Java, SQL,...)

- The run-time environment (DB2, CICS, IMS, Data Warehouse, Internet, Intranet,...)
- The project classification (new development, enhancement, maintenance, strategic IT project,...)
- The project class (large system, interactive database application, standard software, system software, query system, cash system, online/batch proportions of applications,...)
- Complexity of the IT project (data-, code-, and functional complexity, number and type of interfaces,...)
- Regulations for quality and security standards (four eye principle, test concept, software engineering process model,...)
- Restrictions by law, technique, or organization
- Project novelty (First use of new methods, processes, tools, software, languages, platforms, ...)
- Support of the IT project by managers, users, union, ...
- Large number of interfaces or new customers (literature: +25%)
- Project duration (literature: more than 6 months +15%, more than 12 months + 30%, more than 18 months + 50%)
- Clarity of responsibilities in the IT project
- Open-plan office (literature: +25% to +30%)
- Experience of the project leader in estimation
- Skill of project team (experts, beginners, mix)
- Team size (in each project phase)
- Availability and time restriction of people, especially of crucial experts
- Business/industry type (military, banking, avionics, government, ...).

Table 2.1. Factors influencing software engineering estimation

Technology	Product	Development process	Resources
Technical development platform	Functionality	Process organization	Hardware availability
Hardware (and software)	Quality	Software engineering process model	Software availability
Software	Complexity	Methods	Staff availability
Technical standards	Documentation	Project duration	Staff quality
Tools	Restrictions by law	Interfaces	Costs (budget)
Technical requirements	Project classification	Goals	Organizational restrictions
Technical run-time environment	Project class	Organizational development environment	Project calendar

Table 2.1 shows a structured overview of some of such influential factors but cannot compete with the nearly 100–200 such parameters administered in commercially available estimation tools. Only the use of such tools guarantees that

the estimator does not lose the overview when regarding a larger number of parameters for estimation.

Several estimation methods consider some of these factors of influence. The Function Point Method, e.g., uses 14 General System Characteristics (GSC); COCOMO II uses 22 factors, and FiSMA ND21 uses 21 factors for new product development. *Of these factors, the project objectives (goals for quality, scope, schedule, cost) have the most influence on project effort as well as on project success.*

2.1.2 Project Goals and the Devils Square of Project Management

Generally an IT project is characterized by unique conditions requiring special organizational measures (project management, management of crises, risk management) caused by its complexity. It has normally the following characteristics:

- There exists a clearly formulated and reachable goal.
- There exist time, financial, personnel, and/or other constraints as well as a high degree of innovation.
- The project has a clear demarcation to other tasks and projects and has a start date as well as a delivery deadline.

An IT project is a temporary set of activities with the goal to develop and install a software system. *The objectives of an IT project must be absolute and clearly defined, and the achievement of its targets must be measurable.* This is the main success criteria of an IT project. The goals can be differentiated into primary and secondary goals. *Primary goals* are as follows:

1. Quality
2. Size (Quantity)
3. Duration (Time)
4. Costs.

Possible *secondary goals* may be the following:

- A 25% staff reduction in the order management department
- Reduction of the maximum handling time of a customer claim to 24 h.

The primary goals unavoidably compete with each other for the resources of an IT project. Hence, every additional consumption of one resource leads to reduction in the availability of other resources. This effect is known as *the devils square of project management* (see Fig. 2.1). The example in Fig. 2.1 shows how size is reduced in order to gain more quality and reduce costs.

The devils square also highlights that estimation is the basis for a sound planning of quality, functional size, costs, and dates. How can you plan when you do not know the necessary effort? The problem of the project leaders in this context is that management expects them always to minimize costs and time while maximizing size and quality – an impossible task!

2.1.3 Estimation and Quality

The quality of a software product is measured by the degree to which it meets or exceeds the user requirements. The measurement of the functional size for estimation thus becomes of extraordinary significance.

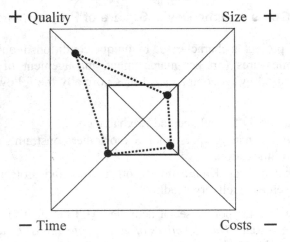

Fig. 2.1. The devils square of project management

The increasing acceptance of IT even in private life leads to increasing demands of high-quality software. This increased *quality consciousness* makes quality one of the most important goals of software development. The PMI (Project Management Institute) identifies quality as the center of the triple constraints triangle consisting of the following as the governing project constraints:

1. Scope (functionality)
2. Cost (budget)
3. Time (duration).

If one of the triple constraints or the quality requirements changes, the other constraints are affected. This directly affects project estimating because software development projects are always limited by budget (cost), time to market (duration), quality, and/or scope (functionality).

For example, once an estimate is made based on a given project scope, quality, budget, and duration, if the scope is increased – then it will affect the other components. Sometimes this is referred to as project tradeoffs because if the project scope changes and there is limited time and cost allocated for the project, the product quality will suffer. Similarly if the quality demands for a project increase after a project estimate is made, then the functionality (scope) must decrease in order to finish the project within the same timeline and cost structure.

There are a number of relevant and proven measures, methods, and techniques for software and software development quality improvement.

Today, quality is no coincidence, but rather it can and must be planned exactly into a product. Today, good quality is built into a product rather than poor quality detected out.

Quality management in IT projects consists of the following tasks:

- Quality planning
- Quality execution
- Quality control (measurement and tracking)
- Quality assurance.

The first two tasks are performed systematically by so-called *constructive quality assurance measures,* which secure quality a priori. Constructive quality assurance measures include the systematic use of methods, development tools, or standardized processes. Quality control is performed by *analytical quality assurance measures* in order to measure adherence to quality requirements or deviations thereof, and if necessary, to correct any gaps or detected defects.

The focus of these tasks centers on constructive quality assurance measures since *prevention is better than defect correction,* or, using a metaphor: *fire prevention is better than fire fighting.*

This premise is accompanied by the requirement to define quality goals for the software development process, which in turn must meet and exceed the quality goals of the software to be developed. Quality attainment is then measured by comparison of the goals for product quality and the actual quality features of the developed software. In IT projects, as part of the requirements, the quality attributes are defined at the start of the IT project, and become part of the input variable set to the estimation equation. This is a direct link to estimation. The ISO/IEC 9126 External Quality Attributes (see Fig. 2.2) identify the major aspects of product quality for the software to be developed, and each major area such as functionality is further subdivided in the ISO/IEC standard into individual quality characteristics.

2.1.4 ISO/IEC 9126 Quality Attributes and IFPUG GSC

The ISO/IEC 9126 Quality Attributes partially overlap with the 14 GSC of the IFPUG Function Point Method, which are used to adjust/modify the Functional

Size Measurement of the software to arrive at the adjusted Function Points for use in estimating. It is therefore obvious that an automatic interface should be created to avoid double work for the project leaders. A large organization developed the following Excel chart, which automatically calculates the quality

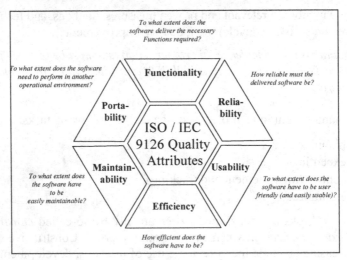

Fig. 2.2. The ISO/IEC 9126 quality attributes

IFPUG GSC's	Value	Adaptability	Usability	Efficiency	Functionality	Maintainability	Correctness	Portability	Stability	Security	Interoperability	Reusability	Reliability
	Value	3	2	2	3	2	2	3	2	3	2	1	2
Data communication	5	1			3		1				1		
Distributed Data Processing	4	2									9		
Performance	4			3	2								
Heavily Used Configuration	5			3						1			
Transaction Rate	0			3	2				1				2
Online Data Entry	5	1	1		3				2				2
End-User Efficiency	4		6										
Online Update	5						5			4			
Complex Processing	4				3		3			1			3
Reusability	2											7	
Installation Ease	4		1				4			2			2
Operational Ease	4						2			6	1		
Multiple Sites	5								8				
Facilitate Change	5	5	1										1
relative meaning		10,0%	8,9%	6,3%	9,8%	7,7%	8,4%	10,5%	7,9%	9,6%	8,4%	5,6%	7,0%
absolute meaning		43	38	27	42	33	36	45	34	41	36	24	30

Value:
High Average Low None
5   4-3   2-1   0   IFPUG
3   2   1   0   Q-

Ratings
High Average Low None
9-7   6-4   3-1   0

abs. rating — Value
45
41 — 3
40
27 — 2
26
6 — 1
5
0 — 0

Fig. 2.3. Mapping of the ISO/IEC quality attributes and IFPUG GSC

Table 2.2. Evaluation of IFPUG GSC and ISO/IEC quality attributes

General system characteristics	Mapped to the priority of the quality attribute
0	= No priority (0)
1 and 2	= Small priority (1)
3	= Medium priority (2)
4 and 5	= High priority (3)

attributes from the GSC and vice versa. The connection between the quality attributes and the GSC was ranked from 1 to 9 by the project team, where the sum of each column is 9. Thus, in Fig. 2.3 the quality attribute *Adaptability* (a quality characteristic in ISO/IEC 9126) is connected with the following IFPUG GSC (see column 1 in Fig. 2.3 and Table 2.2 for the mapping of the values):

- 1/9 with data communication
- 2/9 with distributed data processing
- 1/9 with online data entry
- 5/9 with facilitation of change.

The ISBSG (International Software Benchmarking Standards Group) book titled *Practical Project Estimation, 2nd edition*, identifies two alternative methods of addressing these non-functional or quality requirements for software. The first method identified is the COCOMO II set of factors, and the second is the Finnish Software Measurement Association (FiSMA) situation analysis called New Development 21 (ND21) factors (see www. fisma.fi for details).

A second determination factor, besides the classification of estimation into project controlling, is the consideration of its cybernetic control circuit features.

2.1.5 The Cybernetic Estimation Control Circuit

Estimation can be thought of as a cybernetic control circuit. This is an important feature *since control circuits are directable systems that can be controlled by feedback* that enables them to compensate disturbances influencing them. They are able to proceed in a state of equilibrium (called homeostasis) if there are no disturbances or influences exerted on them from the environment. *With the principal model of the cybernetic control circuit the behavior of complex systems can be understood, explained, and controlled.* For better understanding of the cybernetic control circuit of estimation the concept will be explained in more detail here.

Norbert Wiener coined the term *cybernetics* from the Greek word meaning *steersman*. He defined cybernetics as the science of communication and control in mechanisms, organisms, and society. Cybernetics is a general theory of control, a science of the behavior of adaptive complex systems having the important features of feedback and communication as well as information exchange.

A cybernetic control circuit consists of the following four components:

1. *Controller*: The Controller gets information about measures collected by the measurement component, produces decisions, and delivers objectives to the adjustment component. → In the special case of estimation, the controller delivers an estimate to the adjustment component for reaching this objective.
2. *Adjustment Component* (*Actuator*): The adjustment component accepts input from the controller, chooses measures for the mode of activity, and delivers these adjustment factors as (for the model understandable) signals to the object of control to cause changes in it. → In the special case of estimation, the actuator compares this objective with the knowledge base (historical data) and delivers an improved objective to the object of control.
3. *Object of Control* (*Model*): This is the regulating extension, the model that performs the given measures. It is the component where the cybernetic circuit can de disturbed by factors of influence from the environment. *The shorter is this regulating extension (e.g., time distance: early warning signals), the more modest are the measures for steering of the system.* → In the special case of estimation, the object of control sends notifications and data to the measurement component.
4. *Measurement Component*: The measurement component measures the degree of fulfillment of the objectives and accepts notifications telling it that the state of the model has changed. Data are retrieved from the model and used as feedback passed to the controller to further drive the model. → In the special case of estimation, the measurement component measures the actual state of the model, compares it with the objectives, and informs the controller about the deviations. The controller elaborates from this a new estimation and the circulation starts anew.

The whole process is called *feedback loop* and leads to a flexible balance (*homeostasis*), i.e., the system regulates itself when there are no disturbances affecting it. The user (not necessarily human) is not considered to be a component of the cybernetic control circuit but is part of the controller and constitutes the decision-making function that dynamically directs state changes in the model. Figure 2.4 visualizes the cybernetic control circuit of estimation.

The project tasks together with the objectives, the classification, type and class of the project, and project size are input for the controller where the objectives are defined. Furthermore, the controller produces decisions (output, initial value) – based on the comparison of actual versus planned measures from the measurement component – which are delivered to the actuator for comparison with the knowledge base. The actuator chooses a measure (estimated value) and delivers it to the model. This is the object of control and produces – with influences of outside disturbances from the environment – an actual value. This actual value is sent to the measurement component for measurement of the fulfillment

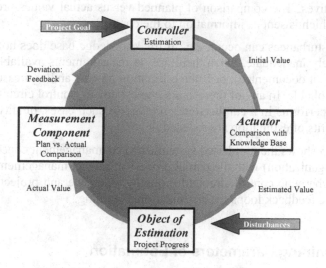

Fig. 2.4. The cybernetic control circuit of estimation

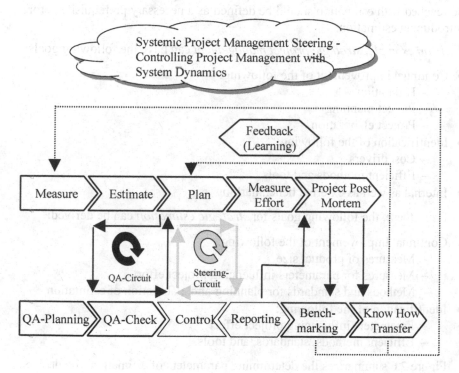

Fig. 2.5. Cybernetic control circuit for estimation

of the objectives. The comparison of planned versus actual values produces a deviation, which is sent as information to the controller.

Severe disturbances can occur, e.g., if the knowledge base does not exist or is qualitatively inadequate, when there are no measurements available (either not done or not documented), or if the estimation process and/or measurements are not controllable. In any of these cases, the cybernetic control circuit is interrupted or it performs in a cumbersome manner. In such cases, quality and the overall benefits of estimation are reduced.

Figure 2.5 shows the tool-based systemic project management concept (realized in an organization) with the partial process of project management and the imbedded cybernetic control circuits for quality assurance and project steering as well as the feedback loops for organizational learning.

2.2 Determining Parameters of Estimation

Strategic estimation is part of strategic project management. Hence, the goals to be reached with estimation should be defined as a necessary prerequisite before introducing estimation.

As an example, strategic project management can have the following goals:

- Continual improvement of the following:
  - Estimation
  - Project planning
  - Project elaboration
- Identification of the following:
  - Cost drivers
  - Efficient methods and tools
- Internal as well as external benchmarking

From these, the following goals for *strategic estimation* can be derived:

- Continual Improvement of the following:
  - Measures of product size
  - Measures for parameters influencing project effort
  - Methods and standards for planning and elaboration of estimation
- Identification of the following:
  - Parameters influencing project effort
  - Efficient methods, standards, and tools.

Figure 2.6 summarizes the determining parameters of estimation, the drivers, constraints, as well as the degrees of freedom. A connection with the devils square of project management can obviously not be neglected.

2.2.1 The Purpose of Estimation

The success of metrics implementation relies on how an organization assesses the principal question: "What (which IT metrics) shall we measure?" After sizing the product (functional size measurement), the effort to be expended shall be estimated in person months (or hours) using the size and additional estimation parameters. Next, the estimated effort is distributed across the phases of the project as the basis for project planning and scheduling. *For the total project plan, an estimate must also be made for the effort for project management and quality assurance. Often the project management and quality assurance efforts are overlooked or forgotten, and this leads to severe miscalculations and underestimating.*

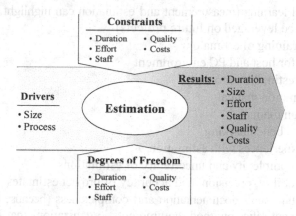

Fig. 2.6. The determining parameters of estimation

Last but not least, estimation contributes to making process improvements measurable. Process capability can be an abstract measure for many factors that influence process improvement. Process capability is a measure of the efficiency of the software development and is measured in effort hours per Function Point, also called PDR (Project Delivery Rate). Putnam and Myers estimate the annual process improvements of organizations with process improvement programs to about 13%. Other authors, including the Software Engineering Institute (SEI), estimate a time span of 2.5–4 years for doubling the process capability of an organization.

The SEI developed a software and systems process maturity model to evaluate the capability of an organization to build software and systems products. Originally, this model was called the Capability Maturity Model (CMM®) for software but today various maturity models for systems, acquisition, and other competencies were combined into what is now known as the Capability Maturity Model Integration or CMMI®. The CMMI® identifies five progressively mature levels of process capability or maturity for an organization, and the average time to ascend from one step or level to the next is ~18 months.

ISO/IEC developed a process improvement framework called SPICE: Software Process Improvement Capability Determination, which is now represented by a series of standards under the umbrella ISO/IEC 15504. CMMI® and SPICE are both examples of process maturity models.

2.2.2 The Goals of Estimation

The following goals can be reached using estimation methods:

- Holistic and integrated estimation process(es) for IT projects
- Organizational learning (measurement and estimation can highlight best practices that can be leveraged on future projects)
- Concept for training of estimators
- Tool support for host and PC environment
- Standardized estimation process
- Detailed estimation manual
- Documentation manual
- Foundation for benchmarking
- Transfer of experiences with estimation
- Reduction of complexity and uncertainty of estimations
- Increased reliability, precision, and accuracy of project estimates
- Improved requirements documentation and completeness (because functional size measurement relies on good requirements, organizations that implement function points often find that their requirements processes necessarily improve to facilitate the size measurement)
- Improvement of estimation exactness.

It does not matter if the IT projects are classified as new development, enhancement, or maintenance – the objectives that can be achieved are the same. Problems may arise when there are goal conflicts, since the estimators tend to think of estimation as being data-centric, whereas the managers are more likely resource-oriented, and the end users or project sponsors are more likely risk-oriented. *Acceptable estimations must consider and address all three perspectives (data-centric, resource-oriented, and risk-oriented).*

2.2.3 The Right Time for Estimation

Determining the right time for estimation is an important consideration for any organization interested in implementing formal estimating procedures. The timing parameter requires a lot of attention since it is the subject of an inherent goal conflict:

Early and precise estimations are necessary and desirable by software custo-mers; however, early estimations are necessarily imprecise and prone to a high degree of uncertainty.

This problem is aggravated by the following effect:
Estimation is done too early and far too seldom!

If one accepts that the precision of estimations at the beginning of an IT project is imperfect and insufficient, and it only increases as the project pro-gresses, then the logical consequence is that multiple estimates are necessary throughout the project. Estimates must be updated and revised whenever impor-tant influencing factors change.

In practice, an estimate is usually only done at the project start, and some-times at a project postmortem. Capers Jones stresses the impact of requirements (scope) creep as causing a 1–3% functional size increase *per month* of project duration.

Additional factors where estimate revisions are necessary include, for example, illness of key staff or resource reallocation. *If such changes are not con-sidered and actualized, the plan made from the original estimation will never be met.* It is critical to revise and repeat the estimation process during project progress especially when there is substantial scope creep or deviations from the project plan. To increase the chance of consensus about the future of the pro-ject, the customer should always be kept informed about changes to the esti-mates (because they reflect changed plans).

Figure 2.7 provides an overview of possible estimation milestones, where milestones 1–7 have the following meaning:

- *Milestone 1: End of Feasibility Study Phase*
  The idea or concept for a new project is constituted. There exists only little information about requirements details and thus Function Points can only be approximated (see chapter "Function Point Prognosis"). Effort estimates can be developed using a tool together with relevant historical data from comparable completed projects. In many companies, the project charter and a preliminary effort estimate are delivered at milestone 1.
- *Milestone 2: Project Start*
  At this point, further information about the project, its resource require-ments, and the possible timeframes exists. Furthermore, the IT project team, the development environment, and the programming language are typically known. Hence, a more detailed estimate derived using an estimating tool is possible.
  There still is not enough information available for a complete Function Point count. Hence, the first Function Point Prognosis should be actualized, and estimation with a tool should be done using the documented assump-tions for the project.

- *Milestone 3: End of Requirements Analysis*
- At milestone 3, there is now sufficient information for a complete Function Point count followed by documentation and estimation with an estimation tool. The GSCs are classified in an estimation conference as previously described.
- The actual data measured to date on the project become input for the estimation tool, and a revised/updated estimate is carried out on this basis. For tracking and organizational learning reasons, this estimate must be compared with the first estimate.
- *Milestones 4–6: End of IT Design until End of Project*
- Counting and Estimation are actualized at least at critical project dates and confirmed on phase transitions. Changes in the IT project become transparent and part of the process, and are documented to capture the data of the experience. Estimates are tracked continually. The actual measured effort is documented in an estimation tool at least at the end of each phase or preferably on a regular (weekly) basis.
- *Milestone 7: Project Postmortem*
- Here the main task is to collect information and experiences at project completion to improve the counting and estimation processes for subsequent projects. (One of the best ways to capture this data is to conduct a workshop about the experiences in this project.)
- In project postmortems the following effort components are frequently neglected: unpaid overtime, effort for project management, effort for quality assurance, effort for administrative tasks (all effort of the IT project) as well as effort of end users and technical specialists not belonging to the core team. To improve and learn from your own completed projects, it is essential to have a record of all expended project effort so that future projects can gain from the knowledge of complete project data.

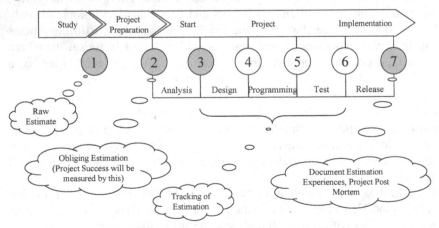

Fig. 2.7. Milestones for estimations in IT projects

The project postmortem must elaborate the realistic amounts for efforts occurring on a one-time basis such as migrations (data conversions) or test drivers (documented separately), as well as effort supplied externally (documented separately). Preferably, this task will be carried out with the assistance of the competence center. It will actualize the metrics for the experience curve as well as IT metrics standards. A competence center will take this data and subsequently use it to determine the productivity measures and other IT metrics. From the viewpoint of estimation the reader is directed to the appendix where we have included a useful checklist for project postmortem of IT projects.

2.2.4 Tracking of Estimates

In its estimation tracking manual, the Software Engineering Laboratory (SEL) of the NASA asks its managers to perform estimates at least six times during the project duration. Each time the estimate for the remaining project work is multiplied with different lower and upper control limits in order to give an interval for the estimate uncertainty at the particular milestone. Table 2.3 shows these multiplication factors.

Table 2.3. Add-ons of the SEL (NASA) for estimate uncertainty

Milestone	Upper control limit	Lower control limit
End of rough requirements concept	×2	×0.5
End of detailed requirements concept	×1.75	×0.57
End of rough IT design	×1.4	×0.71
End of detailed IT design	×1.25	×0.8
End of programming	×1.1	×0.91
End of testing	×1.05	×0.95

For the continuous tracking of estimates, it is advisable to set up a catalogue of continuous activities such as the following:

1. An annual index of applications, projects, and base values to be measured.
2. This registry must only contain objectively measurable data, which must be measured when they occur. In addition to measured values, estimated values must also be recorded. All data must be documented at different aggregation levels to enable later drill down queries into project details. Basic data (esti-mated, planned, and actual) are, e.g., start date, end date, size (in Function Points or SLOC), number of defects, effort by phase, effort of end users, IT and support.
3. For each of these items, a baseline has to be calculated.
4. A comparison of the baseline with the preceding year(s) in order to recognize changes and tendencies.

The following checklist comprises the most important milestones for estimation:

- End of feasibility study
  - Rough estimate based on already known information
  - Depending on estimated project size, add in ~10–30% for each of the following project add-ons: risk, uncertainty, and requirements creep
- Start of project
  - Detailed estimates should be checked by a second estimating professional (e.g., expert estimation). The result becomes the basis for later measurements of the success of the project.
- End of Requirements Analysis
  - Function Point count, project internal estimation conference
- End of each project phase
  - Actualization of the Function Point count due to the requirements creep
- Project postmortem
  - Measurement of success of the IT project
  - Actualization of IT metrics data and repository
  - Workshop for know-how transfer
- Annual baseline and time series.

Project postmortem should be carried out in a meeting documenting all important information about the project, including measures leading to project success as well as those not so successful. *It must be absolutely avoided to search for culprits and attribute blame. Project postmortems are an important prerequisite to foster learning for the future (feed forward).* For this reason, the project postmortem information should be readily available for electronic access.

2.3 Management Summary

Estimation is an essential part of project management and must be regarded in the complete context mentioned earlier. Project management without estimation (often justified because it seems to be too time consuming) is like driving a car without planning to refuel along the way.

Estimation is the foundation of viability assessment of IT projects.

Estimation gets its strategic or long-term character through the capability to provide experiences of the past for the improvement of future estimations. This is part of organizational development whereby lessons of the past are used to master the future (feed forward).

Estimation is the sound foundation of planning and thus also the foundation of project control.

Anyone who does not perform the project management task of estimation could be considered as acting grossly negligent!

In particular, the measurement of project size as a basis for estimation additionally delivers the benefit of providing an objective requirements review for the IT project.

The objectives of an IT project must be absolute and clearly defined, and the achievement of its targets must be measurable. This is the main success criteria of an IT project.

The primary goals unavoidably compete with each other for the resources of an IT project. Hence, every additional consumption of one resource leads to reduction in the availability of other resources. This effect is known as the devils square of project management.

The quality of a software product is measured by the degree to which it meets or exceeds the user requirements. The measurement of the functional size for estimation thus becomes of extraordinary significance.

Today, quality is no coincidence, but rather it can and must be planned exactly into a product. Today good quality is built into a product rather than poor quality detected out.

Estimation can be thought of as a cybernetic control circuit. This is an important feature since control circuits are directable systems that can be controlled by feedback that enables them to compensate disturbances influencing them. They are able to proceed in a state of equilibrium (called homeostasis) if there are no disturbances or influences exerted on them from the environment. With the principal model of the cybernetic control circuit, the behavior of complex systems can be understood, explained, and controlled.

The whole process is called feedback loop and leads to a flexible balance (homeostasis), i.e., the system regulates itself when there are no disturbances affecting it.

The success of metrics implementation relies on how an organization assesses the principal question: *What (which IT metrics) shall we measure?*

For the total project plan, an estimate must also be made for the effort for project management, and quality assurance. Often the project management and quality assurance effort is overlooked or forgotten, and this leads to severe miscalculations and underestimating.

Early and precise estimations are necessary and desirable by software customers; however, early estimations are necessarily imprecise and prone to a high degree of uncertainty.

Estimation is done too early and far too seldom!

Capers Jones stresses the impact of requirements (scope) creep as causing a 1–3% functional size increase per month of project duration.

The project postmortem must elaborate the realistic amounts for efforts occurring on a one-time basis such as migrations (data conversions or test drivers documented separately), as well as effort supplied externally (documented separately). Preferably, this task will be carried out with the assistance of the competence center.

In its estimation tracking manual, the SEL of the NASA asks its managers to perform estimates at least six times during the project duration.

For the continuous tracking of estimates, it is advisable to set up a catalogue of continuous activities.

It must be absolutely avoided to search for culprits and attribute blame. Project postmortems are an important prerequisite to foster learning for the future (feed forward).

3 Prerequisites for Estimation

"Estimation must be performed in a professional manner." *You have already heard this over and over in the previous two chapters; however, the point is so important that is bears repeating*: *Estimating without history is simply an opinion!*

Hence, estimation and the formal process to determine it must be carefully planned. When one takes into consideration that 60–99% of software defects post-production (i.e., in commercial off-the-shelf (COTS) software) can be attributed to poor requirements, one can easily digest the importance of clear requirements and estimation formality as predictors of project success. Besides that, estimating principles and assumptions must be documented for each estimate in order to make sense of the estimate itself. To provide knowledge for laying the fundamentals of estimation, this chapter discusses the information prerequisites (what *MUST* be known) in order to even attempt formal estimation as well as the prerequisites of the process of estimation.

3.1 The Information Basis of Estimation

In order to perform solid estimation, one necessarily needs information about the object of estimation (e.g., WHAT requirements the software product must deliver). Without such information, estimation is only a modified type of Las Vegas-style gambling.

3.1.1 Prerequisites for Estimation

The following rules should be considered when preparing an estimate (sarcastic comment: SURPRISE! yes, estimations should be prepared!):

- An estimate can only be carried out when at least a minimum of project requirements are known. *The clearer the objectives for the software product, the more precise the results will be.*
- *The estimate must be done by persons with sufficient knowledge about the requirements under consideration.* In an ideal situation, the software developers perform this assessment together (or in close cooperation) with the

users and are supported by a competence center. Ideally, this takes the form of an estimation conference. (see Chap. 1: "The Estimation Conference").

- When estimating the project requirements at an early (preliminary estimate) stage, the estimate should not be broken down into too much detail since *the overall application/project requirements should be in the focus.* In other words, the focus of early estimates should be to deliver at least the minimum product within the user constraints of budget (cost), time to market (duration), resources (team size), quality (how *good* the product must be), and scope (functionality to be delivered).
- Because the Function Point Method provides a measure of the functionality of a software product, it cannot be used when estimating on module level or program level, as such granularity is simply not intended by the model. When misused to estimate technologically dependent module- or program-level estimates, the result will be inaccurate. This is similar to using square feet (or square meters) of a floor plan to estimate the amount of time or effort to install wiring in a single wall – it would not result in an accurate micro-level estimate. This is because the square area of a floor plan reflects the size of an entire project or floor plan, and the estimating models based on such areas are unsuitable for use by a particular tradesman working with a small (sub) portion of the work.
- The contributions of the total set of *users* (the definition of user in the context of this book is similar to actors in the context of use cases – being any person or thing that requires particular functionality from software or any person who specifies functional requirements) are often overlooked.
- When using the Function Point Method *the object of estimation has to be seen from the view of the users* (as outlined in the previous point), and not from the view of the IT staff. *This is the most important rule: functional size measurement emphasizes the functional USER requirements, and this point cannot be stressed enough.*

The next paragraphs describe the topics, tasks, and processes necessary to be carried out before the actual estimation is done. Information about the content of effort and about time accounting is discussed, as well as structuring the application to be developed and the documentation of the development environment.

3.1.2 Prerequisites for Estimation of Effort

Before carrying out an estimation, it must be agreed and defined what is the effort to be estimated and how it will be measured.

IBM, e.g., estimates the effort of the following phases 1–4 using the Function Point Method per the International Function Point Users Group (IFPUG) Function Point counting rules:

- Phase 1: Requirements analysis and design of solution
  - Analyze user requirement
  - Define interfaces
  - Evaluate the requirements
  - Develop proposal of organizational solution
- Phase 2: Specification of the application
  - Discuss and agree on user requirements in detail
  - Office desk test, walk through
  - System architecture
  - Hardware-, software- requirements
  - Proposal for technical solution
- Phase 3: Technical development
  - Programming
  - Module test
  - Integration test
- Phase 4: Installation and release of the system
  - System test under productive conditions
  - Release to end user.

Note that the feasibility analysis phase and the installation rollout of the software are NOT part of the phases included in this model. It is critical that the phases of a development project be known both for the project to be estimated AND for any projects used as comparison projects – in order to facilitate an "applies to apples" (consistent) comparison. The ESA database also known as the European Space Agency database uses person months (consisting of 144 person hours per person month) and measures the effort from the delivery of the requirements concept through to acceptance by the customer (i.e., first install).

Whereas COCOMO II uses person months with 152 person hours and measures all project effort, including interface-, management- as well as administration- effort. The importance of these various models to the estimating professional is that the included phases determine the included work effort. As such, we always want to ensure that we are performing an apples to apples comparison in all aspects of the estimating process when we use historical projects as a basis for an estimate.

The ISBSG benchmarking database uses only person hours and assumes the inclusion of overtime work (paid as well as unpaid) and effort of the end users from feasibility study through to delivery (inclusive of training).

3.1.3 Time Accounting

A standardized measurable unit for the effort must be defined in order to compare the development project effort to that of other IT projects. The definition of this base unit of effort, in terms of *hours* – the time accounting, is of central importance. Otherwise, a direct comparison is only possible using hours worked (person hour = 1-hour work of one person without any break).

The project effort is measured in person hours, person months, or person years with the preferable unit being person hours because it entails less subjectivity of units. Two models are shown to demonstrate that comparability is only possible by stating the measurement unit used.

Table 3.1. Example time accounting

Measurement Unit	Model 1	Model 2	
		Gross	Net
1 person month	= 130 person hours	= 160 person hours	= 120 person hours
1 person year	= 1,560 person hours	= 1,920 person hours	= 1,440 person hours

Table 3.1 demonstrates that model 1 is more similar to the net version of model 2 than the gross. Net versions are based on the management experience that staff are usually only available for 70–80% of their overall working hours (about 1,900 h a year) for project work. This will vary worldwide depending on the customs and legal prescriptions of the jurisdiction (e.g., it is standard to work 35 h per week with 6 weeks standard vacation in Finland; however, in the USA the standard work week is a minimum of 40 h with 2–3 weeks standard vacation). The remaining 20–30% of working hours is used for holidays, and work not related directly to the IT project such as training, sickness, information sessions from management, personnel discussions with the boss, reading, etc.

The aforementioned definitions are only two out of many variations. *It is important that a consistent definition for units of work effort be made and communicated.* For example, the reduction of 25% of the gross working time can be defined for the person months. Thus, a person year has 9 effective person-months instead of 12 months (see Table 3.2). Other variations can also be possible based on accounting models. The reduction could be made for the person days (thus a person month has 15 instead of 20 person days, see Table 3.3), or for the person hours (a person day has then 6 instead of 8 working hours, see Table 3.4).

The choice of a suitable variation and unit is not without problems: *the safest is the usage of person hours,* since this is the smallest unit that can be documented, and there does not exist any conversion difference (e.g., in industry a person *year* can vary from 1,680 h (12 months × 4 weeks per month × 35 h per week) to upward of 1,800 h – depending on the jurisdiction or country. Note that these hours are *raw* available hours and do not take into account unproductive (e.g., sickness, vacation, etc.) hours. But the usage of person hours can be uncomfortable on large projects where it is often easier to use person days or person months. A problem occurs when person hours have to be converted into larger units. As Table 3.5 demonstrates, there can be differences of 25% or more depending on the accounting method. If an IT project has been estimated to cost 5 million dollars, a difference of 25% would amount to 1.25 million dollars! Conversely, if person months is used as the *standard* unit of measure, one must use caution to ensure that the appropriate hours per person month are consistently applied.

Choosing one or the other units of measure (person hours or person months) does not cause any problems as long as effort figures are only compared to projects that use the same model. However, it can become dangerous and misleading on contracts with suppliers, external software providers, or with external benchmarking services. It is particularly questionable to use historical data when the underlying, relevant accounting model is unknown.

Hence, effort figures must also supply the units of measure and associated assumptions according to a particular time accounting model – otherwise the effort numbers are rendered useless.

In Tables 3.2–3.5, the following abbreviations are used: *PY* person year, *PM* person month, *PD* person day, *PH* person hour.

Table 3.2. Accounting model 1

	PY	PM	PD	PH
PY	1	9	180	1,440
PM	–	1	20	160
PD	–	–	1	8
PH	–	–	–	1

Table 3.3. Accounting model 2

	PY	PM	PD	PH
PY	1	12	180	1,440
PM	–	1	15	120
PD	–	–	1	8
PH	–	–	–	1

Table 3.4. Accounting model 3

	PY	PM	PD	PH
PY	1	12	240	1,440
PM	–	1	20	120
PD	–	–	1	6
PH	–	–	–	1

Table 3.5. Illustration of how accounting error can occur (given a project with PH = 100,000)

	Model 1	Model 2	Model 3
PH	100,000	100,000	100,000
PD	12,500	12,500	16,667
PM	625	833	833
PY	69	69	69

3.1.4 The Problem of Overtime Work

Another problem arises with overtime work, whether or not it is paid to the workers who perform it, because it is seldom recorded as part of the project hours. Despite the frequency of this situation, the overtime hours are expended as part of the project, but because these are not measured (regardless of whether these are paid), these are neither registered nor included in project effort as part of project postmortems. This problem is exacerbated when using the metric *productivity* as illustrated by the following example: When 10 persons deliver 3,000 Function Points (FP) in 2 years the productivity is 12.5 Function Points per person month, with 240 person months (10 persons × 24 months). If each month is considered as being 120 person hours, and our project team works a total of 50 h per week, but reported only 40, then the true effort was actually 300 person months and thus only a productivity of 10.0 Function Points per person month. Estimations of further projects using the published 12.5 FP/person month will thus be overly optimistic. As such, using this *inflated* delivery rate will lead to unrealistically low estimates, delayed project milestones, premature deadlines and most probably to the ultimate cancellation of the project.

Furthermore, huge amounts of overtime work lead to fatigue, burnout, stress, and its associated follow-up consequences (not only for the team members but also for their families), and this creates more (un)avoidable time delays. In turn, this leads to even more time pressure and higher defect rates. Overall, undocumented (as well as unpaid) overtime work boycotts the benefit of productivity metrics and indirectly negates the benefits of quality metrics.

To use all resources of an organization with full capacity is a short-term strategy that hinders an organization to be able to manage the long-term aspects of its business processes. It can be a formula for failure.

3.1.5 The Definition of the Application Boundary

The boundary of an application determines what is to be sized within the scope of a software application, and as a benefit delivers the context diagram for software interfaces as a byproduct. Together with the actual available objectives and prerequisites, and the assumptions for the project, this boundary must be precisely documented. The application boundary is determined based on the user view and not from a technological focus (see Fig. 3.1).

For enhancement projects, the application boundary must be determined in accordance with the application already installed. If the boundary cannot be exactly determined, it must be estimated. Decisions about where to place the boundary can be assisted by answering the question of whether the data or processes are maintained by the software being enhanceds. The definition of the application boundary is a key component of the IFPUG Function Point Method, as well as other ISO/IEC conformant FSM methods. An added side benefit of identifying the application boundary is its potential reuse as an architecture diagram of the software application in the organizational architecture atlas.

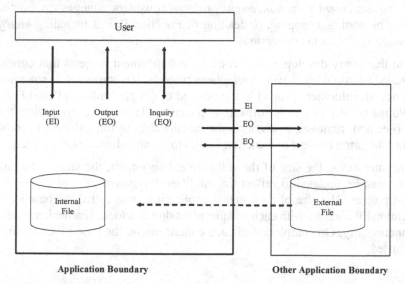

Fig. 3.1. Determination of the application boundary for the IFPUG function point method

3.1.6 The Type of Estimation

When measuring the functional size of software, a project, one has to distinguish between new development projects and enhancement projects. For the majority of FSM methods, a "project" is considered to be the new development or enhancement of one software application at a time. If a business project consists of new development of one or more software applications plus the enhancement of a further one or more software applications, then several separate functional size measurements would be done.

The measurement of the functional size of software for new development projects comprises the size of the functional area worked on (new construction) and results in installed Function Points delivered to the end users at the end of the first release of the software. The project can also include *migration* (data conversion) functionality. To calculate Scope Creep (also called requirements creep), one can take the size of the developed software functionality compared with the Function Point estimate of the size of the software at the start of the project plus the size of any changes during the project. For example, if 1,000 FP was estimated as the software size at the onset of requirements, 1,050 FP was delivered, and a further 50 FP was changed during the project, the scope creep is 100 FP calculated as 1050 FP delivered - 1000 FP estimated + 50 FP changed during the project. To have the correct number of base (application) Function Points at hand, it is important to actualize the Function Point counts during project progress and once the project is complete.

The measurement of enhancement projects considers changes on existing software by adding, changing, or deleting of Function Points including *migration functionality* (data conversions).

Note that many developers will consider enhancement projects that contain only added functionality as *new development* projects. It is important to remember that a new development project in the context of (in particular, IFPUG) Function Points results in a new software application. Thereafter, any project that alters (i.e., add, removes, or changes) the functionality of the software is considered in the same context of Function Points to be an enhancement project.

After measuring the size of the software enhancement, the size of the base system must be updated to reflect the modified functional area of the enhancement project. The size of an installed application, also called the baseline or application FP changes with each enhancement due to added, changed, and deleted functionality. On completion of each enhancement, the base FP count must be adjusted.

3.1.7 Customizing of Standard Software (Packages)

Projects for customizing of standard COTS (commercial off the shelf) software (e.g., ERP – Enterprise Resource Planning – systems, such as Peoplesoft, SAP, etc.) are enhancement projects of a special kind. Clearly, the interfaces to existing legacy applications must be programmed. Typically, these projects deliver software functionality for which the Function Points can be counted. The new or changed interface functionality between the COTS package and the legacy application is usually a part of each application, and is counted as an enhancement to each of the base applications. This means that there will be multiple FP counts for a project that includes installation of the COTS software plus new/changed interfaces from the legacy applications to which the COTS software must send or receive data.

Here, a problem may arise since, due to their extraordinary size and functionality, the standard COTS software packages are usually not counted. Their huge size typically would require a fairly large effort to count all of their functionality when, in fact, organizations often use only part of the functionality or more likely, some of the provided functionality is customized to meet specific user needs. As a result, many organizations cannot justify the additional effort that may be required to find out what functionality is actually relevant to count.

The only solution that can be recommended for these problems is to take these counts of customizations into a separate class of estimations, counting only the functionality for the customization. It is important to note in these situations that the results will not be comparable to other enhancement projects that involve non-packaged solutions.

Morris lists the following essential variations that are relevant to estimation of IT projects where customizing of packaged software is involved:

1. *Implementation*: Parts of standard (packaged, COTS) software that can be used without change.
2. *Customizing*: Parts of standard software that must be changed for the installation.
3. *Conversion*: Parts of existing applications must be altered or changed to meet the requirements of the standard software.
4. *Enhancement*: New functionality must be programmed in addition to installation of the standard software.
5. *Interfaces*: New functionality must be programmed into the standard software in order to secure the interfaces to existing applications.
6. *Release*: Functionality to be developed in further releases.

Function Points can be counted for all these variations. Typically, there is a large number of External Interface Files (EIF) in these cases, which indicate a strong coupling of the standard packaged software with existing applications. Often this indicates a negative influence on the productivity of the IT project. However, when estimating the effort for every other variation mentioned earlier, special metrics and productivity rates must be applied based on historical data of similar projects using that variation.

Coding is generally only a small part of a customization project, and the estimation must consider that there will be additional effort drivers. Note that this is only the second step since the rest of the project must be estimated with other methods. Estimation tools may be beneficial here because they can consider and apply many other factors that influence productivity.

Table 3.6. Standard software implementations

	N	Max.	Mean	Std. Dev.
Number of implemented modules	39	7	3.82	1.48
Number of users of the ERP solution	39	1,500	217.46	364.23
Modifications (expressed in SLOC)	39	5,000	227.95	841.70
Number of interfaces	39	100	12.10	20.39
Number of local offices	39	62	4.26	9.98

Table 3.7. Standard packaged software implementation effort and duration

Note: At the time of the survey, 1 (Euro) € = ~1.20 US$	N	Mean	Max.	Std. Dev.
Duration in weeks	39	43.05	156.00	29.45
Total effort in person years	39	4.77	87.21	17.85
Total costs of implementation (€)	39	1,477,191.39	14,534,566.83	2,717,536.03
Costs of software (€)	39	360,985.42	5,813,826.73	977,172.01
Costs of necessary hardware (€)	39	267,121.14	4,360,370.05	743,279.43
Costs of consultants for implementation (€)	39	518,547.17	5,813,826.73	996,686.46

Experience shows that estimating projects involving package customization where custom software is written to integrate the standard software is mostly performed bottom–up. *For these projects, we recommend the development of estimation checklists.*

Stefan Koch from the Wirtschaftsuniversität Wien in Austria presented at the MetriKon 2005 conference the results of a survey of 39 Austrian organizations (mostly small or medium sized, and a few large ones). These organizations had implemented standard software and were mostly from production and commercial businesses. Almost two-thirds of the companies surveyed reported using SAP (61.5%) or BaaN (23.1%), followed by Oracle, Xal, and Navision with about 7% each. Table 3.6 shows the descriptive statistics of Koch's survey.

The more interesting results of the survey pertain to the analysis of the implementation effort and duration as displayed in Table 3.7. Remarkably, only three organizations performed the implementation without the aid of consultants.

3.1.8 Documentation of the Development Environment

Variations in productivity can be evaluated to compare the estimation results of different development projects. *Note that as a prerequisite to comparing estimates it is necessary to document the environmental and situational conditions under which the IT project is developed.* We recommend that the following details be documented at a minimum:

- Milestone and objective of the estimation, e.g., milstone = requirements completion; objective = estimate effort to complete (install) the software.

- Novelty of project, and any constraints, e.g., first usage of a new development environment. (The estimate would likely include additional effort to compensate for the team's learning curve).
- Type of estimate, e.g., postimplementation confirmation of the size and complexity of a new software application (after implementation).
- Definition of the boundaries of the application (for functional size measurement).
- The type of the software to be developed, e.g., online data entry system or data warehouse system.
- The programming language(s) to be used.
- The operating system(s) on which the software will be used.
- Skill levels or expertise of the development team with the environment (software, hardware, subject matter, etc). This can be reported in number of months or alternatively in a nominal scale such as beginner, expert, mix.
- Degree of participation of end users, e.g., number of persons from the user community who fully participated in the project.
- Project organization, e.g., centralized, decentralized, and geographically dispersed.
- Tools and techniques used, e.g., object-oriented programming, CASE (Computer Aided Software Engineering) tools, and code inspections done by quality assurance teams.
- Classification of comparable historical figures, e.g., description of any sample set from ISBSG or other database used for productivity rates.
- Nonstandard development tasks that were required, e.g., one-off efforts for data migrations or data conversions, or externally sourced development support.

Together, this documentation aims to describe the development environment used in the organization as precisely as possible.

For IT projects that do not use the general development standards (methods, regulations, tools, development environment), additions or reductions of effort must be applied during the estimating process to account for such differences and arrive at an appropriately adjusted estimate. Such modifications are usually determined by the estimator(s), and his/her assumptions must be justified and documented in order to create an effective historical record.

Usually, an estimate is done at the end of the requirements phase as part of the project. It is recommended that this be done in an estimation conference where the influencing factors can be discussed and classified by members of the project team. In practice, we have experienced that spreadsheets or other counting tools were valuable to document measurements of size and effort estimates.

When performing project estimates, do not forget to include effort for project management, and quality assurance efforts, as well as realistic allowances for uncertainty, risks, and requirements scope creep. The result should then be presented as a range of estimates addressing both worst-case and best-case scenarios.

3.1.9 Validation of Estimates

To evaluate the long-term trends about projects and their activities, all experiences about estimates must be documented *and* available to be used for future, similar project estimates.

To capture these experience factors, it has to be decided ahead of time that the actual data will be collected and measured according to the plans. Initially, when an organization is getting started with its first project estimate, one can only rely on one's own practical experience. However, once a number of completed projects have their experience information collected and documented, future estimates can learn from and be improved by the historical data.

Some companies have implemented a formal competence center that collects the project data (documentation and estimates as described previously) to create an experience database. When there is a need for a future estimate (feed forward) this database allows the systematic retrieval of data of relevant historical estimates.

Function Point counts and their associated estimates should be checked and calibrated for validity after documentation. Estimates done using an estimation tool such as Checkpoint/KnowledgePLAN®, ExperiencePro®, or others, should be checked at least once after performing the first estimate. This is because all tools assume a *standard* set of development environment conditions. If the resultant estimate is too low or too high due to specific environmental conditions, the tool will continue to underestimate or overestimate future projects unless the organization calibrates the results to its own environment. If estimation is done manually or without a tool, the evaluated parameters involved in the estimate should be documented.

Thereafter, counts and estimates should be quality assured by a third person (ideally from the competence center). Only then can the counts/estimates be considered as valid and qualified as sound counts/estimations. For this quality assurance activity, a checklist (see appendix) can be used.

3.2 The Process of Estimation

The principal process of estimation is shown in Fig. 3.2.

For the purpose of control and transparency of estimation, the following information is a prerequisite to the preparation. of an estimate.

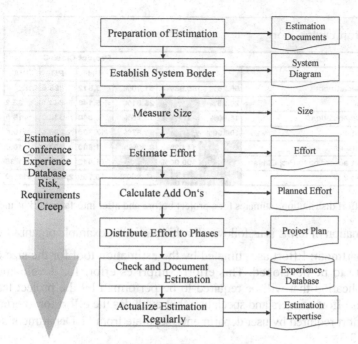

Fig. 3.2. The process of estimation

3.2.1. Distribution of Estimated Effort Across Project Phases

Using an Excel spreadsheet, the distribution of the estimated effort of various project phases can be calculated using the Percentage Method. A corporate solution, e.g., would ask for following inputs:

1. Effort as estimated
2. Effort for interfaces (e.g., computing center, other projects) estimated individually, or by an estimation tool
3. Project team size for each phase
4. Project team size of end users and specialists for each phase
5. Figure 3.3 shows an example of such a standard. In the first column, the estimated effort for development and users (effort 1) is broken down into the three partial efforts for IT department, user, and IT Organization. After input of the effort for interfaces, the overall project-related effort will be calculated and the appropriate Project Class will be determined depending on the overall effort as described later (Project Class C in this case). The effort is shown in person hours (PH), person days (PD), and person months (PM).

Effort Distribution						
				Project Class C		
				PH	PD	PM
IT-Department	55.75%	85.98%	51.10%	9,812	1,226.5	61.3
User	29.25%		26.81%	5,148	643.5	32.2
IT-Organization	15.00%		13.75%	2,640	330.0	16.5
Effort 1	100.00%		91.67%	17,600	2,200.0	110.0
Interfaces		14.02%	8.33%	1,600	200.0	10.0
Effort according to Proj.Class		100.00%		11,412	142.5	71.35
Effort 2			100.00%	19,200	2,400.0	120.0

Fig. 3.3. Effort distribution estimates for a project before and after interface work is included

The explanation of terms is as follows (for this particular example organization):

- IT Department: Effort as estimated by the estimation tool for the size of the software to be developed. This effort comprises effort for development of the application that will be required to be performed by the project team: it includes effort of users and specialists, but excludes the effort for interfaces.
- User effort required by user departments, separate from IT Department's effort in Fig. 3.3.
- IT Organization: Effort to be performed by other departments, specialists, project management, quality assurance, and consultancy (not already included in the two categories in Fig. 3.3).
- Effort 1: Effort accomplished by the IT team (consisting of people from all three groups in Fig. 3.3), comprising all requirements and design tasks, programming and testing-related tasks, as well as effort for project management and quality assurance.
- Interfaces: Effort for interfaces required in other applications or departments that have to change their systems or processes for the integration of the new project.
- Effort according to Project Class: The Project Class relevant effort is the sum of effort accomplished by the IT team plus the effort for interfaces. It determines the Project Class that is used for planning the organizational structure of the project.
- Effort 2: This is the sum of Effort 1 and Interface effort.

Figure 3.4 is used to determine the phase relevant effort for the IT staff and users. The project duration is computed by dividing the phase effort by the team size for the phase. The percentages shown in both tables were determined by the competence center in an actual large organization, which also documented and maintained project data in a central experience repository.

	Project		IT-Core Project				User				
Phase	Percent. Phase	Effort (PM)	Percent. Phase	FTE	Effort (PM)	Duration (Month)	Percent. Phase	FTE	Effort (PM)	Duration (Month)	Duration (Month)
Req. Anal.	24.0%	26.40	11.00%	5	12.10	3.23	10.50%	7	11.55	2.20	3.67
Design	21.5%	23.65	15.05%	6	16.56	3.68	3.05%	5	3.36	0.89	3.68
Coding	25.5%	28.05	19.50%	7	21.45	4.09	3.30%	3	3.63	1.61	4.09
Test	14.5%	15.95	6.80%	4	7.48	2.49	5.70%	2	6.27	4.18	4.18
Integr. Test	14.5%	15.95	3.40%	3	3.74	1.66	6.70%	3	7.37	3.28	3.28
Sum	100.0%	100.00	55.75%	25	61.33	15.15	29.25%	20	32.18	12.16	18.89

Fig. 3.4. Phase relevant effort

It is important to mention the work of Ross Jeffrey who states that the work effort to develop software grows linearly up to a project size of ~10 person years (about 125–300 FPs) and exponentially thereafter.

A comparison of the ISBSG surveys from 1997 and 2002 shows that the percentage of effort in the planning phase for IT projects appears to have decreased from 10% to 5%, and that the percentage of effort for installation has decreased from more than 50% to 5%. Correspondingly, the percentage of effort for programming increased from less than 10% to more than 10%. David Dery and Alain Abran presented at the IWSM 2005 (International Workshop on Software Measurement) their research of the ISBSG benchmarking data base (release 9, 2005), indicating that only 350 of the 2,562 projects had effort recorded for all 5 phases (PSBTI: planning, specification, build, test, implementation) while only 41 of these had detailed and credible data. Table 3.8 shows the distribution of effort across the five phases that can also be used to allocate phase effort using the Percentage Method.

The distribution of the estimated total effort across the project phases and to the teams involved is a necessary prerequisite for sound resource planning. In addition, information about costs, effort, schedule, and staff is needed.

Table 3.8. Effort by project phase distribution in ISBSG release 9, 2005

Number of Projects: Phase	Percentage				
	P	S	B	T	I
41 with credible data	9.1	24.7	39.1	19.7	7.3
34 with high effort in S	0.1	98.5	0.7	0.5	0.2
62 without outliers and unusual patterns and only effort in phases PSBT	11.2	18.3	34.6	35.9	0
3 with only effort in phases SBTI	0	27.6	49.0	15.3	8.1

3.2.2 The Documentation of Project Estimates

In order not to lose the estimating experiences for IT projects, it is critical to collect, interpret, and administer the data centrally. Without a central experience repository, it becomes difficult, if not impossible, to maintain the necessary volume and diversity of documentation required to consistently estimate future IT projects. These tasks are ideally performed by a competence center and can be greatly assisted by text processing and graphics software.

The following documents are necessary for a complete documentation of an IT project and its estimates:

- Estimation Log (text software)
    - This log contains the names of persons performing the estimate, dates and milestones of each estimate, references to existing information, documents, agreements, assumptions, special requirements, constraints, etc.
- Software Boundary Diagram (graphics software)
    - Architectural diagrams of the object of estimation (IT software) including files, logical data model, interfaces, processes (dialog steps and screens), batch processes, object models, etc.
- Reports of functional size measurement details (Function Point counts) and estimates from estimating tools
    - Containing information about functional size, input and output data, screens, reports, objects, classes, processes, etc.
- Copies of documents from the IT project
    - Necessary prerequisites for the count and/or estimation, e.g., dialogue structure, layouts of screens, reports, html pages, etc. (may be kept online)
- Results from estimation tools
    - Containing productivity metrics and quality metrics, proposals for planning, and diverse scenarios of an estimation.

Such an approach is beneficial in order to gain access to all information when analyzing the estimates done for an IT project. For an inter-project view, this approach provides the advantage that one can see how similar IT projects were classified, and what were the assumptions and the values of some of the soft parameters of estimation.

To get started, one can manually collect and maintain the assessments of all parameters of the first estimates using an Excel spreadsheet. Estimation tools like, e.g., Checkpoint/KnowledgePLAN® administer in excess of 220 parameters when performing an estimate. Such sophisticated estimating tools as this demonstrates that soon, after about five projects, this task can no longer be done manually.

An example of advantages of professional documentation of estimates (for advanced readers) is the fact that it can be used to automatically transfer data into existing tools, for example, KnowledgePLAN® or Experience® Pro software. To automate this process, an Excel visual basic application can be developed to import existing data that may already be administered in the tool.

This can be done by using the portfolio concept of Checkpoint/ Knowledge-PLAN. A new portfolio with the IT projects to be compared will be created and exported to Excel. This export is not very readable – as usual in such cases. Using macros the data have to be automatically adjusted and formatted. Importing the data to Excel allows using all visualizing features of Excel. Important data can thus be shown in diagrams, e.g.

- Size of application/project (Function Points, or in some cases, SLOC)
- Effort (hours or person months)
- Productivity (Function Points per person month or per hour, see following Fig. 3.5)
- Quality (corrected and delivered defects)
- Risk evaluation
- Soft parameters (team, technology, process, environment).

Note: As profiled in the ISBSG publication, Practical Project Estimation: there are multiple ways to evaluate these parameters. Three such ways include: the Finnish Software Measurement Association (www.fisma.fi) and its ND21 (New Development 21 factors), the IFPUG Value Adjustment Factor (VAF), and the COCOMO II factors (http://sunset.usc.edu/csse/tools/index. html)

Within minutes, a presentable interproject documentation can be obtained from the documented data.

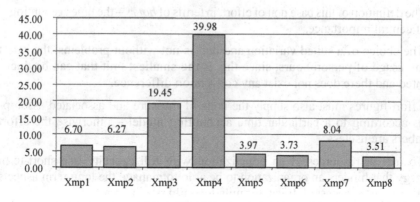

Fig. 3.5. Comparison of productivity of eight IT projects

3.3 Management Summary

Estimation must be performed in a professional manner.

Estimating without history is simply an opinion!

To perform solid estimation, one necessarily needs information about the object of estimation (e.g., WHAT requirements the software product must deliver). Without such information, estimation is only a modified type of Las Vegas-style gambling.

Estimations should be prepared!

An estimate can only be carried out when at least a minimum of project requirements are known. The clearer the objectives for the software product, the more precise the results will be.

The estimate must be done by persons with sufficient knowledge about the requirements under consideration.

When estimating the project requirements at an early (preliminary estimate) stage, the estimate should not be broken down into too much detail since the overall application/project requirements should be in the focus.

When using the Function Point Method the object of estimation has to be seen from the view of the users (as outlined in the previous point), and not the view of the IT staff. This is the most important rule: functional size measurement emphasizes the functional USER requirements, and this point cannot be stressed enough.

Before carrying out an estimation, it must be agreed and defined what is the effort to be estimated and how it will be measured.

A standardized measurable unit for the effort must be defined in order to compare the development project effort to that of other IT projects.

The definition of this base unit of effort, in terms of *hours* – the time accounting – is of central importance.

The choice of a suited variation and unit is not without problems: the safest is the usage of person hours, since this is the smallest unit that can be documented and there does not exist any conversion difference.

Effort figures must also supply the units of measure and associated assumptions according to a particular time accounting model – otherwise the effort numbers are useless.

To use all resources of an organization with full capacity is a short-term strategy that hinders an organization to be able to manage the long-term aspects of its business processes. It is a formula for failure.

The boundary of an application determines what is to be counted, and as a benefit delivers the context diagram for software interfaces as a byproduct. Together with the actual available objectives and prerequisites, and the assumptions for the project, this boundary must be precisely documented.

The application boundary is determined based on the user view and not from a technological focus.

For enhancement projects, the application boundary must be determined in accordance with the application already installed.

The definition of the application boundary is a key component of the Function Point Method.

An added side benefit of identifying the application boundary is its potential reuse as an architecture diagram of the software application in the organizational architecture atlas.

When measuring a project's size, one has to distinguish between new development projects and enhancement projects.

The measurement of enhancement projects considers changes on existing software by adding, changing, or deleting of Function Points including migration functionality (data conversions).

Projects for customizing of standard COTS software (e.g., ERP systems, such as Peoplesoft, SAP, etc.) are enhancement projects of a special kind. Clearly, the interfaces to existing legacy applications must be programmed. Typically, these projects deliver software functionality for which the Function Points can be counted. The new or changed interface functionality between the COTS package and the legacy application is usually a part of each application, and is counted as an enhancement to each of the base applications.

As a prerequisite to comparing estimates it is necessary to document the environmental and situational conditions under which the IT project is developed.

Together, this documentation aims to describe the development environment used in the organization as precisely as possible.

When performing project estimates, do not forget to include effort for project management, and quality assurance efforts, as well as realistic allowances for uncertainty, risks, and requirements scope creep. The result should then be presented as a range of estimates addressing both worst-case and best-case scenarios.

To capture these experience factors, it has to be decided ahead of time that the actual data will be collected and measured according to the plans.

Some companies have implemented a formal competence center that collects the project data (documentation and estimates as described previously) to create an experience database.

Function Point counts and their associated estimates should be checked and calibrated for validity after documentation.

Thereafter, counts and estimates should be quality assured by a third person (ideally from the competence center). Only then can the counts/estimates be considered as valid and qualified as sound counts/estimations.

Using an Excel spreadsheet, the distribution of the estimated effort of various project phases can be calculated using the Percentage Method.

It is important to mention the work of Ross Jeffrey who states that the work effort to develop software grows linearly up to a project size of ~10 person years (about 125–300 FPs) and exponentially thereafter.

In order not to lose the estimating experiences for IT projects, it is critical to collect, interpret, and administer the data centrally.

4 The Implementation of Estimation

The implementation of estimation is an innovative project and as such, it must be planned and performed with as much rigor as any other formal IT project. The estimation process is the foundation for successful communication as well as for monitoring and improvement of the project management processes. As in all innovative projects, it is important to take notice of and plan for acceptance issues, that is, for resistance to occur.

In Europe, we speak of the "king's road," which is the means to accomplish the best outcomes. This means that the road to gain acceptance in any innovative or new endeavor consists of information, training, and participation of all involved persons. In addition, there is need for time to pass in order to foster awareness for the innovations. If this cornerstone is omitted during the implementation of an IT metrics program, *then it has a good chance, as proven by 80% of all IT metrics initiatives (Dekkers 1999), to be abandoned early and without success. An IT metrics program is a strategic project and should be viewed as such. Otherwise, if the project is perceived as extra overhead, its chances of success are minimized.*

A roadmap for successful implementation is illustrated in Fig. 4.1. Estimation should consider the following stations (see Fig. 4.1).

1. Building the foundation: This is where the Goal, Question, Metric model of Basili, and later Van Solingen and Berghout fits. We have adapted the method here in our roadmap:
   (a) Goals: First define the goals for estimation and propagate them. Define a standard process. Be informed and gain a market overview. Search for projects with which to start the metrics initiative. The best ones to start with are typically the strategic projects with at least 3 months duration and more than one person-year of effort, so that the implementation of estimation can show the benefits. The American author of this book asserts that the Goals of the estimation process must be "SMART," which is an acronym that stands for the following:
   - *Strategic* (that is, the goal must be important to the organization)
   - *Measurable* (that is, the goal must be to measurably improve estimation)
   - *Actionable* (that is, the goal must be something that the project team can act on)

- *Realistic* (that is, the goal to improve estimating must be seen as something achievable)
- *Time-bounded* (that is, there must be a definitive time frame in which to achieve the goal).

(b) Question: To achieve a goal (such as, for example, increase the accuracy of project estimates by 15% until 31st December), we need to ask a minimum of three questions:

1. How good is our estimating currently?
2. How good is our estimating when we implement the estimation process?
3. Are we achieving the goal? (And why or why not?)

(c) Metrics: To answer the questions to meet the goals of estimation, there needs to be measures in place as outlined previously to track our achievements. Functional size measurement (or in some cases lines of code) must be used to measure software size, effort units (and what is included within them) must be consistent, and delivery rates must be standardized.

2. Strategic planning: Foster the transition by training about estimation, which assists in the creation of awareness and understanding, as well as to motivate and increase the expertise of those who will be involved. This is very helpful for knowledge transfer with other stakeholders and to eliminate the fears of the people involved. Important considerations include:

(a) Stay on course: Manage resistance and document first experiences. Check consistency by means of inspections. Note that resistance is the natural response to change and if it does not manifest itself directly to you, be assured that there is resistance to the change – it is simply not being expressed overtly. It is better to watch for and address the resistance during the early stages of implementing estimation rather than have it fester and derail the entire process later on.

(b) Improve the processes by development of standards and IT metrics knowledge transfer and comparison with others who have successfully gained from estimation (e.g., ISBSG (International Software Benchmarking Standards Group) or other corporations).

3. Implementation: This is accomplished by planning, budgeting, scheduling, and resource coordination. To succeed, the project must have committed resources dedicated to the development and implementation of the estimating process.

4. Establish precedence.

(a) Define an appropriate structure, process, methods and tools to support estimation.

(b) Establish the concept by beginning to apply the process on selected IT projects.

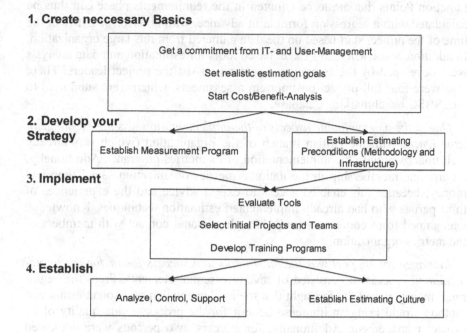

1. Create neccessary Basics

Get a commitment from IT- and User-Management

Set realistic estimation goals

Start Cost/Benefit-Analysis

2. Develop your Strategy

Establish Measurement Program

Establish Estimating Preconditions (Methodology and Infrastructure)

3. Implement

Evaluate Tools

Select initial Projects and Teams

Develop Training Programs

4. Establish

Analyze, Control, Support

Establish Estimating Culture

Fig. 4.1. A roadmap for successful implementation of estimation

4.1 Report About a Successful Implementation

A successful implementation in a large insurance organization with approximately 500 IT developers was done over a 3 year period by two full-time persons who worked as the competence center. During the implementation process, an estimating method and tools were chosen, a number of presentations for managers and project leaders were given, an estimation manual was developed, and about 90 developers attended training sessions. As a result, at least one person in each development team was trained in function point counting and estimation principles. The function point counting of all historic applications was performed with tool-support and with assistance of the competence center. The two person competence center team coached all function point counts and assisted the project leaders with assembling tool-based documentation. Because the IT projects were in various stages of completion when we began the initiative, in some cases there already existed an estimate. In one large project, a subsequent estimate was done after a year, and therefore, the requirements creep could be measured.

Data analysis enabled the development of a function point prognosis for the early estimation of Function Points, which became the basis for subsequent estimates using only the number of inputs and outputs of new software. The

Function Points that are to be counted in the requirements phase can thus be calculated with a regression formula in advance, with an error of ±15% at the time of the project start based on the data gathered from this large organization. In addition, some Microsoft Excel based tools for estimation and data analysis were developed by the competence center to assist the project leaders. There also were four full project postmortem assessments, which were submitted to the ISBSG benchmarking database.

One of the most valuable aspects of the implementation was the exchange of experiences with the British branch of the organization (which was already well underway with the implementation of its metrics program). Additionally, a corporate membership in the national metrics organization saved time and money, because this enabled access to expert advice and the experiences of third parties who had already implemented estimation techniques. Knowledge was gained from conferences and through personal contact with members of the metrics organization.

Management support was the most important success factor for the implementation process. It consisted of several essential elements. From the beginning, managers had the foresight that the implementation of a sound estimation method would bring an immense benefit for the processes and quality of IT project management. Additionally, for 3 years, two persons were dedicated (one full time, the other part time) to gain the knowledge to build up a competence center. This competence center worked to ensure that the developers and project leaders were involved in meetings and presentations, and this was an important part of creating an estimation culture. After a 2-year break (when the competence center had got another task: to install a new project management tool with time accounting since the old tool had a Y2K collapse), another two part-time employees joined the competence center to restart the slowed down process.

Groups of developers were trained in function point analysis (FPA). The three-day training for each group of developers was always done by (the same) external consultants. Manpower bottlenecks in function point counting were also alleviated with the aid of external consultants.

After 2 years, the goal of counting all historical applications was reached: 98 applications with a total of 150,000 Function Points were in the portfolio – not including packaged software. A byproduct of counting the portfolio was the recognition that the documentation of the Function Point counts in the Function Point Workbench® repository software, enabled the organization to quickly and easily find the Function Point counts for small maintenance tasks. Thus, productivity metrics for applications (support rates), as well as for projects and maintenance tasks, could also be implemented. A metrics database and a function point baseline were established and are still in frequent use today.

The 98 applications could be ordered by size into six groups:

- Three in the range between 9,000 and 10,000 Function Points
- Three in the range of 6,000–7,000 Function Points
- Six in the range of 4,000–6,000 Function Points
- Fifteen in the range of 2,000–4,000 Function Points
- Twelve in the range of 1,000–2,000 Function Points
- The 59 remaining applications had a size of less than 1,000 Function Points.

During the first year after the establishment of the baseline the following increases in productivity were measured:

- Projects (Costs >400,000 US-$): 8.3%
- Enhancements (Costs <400,000 US-$): 4.1%
- Corrections (Enhancements without change of Function Points): 3.1%.

The publication of such positive key experiences can help to foster the acceptance of metrics programs in organizations. But these figures are very imprecise, since the baseline at the beginning of such initiatives can be inconsistent due to the novelty of both the measurements and the data collection processes. With the results obtained, 55% of the baseline applications were used to calculate the productivity of enhancements and corrections. For the productivity measurement of projects in the baseline 11 projects were included in the calculations, and in the following year there were 17 projects included. The productivity of enhancement projects was measured considering a sample size of 10% of all enhancements.

The implementation breakthrough came with the final function point counting of all applications. The achievement of this goal was connected with 20% of the annual bonus of the managers of each development department. This led to a huge number of questions from project managers. Experiences in the British organization were similar. They were able to increase the productivity of application development in 1 year from 11 to 13 function points per person-month because their goal was also connected with the financial bonus of the project managers.

Continuous questions from management increased the awareness of managers and project managers for estimation. They realized that function point counting and estimation were more and more integrated in the project life cycle, and the process of counting was no longer neglected or viewed as overhead. The competence center accompanied the whole implementation process with many presentations, discussions, reports, and work on routine tasks.

In the estimation tool, along with the function point counts, there were also 32 project estimates:

- Twelve were new development projects (three host, nine PC)
- Twenty were enhancements (15 host, 1 PC, 4 Client/Server)
- Ten were project postmortems (final estimate).

Within 2 further years there were 45 projects in the estimation tool:

- Seventeen new development projects (4 host, 13 PC)
- Twenty-six enhancements (21 host, 4 Client/Server, 1 PC)
- Two maintenance (both host, 715 and 335 Function Points).

There are only a few technical challenges associated with the successful implementation of software measurement, but there are many psychological challenges. The following pages introduce an empirical survey of positive and negative aspects of measurement.

4.2 Positive and Negative Aspects of Software Measurement

Hall et al. show an interesting empirical survey of 13 groups of developers, 12 groups of project managers, and 4 groups of senior managers in 11 associations conducted between October 1999 and March 2000. Her team interviewed the groups and collected both positive and negative opinions relating to the use of IT metrics. Their joint result is that the majority of the positive aspects benefit the project managers more than the developers, as manifested by the declaration of one developer: "if any of us came up with a workable approach to metrics we would become very rich."

Table 4.1 shows that the overwhelmingly positive perception of measurement cited by developer groups was that measurement data allows progress to be tracked (69%) and that it improves planning and estimation (38%).

Project managers and senior managers have a more positive view of IT metrics as depicted in Table 4.2. Project managers favor the use of IT metrics for estimation purposes (P1, P2, P5) and for the identification of specific problems (P3).

Three negative aspects of software measurement were mentioned by 38% of the developers:

- Developers are often not informed/do not know if and how the measured data are used.
- There is no feedback about the measured data.
- Data collection is time consuming for the developers (which was also confirmed by 67% of the project managers). It is interesting that this insight did not lead to the requirement for automatic measurement.

Tables 4.3 and 4.4 demonstrate that 23% of the developers disliked the extra effort for data collection and the rather scarce presentation of the results. About 60% of the project managers said that they had difficulties in identifying and knowing whether they were collecting and reporting the right data.

Table 4.1. Perceived general positive aspects of software measurement as reported by Hall et al.

	Benefits of software measurement	Percentage of responses by group		
		Developers	Project managers	Senior managers
P1	Know whether the right things are being done	23	25	50
P2	Finding out what is good and what is bad	23	58	50
P3	Identify problems	8	42	25
P4	Support/improve planning and estimating	38	25	25
P5	Track progress	69	58	50
P6	Makes what you are saying more substantial	15	8	50
P7	Provides feedback to people	8	25	25

Table 4.2. Favorite aspects of software measurement as reported by Hall et al.

	Favorite aspects of software measurement	Percentage of responses by group		
		Developers	Project managers	Senior managers
B1	Can target effort into things (that are) not doing so well	8	8	25
B2	A check that what you are doing is right	15	17	50
B3	People can not argue	8	25	0
B4	The confidence they give	8	17	50

Table 4.3. Perceived general negative aspects of software measurement as reported by Hall et al.

	General negative aspects of software measurement	Percentage of responses by group		
		Developers	Project managers	Senior managers
N1	Hard to measure what you want to measure	15	25	0
N2	Do not know how or if the data is being used	38	8	0
N3	No feedback from the data	38	8	0
N4	Detracts from the main engineering job	8	8	50
N5	Difficult to collect, analyze and use the right measures	23	58	50
N6	Time consuming to collect the data	38	67	25
N7	They must be used fort the right reason	15	33	50
N8	There must be integrity in the data	15	17	25
N9	They can be used against people	0	0	25

A quarter of the developers also added that software measures do not always measure what you want them to measure.

Senior mangers, unsurprisingly, had different views about software metrics. Their negative perceptions centered primarily on the following (see Table 4.3):

- Data collection detracts from the main engineering job.
- It is difficult to collect, analyze, and use the right measures.

As we have stated before, software measurement must be used for the right reason and goals must be aligned with the initiative.

A quarter of the senior management commented that measurement is time consuming and that it is important not to use the data against people. It is interesting that none of the other two groups identified these negative issues in the study. We can speculate on a variety of reasons for this: Perhaps the developers and project managers involved in the survey had not experienced measurement being used in this way and so it did not occur to them as a problem, or they did not perceive data being used in this way as problematic. In the American author's consulting experience, developers often express outward resistance to software metrics based on the fear that management may punish the messengers if the resultant data are not favorable. The psychology of measurement and its impact on those involved is an important aspect of software metrics implementation.

Hall's research further reported that the least favorite rated aspects of software measurement included the following (see Table 4.4):

Table 4.4. Least favorite aspects of software measurement as reported by Hall et al.

Least favorite aspects of software measurement	Percentage of groups		
	Developers	Project managers	Senior managers
L1 Extra work	23	8	0
L2 Difficult to compare data across systems or projects	0	25	0
L3 Can be misunderstood	15	8	25
L4 Not used enough	8	17	25
L5 Poorly presented data	23	17	50
L6 Data too abstract to use easily	15	17	0
L7 Poor quality data	15	25	0

- Poorly presented data
- Difficult to compare data across systems or projects
- Poor quality data
- Can be misunderstood
- Not used enough.

Hall's research can be summarized as follows:

All positive aspects fell into the following three categories:

- Assessment (P1, P2, P3)
- Planning (P4, P5)
- Decision support (P8)

All negative aspects fell into the following three categories:

- Implementation (N2, N3, N7, N8)
- Time and effort (N4, N6)
- Measurement immanent difficulties (N1, N5).

When implementing a new estimating process in your own organization, it is important to keep these issues in mind. Any of these issues can be directly managed by doing forward planning before implementing software measurement.

The following pages introduce answers to frequently asked questions about estimation and discuss the benefits of a competence center.

4.3 Frequently Asked Questions

The following topics are asked regularly in connection with the implementation of estimation in an organization:

1. How much effort does it take to implement a formal estimation process?
2. When is the right time for implementation of estimation?
3. What are the pros and cons of a competence center?

4.3.1 The Effort for Estimation

The recommended method for implementing estimation is to use a pilot project approach. The effort of this pilot project through to full scale implementation in a large organization can be planned to be approximately 2 person years. The process of gaining estimation knowledge, the integration of estimation into the processes of the software development model of the organization until consequent organization, and usage of IT metrics for continual improvement may possibly consume about another 2 person years.

A general rule of thumb that we use (garnered from personal experiences and published literature) is that the effort for estimation consumes about 0.5–1% of the total IT budget. This means that for 100 developers there should be at least a half FTE (Full Time Equivalent) budgeted for collection and analysis of metrics for estimations. During the process of implementation of a metrics program, the effort may well be as double as much – at least until estimation becomes the way of doing business.

Counter argument: Often, costs are cited as an argument against systematic and sound estimation practices. Considering the cost of large projects often being in the range of tens of million of USD or €, one can argue:

All effort that is necessary to implement and foster sound methods of software estimation and measurement is quickly surpassed by the costs of a single failed IT project.

4.3.2 The Right Time to Implement a Formal Estimation Process

The right time for implementation depends mainly on the state of the IT project "chaos," that is, if customers are complaining about late projects that are overbudget and do not meet their needs, then the time is ripe for formal estimation! However, if the situation is that customers do not care about late delivery (yes, this does happen!), and management is unconcerned about budget amounts (we have seen this especially on internal projects), and basic processes are not in place for requirements gathering, then it is probably premature to implement estimation processes. For example, it makes little sense for an organization assessed at a CMMI® level 0 (initial) to implement formal estimation when there are many other more urgent processes that need to be put into place first.

The minimum requirement for successful implementation of estimation is that there is a standardized software development life cycle (SDLC) and standardized work effort reporting. If every project does their own style of project tracking (i.e., Overtime in/out, start, and stop points on the projects vary, different team definitions are in place, etc.) then project hours will be disparate and uncomparable across projects. As such, benchmarking and estimating will result in inconsistent results. Reliance on such inconsistencies under the guise of real, accurate data will lead to the wrong decision making and the wrong conclusions – definitely not the goals of a formal estimation process!

Once the prerequisite processes (requirements processes and work effort tracking) are in place, then estimating is practically always chosen too late. A good timing is when the established organizational processes for software development are to be improved or when customers or management are concerned about late or overbudget software delivery. Hence, one has the chance to integrate the necessary tasks for estimation directly.

But the guiding principle has to be–start now if you have the prerequisites in place! Follow the Goal/Question/Metric approach if you are in doubt about what you can gain from formal estimating processes: if your goals are to get the requirements right or at least document them in the first place, then you know that you have got work to do before you can look at formal estimating.

This guarantees that the quality of software development is safeguarded and the teams involved do not waste their time pursuing goals that are unattainable (think of a CMMI® level 0 company trying to achieve a level 3 rating in 6 months. This is similar to a second grade student who is learning to read attempting to write a master's dissertation by the end of the school year). Estimation is a nontrivial process and it makes sense to ensure a good chance of success before one gets started with implementation! *However, once you have established that this is a good time for estimation implementation* and you have the support of senior management, the collection of experience and the according cybernetic learning circuit can be started anytime.

4.3.3 The Pros and Cons of a Competence Center

Practical experience bears out that it is useful to have a centralized source of support, with qualified and competent personnel available to assist the organization with estimation. To gain the benefits of an estimating process, it is important that the collected data be accurate, consistent, and reliable and the best way to accomplish this is through a central competence center for a number of reasons:

- The processes of counting the software functional size, collecting the project documentation, and recording other software project attributes in order to do an estimate is nontrivial. As such, it makes sense to have a central place where data can be verified and centrally stored.
- The estimating process is not something that the project managers will perform on a daily basis, but rather at the time of milestone completion (as specified by the process) or when major scope change occurs or is proposed. This means that project managers will not perform the process frequently and their knowledge cannot be expected to stay current and up-to-date without support of a group for whom it is the core competency. The competence center can hone their skills and stay current with functional size measurement and the estimating processes because they perform the analysis and process for the entire IT organization (this is similar to having a specialized group of tax accountants in house – instead of having everyone practice tax accounting once a year it is more feasible and reliable to have it performed by a group for whom it is their specialization).
- A competence center is the only guarantee for central collection, documentation, and analysis of the gained estimation experience in order to learn the most from it. *The build-up of an experience or metrics data-base and the development of standards for the improvement of the knowledge base with tool support are necessary and important steps as outlined previously.*

Such a competence center can support the dissemination of experiences through continuous publication of results, experiences, reports from conferences, knowledge exchange with other organizations, and literature and new publications about estimation. This improves the communication about the estimation process and fosters better acceptance since the people feel more informed and involved than if there was no central source of information.

Some of the benefits of a competence center include the following:

- *A growing knowledge bank of experience in estimation*: Experienced experts are always available in the organization for all questions about estimation. Often, certified function point counters (CFPS, certified function point specialists) are among them.
- *Independent estimates*: A competence center is independent of the projects that are to be estimated, and therefore does not have a vested interest in over or underestimating projects to protect their team.
- *Collection of experiences:* Historical data can be consistently collected in an experience or metrics database and process improvements can be made based on new knowledge from data analysis.

However, as with any new corporate decisions, there can also be reasons why estimation should not be done by a competence center. While specialists for estimation are a scarce resource and should concentrate on estimating work instead of projects, project managers are in closer contact with the projects themselves and can better gauge the expectations of the users.

Table 4.5. Function point coordinator role description.

Function point coordinator role description	
Position in organization	Decentralized. Reports to the IT department and interfaces with the Competence Center and the estimation coordinator
Responsibility	Planning, scheduling, and overseeing the FP counts for the department; measurement of productivity baseline for department
Coordination	Planning and organization of application, project, and maintenance task FP counts
Quality assurance	Planning and organization of quality assurance of the FP counts by the department
Tasks	Administration of the FP counts of his department: applications, projects, maintenance tasks
	Annual actualization of the application counts and the associated Function Point repository files
Controlling	Oversight of FP counts, the estimation tool, and productivity metrics
Communication	Communication with colleagues, managers, and the competence center
Necessary knowledge	Function Point plus estimation tool knowledge
Necessary skills	Ability to communicate well and understand the role of project vs. metrics team members. Well versed in the FP and estimating processes and coordination

Table 4.6. Function point counter role description.

Function point counter role description	
Position in organization	Reports to IT department and Function Point Coordinator works with project team members to perform FP counts of software
Responsibility	FP counting for his department: application, project and maintenance task counts
Coordination	Minimal. May need to coordinate with different application specialists if multiple applications are involved for a project
Quality assurance	Counts should comply with internal and external quality standards as set by the competence center
Tasks	FP counting and documentation in the Function Point repository software
Controlling	Peer review of counts done by other counters on an as-required basis
Communication	Communication with function point coordinator and other FP counters
Necessary knowledge	Two day Function Point course and estimating process knowledge
Necessary skills	FP counting and estimation tool proficiency

Table 4.7. Estimation coordinator role description.

Estimation coordinator role description	
Position in organization	Reports to IT department and coordinates with Function Point Coordinator and competence center
Responsibility	Planning and performing estimates for projects and maintenance tasks (based on FP counts and project attributes provided by FP coordinator) and providing them to the project managers and reporting them to the Competence Center
Coordination	Planning, scheduling, and performance of estimates with FP coordinator, project teams, and competence center
Quality assurance	Planning and quality assurance for the estimates before sending to project managers and the competence center
Tasks	Administration and updates to estimates within the department at project milestones and at specified intervals for maintenance tasks
Controlling	Controlling of the estimates and their distribution within the department and controlling access to data within the estimation tool
Communication	Communication with colleagues, managers, and the competence center
Necessary knowledge	Function Point overview course and in-depth estimation course
Necessary skills	Knowledge about the Function Point Counting process (performed by FP counter) together with estimation process and estimating tool proficiency

This is the reason for a hybrid alternative, where qualified individuals would work decentrally as the estimation coordinator of their department. These co-ordinators are then responsible to coordinate and schedule the estimations and function point counts within their department, to plan and elaborate the necessary measures and indicators, and work with the central group to calculate metrics. These estimation coordinators are thus the ideal partners for a small competence center. This accomplished the best of both worlds where there is core, centralized specialization in metrics, process and data consistency together with decentralized estimating process knowledge spread throughout the IT department.

Tables 4.5 through 4.7 show possible role descriptions for a Function Point coordinator and a Function Point counter, as well as for an estimation coordinator.

4.4 Acceptance Challenges

As we have touched on previously, it is commonplace for the implementation of new methods and processes to encounter acceptance problems. We again refer to the king's road analogy: *This challenge can only be met with walking down the three-lane king's road to implementation of innovations: the three lanes being provision of intensive (and consistent) information, qualified training (at the right time), and enlisting the active participation of all involved persons!*

The implementation of estimation is the most difficult in organizations that exceed 100 developers. As such, one encounters in large organizations the most resistance from project leaders since the purported benefits and gains to be made from estimating are mostly on the management side. Experience with the large corporation to which we have repeatedly mentioned shows that even the well-trained project staff performed FP counts without argument but only if they were specifically assigned to do so. FP counting and estimating will not be performed unless it is built into the project manager's processes. Unless the project leader has planned these tasks *into* the project plan, which is the most critical point, it will be seen as overhead and conveniently (even if unconsciously) forgotten!

4.4.1 Counter the Counterarguments

While this sounds like a circular reference, we are talking here about addressing the resistance to estimating with solid information to the contrary. And it must be *factual information,* not hype! A typical killer argument against formal estimation is a "lack of time" ("we have to do more important things than to collect data or perform estimates" or "we must reach the deadline" or else!). The way to address this concern is threefold.

1. In the authors' experience, even for larger IT projects, a full-blown estimate complete with a high level FP count of the software size can be done in a matter of a couple of days. *Medium and smaller projects can normally be estimated within half a day or a day* (with the aid of a competence center). This is a small effort compared to the whole project size. Only for large and extra-large IT projects (more than 100 person years) might this effort be double or triple.

   If you cannot estimate what is to be done, the question is how can you do it at all? Normally, an IT project should have the necessary and current information for measurement and estimation readily available. If this is not the case see point 3. In any case compared to the overall project effort, the effort for the estimation is negligible especially considering that close to 40% (or more) of software development effort on a project is due to rework. Perhaps if we spent more time figuring out exactly what it is the project is intended to deliver (solid, countable requirements), we would have less to do over! Estimation supports this goal!

   If there is truly a lack of time, it has to be stated that there are (time) problems in a very early stage of that project. Thus the project leader should be asked if he should not stop the project before starting it, since experience shows that time will become scarcer (not more prevalent) as the project progresses.

2. *It is a high risk not to quantify the project size* especially because if one does not know what is in the project (i.e., enough to quantify the requirements) then how can development proceed? In North America there is a joke about a project manager saying to his team "You guys just start coding and I'll go talk to the customer about their requirements." This might seem outlandish in light of the incredible millions (and billions) of dollars spent on software development, yet it is too close for comfort to the situation on many software projects today.

3. The effort for the measurement and estimation increases significantly when the project team has to search for the necessary documentation or they cannot find it since it does not exist. The discovery that a project is deficient of basic requirements and database diagram documentation is critical to know and this allows management the opportunity to increase the quality of project documentation to an acceptable level. This is similar to the statement (which is more common than not) that the "necessary documentation is not up to date or is incomplete." This illustrates that measurement and estimation can have a quality assurance benefit as a side effect.

   The effort for fixing such deficits in project documentation is sometimes erroneously accounted for as being estimation effort. In reality, this is an excuse – the effort is actually effort that should have been expended in the first place but was a neglected documentation task. One might actually consider this "extra" effort of upgrading the documentation to the acceptable level as rework! However, the misguided notion that we need to complete documentation (supposedly otherwise not needed) again fosters the prejudice that estimation takes too much effort. Do not be swayed by detractors who insist that this is the situation. Re-read these three points so that you will have ready information to counter this argument!

Further obstacles for the dissemination of software measurement and estimation are deficits in usability, relevance, end user efficiency, and the poor presentation of IT metrics. Other obstacles are lack of discipline and the chaotic nature of many IT organizations. As we discussed in the previous section, sometimes an organization is too immature from a process maturity standpoint (i.e., level 0 or level 1 on the CMMI® or SPICE maturity scales) to even consider formal estimation processes. Once you have assessed the timing for estimation and determined that the time is right, do not allow detractors to convince you that you were incorrect. Enlist the aid of management to support you in the implementation!

In many organizations the dissemination of estimation methods that are used in one department fails in other departments (particularly in very large geographically dispersed IT organizations) because of the *"not invented here" syndrome*. This syndrome exists internationally and leads to the habit that nobody is responsive to proven process improvements, or that valuable ideas are ignored or repulsed in order to use politically correct, but less valuable, methods.

On the other hand, what also occurs is that the newest trends in software development are copied just because they are the "flavor of the week," and they are then propagated fast and furiously in blind adaptation. This is often found with the newest and greatest (or so their marketing representatives assert) tools and software. However, the existence of a realistic and positive effect on project performance is not evaluated and as a result the promised benefits are never fully realized.

It is amazing to realize that as humans we are quick to reject new and proven ideas just because they might not have been invented here, yet we are quick to embrace the unproven new project "toys" just so that we will be as "cool as the other kids on the block."

We have seen this in practice far too often, where the demand to deliver software solutions faster and cheaper leads to a tendency to start with a "quick and dirty" programming approach even before the requirements of the end users are understood correctly. This again leads to lower software product quality and increased rework.

Acceptance problems can also be solved by experts in the domain who have successfully been through the processes before (i.e., *consultants*). At the beginning of the process implementation, their assistance is a *conditio sine qua non* to start quickly and effectively with the right concept for estimation. One caution to bear in mind here, however, is that problems can arise if the dependence on consultants in the beginning is too great because the staff may feel that management does not have enough confidence in them to implement the processes themselves.

One positive aspect of consultants, however, is that management listens more readily to consultants (gurus) than to their own people. This is a common source of frustration for internal professionals (we used to say "here, you move the consultant's mouth and I'll say the words" in jest when we encountered a consultant who knew less than us). There is the additional danger that too much knowledge will be lost to the organization if it is not properly transferred to the employees before the consultants leave. Do not let this happen to your organization – ensure that any consultants you bring in to assist with estimation are "part" of the process not THE process. Shortcuts where consultants leave before knowledge is transferred mostly happen for time- and cost-saving reasons. However, the cost of having knowledge walk out the door with your consultants is far higher than paying them for the time to transfer the knowledge!

4.4.2 Resistance

An effect often overlooked in establishing project control is the impact on the people involved. Software is developed by engineers, and not by machines, yet we end up routinely treating developers (and project teams) like inanimate objects. *Although introducing metrics typically means a cultural change to all involved parties, the focus is too often only on tools and definitions.* If faults, efficiency, or task completion are measured, it is not some abstract product that is involved, it is the practitioners who know that they will be compared to others. People at all levels are sufficiently intelligent and experienced to know when the truth is being obscured.

Introducing measurement and analysis will change behavior, potentially in dysfunctional ways. Knowing the benefits of metrics for better project management or for steering the course of improvement initiatives does not at all imply that people will readily buy into the decision to participate in measurement. In fact, using words such as "productivity" leads to the implication that somehow people need to be measured. Clear explanation of the motivation–from the beginning–to provide the whole picture is far better than superficial statements about project benefits. State the goals emphatically, clearly, and consistently. If the rationale behind better estimation is to ward off potential outsourcing, say so! If you try to pretend it is not so using flaky or contrived excuses for the new processes, morale will suffer and people will start to print off their resumes in anticipation of the very outsourcing you denied.

The lack of acceptance of new things is a natural element of being human. Rejecting the resistance or denying it exists can exacerbate the situation and can lead to a general behavior of resistance (the money is out of another pocket!). Resistance takes various forms, such as the following:

- Passive resistance
- Work (only) on order also known as work to rule
- Active resistance
- Giving notice to leave or threatening to do so
- Outright rebellion (where the resistance becomes the focus of work rather than performing the work itself)

Tom DeMarco distinguished seven kinds of resistant people:

1. Blind loyalists (they ask no questions)
2. Critical convinced
3. Skeptics ("prove it to me")
4. Passive observers ("what's in it for me?")
5. Opponents (they fear change and how it will affect them and their jobs)
6. Enemies (they fear lack of power and a further erosion of the power they currently perceive they have)
7. Militant enemies (they undermine and destroy your plans).

Hence it is recommended to collect a repertoire of behavioral arguments – in addition to some slogans – that can readily help you to oppose resistance, as shown in Table 4.8.

Table 4.8. Tackling the many forms of resistance.

Resistance	
. . . is natural and unavoidable!	Expect resistance!
. . . is often hidden!	Find resistance!
. . . has many causes!	Understand resistance!
. . . discusses the hesitations, not the arguments!	Confront resistance!
. . . can be fought in many ways!	Manage resistance!

It must be said explicitly that there is an immense interdependency between motivation and acceptance. *Therefore, a major success factor for the implementation of measurement and estimation is the construction (or realignment in some cases) of a well planned motivation or reward system.* It should have the goal to positively influence the people for active cooperation and, last but not least, to identify the individual processes or techniques. In some organizations the existing reward system gives credit to dysfunctional behaviors (such as when project managers hide project effort in order to "fake" an on-time delivery) and these need to be realigned to incent the desirable new behaviors. If the old reward system stays in place without adjustment, then people will continue to behave in the manner in which they receive the most reward, which can severely undermine the estimation initiative!

The three most important columns of such a motivational system are information, training, and participation, the so-called three lane king's road for introduction of innovations or new processes. This recommendation cannot be stressed enough.

Plan to position metrics from the beginning as a management tool for improvement and state that one of the targets is to improve efficiency in the competitive environment. Make explicit what the results will be used for and how they will be measured. When used for competition and benchmarking, first stimulate that people work with their measurements and start improving later on. For instance, if faults are counted for the first time over the life cycle, establish a task force with representatives from different levels to investigate results from the viewpoint of root cause analysis and criticality reduction. *Ensure that people are not punished for reporting true data!* Remember that data are the status quo of the current situation and the worse the current situation, the more opportunities for process improvement exist.

Management must be on-board to support a new or realigned reward system that gives positive motivation (and rewards) to compliance with the new processes rather than the old. *Remember that people will generally follow the path of least resistance.* So if the cost of compliance with a new process is less than the cost of non-compliance, you have a positive balance. Conversely, if it costs more (in terms of time, energy, overtime, punishment, or lack of bonuses) to change and comply with the new process than to simply stay doing the status quo, then you will be fighting an uphill battle. In this situation, when management questions why people are not following the new process, the response will generally be it is too hard or takes too much time or gets in the way, and your whole initiative can be derailed quickly. Make sure that people are encouraged to adopt the new desired behavior through motivational incentives!

Educate your senior management. Uneducated or negligent managers tend to use metrics recklessly. It is important to forewarn your management not to make decisions from metrics without reasoning about their context. For example, if there are many defects reported against a newly delivered software component, negligent managers would errantly conclude that the designer does not know his job. More often, however, the valid conclusion is that a specific piece of software is error-prone because of high complexity, or because of instability of legacy code, one area breaks when another area is fixed.

Restricted visibility but appropriate access to the metrics (and raw data) helps in creating credibility among practitioners, especially in the beginning when the data analysis is getting started. For instance, progress or defects on a component maintained by an individual engineer could be misconstrued or misrepresented and is not the type of information to be propagated across the enterprise. It is often helpful to change one's perspective towards the one providing raw data: is the data collection activity adding value to her daily work? Statistical issues might not automatically align with emotional priorities. Especially with metrics, remember that the perception becomes reality in absence of facts to the contrary!

A competence center can also greatly assist with this aspect of measurement. Rather than reporting raw data or statistics, the competence center can do analysis where causal analysis is conclusive. What this means is that the chart should lead readers to understand the rationale (reasons) that explain the data. If a chart leads managers or other readers to draw the wrong conclusion from the data, then it could be considered negligence on the part of the analyst who presented the data on the chart. *Too often, a chart is presented where the data presentation misleads the reader to a wrong conclusion,* for example, if many projects of different types and their relative delivery rates are presented as a bar chart, it will provide readers with little clue of the reasons for the differences. However, if the chart presents mainframe vs. pc based new development projects, one may more appropriately conclude that one development platform is more conductive to speedy delivery than the other. *One should never present data in any chart where the interpretation of the data would lead one to the wrong conclusion!* Rather, take care to report what the data means (through analysis) and then figure out how to present the data to say exactly what should be concluded. For example, rather than presenting a bar chart showing the productivity or delivery rates in FP/hour across various (disparate and unalike) projects (which would lead to the questions of "who works on the low productivity projects?"), it is better practice to cluster the projects that are alike using a particular toolset and present them against those using a different toolset to depict that it is the toolset that makes the difference (which it is!) rather than the individuals who worked on a particular project.

Good communication is necessary in every business to be successful, to reduce friction, and foster teamwork, whether it is from engineer to manager, manager to engineer, or engineer to engineer. The 2004 edition of the Project Management Body of Knowledge (PMBOK) asserts that communication accounts for approximately 80% of a project manager's job. It is relatively easy for software functions to be relegated to a low priority in a company focused on other aspects of its products (such as in an insurance company or a bank). However, software engineers need to speak out clearly and be heard if they want to be understood by management. *Communication requires effort on the part of all parties.* In the case of management and software developers, both sides need to learn how to address each other's real needs. Management does not care for techno-babble, while engineers are easily bored with capitalization or depreciation questions regarding their software. Keeping this in mind while preparing data analysis or trend charts is essential for driving positive decision making and process improvement. Remember the needs of the audience and make sure that the right message comes across before you distribute any data.

4.4.3 Information and Participation

Correct information policy demands that project leaders and project team members get frequent and timely information about the goals of the estimation process and the desired effects of the implementation of the new estimation methods. For this reason, a competence center can, for example, publish its own newsletter, and can regularly inform readers about the actual results and the work performed by the competence center. It can also use the estimation training sessions to inform the participants about actual measures and real life results.

It is also important that experiences are exchanged with other organizations and between departments in order not to become mired in one's own problems. In some companies, this is referred to as "tunnel vision" and can result in fixation on a single perceived deficiency, which may not be at all pertinent to fix in the context of customers or the industry. The participation in conferences like the annual SEPG (Software Engineering Process Group, a concept of the US based Software Engineering Institute) conferences, local SPIN (Software Process Improvement Network, with many worldwide chapters supported by the Software Engineering Institute) meetings, the IWSM (International Workshop on Software Measurement convened by the University of Magdeburg and the University of Quebec at Montreal), or those organized by the national metrics organizations such as the International Function Point Users Group (IFPUG), or MAIN (Metrics Association's International Network) offers the opportunity to learn from other organizations that face similar problems. This allows one to participate and benefit from other experiences (see positive examples) and help to avoid pitfalls in implementation of measurement and estimation. Often useful contacts can be made that might lead to an exchange of experiences with colleagues after such conferences.

The next logical step on the way to acceptance is participation. *The goal of participation is the creation of widespread cooperation of all involved persons, and leading to active teamwork.* For this reason, it is of immense importance to avoid blindly import existing processes from another organization or another department. Instead, elaborate an adaptation according to the requirements of your own organization and in dialogue with those who will be involved. This can typically be done with the aid of a neutral (external) consultant together with the staff, as a pilot project. Hopefully, these initial adopter team members will go on to become the promoters of the new methods and processes. Figure 4.2 highlights some of the problems during the implementation of an estimation and measurement program.

Besides acceptance problems, there are a number of other challenges associated with the implementation of estimation and measurement. *The focus should be that processes are measured, not people.* If one does not follow this rule and keep it as the focus, the motivation of the staff will be undermined and the honesty of estimation cannot be fostered. Measurement and estimation should be integrated into the existing SDLC. Otherwise, if project teams must stop what they are doing to comply with the (extra) necessary tasks, data collection and the new tasks will be regarded as overhead. *The most important critical success factor is the visible and sustained support from management.* If there is a real or perceived lack of support from management, then project leaders will neglect the necessary tasks for measurement and estimation. Such disregard will not only delay the implementation process, but it will undermine the compliance and acceptance of the whole initiative.

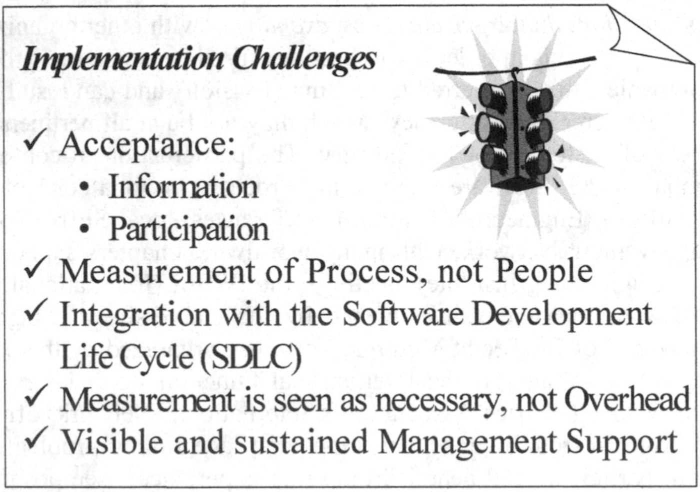

Implementation Challenges

✓ Acceptance:
  • Information
  • Participation
✓ Measurement of Process, not People
✓ Integration with the Software Development Life Cycle (SDLC)
✓ Measurement is seen as necessary, not Overhead
✓ Visible and sustained Management Support

Fig. 4.2. Implementation challenges.

The aforementioned formal estimation process is intended to deliver a clear picture about the strengths and weaknesses of the software development processes of an IT project. Capers Jones calls this the diagnosis. The strategic estimation takes this diagnosis as a starting point for the planning of measures for process improvement. Note that the intention of process improvement is to minimize and eliminate the areas of process weaknesses while intensifying and disseminating the strengths of the software development processes.

In doing this one must not forget that estimation and measurement and process improvement are not instantaneous. The decisions for performing such measures and its effects take time! Critics of such measures repeatedly say that estimation in this form does not pay, but:

A solid and profound estimation on operational and strategic level in connection with an adequate controlling of projects is the starting point of an improvement process that can be verified by measurable data.

4.5 Goals for an Estimation Process

Before the implementation of an estimation program goals must be clearly defined. Figure 4.3 shows an example of the high level goals of a large organization.

Goals

✓ Integrated Estimation Process
✓ Metrics as Basis for Benchmarking
✓ Tools Supporting the Estimation Process
✓ Comprehensive Documented Estimation Manual
✓ Estimating Training for Project leaders
✓ Exchange of Experiences about Estimations
✓ Reduction of Complexity and Uncertainty of Estimate
✓ Improvement of Precision of Estimates
✓ Consulting and Cooperation in Projects

Fig. 4.3: Goals for Implementation of Estimation

Note that these goals do not comply with the "SMART" acronym presented for goals when we discussed the Goal/Question/Metric approach to measurement presented on the second page of this chapter (Smart, Measurable, Actionable, Realistic, and Time Bounded). However, as high level initial goals, they represent the strategic goals for formal estimation. By selecting the most critical of the goals and drilling down to SMART goals, then questions, the appropriate metrics can be developed and planned for. The metrics stage is where many engineers get excited because it involves statistics and equations, but do not let the enthusiasm dissuade you from properly planning the goals and questions before diving in to which metrics and measures to collect.

Once the questions (how good is our estimating today? How good is it with the new estimating process? What is the difference? How can we improve the process to get better?) are assessed, the metrics can be defined as to which data are needed to measure to reach these goals. Figure 4.4 also shows as an example the measures developed to meet the goals of a large organization.

The large organization in question implemented formal estimation and measurement following the guidelines of Figs. 4.3 and 4.4. Two years after the start of the metrics initiative, the first results proved that the initiative was accepted and on its way to success (see Fig. 4.5).

Data Measured   per Project

✍ Project Size in Function Points
   as well as all details of Counts
✍ By Phase of the Software Development
   Lifecycle
   • Total Development Effort in Person Months or hrs
   • Effort for Project Management and
     Quality Assurance
✍ Quality Characteristics and Quality Metrics in
   Connection with the IFPUG-GSC's, or other assessment of
   non-functional requirement such as FiSMA's ND21
   or COCOMO II factors
✍ Quality- and Productivity Metrics based on
   Function Points (in some situations KLOCs)
✍ Risk Plan and Risk Metrics

Fig. 4.4. Measured data per project

Actual Results at example organization

✓ Training conducted for Function Point Workbench and
  Checkpoint/KPlan for Windows
   • Competence-Center-Staff
   • 25 Project Leaders
✓ 16 counted Projects with 25,000 Function Points
✓ Regular Inspections and Reviews
✓ Metrics for early Estimations
✓ Regular Knowledge Transfer

Fig. 4.5. Actual results

One IT organization reported about the development of a one-day estimation course and following training of some thousand persons. There were about 50 certified function point specialists (CFPS) within the staff.

One key deliverable was an estimation manual as the standard for process users and training material. Other organizations saw more on time delivery and better estimates leading to increased project control and satisfied customers. The training materials are an important prerequisite component to rolling out a metrics initiative in an organization, beyond the pilot project. This task can be combined with solving the problem of nonexisting historical data by counting and estimating finished projects according to the manual for testing it.

4.6 Counting of Historical Projects

The majority of software development in large organizations deals with enhancement projects. The development of large new software systems from scratch is more an exception than the rule. To effectively and efficiently count the functional size of enhancement projects, it often makes sense to first measure the size of the system to be enhanced. Figure 4.6 shows the central significance of the measurement of the size of the system to be enhanced. This can also help to solve the problem of missing historical data. However, it is not always financially possible to first measure the entire portfolio application size and in those cases, enhancement projects must assess and evaluate the extent of enhancement of the application even before beginning the FP enhancement count.

In the situation of the large organization we cite, management decided it was worthwhile to perform functional size measurement (function point counting) of the entire portfolio so that support and maintenance ratios could be established. As a result, the funding for FP counting of all applications was a part of their formal estimation process implementation.

Before one can estimate the work effort for an enhancement project, the functional size of the enhancement must be measured in terms of the functions to be deleted (i.e., removed from the software's functionality), changed (i.e., renovated or modified), and new development (added functionality) must be sized and the result input into the estimation tool. In addition, the functional size is often considered relative to the size of the system to be enhanced. Also migration functionality (data conversions) must be taken into account.

Migrations (data conversions) are a solitary task of the project that does not change the functional size of the application but it takes effort to do. Migrations are generally part of a project and result in a small number of Function Points (only some EIs, in extreme cases only one EI). To properly gauge the correct proportion of the migration effort (as estimated) from the whole effort of the project, one has to do the estimation twice: once with the migration and then again without including the size of the migration functionality. The difference can then be (hopefully) made responsible for the migration, since the effort evolves "on top."

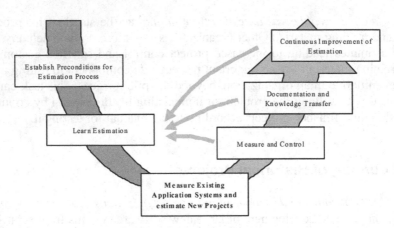

Fig. 4.6. Measurement of historical data.

A complete FP count of historical applications is sometimes not possible in cases where there is missing documentation. For these situations, if it is deemed that the portfolio size is necessary, approximations can be made with backfiring (see according chapter), whereby one derives the functional size-based on conclusions from source lines of code counts (SLOC) and code complexity (language level) of the application. This should be used with extreme caution as the functional size of the software in FP does not often have a linear correlation to the application's physical size in terms of its lines of code. Nonetheless, we present the information in a separate chapter for those who require a rough, "ballpark" approximation of functionality.

4.7 Estimation as an Early Warning System

Today, management often reacts more than they act in software development. As such, estimation processes can work as a kind of an early warning system that could – as in Industrial production processes – define tolerances for an IT project. If the project progresses within the estimated (statistically process controlled) borders, it should be finished successfully. Earned value management (EVM) as outlined in the PMBOK uses estimates against progress to-date to gauge the projected success (and anticipated over-budget or over-time results) of a project.

A prerequisite for an early warning system is the production of project progress reports. This requires constitution of a regular and consequent reporting process. In the start up phase, quarterly or half year reports should be planned for giving an overview about the actual status of all projects under way. Besides this, it is recommended that an annual report be delivered, showing the following:

1. An evaluation of the past year's development processes
2. Possible causes for project crises
3. Goals with according measures for the coming year for improvement of the software development in relation to the current year results.

Examples:

- *Goal:* Improvement of precision of the first obligatory estimation of a project to ±20% by 31 December.
  - o *Action:* development of a metrics data base
- *Goal:* Improvement of the productivity of IT projects of a particular kind to 13 Function Points per person month by 31 December.
  - o *Action:* training of the development staff for improvement of skills
- *Goal:* Improvement of the effectivity of defect correction of IT projects of a particular type to 80% by 31 December.
  - o *Action:* Installation of a test tool and associated training of staff.

Naturally, many causes for project crises and also typical cost drivers are known. It is known, for example, that documentation or tasks for quality assurance have an extraordinary influence on project effort. It is also known that these measures result in a positive influence (reduction) on the resultant maintenance effort for the application. What is not known are simply the answers to such crucial questions, as for example, *"How much should I invest on effort for quality assurance tasks to optimally improve quality on the one hand, but not detrimentally decrease the productivity on the other hand?"* In other words, what is the point of "just enough quality" to result in a positive benefit that is not offset by the negative result to productivity (break even analysis of cost vs. benefits). In this case, simulations of different scenarios of an estimation can support better decisions. Only a consequent measurement and follow up documentation of such information enables us to find answers to such questions. Examples are the following:

- Investigations of the Government Accounting Office in the USA showed that 47% of the dollars spent for software development of public administration was for software that was never used. A further 29% was spent for software that later required heavy improvement; a further 3% was spent on software that required minor later improvement. Result: only 21% was for software that was delivered to specification.
- The Department of Trade in England reported out of a sample size of 200 projects from all industrial branches, 55% were over-budget and 66% were delivered late. A similar investigation of the Government Accounting Office in the USA reported comparable figures of 50% and 60%, respectively.

To regain control about runaway projects in the cases of project crises, the project leader should consider the following steps:

1. *Clarify the project goals.* This is the most important but most difficult aspect to measure. Ambiguous project goals are one of the most frequent causes of project cancellation.
2. *Distinguish clearly between tasks and steps.* In many projects in crises the "meat balls in spaghetti" were not recognizable.
3. *Clarify the degree of completion.* Mostly this involves measures to obtain a milestone trend analysis, as well as the project status analysis. Often these two valuable tools are not used for controlling of projects.
4. *Measure project progress.* Here the results of step 2 and measurement of the size of the software to be developed can be applied.
5. *Management by exception.* Identification of critical tasks and their prioritized elaboration.

4.8 Management Summary

The implementation of estimation is an innovative project and as such, it must be planned and performed with as much rigor as any other formal IT project. The estimation process is the foundation for successful communication as well as for monitoring and improvement of project management processes. As in all innovative projects, it is important to take notice of and plan for acceptance issues, that is, for resistance to occur.

In Europe, we speak of the king's road, which is the means to accomplish the best outcomes. This means that the road to gain acceptance in any innovative or new endeavor consists of information, training, and participation of all involved persons. In addition, there is need for time to pass in order to foster awareness for the innovations.

A successful implementation in a large organization with approximately 500 IT developers was done over a 3 year period by two full time persons who worked as the competence center.

Management support was the most important success factor for the implementation process.

The publication of such positive key experiences can help to foster the acceptance of metrics programs in organizations.

The implementation breakthrough came with the final function point counting of all applications.

Continuous questions from management increased the awareness of managers and project managers for estimation. They realized that function point counting and estimation were more and more integrated in the project life cycle, and the process of counting was no longer neglected or viewed as overhead. The competence center accompanied the whole implementation process with many presentations, discussions, reports, and work on routine tasks.

There are only a few technical challenges associated with the successful implementation of software measurement, but there are many psychological challenges.

The recommended method for implementing estimation is to use a pilot project approach. The effort of this pilot project through to full scale implementation in a large organization can be planned to be approximately 2 person years. The process of gaining estimation knowledge, the integration of estimation into the processes of the software development model of the organization until consequent organization, and usage of IT metrics for continual improvement may possibly consume about another 2 person years.

Counter argument: Often, costs are cited as an argument against systematic and sound estimation practices. Considering the cost of large projects often being in the range of two digits of millions one can argue against.

Only one failed IT project costs more than all effort that is necessary to implement and foster sound methods of software estimation and measurement.

The right time for implementation depends mainly on the state of the IT project "chaos," that is, if customers are complaining about late projects that are overbudget and do not meet their needs, then the time is ripe for formal estimation!

But the guiding principle has to be as follows: start now if you have the prerequisites in place!

The build-up of an experience or metrics database and the development of standards for the improvement of the knowledge base with tool support are necessary and important steps.

A competence center can support the dissemination of experiences through continuous publication of results, experiences, reports from conferences, knowledge exchange with other organizations, and literature and new publications about estimation. This improves the communication about the estimation process and fosters better acceptance since the people feel more informed and involved than if there was no central source of information.

However, as with any new corporate decisions, there can also be reasons why estimation should not be done by a competence center. This is the reason for a hybrid alternative, where qualified individuals would work decentrally as the estimation coordinator of their department.

As we have touched on previously, it is commonplace for the implementation of new methods and processes to encounter acceptance problems. We again refer to the king's road analogy: This challenge can only be met with walking down the three-lane king's road to implementation of innovations: the three lanes being provision of intensive (and consistent) information, qualified training (at the right time), and enlisting the active participation of all involved persons!

One encounters in large organizations the most resistance from project leaders since the purported benefits and gains to be made from estimating are mostly on the management side. Experience with the large corporation to which we have repeatedly mentioned shows that even the well-trained project staff performed FP counts without argument but only if they were specifically assigned to do so.

FP counting and estimating will not be performed unless it is built into the project manager's processes. Unless the project leader has planned these tasks *into* the project plan, which is the most critical point, it will be seen as over-head and conveniently (even if unconsciously) forgotten!

A typical killer argument against formal estimation is a "lack of time" ("we have to do more important things than to collect data or perform estimates" or "we must reach the deadline" or else!). The way to address this concern is threefold.

1. In the authors' experience, even for larger IT projects, a full-blown esti-mate complete with a high level FP count of the software size, can be done in a matter of a couple of days.
2. If there is truly a lack of time, it has to be stated that there are (time) prob-lems in a very early stage of that project.
3. The effort for the measurement and estimation increases significantly when the project team has to search for the necessary documentation or they cannot find it since it does not exist.

This illustrates that measurement and estimation can have a quality assur-ance benefit as a side effect. The effort for fixing such deficits in project docu-mentation is sometimes erroneously accounted for as being estimation effort. In reality, this is an excuse – the effort is actually effort that should have been expended in the first place but was a neglected documentation task.

In many organizations, the dissemination of estimation methods that are used in one department fails in other departments (particularly in very large geo-graphically dispersed IT organizations) because of the "not invented here" syndrome.

Although introducing metrics typically means a cultural change to all invol-ved parties, the focus is too often only on tools and definitions.

Introducing measurement and analysis will change behavior, potentially in dysfunctional ways.

Hence it is recommended to collect a repertoire of behavioral arguments – in addition to some slogans – that can readily help you to oppose resistance.

It must be said explicitly that there is an immense interdependency between motivation and acceptance. Therefore, a major success factor for the implementation of measurement and estimation is the construction (or realignment in some cases) of a well planned motivation or reward system.

Plan to position metrics from the beginning as a management tool for improvement and state that one of the targets is to improve efficiency in the competitive environment. Make explicit what the results will be used for and how they will be measured.

Good communication is necessary in every business to be successful, to reduce friction, and foster teamwork, whether it is from engineer to manager, manager to engineer, or engineer to engineer.

Correct information policy demands that project leaders and project team members get frequent and timely information about the goals of the estimation process and the desired effects of the implementation of the new estimation methods.

It is also important that experiences are exchanged with other organizations and between departments in order not to become mired in one's own problems.

The next logical step on the way to acceptance is participation. The goal of participation is the creation of widespread cooperation of all involved persons, and leading to active teamwork.

The focus should be that processes are measured, not persons.

A solid and profound estimation on operational and strategic level in connection with an adequate controlling of projects is the starting point of an improvement process that can be verified by measurable data.

One key deliverable was an estimation manual as the standard for process users and training material.

Before one can estimate the work effort for an enhancement project, the functional size of the enhancement must be measured.

A prerequisite for an early warning system is the production of project progress reports. This requires constitution of a regular and consequent reporting process.

5 Estimation Methods

Today, there are several popular different approaches available for estimating software project work effort and cost. These models range from overly simplistic models (that rely on straight linear equations) to incredibly complex algorithm-based models. While commercially available products promise the magic elixir to solve estimation problems, and a range of public methods state similar claims, the truth is that most are based on a variation of the same underlying principles that relate the software product size (scope), quality, technology to time constraints. Four major types of software estimating models are prevalent:

- Models that require estimated technical size (Those based on source lines of code (SLOC))
- Models based on early estimates of functional size (FP shortcut-based)
- Models based on functional size of the software product (FSM based models)
- Those based on some other sizing mechanism such as analogy or counts of screens
- Hybrids of the above.

The principal steps of the process of estimation (see Fig. 5.1) start with a measurement of the size of software to be developed, *delivering a numerical value for the size of the object of estimation.* Using the functional size value for each piece of software, together with the environmental (situational and technical) and nonfunctional factors (quality constraints) for the software, the work effort estimate can be determined. Depending on the sophistication of the particular estimating model your organization selects, the estimation process can require anywhere from a few input variables to 200 or more. If there are several software applications involved in the project, there will be several function point counts required (at least one per "piece of software" or application being developed or enhanced), and subsequently there may be several estimates developed. The overall project work effort is typically the sum of all the component effort estimates. Note, however, that due to task and team dependencies, the overall project duration will not necessarily equate to the number of work effort hours divided strictly by the number of team members. Remember Fred Brooks' *Mythical Man Month* – one cannot create a baby in 1 month using nine women!

The next step after estimating the project work effort is usually to calculate a cost value from the effort using a metric such as US-$ per hour for the project or for classes of human resources. Again a note is in order: keep in mind that the project cost may include burdened (fully loaded with vacation and other benefits) or nonburdened labor rates, hardware and software acquisition costs, and other costs. It is important to be consistent with cost categories when comparing cost categories per FP at a later stage of the project.

In the simplest case to determine a preliminary estimate of project duration, the total work effort is apportioned across the various SDLC phases of an IT project using a Percentage of time per phase Method. The above mentioned estimate of *the total effort can be compared with the estimation calculated by the Percentage Method*, post project completion by using the actual measured effort of the first phase of the IT project, and calculating from this the total effort using the proportion percentage for this phase.

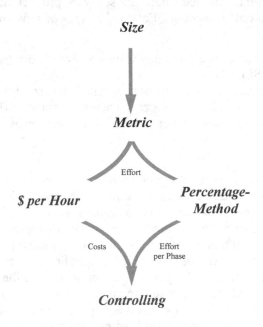

Fig. 5.1. Steps of the process of estimation

5.1 The Challenges of Estimation Methods

There exist many known and profound estimation methods. In an older German book, Noth/Kretzschmar compared some estimation methods and found *that Function Point based estimating performed best in their benchmark*. This is not to say that Function Points alone can produce a work effort estimate, but rather that his method was based on determining the FP count (functional size) and then using it and other input parameters to estimate the effort. This old statement is as valid today as it was at the time of its publication because nothing has changed much since then.

The cited method on which the effort was estimated using FP is relatively widely known worldwide among those knowledgeable in functional size measurement. IFPUG's FP method is a de facto standard and is the most widespread and best accepted method for measurement of the functional size of software. At the time of this printing, there is an ISO/IEC standard 20926: IFPUG 4.1 unadjusted Function Point Counting Method, in place within ISO/IEC. Future releases will be coordinated with ISO/IEC.

Because functional size measurement is becoming more commonly used (even though overall adoption or use of any measurement in software at all is limited to a mere 1–2% of the overall software development community), we have dedicated two special chapters in this book to Functional Size Measurement rather than deal with the extensive topic here.

Another formal estimating method in widespread use (particularly with in the U.S. government) is called the *COCOMO II* (COnstructive COst MOdel, which is SLOC based). COCOMO II is the invention of Barry Boehm, who established the Center for Systems and Software Engineering at the University of Southern California (see the website at http://csse.usc.edu/csse/). Boehm and his colleagues introduced the first COCOMO model in the early 1980's. Since its first incarnation the model has undergone continuous refinement to COCOMO II based on industry input. Dr. Boehm now has a number of COCOMO II models available for which there are both commercial and free automated tool support.

Practically, Function Points and SLOC are two principles used for measuring the size of the object of estimation (the software product size) and for calculating the effort needed to develop it.

In 2002, the IT department of an international insurance company in Germany elaborated an international survey about the usage of methods for measurement of size and received the following answers from 16 organizations worldwide:

- Three of the organizations measure effort
- Two measure Function Points (FP)
- Six measure a combination of effort and FP
- Two measure a combination of SLOC and FP and
- Two do not measure size at all.

The problems of the SLOC methods are that SLOC can only be measured in a late phase of a project's progress (after coding is complete) and when the majority of software development is already complete (coding is approximately 10% to 40% of the effort of system development). At the coding phase there are some KSLOC (Kilo-SLOC) methods available for effort estimation of the component tests and integration tests. In addition to the lateness of data availability of SLOC counts, there is a complication that the standards for counting of the SLOC must clearly be defined (e.g., how are SLOC counted in different programming languages?). At this point, comparability can fail when there are different or unknown counting rules leading to inconsistent results. For this reason, the IEEE (The Institute of Electrical & Electronics Engineers, Inc., one of the two large US organizations for software specialists, http://computer.org) developed its IEEE Standard 1045 for counting of SLOC.

The paradox of the Assembler equivalent (see chapter "Backfiring") is a doubtless argument against the SLOC methods: the mightier a programming language, the less SLOC are necessary for the programming of certain functionality. *This can lead to the wrong conclusions! In light of falling productivity (less lines of code per hour) there is a growing level of efficiency (i.e., more functionality produced in less time)!* Albeit the SLOC methods are of minimal use for early estimating, they are still used extensively in US-based large governmental software development. SLOC based estimation is defended by the argument that the development is often repeatable, homogeneous, and there is a large historical base of SLOC counts (e.g., a "cookie-cutter environment" where the same types of software projects are done repeatedly). In such an environment, the argument is that there exist no better metrics than those based on years of repeatable projects where they have recorded the actual historical effort by SLOC counts. Some of the governmental organizations (e.g., the United States Department of Defense agencies) have recently toyed with function point-based estimating when new technology is introduced, or multiple platform new development is involved.

Organizations mired in engineering businesses also often rely on business SLOC counts as their sole measure for software size. These measures are by definition dependent on the technology used in development, and are not readily comparable from one programming language to another. Nevertheless, there is no convincing professionals who see their SLOC counts as a special solution that rewards larger amounts of programming code as a better representation of their engineering problem to be solved. In North America there is an old adage: *You can lead a horse to water, but you cannot make him drink.* This is the same thing for people – they will do what they want in spite of better methods, partly because of the comfort level with the tried and familiar, and partly due to the acceptance issues we have already covered. It is worth noting that Capers Jones and other leading metrics specialists do not rely on SLOC methods to compute the size of software.

The advantage of Functional Size Measurement based estimation Methods is that they can be used early (in the requirements phase) in the software development life cycle. In addition to the IFPUG functional size measurement method that is an ISO/IEC standard 29026, there are four functional size measurement methods (FSMM) recognized by ISO/IEC as being conformant with the mandatory provisions of the Functional Size Measurement definition of concepts standard (ISO/IEC 14143-1). All of these FSMM's are described in a subsequent chapter.

- The Mark II Method (ISO/IEC 20968)
- The NESMA Method (ISO/IEC 24570)
- The FiSMA (Finnish Software Measurement Association) Method (ISO/IEC 29881)
- The COSMIC Method (ISO/IEC 19761).

Besides these standards, trainings, user-groups, consultants, and benchmarks are established and the organizations using the methods get valuable results. Function Points are appreciated for performing benchmarks, for comparing projects, departments, organizations, business areas, or countries, or for measurement of software quality and productivity. Other methods of sizing software aside from SLOC and functional size measurement methods are also available in industry. These somewhat experimental sizing approaches are also profiled in a separate chapter in this book, and include:

- The Use Case Point method
- The Data Point method
- The Object Point method
- The Feature Point method
- The 3D FPM
- Other lesser known variations.

The problems associated with users of functional size measurement include that the requirements are not detailed enough after project start and that the IFPUG base functional component complexity factors (e.g., 1 ILF low = 7 FP) are continuously the object of debates (for reason of their origins and that the measurement scales are discrete rather than continuous). The IFPUG 4.1 unadjusted method was published as an ISO/IEC standard: 20926:2003 IFPUG 4.1 Unadjusted FP Method.

Note: The International Organization for Standardization (ISO) in its standard ISO/IEC 14143-1:2007 has two definitions that are pertinent to mentioned here:

- *"Functional Size" is defined as a size of the software derived by quantifying the Functional User Requirements.*
- *Functional User Requirements are defined as a subset of the User Requirements that describe what the software shall do, in terms of tasks and services.*

According to ISO, this means that functional size must purely reflect what the software must do, and exclude nonfunctional or technical characteristics.

This is why the ISO/IEC version of the IFPUG standard is "unadjusted," and excludes the adjustment of the Value Adjustment Factor.

Several of the non-ISO/IEC methods listed above (object points, data points, use case points, etc.) would not meet the requirements for measuring functional size due to the reason that they include aspects of the technical environment (OO e.g.) in their measurement.

Function point-based methods are superior to SLOC-based methods for hybrid technology environments (in particular). Besides this, the standards, trainings, user-groups, consultants- and benchmarks are established, and the organizations using function point-based estimating methods prove that they get valuable results. Function Points are appreciated for performing benchmarks, for comparing projects, departments, organizations, business areas, or countries, or for measurement of software quality and productivity.

The issues related to adoption of IFPUG function point counting typically occur when the requirements are not detailed enough after project start, and there is also concern that the IFPUG complexity factors (e.g., 1 ILF low = 7 FP) are continuous object of debates for reason of their origin as well as being fixed and have not changed since the introduction of the method in 1984. The acceptance of function point-based estimating is low in the noncommercial (typically government) environment of software development, since its sensibility for technical and other complexity (very low or very high complexity of transactions) is low. This leads to a follow-on debate about the value of the 14 GSCs of the IFPUG Method, as well as to the CPLX Adjustment Factor of COCOMO II.

Purists of *the object-oriented paradigm* often use the killer phrase that functional size based estimation methods are not suited for object-oriented system development. In numerous discussions with such purists, the German author discovered that their opinions were typically based on theory since none had actually tried to use a non-OO specific estimation method to estimate an actual OO project. The opinions were based on the supposition that, in particular, function point-based methods of estimating could not be as good as OO-specific methods because they did not take into account OO-specific artifacts.

To support the premise that Function Point Analysis can be universally applied to functional user requirements regardless of the implementation or design method (i.e., object-oriented development), the IFPUG has published several case studies (which are updated with each new release of its counting practices manual). One of the case studies, currently named "Case study 3," illustrates a Function Point count in an object-oriented environment. At international metrics congresses (MAIN, IWSM, IFPUG, ISBSG, SEPG, SMEF, etc.) there are also many reports where success stories about functional size measurement in object-oriented environments are presented. *Hence it is possible to estimate the effort of object-oriented system development using functional size measurement together with solid historical data from such projects and earnest endeavor using the known estimation methods* (see also the chapters about object-oriented metrics).

Mathematicians attest that it really does not make sense to measure the "length of algorithms" (when performing functional size measurement), since anytime someone can develop a new and shorter algorithm for the solution of a problem. Hence, according to the mathematicians, the length of an algorithm depends more on the actual solution as on the problem to be solved (see also the chapter about McCabe's Complexity Design Metric). Furthermore, the length of an algorithm coded in a special programming language has little relation to the functional requirements to be solved. And the length of an algorithm is more a measure of the programming skills of the programmer and thus depends on a person. Programming itself is essentially a translation task and hence easier than the discovery of an algorithm. The most effort arises from the requirements of rigorous testing. For all these reasons, the measurement of the functional size of very algorithmic software is still a challenge today.

Two of the ISO conformant functional size measurement methods, ISO/IEC 29881:FiSMA 1.1 and ISO/IEC 19761:COSMIC-FFP, do take into account counting of algorithms in their methodology. COSMIC does so as part of the functionality, while the FiSMA 1.1 method includes a set of identifiable independent algorithmic services in their base functional components used to determine the functional size. To-date, the IFPUG Method, the Mark II Method, and the NESMA Method consider algorithms and their complexity to be either nonfunctional requirements or to simply contribute data elements to another elementary process (function) that they count. Whether it is better to independently count algorithms as explicitly functional or nonfunctional is a matter of expert opinion or of the methodology chosen for the functional sizing. (Note that the "Feature Point" method originally developed by Capers Jones in the 1990s added "Algorithms" as a sixth base functional component to be counted in addition to the five functional components of the IFPUG Method. While Capers Jones has stepped away from endorsing Feature Points in favor of the updated IFPUG Method, there are still proponents who adhere to his Feature Point method.).

Hand in hand with estimation goes *the usage of tools* that is described in a special chapter of this book because of its importance where we discuss only the methods used in the tools and provide a list of available tools. The more commonly used functional size measurement methods are usually supported by a broader variety of software estimating tools compared to less disseminated methods. However, beware that the quality of the data used to generate estimates as well as the match to your organization's needs are more important than the number of tools. For example, many of the estimating tools rely on a database of SLOC sizing values that are "backfired" into function points based on using a language level multiplier that divides the number of SLOC by a constant to derive the function point size. See the chapter on usage of tools for further information.

We define a software estimation process as *"a method with detailed regulations and standards that is effectively supported by tools."* Two examples illustrate an estimation process:

Example 1:
In a large organization, for example, the following estimation process is installed:

Methods:
- International standardized size measurement method IFPUG (current release)
- A Certified Function Point Specialist (CFPS) in the central competence center
- Quality- and risk-metrics
- A bimonthly internal newsletter for the project leaders, published by the competence center

Tools:
- Function Point Workbench (LAN-Version) from Charismatek, Australia
- Knowledge PLAN (formerly Checkpoint) from SPR (Software Productivity Research, founded by Capers Jones) in Burlington, Massachusetts
- Excel charts for different metrics
- All documents, standards, and tools publicly available in Intranet and LAN

Example 2:
In a large governmental organization, for example, the following estimation process is installed:

Methods:
- International standardized size measurement method FiSMA 1.1
- Qualified and knowledgeable measurement specialist in the central competence center
- Quality- and risk-metrics
- A monthly progress report of each project's FP completion (in % delivered) for the customer organization and project leaders, published by the measurement specialist on the project

Tools:
- Experience® Pro software from 4SUM Partners, Finland which houses the function point details, maps progress, controls scope and produces reports
- Microsoft Word is used to produce the standard written project progress report

A challenge to estimating methods overall is the low degree of dissemination and serious consideration granted to the estimating theme by researchers, scientists, and educational institutions. Two noted German authors, Achim Kindler and Wolfram von Schneyder, address the lack of widespread acceptance and support of estimation as a serious discipline:

"In project management it is typical to find that the basic methods such as Delphi and the Three Point method (for estimating) are described. Regrettably, project management (and its associated estimating tasks) is not acknowledged as a science and thus shows up only as an exception in universities. The low priority of estimation in science shows up also in research."

Estimation in academic studies as well as in training and literature is often dealt with at a peripheral level in that it is mentioned as a necessary task to be done with the existing methods and processes (with no mention of its importance or how to do it properly). This impression is also valid for monographs and literature about project management as, for example, the ISO/IEC 17024 Standard conform 4-Level Certification System (4LC) of the IPMA (International Project Management Association, http://www.ipma.ch) or the PMBOK Guide (Project Management Body of Knowledge, PMI – Project Management Institute http://www.pmi.org).

It is common in large- and medium-sized organizations for there to be a series of project management manuals and standards with regulations how to proceed in projects. However,

- These standards mostly give mandate that estimation has to be done (without any hint how to do this).
- If there are detailed descriptions about how to perform estimating, it is based on a theoretical premise that the organization is sufficiently equipped with all the information outlined – this is seldom the case. In other words, the estimation procedures are sound; however, it is impossible to enact them in practice because of, for example, nonexistent historical data, inapplicable project types in the model (that do not match the reality of the types of projects being done), or changed organizational structures.

Should you purchase a commercial tool or rely on a publicly available model to do your estimating? The answer depends on a number of factors, including size of your estimating initiative, your organization's maturity level and the sophistication required by a tool (i.e., giving a CMMI® Level 1 organization a CMMI® Level 5 tool to do estimates will lead to frustrating results and a poor investment. Morale will suffer and resistance will grow – the tool must match the needs!), the budget for estimation support, data quality (of the historical experience database provided in some tools), accuracy required, and the fit to your organization's needs.

While commercially available products generally feature a larger historical experience database than those that are publicly available, it is important to know how the model actually works and how good the quality of the collected data really is. You may have heard the saying: *A fool with a tool is still a fool!* And this adage applies if you do not take the time to research the estimating model that will best fit with your goals.

5.2 Determination of the Effort

The result of a work effort estimation is a figure for the human resource effort that characterizes the development or enhancement of the software system (or a part of it). Work effort is generally estimated in units of *person month* (PM) or derived measures, for example, person year (PY), person day (PD), or person hours (PH). It was synonymously called man month or staff month in older publications.

The usage of estimation processes, for example, with *experience curves or estimation equations* implies the existence of mathematical functions for calculation of effort, and can seduce one to the wrong conclusion by assuming that exact results can be calculated. This is not true! Remember the adage that garbage in equals garbage out – and if one uses approximate or rough values for input variables in an estimating equation, the results will be even more approximate, and never more accurate than the least accurate input value.

After determination of the size of an application, for example, by counting Function Points, one tries to find an applicable relationship between the functional size and the work effort for software development. Two such relationships include the following:

- Size-based estimates
- Heuristic estimates.

Some of the heuristic methods are described in the chapter *Overview of Methods*. The size-based methods can be divided into three categories:

- Estimation with an experience curve
- Estimation with an estimation equation
- Estimation with an expert system
- In addition, the often-discussed method of backfiring will be addressed.

5.2.1 Estimation Based on an Experience Curve

Project postmortems or retrospectives should provide actual project work effort figures in at least person months, and the actual project delivery size in Function Points for each project. Using this data in statistical regression analysis, one can calculate an "experience curve." Once there are at least five high quality data points for similar projects (same hardware platform, same development language, similar team size, same business area, and same application type), one can build a table from this curve showing the relation between person months and Function Points. Subsequently, when the Function Points for a new project are counted, one can estimate the project work effort from the table or can calculate it using the regression formula.

Obviously, the validity of the table and the equation is better if the projects are fairly homogeneous. A further point to note is that the effort recorded for the project postmortems must be measured in a standardized form (using a standard definition of what constitutes "project work effort") according to the time accounting practices in place.

When performing the regression analysis, one should also check to ensure that the usage of the (simpler) regula falsi (linear interpolation between data points) leads to acceptable results. Depending on the scatter of the data between projects, one of the methods (table or regression equation) will deliver better results. Figure 5.2 shows an example of an experience curve from IBM.

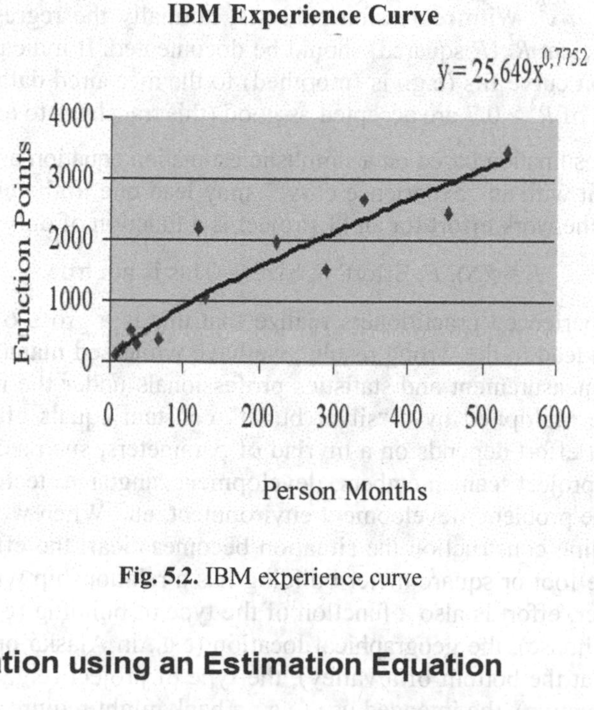

IBM Experience Curve

$$y = 25,649x^{0.7752}$$

Fig. 5.2. IBM experience curve

5.2.2 Estimation using an Estimation Equation

Estimation using standard equations relies on established industry relationships between effort parameters that has been proven to strongly influence the productivity of software development. At least 50 or more such methods abound in software tools and published literature. Two of the most popular traditional models are (1) the Monte Carlo distribution equation used by Larry Putnam who established Quantitative Software Measurement (QSM) and developed the SLIM (Software Life Cycle Management) estimating model; and (2) COCOMO II developed by Barry Boehm at the University of Southern California, which is also based on a Monte Carlo distribution of work effort throughout a software development project.

The majority of effort estimation equations follow the general form $y = f(x_1, x_2, x_3,...)$, where y is the estimated work effort and x_i are the input parameters influencing the effort. When IFPUG or another functional size measurement method is used to determine the size of the software to be developed or enhanced, the work effort equations most commonly used are in the form $y = a*x^b$, with a and b calculated by a regression analysis process, y is the estimated work effort, and x is the functional size. The exponent b varies normally between 0.5 and 1.5. Researcher Horst Zuse proved mathematically in his paper (Zuse 2005) about the Halstead complexity metric that the only mathematically correct and valid prediction models related to software estimating are of the form $y = a*x^b$. With regression analysis, normally the regression- or reliability-coefficient R^2 (R squared) should be documented. It indicates how good the regression curve fits (e.g., is smoothed) to the measured data points. Generally values of $R^2 > 0.7$ are accepted as good (this translates to an $R > 84\%$).

Note that estimation based on a simplistic estimation equation as well as those based on a fit with an "experience curve" may lead one to the erroneous conclusion that the work effort for an IT project is a function of only one variable:

$$E = f(S), E, \text{Effort}, S, \text{Size.} - \text{This is not true!}$$

While experienced practitioners realize that this is a gross oversimplification that can lead to the wrong results, we have witnessed managers and even specialized measurement and statistics professionals under the misguided belief that size multiplied by a "silver bullet" constant equals effort. Software development effort depends on a myriad of parameters, such as, for example, the skill of project team members, development language, technology, complexity of the problem, development environment, etc. When we use the analogy of building construction the situation becomes clear: the effort to build a 1,000 square foot or square meter building has a relationship with the overall size; however, effort is also a function of the type of building (e.g., an aircraft hangar or a house), the geographical location (e.g., in Alaska or in Germany, on a hill or at the bottom of a valley), the type of project (e.g., new or renovated construction), the intended use (e.g., a bank might require a more secure building than a grain silo), and the type of construction (e.g., custom built from scratch vs. using a prefabricated log cabin kit, or a premanufactured set of connectable trailer units).

Now, when we apply the analogy to software development, the effort to develop a 1,000 FP piece of software has a relationship with the overall size; however, the effort is also a function of the type of software (e.g., avionics software or banking software or pacemaker software), the location of the development team (e.g., if ½ the team is in India and ½ the team is in the US, as opposed to an entire team in the same location), the type of project (e.g., new development or enhancement or conversion of existing software), the intended use (e.g., a single user vs. tens of thousands of users), the quality or nonfunctional requirements (including the ISO/IEC 9126 quality attributes plus accuracy, performance, etc.).

Barry Boehm remarked on the impact that can be caused by nonfunctional requirements: "A tiny change in NFRs (nonfunctional requirements) can cause a huge change in the cost" (Boehm 2005, in the preface). Boehm went on to cite the tripling of a $10 million [USD] project to $30 million [USD] when the response time (of a NFR) went from four seconds to one. It is important to document assumptions for NFRs, especially if project complexity is likely to increase.

For this reason one must suggest that the effort of an IT project depends on many variables:

$$E = f(x_1, x_2, x_3, \ldots).$$

The International Software Benchmarking Standards Group (ISBSG) is a not-for-profit consortium of software measurement organizations and maintains one of the world's leading software measurement repositories of actual project data – based primarily on function points (functional size measurement of projects) and other project data (including software development effort, complexity, defects, etc.). Currently, the database is the only publicly accessible database housing over 4,000 projects from over 20 countries, and it is growing weekly. The ISBSG scrubs the data submitted from companies around the world, anonymizes it (removes the unique company identifies), analyzes the data, and then makes it available for public purchase (at a cost-recovery price).

The analysis of the ISBSG data results in experience curve equations published by the ISBSG in the form of such books as *Practical Project Estimation* (Hill 2005) and *The Software Compendium* (ISBSG 2002). The American author of this book contributed chapters to the *Practical Project Estimation* book. The reader is encouraged to explore the latest releases of the ISBSG resources and available publications. (See www.ISBSG.org.) The experience curves published by the ISBSG follow the same form as the equation above. The four largest drivers of effort found by the ISBSG include business sector, application type, hardware platform, and development language.

5.2.3 Estimation with an Expert System

The third variation of estimation methods aside from experience curves and estimation equations is a knowledge based expert system. This method of estimation relies on a database of historical knowledge stored in a standardized form, often within a specialized software package. While there are close to a hundred software packages that promise accurate estimates for work effort and cost that range from the simplistic to the obscenely complex (with price tags that also range widely), the reader is cautioned to make sure that any expert system they purchase *meets their specific corporate needs*, just because the package promises to deliver accurate results does not necessarily mean it suits your particular organization or the way you may develop software. We have included a section on tool support in this book; however, we only endorse those with which we have had personal and positive results at our organizations.

When an effort estimate is desired, many of the tools require, at a minimum, software size as an input variable. While size is a driver of effort and cost, remember from the preceding paragraphs that it is not the only driver! When inputting size, these expert estimating systems ask for it in either SLOC or in IFPUG Function Points (FP). A few will accept number of screens, sizing by analogy (based on past projects that are "similar"), or one of the other ISO conformant functional sizing units (FiSMA, NESMA, Mark II, or COSMIC), and other sizing units (such as the once popular Feature Points). Be aware that for the simplest expert system for which size is the only explicit input value, this means that all of the other input variables (such as type of project, development language, business area, etc.) will be considered to be average values and that the resultant estimate will be a high level guess based purely on the project raw size. Note that it is important to know whether the expert system asks for adjusted or unadjusted function point size in the case of IFPUG, and older Mark II, or NESMA function points, which can cause a variation of up to ±35% (for IFPUG counts) relative to the raw unadjusted FP count. Note also that this type of high level estimate based purely on the FP size is similar to saying "How much will it cost to build a 1,000 square foot building?" without any consideration of the type of building, geographic location, number of floors, construction approach, etc. So be *very careful* when using such a coarse estimating method, and especially careful if the expert system gives you an estimate that appears to be precise! (Again think of putting 1,000 square feet into a construction estimating model and getting out a number that includes decimals after the hours such as 10,506.92 h!!! It would be absolutely ridiculous for a builder to report back such a figure to a prospective client – yet the same thing happens in software estimating all the time! Someone guesses that a piece of software is "about" 500 FP and puts it into an expert system to discover that the tool estimates 5062.86 h to build whatever it might be, and then has the ignorance to report that to management! Not only is the tool performing a disservice by giving a too-precise guesstimate, the user is misleading management by reporting this guesstimate as if it is a precise estimate.)

Remember a fool with a tool is still a fool!

Now that we have got that out of the way, let us look at doing estimates based on more than a pure raw number for size. As such, detailed estimations require more details to be input, such as

- Information about the complexity of the software (nonfunctional requirements and constraints)
- The business area
- The type of project (new development, enhancement, conversion, etc.)
- Information about the skills of the project team
- The programming language(s) to be used
- The hardware platform(s)
- The methodology
- Etc.

The principle behind the process of estimation with an expert system is simplified as shown in Fig. 5.3. If an organization already has a historical base of measured actual effort, some tools will allow you to enter this information to augment their "experience" database. Whether or not the tool accepts your own historical data to alter their expert system or as a comparison against the estimates they generate is a matter of each particular tool. In our experience, your own organization history of actual completed projects can often be a better (or at least as good) estimator as a theoretical model. This is especially true if the expert system model has not been calibrated to your own organizational practices. (A good exercise for this is to take one of your completed projects and its actual size, complexity, and other characteristics and run them through the tool as if you were doing an estimate. Then compare the estimated work effort to your actual work effort it took to do the project in reality; if the numbers are far apart, then you know that the tool needs to be calibrated to your own environment. If you do not calibrate the tool, you will consistently end up with estimates that are based solely on the tool defaults and will be either too high or too low compared to your actuals.)

An example of an expert system for which the German author of this book has extensive experience is SPR KnowledgePLAN (formerly known as Checkpoint). The American author has experience using Experience® Pro by 4SUM Partners, SLIM (and Estimate Express) by QSM, as well as a number of other expert systems. Experience® Pro includes the ISBSG current database release as one of its estimating databases (the full database as well as an ISBSG subset with only the highest quality "A" projects) to augment its proprietary database of completed projects. SPR is also in the process of including ISBSG data in the KnowledgePLAN tool, as are several other tool vendors. It is not known at the time of this writing whether the SLIM tool suite intends to utilize the ISBSG database as part of their expert system data.

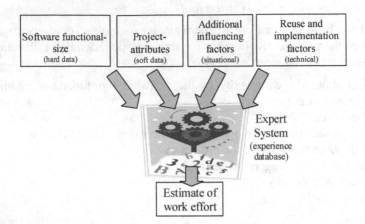

Estimation comprises:
1.   Measurement of the (functional) size
2.   Analysis and evaluation of project attributes and additional influencing factors
3.   Input of reuse and other implementation (build) specific factors
3.   Rules, how 1. and 2. and 3. will be correlated

Fig. 5.3. Estimation with an expert system

The advantage of such expert systems is obvious: The knowledge base can be administrated from a central competence center, enabling the user to access a substantially larger database than if he would only use his own projects with an experience curve. Currently, the knowledgebase of KnowledgePLAN contains historical data of about 6,700 projects, Experience® Pro includes almost 1,000 projects as well as the 4,000+ of the ISBSG database. The SLIM Suite of tools relies on Monte Carlo simulation equations as the basis for its experience data in addition to customized databases that can be provided using the SLIM Metrics tool based on an organization's own data.

5.2.4 Backfiring

At times it is necessary to replace a legacy application and obtain an estimate of the work effort to redevelop the same set of functionality. As such, one can typically use existing documentation (user manuals or other document that describes the functionality provided by the software) to count the FP size for input into one of the previous estimation models. But what if there is no documentation or the documentation is so out of date to render it useless? In such a case, one can do a rough approximation of the FP size if the number of SLOC is known along with the development language(s) used. The SLOC can then be divided by a language specific constant (such as 25 SLOC of COBOL code per FP) to arrive at an approximate number of FP. This method of estimating the functional size of software is called "backfiring" and its use is discouraged unless there is no other way to approximate the software size. The reason that it is discouraged is that the results can vary from hand counted FP by up to 400% according to comparisons done in industry. For a more detailed discussion of the issues and considerations involved in Backfiring, see Dekkers' article *Using "Backfiring" to Accurately Size Software – More Wishful Thinking than Science?* a copy of which is available in PDF format by emailing the American author.

So you need an approximation and have exhausted all other options – the functionality can be at least approximated by backfiring. This method is often passionately discussed (see also the last paragraph of this chapter) between advocates of SLOC and Function Points, since Function Points and SLOC are not equivalent, but sometimes are considered to be complementary to each other.

Backfiring concludes that the functionality (in Function Points) can be inferred from the source code size (in SLOC).

History of Backfiring

Since the size of a software's code depends on the programming language, IBM first introduced language levels intended to describe how many Assembler statements are, on average, necessary to program the functionality of a statement in the chosen programming language. Table 5.1 shows the Assembler equivalents for some programming languages.

Soon further research started in search of a second conversion that would answer the question of how many SLOC are necessary to code one Function Point. Capers Jones called this second conversion (level) the average expansion rate. Table 5.2 gives an overview of some known programming languages and their expansion rate.

Backfiring Today

Since publishing Table 5.2 in the 1990s, SPR and Capers Jones have refined and expanded their backfiring conversion table to include over 700 programming languages together with upper and lower bounds to help qualify the SLOC to FP conversion factors. It is offered to clients and visitors on their website at www.spr.com (Language Level table).

To illustrate a simple example of backfiring using Table 5.2, let us consider that we have an application with 10,000 SLOC of ANSI COBOL 85 code. Using the conversion factor is 107, the FP can be backfire approximated at other

Table. 5.1. IBM's language level equivalents to 1 SLOC in Assembler

Programming language	Assembler equivalent
ABAP/4	20.00
Access	8.50
ANSI COBOL 74	3.00
ANSI COBOL 85	3.50
Microfocus Cobol	4.00
Basic assembly	1.00
Macro assembly	1.50
C	2.50
C++	6.00
Symantec C++	11.00
Visual C++	9.50
CICS	7.00
IBM CICS/VS	8.00
Clipper	17.00
Cold Fusion	18.00
EIFFEL	15.00
Excel 3–4	55.00
Excel 5	57.00
Focus	8.00
Fortran	3.00
Fortran 90	4.00
Framework	50.00
HTML 4.0	24.00
Interpreted Basic	3.00
Java, JavaScript	6.00
LISP	5.00
Lotus Notes	15.00
ORACLE	8.00
Programming Generators	20,00
SAS	10.00
SmallTalk, SmallTalk/V	15.00
ANSI SQL	25.00
Visual Basic 2	9.00

$$FP = (10{,}000\ SLOC)/107 = 93\ \text{Function Points.}$$

consultants and measurement practitioners have published their own conversion factors that vary from the SPR table, sometimes considerably.

For example, for COBOL,
1 FP = 145 SLOC COBOL (John Barnes Consulting, England),
1 FP = 105 SLOC COBOL ±40% (SPR, Burlington, MA).

Regarding the issue of code complexity, *Capers Jones stated that very complex code needs generally more Function Points per SLOC compared to extremely simple code.* While he is not an advocate of backfiring, he does recommend this additional step to those who use the method: after determining the size the

Table 5.2. Average expansion rate

Programming language	Average expansion rate (SLOC per FP)
Basic Assembler	320
Macro assembly	213
C	128
ANSI COBOL 74	107
Fortran	107
Interpreted Basic	107
ANSI COBOL 85	107
Fortran 90	80
Microfocus Cobol	80
LISP	64
C++	55
CICS	46
IBM CICS/VS	40
ORACLE	40
Visual Basic 2	35
Visual C++	34
SAS	32
Symantec C++	29
EIFFEL	21
SmallTalk/V	21
ABAP/4	16
Program generators	16
ANSI SQL	13
Excel 3-4	6

above calculated value is divided by a *code size adjustment factor* as presented in Table 5.3. If, for example, the above-mentioned application had a complexity sum of "6," Table 5.3 shows a corresponding value of 0.85. This would adjust the FP size accordingly:

$$FP = (10,000 \text{ SLOC})/(107 \times 0.85) = 110 \text{ Function Points.}$$

This means that the application has a less than average complexity. In other words, more functionality can be programmed per SLOC.

One more cautionary note about SLOC-based measures: Albeit measurements with source code need always special attention, backfiring is often the only chance to approximate the functionality of legacy systems. While some may argue with this, we have found that sometimes an imprecise estimate is better than none at all. Some projects have been immediately cancelled when the "ballpark" guesstimates based on SLOC backfired into FP and expert systems have been way out of their budget. Often the recognition that the customer cannot afford to redevelop a system is enough reason for them to live with software that was adequately working in the first place. Think – pet projects!

Table 5.3. Code size adjustment factor

Sum of problem-, code- and data complexity	Code size adjustment factor
3	0.70
4	0.75
5	0.80
6	0.85
7	0.90
8	0.95
9	1.00
10	1.05
11	1.10
12	1.15
13	1.20
14	1.25
15	1.30

And there are users who made good experiences with backfiring. A prerequisite is a homogeneous and stable development environment. SLOC-based estimates can be used very well for migrations (data conversions), since there is typically little functionality that is changed. Additionally, there is also the reverse use of backfiring when an estimating tool will only take in SLOC estimates for the software size. In those cases, a FP estimate is sometimes done and the SLOC is then estimated by "front firing" or multiplying the FP by SLOC conversion factor instead of dividing it.

When using backfiring for calculation of Function Points from SLOC and vice versa one has to regard in any case that the SLOCs are counted, which belong to certain Function Points. Only then can a reliable calculation factor be derived (i.e., does not include SLOC that is used entirely in the back-ground or across multiple applications unless it is used to deliver specific functionality).

A prerequisite for backfiring is that historical data are available. When counting SLOC it is important for comparisons if the SLOC are counted from physical or logical source code, as well as how compiler declarations and data declarations are considered. Counting SLOC makes no sense at all when using generators. Consensus is that commentary lines are not counted, since that would lead to the fact that programmers would document their code worse. A good recommendation is to count according to the IEEE Standard 1045.

Generally, SLOC are seen as a technical or physical measure and Function Points as a functional measure. Hence believing on backfiring implicates believe that a technical measure is also a functional measure. That is why backfiring is a heavily debated method, and it ties into the overall function point vs. SLOC debate that has no clear end in sight.

5.3 Overview of Methods

Estimation methods can be characterized by *areas of application* and *radius of action*. This results from different utilization during the process of system development and from the requirements of the involved persons and instances. From many documented estimation methods, the following ones are a little bit more known and thus are presented here in a few words. Because we have devoted an entire chapter to the size-based FSMs of estimation, we do not specifically address them in this chapter.

5.3.1 Heuristic Methods

Heuristic means "grown by experience." We use this term to describe those methods that are both simple and practical, for example, the Pi Times Thumb Method or Percentage Method, as well as or methods developed internally by organizations. The latter are primarily applicable to the organizations that developed them, and in some cases, they may not be suitable for usage elsewhere. We include them here because they are examples that depict how one can initiate organization specific methods. The disadvantage of such organizational solutions is naturally that they lack comparability.

The Expert Estimation

This method is likely the most used estimation method worldwide because it relies on one's own personal experiences in software development and is therefore based in reality and has a sense of comfort (termed at times, expertise). This is no more than estimation done by one or more persons with expertise (at whatever level). All other heuristic methods simply pertain to measures intended to improve on such Expert Estimations.

The Delphi Method

The Delphi Method involves asking multiple Experts for their estimation of effort. The results are compiled and sent back to the experts anonymously, and they are asked for an improved estimation regarding the answers. After several iterations, the results generally converge towards a similar estimate.

The Pi Times Thumb Method (Three Point Method)

This method, also called Three Point Method, is part of the PERT network technique. In its most simple variant it works with two figures: the average from a worst case (most pessimistic) and a best case (most optimistic) estimate. When three estimates are involved, there exist the following variants: A quarter of a worst case plus a quarter of a best case and half of a realistic expected estimation. Or put another way is the worst case estimate plus the best case estimate plus four times the most likely (expected) estimation, divided by six. This can be done using estimates from one project leader or by asking several persons and calculating the average of their estimates. Of course, better results emerge when those doing the estimates have some expertise in the type of projects being estimated. They should also be asked how they might change the estimate if a less experienced person would perform the work. The most beneficial situation is when the estimator(s) have fresh experience from a similar task or set of tasks, so that they do not rely on pure memory. The best case is when there are naturally measured data available to support this estimation.

The disadvantage of such methods is that estimates depend on subjective evaluations and mostly undocumented recollections of historical task effort. *The documentation of premises and the environment of estimation, the persons involved, and assumptions made during the estimation are all necessary prerequisites if there is to be any lessons learned or experience gained for future estimates of this type.*

The effort to conduct this type of estimating is often better spent by doing standard estimation using one of the more formal methods. At least the effort is not larger using a formal method, and it provides a lot of benefits as, for example, interorganizational comparability, and increases the potential accuracy of the estimate. Our recommendation if your organization demands a heuristic estimating method is to supplement it with a second method of estimating so that the estimate has the benefit of the experiences of third parties (e.g., benchmarking).

The Analogy Method

The Analogy Method estimates the effort by comparing the new development with historical projects, by relying on postmortems (sometimes called retrospectives) regarding certain aspects of the project. Possible criteria include the size of deliverables in SLOC or number of programs of a software product. The challenge with this method is to find enough "similar projects" that are comparable with the one you need to estimate. Projects are per se solitary with the implication that comparability is the exception.

Example of how to use the Analogy Method in practice:

1. First develop a raw model showing the user and technical requirements of the system to be developed.
2. Search for similar projects already completed by using organizational project postmortems.

3. Once you find one or more similar projects, compare the features between your project and the analogous project(s) to estimate the size of the deliverables of the planned system development and the development productivity.
4. The team size is calculated by dividing the estimated size of deliverables by the estimated development productivity.

The Relation Method

Using the Relation Method, the effort is estimated similar to the Analogy Method by comparing the system with completed project postmortems. The only difference in the relation method is that the comparison is done using indices where the basic index (=100) characterizes the normal measure, the average. For the Relation Method, the same remarks are valid as for the Analogy Method. The usage of indices implies that estimations can be calculated exactly thus distracting from the uncertainty, which is imminent in estimation methods.

Example of how to use the Relation Method in practice:

1. Definition of the partial indices
2. Determine the basic index 100
3. Evaluation of the program to be developed regarding the indices
4. Calculate the effort for the new development based on the evaluation in 3.

In the following example (see Table 5.4) the programming language COBOL is used with the basic index 100 for programmers with a programming experience of 3 years. Compared to these, projects with programming language PL/1 would be calculated with 15% less and Assembler projects would be calculated as needing 30% more effort.

Table 5.4. Part of an index table for estimating with the relation method

Indices	Index (%)				
	70	85	100	115	130
Programming language	RPG	PL/1	COBOL	–	Assembler
Programming experience	More than 5 years		3 years		Less than 1 year

The Weights Method

Weights methods associate objective and subjective factors that influence systems development with certain weights. The weight should relate to the relative influence on the effort of the specific factor. These influences are estimated and then multiplied by the weight. The total effort is calculated as sum of the component results. A prerequisite for using such weighting methods is availability of measurement data for elaboration of the weights in the formula.

Example 1 for how to use the Weights Method:

The "Time Cost Planning Method" (a specific instance of the Weights Method developed by a large IT department of a worldwide operating industrial organization) is suitable for performing estimates at the end of the requirements analysis. It estimates the effort for the team from the rough IT design until the end of testing. The basic formula is

Programming time = (file factor + run time factor)(problem knowledge factor + knowledge experience factor).

After add ons for organizational effort and an allowance for time slack during the project, we arrive at estimated effort for programming of each task. This estimate calculation is done for every task in the project work breakdown structure according to the software development processes (per the lifecycle model chosen) and organizational specific regulations. The size of the tasks should not exceed 1,000–1,500 Cobol statements (the equivalent effort of approximately three person months). The classification of each task is done with tables provided to the estimator (see Table 5.5).

This method is a bit antiquated and is fairly inflexible to consider actual influences, especially when there are ranges in the transactional processing and database processing involved between projects. However, it still can add value (as a second estimating method) and the equation can be adapted with some effort (using analogies) to modern software development environments. It was developed in the early 1970s based on the IBM Manual Method, and was checked in 1984 from Noth and Kretzschmar in the early 1980s showing up to a 300% difference between early estimation and the actual effort.

Example 2 for the Weights Method: The EGW Method

The EGW method was developed in the early eighties and got its name from the developers: End, Gotthardt, and Winkelmann. It calculates the total effort by adding the estimated functional effort to the estimated IT technical effort using the formulae

Total effort = functional effort + IT technical effort,

Functional effort = FS × FO × FE, with

FS = Functional Size
FO = Functional and Organizational Tasks
FE = Functional Experience
FS is the functional size measured by the number of user functions or functional tasks. FE regards the relation between required and existing skills.

Table 5.5. Example of a weight table used for a specific organization

Time effort for the organization			
Kind of effort	Stage	Stages of Effort	
Organization of phases		No Effort	0
Standards, determination of conventions		Small Effort	1
Reading of rough/detailed requirements concept		Medium Effort	2
IT-technical analysis		Large Effort	3
Becoming familiar with existing software		Extra Large Effort	4
Not to be anticipated changes of user requirements			
Elaboration of test data			
Support for data migration			
Sum:			

Table 5.6. Table for determination of FE

Existing experience	Necessary experience		
	Low	Average	High
Fair knowledge of the application area and project experience	1.00	1.00	1.05
Knowledge of the application area and project experience	1.00	1.10	1.15
No knowledge of the application area but project experience	1.05	1.15	1.25
No knowledge of the application area and no project experience	1.15	1.30	1.50

Table 5.6 shows an example for some factors.

$$\text{IT technical effort} = PS \times CP \times PE \times OC \times DR \times PL,$$

PS = Program Size
CP = Complexity of Programming Tasks
PE = Programming Experience
OC = Organizational Complexity
DR = Degree of Reuse
PL = Programming Language

The Percentage Method

The Percentage Method distributes the costs relative to phases or tasks, is quite easy to use, and can be used in parallel with other estimation methods. It is the only process-oriented estimation method, and is based on the (in some organizations antiquated) waterfall model that divides a project into sequential (and somewhat overlapping) phases. In theory, each phase starts only when the predecessor phase is finished. *A "bonmot" is that the design phase is declared to be finished when the project team has consumed the planned time or the budget.*

Frederick Brooks in his famous and timeless book *The Mythical Man Month* recommended the following ratios as rules of thumb:

- 1/3 <of project work effort allocated to> planning
- 1/6 <of project work effort allocated to> programming
- 1/4 <of project work effort allocated to> component test and early system test
- 1/4 <of project work effort allocated to> system test (integration testing).

The effort of the entire project or of a single phase of the development process can be estimated by using the actual measured effort spent up to the point at which estimation is done (assuming that the planning is complete at that point). For example, planning using Brooks' rules is 33% of the total project effort; therefore, the total effort can be derived to be three times that effort. A prerequisite to the use of the Percentage Method is to analyze your own organization as the variation between Brooks' ratios and your own can negate the ratios. Calibration to one's own organization and recurring factors in the development environment are always more relevant and useful than theoretical models. Remember:

History is always a better predictor of future performance than theoretical models!

Table 5.7. Example of mapping the ISO/IEC 12207 life cycle phases to ISBSG

Phase Nr.	Steps in ISO 12207 – Software engineering lifecycle processes	ISBSG phase	ISBSG phase percentage
0		Plan (Feasibility Study)	5%
1	Requirements analysis	Specification	23%
2	System requirements analysis		
3	System architectural design		
4	Software requirements analysis		
5	Software design	Design (Plan)	
6	Software construction (code and unit test)	Coding	41%
7	Software integration		
8	Software test	Test	22%
9	System integration		
10	System test		
11	Software installation	Implementation	9%
12	User support		

The ISO/IEC Standard 12207 (prior to the 2007 version that integrated software and systems distinguishes 12 phases for "standard" software development. ISBSG has reduced this down to five phases. Table 5.7 shows the relative percentages calculated from the ISBSG benchmarking data-base (release 7) on the basis of 404 projects.

The ISBSG database contains further details of the Percentage Method (see *Practical Project Estimation* featuring the American author). It includes breakdowns specific to diverse criteria such as, for example, new development vs. enhancement vs. redevelopment etc. See also our later chapter in this book about benchmarking.

5.3.2 Size-Based Methods

Since functional size-based measurements are so important, we have dedicated several special chapters to functional size measurement methods and variants. Here we present only the method of parametric-based estimation equations featuring SLIM, COCOMO II, and the Multiplicator method.

Parametric-Based Estimating Equations

Parametric-based estimating equations rely on the input of a measured size (e.g., KSLOC or FP) into a standard estimation equation that follows a parametric approach such as Monte Carlo simulation. Depending on the degree of detail available, the models may employ different estimation formulas for different complex applications. To achieve this, the stronger effort-influencing parameters are used as independent variables. The validity of the formulas used in the models should be calibrated to ensure conformity with one's own organizational data. The typical estimation formula is of the following form:

$$Y = f(X_n),$$

where Y = the dependant variable such as effort, duration, or cost,
and X_n = the independent variable(s), for example, programming language, number of subprograms, application size, etc.

Example: The Formula used in the SLIM suite of tools (www.qsm.com).

The SLIM Method from QSM, Inc. (Putnam and Myers 1992) estimates the effort for software development based on the software life cycle starting at project initiation through to implementation of the system. Putnam found a repeatable, functional relationship between system size, the development work effort, and project duration:

$$\text{Development effort} = E = S \times 3/(Ck \times 3 \times td \times 4),$$

Legend:
E = work effort for the software development life cycle in person years
S = the expected system size measured by KSLOC
Ck = technological stage of the development organization
Td = development duration in years.

For Ck, for example, following empirical values were found:

$Ck = 8$ for systems with many interactions
$Ck = 15$ for stand alone systems
$Ck = 27$ for partial systems of large systems.
(Note: This formula can be retrieved from the following URL: http://ivs.cs.uni-magdeburg.de/sw-eng/us/java/sweq).

Putnam's company, QSM, developed their software estimating tool SLIM that relies on this equation plus a growing database of projects (http://www.qsm.com/database.html). According to an email received by the authors from Larry Putnam, Jr.: "The numbers change as we continue to collect project data (250–500 per year). Every 18–24 months we analyze the most recent data in the major application categories, and do statistical fits that are updated in the products. The SLIM-DataManager is the metrics repository product that stores the historic data. SLIM-Metrics is the analytical tool that allows the user to do queries against the database and do statistical analysis of the data. All the products in the SLIM-Suite have the QSM database information contained in them."

Example: COCOMO II

COCOMO was originally published in 1981 in Barry W. Boehm's book *Software Engineering Economics*. Through years of refinement and practical enhancements (based on industrial participation), COCOMO II emerged and was featured in Boehm's 2000 book: *Software Cost Estimation with COCOMO II*. The earlier COCOMO model and the COCOMO II model are both based on the Weights method and parametric-based equations. COCOMO II distinguishes three levels of software development:

1. Organic: relatively small teams develop in known environment. Product size <50 KSLOC.
2. Semidetached: Situation between 1 and 3. Medium complex software projects <300 KSLOC.
3. Embedded: development is restricted by time and costs, complex software projects

Table 5.8 illustrates the corresponding COCOMO II estimation equations.

Table 5.8. Example COCOMO II

COCOMO II mode	Organic mode effort	Semidetached and embedded mode effort
Small SW project	PM = 2.4 × (KSLOC) × 1.05	PM = 3.2 × (KSLOC) × 1.05
Medium SW project	PM = 3.0 × (KSLOC) × 1.12	
Large SW project	PM = 3.6 × (KSLOC) × 1.20	PM = 2.8 × (KSLOC) × 1.20

Generally the following formula holds:

$$PM = a \times (KSLOC) \times b \times c_i,$$

where $i = 1,...,15$; PM = work effort expressed in person months
a and b = constants
c_i = cost factors.

Boehm defines a person month as 152 net working hours (i.e., holidays, sickness, and other nonproject related work excluded). Again, this formula is available from the following URL: http://ivs.cs.uni-magdeburg.de/sw-eng/us/java/COCOMO/index.js.shtml. Barry W. Boehm's COCOMO II tool is based on approximately 8,000 completed projects in its database.

In addition to the three modes, COCOMO II uses three submodels:

1. Application Composition Model
   For software development in ICASE environment (Integrated Computer Aided Software Engineering) with a high degree of automation. The size of the projects is measured in Application Points. It is often used in early project phases and during prototyping.
2. Early Design Model
   Also used in early project phases for evaluation of architectural alternatives and/or incremental development strategies. The size of the projects is measured in KSLOC or unadjusted Function Points.
3. Post Architecture Model
   Based on the Application Composition Model but much more detailed. It is used after the design phase. The size of the projects is also measured in KSLOC or unadjusted Function Points. The Post Architecture Model regards 17 cost drivers.

A Freeware estimation tool for COCOMO II can be downloaded from the University of Southern California's URL http://sunset.usc.edu.

Since COCOMO II is widely used (particularly in the large government and defense contractor industries in the United States and elsewhere), there exists a wide number of variants. Andreas Schmietendorf and Reiner Dumke (MetriKon 2003) reported the following:

- COPSEMO (Constructive Phased Schedule and Effort Model) for cost estimation of each of the development phases
- CORADMO (Constructive RAD Model) for support of RAD (Rapid Application Development)
- COCOTS (Constructive COTS) for estimation of effort to customize COTS (Commercial Off The Shelf Packages) such as ERP systems like SAP® or PeopleSoft®)
- COQUALMO (Constructive Quality Model) for general estimation of quality based on defects introduced during each of the development phases
- COPROMO for estimation of productivity according to CORADMO and COPSEMO (above) for phase scaled productivity evaluation
- Expert COCOMO for risk assessment of projects.

Parametric-Based Estimating Equations in Practice

A benchmarking-type experiment for which results were presented at the IWSM 2005 (International Workshop on Software Measurement) congress, Ton Dekkers compared the estimates for a project done conventionally (i.e. with expert estimates) and in-parallel using the ISBSG Reality Checker (also the online version showing slight difference) and estimates done using the QSM software estimating tool SLIM (also with 2 simulations). The project size was estimated at 540 Function Points to be developed on a mainframe platform. The project was in the domain of business applications and the programming language was assumed to be third generation language COBOL. The results are shown in Table 5.9.

Table 5.9. Results of various estimating methods for a 500 FP software project

Estimating approach	Duration	Cost	Peak staff
Conventional estimate	10 months	1 million Euro	–
ISBSG Reality Checker v3.0-R9	9.5–23 months	Range between 656 thousand and 2 million Euro	–
ISBSG Reality Checker Online (based on R9)	30.5% of the database projects delivered in 10 months, median 14.6 months	72% of the database projects delivered with expected cost	–
QSM SLIM 6.1 quick estimate	12.8 months	1.2 million Euro	8.5 persons
QSM SLIM 6.1 simulation with restrained duration	10 months	3.3 million Euro	30 persons
SLIM 6.1 simulation with restrained costs	13.5 months	1 million Euro	6.7 persons

The size of an application is, without doubt, a major driver of project work effort but, as mentioned already numerous times in this book, it is not the only one. Considering this, we present the next estimation variant: the Multiplicator Method.

The Multiplicator Method

The costs of a new project can be calculated by multiplying the estimated number of units with predetermined effort per unit (based on historical actual ratios). In this way, the average programming productivity is multiplied by the estimated SLOC. A variant of the Multiplicator Method is the Wolverton Method, which refines the effort per unit figures by the type of software and the degree of complexity.

Example: The Mutliplicator Method

A consultancy derives a ratio of "1,200 instructions per month" (1,200 SLOC per month) for an average programmer based on an assessment of the average delivery rates on their historical projects for which data are available. Their costs per person month are determined to be $9,000 USD.

Using these values = Costs per instruction = $9,000 USD divided by 1,200 = $7.50 USD per SLOC.

Now, to estimate the cost for a similar program with an estimated 5,000 SLOC:
Cost = 5,000 SLOC × $7.50 USD per SLOC = $37,500 USD.

Example: The Wolverton Method

Taking the multiplicator method above, the Wolverton refinements (see Table 5.10) provides a more differentiated result. For example, considering the example used in the Multiplicator method above:

Cost of 5,000 SLOC with an average complexity and type C software = 5,000 SLOC × $24 USD per SLOC = $120,000 USD.

Table 5.10. Costs in US-$ per instruction stratified by type of software and degree of complexity (Wolverton 1974)

Degree of complexity	Type of software (specific types)					
	A	B	C	D	E	F
Simple	15	17	18	21	24	75
Average	20	23	24	27	31	75
Complex	23	26	27	30	35	75

5.4 Evaluation of an Estimation Method

Cost estimators and software developers alike need estimating methods that deliver reliable estimates that cover their entire software development life cycle. To reach this goal, different authors have published requirements catalogues to assist in evaluating estimation methods. Noth and Kretzschmar published such a catalog, which also contains criteria gathered from other authors and enriched by their own experiences.

The criteria for evaluating which estimating method is best for your organization falls into three categories:

1. User comfort
2. Project management
3. Quality of result.

5.4.1 User Comfort

Considering the user comfort with an estimating method involves the following criteria:

- Usability (ease of use)
- Ease to learn
- Effort to arrive at an estimate
- Tool support
- Transparency.

The method should be *usable* without having to do too much preparation in advance (e.g., collection of historical data from project postmortems). It is beneficial when existing documentation can be used, (e.g., the existing requirement documents can be used to derive the functional size, or the existing SLOC can be counted).

The method should also be easy to learn and master after a number of uses. If the estimating method requires hundreds of inputs that must be gathered using new processes, it is unlikely that the effort to do so will be cost effective. In other words, if it takes longer to perform the estimation than it does to actually do the work (of software development) then the method is not a good fit. This is also a measure of the efficiency and profitability of the method for your usage.

It should be easily possible to evaluate the *level of tool support* for a given estimating method. A market review (or internet search) can provide a quick answer to this question.

The acceptance of an estimation method grows with automated support. This is an essential element behind motivation of the estimators and the efficiency of the estimation method. On the one hand, it is difficult to be taken seriously when one must do manual (pencil and paper) calculations in IT management meeting, especially when project leaders want to do "what-if" analysis by changing project parameters to see the results on the estimates. On the other hand, it is also important for a tool to support a valid method that CAN be done by hand, but it is more convenient that it is automated. Remember the adage:

A fool with a tool is still a fool! (In other words, a fool with a tool can get to the wrong answer more quickly but with better graphs than the fool without.)

Transparency of the estimating equation is also an important criterion on which to judge an estimating method. If the tool becomes a "Black Box" into which input criteria is entered, and through a magical transformation an estimate emerges, there will be a lack of trust on the part of both the customer (acquiring the software) and the supplier. It is important that the method of transforming the input variables into an output estimate be easily seen (especially for the customer) so that the result can be trusted. Again an American adage holds:

Trust, but verify!

In other words, without revealing the innermost estimating "secrets" any estimating method worth using will be transparent about the object of estimation and the general approach used to estimate the work effort to develop it.

5.4.2 Project Management

The evaluation of the category Project Management consists of the following criteria:

- Early applicability
- Structuredness
- Ability to iterate the results for better estimates
- Sensitivity analysis.

Early applicability means that the method can be used for early estimates when the core minimum of input parameters (influential factors) is known. Some methods pride themselves at being able to be applied early in the development lifecycle, while others do not. It is important to use a method that is consistent with the phase or point at which you want to use it to develop estimates.

Structuredness refers to the fact that the result of the calculation should be structured to the same level as the chosen work breakdown structure. It is not feasible to use a method that gives only a single value for an overall software development effort if your project management requires a breakdown to the level of their work breakdown structure tasks. Conversely, if an estimating method provides you with estimates that are much too granular to be applicable (i.e., multiple decimal places in hours estimated by task before requirements), then you should be wary of the "perceived" precision that simply cannot exist despite the fact that they come out of a "sophisticated tool". Correct alignment of an estimating tool to its desired support of project management activities is important. Not every estimating tool suits every organization – examine your requirements for estimating *before* choosing the estimating method.

Ability to iterate the results for better estimates aims at usability of the estimation method repeatedly at multiple times during the project. Hence one can monitor and track variances of the estimates developed at different phases of the development. The estimates should converge to the center (i.e., become more reliable and accurate) as more information becomes known during the project. This criterion is especially important on projects involving the management of complex dynamic systems (as, e.g., software development projects) that are mission critical. Note that the weekly newspaper reports of publicly tendered software development projects that are now in excess of their original estimates by hundreds of percentages have not used an estimating model based on reality, or the information used to generate the original estimates was too vague to be of practical use. While one would think that our industry would learn from its experience when subsequent projects are undertaken, it seems that history has a way of repeating itself. In the words of Albert Einstein:

- *Insanity is doing the same thing over and over again and expecting different results.*
- If we do not change how we do estimates after grossly over- or under-estimating a prior project, then we are in Einstein's words: insane.

System Dynamics research led to the understanding that complex dynamic systems tend in critical situations to deliver abnormally quick changing and strong measurements. Early warning signs such as these can only be recognized, and therefore acted upon, if measurements are taken repeatedly as the project progresses.

Last, but not least, the method should enable *sensitivity analysis* or have them integrated into the overall model.

5.4.3 Quality of Result

This category comprises following requirements:

- Exactness
- Traceability
- Evaluation
- Influence
- Number of parameters
- Objectivity
- Stability
- Defect localization
- Flexibility
- Adaptability.

Exactness measures the difference between a former estimate and the resultant actual measurement during project progress. *This aims to address the problem of the precision of estimation.*

An estimate is *traceable* if a third party can understand and repeat the calculation. It must be clearly understood why certain evaluations and/or assumptions were made.

Evaluation requires that those influencing factors used (available) at the time of the estimation need to be evaluated (i.e., they are objectively measurable) at this stage of project progress. The factors must also be available when comparing the actual effort at project postmortem to enable the organization to learn (i.e., make process improvements based on finding out which factors changed during the projects). *Influence* means that the influencing factors are also relevant to the project and that they can be measured quantitatively or qualitatively.

The number of parameters fits in with usability (from the previous section) and also comprises the requirement that all of the factors used in the calculations should be ones that directly influence the estimate (i.e., the estimating model does not ask for irrelevant or superfluous information).

To reach *objectivity*, the majority of variables used in the estimation must rely on objective rather than subjective (i.e., opinion only) evaluation.

Stability is reached when the influence of the factors does not exceed the measurable influence. Estimates prepared using the same input data and the same method must deliver the same result.

Defect localization is the attribute that reflects whether the estimation method recognizes when influences are evaluated incorrectly (i.e., there are checks and balances to detect incorrect data entries or conflicting data).

The method should be *flexible to be used* in different development environments and for all types of development projects without major alteration.

Adaptability refers to the ability of a method to react (and consider the influence) of changed conditions.

Other requirement catalogues contain similar criteria with slight differences. Be aware that because of the range of requirements for estimating tools, one *requirement catalogue published in academic literature may contradict others in practical usage.*

5.4.4 Precision of Estimation Methods

At the end of 1981, the Institute for Management of the Free University of Berlin asked the IT managers from a number of large organizations and software consultancies to evaluate the estimating methods they used:

Question: How would you rate the precision of the software development estimating methods you use?

Answer: By a large margin, the estimators lacked trust in the estimates produced out of their estimating methods. The majority of IT managers admitted that their estimates were of the actual effort by up to 300%. A full 70% conceded that their best estimates ranged from 10 to 50% off from the actual effort, and rarely they were on the lower (10%) end of the scale. Almost 10% admitted that their estimates were routinely out by at least 100% or more.

When pressed for the reasons for these deviations, IT managers typically said that the requirements changed during the project and that the objectives and goals were not precise enough. But, more than half of those surveyed (61%) claimed that their estimation methods and processes were insufficient to perform accurate estimates.

A test of the various estimation methods used confirmed the concerns of these IT managers since most of their methods could not meet even the basic criteria listed in the previous section.

Note that these results must also be taken with a grain of skepticism because a mere 20% of software developers industry-wide use any form of structured estimating and only a small number of them have experience with solid estimation methods.

In this light, it is interesting that the traditional criticism of the FPM focused on the argument that different Function Point counters arrived at a different number of Function Points, and therefore, somehow the function point measure is subjective. In an effort to counter this argument, the UKSMA (United Kingdom Software Metrics Association) performed an experiment. They conducted a "blind" test based on a case study whose functional size was determined by expert counters to be 139 Mark II Function Points. Taking two groups of function point counters:

- Group 1: new estimators with only two days training and meager experience and expertise, and
- Group 2: experienced Mark II counting experts with more than 4 years experience.

When checking the resultant functional sizes that each group came up with, the new estimators had a variance of ±26%, while the experts varied in their estimates by ±13%.This lead to some improvements in the Mark II counting manual. New experiments after the improvements produced a variance of 5% for the experts. Similar results (with a 3.4% deviation) were reported in an assessment of Function Point counts done by Compass Consulting on a large IT department of an international organization. This is a minor variance considering that the size of the assessment was 9,000 Function Points across a wide number of pieces of software.

Caper Jones wrote in his book *Software Quality* in 1997 that research at M.I.T. (Massachusetts Institute of Technology) on behalf of IFPUG confirmed that CFPS varied in their results by a mere ±10%. It is important to realize that a focus on size to the detriment of the accuracy of other input variables delivers inaccurate results NOT due to the FP counts but due to the least accurate input variable.

Remember that any estimate can only be as accurate as its least accurate input variable!

A benchmarking study based on function points conducted by Gartner Group for an Asian customer (not publicly available) was subsequently critically examined by a group of in-house customer FP counters. Using IFPUG 4.1 rules as their basis for counting, the result was that the Gartner-estimated Function Points counts were underestimated on average by 22% (band width from 9 to 34%). Again, before "throwing the baby out with the bathwater" (a North American saying), it is important to realize that Function Point counting is more consistent than many of the other inputs to the estimating models.

Barbara Kitchenham attests that the complexity of software systems in and of itself can cause major differences in resultant estimates. The worse the quality of the data (or the increased ignorance of the influence of nonfunctional requirements), the worse the outcome and reliability of the estimate on which it is based.

Many organizations measure (if at all) their actual project work effort to a precision of ±20%, which translates into ±1 h and 36 min for an average 8-h working day. This means that the functional size measurement, especially if done by an expert, is more precise and is a viable and reliable measure of software size, and is definitely suitable for use during the requirements analysis, and for use to measure the output of outsourcing contracts, and in benchmarking. If this precision and consistency can be preserved, there can be more effort allocated in the future for the measurement of actual data such as actual work effort, unplanned overtime work, defects, etc.

Carlos Granja and Angel Oller presented at the IWSM/MetriKon 2004 a case study comparing estimates on three projects done by three groups who addressed the same problem from different perspectives:

- Group 1 used a Linux platform and a Posgre database
- Group 2 used Windows Professional XP (W) and an Oracle database (O)
- Group 3 used a reutilization approach, and also W and O.

The Functional sizes of the projects (in FP) were first measured during the analysis phase, after use cases were completed. A second Function Point measurement was done after implementation by backfiring from SLOC according to Brian J. Dreger's 1983 method. The following precision was observed (see Table 5.11):

Table 5.11. Precision of estimation in the Granja/Oller case study

	Estimated FP	Implemented FP	Deviation (%)
Group 1	78.57	50.28	36
Group 2	96.72	73.72	24
Group 3	97.85	35.79	63

As can be seen from Table 5.11, the *size was always underestimated.*

Note that the implied precision (two decimal places) of each of the estimated and implemented Function Point counts as reported leads one to the belief that functional size is a precise value. This is not the case as the components that are used to create the FP counts are based on whole numbers. Nonetheless, this study simply reports the relative accuracy (not precision) of the case study and shows that functional size measurement can be used effectively as an estimate of the resultant implemented size of a piece of software.

The working group "Precision of Estimations"of the German metrics organization DASMA reports that the ISBSG did research using more than 400 selected projects in its database (release 9) concerning the precision of effort, costs, size, and duration. The results are shown in Table 5.12.

Table 5.12. ISBSG study: Precision of costs, size, and duration based on 400 completed projects

	Effort	Costs	Size	Duration
Number of projects	200	86	130	222
Higher/earlier than estimated by >10%	19%	16%	12%	4.5%
	(38 projects)	(14 projects)	(16 projects)	(10 projects)
Exact estimation (<±10%)	23.5%	49%	50%	51.5%
	(47 projects)	(42 projects)	(65 projects)	(114 projects)
Lower/later than estimated by >10%	57.5%	35%	38%	44%
	(115 project)	(30 projects)	(49 projects)	(98 projects)

Table 5.12 shows that about half of the projects are estimated within a range of 10%. In most cases, the effort was underestimated.

5.5 Management Summary

The principal steps of the process of estimation start with a measurement of the functional size of each piece of software to be developed, delivering a numerical value for the size of the object of estimation.

Using the functional size (FP count) value for each piece of software, together with the environmental (situational and technical) and nonfunctional factors (quality constraints) for the software, the work effort estimate can be determined.

The next step after estimating the project work effort is usually to calculate a cost value from the effort using a metric-like US-$ per hour for the project.

In the simplest case to determine a preliminary estimate of project duration, the total work effort is apportioned across the various SDLC phases of an IT project using a Percentage of time per phase Method.

The above mentioned estimate of the total effort can be compared with the estimation calculated by the Percentage Method, post project completion by using the actual measured effort of the first phase of the IT project, and calculating from this the total effort using the proportion percentage for this phase.

Practically, Function Points and SLOC are two principles used for measuring the size of the object of estimation (the software product size) and for calculating the effort needed to develop it.

The problems of the SLOC methods are that SLOC can be measured only in a late phase of a project's progress (after coding is complete) and when the majority of software development is already complete (coding is approximately about 10% of the effort of system development).

The paradox of the Assembler equivalent (see Chap. Backfiring) is a doubtless argument against the SLOC methods: the mightier a programming language, the less SLOC are necessary for the programming of certain functionality.

The advantage of Functional Size Measurement Methods is that they can be used early (in the requirements phase) in the software development life cycle. In addition to the IFPUG FPM, there exist some established variants (some of which are ISO conformant been published as ISO/IEC standards) of it.

The problems of the FPM are that the requirements are not detailed enough after project start and that the IFPUG complexity factors (e.g., 1 ILF low = 7 FP) are a continuous object of debates (for reason of their origin and being antique).

The problems of the FPM occur when the requirements are not detailed enough after project start.

Purists of the object-oriented paradigm often use the killer phrase that these estimation methods are not suited for object-oriented system development.

It is possible to estimate the effort of object-oriented system development using functional size measurement together with solid historical data from such projects and earnest endeavor using the known estimation methods.

Mathematicians attest that it really does not make sense to measure the "length of algorithms" (when performing functional size measurement), since anytime someone can develop a new and shorter algorithm for the solution of a problem.

Hand in hand with estimation goes the usage of tools.

We define a software estimation process as "a method with detailed regulations and standards that is effectively supported by tools."

A challenge to estimating methods overall is the low degree of dissemination and serious consideration granted to the estimating theme by researchers, scientists, and educational institutions.

Estimation in academic studies as well as in training and literature is often dealt with at a peripheral level in that it is mentioned as a necessary task to be done with the existing methods and processes (with no mention of its importance or how to do it properly). This impression is also valid for monographs and literature about project management.

The result of a work effort estimation is a figure for the human resource effort that characterizes the development or enhancement of the software system (or a part of it).

The usage of estimation processes, for example, with experience curves or estimation equations implies the existence of mathematical functions for calculation of effort, and can seduce one to the wrong conclusion by assuming that exact results can be calculated.

After determination of the size of an application, for example, by counting Function Points, one tries to find an applicable relationship between the functional size and the work effort for software development.

Using size measures in statistical regression analysis, one can calculate an "experience curve."

The majority of effort estimation equations follow the general form $y = f(x_1, x_2, x_3, \ldots)$, where y is the estimated work effort and x_i are the input parameters influencing the effort. When IFPUG or another functional size measurement method is used to determine the size of the software to be developed or enhanced, the work effort equations most commonly used are in the form $y = ax^b$, with a and b calculated by a regression analysis process, y is the estimated work effort, and x is the functional size.

The third variation of estimation methods aside from experience curves and estimation equations is a knowledge-based expert system.

So you need an approximation and have exhausted all other options – the functionality can be at least approximated by backfiring.

Regarding the issue of code complexity, Capers Jones stated that very complex code needs generally more Function Points per SLOC compared to extremely simple code.

When using backfiring for calculation of Function Points from SLOC and vice versa, one has to regard in any case that the SLOCs are counted which belong to certain Function Points. Only then can a reliable calculation factor be derived.

Generally, SLOC are seen as a technical or physical measure and Function Points as a functional measure.

The expert estimation method is likely the most used estimation method worldwide because it relies on one's own personal experiences in software development and is therefore based on reality and has a sense of comfort (termed at times, expertise).

The disadvantage of such methods is that estimates depend on subjective evaluations and mostly undocumented recollections of historical task effort. The documentation of premises and the environment of estimation, the persons involved, and assumptions made during the estimation are all necessary pre-requisites if there is to be any lessons learned or experience gained for future estimates of this type.

The effort to conduct this type of estimation is often better spent by doing standard estimation using one of the more formal methods. At least the effort is not larger using a formal method, and it provides a lot of benefits as, for example, interorganizational comparability, and increases the potential accuracy of the estimate.

The Analogy Method estimates the effort by comparing the new development with historical projects, by relying on postmortems (sometimes called retrospectives) regarding certain aspects of the project.

Using the Relation Method the effort is estimated similar to the Analogy Method by comparing the system with completed project postmortems. The only difference in the relation method is that the comparison is done using indices.

Weights methods associate objective and subjective factors that influence systems development with certain weights.

The Percentage Method distributes the costs relative to phases or tasks, is quite easy to use, and can be used in parallel with other estimation methods. It is the only process-oriented estimation method.

The effort of the entire project or of a single phase of the development process can be estimated by using the actual measured effort spent up to the point at which estimation is done (assuming that the planning is complete at that point).

History is always a better predictor of future performance than theoretical models!

The SLIM Method from L.H. Putnam (Putnam and Myers 1992) estimates the effort for software development based on the software life cycle starting at project initiation through to implementation of the system.

The size of an application is, without doubt, a major driver of project work effort but, as mentioned already numerous times in this book, it is not the only one.

The acceptance of an estimation method grows with automated support. This is an essential element behind motivation of the estimators and the efficiency of the estimation method. It is difficult to be taken seriously when one must do manual (pencil and paper) calculations in IT management meeting.

System Dynamics research led to the understanding that complex dynamic systems tend in critical situations to deliver abnormally quick and strong measurements. Early warning signs such as these can only be recognized, and therefore acted upon, if measurements are taken repeatedly as the project progresses.

An estimate is traceable if a third party can understand and repeat the calculation. It must be clearly understood why certain evaluations and/or assumptions were made.

Remember that any estimate can only be as accurate as its least accurate input variable!

Barbara Kitchenham attests that the complexity of software systems in and of itself can cause major differences in resultant estimates.

6 Estimating Maintenance Effort

Project estimation usually does not include lifetime (or even the first year) of maintenance effort. The lifetime maintenance costs, however, typically exceed the original application development effort by up to 10 times. Software maintenance is often defined as the correction or modification of a software product after delivery, to correct faults, to improve performance or other attributes, or to adapt the product to a changed environment. *Practical experience shows that IT systems live longer than expected, with the recent case-in-point being the Year 2000 conversion of applications originally intended to be replaced during the 1980s, but surviving through to the turn of the century.*

It is a common practice that the costs for maintenance are accumulated during the lifetime of a system without controlling the amount and without differentiating between the different kinds of costs. Yet, the maintenance and support area can be prone to inefficiencies (i.e., cost excesses) and the lack of consistent processes, resulting in IT spending that is not only misunderstood, but many time uncontrolled.

Capers Jones states (Jones 2007): "The word *maintenance* is surprisingly ambiguous in a software context. In normal usage it can span some 23 forms of modification to existing applications. The two most common meanings of the word maintenance include the following:

1. Defect repairs
2. Enhancements or adding new features to existing software applications".

Using a supermarket analogy: The shopper is astonished at how many cheap goods fit into a shopping basket (i.e., in software, this is akin to comparable maintenance requirements) but accumulates to a large sum when all items are rung up at the cash register. While the grocery shopper can remove items and reduce the overall costs, this is not the case with software maintenance where the work done before production cannot be corrected (or done more correctly) after the products are released. In software, many smaller defects lead to large costs postproduction.

Note that the International Function Point User Group (IFPUG) definition holds that software maintenance does not change the functionality of an application. If a project results in new/changed/deleted functionality, it is classified by IFPUG as an "enhancement" project.

6.1 International Standards for Software Maintenance

There are two main sources of maintenance standards:

- ISO/IEC standards
- Other standards.

  Besides these we present in the first paragraph of this chapter a short overview of the following standards:

- FiSMA: Finnish Software Measurement Association
- IFPUG: International Function Point Users Group
- NESMA: Netherlands Software Metrieken Gebruikers Associatie
- UKSMA: United Kingdom Software Metrics Association.

6.1.1 ISO/IEC standards

At least two ISO/IEC standards exist to provide direction for software maintenance:

- ISO/IEC 14764: Software Engineering: Software Maintenance
- ISO/IEC 9126-3: Software Measurement: Quality In Use (metrics).

6.1.2 FiSMA: Finnish Software Measurement Association

The FiSMA published their MT22 situation analysis for maintenance and support, which is composed of 22 standard productivity factors that influence the amount of effort to maintain a particular piece of software. MT22 is classified into six organization factors, five process factors, six product factors, and five people factors.This situation analysis is freely available from www.fisma.fi and can also be found in the Appendix of this book. The purpose of this method is to help to estimate annual maintenance and modification projects.

6.1.3 IFPUG: International Function Point Users Group

In January 2004, IFPUG published its Counting Practices Manual (CPM) Release 4.2, which contained in Part 2, Chap. 4 Enhancement Projects and Maintenance Activity. This chapter provides guidance to practitioners of Functional Size Measurement to discern between maintenance projects for which there may or may not be function points, and enhancement projects for which there is typically functional change.

IFPUG states, "Once an application has been developed and installed, it must then be maintained (modified) in order for it to continue to meet the needs of an ever-changing business and technical environment. This maintenance includes a wide range of activities that are performed during this phase of the application life cycle, some of which involve functional changes that are applicable to FPA."

The chapter goes on to use the IEEE (Institute of Electrical and Electronics Engineers) definitions for maintenance based on three categories:

- *Adaptive Maintenance*: Software maintenance performed to make a computer program usable in a changed environment.
- *Corrective Maintenance*: Software maintenance performed to correct faults in hardware or software.
- *Perfective Maintenance*: Software maintenance performed to improve the performance, maintainability or other attributes of a computer program.

Further, IFPUG states, "While the body of this chapter has provided Function Point Counting hints and guidelines for enhancements to existing applications, there is no industry-wide standard for consistent classification of activities that fall within the above categories. This section provides a framework based on common industry experience from which to evaluate the applicability of FPA in the support of installed applications. Since maintenance and support activities are subject to inconsistent reporting, locally developed guidelines should address these areas. The following are some of the more commonly encountered activities, with suggested handling relative to FPA.

For example, a project involving only upgrades from one platform, language, or technical environment to another, with no change in user functionality, should not be subject to an enhancement function point (EFP) count."

IFPUG goes on to outline the various application maintenance and support activities as presented in Table 6.1.

Table 6.1. IFPUG categories of maintenance and their relationship with function points

Type of maintenance and support activity	Description
Maintenance Requests	Regardless of duration or level of work effort required, it is the type of activity that determines how the work is classified. Function Point Analysis should not be used to size perfective or corrective maintenance work. Corrective maintenance should be charged to the development or enhancement project that introduced the defects. Perfective maintenance should not be charged to any development or enhancement projects.

(Continued)

Table 6.1. *(Cont.)*

There may be a tendency to track some enhancement functionality as maintenance work, but that work should be monitored and reported separately. The usual rationale for inclusion is for either immediacy or expediency. Organizations often provide a fast path for small enhancement requests, usually 40 h or less, in order to reduce the overhead burden on the project. When business requirements are affected, Function Point Analysis should be applied at least for results measurement.

If a release contains a mix of adaptive, corrective, and/or perfective maintenance requirements, care must be exercised in separation of work effort, since the latter two categories contribute zero function points to the business. While such work effort segregation may be relatively easy during the construction phase, depending on the level of granularity in effort tracking, it is generally more difficult during most final test phases. One possible approach would be an apportionment of the entire release based on proportional content.

Activity	Within enhancement counting scope
Correction of production errors ("break/fix")	No
Perfective or preventative maintenance	No
Platform upgrades, new system software releases	No
Project with both fixes and enhancements	Partially

On-Demand (Ad Hoc) Requests (for definition see Glossary of IFPUG CPM 4.1, 1999)

Functionality that is provided to the end user in the form of one-time/on-demand reports and data extracts is certainly countable. The decision to count should be made based on whether the functions will be maintained and the business need that the function point count will meet. It must be noted that this discussion is limited to reports/extracts produced by I/S Development and does not cover user generated Ad Hoc reports or queries. It should be noted that the methodology to produce ad hoc reports is usually not as rigorous as for a full enhancement project. Therefore, care should be taken when comparing the relative costs of such work with those of general enhancement activity.

Activity	Within enhancement counting scope
One-time reports	Local convention
Table updates	No
Special job setup	No
Data correction	No
Mass data changes	Yes, as conversion if associated with a project.

End User Support

Any nonproject work effort related to activities classified as "not countable" should be charged to a labor classification other than

(Continued)

New Development or Enhancement. For Preliminary Estimation or Feasibility Studies, the problem is that user requirements are not yet well defined. Also, a project at either stage is usually not yet funded (and may never be funded). At best, a Rough Order of Magnitude (ROM) function point estimate can be determined, but no quantitative measurements should be applied at this point. Any resulting number is for budget and planning purposes only. General nonproject user support activities, such as answering "what-if" questions and helping users, should not be subject to Function Point Analysis.

Activity	Within enhancement counting scope
Preliminary estimation or feasibility analysis	At best, ROM
Answering "what if" questions	No
General nonproject client support	No
Help desk support	Partially

6.1.4 NESMA: Netherlands Software Metrieken Gebruikers Associatie

In 2001, NESMA published their *Function Point Analysis for Software Enhancement Guidelines Version 1.0*, (Downloadable from http://www.nesma.nl/download/FPA).

In this document, NESMA developed a measure (with special weighted impact factors) called *Test Function Points (TFP) and Enhancement Function Points (EFP)* for calculating the total enhancement effort including testing:

$$E = (\text{EFP} \times \text{hours per EFP}) + (\text{TFP} \times \text{hours per TFP}),$$

where E is the total enhancement effort in hours, EFP is the enhancement FP count in NESMA FP, TFP is the testing FP count in NESMA FP, hours per EFP and hours per TFP are measured effort.

6.1.5 UKSMA: United Kingdom Software Metrics Association

In July 2001, UKSMA together with the International Software Benchmarking Standards Group (ISBSG) published (as part of the UKSMA Quality Measurement Standards) their standard *Measuring Software Maintenance and Support, Version 0.5 Draft* (available for free download from the URL: http://www.uksma.co.uk).

This standard distinguishes between maintenance, support, and operations work as distinct from development or enhancement (see Table 6.2).

Table 6.2. The UKSMA activity based model of support and maintenance

Type of work activity	Definition
Development (1)	Development – as defined in IFPUG 4.1
Enhancement (2)	Enhancement
	– As defined in IFPUG 4.1
	– ≥5 person days effort – changes the functionality
Maintenance (3) and	(3) Maintenance: can be
Support (4)	– Corrective maintenance
	– Perfective maintenance
	– Preventative maintenance
	– Adaptive maintenance (≤5 person days effort) –
	may change the functionality!
	(4) Ad hoc help desk responses
	– Problem analysis
	– Decommissioning
Operations (5)	(5) System administration
	– Deployment/rollout
	– Database management
	– Information retrieval support

The aim of the standard is to define the measures from which up to 23 metrics could be derived, including the following:

- Productivity: Function Points supported per person year
- Departmental Proportion for Minor Enhancements (D): maintenance effort (ME) divided by support effort devoted to minor enhancements (SE) per department, expressed in percent. The formula is $D = \text{ME}/\text{SE} \times 100\%$
- Proportion of Application Minor Enhancements (AME): Departmental effort for minor enhancements (ME) divided by the sum of maintenance effort and support effort (ME + SE), expressed in percent. The formula is $\text{AME} = \text{ME}/(\text{ME} + \text{SE}) \times 100\%$

6.2 Enhancement Projects

In some organizations, the maintenance and enhancement activities are well defined and separate pieces of work. In such organizations, work done to fix defects (corrective maintenance), make it run better (perfective maintenance), or prevent future business issues (preventative maintenance including upgrades to new releases of packaged components) are all considered to be categorized as *maintenance and support* that does not change the functionality of the application. Work that results in new or modified functionality (by user request) is typically categorized as *adaptive (maintenance)* or enhancement that is managed more as a project or service request (SR) and typically would involve modifications to the application functionality. However, this seemingly simple way of categorizing work is often anything but simple.

The American author has direct experience where a large organization categorized work to an SR by estimated effort hours – if it exceeded 50 h it was put to an SR, otherwise it was considered production systems support (i.e., maintenance). The organization decided to use function points to measure the size of enhancement projects (i.e., SRs) and simply record straight hours for maintenance work. The result was that there were many SRs that had no functionality change (i.e., zero function points) – even though they were assumed to be *enhancement* projects.

Capers Jones published (in *Estimating Software Costs*, 3rd ed., 2007) a table outlining 23 types of work that are variously considered to be maintenance or enhancement (see Table 6.3).

Table 6.3. Major kinds of work performed under the generic term "maintenance" (Jones 2007)

1. Major enhancements (new features of >20 function points)
2. Minor enhancements (new features of <5 function points)
3. Maintenance (repairing defects for good will)
4. Warranty repairs (repairing defects under formal contract)
5. Customer support (responding to client phone calls or problem reports)
6. Error-prone module removal (eliminating very troublesome code segments)
7. Mandatory changes (required or statutory changes)
8. Complexity or structural analysis (charting control flow plus complexity metrics)
9. Code restructuring (reducing cyclomatic and essential complexity)
10. Optimization (increasing performance or throughput)
11. Migration (moving software from one platform to another)
12. Conversion (Changing the interface or file structure)
13. Reverse engineering (extracting latent design information from code)
14. Reengineering (transforming legacy application to client-server form)
15. Dead code removal (removing segments no longer utilized)
16. Dormant application elimination (archiving unused software)
17. Nationalization (modifying software for international use)
18. Mass updates such as Euro or Year 2000 Repairs
19. Refactoring or reprogramming applications to improve clarity
20. Retirement (withdrawing an application from active service)
21. Field service (sending maintenance members to client locations)
22. Reporting bugs or defects to software vendors
23. Installing updates received from software vendors

There is a critical difference between the definition of the word enhancement in the IT and customer world (where anything that makes the application run better, makes it easier to use, reformats screens, or adds function is categorized as an enhancement by the users) compared to the definition in the functional size measurement world (where enhancement means "functional" change).

Table 6.4. ISBSG function point component percentage profile for enhancement projects

Functionality	Added	Changed	Deleted	Total
N (number of projects, overlapping)	408	306	83	454
EI (%)	31.9	37.8	38.0	34.4
EO (%)	31.4	25.9	35.1	29.4
EQ (%)	13.5	16.0	10.7	14.1
ILF (%)	15.6	18.0	11.1	16.5
EIF (%)	7.5	2.3	5.1	5.6
Totals (%)	55.3	42.0	2.7	

Table 6.5. Analyses of changes in enhancement projects

Enhancement project functionality	N (number of projects)	Percentage
Only added functions	143	31.5
Only changed functions	46	10.1
Added and changed functions	183	40.3
Added and deleted functions	5	1.1
Added, changed and deleted functions	77	17.0
Total	454	100.0

The ISBSG database (The Metrics Compendium, ISBSG 2002) contains slightly more new development projects (60%) than enhancement projects (40%), of which the following function point profile was published based on a sample size of 454 IFPUG 4.0 Function Point Enhancement projects (see Tables 6.4 and 6.5).

FP percentages of enhancement projects in the ISBSG database release 10 (2007), which contains 4,106 completed software projects:

The ISBSG Database release 10 from 2007 has 59% enhancement projects, 39% new development projects, and 2% redevelopment projects.

When counting the Function Points for software enhancements, one must remember the *domino effect*, that is, that a functional change to an ILF typically also causes a change to the elementary functions that use it (e.g., add, change, delete, and potentially query functions). All elementary functions need to be considered that have relationships to other functions (e.g., functions may also be related via interfaces).

Nevertheless, when considering software maintenance, remember that the functional size measurement definitions indicate that maintenance does not alter the system size in Function Points. If a project does alter the functionality of an application, it is typically considered not to be maintenance per se, but an enhancement instead.

6.3 Software Metrics for Maintenance

Referring again to the analogy of the supermarket-shopping basket, we can direct our attention to measures that can aid us in the estimation of maintenance effort. The aim is to develop measures and threshold figures to determine if the amount of effort hours could exceed the costs of redevelopment of the software. *Often it is not considered that software – like other products or goods – ages over time and that preventive maintenance and eventual replacement (redevelopment) of software will someday be necessary.*

There is broad consensus in the metrics community that annual support ratios (i.e., how many FP can be supported by one person in one year) depends on the same factors as software productivity (as previously discussed). As such, maintenance effort is a function of software size, plus a myriad of other factors, including the type of software and development language.

The COCOMO-M(aintenance) Model and SLIM model for maintenance both rely on only one parameter related to maintenance, while PRICE-S, SEER-SEM, KnowledgePlan, and Experience® Pro all use multiple parameters for their maintenance models.

Some of the dominant parameters related to maintenance are shown in Table 6.6 (see Abran et al., 2002).

Table 6.6. Factors influencing software support rates

Dominant parameters influencing software support rates
Type of application
Programming language
Age of software
Quality of existing documentation
Necessity of a complete system test
Restrictions in availability of resources
Functional complexity
Technical complexity
Degree of reuse

Note: For readers interested in further academic research in this area (some of it experimental and inconclusive) refer to the University of Quebec at Montreal studies including the following:

- The above mentioned field study of Abran et al. conducted at the University of Quebec at Montreal showed as result a positive, but weak relationship between application size and effort.
- Further research of this same data (Tran Cao et al., 2004) outlined a field study to investigate how cyclomatic complexity, together with the number of data groups and COSMIC Function Points affected the maintenance effort.

- *Abran and Robillard* (1996), about 21 maintenance projects of the Management Information Systems (MIS) type with larger functional enhancements. The average effort for these projects was more than 2,200 person hours or 332 person days. The authors found a strong ($R^2 = 0.81$) statistical relationship between size and effort. The data were from an organization that was known to deliver its projects successfully on time, in costs, in functionality, and in quality. The organization had by the beginning of the 1990s reached CMMI® level 3 with an evidentially strong quantitative management of the Key Performance Indicators (KPI) on CMMI® level 5), or
- *Abran and Nguyenkim* (1993), study of an organization with strong data collection and effort records. The projects involved smaller maintenance tasks that were all performed by one person only. The average effort per maintenance task was 37 h with a minimum of 27 h and a maximum of 52 h for corrective maintenance), or

Zuse collected the following metrics that can be used when estimating maintenance effort:

- Number of defects occurring after delivery. Often the measurements are performed during 6 months after delivery
- Number of changes or change requests
- Effort for defect search and correction
- Defect density (recorded as defects per Function Point)
- Mean time until defect occurrence (similar to mean time between failures)
- Software Maturity Index (SMI), defined as difference between the number of modules/functions of the actual release (R) minus the number of modules/functions changed, added, and deleted in the previous release (P). This difference is divided by the number of modules/functions of the actual release:

$$SMI = (R - P)/R.$$

This list can be enhanced with the following metric:

- Maintenance hours per installed Function Point. If this figure is very high, (or remarkably higher than for other applications), reengineering or new development should be considered.

From all of the research and industrial findings, we can conclude that a simple counting of the maintenance tasks and the defect reports can hint at where there are error-prone modules, and can furthermore deliver information for making decisions about the future enhancement of modules/functions. Such metrics and results from collections of relevant data can provide information on best practices and know-how collection of organizations and estimation of future maintenance tasks.

Two aspects should be considered when considering maintenance metrics:

- Estimation of maintenance effort after delivery of the application (perhaps by type of maintenance)
- Estimation of (single) maintenance tasks.

6.4 Estimation of Maintenance Effort after Delivery

From the beginning of the 1990s, Großjohann (1994) at Volkswagen AG (VW) used a VW-specific variant of the Function Point Method to estimate the service effort for IT systems. He calculated the relationship between the service year and the hours per Function Point per year (service factor). This resulted in a "bathtub" curve (see Fig. 6.1), the name derived from the shape of the curve. The relationship was calculated by the formula (S, service factor; Y, service year):

$$S(Y) = 1.604 - 0.37268Y + 0.04684Y^2 - 0.00166Y^3.$$

The total effort to support the complete life cycle of an application (ST) is calculated according to the following formula:

$$ST = FP \times S(Y - 0.5) \times B(Y).$$

In this formula $B(Y)$ represents the influential factors (skills, number of users, system-specific and environment-specific parameters) correlating to the service year. This total effort is divided into the following:

- Maintenance 65%
- User support 25%
- Production 10%.

Note that if maintenance budgets are reduced below the minimum level required to keep the application up and running per the user specifications (production system support), problems and user satisfaction issues will occur. It is

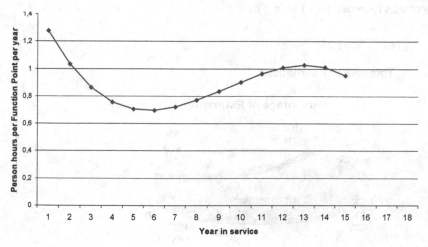

Fig. 6.1. "Bathtub" curve for postdelivery support of applications at Volkswagen AG, 1994

every user's right to expect (and demand) at a minimum, correct and up-to-standard functionality of their software system. Without an adequate level of funding, this cannot be guaranteed.

Enhancement projects that add, change, or delete the functionality of the application are not included in this formula, and such effort (not included in the maintenance effort) must therefore be added separately to the estimate.

6.5 Estimation of Small Changes

Small changes for maintenance reasons are sometimes necessary to meet legal, technical, or organizational requirements, as well as for defect correction. In an international insurance company in Germany these small changes due to maintenance reasons are called "maintenance tasks". Typically, the effort for such maintenance tasks is less than 3 person months, and therefore, the effort to do a Function Point count is usually unfeasible – especially if the Function Point documentation is not readily available.

The estimation Competence Center within the IT department of an international insurance company in Germany worked with a number of experienced project leaders to develop an Excel spreadsheet containing typical tasks for such small changes caused by maintenance reasons and the parameters that were considered to be influential for each. Each factor was correlated with an estimated effort for estimation, which could be changed by ±100%. During the first 2 years, five of the application deve-lopment departments performed more than 220 estimates based on these spreadsheets (see Fig. 6.2), and for more than 90 of these projects, the actual effort expended at the end of the project was recorded (see Fig. 6.3).

Field Test (1)

● Totally 229 Estimations

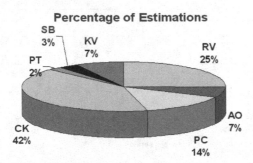

Fig. 6.2. Estimates of small changes due to maintenance reasons (using the Excel spreadsheets) ordered by Application Development Department during the first 2 years

Field Test (2)

● Totally 93 Estimations with Actual Effort

Percentage Actual Effort

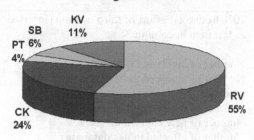

Fig. 6.3. Comparison of effort for small changes due to maintenance reasons estimated with the Excel spreadsheets to actual effort, for 93 projects during first 2 years

Based on the results depicted in Fig. 6.3, corrections were made to the estimating assumptions in the Excel spreadsheets. On average, these *corrections* resulted in a reduction to the formerly estimated efforts by 44%.

Example: Excel Spreadsheet for estimating the effort of Host Maintenance Tasks.

Table 6.7 shows the revised Excel estimating spreadsheet for host maintenance tasks.

Three experiences for this pilot project were interesting:

1. During the pilot phase in three of the departments, the existence of the estimation spreadsheets was discovered by colleagues from four of the other application development departments. This resulted in the pleasant surprise that a total of seven departments participated and made their data available at the end of the pilot phase.
2. As a follow-up to this initial 2 year activity and spreadsheet revision, several other departments developed their own specific variations of the spreadsheets (e.g., for data warehouse applications), which were later approved and published as part of the standard set of estimating spreadsheets by the Competence Center.
3. One experienced senior manager contradicted the previously stated opinion by the Competence Center that the effort for a Function Point count could not be economically justified in the case of small changes. Not only did he conduct FP counts on his projects, he presented his count data and demonstrated that it was no grand effort to do so as part of the effort estimating process. As such, for easily documented FP counts, management subsequently demanded that all other departments count

Table 6.7. The estimation spreadsheet used to estimate effort of small changes due to maintenance reasons in host environment

Parameters	Counted item	Effort in person days (PD), 1 PD = 8 Person Hours
Project management (coordination)	10% from total effort of third column (inserted as last item in column 3)	
Discussions	Number of involved IT persons	0.2 PD
	Number of involved users of the insurance branches	0.3 PD
	Number of involved interfaces	0.4 PD
Databases	Number of new tables/databases	3 PD
	Number of affected tables/databases	2.5 PD
Programs	Number of trivial program changes	0.1 PD
	Number of small program changes	0.3 PD
	Number of "normal" (average) program changes	3.0 PD
	Number of large program changes	5.0 PD
	Number of all programs to be changed	0.1 PD
Other elements	Number of affected Program Status Blocks (PSBs)	0.2 PD
	Number of new or to be changed production jobs	0.7 PD
	Number of changed layouts	0.3 PD
Documentation	Number of affected pages of system documentation	0.3 PD
	Number of new pages of system documentation to be written	0.3 PD
Test	Number of new test cases to be defined	0.1 PD
	Number of existing test cases that must be verified	0.05 PD
	Amount of IT testing effort	0.8 PD
	Number of test cycles for end user testing	2.8 PD

and organize their Function Point counts in a similar manner. In response, the Competence Center developed an additional small Excel spreadsheet that became known as the "FP Counting Sheet" (see Table 6.8). Today, for those estimates for which a quick FP count can be readily obtained, this counting sheet accompanies each small customer change order due to maintenance reasons and ask for an estimate of how many Function Points will be added, changed, or deleted as part of the order.

Today, all of the measures collected are recorded and documented in the metrics database so that they can be used for ongoing project tracking and for the future development of metrics.

Table 6.8. The FP counting spreadsheet for small customer change orders

Customer M. Orders	Several S. col. C. A. data (order # and status, account #, AS #, FP counter name, actual effort in hours)	# of F. CHG	# of FPs for F changed	# of F. NEW	# of FPs for NEW F.	# of F. DEL	# of FP's for DEL F.	Total # of FP's (sum of FP col.) for this order
Release 04/2008								
Order 1								
Order 1								
Order 1								
Order 2								
Order 3								
...								
Total for Release 04								
Release 09/2008								
Order 1								
Order 2								
Order 3								
...								
Total for Release 09								
Total of all releases and orders for the year								

Abbreviations: M. Maintenance orders, *S.* spreadsheet, *col.* columns, *C.* containing, *A.* administrative, *AS.* application system, *F.* Functions, # Number

Example: PC estimating spreadsheet for small customer change orders due to maintenance reasons

The department involved in PC-based application development uses a modified version of this Excel sheet. It can be easily modified (tailored) by the project leaders and is widely accepted. Table 6.9 shows this variant.

Both Tables 6.8 and 6.9 depict possible heuristic estimation methods based on practical experience correlated with actual historical data. The spreadsheets and the values they include are not necessarily transferable to other organizations directly, at least not 1.1 because they were specifically developed to be

Table 6.9. The estimating spreadsheet as tailored for PC-based small customer change orders

Parameters		Effort in person days (PD), 1 PD = 8 Person Hours
Project Management (Coordination)	10% of the total effort	
Discussions	Number of involved IT persons	1.0 PD
	Number of involved users of insurance branches	1.0 PD
	Number of involved existing interfaces	2.0 PD
	Number of involved new interfaces	5.0 PD
	Number of discussions with computing center	5.0 PD
Concept (data model, data search, processes, authorizations, security system, DB2)	Number of complexity 1	5.0 PD
	Number of complexity 2	10.0 PD
	Number of complexity 3	20.0 PD
Coding	Number of data searches of complexity 1	2.0 PD
	Number of data searches of complexity 2	5.0 PD
	Number of data searches of complexity 3	10.0 PD
	Number of functional interface integrations (Security, memo routing, ...)	5.0 PD
	Number of data migrations	5.0 PD
	Number of search algorithms	5.0 PD
	Number of functionality (folders, business processes, ...) of complexity 1	1.0 PD
	Number of functionality (folders, business processes, ...) of complexity 2	2.0 PD
	Number of functionality (folders, business processes, ...) of complexity 3	3.0 PD
	Number of reports, printouts, listings of complexity 1	0.5 PD
	Number of reports, printouts, listings of complexity 2	2.0 PD
	Number of reports, printouts, listings of complexity 3	5.0 PD
	Number of graphics	1.0 PD
	Number of administration dialogues for meta data/key tables	2.0 PD
	Number of others complexity 1	2.0 PD
	Number of others complexity 2	5.0 PD
	Number of others complexity 3	10.0 PD

(Continued)

Data Storage	Number of host tables small (≤10 data fields)	0.1 PD
	Number of host tables medium (≤30 data fields)	0.5 PD
	Number of host tables large (>30 data fields)	1.0 PD
	Number of local data base tables small (≤10 data fields)	0.1 PD
	Number of local data base tables medium (≤30 data fields)	0.2 PD
	Number of local data base tables large (>30 data fields)	0.3 PD
	Number of server data base tables small (≤10 data fields)	0.1 PD
	Number of server data base tables medium (≤30 data fields)	0.3 PD
	Number of server data base tables g large (>30 data fields)	0.5 PD
Techniques	Number of existing technical elements easy	0.5 PD
	Number of existing technical elements medium	2.0 PD
	Number of existing technical elements complex	5.0 PD
	Number of new technical elements easy	1.0 PD
	Number of existing technical elements medium	5.0 PD
	Number of existing technical elements complex	10.0 PD
Tuning	Number of tuning measures	5.0 PD
Installation /Release	Number of installations complexity 1	1.0 PD
	Number of installations complexity 2	2.0 PD
	Number of installations complexity 3	3.0 PD
	Number of releases complexity 1	1.0 PD
	Number of releases complexity 2	2.0 PD
	Number of releases complexity 3	3.0 PD
	Number of supports for installations by computing center	5.0 PD
	Number of concerned formats	0.3 PD
Documentation	10% of the total development effort	
Test	Program system test, 20% of the total development effort	
	Functional integration test, 30% of the total development effort without project management, test and project post mortem	
Project post mortem	5% of the total development effort	

used by IT application development teams within a certain business area and software development environment. In particular, while the effort hours allocated in person days may be typical for the individual environment of this large company, they will be different for others. Nonetheless, these models can be understood as a basic concept that could be adapted to your own environment.

They are presented here to provide readers with some easy and practical ideas to get started.

These MS Excel-based estimation spreadsheets for small customer change orders due to maintenance reasons were made available to the project leaders via the corporate local-area-network (LAN). As these spreadsheets increased in popularity within the organization, they were used to develop several hundred estimates every year. A formal Cold Fusion application was later developed to increase user comfort and add flexibility for actualization of the parameters, as well as providing an easier way to collect and report the corporate metrics.

6.6 Management Summary

Project estimation usually does not include lifetime (or even the first year) of maintenance effort. The lifetime maintenance costs, however, typically exceed the original application development effort by up to 10 times.

Practical experience shows that IT systems live longer than expected.

Note that the IFPUG definition holds that software maintenance does not change the functionality of an application. If a project results in new/changed/ deleted functionality, it is classified by IFPUG as an "enhancement" project.

There is a critical difference between the definition of the word "enhance- ment" in the IT and customer world (where anything that makes the applica- tion run better, makes it easier to use, reformats screens, or adds function is categorized as an enhancement by the users) compared to the definition in the functional size measurement world (where enhancement means "functional" change).

When counting the Function Points for software enhancements, one must remember the "domino effect," that is, that a functional change to an ILF typically also causes a change to the elementary functions that use it (e.g., add, change, delete, and potentially query functions).

Often it is not considered that software – like other products or goods – ages over time and that preventive maintenance and eventual replacement (rede- velopment) of software will someday be necessary.

There is broad consensus in the metrics community that annual support ratios (i.e., how many FP can be supported by one person in one year) depends on the same factors as software productivity (as previously discussed).

From all of the research and industrial findings, we can conclude that a sim- ple counting of the maintenance tasks and the defect reports can hint at where there are error-prone modules, and can furthermore deliver information for making decisions about the future enhancement of modules/functions.

Such metrics and results from collections of relevant data can provide information on best practices and know-how collection of organizations and estimation of future maintenance tasks.

Note that if maintenance budgets are reduced below the minimum level required to keep the application up and running per the user specifications (production system support), problems and user satisfaction issues will occur.

7 Software Measurement and Metrics: Fundamentals

Only 20% of all metrics programs are successful. (Howard Rubin)

Software metrics are useful to measure both the process to develop and the ultimate product characteristics associated with software development. We differentiate between the word "measure" and the word "metric" (or indicator) although these terms are frequently confused in general practice.

Depending on their roles in an organization, different people focus on different metrics (see Table 7.1).

Table 7.1. Metrics viewpoints

Participant	Interests	Goal	Metric
Manager	Economic	Costs, dates	Effort, quality
Developer	Technical	Development environment	Size, complexity
End user	Social	Usability	Functionality
Estimator	Economic	Costs, effort, dates	Effort, budget, project size, duration
Project manager	Technical	Effort, dates, size, complexity	Earned value, progress to date, impact of change

The relevance of software and systems measurement has increased over the past decades; however, the interest in establishing a sustainable software measurement program appears to follow some sort of cyclical trend where waves of commitment surge to a frenzy at times, then wanes to barely a whisper – almost a "management flavor of the month." In the 1960s and 1970s the focus for IT was on product evaluation in the 1980s and 1990s it was on process evaluation and quality initiatives, and changed in the 1990s to measurement process integration. Today, for measurement to succeed, it must provide a positive return on investment with a direct tie to improvement of the business (the "bottom line" finances so to speak) - not simply to the IT department.

Philip Theden distinguishes *three characteristics of metrics*:

- *Information character:* where metrics permit one to make judgments about important subjects and relationships in organizations.
- *Quantifiability:* where subjects and relationships between them are measured on a standard scale.
- *Specific form of information:* where complicated structures and processes can be presented in relatively simple ways through a specific form of metrics.

This chapter provides an overview about the potential use of software metrics.

7.1 Terminology

One generally distinguishes between basic measures (measures) and metrics. Often the term *indicator* is incorrectly used interchangeably with the word *metrics*. Definitions are included in the sections that follow.

7.1.1 Formal Definitions

To define our use of terms here, we went to the comprehensive source for software engineering terminology: the Software and Systems Vocabulary website of the IEEE Computer Society which contains a consolidated vocabulary of terms used in ISO/IEC standards and IEEE standards.

http://pascal.computer.org/sev_display/index.action.The definitions for measure, metric, indicator, and value are listed below:

Measures:

1. Variables for which a value is assigned as the result of measurement *(ISO/IEC 25000:2005 Software Engineering – Software product Quality Requirements and Evaluation (SQuaRE) – Guide to SQuaRE, 4.32)*
2. Make a measurement *(ISO/IEC 25000:2005 Software Engineering – Software product Quality Requirements and Evaluation (SQuaRE) – Guide to SQuaRE, 4.33)*
3. A way to ascertain or appraise value by comparing it to a norm *(IEEE 1061–1998 (R2004) IEEE Standard for Software Quality Metrics Methodology, 2.6)*
4. To apply a metric *(IEEE 1061-1998 (R2004) IEEE Standard for Software Quality Metrics Methodology, 2.6)*
5. A number that assigns relative value *(ISO/IEC 20926:2003 Software engineering – IFPUG 4.1 Unadjusted functional size measurement method – Counting practices manual)*

6. *To ascertain or appraise by comparing to a standard* (ISO/IEC 20926:2003 *Software engineering – IFPUG 4.1 Unadjusted functional size measurement method – Counting practices manual*)
7. The number or category assigned to an attribute of an entity by making a *measurement* (ISO/IEC 14598-1:1999 Information technology – *Software product evaluation – Part 1: General overview, 4.18*)
8. A quantitative assessment of the degree to which a software product or process possesses a given attribute *(IEEE 982.1-1988 IEEE Standard Dictionary of Measures to Produce Reliable Software, 2)*

Metric:

1. A combination of two or more measures or attributes *(ISO/IEC 20926: 2003 Software engineering – IFPUG 4.1 Unadjusted functional size measurement method – Counting practices manual)*
2. A quantitative measure of the degree to which a system, component, or process possesses a given attribute *(ISO/IEC 24765, Systems and Software Engineering Vocabulary)*
3. The defined measurement method and the measurement scale *(ISO/IEC 14598-1:1999 Information technology – Software product evaluation – Part 1: General overview, 4.2)*
4. A quantitative scale and method which can be used to determine the value a sub-characteristic takes for a specific software product *(ISO/IEC 14102:1995 Information technology – Guideline for the evaluation and selection of CASE tools, 3.1.6). Note:* The term metric is used in place of the term software quality metric. *See also* software quality metric

Indicator:

1. Measure that provides an estimate or evaluation of specified attributes derived from a model with respect to defined information needs *(ISO/IEC 25000:2005 Software Engineering – Software product Quality Requirements and Evaluation (SQuaRE) – Guide to SQuaRE, 4.24)*
2. A measure that can be used to estimate or predict another measure *(ISO/IEC 14598-1:1999 Information technology – Software product evaluation – Part 1: General overview, 4.11)*
3. A device or variable that can be set to a prescribed state based on the results of a process or the occurrence of a specified condition *(ISO/IEC 24765, Systems and Software Engineering Vocabulary). Note,* for example, a flag or semaphore

Value:

1. Number or category assigned to an attribute of an entity by making a measurement *(ISO/IEC 25000:2005 Software Engineering – Software product Quality Requirements and Evaluation (SQuaRE) – Guide to SQuaRE, 4.63)*

2. Numerical or categorical result assigned to a base measure, derived measure, or indicator *(ISO/IEC 15939:2002 Software engineering –Software measurement process, 3.41)*
3. An entity that may be a possible actual parameter in a request *(ISO/IEC 19500-2:2003 Information technology – Open Distributed Processing – Part 2: General Inter-ORB Protocol (GIOP)/Internet Inter-ORB Protocol (IIOP), 3.2.26)*
4. Magnitude of a particular quantity, generally expressed as a unit of measurement multiplied by a number *(ISO/IEC 19761:2003 Software engineering – COSMIC-FFP – A functional size measurement method, 3.3)*

These definitions are *copyrighted* © 2006 by the IEEE. The reader is granted permission to copy the definition as long as the statement "Copyright © 2006, IEEE. Used by permission." remains with the definition. All other rights are reserved.

7.1.2 Basic Measures (Measures)

Measures are used to assist in business operations, especially in reporting, controlling, and quality planning; Measures are quantifiable figures derived from a product, a process, or a resource. By definition, measures are quantitative, and in the software and systems development industry, they can be applied to applications and projects, and other initiatives. Measures should be documented and often are instantiated with estimated, planned, and actual values. Examples of measures include start and end dates, software functional size, effort, and defects. Effort values can typically be detailed further by phase (proportion of effort by phase) and by other breakdowns, including type of resource (e.g., by end users, IT core team, technical support and interfaces, and proportions thereof). Measures are also called "absolute measures" because they can be taken directly from business data without requiring calculations.

7.1.3 Metrics

Metrics are used to evaluate applications, projects, products, and processes, and they enable a quantitative comparison with other products, processes, applications, and IT projects. Metrics typically facilitate a common denominator type of comparison between two or more observed measures.

Metrics are most often calculated from (basic) measures or their combinations and are typically compared with a baseline or an expected result. Sometimes they are more precisely called relative metrics since they bring absolute figures in a relation to each other. Their actual and estimated values have to be measured incidentally and must be documented on several aggregation levels to allow for drilling down into more detailed data.

Metrics should deliver "orientation support," that is, direction, for planning and management of the key production processes in an organization. Therefore, appropriate metrics can be the critical success factors of organizational management.

In this book, we present metrics that are often found in literature or as argumented proofs used in the software market. A measurement (or metrics) system must continuously be fostered, administered, and enhanced to ensure its ongoing sustainability. To ensure that there will be a future collection of detailed, actual values of (basic) measures and metrics, one requires (as a prerequisite) current catalogues of applications to be measured on an annual basis.

7.1.4 Indicators

Indicators compare a metric to a baseline or to an anticipated result. They are also sometimes called coefficients. Indicators are collected over a time period to derive trends – often these can serve as early warning indicators. According to David Card (1997), an indicator consists of a measured variable, a goal (expected by historic experience, industrial average, or best practice), and an analysis technique, allowing a comparison between measurement and goal. It is the comparison between the measurement and the goal that permits one to recognize if some action has to be performed.

According to Teade Punter, an indicator is a visualization of a metric or a model where raw data are aggregated. Indicators are used to present measured data in a manner that useful information can be derived from them. Table 7.2 gives a short overview of categories of metrics.

Dueck (2003) presented the following view in his regular column in the magazine Informatik Spektrum of the German GI (Gesellschaft für Informatik e.V.) in order to foster awareness of software metrics. He describes how many things that we believe we can measure are really indicators based on other measures. Other important thoughts of him include:

"A measurement is for me a kind of statement. If the clinical thermometer indicates 38 degrees (centigrade), then it is 38 degrees. The number of publications is an indicator of research efficiency, but not a measurement of it. Frequency of citation or keynote payments is also only indicators, not measures. An indicator delivers only evidence for a real fact. It does not prove *it* as, for example, a measurement could do. We often measure not what is reality when measuring, but only indicators. Since we measured the indicator very correctly and objectively, we often take the indicator as reality. But no matter what, it is only an indicator!"

There are as many opinions about metrics as there are metrics. However, four governing opinions abound about indicators.

Table 7.2. Overview of metrics types

Metric	Description	Forms	Examples
Absolute metrics	Basic measures manipulated to provide new information as metrics	Single data sums, averages, differences,	Start- and end-dates, software size, effort in person hours
Relative metrics	Relative data, structuring data, relational data, relating several absolute measures together	Factorial figures, relationships, derived data	Percentages of Function Points attributable to EIs compared to the total size of the software
Coefficients	Indicators, maximum, average, and Minimum, calculated from other metrics on a time series basis and used for comparison	Measured data chronicled over time, metrics	The relation of IT effort to total business
Index figures	Figures for general presentation of many changes of organizational data	Percentages, single figures indexed, basic values (mostly 100)	Annual increase in productivity

Opinion 1: "What you can't measure, you can't manage." Organizations that hold this opinion are typically dominated by managers seeking easy-to-measure indicators that will equip them to drive their world in a certain direction. Indicators for these managers include, for example, the index of customer satisfaction, the sum of third party investments. Management imports these indicators into Excel tables stating: "more!" (or concerning costs etc. "less!"). Experiences of the authors show that managers want these indicators quickly, no matter how right or wrong they may be. Another twist on this is how to lie with statistics, also known as "just give me the numbers and I'll make them say whatever I want." This is not a productive environment for a measurement program.

Opinion 2: People whose behavior is driven by indicators bitterly complain that indicators do not tell the truth and do not reflect reality. They cite published studies that were subsequently proven to be falsified. Organizations where cynicism is the mode d'etre (the way to be) will have difficulty with implementing a realistic measurement program.

Opinion 3: We all secretly know the difference between indicator and measurement. We better try to escape now before everyone become an expert on the subject. We publish citations of each other to gain acknowledgement. We make fifty papers out of one idea. All of these tricks for survival use the difference between an indicator and a measurement. The tricks optimize the sharply measured indicators. The essential is lost since the indicators do not touch it at all.

Opinion 4: "Measurement is characterized by the despair about the distraction of the attention from reality. Indicator driven management by "Quick! More!" paints a picture in my mind about people who are lazy and must be urged on trot."

7.1.5 Metrics

These seems to be a widespread misunderstanding that by simply collecting and reporting data is the same as implementing a metrics initiative. This is one of the dominant reasons that software measurement often fails – the collected data has little relationship to corporate goals, and ends up being a tawdry mixture of disparate data points – that practitioners hope to compile into "information" with meaning.

In the American author's experience of teaching Goal/Question/Metric workshops and also implementing software measurement programs in Fortune 500 companies, one of the biggest mistakes that corporations make is failing to plan a goal-driven measurement program (Dekkers 1999). Goal-driven measurement (also called the Goal-Question-Metric (GQM) approach by Dr. Victor Basili) is built by starting with the sustainable strategic goals for measurement, then once those are set, moves to the Question part where the answers to said questions will determine the decisions to be made to move towards the goals, and then the metrics are determined solely in support of the questions they must answer.

This sounds like a sane, straightforward approach, yet the majority of companies who embark on a measurement initiative will approach the process completely backwards: they will first try to figure out what measures and metrics to collect, then try to figure out what decisions they can make based on the data they collect, and then hope that somehow, someway the decisions and metrics will support the corporate objectives and move their division towards their attainment.

The American author often emphasizes particular points in her workshops by using analogies from other industries or real life situations. To explain the concepts of GQM, here is one such analogy: "if I (living here in Florida) were to invite a group of 20 of you for dinner to my home, and all of you agree to attend, I should be able to clarify my goals – to provide ample and varied food and drink for 20 people of various gourmet likes and dislikes. Now if this was a measurement program instead of a dinner party, I would then go straight to the grocery store and start shopping for ingredients. After selecting suitable and not-too-expensive ingredients I would pay for them, go home, and then say, "I sure hope that I can cook up a great evening set of food platters with all the stuff I just bought." Completely backwards isn't it? I should have started with the goal, chosen some recipes (questions), made a list, and then (and only then) gone shopping for ingredients (the metrics in a software measurement program). In software measurement, too often people try to "cook something up" with all the data that has been collected, yet the data are all at different or uncomparable levels, and not of the right kind. So, to go back to the analogy, it does not matter if I have a pantry full of ingredients (collected data) if I cannot use it in a meaningful way."

The Software Engineering Institute (SEI) in the US endorses goal-driven-measurement in their training programs, as does the ISO/IEC 15939 standard: Software mea-surement framework, which was built on the basis of Practical Software and Systems Measurement (PSM) initiative out of the US Department of Defense (see www.psmsc.com for details). Today, the SEI has added an "I" to their GQM offerings to make it GQIM - Goal Question Indicator Metrics, likely in part to ensure that the resultant measures and metrics provide targeted and indicative answers to the questions.

Fenton (1991) found four different definitions for a metric:

• A figure derived from a product, process, or resource
• A scale for measurements
• An identifiable attribute
• A theoretic, data-driven model describing a variable as a function of an independent variable.

A software quality metric is a function mapping of a software unit onto a figure. This calculated value could be interpreted as degree of fulfillment of a quality characteristic of the software unit. A quality characteristic is, at first thought, a lack of defects, efficiency, user comfort, maintainability, etc. and, according to the CMMI®, also includes process related quality characteristics as, for example, productivity or fulfillment of plan. Thus, software quality metrics must be able to derive figures from software development that are related to the aforementioned quality characteristics.

The supporting structure for a metrics system includes automated tools for estimation and project control and the retained knowledge in these tools or in metrics databases.

The following adage should be remembered:

No single metric can provide wisdom!

This statement tells us that, like estimation methods, there should always be several metrics considered to control an organization. On the one hand, metrics can be similar to pieces of a puzzle: they individually contain pieces of information, but their true value lies in evaluating them in terms of their context and the relationship with other data. On the other hand, metrics form an integral part of the total picture and, like a puzzle, one must go one step ahead to view the whole before the meaning of each part can be understood. A metrics initiative when integrated with the organization can deliver insight about gaps in organizational processes and help to kick start improvement initiatives.

7.2 Goals and Benefits of Metrics

Even in a major international insurance company well acquainted with the benefits of metrics in the core business, it was a tough business to sell the benefits of software metrics. With appropriate and targeted metrics, data are collected and analyzed, which relate to the software product and the development process and support effective management. The first objective is to identify the actual state of the processes and/or product. The Capability Maturity Model Integration (CMMI®) of the SEI includes the process area: measurement and analysis at maturity level 2.

7.2.1 Goals of Metrics

Goldensen et al. from the SEMA Group (Software Engineering Measurement and Analysis Group) of the Software Engineering Institute (SEI) at Carnegie Melon University states that the following goals can be achieved with a good metrics program:

- To establish a common understanding throughout the organization.
- To determine the information requirements of the organization and management processes.
- To identify or develop a reasonable selection of measures according to the information requirements.
- To identify and accomplish the activities for measurement.
- To collect, store, analyze, and interpret the results of measurement.
- To use measurement results for decision support as well as as a basis for communication.
- To evaluated and communicate the measurement process to the process owner.

The analysis of metrics and the resultant reports are the most important processes of a metrics initiative. Pure collection of metrics seldom leads to success.

It should be remembered that metrics measure only aspects about software products or processes, but never individual people. Ignoring this critical rule most certainly leads to damage control and ultimately the failure of a measurement program. Moreover, metrics must be seen in a larger context. In addition, management must be sensitive to the fact that there are many reasons for differences in metrics results.

Two important concepts are critical to keep in mind:

1. People can make or break a measurement program. Paul Goodman in his 1993 book Practical Implementation of Software Metrics stated in the closing pages: you might be surprised to find out just how big a part people play in the success or failure of a measurement program. It is critical to include people in the planning and implementation of the measurement program.

2. Metrics data reflect the current state and are passive. There is no such thing as good data or bad data – there is only data and data are the status quo of the current process or product. As such, when management asks their staff to collect and report metrics, they must also understand that the worse the current data are, the more opportunity there is for process improvement. The adage "don't shoot the messenger" is especially true here when software personnel report their data.

Metrics can be a mighty tool to determine quality and improvements in comparison to a goal.

7.2.2 Benefits of Metrics

Metrics use measurements of the past to give guidance for future directions (feed forward). Measurement should establish a basis for estimating and controlling project progress. Continual observation of the collected metrics on ongoing projects enables us to collect experience factors that can be used to meet goal commitments. A continuous comparison of planned to actual values can help to find weaknesses in the software development process and can enable process improvement. *The benefit of metrics cannot be measured by the cost of installation, but on the costs of not having a working metrics system in place.*

Goldensen states that metrics provide support for the project leader, mainly by answering the following questions:

- Are there problems emerging on my project?
- If so, what effects will they have?
- What is the root cause of the problem(s)?
- Can I trust my data?
- What alternatives do I have to mitigate the problem(s)?
- What measures should be collected?
- When can I expect results?

The example of a project metrics report with fictitious values depicts a practical use of metrics (see Table 7.3).

Table 7.3. **Example** project metrics report

Metrics Category	Metric	Formula	Calculation	Comparable Projects	Industrial Average
Efficiency of development process	Project delivery rate (PDR)	Effort/size	1,000 h/100 FP = 10 h/FP	8.0 h/FP	10.0 h/FP
Churn (process rework)	Percent rework	Rework hours/effort hours	6,500/13,000 = 50%	55%	45%
Testing process effectiveness	Defect removal effectiveness	Number of found defects /number of pre + post production defects (90 days)	300/400 × 100% = 75%	75%	85%
Product quality	Defect denity	Number of found defects/ FP	20 defects/100 FP = 2 def/FP	0.4 defects/FP	0.3 defects/ FP
Product enhancement	Degree of enhancement per year	Annual FP enhancement projects/FP base	250/1,000 × 100% = 25%	35%	28%
Unit cost	Cost ratio	Cost/FP	$1,800/FP	$1,700/FP	$1,100/FP
Time to market	Duration delivery rate	(End date – Start date)/FP	180 days/100 FP = 1.8 days/FP	2.3 days/FP	3 days/FP

Metrics facilitate objective analysis of the challenges with processes, and also enables early risk recognition that can support mitigation of those risks. Metrics should improve communication between project team members and also between the project team and the project steering committee and other stakeholders.

Furthermore, metrics can be used to develop rules of thumb and are beneficial for objective planning and estimation. When metrics are used as standards, they provide a common understanding of software measurement that the staff can understand and can use as a basis for process improvement. Appropriate measurement makes the process of software development transparent so that it can be evaluated. A properly planned and implemented measurement program can be evaluated and, through corrective action can improve the quality of software products and processes.

Metrics can also be used to manage contracting and outsourced software development. Critical success factors for this area of application include the following:

- Up-to-date and exacting definition of requirements. This helps to minimize risks for both parties in the contract
- Appropriate and just-in-time training to empower the project team to succeed on the project
- Support before and after the implementation to ensure the long-term product success.

Successfully introducing a metrics initiative requires committed management support. Furthermore, the people who will be responsible for metrics implementation (i.e., function point counters, data gatherers, analysts) must be chosen carefully and receive training. It is a measurement prerequisite to engage the right human resources with the right skills to lead and drive the measurement program. The minimum skills include a positive attitude about software measurement, a curiosity and vision that measurement can make a difference, knowledge about process and product improvement, analytical skills, attention to detail, willingness to learn, and excellent communication skills.

7.3 Start and Implementation of a Metrics Initiative

The implementation of a metrics initiative needs time, committed resources, projects, and measured data. Silveira recommends that metrics initiatives should embrace the following concepts to be successful:

- Do not measure individuals
- Avoid "Big Bang" implementation
- Committed support by management
- Discussions, forums, frequent, and open communication
- Information meetings at least monthly.

Another prerequisite for a successful metrics initiative is an organization that fosters positive change and encourages individual innovations. We recommend implementing a Competence Center to provide recommendations to decentralized experts and project leaders to collect and analyze data, develop, refine, and analyze metrics. The competence center should be tasked with developing the metrics "experience" database to support future projects based on similar historical experiences. Improvements in IT take the following forms: better control of project progress and decision-making based on measured facts.

The following list of success *secrets* apply for measurement (Dekkers 1999):

1. Set solid objectives and plans for measurement
2. Make the measurement program part of the process – not a management pet project

3. Gain a thorough understanding of what measurement is all about – including benefits and limitations
4. Focus on the cultural issues
5. Create a safe environment to collect and report true data
6. A predisposition to change
7. A complementary suite of measures.

7.3.1 Establishing a Metrics Initiative

The process of establishing a metrics initiative evolves in six steps (see Fig. 7.1). This model was used by the ISO/IEC working group for the Measurement Process Framework (for software and systems measurement): ISO/IEC 15939.

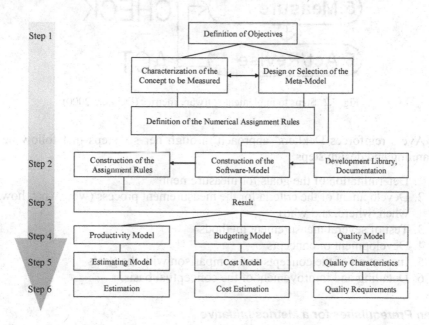

Fig. 7.1. Steps to establish a metrics initiative

A modification of the well known total quality management Plan-Do-Check-Act (PDCA) model can be effective for measurement program implementation. The American author conducts workshops titled: Guide to Software Measurement Start-up, 2000 (see Fig. 7.2):

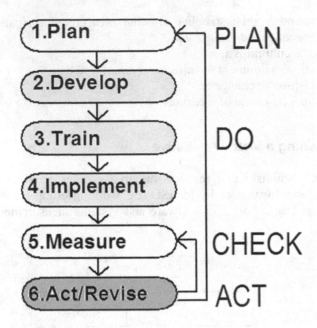

Fig. 7.2. Steps to implement software metrics (Dekkers 2000)

Ayers reinforces Dekkers' approach through her six steps that follow her planning and design steps:

1. Determination of the goals for measurement
2. Development of the criteria for the measurement process (why, what, how, when, where, and who)
3. Test of several measurement methods
4. Development of concepts
5. Inspection of the concepts and comparison with the goals
6. Detailing and improvement of the conceptual basis.

Ten Prerequisites for a Metrics Initiative

The establishment of a metrics initiative constitutes a change of the organizational culture. If management is not committed to measurement as part of the new way of doing business, the chances for its success will be limited. Even with management support, measurement may not succeed unless the involved staff is willing to support it or if they do not understand why they should make the effort. If staff suspect that measurement is a new management way to control their productivity, measurement will not succeed. As we have mentioned elsewhere, the king's road to acceptance of innovations can guide the initiative to success through information, training, and participation of the involved staff.

From the beginning, the metrics initiative should not be sold as an easy task for delivering the organization important benefits, rather it needs to be marketed as one part of a continuous improvement process. If an organization is in a state of chaos, immaturity (i.e., level zero on the Capability Maturity Model Integration's five level maturity scale), or if it is in a state of continuous organizational change, a metrics initiative can hardly be established. Metrics need a stable environment (even if not terribly mature) in order to have a chance of success.

A lack of tool support can bring with it problems with acceptance, that is, one cannot implement a robust and plausible measurement program on purely paper and pencil. Tool support and committed resources show the organization that you are serious about measurement!

Nonetheless, in spite of all these challenges, never believe that your metrics initiative is truly dead (i.e., management has "pulled the plug" on funding) until you read about it in a public announcement or newspaper!

The following real-life international experiences partly overlap the afore-mentioned and demonstrate which factors were truly indispensable for the success of the large scale international metrics initiative. There are also some practical hints for transfer in the own organization. Prerequisites cited by Dekkers (2002) in *How and When Can Functional Size Fit with a Measurement Program?* include the following:

- Continuous and effective marketing as support for the physical, intellectual, and especially cultural change associated with measurement
- Secure the availability of the data to anticipate the uncertainty of the staff
- External support for training and consulting to minimize start-up errors and to gain knowledge-transfer to build internal expertise
- Realistic goals and plans supported by management
- Being prepared and willing for change
- A defined choice of metrics implemented in bite-size-pieces incrementally (the German author: "an elephant can only be eaten in slices")
- Accurate, actual and consistent data to support decision-making.

Mah agrees with the SEI by recommending that an organization start out with the *four core metrics: size (scope), effort, duration, and quality*. The first step is then to establish a baseline for productivity to answer the managerial question about the capacity of a development department. Why these four core metrics? Many projects are only managed by milestones and effort, even though scope (per the functional size) and quality (defects and other measures) are also equally critical elements. Measurement can be implemented in a pilot projects; however, such projects should have (according to Mah) at least 3 months duration, comprise at least 12 person months effort, and be considered of high level importance for the organization.

Russac recommends the following rules to maximize the success of a metrics initiative:

- Metrics must be integrated with existing processes.
- Metrics must be part of the organizational culture.
- Measured data must be collected on a project level and aggregated on an organizational level for reporting.
- Measured data must be exact, repeatable, and consistent.
- In the beginning, only a few metrics should be implemented.
- For benchmarking with other organizations, only industrial standards should be used.
- A metrics database should be installed.
- A metrics initiative must be simple and consistent.
- Metrics should be used for decision support, goal setting, and process improvement.
- Results must be timely and be communicated adequately.
- Support must be committed from management.
- Metric specialists must be chosen according to their qualification and not according to their availability.
- All those involved in measurement should get training.
- Metrics must change and evolve as much as the organization grows.
- Metrics must be fostered in the organization.
- Metrics must be used positively and not to measure individual persons.

All this expert knowledge shows that metrics should never be introduced and used half-heartedly!

Ten Factors to Consider When Choosing a Measure

Dekkers and McQuaid (2002, pp 33–39) analyzed the measurement model recommended by Kaner et al. He stated that the theory underlying a measurement must take into account a set of ten questions as shown in Table 7.4 (Kaner 2002).

Table 7.4. Kaner's 10 considerations for selecting a measure

Number	Factor for consideration	Description	Example
1	Purpose of this measure	What are you trying to measure?	Size, quality, effort
2	Scope of this measure	What range of applicability you want to cover with the method, the wider the range of issues that can be affected by the measure. The purpose must be closely mapped to the scope of the measure.	

(Continued)

3	What attribute are we trying to measure	You need a clear idea of the specifics of what you are trying to measure, so your measure will have a strong relationship to your purpose and scope.	Software quality = functionality? Portability? Usability? etc.
4	Natural scale of the attribute	We might measure a person's height in inches, but what units should we use for extent of testing? Are the attribute's mathematical properties rational, interval, ordinal, nominal, or absolute? You must preserve the ratio relationship to make measurement meaningful.	
5	Natural variability	When measuring two supposedly identical items, some of their characteristics are probably slightly different. The attribute itself is likely subject to random fluctuations, so we need a model or equation describing the natural variation of the attribute.	For example, what model can deal with why a tester may find more defects on one day than on another?
6	What instrument to measure	Examples include trying to measure the extent of testing with a coverage program, or counting the number of defects found.	
7	Natural scale of the instrument	Whether the mathematical properties of measures taken with the instruments are rational, interval, ordinal, nominal, or absolute.	For example, bug counts are absolute.
8	Natural variability of the readings	This is normally studied in terms of "measurement error." We need a theory for the variation associated with using and reading the instrument. The act of taking measurements, using the instrument, carries random fluctuations, so even though you record your result as precisely as you can, there may be error and variability.	
9	Relationship of the attribute to the instrument	What is your basis for saying that this instrument measures this attribute well? What mechanism causes an increase in the reading as a function of an increase in the attribute? If we increase the	

(Continued)

		attribute by 20%, what will show up in the next measurement? It might be the model or equation relating the attribute to the instrument	
10	Natural and foreseeable side effects of using this instrument	When people realize that you are measuring something, how will they change their behavior to make the numbers look better or to provide you with the data you desire?	For example, we could drive people to decrease the bug count, but it might make the testers much less effective.

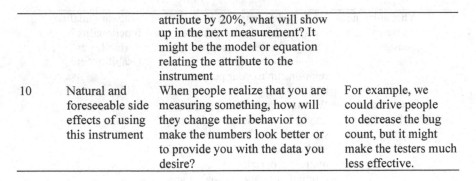

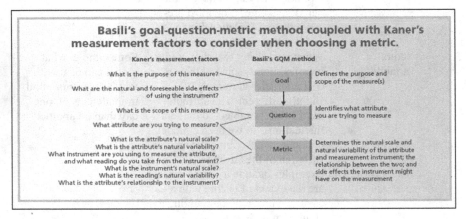

Fig. 7.3. Basili's GQM and Kaner's factors for choosing a metric (Dekkers et al. 2002)

Combining the GQM method and the Kaner's model, Dekkers and McQuaid (2002) produced Fig. 7.3.

7.3.2 Establishing a Metrics Database

The best basis for estimation is a metrics experience database. Hence metrics and collected measures should be available in an automated database. Often they are implemented using one or more software tools. For example, the function point details may be stored in a tool such as the Function Point Workbench, in combination with time reporting systems, problem tracking tools, or source code checkers. Experience® Pro, a software estimating and scope management tool, allows for estimates and actuals together with project characteristics and situation analysis factors to be stored in an experience database within the tool. Other tools may also be available depending on your specific organizational needs to store the measures and metrics. See the chapter on Tools for further details.

Experience shows that on average 5–10 years worth of historical project data are necessary before an organization has elaborated such a central repository housing the collection of information about estimates and actual project values. The benefits for an organization are plentiful according to Beckett and Llorence:

- With the development of one's own experience database, the organization gains estimation know-how and data (expertise) is always available.
- The database can be used to generate or derive project independent "neutral" estimates.
- Historical experience data are available and enable more precise estimates than pure wishful thinking.
- The knowledge that estimation is done professionally with the aid of the database reduces the project risk for the customer.

A metrics database that is too complex in the beginning will hinder a metrics initiative more than it will support it. Therefore, one should start with a core set of metrics targeted to answer the questions necessary to gauge the progress towards the goals (see GQM based measurement programs earlier in this chapter). This also requires collecting further information in a repository:

- Project
    - Project ID and name
    - Responsible project leader and department
- Project Management
    - Start date (estimated, planned, actual)
    - End date (estimated, planned, actual)
    - Duration (estimated, planned, actual)
    - Effort by phase (estimated, planned, actual)
    - Cost (estimated, planned, actual)
    - Special information
- Product
    - Function Points with all detailed information (estimated, planned, actual)
    - Defects (actual by phase)
    - Logical lines of code (estimated, planned, actual)
- Process
    - Programming languages and their proportions
    - Software architecture
    - Hardware architecture
    - Percentage of reuse
    - Proportions allocated to each project phase
    - Proportions of end users, IT, technical support, and interfaces.

To be effective, a metrics database must contain data on actual completed projects and their attributes. This means that a formal process must be established for transferring data from historical files. One challenge for database administration is that the important factors in the metrics database can change over time. Therefore, the definitions of the metrics based on such factors also can change, and comparisons in time series can be rendered unreasonable. For this reason, a database historical mapping over time is also important.

In 2002, the IT department of an international insurance company in Germany sent out an international request for information about the usage of metrics by email to the CRIM listserv members and the mailing lists of international metrics organizations, and received answers from 24 organizations all over the world. The answers were varied:

- Four of the organizations did calculations of productivity in FP per effort or per cost (budget, planning).
- Three of the organizations did calculations of the efficiency in effort per FP (PDR) or they used Balanced Scorecards or did not answer or did not use metrics at all.
- Two of the organizations used Compass Analysis to do their metrics.
- One organization calculated the quality in defects per FP and another one measured only if their projects were delivered on time, on budget, or on specification (OTOBOS).

Finck and Hampp presented an analogue survey and compared it with the 24 organization study above, and with the ESMIT survey (2003) by Löper and Zehle of Sweden. Finck and Hampp encountered 21 valid answers and interviewed 7 of those organizations. Their overview is shown in Table 7.5.

Table 7.5. Fink and Hampp's consolidated overview of surveys

Metrics used	Percentage of answers in		
	This survey	The ESMIT survey	The above survey
Effort	100%		53%
Costs	95%		12%
Duration	90%		
Productivity	50%		24%
SLOC	45%	46%	18%
Function points	20%	11%	59%
McCabe's complexity metric	10%	9%	
Halstead metric	0%	4%	
OO metrics	10%	6%	
Number of defects	60%		

7.3.3 The Structure of a Metrics System

A metrics "system" consists of basic measures and metrics related to these basic measures in an appropriate way. Figure 7.4 shows the basic structure of

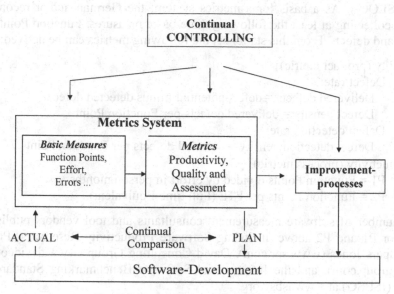

Fig. 7.4. Basic structure of a metrics system

a metrics system. A solid metrics system is analogous to a cybernetic control circuit, where the controlling activities can clearly be recognized.

A simple list of topic areas for which software development measurement should collect metrics includes (Weller 2002) the following:

• Precision of estimation regarding dates and effort
• Product quality at delivery
• Defect removal efficiency (number of defects in requirements divided by total number of defects)
• Inspections
• Testing
• Number of problems reported by the customer
• Estimation of maintenance
• Frequency of inspections and meetings
• Effort proportions per project phase
• Frequency of help desk calls.

Of course not all of these measurement areas are even examined, or collected from every organization.

The six most common core measures (depending on the author 4–6 core metrics are mentioned) are scope (sized in Function Points), effort (in hours or person months), quality (typically measured as defects), cost (in USD or € or currency unit), duration (in days or months), and physical size (source lines of code (SLOC)). As a basis for a metrics system, the German author recommends collecting at least the following three basic measures: Function Points, effort, and defects. From this starter set the following metrics can be derived:

- Quality (product metric)
  - o Defect rate:
    Delivered defects = defect potential minus detected defects
    Defect density = delivered defects per Function Point
  - o Defect detection rate:
    Defect detection density = detected defects per Function Point
- Productivity (process metric)
  - o P1 = Function Points divided by effort in person months
  - o P2 = Function Points per FTE (Full time Equivalent).

A number of software measurement consultants and tool vendors publish rates for P1 and P2 above, including Software Productivity Research (SPR) and Capers Jones (www.spr.com), David Consulting Group (www.davidconsultinggroup.com), and the International Software Benchmarking Standards Group (ISBSG) at www.isbsg.org.

The definition of suitable measures and the processes to collect and analyze them can be a time consuming process. While the American author advocates a GQM approach that is mandatory to ensure the measurement system is targeted, the German author's experiences in organizations show that partial success is possible with systems that simply begin measurement by collecting function points, effort, and defects. After measuring in an organization a productivity of x FP per pm (Function Points per person month), for example, the goals for the project leaders were set to $(x + 3)$ FP per pm for the subsequent projects. With a bonus system put into place, motivation was fostered and a degree of success was achieved. The agreed productivity was reached within 12 months. Literature tells us that productivity can vary by a factor of ten.

Capers Jones writes that the productivity in Europe is less than that in the United States purely for the reason that Europe observes more holidays and vacation days. This is apparent when person months are used as the measure of effort. For this reason and because of varying definitions of hours per person month, we recommend reporting and collecting effort in units of hours.

Quality and productivity are in strong connection with process, persons, and technology. Improvement concerning these three dimensions (process, people, and technology) leads to increased quality and productivity. Jones further mentions in his comparison across countries that Japan, India, Norway, and Sweden have extraordinary good quality compared to the United States. There may be a number of factors for this, including mandated quality levels or standards.

From the parameters influencing process improvement project duration and project size proved to be especially flexible. When dealing with a stable size (solid requirements), condensed project schedules to reduce the overall time-to-market (duration) costs more money and delivers lower quality (think of this similar to squeezing a balloon to reduce its diameter). A longer duration enables the team to produce higher quality but typically delays the usability of the required functionality. On the other hand, reduced scope (project size) can provide a better chance to deliver important functionality earlier. Normally, functionality is decreased in order to reach the overly optimistic milestones on time. The other factors for improvement of processes such as staff, cost, and quality are less flexible. This is caused by the devils square of project management. Note: the devils' square depicts the effect that the primary goals (costs, size, time, and quality) of an IT project unavoidably compete with each other for the resources of the project. Hence, every additional consumption of one resource leads to reductions of other resources.

It is also important to track change metrics in terms of thresholds and limits, or to define them to gain improvements for the metrics initiative. Metrics related to project change measure the differences between estimation and actual values measured (like, for example, the change of cost, effort, or duration), as well as requirements creep or relationships in changes of quality (e.g., defect detection rate: defects at delivery divided by total number of defects), or rework proportions (percentage of rework). The last three mentioned metrics related to change can help to identify and manage risks. These measures are more difficult to measure than the first three ones listed.

Galorath distinguishes between planning metrics and tracking metrics:

- *Planning metrics* support planning of successful projects. They are strongly connected with the goal and the size of projects. The size is the key metric of the planning metrics.
- *Tracking metrics* support successful management of projects. Planning metrics often serve both goals.

One of the best-known tracking metrics is the *Earned Value Method* that explores two basic questions:

1. Is the actual (consumed) effort at the time of measurement being consumed at a rate adequate to deliver the planned project?
2. Is the actual money spent to date less than or equal to the money budgeted for the project to get to this point of delivery?

If both questions can be answered "yes" then the project is typically on-track. If the answer is "no" in both cases, then the Project has severe problems of being overbudget and behind schedule .

If the first question is answered with no and the second with yes, then the productivity is less than expected. This may be caused by different reasons, and if a project becomes more than 15% late it will never catch up. If the project connot recover quickly enough, the project most likely will be delivered later than planned and cost more than it was budgeted.

If the first question is answered yes and the second with no then it may be that the motivation of the project team has been supported by incentives or that planning was too conservative.

The challenge of the Earned Value Method is the exact measurement of the degree of completion. This can be supported by milestones for different degrees of completion. Just asking the staff to which degree they finished their task leads to the famous *90% finished syndrome*. The degree of completion is always overestimated and then during a long time in the 90% stage. To avoid this problem it is psychologically better to ask the involved staff how many effort they estimate for completion of their task. Using the already consumed (measured) effort the degree of completion can easily be calculated.

Figure 7.5 depicts some strong Earned Value Method statements from McKinlay's (2006) IPMA/ICEC presentation.

 Analysis of over 500 completed contracts – when a contract is more than 15%-20% complete:

➤ The **absolute** overrun at completion will not be less than the overrun to date

➤ The **%** overrun at completion will be greater than the **%** overrun to date

➤ The CPI does not change (by more than 10%) and almost always deteriorates

With 95% confidence

Christensen, David S. 1993. "An Analysis of Cost Overruns on Defense Acquisition Contracts." *Project Management Journal* 3:43-48 (September).

Mary McKinlay Projects Ltd

Fig. 7.5. Earned Value Method figures (McKinlay 2006)

Other tracking metrics are defect measurements, which can be accomplished in any phase of the project, but mostly in testing (defect metrics). A widely accepted categorization of metrics distinguishes between the product and the process of software development. In this system, Galorath's planning metrics fit better in the product metrics and his tracking metrics more likely to the process metrics.

Besides that the project metrics are often viewed separate from these two categories, neglecting the fact that they can also be seen from process or tracking view. The difference is only that the metrics derived show other values since projects also have effort for software parts to be enhanced. This effort is related to little or no functional software size at all because the "user functionality" has not changed, similar to how software maintenance is handled.

How important a reasonable choice of metrics is can be shown with the definition of two tongue-in-cheek project measures, also published by Galorath:

The Pizza Metric: The count of the empty pizza boxes in the team area is a measure of project delay, since people would not eat consistently at their workplace if the project was on time.

The Aspirin Metric: A jar of headache tablets is supplied for the team, and the tablets remaining are regularly counted. The higher the number of tablets consumed the less motivated (and more under stress) is the team.

7.4 Management Summary

Software metrics are useful to measure both the process to develop and the ultimate product characteristics associated with software development.

One generally distinguishes between basic measures (measures) and metrics. Often the term "indicators" is incorrectly used interchangeably with the word "metrics."

Measures are used to assist in business operations, especially in reporting, controlling, and quality planning; Measures are quantifiable figures derived from a product, a process, or a resource.

Metrics are used to evaluate applications, projects, products, and processes, and they enable a quantitative comparison with other products, processes, applications, and IT projects. Metrics typically facilitate a common denominator type of comparison between two or more observed measures.

Metrics are most often calculated from (basic) measures or their combinations and are typically compared with a baseline or an expected result.

Metrics should deliver "orientation support," that is, direction, for planning and management of the key production processes in an organization. Therefore, appropriate metrics can be the critical success factors of organizational management.

Indicators compare a metric to a baseline or to an anticipated. They are also sometimes called coefficients.

A widespread misunderstanding is that just collecting and reporting of data is the same as implementing a metrics initiative.

A software quality metric is a function mapping of a software unit onto a figure.

The supporting structure for a metrics system includes automated tools for estimation and project control and the retained knowledge in these tools or in metrics databases.

No single metric can provide wisdom!

It should be remembered that metrics measure only aspects about software products or processes, but never individual people. Ignoring this critical rule most certainly leads to damage control and ultimately the failure of a measurement program.

People can make or break a measurement program.

Metrics data reflect the current state and are passive.

Metrics can be a mighty tool to determine quality and improvements in comparison to a goal.

Metrics use measurements of the past to give guidance of future directions (feed forward).

The benefit of metrics cannot be measured by the cost of installation, but on the costs of not having a working metrics system in place.

Metrics facilitate objective analysis of the challenges with processes, and also enables early risk recognition that can support for mitigation of those risks.

Furthermore, metrics can be used to develop rules of thumb and are beneficial for objective planning and estimation.

Metrics can also be used to manage contracting and outsourced software development.

Successfully introducing a metrics initiative requires committed management support.

The implementation of a metrics initiative needs time, committed resources, projects, and measured data.

Another prerequisite for a successful metrics initiative is an organization that fosters positive change and encourages individual innovations.

The establishment of a metrics initiative constitutes a change of the organizational culture.

From the beginning, the metrics initiative should not be sold as an easy task for delivering the organization important benefits, rather it needs to be marketed as one part of a continuous improvement process.

A lack of tool support can bring with it problems with acceptance, that is, one cannot implement a robust and plausible measurement program on purely paper and pencil.

Nonetheless, in spite of all these challenges, never believe that your metrics initiative is truly dead (i.e., management has "pulled the plug" on funding) – until you read about it in a public announcement or newspaper!

Mah agrees with the SEI by recommending that an organization start out with the four core metrics: size (scope), effort, duration, and quality.

All this expert knowledge shows that metrics should never be introduced and used half-heartedly!

The best basis for estimation is a metrics experience database.

Experience shows that on average 5–10 years worth of historical project data are necessary before an organization has elaborated such a central repository housing the collection of information about estimates and actual project values.

The knowledge that estimation is done professionally with the aid of the database reduces the project risk for the customer.

A metrics database that is too complex in the beginning will hinder a metrics initiative more than it will support it. Therefore, one should start with a core set of metrics.

To be effective, a metrics database must contain data on actual completed projects and their attributes.

A metrics "system" consists of basic measures and metrics related to these basic measures in an appropriate way.

The six most common core measures (depending on the author 4–6 core metrics are mentioned) are scope (sized in Function Points), effort (in hours or person months), quality (typically measured as defects), cost (in USD or € or currency unit), duration (in days or months), and physical size (SLOC).

The definition of suitable measures and the processes to collect and analyze them can be a time consuming process.

Quality and productivity are in strong connection with process, persons, and technology.

It is also important to track change metrics in terms of thresholds and limits, or to define them to gain improvements for the metrics initiative.

One of the best-known tracking metrics is the Earned Value Method.

The challenge of the Earned Value Method is the exact measurement of the degree of completion.

Just asking the staff to which degree they finished their task leads to the famous 90% finished syndrome.

Other tracking metrics are defect measurements, which can be accomplished in any phase of the project, but mostly in testing (defect metrics).

8 Product- and Process- Metrics

Basically one distinguishes between product metrics and process metrics. The distinction is not always unambiguous since some metrics are used to evaluate both products and processes. Even so, at times, the product and processes are viewed so separately that it is almost as if there are two different worlds each with their own special scientific *community*. When discussing software development processes, there are several models that are representative: the waterfall model, the spiral model, prototyping, agile methods, object-oriented, and entity-based process models.

Table 8.1 gives an overview of the product metrics and process metrics dealt with in this chapter. Product metrics can additionally be separated into external metrics (functionality or cost related) or internal metrics (e.g., size or complexity related). Similar to quality metrics, product metrics can be divided into direct metrics (quality attributes related) or indirect metrics (quality criteria related).

Table 8.1. Examples of product and process measures and metrics

Product metrics	Measure or metric	Suitable basic measures	Suitable metrics	Examples
	Size	Function Points (FP); source lines of code (SLOC or KSLOC – kilo SLOC) of applications	Functional size per application; technical size per application	Average FP per application, average SLOC per application
	Quality	Defects and size of applications	Defect density	Defects per FP after delivery, defects per SLOC (KSLOC) after delivery
	Documentation	Pages and documents	Number of pages per document	Number of pages per requirements document, and per module of specification
	System complexity	Complexity and modules	Structural components per module	Data per module

(Continued)

Table 8.1. *(Cont.)*

Process metrics	Measure or metric	Suitable basic measures	Suitable metrics	Examples
	Effort	Expended team effort hours	Effort for system development	Effort per project or project phase
	Quality	Defect density for project or phase		Defects per FP
	Project delivery rate (PDR)	Effort and size	Effort (hours) per unit size (FP)	Hours/FP
	Costs	Costs and size	Costs per unit of size	Dollar per FP
	Duration	Duration and size	Size per unit of duration	FP per month (or per day) of project duration
	Efficiency	Effort and size	IT work unit per unit size	Hours effort per FP

8.1 Product Metrics

Product metrics relate directly to the result of a software development proc-ess. Important features of the product that are often measured include but are not limited to: size, quality, user requirements, product growth, and user com-fort. Product measures (that can be used in product metrics) are, for example, as follows:

- Architectural measures (e.g., number of components, layers, coupling)
- Quality measures (functionality, portability, reliability, usability, maintain-ability, and performance)
- Functional size (and technical size)
- Documentation
- Software and System complexity (both structural and data related).

8.1.1 Size of the Software Product

The result of a functional size measurement of a piece of software is normally a measure of the size of an installed application or the size of software reno-vated (enhanced). Note that adjusted Function Points are a size and complexity metric, but unadjusted FP reflect functional size (without the complexity ad-justment). The value adjustment factor currently or previously present in the original models for some of the FSM methods, actually takes the functional size (raw or unadjusted FP) and modifies/adjusts it by the impact of a method-specific number of nonfunctional characteristics. Therefore, adjusted Function Points could be called a metric, whereas unadjusted Function Points are a

measure. There are at least three different product sizes that occur in practice –
each offering a different view of the product:

- *Technical size* is based on the physical size of the developed code in units of
thousand lines of source code or KSLOC (kilo source lines of code). These
are sometimes called source metrics in models such as COCOMO II or the
Wolverton method.
- *Functional size* (*functionality* in units of functional size, e.g., IFPUG FP,
FiSMA fp, NESMA fp, COSMIC fp, Mark II fp, etc.)
- *Methodology specific size* (such as object points, use case points, others).
Various product sizes are sometimes necessary for facilitating comparison
of large and small projects, which may have previously been sized with one
of these views. They can also be useful indicators as input to estimate the
project effort for subsequent development of similar products.

8.1.2 Source Code Metrics

Source code measures and metrics vary from module cohesion and proportion of
comment lines to object-oriented measures such as number of parameters, depth
of inheritance, number of instances, inherited methods, and abstract classes.

Simon and Simon (2005) reported how reactionary behavior of developers
emerged after introducing source code metrics in an organization, and how
they introduced incentives to overcome the behaviors. They categorized the
reactions of developers into behaviors of five types:

1. *Optimism strategy.* The developers used phrases such as "we are professionals," "we use tool xyz and technology abc," and when they were
confronted with the data, said things like: "it cannot be as bad as this,"
"that's not actual performance, the next version is better." To overcome
this, developers were encouraged to participate in the development of the
source code metrics, and were shown that high (or low) quality can
be proven based on the measures. Developers became motivated to improve the overall work based on the metrics.
2. *Delegation strategy.* The developers argued initially that the purchased
software was defective and not their in-house developed software. (They
delegated blame to the purchased software.) To overcome this, the developers were shown that the source code metrics make all errors transparent
regardless of the sources. The simple act of separating out the purchased
from the in-house software allowed visibility on the quality, and allowed
the defects to be allocated to the appropriate software. As such, developers
assumed responsibility for quality and risks occurring in their own code.
3. *Automation strategy.* The developers believed that the complete code
could be generated by tools automatically, and therefore defects were not
their fault. This was overcome by demonstrating that the application of

source code metrics could insight into which parts of code truly can be generated automatically, and which parts cannot.

4. *Special subject strategy.* The developers attested that their tools, technology, and methods are so specific that they are outside the area of applicability of source code metrics. This was overcome by showing that the tools and metrics can be integrated smoothly in the development environment.

5. *The rabbit and hedgehog strategy.* The developers said things such as "we already have the concepts in place," "we have already invented that," "this concept is already used in practices," which ultimately led to decisions to custom-deliver software instead of purchasing existing products. This behavior was overcome by questioning, which ultimately led to answers that the concepts under consideration had only been piloted or were not a general practice of the organization.

Simon and Simon recommended that no matter what strategy was observed, good cooperation must be fostered with developers when implementing metrics, so that they are not driven into a defensive position, feeling like they are being attacked. They have to be convinced that measurement is worthwhile to highlight improvement areas in their process and with the product. In addition, their expertise should be used constructively in the metrics design to increase the chances of metrics program success.

8.1.3 Source Lines of Code

The measurement of source lines of code (SLOC) is widespread in certain segments of the IT industry, but not without challenges. The advantage of SLOC counts is that they for applications already in place, they are readily available, take a minimum of labor to compile, and supporters state that they can be used for very different software systems (real-time systems, system software, and commercial software) – especially where the technology is homogeneous, and the projects are to be identical to prior projects. The problem with then trying to do SLOC-based estimating is that the SLOC numbers can only be estimated before coding, and until the programming is complete, there are no SLOC *counts*. Furthermore, there is a problem that the number of program lines can vary depending on the programming language, programmer ('spaghetti' code amounts to a higher SLOC count) and inconsistencies of how to count SLOC (logical source lines of code?). This leads to a paradox (see Table 8.2),.

As Table 8.2 demonstrates, a project done using Assembler as the source code language, would appear to be more productive (measured in SLOC per person month) as the same project done using Ada as the programming language. This leads to the request to normalize all programming languages to a base Assembler level (so-called *Assembler equivalent*). This Assembler equivalent is also used for backfiring SLOC into Function Points.

Table 8.2. Paradox of SLOC metrics

	Assembler version	Ada version
Source lines of code (SLOC)	100.000	25.000
Effort (person months)		
Requirements Specification	10	10
Design	25	25
Coding	100	20
Documentation	15	15
Integration and Test	25	15
Management	25	15
Total effort (person months)	200	100
Total costs ($)	1,000,000	500,000
Costs($)/SLOC	10	20
Productivity (SLOC/person month)	500	250

One of the great challenges using SLOC-based sizing is to document clearly how the SLOC have been counted. The users principally agree that comment lines, empty lines, and lines that span across several lines for readability are not counted, or would not increase the count (they are inserted for better readability of the source code). The *IEEE Standard 1045 for counting SLOC was developed by the Institute of Electrical & Electronics Engineers, Inc.*

SLOC is ineffective to be used to measure project productivity since more than half of the software development effort belongs to noncoding-related tasks.

8.1.4 Functional Size

Functional size of the software reflects a size of the functional user requirements (i.e., what functions the software must perform). This size is easier for customers to relate to because the focus is on the functionality to be delivered to the users, and not on how it is developed. Users are less interested in which manner, with which programming language, and how many SLOC a software product may contain than they are in what functionality they will receive. Since functionality is independent of the programming language, the aforementioned paradox of SLOC does not appear when using Function Points.

The International Organization for Standardization and Electrotechnical Commission (ISO/IEC) has standardized five worldwide functional size measurement (FSM) method standards (IFPUG, COSMIC, FiSMA, Mark II, and NESMA). Regardless of the specific FSM method is selected, FSM can be used to estimate the functional size of software early in the development process, and then measure the functional size as soon as the requirements analysis is finished.

Functional size can be updated after each phase of the development and after each change of the user requirements, similar to updating a floor plan after each stage of construction completion and then counting the resultant square foot size. Typically the functional sizing is done manually (using the various method standards), and can be supported by various commercial software tools. The project leader or someone from the competence center, both with the user perspective in mind, should be responsible for the counting.

Automatic counting of Function Points (a functionality provided by some commercial software tools) should always be augmented with a review by someone experienced in functional size measurement of the method being used in the tool. (This is similar to needing to know the basic mathematical times tables before using a calculator – one must be able to discern mistakes made by the machine – at least from a sanity point of view, should there be errors made.) Automated counting from physically implemented code contradicts the premise of the Function Point methodology to count everything from the user view point. When counting automatically from implemented code, the Function Points are typically derived from coded modules developed many times based on technical or physical implementation reasons, i.e., from the physical rather than from the logical data model. While using a physical code or function counter may speed up the time to arrive at a numerical value for the functional size, the benefit of early usage of Function Points during the development life cycle is lost since automatic counting can only be done when the code is finished – near the end of the project.

There are several Function Points counting software tools that can purportedly count based on the logical models such as use case or object models, but the degree to which these can emulate manual counting is not known. More often, it is our experience that such tools can produce an excellent set of candidate elementary processes (but do not eliminate duplicate funtions) that can be used by Function Point practitioners to save time with the manual interpretation of the user requirements into functional components.

Regardless of the type of automated counting tool, the rules must be documented thoroughly in terms of how the automatic counting is performed, and the tools can assist with the identification of candidate elementary processes and logical files to save time and energy, especially with poorly documented or aging legacy applications.

The IFPUG has a three-tiered certification scheme for counting-related software tools (IFPUG, 2008):

- Type 1: Software supports Function Point data collection and calculation functionality. The user performs the count manually, and the software acts as a data repository of the data, and performs the appropriate Function Point calculations.
- Type 2: Software supports Function Point data collection and calculation functionality, where the user and the software determine the Function Point

count interactively. The user answers questions presented by the software, and based on the answers, the software determines the type of elementary process (if any), records it, and performs the appropriate calculations.

- Type 3: Software carries out an automatic Function Point count of an application using multiple sources of information such as the application software, database management system, and stored descriptions from software design and development tools. The software records the count and performs appropriate calculations. The user may enter some data interactively, but his or her involvement during the count is minimal. Software type 3 instructions and criteria are currently under review by the IFPUG board of directors.

Based on the type 3 description, there is no automated counting software currently certified by IFPUG as being of type 3. Any such software usually keeps the business rules for such software secret for proprietary reasons.

8.1.5 Project Size Categories

Generally, projects can be categorized into a small number of size categories, and there are several classification schemes available that vary according to the originator. The most typical categories include small, medium, large, and extra large in terms of the number of functional size measurement units.

Table 8.3. Development and enhancement project size categories (Natale et al., 2004), uFP is unadjusted FP

Project size category	New development (uFP)	Enhancement (uFP)
Very small	0–150	0–60
Small	150–300	60–120
Medium	300–600	120–240
Large	600–1,200	480–2,000
Very large	1,200–5,000	>2,000
Extremely large	>5,000	

Most commonly, there are small or medium projects, followed by large projects (that are usually only successful with high productivity tools), and even fewer extra large projects (most commonly these are Enterprise Resource Planning (ERP) programs that include PeopleSoft or SAP software implementation projects). Such categorizations are always subjective and as a result are different in different organizations.

Natale et al. presented research done with GUFPI-ISMA (see Table 8.3) based on the ISBSG Benchmark CD Release 8 (R8). It shows distribution analysis of new development and enhancement projects, and obtained the project size classifications presented in Table 8.3.

Table 8.4. Rule's (2005) relative size scale

Rule's categorization of size	Abbreviation	Project size (IFPUG uFP)
Extra-extra-small	XXS	>0 and <10
Extra-small	XS	>10 and <30
Small	S	>30 and <100
Medium 1	M1	>100 and <300
Medium 2	M2	>300 and <1,000
Large	L	>1,000 and <3,000
Extra-large	XL	>3,000 and <9,000
Extra-extra-large	XXL	>9,000 and <18,000
Extra-extra-extra-large	XXXL	>18,000

Rule (2005) presented his categorization of software size based on evaluation of the same ISBSG database r8 as shown in Table 8.4.

Figure 8.1 shows that the project size variation is consistent irrespective of the functional size measurement method. Note that NESMA and FiSMA functional size measurement units were not evaluated, but it is reasonable to assume that projects measured with those two methods would be consistent with these results.

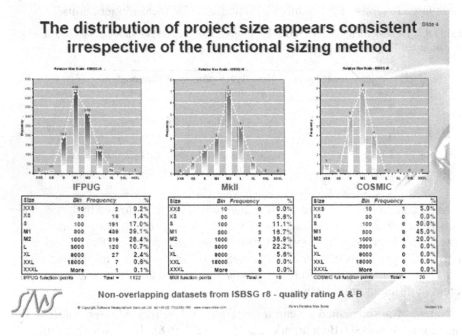

Fig. 8.1. Distribution of project size in ISBSG r8 database for IFPUG, Mark II, and COSMIC units of measure (Rule, 2005)

Note: Because of their ISO/IEC status and worldwide usage, the IFPUG Function Point Method is dealt with in a separate chapter in this book, with the remaining four FSM methods also in a separate chapter following the IFPUG chapter.

Since both methods, Function Point-based estimating and COCOMO II (KSLOC-based estimating), are used internationally there is a demand for conversion factors for backfiring. Such conversion factors provide an average number of Function Points per non-commented source line of code, and only make sense if they are measured in the same environment on similar types of applications. This means that only for similar projects in the same organization can reliable estimates for Function Points (based on lines of code) or for lines of code (based on Function Points) be done with calculated conversion factors, derived from historic counts. In all other cases, such conversion factors should only be used as rough rules of thumb and for raw quality assurance (see also the chapter about backfiring).

Because *industry* conversion rates take an average value for KSLOC to FP or vice versa, manual counts of Function Points will not be the same as the backfired count. Consider this analogy: if there was an average conversion rate for the number of pieces of drywall (wall materials) per square foot in a building, we would expect that the ratios would vary based on whether the building had cathedral ceilings (more wall space per square foot) or it pertained to a manufactured home (less wall space per square foot). If we were to derive the approximate square foot size of an entire village, the variations between the drywall pieces per square foot would be trivial because the law of large numbers would average out. A similar concept holds for software: backfiring works for an entire portfolio because some applications will have more FP per KSLOC, others will have less, and the *average* will end up typically close to the backfiring conversion rate. *Dekkers and Gunter warned against relying on back-firing conversion rates because of the variations that can occur between the actual functionality and SLOC.*

8.2 Software Quality

The quality of software products can be measured by staff and by the customer. It is both a measure of the product to be developed, as well as a measure of the software process. Thus, two different viewpoints of quality can be measured, and it is important to distinguish between the measure of quality of the process and of the product. Product quality is typically measured in terms of the length of time between occurrences of defects (mean time between failures) or defect density (defects per delivered Function Point); process quality is typically measured as defects over time (e.g. defect per time unit) or defects per phase. Furthermore, it is differentiated between the severity of defects, customer claims, and the measurement of customer satisfaction. Quality has a variety of definitions, and therefore there is a variety of metrics to reflect the different viewpoints. The International Organization for Standardization (ISO) working group on software and systems quality metrics (ISO/IEC JTC1 SC7 WG6) published ISO/IEC 9126 in three parts:

- 9126-1 Internal attributes of quality
- 9126-2 External attributes of quality
- 9126-3 Quality in use.

In the past couple of years, this quality standard has been integrated in a wide suite of software and systems quality standards currently under development (which will replace the 9126 series). This new ISO/IEC 25000 series of standards is called SQuaRE (*S*oftware product *qua*lity *r*equirements and *e*valuation).

Internal quality attributes are intrinsic to the software and can be measured by the developer himself/herself. External quality attributes are a function of the product and are measured by the customer. Quality in use is based on the product and also can be measured by the customer use.

The product quality can be improved very early in the software life cycle by performing reviews and inspections, enlarged test effort, and early defect removal. Table 8.5 demonstrates the relationship between a quality model (not the ISO/IEC 9126 quality model but rather a corporate quality model) and quality metrics.

Table 8.5. Relationship between a quality model and quality metrics

Component of quality model	Quality characteristic	Description	Measure or metric
Usability	Functionality	How well the product meets the required functionality	Functional completeness, transparency of requirements
		Consistency	Degree of contradiction
	Stability	Correctness	Test coverage, review coverage, defect rate, module test coverage
		Reliability	Stability against changes, defect stability, degree of availability, mean time to failure
		Safety	Degree of safety
		Robustness	Test case coverage, degree of robustness
		Feasibility	Completeness of documentation
		Efficiency	Storage efficiency, performance
	User comfort		Time for training, user contentment, help texts, size, CUA conformity

(Continued)

Ease of administration	Maintainability	System complexity, depths of structure, number of functions and parameters, effort for error removal, proportion of comments in code, module size
	Verifiability	Degree of verifiability
Utilization	Portability	Degree of portability
	Reusability	Degree of reuse, degree of reuse production

In the chapter "Estimation Fundamentals, Estimation and Quality" an Excel chart is provided for mapping and conversion of the 14 General Systems Characteristics (GSCs) of the value adjustment factor optionally used in the IFPUG function point method into the ISO/IEC 9126 Quality Attributes and vice versa.

8.2.1 Defect Metrics

Defect metrics are a subset of quality metrics. Theories abound in research and academia about defect prediction; however, actual defect metrics are less prevalent. When defect metrics are released, they are published scarcely and typically reflect only successful projects. An organization must have reached a certain level of organizational process maturity in order to understand the importance of localizing and documenting defects before delivering software to its customers. For example, one of the organizational maturity models: the Capability Model Integration (CMMI®) from the Software Engineering Institute introduces Measurement and Analysis as a process area at level 2 of the maturity model. Organizations with a higher degree of maturity (level 2 and higher) often also have lower defect rates.

According to Bierfert (2002) defects must be the following:

- Localized, administrated, and removed
- Defined beforehand
- Systematically explained.

The main benefit of defect metrics is the prediction of (future) defect rates. These rates become the thresholds for comparison of measurements of actual software quality. The following list identifies the most common defect-based metrics:

- Defect density: Number of defects per KSLOC or per function point. The number of defects increase (through a relationship that is more than linear) with the size of the software. Note that defect density per KSLOC can again be misleading - the larger the number of KSLOC, the higher quality is implied, when in fact, it may simply be that the code is not written tightly and extraneous lines of code may contribute to the illusion of higher quality.

Again industry gurus such as Capers Jones join us in discouraging the use of SLOC based quality or productivity metrics in favor of FSM based ones.

- Defect ratios: Number of defects by:
  - Detection phase: that is, where the defect was discovered (requirements, design, coding, test, installation, postdelivery)
  - Injection phase: i.e., where the defect was injected (requirements, design, coding, test, installation, postdelivery)
  - Type of testing (specification-, design-, module-, system-, integration-test)
  - Causes, origin (functional, interfaces, ambiguity, data)
  - Severity of defect (according to the four defect severity levels)
  - Size of the software to be developed (in Function Points or lines of code).

Jones (2007) defines the defect potential as "the life-cycle total of errors that must be eliminated. The defect potential will be reduced by somewhere between 85 percent (approximate industry norms) and 99 percent (best-in-class results) prior to actual delivery of the software to clients. Thus the number of delivered defects is only a small fraction of the overall defect potential. Testing has a surprisingly low efficiency in actually finding bugs. Most forms of testing will find less than one bug or defect out of every three that are present. The implication of this fact means that a series of between 6 and 12 consecutive defect-removal operations must be utilized to achieve very high-quality levels." Jones then added a rule of thumb for sizing defect-removal efficiency for test steps: "Each software test step will find and remove 30 percent of the bugs that are present."

Jones (1994) reported that the standard for defect rates in the USA is approximately five defects per function point where about 85% of the defects are removed during software development. This implies that approximately 0.75 defects per function point are delivered in production software (15% undetected × 5 defects/ FP).

Jones also reported that best performers are able to improve their defect rate to three defects per function point predelivery and the defect removal rate to 95%. A summary of Jones' research into defect potential is shown in Table 8.6.

Table 8.6. Defect potential per phase according to Jones (1994)

Defects in	Defect density (defects/Function Point)
Requirements	1.0
Specification	1.25
Coding	1.75
User documentation	0.6
Bad fixes (new defects caused by defect removal)	0.4
Total	5.0

Lucent Technologies' Lubashevsky (2002) demonstrated the defect numbers by severity level that was tracked for the development of an object-oriented communication system (with a size of about 1,800 function points). See Table 8.7 for details.

Grady (1992) of Hewlett-Packard supposed that about one-third of the effort for new software development of software is used for defect removal. One psychological effect is important: if a large number of defects are found, the defect detection rate decreases. This is often regarded as a quality improvement but leads to more delivered defects in contrary. But it may also be that the testers become frustrated and reduce their attention to detecting further defects.

Table 8.7. Defect measures according to the four defect severity levels (Lubashevsky, 2002)

	Defect severity level	Potential defects	Industry standard	Detected defects (before delivery)	Difference between industrial standard and detected defects
Increasing severity →	1. System failure	87	103	67	22–35
	2. Defect main functions	408	516	359	14–30
	3. Defect subfunctions	1,185	1,446	1,076	10–25
	4. Superficial defects	945	1,034	742	27–28
	Total	2,626	3,098	2,244	17–28

A known effect is that defect rates correlate with schedule pressure. Highly stressed people are naturally unable to produce the highest quality software. This has been proven to hold especially when a large amount of overtime is required over a prolonged period of time.

For an extensive discussion on defect categories, defect prediction, and quality measurement, we refer the reader to Stutzke (2005).

Rösler (2005) experimented with Fagan/Gilb style inspections and reported that review teams find close to 95% of the defects during the individual checking phase, with the remainder of predelivery defects found during the formal review as long as double-checking was done. Without the double-checking (two or more professionals checking the same code), he reported that only 80% of the defects will be found. The research was based on work with 92 professionals in 13 review workshops conducted between October 2004 and September 2005. Conclusions included the following measures:

- Individual checking was possible for 100–150 NSLOCs (noncomment SLOC) per hour.
- Proper review of text documents required ~1 h per page (about 300 words per page), with ±0.8 pages.

- Participants found *minor defects* in a typical specification at an average rate of 9.8 pages per hour. 93% (86 persons) estimated that they would need 9.7 times longer to find *major defects.*
- Theoretical research suggested a reading speed of 48 pages per hour. Participants confirmed *a reading speed* average of 49.4 pages per hour.

Further, Rösler summarized his findings with the following rules of thumb:

- Professionals can read ~50 pages per hour, but can check (for defects) only one page per hour.
- Any manual defect detection method will find about 3–5% of the defects.

Since the defect density (defects per function point) is one of the most important FP-based quality metrics, it is further discussed in the following paragraph.

8.2.2 Function Points and Defects

A familiar rule of thumb is that on average, there is ~80% of project effort spent on unplanned defect removal for defects elaborated earlier in the project. This is one of the reasons why early defect removal brings immense economic benefits. The other reason is that lower defect density results in a reduction of rework. Rework accounts for ~40% of software development effort according to Nelson (1999).

Thus, it is important to measure and implement defect tracking and reporting during the software development life cycle. As mentioned previously, there are many measures mentioned in the literature for this task, and also in several estimation tools (see the chapter on tools.)

The figures published in literature are typically devoid of solutions since there is little information provided about the environment and phase concepts, etc. As such, the basis for comparability across projects is missing, and the published data are spread across huge bandwidths.

In contrast to the literature, the ISBSG published in its report of June 2002 the defect metrics shown in Table 8.8 on the basis of 189 projects that had reliable records regarding defects.The United Kingdom Software Metrics Association together with the ISBSG, published in 2000 the *Quality Standards: Defect Measurement Manual* (UKSMA and ISBSG, 2000). A general part with definitions and categorizations assists with defect comparisons and clarifications (especially in benchmarking environment), and for the implementation of defect metrics in organizations.

There are three important experiences that should be regarded as general rules:

1. Defect removal itself produces new defects (so called *bad fixes*).
2. Delivered software always contains defects (called *latent defects*).

It cannot be proven that there are no defects, only that there are defects (Dijkstra).

Table 8.8. Defect metrics by various categories from the ISBSG Software Metrics Compendium (2002)

ISBSG projects from Software Metrics Compendium (June 2002)	N (No. of projects reporting nonzero defects)	Defects per 1,000 FP		N (No. of projects reporting zero defects)
By level of defects:		Mean	Median	
With minor defects	105	0.043	0.017	64
With major defects	83	0.019	0.006	83
With extreme defects	16	0.011	0.006	121
Total all defects	*133*	*0.047*	*0.018*	*56*
By organization type:				
Financial	50	0.078	0.27	14
Public administration	22	0.039	0.022	9
Service	12	0.014	0.013	6
Production	14	0.046	0.013	5
Total all types	*98*			*34*
By application type:				
Transactional systems	59	0.073	0.023	17
MIS	31	0.024	0.016	14
Office communication	11	0.18	0.019	4
Decision aid systems	5	0.008	0.011	2
Process computing	6	0.093	0.023	1
Total all types	*112*			*38*
By development type:				
New development	73	0.043	0.016	16
Redevelopment	4	0.017	0.028	0
Enhancement	56	0.054	0.022	39
Total all types	*133*			*55*
By platform type:				
Mainframe	73	0.068	0.022	47
Midrange	34	0.019	0.014	3
PC	20	0.016	0.015	6
Total all types	*132*			*56*
By language type:				
3GL languages	57	0.039	0.023	24
4GL languages	54	0.028	0.013	23
Program generators	19	0.131	0.024	6
Total all types	*130*			*53*

One practical experience relating to the third rule was that a development team once declared the test phase to be finished (earlier than planned) since *all potential defects were found and removed*. This naturally contradicts the first two rules.

8.3 Documentation

There are generally two types of documentation, developer- and user- documentation. In the following discussion, the focus is on user documentation, particularly those manuals written to aid in the use and maintenance of programs.

Documentation is often the stepchild of application development, since the effort for it is typically not explicitly planned and it is the first task to be omitted when there is excessive time pressure. However, every stakeholder of the project depends on complete, correct, and actual documentation to facilitate user satisfaction and knowledge.

Boehm (2000) suggests a rule of thumb effort of two person hours per page of documentation for small projects, and double that amount for large projects. Documentation can have a negative effect on project productivity, and a positive effect on the quality and customer satisfaction of the project, due to the devils square of project management. Note: the devils square depicts how the primary goals (costs, size, time, and quality) of an IT project unavoidably compete with each other for the resources of the project. Hence, every additional consumption of one resource leads to reduction in the availability of other resources.

What about metrics for documentation? A simple kind of metrics is based on using the statistical functions that are part of standard text software for counting the number of characters, words, and pages of the documentation (manuals) per week from start of the documentation development.

8.4 System Complexity

System complexity is a basic feature of software, and measures of it reflect the relative simplicity of the system design. System complexity consists of several interacting components:

- Problem complexity
- Technical complexity
- Structural complexity
- Data complexity.

Increased problem complexity and structural complexity increase the perceived system complexity, whereas increased technical complexity and data complexity actually reduce the perceived system complexity. Therefore, increased structural complexity is associated with increased problem complexity, and structural complexity decreases with increased technical complexity. Figure 8.2 depicts these interactions.

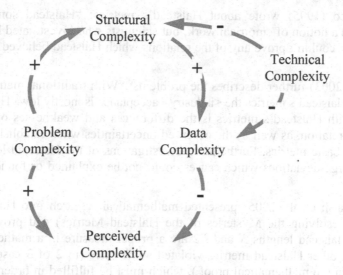

Fig. 8.2. Interactions of the components of system complexity

8.4.1 Structural and Data Complexity

System complexity in a narrow sense is calculated as the sum of structural complexity and data complexity, together with a count of the number of interfaces between the different system components.

The following formulae apply:

$$\text{Structural Complexity (SC)} = \text{Sum } (F^2(i))/N$$
$$\text{Data Complexity (DC)} = \text{Sum } (V(i)/(F(i) + 1))/N$$

where
N = number of modules without library- and system- modules
$F(i)$ = Fan out of the ith module (number of modules calling the ith module)
$V(i)$ = Number of I/O variables of the ith module (module parameter).

8.4.2 Halstead's Metrics

Halstead's metrics are used to measure code complexity. They were introduced in 1977 and calculate code complexity metrics based on the program length (N), the sum of operators ($N1$, comparisons, arithmetic operations, alternatives, loops, reads, writes), and the number of operations ($N2$, variables, constants, marks, records, unions, etc.). The Halstead metrics can then be correlated to the number of defects to provide a metrics of product quality.

The main advantage of the Halstead length (part of the overall Halstead calculation) is that it can be estimated in a simple manner. Compared with the SLOC metrics they can thus already be used in early phases of the software development process.

DeMarco (1995) wrote about Halstead's metrics: "Halstead sometimes mentioned a notion of empirical work, but scientists who investigated his data thoroughly couldn't prove any of the relations which Halstead believed to have observed."

Wolle (2003) further describes the problems: "With traditional metrics like SLOC or Halstead's metrics the <industry> acceptance is mostly low. The cause for this with Halstead's metrics is the differences and weaknesses of origin and interpretation, as well as the observed uncertainties when establishing the according basic metrics. Furthermore investigations of the Halstead length N showed large deviations which causes could not be explained or found in the details."

Al Qutaish et al. (2005) presented mathematical research into Halstead's metrics (Resolving the Mysteries of the Halstead Metrics) and proved that only the Halstead lengths N and $N2$ are a proper measure in a mathematical sense. All other Halstead metrics violated some rules (in 2 of 3 cases to be regarded in the mathematical proof), which must be fulfilled in order to be a true metric (in mathematical sense). In the best case (of the three), they can be reduced to N or $N2$ (the measures E and V converge to N, the measure D converges to $N2$ under certain conditions for large projects).

Nonetheless, Halstead's metrics are incorporated into a number of software measurement tools, but their usefulness and mathematical soundness are still under debate.

8.4.3 McCabe's Cyclomatic Complexity

The McCabe's Complexity Design Metric, also called *cyclomatic complexity,* quantifies the control flow within a program by counting the independent paths on a control flow graph that indicates a certain degree of well structuredness of an application. McCabe's metrics are calculated by counting the number of *edges* (conditional statements) minus knots (the intersections) plus not connected components times two. Thus, the McCabe's cyclomatic complexity increases with the number of branches through a program.

Stutzke (2005) states that a simpler way to calculate McCabe's cyclomatic complexity is to count all of the conditional statements in a module or procedure and add 1.

McCabe's metric is often used as an indicator for potential quality problems because it gauges the difficulty of understanding a program. It is also a measure for the number of test cases. From practical experience (and reinforced by literature), those modules with a cyclomatic complexity higher than 10 tend to be prone to higher defect rates. It has been heavily discussed in literature whether or not this metric can be transferred from modules to whole classes.

Büren and Hopf (2002) declared that McCabe's cyclomatic complexity metric is sometimes viewed as controversial because it is seen as a theoretical figure without solid practical benefits or meaning.

DeMarco (1995) published the same devastating judgment about McCabe's cyclomatic complexity stating: "nevertheless this metric is widely unproven albeit it is intuitively intelligible (McCabe's original publication is mostly empirical)".

Abran et al. (2004) published a detailed analysis of the McCabe Cyclomatic Complexity, highlighting, in particular, some misconceptions underlying the measurement approach. The research also pointed out the necessity to have well-grounded definitions and models for the measurement methods that practitioners apply in the software industry.

Nonetheless, various literature outlines different levels of *acceptable* McCabe's cyclomatic complexity. As mentioned earlier, a McCabe's cyclomatic complexity metric equal to 10 or higher is generally considered to be the threshold above which the code may be too complex. Error-prone modules typically score higher than 10, and the use of McCabe's cyclomatic complexity may indicate potential candidates for redevelopment.

8.5 Process Metrics

Process metrics relate to the software development process, comprising the activities, methods, and standards used.

Process metrics consist of the following:

- Maturity- and defect- metrics
- Management metrics
- Team resourcing and method metrics, e.g., productivity metrics based on effort, cost, milestone dates, duration
- Life cycle metrics
- Metrics for measuring project progress
- Metrics for measuring project dynamics, e.g., change requests, requirements scope creep
- Metrics for tracking team morale.

The remainder of this section further explains the various methods available to *estimate* measures and metrics including work effort, productivity, project delivery rate (PDR), efficiency, cost, and duration. Additional statistical data (actuals) related to these metrics can also be found in the chapter on benchmarking.

8.5.1 Work Effort

Work effort is the sum total of the actual time worked by all project team members including necessary training, but not including holidays, days of sickness, or other nonworked days. For further analysis of work effort, refer to the chapter "Time Accounting," which addresses key concepts such as the calculation of person month from person hours.

The measurement of actual work effort is typically done using a project management tool or a time reporting system. In these tools, specific resources and the planned and actual effort are related to project tasks. Team members report their actual working hours for project tasks, and the automated tool collects and summarizes the team time reports automatically at different levels, tasks, task groups, subprojects, and projects. The measured effort is reported and updated in the project plan, and also used in the estimation tool for updating and comparing with the estimate(s). Changes (and deviations) from the plan should be reported as part of the project status.

There are many rules of thumb for deriving work effort estimates as published in literature. One such source is the ISBSGSoftware Metrics Compendium (2002), which provides data analysis and resultant formulas for work effort etimates (see Table 8.9).

Table 8.9. ISBSG Software Metrics Compendium effort equations

Project platform	Number of projects	Effort estimate (effort in person hours)
All platforms	605 projects	$\text{Effort} = 27.0 \times \text{FP}^{0.438}$
Mainframe	197 projects	$\text{Effort} = 16.0 \times \text{FP}^{0.892}$
Midrange	105 projects	$\text{Effort} = 35.6 \times \text{FP}^{0.774}$
PC	105 projects	$\text{Effort} = 24.2 \times \text{FP}^{0.725}$

8.5.2 Productivity

Productivity is the most popular and also the most misunderstood management metric. Productivity is the ratio of the software development process output (FP size) divided by the input resources (work effort hours or person months).

Productivity should not be confused with Project Delivery Rate or PDR, which is a metric that reflects the number of input resources (in effort hours) that it takes to produce one unit of output (FP of the software delivered). As such, PDR is measured in units of hours per FP.

Units for productivity are Function Points per person month or per person hour. The successful calculation of productivity depends on accurate measurement of the output software size, as well as the actual work effort expended. Putnam and Myers (2002) define Productivity (P) as

$$P = \text{Size}/(\text{effort}^a \times \text{duration}^b),$$

where a and b are exponents.

Productivity is expressed in units of Function Points or SLOC per person month (or person hour).

Table 8.10 demonstrates how productivity (P) was defined and calculated in an organization for projects, change orders, and maintenance activity in order to achieve comparable measurements.

Table 8.10. Productivity metrics for various types of software and systems development (or maintenance) work

Productivity metric $(P = S/E)$	Standard	Measure effort (E)	Measure size (S)	Goal/benefit
Project	Projects ≥US$100 K	Total project effort (IT + users + com puting cen- ter + external staff)	Function Points for the project (according to IFPUG)	Measurement of productivity of projects; improvement of future project estimates
Change order (enhancement)	Orders <US$100 K	Total effort of the order effort (IT + users + computing center + external staff)	Function Points for the order enhancement (according to IFPUG)	Measurement of productivity of change orders; improvement of future change order estimates
Maintenance	Operations and support	Sum of all IT effort expended on maintaining each application for the year	Function Point size of the base application (according to IFPUG) at end of the year	Measurement of support productivity

A prerequisite for measuring productivity is that the resultant metrics are based on measures of the processes (often on phase level). This requires that the organization has already reached the CMMI® maturity level 2 (SEI, 2006) indicating that the processes (in this case software measurement and analysis) are defined and used responsibly. At maturity level 3 and higher, the process- and product-metrics are measured with repeatable and comparable results.

Productivity rates vary widely across different organizations and application areas, as well as development environments. Research shows that more than 100 factors can influence the productivity rate. (It is critical to note that the effort figure used in the calculation of productivity must capture a consistent definition of work effort. See the chapter on work effort for a full discussion on the importance of consistency as a pre-requisite to being able to do "apples to apples" comparisons between projects.)

Another measure related to the productivity of the software development processes is the *percentage of rework* compared with total project effort. In this regard, rework must be defined exactly. Rework usually means the process to remove, correct, or repeat results of a former phase that are not due to the changed requirements of the customer. IEEE Computer Society (2008) defines rework as follows:

Rework: action taken to bring a defective or nonconforming component into compliance with requirements or specifications. (*Source: A Guide to the Project Management Body of Knowledge (PMBOK® Guide) – Third Edition*). Project managers commonly regard productivity measurement with major skepticism since it can easily be misused to compare dissimilar projects, and can be misused to report the resulting efficiency of the project team and its project manager. This is nonsensical because such a comparison is only valid if all parameters influencing the software development process are identical, and if the project team and project manager have sole control to influence (and change) the project parameters. Another way to think of this is to compare it to building construction where FP of the project is akin to the construction square foot area. It would not make sense to compare the productivity (square feet built per person hour) of a construction crew working on a hospital to that of a project building a house. Yes, there are numbers that can be calculated and compared; however, it makes little sense to do the comparison and then to report that the hospital crew is *less productive per square foot*. The same thing goes for software development: it makes no sense to compare the productivity for a new development project where a commercial off-the-shelf (COTS) package is installed to the productivity of a project where specialized custom software is developed to meet the needs of a new innovative business area.

One must be very careful to compare like projects to like (apples to apples as we have said several times before). Misusing *productivity* to reward or penalize individuals or teams can damage the team morale and ultimately lead to resistance, boycotting of the measurement methods, and a general distrust of the entire measurement program and its management. *Productivity must never be deemed as the productivity of a single person or team!*

DeMarco says: "The paradox of productivity is, that productivity and benefit conflict each other. Maximizing benefit is only possible with alacrity for risks and going new ways. Improvement of productivity needs as a prerequisite confidence and repetition."

Nonetheless, even though it is understood now that productivity is a function of the functional size (relatively based on the category of size: small/medium/large, etc.), the quality requirements, and the technical implementation (tools, skills, techniques, methods, programming language, organization type, platform, etc.), there are many published *rules of thumb* prevalent in literature. One must be careful to understand the rationale behind each rule of thumb and the limitations (and potential damage) that could result from its misuse.

8.5.3 PDR

The ISBSG routinely publishes in its analysis of the most current database as a formal report called a *Benchmark*. The most recent Benchmark r10 was released in March 2008, and it pertains to the analysis of ISBSG CD Repository 10 (with 4,106 projects). One of the most regarded (outside Europe) metrics published there is the Project Delivery Rate or PDR, measured in hours per Function Point (a metric for efficiency).

Shepperd et al. (2006) reported his research findings about PDR based on data from 661 projects of the Finnish Experience database. The mean PDR across all projects (without discernment of type of project) was 7.5 h/FP, and the median value was 6.3 h/FP.

Shepperd extended the analysis to stratification by project type (see Table 8.11) and organization type (see Table 8.12)..

Table 8.11. PDR by project type from Finnish Experience Database (Shepperd et al., 2006)

Project type	N (number of projects)	Mean PDR (hours per FP)	Median PDR (hours per FP)
Enhancement	70	7.913	6.551
Maintenance	96	6.545	5.815
New development	478	7.720	6.506
Other	17	4.499	3.967

The variance analysis showed that the project type has a significant impact on the PDR. The PDRs for enhancements and new developments are surprisingly similar as can be seen from Table 8.11, but the variation of PDR between new development and other (nonenhancement, nonmaintenance) work was striking.

The variance analysis showed that organization type also had a significant impact on PDR. As can be seen from Table 8.12, the organization types separate into two groups with banking, CT, and insurance being less efficient (higher PDR) than similar work done in the remaining organization types. *This implies that when working with productivity estimates, one must be well aware of the type of organization with which data is being compared.*

ISBSG Benchmark release 10 (ISBSG, 2008) reports the mean and median PDR for new development and enhancement for Web development and non-Web development. The results are presented in Table 8.13.

From the PDR, one can derive the productivity in FP per person month by dividing it for example, by 120 h per person month (net working hours per month) and then inverting the resultant ratio

Table 8.12. PDR by organization type from Finnish Experience Database (Shepperd et al., 2006)

Organization type	N (number of projects	Mean PDR (hours per FP)	Median PDR (hours per FP)
Banking	137	9.657	7.651
CT	23	9.805	6.573
Insurance	285	8.010	7.018
Manufacturing	60	4.574	3.989
Other	23	5.333	4.275
Public administration	105	5.439	4.649
Retail	28	5.317	4.600

Table 8.13. PDR by type of project and Web- or non-Web-based development (ISBSG, 2008)

Type of project	Web development			Non-Web development		
	N	Mean PDR (h/FP)	Median PDR (h/FP)	N	Mean PDR (h/FP)	Median PDR (h/FP)
New development	122	10.7	7.6	359	14.9	8.3
Enhancement	148	4.3	3.0	777	5.7	4.3

The average of 421 projects of the ISBSG Software Metrics Compendium (ISBSG, 2002) reports an overall (nonstratified) average PDR of 15.1h per Function Point (with the median value = 11.2 h per Function Point).

Each ISBSG Benchmark Report and the Software Metrics Compendium (2002) analyze various different aspects of software development including, for example, the application area, team size, type of project, application type, data base type, programming language, etc. The Software Metrics Compendium provided the following conclusions (ISBSG, 2002):

Projects with Worse Efficiency

- The PDR (hours per Function Point) in North America is higher (i.e.,it takes more hours to produce one Function Point) as compared with European or Asian countries.
- The PDR of Client-Server projects is higher (more hours per FP) as compared with other projects.
- The PDR is higher (more hours per FP) in projects using formal methods. The ISBSG suggests that this effect may arise since methods are used more in large organizations and on larger projects where there are many stakeholders and many interfaces between projects.
- The PDR is higher (more hours per FP) in projects using process modeling or business area modeling.

Projects with Better Efficiency

- The PDR is lower (less hours to produce one FP) for team sizes from one to four persons, as compared with teams of five to eight persons. (Statement by the ISBSG: Team size is one of the most influential factors for productivity.) This is also valid regarding the experience of teams.
- The PDR of new development projects is lower than that for enhancements when each project is between 2,000 and 3,000 FPs.
- In staged software development the PDR goes down (i.e., the delivery improves) after the first phase (requirements).
- The PDR of development of management information systems (MIS) is lower (i.e., better) than that to develop transactional systems.
- The PDR of single user systems is lower (i.e., better) than for multiuser systems. This is also valid for single/multiuser projects.
- The PDR for projects using Access databases is less (i.e., better) than that using other databases. This was also valid for comparisons of Access to other programming languages.
- Projects where the programming language is a fourth generation language (4GL) have a lower PDR (i.e., better delivery) than projects where a third generation language (3GL) is used.
- The PDR is lower when using Upper Case Tools.
- The PDR is lower when using prototyping, rapid application development (RAD), and object-oriented analysis (OOA).

8.5.4 Efficiency

Efficiency means how quickly project goals can be reached. Rubin (2002) defines efficiency of an IT development department as the throughput or IT work units as work effort hours necessary to implement one Function Point. With an average productivity of 88 FPs per person year (for the average US-based software and systems developer) as quoted in the Worldwide IT Trends and Benchmark Report, 1,824 working hours per person year result in the IT work unit to be 20.7 h. That means that every hour effort relates to 0.05 IT work units (the inverse of 20.7 h) on average.

With IT work units completed tasks are counted to measure project progress. This is to avoid the 90% finished syndrome. The IT work unit is often used as a basis for outsourcing and software contracts.

This metric has two disadvantages: First, the partially completed tasks are not counted and second all tasks are weighted equally regardless of any differences in the complexity or difficulties encountered during development.

Generally, the measure for efficiency is the effort per FP, also called PDR or project delivery rate (hours per Function Point). As a measure of processes, it is sometimes called *process capability*.

8.5.5 Cost

Cost metrics (also called CER = *Cost Estimation Relationship*) need associated and appropriate experience databases with expert knowledge as a prerequisite. For industrial projects in the USA, particularly for military software projects, there is generally applicable data available. Note that the data may not be optimum; however, it may assist with creating a historical database from which beginning comparisons can be made.

Similar to the discussion of productivity and work effort, it is critical to compare apples to apples. Before using any historical cost data, one must know what costs were included (i.e., hardware, software, effort, contracts, etc.), and which were explicitly excluded. With cost, it is also important to know whether costs were burdened (e.g., taking into account organizational resource costs such as vacation, benefits, nonproductive hours, overtime, etc.).

Some software and systems development estimating tools are available in many variants – each suited to a particular configuration of how an organization chooses to perform costing and subsequent analysis. Therefore, it is not surprising to find many variants of the PRICE-S cost estimation model, the many COCOMO II variants, and the SEER-SEM variants by Galorath at installations across the USA, and also in specific industries in Europe. Other automated tools allow the user to define (to varying degrees depending on the tool) stratifications and variations of cost models that can be set by means of user parameters. There is no single correct way to do project costing; however, it is critical that the assumptions and included components of cost be transparent and available in order to perform comparisons between projects, or create cost estimates for future projects.

Project costs can comprise combinations of hardware costs of components, microelectronic components, life cycle costs of software and systems development (typically from requirements to preparation for installation or beyond), packaged or other software tools, costs of training, overtime hours, contracted resources, systems integration costs, and software life cycle costs. One source of freely downloadable information about project cost estimating can be found in the freely downloadable 183 page book: *National Aeronautics and Space Administration (NASA) Cost Estimating Handbook* (NASA, 2002) available from http://eclipse99.ksc.nasa.gov/shuttle/nexgen/Nexgen_Downloads/NASA_CEH_Final_Production_Copy_April_2002.pdf or from Carol Dekkers' website at www.qualityplustech.com.

For information regarding COCOMO II (Constructive Cost Model II) and its variations, visit the University of Southern California's Center for Systems and Software Engineering at http://sunset.usc.edu/.

Cost is the most important factor for the go/no go *decision to proceed with a software and systems development program or project. Cost overruns can lead to project failure or cancelation before the work is completed, and it can lead to dissatisfied customers.*

According to the Standish Group CHAOS Report (2003), cost overruns exceed their budgeted amount in over 15% of the projects. The report also showed that successfully completed projects exceeded their budgets on average by 43%.

The ISBSG database contains a rather insignificant number of projects with reliable cost data (less than 10% and cost data is not even included in the distributed data repository), due to a number of inherent problems with *reported project cost*. As such, we will not pursue cost data based on ISBSG projects. Among the inherent issues with reported project cost are the following:

- Fluctuating currency conversion rates. Project cost data is reported in US dollars; however, with projects reported from over 20 countries and worldwide fluctuations in currency that have varied by ~100% over the past decade, reconciling the cost structures is almost impossible.
- Cost varies depending on who reports it – the customer (acquirer) of the software or the supplier (developer).
- Cost is far more unreliable than reported work effort because there are many more inclusions and exclusions related to cost that may not be explicitly defined. (Work effort must also be defined and consistently reported as discussed earlier.)
- Most project managers are responsible for reporting and tracking work effort figures for their team, but this is not typically the case for project costs.
- Even within the same organization for the same project, there are often various cost figures discussed: original budget, capital acquisition costs, labor costs, derived cost (total work effort hours multiplied by an average cost per hour), etc. There is no single consistent definition of project cost.

Jones (2007) agrees with the inherent dangers of using global cost figures and states: "Indeed the impact is so significant that it is quite unsafe and harzardous to use *average cost per Function Point* for any business purpose unless the average in question is taken from information that meets the following restrictions: similar companies; similar geographic region; similar staffing patterns; similar work habits; similar burden rate structures. Cost data is far too variable for more global averages to be valid for specific projects or estimating purposes."

In terms of an *average cost per Function Point* there are published variations that can assist in providing a *ballpark* cost range for preliminary budgeting purposes. On page 331 of his 2007 book: *Estimating Software Costs: Bringing Realism to Estimating*, 2nd edition, Jones provided a table of the average US cost per Function Point from 2007 (both burdened and unburdened rates). The following Table 8.14 is an excerpt from Jones' table:

Jones (2002) also published that software development costs in Western Europe are on average US$1,500/FP compared with ~US$350/FP and even less in Eastern Europe.

Note: *The reader is forewarned, however, to be cautious with any average cost per Function Point figures* for reasons mentioned earlier, plus one additional: just as one would never rely on *industry published averages for building on a $ per square foot basis* – especially without knowing the context for the cost (i.e., not knowing whether the $ per square foot is for an existing house, or new construction of a hospital where land clearing will be required). Cost is the most important factor that must be fully understood before any industry or other cost ratios are used!

Table 8.14. Capers Jones, (2007) US cost per FP in 2007

Type of development	Unburdened $/FP	Burdened $/FP
Web	$145	$232
MIS	$1,053	$1,684
Outsource	$890	$2,671
Commercial	$1,281	$2,049
Systems	$1,733	$2,773
Military	$2,601	$8,453
Average	$1,284	$2,977

Authors' note: Remember that you need to know the details behind the costs before you can reliably use these figures.

For this reason, the reader is urged to obtain the Jones (2007) book for a full discussion about the context and what is included in the cost figures BEFORE negligently applying the figures in the previous Table 8.14. (See references for further details).

Norman R. Augustine (1980, former Lockheed Martin Corporation chairman; further details of this quotation are regretfully no longer available at the time of this new edition) recommended a correction factor should be applied to estimated costs with every incremental cost estimate to avoid cost overruns. He discovered that his equation worked especially well for aviation projects:

$$K = 1 + 0.8/(1 + 8\,d^3)$$

where K = the correction factor, d = percent of project duration already elapsed (i.e., $d = 0$ at project initiation and $d = 1$ at project postmortem).

8.5.6 Project Duration

There are many rules of thumb for predicting project duration as published in literature. The most important might be that the longer the duration is anticipated to be, the more imprecise will be the estimate. The project duration is a prerequisite for scheduling (time planning) and resource planning and allocation. In addition, project duration (especially when it is compressed) can also influence project quality. Besides that, the requirements (scope) creep can have negative influence on the project duration because the more functionality one attempts to put into an existing schedule, the longer the duration turns out to be. There is also the concept of Fred Brooks' *Mythical Man Month*, which states that adding people onto an already late project will make it even later (and thus, prolong, rather than shorten the project duration).

The ISBSG release 8 (2004) based on 662 projects (all platforms) presented the following regression formula for duration:

$$\text{Duration} = 0.38\text{Effort}^{0.370}, \text{ with } R^2 = 0.39,$$

where effort is in person hours (The reader should be aware of the low correlation coefficient).

The ISBSG Benchmark r10 (2008) published the following figures related to duration (see Table 8.15):

Table 8.15. Duration averages (ISBSG, 2008)

Type of Project	Web development			Non-Web development		
	N	Mean duration (months)	Median duration (months)	N	Mean duration (months)	Median duration (months)
New development	118	6.6	5.8	329	8.9	6.9
Enhancement	197	13.4	7.0	1,110	22.9	13.6

Note: N=number of projects.

Boehm (2000) published Table 8.16 showing the relationship between duration and work effort using COCOMO II:

Table 8.16. Boehm's COCOMO II based equations for project duration (2000)

Complexity of project	Optimal duration
Simple software projects	$2.5\text{PM}^{0.38}$
Medium software projects	$2.5\text{PM}^{0.35}$
Complex software projects	$2.5\text{PM}^{0.32}$

Note: PM = person months with 152 working hours.

The duration can be compressed by 25% (until 75% of the optimal duration) according to the COCOMO II model, if accordingly more staff will work on the product. Further compression is not possible because beyond this point, the duration actually increases with more staff as mentioned previously.

An additional, frequently found equation in published literature (source unknown) also calculates the optimal project duration (D) and number of persons (N) relative to effort (PM = person months):

$$D = PM^{0.5}$$

$$N = PM^{0.5}$$

When using the metric project duration it must be clearly defined what are the conditions to be fulfilled for calling the project complete, or under what conditions the project postmortem has been reached.

In the chapter "Benchmarking of IT Projects, Factors influenced by the Organization" we have included additional data from the ISBSG benchmarking database regarding duration and team size.

8.6 Management Summary

Basically, one distinguishes between product metrics and process metrics.

Product metrics relate directly to the result of a software development process.

The result of a functional size measurement of a piece of software is normally a measure for the size of an installed application.

The measurement of SLOC is widespread but not without challenges.

SLOC cannot be used to measure project productivity since more than half of the software development effort belongs to noncoding-related tasks.

Functional size of the software reflects a size of the functional user requirements (i.e., what functions the software must perform).

Function size can be updated after each phase of the development and after each change of the user requirements.

Automated counting from physically implemented code contradicts the premise of the Function Point methodology to count everything from the user view.

The IFPUG has a three-tiered certification for Function Point counting related software tools.

Dekkers and Gunter warned against relying on backfiring conversion rates because of the variations that can occur between the actual functionality and SLOC.

The quality of software products can be measured by staff and by the customer. It is both a measure of the product to be developed, as well as a measure of the software process.

The product quality can be improved very early in the software life cycle by performing reviews and inspections, enlarged test effort, and early defect removal.

Defect metrics are a subset of quality metrics.

The main benefit of defect metrics is the prediction of (future) defect rates. These rates become the thresholds for comparison of measurements of actual software quality.

Testing has a surprisingly low efficiency in actually finding bugs. Most forms of testing will find less than one bug or defect out of every three that are present.

Grady (1992) of Hewlett-Packard supposed that about one-third of the effort for new software development is used for defect removal.

A known effect is that defect rates correlate with schedule pressure. Highly stressed people are naturally unable to produce the highest quality software. This has been proven to hold especially when a large amount of overtime is required over a prolonged period of time.

Rösler (2005) experimented with Fagan/Gilb style inspections and reported that review teams find close to 80% of the defects during the individual checking phase.

There are three important experiences that should be regarded as general rules: Defect removal itself produces new defects (so called *bad fixes*); delivered software always contains defects (called *latent defects*); it cannot be proven that there are no defects, only that there are defects (Dijkstra).

Documentation is often the stepchild of application development, since the effort for it is typically not explicitly planned and it is the first task to be omitted when there is excessive time pressure.

Boehm (2000) suggests a rule of thumb effort of 2 person hours per page of documentation for small projects, and double that amount for large projects.

Documentation can have a negative effect on project productivity, and a positive effect on the quality and customer satisfaction of the project.

System complexity is a basic feature of software and measures of it reflect the relative simplicity of the system design.

Halstead's metrics are used to measure code complexity.

The McCabe's Complexity Design Metric, also called cyclomatic complexity, quantifies the control flow within a program by counting the independent paths on a control flow graph that indicates a certain degree of well structured-ness of an application.

McCabe's metric is often used as an indicator for potential quality problems because it gauges the difficulty of understanding a program. It is also a measure for the number of test cases.

Process metrics relate to the software development process, comprising the activities, methods, and standards used.

Productivity is the most popular and also the most misunderstood management metric. Productivity is the ratio of the software development process output (FP size) divided by the input resources (work effort hours or person months).

A prerequisite for measuring productivity is that the resultant metrics are based on measures of the processes (often on phase level). This requires that the organization has already reached the CMMI® maturity level 2.

Productivity rates vary widely across different organizations and application areas, as well as development environments. Research shows that more than 100 factors can influence the productivity rate.

Rework: Action taken to bring a defective or nonconforming component into compliance with requirements or specifications.

Project managers commonly regard productivity measurement with major skepticism since it can easily be misused to compare dissimilar projects, and can be misused to report the resulting efficiency of the project team and its project manager.

Productivity must never be deemed as the productivity of a single person or team!

DeMarco says: "The paradox of productivity is, that productivity and benefit conflict each other. Maximizing benefit is only possible with alacrity for risks and going new ways. Improvement of productivity needs as a prerequisite confidence and repetition."

One of the most regarded (outside Europe) metrics published is the PDR, measured in hours per Function Point (a metric for efficiency).

The variance analysis showed that the project type has a significant impact on the PDR.

The variance analysis showed that organization type also had a significant impact on PDR.

When working with productivity estimates, one must be well aware of the type of organization with which data is being compared.

From the PDR, one can derive the productivity in FP per person month by dividing it with 120 h per person month (net working hours per month) and then inverting the resultant ratio.

Efficiency means how quickly project goals can be reached.

Generally, the measure for efficiency is the effort per FP, also called PDR (hours per Function Point). As a measure of processes, it is sometimes called process capability

Cost metrics (also called CER) need associated and appropriate experience databases with expert knowledge as a prerequisite.

Cost is the most important factor for the *go/no go* decision to proceed with a software and systems development program or project. Cost overruns can lead to project failure or cancellation before the work is completed, and it can lead to dissatisfied customers.

The reader is forewarned, however, to be cautious with any average cost per Function Point figures.

The project duration is a prerequisite for scheduling (time planning) and resource planning and allocation. In addition, project duration (especially when it is compressed) can also influence project quality.

When using the metric *project duration* it must be clearly defined what are the conditions to be fulfilled for calling the project complete, or under what conditions the project postmortem has been reached.

9 Object-Oriented Metrics

The object-oriented paradigm shows some peculiarities when compared with traditional software development. This is particularly apparent when one considers that object-oriented system development supports prototyping, and uses its own object-oriented programming languages and tools. In addition, there are terms specific to object-oriented development including the following:

- Attributes and classes of objects: Data and its states are stored. Attributes define the data that characterize classes.
- Classes with attributes and methods: These are essential factors for describing and structuring software programs. Classes define the variables and methods common to all objects of a certain class.
- Cohesion: Is a measure of how logically related are the parts of an individual component (class) to each other, and to the overall component.
- Coupling: Is a measure of the strength of the connection between any two system components such as classes.
- Interfaces: These are lists of methods.
- Inheritance: Is the process by which one object acquires characteristics from one or more other objects.
- Message: Means of communication and interaction between objects.
- Method: Operations that manipulate or process data.
- Objects: These are instances of classes.
- Object identity: Objects are unique and have a storage address.
- Polymorphism: Allows a single name to be used for more than one related purpose, which is technically different.

Practitioners and developers who use object-oriented methods often purport that functional size measurement is not appropriate to size the functional user requirements in object-oriented environments. However, research by Fetcke et al. delivered a concept for counting function points for object-oriented projects involving the Jacobsen method, and additionally provided concrete rules to do so. In addition, presentations by Abran et al. reinforce the applicability of functional size measurement to measure the size of software developed using object-oriented approaches.

Additionally, the IFPUG has made available a detailed case study (case study 3) illustrating how to count function points in an object-oriented environment where both an OOA part (object-oriented analysis) and an OOD part (object-oriented design) are involved.

Classes are typically candidates for ILFs or EIFs, while subgroups are RETs of such, and attributes are DETs. Objects themselves may be candidates for EIs, EOs, and EQs. In OOD, Function Points already counted in OOA are not counted again, but rather the size at OOD only increases if there is new functionality identified at OOD (not typically). *Use cases are an artifact of object-oriented development that identifies functionality from the user viewpoint, and therefore it is easy to count FP from use cases.*

Object-oriented systems development claims the following design principles:

- Data abstraction
- Information hiding (Parnas' law: "Only what is hidden can be changed without risk.")
- Modularization by data encapsulation and well-defined interfaces
- Dynamicism and flexibility by instantiation
- Reuse of code by inheritance and aggregation.

The final two design principles objectively distinguish object-oriented development uniquely from its predecessors (object-oriented languages).

Sneed (1996) characterized the relationship between object-oriented software components as shown in Table 9.1.

Table 9.1. Components of object-oriented software according to Sneed (1996)

Objects	Build	Classes
Objects	Have (are composed of)	Attributes
Objects	Inherit	Attributes
Objects	Have (are composed of)	Methods
Objects	Inherit	Methods
Objects	Send	Messages
Objects	Receive	Messages
Messages	Are	Data
Messages	Are	Relations

Generally, object-oriented metrics are characterized by unclear definitions, and they are not based on extensive structures, contravening the prerequisite rule for a *good* metric. *Object-oriented software metrics are often used to measure complexity, maintenance, and clarity. As such, object-oriented metrics are mostly quality metrics* and can be categorized into the following three groups:

- System metrics, e.g., number of files, classes, and inheritance trees
- Tree metrics, e.g., number of children (NOC) or classes
- Class metrics, e.g., number of methods.

Peter Rosner et al. state that object-oriented metrics are used mainly to understand to which extent the concepts of object orientation are realized in a system as evaluated at the class, method, and system levels. Henderson-Sellers (1996) calls attributes that contribute to the total complexity as programmer's attribute.

These metrics can be used to evaluate the changeability and modularization ability of a system. As such, object-oriented metrics can support decisions regarding the future development of a system.

The results of factorial analyses concluded that the metrics suite could be reduced to five relevant and quantifiable measures for evaluating the size and complexity of object-oriented software:

- The number of weighted methods per class (WMC) is an indicator of system size. The weight in this case is caused by the complexity of the respective method
- The depth of the inheritance tree measures the complexity of the system design
- The NOC is a measure of the reusability of a class
- The degree of coupling between classes indicates the degree to which the classes are independent. This is an important indicator for understanding classes and their division into subclasses. Strong coupling indicates a malpractice of modular design
- The response behavior of a class.

An interesting result was that with the factorial analyses in neither of the two categories, tree- and class- metrics, could a relationship be found between Source Lines of Code and the depth of classes. (However, there are a number of metrics based on relationships between them).

Gupta and Gupta (1996) characterized *Object Points* as having a structure similar to the function point counting rules. However, object points are based on counting objects instead of user functionality. Object Points derive complexity from effective attributes as well as from instances and message connections.

9.1 Examples of Object-Oriented Metrics

More than 200 different object-oriented metrics have been propagated over the past two decades. Zuse (1997) has identified more than 130 of them in *A Framework for Software Measurement* (p. 568) and has partially characterized them. In this chapter, we present more than eight examples focusing on some of the early and renowned metrics as well as showing some actual examples from studies presented in recent international metrics congresses.

9.1.1 Design metrics by Lorenz (1993)

Lorenz identified and quantified design metrics:

- System level (e.g., number of files, classes, and inheritance trees)
- Prototype classes typically consist of 10–15 methods, with 5–10 SLOC of C++ each, and require an average of 5 person days of development effort
- Production classes typically consist of 20–30 methods, with 10–20 SLOC of C++ each, and require an average of 30–40 person days effort for development
- With more than 20 methods per class, there is too much functionality in too few classes
- C++ systems produce 2–3 times more source lines of code as SmallTalk systems
- The system complexity evolves mainly from the number of different message types that are sent or received
- Class metrics (e.g., the number of methods) to measure the complexity of a system
- The average size of a method is 8 SLOC for SmallTalk and 24 SLOC for C++
- Methods with more than 12 SLOC in SmallTalk or 36 SLOC in C++ should be redesigned
- An average class consists of six object attributes or instance variables.
- Attributes require about 2 person hours development time; methods require about 10 person hours.

9.1.2 The Metrics Suite from Chidamber and Kemerer, 1994

A de facto standard is the often used Metrics Suite from Chidamber and Kemerer consisting of six metrics (see Table 9.2). This catalogue is also called MOOSE (Metrics Suite for Object-Oriented Software Engineering).

Table 9.2. The Metrics Suite (MOOSE) from Chidamber and Kemerer

Metric	Explanation
WMC	Number of methods of a certain class without inherited methods (the weight is mostly 1)
Depth of Inheritance Tree (DIT)	Maximal depth of a certain class in an inheritance structure (root = 0)
NOC	Number of direct subclasses of a certain class
Coupling Between Object Classes (CBO)	Number of couplings between a certain class and all other classes
Response Set for a Class (RFC)	Number of methods that can be performed by a certain class regarding a received message
Lack of Cohesion Metric (LCOM)	Number of disjunctive method pairs (i.e., there exist no *shared* instance variables) of a certain class

9.1.3 Capers Jones' Object-Oriented Cost, Defect, and Productivity Metrics

Jones measured a piece of PBX (Private Branch eXchange) Switching software for telephone switching in large hotels and administrations, in eight programming languages using his estimating tool KnowledgePlan™. He estimated the effort based on 132 person hours per person month (22 person days per person month × 6 productive hours per person day). The anticipated system has an estimated size of 1,500 function points. KnowledgePlan™ results are presented in Table 9.3.

It can easily be seen that the productivity in SLOC/PM decreases as the productivity in FP/PM increases. This is not a surprising result; it represents the paradox – increase in costs per SLOC toward the higher programming languages. *For this reason and others, Capers Jones calls the use of SLOC metrics a management malpractice.*

It can also be observed that use of object-oriented programming languages reduces the number of detected defects.

Capers Jones summarizes: Object-oriented programming languages are beneficial for improving software quality as well as the productivity of software development. Neither one of these can be measured with SLOC-based metrics.

9.1.4 The survey of Xenos et al.

Dr. Michael Xenos and his coauthors from Patras, Greece collected more than 80 object-oriented metrics (Xenos et al., 2000) from Object Pascal, C++, and Java systematically. Their list comprises the following:

- Twenty-eight traditional metrics, which can also be used in object-oriented environments
- Sixty-one dedicated object-oriented metrics in 5 categories:
  - Twenty-five class metrics relating to complexity, size, methods, attributes, and cohesion
  - Four method metrics
  - Three coupling metrics
  - Sixteen inheritance metrics relating to reuse of methods, multiple inheritance, DIT, NOC, and number of predecessors
  - Thirteen system metrics.

All together, the team discovered more than 200 dedicated object-oriented metrics, and more than 300 references showing the same or similar metrics. In addition, they discovered with regret the existence of 16 metametrics that are only published to date in the Greek language.

Table 9.3. Capers Jones' object-oriented cost, defect, and productivity metrics

Language		Structured Programming						Object-oriented	
		Assembler	C	CHILL	PASCAL	Ada 93	Ada 9x	C++	Small-Talk
Size	FP	1,500	1,500	1,500	1,500	1,500	1,500	1,500	1,500
	KSLOC	376	206	158	118	93	78	38	28
	SLOC/FP	250	137	105	79	62	52	25	19
Effort in person months (PM)	Requirement	10.5	10.5	10.5	10.5	10.5	10.5	10.5	10.5
	Design	61.5	61.5	61.5	61.5	61.5	61.5	44.5	36.5
	Coding	317	117	67	51	35	21	9	5
	Integration and test	295	159	116	97	82	67	50	40
	Documentation	40	40	40	40	40	40	40	40
	Management	108	57	44	39	35	30	23	19
	Sum	832	445	339	299	264	230	177	151
SLOC/PM		451	462	339	299	264	230	177	151
FP/PM		1.80	3.37	4.42	5.01	5.68	6.52	8.47	9.99
Hours/FP		73.21	39.16	29.93	26.31	23.23	20.24	15.58	13.29
Costs	Costs (C) in million US-$	8.32	4.45	3.39	2.99	2.64	2.30	1.77	1.51
	C/SLOC in US$	22.13	21.60	21.45	25.33	28.39	29.49	46.58	53.93
	C/FP in US$	5,547	2,966	2,260	1,993	1,760	1,533	1,180	1,007
Defects	Defect potential	8,635	3,812	2,726	2,247	1,775	1,397	1,092	959
	Defect removal rate	90.9	89.1	87.5	86.7	85.5	83.5	80.9	79.4
	Delivered defects (DD)	786	415	342	295	258	230	208	198
	DD/KSLOC	2.09	2.01	2.26	2.50	2.77	2.94	5.47	7.07
	DD/FP	0.52	0.29	0.23	0.20	0.17	0.15	0.14	0.13

9.1.5 Metrics for Defects and Size by Cartwright and Shepperd

Cartwright and Shepperd (formerly of Bournemouth University, England) (1997) researched the relationship between events and defects, and between states and size, based on analysis of a large telecommunication system (133 KSLOC developed using C++ in an OOA environment). Using the Shlaer and Mellor method, they developed following formulae (with very strong R^2 regression coefficients):

$$C = 0.42 \times E - 0.58; R^2 = 0.872$$

$$S = 170.68St + 1,101.01; R^2 = 0.966$$

where C = number of changes reported in the configuration management system (= class defect counts), E = number of events per class, S = size of class in SLOC, and St = states.

Because of the strength of R^2 values, the equations successfully predicted defects and the size of programs. Cartwright and Shepperd found it difficult to use their data for the complete metrics suite of Chidamber and Kemerer, and instead decided to count the events, states, changes, and SLOC from which they could derive their formulae.

9.1.6 Methods for Size from Catherwood et al.

Bill Catherwood and Monica Sood (Catherwood et al., 1997) from AMS Management Systems, together with Frank Armour of George Mason University, developed the following object-oriented metrics:

- Based on use cases
  - Number of objects (#O) per Function Point (FP):
    #O = 1.159FP; standard deviation = 0.045
  - Number of methods (#M) per Function Point (FP):
    #M = 18.182FP; standard deviation = 8.444
- Based on counts after implementation:
  - Number of objects (#OF) per Function Point (FP):
    #OF = 0.380FP; standard deviation = 0.120
  - Number of methods (#MF) per Function Point (FP):
    #MF = 4.955FP; standard deviation = 0.951
- (Note that when a system developed with Powerbuilder was removed from the sample, the standard deviation was lower)
- Number of Methods based on use cases

#MU per Function Point (FP):
#MU = 23.692FP; standard deviation = 0.571
o Number of methods after implementation
#MI = 5.287FP; standard deviation = 0.588.

The authors reported that they could use these metrics successfully to estimate the program sizes for other object-oriented developed applications.

9.1.7 Class Metrics from Silvia Regina Vergilio and Chaves

Silvia Regina Vergilio and Chaves (2000) from the Federal University of Parana,
Brazil, investigated software test metrics of C++ programs developed using the
IBM/Rational Rose tool. The team collected basic measures shown in Table 9.4
and found that the number of methods and attributes were of greater significance.

These measures can easily be used to derive additional object-oriented metrics
as is depicted in Table 9.5.

Table 9.4. Basic measures of C++ programs

System	Number of methods	Number of attributes	Number of classes	Number of messages sent or received
1	40	91	7	49
2	223	168	16	102
3	70	40	7	53
4	17	104	7	48
5	18	239	17	123

Table 9.5. Metrics derived from basic measures of C++ programs

System	Number of attributes per method	Number of methods per class
1	2.275	5.7
2	0.75	13.9
3	0.57	10.0
4	6.12	2.4
5	13.28	1.1
Average	1.74	6.8

9.1.8 Use Case Points

Piotr Habela et al. (2005) present their experiences with Use Case Points (developed by G. Karner in 1993) as follows:

- In contrast to other measurement methods, Use Case Points directly refers to the notions we assume to use for requirements modeling (that is the use case model and class model).
- The Use Case Points methodology assumes classification of use cases into three groups, based on their roughly determined size or complexity. The criteria are either the number of interaction steps in a use case scenario or the number of (domain model) classes involved in its processing. Based on that classification, each use case is assigned a number of 5, 10, or 15 Use Case Points.
- Interestingly, the method suggests that the use cases connected through an *uses* or an *extends* relationship (that is, not connected directly with the actor) should not be counted.
- The count of the number of actors contributes to the Use Case Points, though their impact is smaller. Actors are assigned a value equal to 1, 2, or 3 points each, depending on whether they access system through local API (1), through textual interface or network (2), or through a graphical user interface (3). Note that in effect at this stage, a rather nonfunctional characteristic (actor complexity) was already introduced.
- The Use Case Point methodology focuses attention on the nonfunctional factors. It adopts (with minor changes) a set of factors similar to the Value Adjustment Factors (VAF) that are available for the IFPUG-FPA method. In addition, Use Case Points relies on a set of environmental factors (EF) that can potentially influence a given organization's productivity. The factors, using method-prescribed weights, are applied to the counted number of Use Case Points, transforming the unadjusted Use Case Points into the result expressed in (adjusted) Use Case Points.
- There are advantages and disadvantages to the Use Case Point approach. There are two major advantages:
  1. The method is directly applicable to the assumed form of requirements document.
  2. The way that functional size is counted does not enforce full refinement of use case scenarios.
- There are four major disadvantages of the Use Case Point approach:
  1. The Use Case Points method lacks any official status as a standard.
  2. The technical complexity factors are potentially inadequate.
  3. The style of use case can impact the measured size.
  4. The relationship between use case points and work effort relies on a small number of constants of hours per use case point (i.e., 20) to calculate the project hours from use case points. This(these) constants are not supported with any statistically valid historical data.

9.1.9 Further Examples of Object-Oriented Measures and Metrics

Examples of quantitative and qualitative object-oriented metrics proposed by other authors include the following:

- System level: (measures)
  - The number of classes, functions, and class interactions
  - The number of instance variables and methods
  - The number of files and inheritance trees
  - The number of data variables
  - The class depth
- Tree metrics
  - The depth of the inheritance tree as indicator of the inheritance complexity (measured by the number of classes between the inheriting and the parent class)
  - The number of siblings or subclasses for each class as an indicator for the degree of reuse
  - The number of class hierarchies
- Class measures and metrics:
  - The average size of a method is 5 SLOC for SmallTalk or 15 SLOC for C++
  - A message should not have more than three parameters
  - The number of methods in a class
  - The number of external methods, which are used from a given method
  - The degree of coupling or interactions between classes as an indicator of interface complexity. A coupling is the usage of a method from another class by a method of a certain class
  - The response behavior of a class as a measure for the degree of polymorphism. This is measured by the number of different methods that can react to a message (these are the potential goals of the message)
  - The deficit of cohesion between the methods, or the number of dissimilar methods provide quantitative measure of the cohesion or diversity of class.

9.2 Projects that were Developed Using Object-Oriented Approaches in the ISBSG Benchmarking Database

In the Benchmark r10 (*ISBSG*, 2008), there are 33% of projects (1,345 of 4,106 projects) that indicated that specific techniques were used: there are 620 of 1,238 projects with specific development methods and 10% of it developed with OOA and 13% developed with OOD (these are 64 or 81, respectively). Together it is 23% with increasing trend over the last years (20% in release 6 – OOA 9% and OOD 11%).

Table 9.6 shows the project delivery rate (PDR; higher PDR = lower productivity) in the Benchmark r10 (2008).

Table 9.6. Project delivery rate (PDR) of object-oriented projects in the ISBSG benchmarking database

PDR		OOA	Not OOA	OOD	Not OOD
Total	Number of projects:	52	1,046	42	1,056
Median		12.1	10.0		

OOA object-oriented analysis, *OOD* object-oriented design

9.3 Function Points and Object-Oriented System Development

A wide range of research has been done to apply functional size measurement to object-oriented software development:

- *The IFPUG Case Study 3* used object models where the methods of the classes are identical to the methods used in the requirements concept. *Thus, the methods can directly be counted as transactions.*
- *Whitmire* (1992) developed a proposal based on a class diagram showing the message traffic between classes. He counted each class as an ILF and counted the message crossing the boundary of the system as transactions. There were no EIFs counted because there was no direct access to externally administered data.
- *The Australian Metrics Organization, ASMA* (1994), developed an approach similar to that of Whitmire. ASMA counted methods delivered from objects to the user as elementary processes (EI, EO, or EQ). The complexity of the methods was measured based on the attributes used and communicated. Objects were counted as ILFs, and their complexity was defined by the attributes.
- *Antoniol et al.* (*1998*) published an *object-oriented Function Point Method* with counting regulations based on a static object model. The method appears to be flexible and adaptable to organization-specific environments; however, it does not discern between the functional components: EI, EO, and EQ. Instead, the transactional function types are defined as generic method requests between objects.
- *Pastor et al.* (*2001*) published very detailed Function Point counting regulations for the object model, functional model, and dynamic model of an object-oriented system development with the OASIS tool, allowing automatic counting.

9.3.1 IFPUG Function Points and OOA According to the Jacobsen Approach

Fetcke et al. (1998) counted three projects using IFPUG function points per "Function Points of an object-oriented analysis according to the Jacobsen method." The results of their experience are presented in Table 9.7.

Table 9.7. Results of applying functional size measurement on OOA projects (Fetcke, 1998)

Functional Component	Object-oriented artifact or concept
System boundaries	Actors represent the user and other applications. Use cases represent the functionality. Actors representing systems or hardware are not regarded as users.
Evaluation of logical transactions	Different interaction flows in a use case represent candidate elementary processes (EI, EO, and/or EQ). Abstract use cases are not regarded. Object attributes are DETs. FTRs are counted per reference object (ILF or EIF) of the counted files.
Evaluation of logical files	Data entities of Domain objects represent ILFs or EIFs. Entity objects are also candidates for ILFs or EIFs. Object attributes are DETs. RETs are counted according to the user view.

9.3.2 IFPUG Function Points and UML

Myerson (1999) of South Africa reported on experiences in an UML (Unified Modeling Language) environment of a leading South African Bank. The UML components of the Function Point components were deemed to be related as shown in Table 9.8.

Table 9.8. Proposed approach for translating UML components into Function Point components (Myerson, 1999)

UML component	IFPUG Function Point component
Use cases	EIs or EQs
Primary actors	EIFs
Secondary actors	EOs
Kernal Business Objects	ILFs

To evaluate the relative complexity of each functional component, Meyerson attempted to derive metrics from the following information to categorize the complexity level: low, average, or high.

- For use cases
  - Event inputs and outputs
  - The number of alternative flows
  - The number of steps in alternative flows
  - The number of actors involved in a process
  - The number of nonleaf processes

- For Domain Objects
  - The number of attributes
  - The number of checks for input attributes or objects
  - The number of external keys (relations).

Note: The American author does not endorse the approach posed by Myerson in the immediately prior table, particularly in the rows where a use case equates to an EI or EQ (it could also be related to multiple EIs, EOs, and/or EQs depending on the granularity of use cases). In addition, there are other rows where we do not agree; however, we do not endorse, but rather simply present these ideas.

Uemura et al. (1999) published detailed Function Point counting rules to be used with UML- based specifications. The team counted the design specifications of the Rational Rose development tool as EIs.

Iorio (2004) presented similar experience reports at the 2004 Software Measurement European Forum in Rome.

9.3.3 COSMIC and UML

Azzouz and Abran (2004) published a comparison of COSMIC and UML concepts with a mapping to the Rational Unified Process (RUP). Two COSMIC concepts had no direct relationship to any UML equivalent. The research results are presented in Table 9.9.

Table 9.9. COSMIC and UML equivalences in the Rational Unified Process – RUP (Azzouz et al., 2004)

COSMIC concept	UML equivalent	Remark
Software boundary	Use case diagram	
Software layer	No UML equivalent	Must be elaborated manually
User	UML actor	
Functional process	Use case	
Data movement	Operation (message)	
Trigger (starting event)	No UML equivalent	A new UML icon for triggering events was introduced in order to distinguish it from messages
Data group	UML class	
Data attribute	Class attribute	

Habela et al. (2005) summarized their experiences with applying COSMIC to object-oriented application development:

- Significant differences in complexity were observed depending on the required system's architecture. The COSMIC tier concepts help to overcome this issue.

- A second issue concerned the variation in the complexity of data groups (i.e., entities) processed in the systems we analyzed. This led us to base our COSMIC counts on the observed data attributes rather than on data group units. For future users of this approach, it is easier to point out the attributes than name the data groups of which such attributes are a part.
- To provide the information about data movements that we needed to measure using COSMIC, we need to take a rather system- or design-oriented view of the use case model.
- In order not to lose sight of the general picture, we kept in our use case template some business-oriented specification elements.
- Some variation was introduced because of the relationships between use cases. This typically results in a number of use cases that are not self-contained when considered separately from those use cases to which they are attached. An intuitive rule of the method is that a functional process must at least consist of two data movements to provide functionality to its user. Namely, some triggering input (entry) and at least an output (exit) or registration (write) of information should be present. When dealing with abstract use cases, this assumption must be revised. Therefore, the aforementioned rule should be applied to verify complete use case instances rather than to separate use cases.
- The only place where we diverged from the COSMIC rules was in our treatment of the triggering events. Since we considered that there is a difference in the complexity between a flow that simply triggers a function, and an initial flow that provides some input data attributes, we assume counting the functionality only in the latter case.

9.4 Management Summary

Practitioners and developers who use object-oriented methods often purport that functional size measurement is not appropriate to size the functional user requirements in object-oriented environments. However, research by Fetcke et al. delivered a concept for counting function points for object-oriented projects involving the Jacobsen method, and additionally provided concrete rules to do so.

Additionally, the IFPUG has made available a detailed case study (case study 3) illustrating how to count function point in an object-oriented environment where both an OOA part and an OOD part are involved.

Classes are typically candidates for ILFs or EIFs, while subgroups are RETs of such, and attributes are DETs.

Objects themselves may be candidates for EIs, EOs, and EQs. In OOD, Function Points already counted in OOA are not counted again, but rather the size at OOD only increases if there is new functionality identified at OOD (not typically).

Use cases are an artifact of object-oriented development that identifies functionality from the user viewpoint, and therefore it is easy to count FP from use cases.

Object-oriented software metrics are often used to measure complexity, maintenance, and clarity. As such, object-oriented metrics are mostly quality metrics.

The results of factorial analyses concluded that the metrics suite could be reduced to five relevant and quantifiable measures for evaluating the size and complexity of object-oriented software.

A de facto standard is the often used Metrics Suite from Chidamber and Kemerer, consisting of six metrics.

Capers Jones calls the use of SLOC metrics a management malpractice.

Capers Jones summarizes: Object-oriented programming languages are beneficial for improving software quality as well as the productivity of software development. Neither one of these can be measured with SLOC-based metrics.

There are two major advantages of the Use Case Point approach: the method is directly applicable to the assumed form of requirements document; the way that functional size is counted does not enforce full refinement of use case scenarios.

There are three major disadvantages of the Use Case Point approach: the Use Case Points method lacks any official status as a standard, the technical complexity factors are potentially inadequate, and the style of use case can impact the measured size.

10 Measurement Communities and Resources

Software measurement is not easy. The majority, over 80% of measurement programs, fail to deliver actual performance improvements for numerous reasons, as we outline in this book. This chapter is intended to familiarize you with useful international standards, to guide you with benchmarking and consulting resources, and to assist you to navigate the quagmire of software measurement standards and communities throughout the world.

In general, there are three main types of measurement standards related to software and systems:

- Standards that define measures
- Standards that present measurement methods (in particular Functional Size Measurement Method standards)
- Standards that regulate how to perform measurements.

Such standards in the area of functional size measurement have evolved and have been available for a number of years from the Geneva based International Organization for Standardization (ISO) and the International Electrotechnical Commission (IEC) joint technical committee 1, subcommittee 7: Software and Systems Engineering (ISO/IEC JTC1 SC7), especially through the standard suite of standards ISO/IEC 14143 Parts 1–6, and through a series of standards for each of the major Functional Size Measurement Method standards as listed later. The final standard in the suite is ISO/IEC 14143-6:2007 Guide to Functional Size Measurement (FSM) Usage.

All standards are current as of this publication; however, since ISO/IEC JTC1 standards are valid for a period of only 5 years at a time, the reader is encouraged to contact your national standards body or ISO/IEC for the most up-to-date standard available. Currently, there are five Functional Size Measurement Method standards that are ISO/IEC recognized as conforming to the Functional Size Measurement definitional standard:

ISO/IEC 14143-1: 2007 – Functional Size Measurement: Definition of concepts. Each standard went through a rigorous process within ISO/IEC JTC1 to become an accepted standard, the first four using the ISO/IEC Publicly Available Standard (PAS) transposition process, while the last one (COSMIC) utilized the regular ISO/IEC JTC1 SC7 process because it was not, at the time of standardization, supported by a stable international user or industry organization.

The most popular and in-use functional sizing methods have now been standardized by ISO/IEC as outlined in the next section, as well as regulation and definitional standards pertaining to measurement frameworks.

Besides ISO, we also briefly examine three other important standards: the Capability Maturity Model Integration (CMMI®), the Goal Question Metric method (GQM), and the Balanced Scorecard.

As far as measurement organizations or communities, we have concentrated on those communities that most actively cooperate and organize international software measurement conferences. The list is far from complete but is intended to aid the reader to gain insight into the current and past international cooperation. The selection of the metrics organizations is sorted alphabetically.

10.1 The ISO Standards

Within the ISO/IEC JTC1/SC7 Working Group 12 (WG12), a series of standards has been developed for the definition, design, and verification of software Functional Size Measurement (FSM) methods: ISO/IEC 14143. Initiated as a working group in 1994, WG12 developed a total of six standards in the 14143 suite, and was instrumental in standardizing all of the ISO-conformant Functional Size Measurement Method standards. This series of standards was developed because in the early 1990s, there were already over 30 variants of FSM methods, but there was no recognized set of definitions or criteria on which to assess them.

The benefits of the ISO suite of standards are as follows:

- The basic principles for FSM are defined and stabilized.
- Standards exist for checking if a metric conforms to the definition of a functional size measurement metric.
- It is the only forum where national experts from over 30 nations collaborate.

The pitfalls of the ISO suite of standards are as follows:

- It is a metastandard (framework).
- Because the standards are limited to Functional Size Measurement, they do not address the problems with or the impact of technical- and quality-requirements in estimating or their usage together with functional size.
- The standardization process is slow (voluntary members, regulations, protocols, etc.)

Figure 10.1 gives an overview of the ISO/IEC JTC1 SC7 framework for measurement standards.

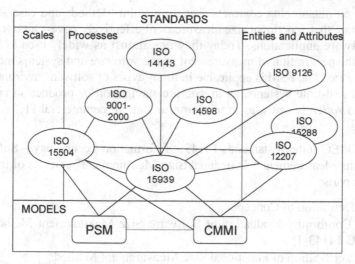

Fig. 10.1. The ISO/IEC JTC1 SC7 framework for software and systems measurement

The following list includes some of the most important software and systems related measurement standards:

- ISO 9000 Quality Management and Quality Assurance.
- ISO 9001 Quality Management.
- ISO/IEC 9126 Quality Attributes (Parts 1–3 cover Internal, External, and Quality in use measures). Note that ISO/IEC 9126 is being replaced with the new ISO/IEC 25000 *SQUARE* series of standards currently under development in SC7's Working Group 6 (WG6).
- ISO/IEC 12207 Software and Systems Life Cycle Processes (harmonized for software and systems).
- ISO 14000 Environmental Management.
- ISO/IEC 14143 Information Technology – Software Measurement – Functional Size Measurement (six standards).
- ISO 14756 Measurement and Rating of Performance of Computer-Based Software Systems.
- ISO/IEC 15504 Information Technology – Software Process Assessment.
- ISO/IEC 15939 Software Measurement Process.
- ISO/IEC 19761 COSMIC Full Function Points version 2.1.
- ISO/IEC 20926 IFPUG Function Point Unadjusted Method version 4.1.
- ISO/IEC 20968 Mark II Function Points.
- ISO/IEC 24570 NESMA Function Points.
- ISO/IEC 29881 FiSMA 1.1 Functional Size Measurement Method.

The standards and usage of Functional Size Measurement have increased over recent years, as measurement has become a mandatory contract provision especially on outsourcing contracts. Function Point Methods and case studies now illustrate that functional size measurement effectively covers a large variety of software applications. Today they are almost as widely used as LOC; however, the penetration of measurement in the software and systems industry is still a meager 1%. FSM is applicable in many types of software environments from *hard* real-time systems, as in satellite navigation or production control systems, to *softer* systems, as in telecommunication, commercial IT, or batch processing.

The ISO/IEC suite of standards 14143: "Information Technology – Software and Systems Measurement – Functional Size Measurement" consists of the following six parts:

- Part 1: Definition of Concepts
- Part 2: Conformity Evaluation of Software Size Measurement Methods to ISO/IEC 14143-1
- Part 3: Verification of Functional Size Measurement Methods
- Part 4: Reference Model
- Part 5: Determination of Functional Domains for Use with Functional Size Measurement
- Part 6: Guide for Use of ISO/IEC 14143 Series and Related International Standards.

Measurement of the functional size of software is an essential part of the measurement of user *requirements*, but it only measures the size of the functional user requirements (*what* the software must do in terms of business processes and tasks). It is critical to remember that the functional user requirements are a subset of the user requirements, and as such, estimates of cost and work effort must take those requirements also into consideration. These other types of user requirements (called nonfunctional and technical requirements) are not measured by functional size. As such, other types of measures may be necessary when estimating software effort in addition to functional size. Examples of such metrics include, for example, response time behavior and transaction rate, reliability (availability, error tolerance, integrity, etc.), portability, maintainability, and efficiency, just to mention a few. There is not a universally accepted general set of measures or standards to cover these requirements; however, ISO/IEC's JTC1 SC7 Working Group 6 is developing a set of quality measurement standards (called SQUARE) to replace the current ISO/IEC 9126 standard. Currently 9126 is published with three parts that set out measures for software quality (internal quality, external quality, and quality in use). Note that product quality in the context of ISO/IEC 9126 falls into six distinct categories:

- Usability (how usable is the software)
- Reliability (mean time to failure is one metric)

- Functionality (how well does the software meet the functional requirements)
- Portability (how well does the software meet the user needs for portability)
- Efficiency (how well does it perform what it is supposed to do)
- Maintainability (how easy is the software to maintain and fix).

Benefits of the ISO/IEC standards are that they consolidate the knowledge of best practices from metrics experts from all over the world. (Note that for non-functional requirements there are also at least three additional models available including the COCOMO II productivity factors, the FiSMA ND21 (new development) 21 situation analysis (productivity factors) and the General systems characteristics (GSC) in the IFPUG FP method.

10.2 The Capability Maturity Model Integration

The CMMI® of the SEI (Software Engineering Institute) at Carnegie Mellon University in Pittsburgh, PA, is a five level process maturity model (see Fig. 10.2) for Software Process Improvement (SPI). CMM® and CMMI® are registered trademarks of the SEI at Carnegie Mellon University, Pittsburgh, PA, USA. The latest version of the CMMI® manual can be downloaded without charge from the CMMI® homepage of the SEI (http://www.sei.cmu.edu). The SEI was founded in 1994 by the American Congress, funded by the United States DoD (Department of Defense), and hosted at the Carnegie Mellon University.

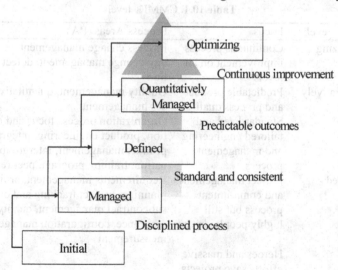

Fig. 10.2. The five levels of the CMMI® (source: www.sei.cmu.edu). (Note that level 1 is initial and progress up an integer level at a time to the highest level 5 which is the optimizing level)

The CMMI® model superceded the earlier Capability Maturity Model (CMM®) for software, and combined a number of variants of process maturity models (e.g., CMM® for acquisition, CMM® for systems, etc.), with an eye to integrating these models. The CMM® and later the CMMI® currently in use were created by the SEI as a basis to improve the state of the defense software engineering world. They provide an improvement framework for process maturity, and as a consequence, quality and predictability.

Table 10.1 explains the five levels in more detail.

A weak point of the earlier versions was that they lacked a central discussion of metrics. In the current CMMI®, measurement and quantitative methods are mentioned throughout, and specifically as a process area (PA) to achieve maturity level 2.

Software measurements is of such importance that the US Department of Defense (DoD) demands explicit planning and tracking of metrics on every project.

ISO/IEC 15939 was developed on the basis of the SEI-supported Practical Software and Systems Measurement (PSM), which provides additional support for developing and creating sustainable goal-driven measurement. (See www.psmsc.com to download the current version of PSM at no charge.) Besides the CMMI®, we direct the reader to the Recommended Approach of the NASA on measurement.

Table 10.1. CMMI® levels

CMMI® Level	Focus	Process Areas (PA)
5 Optimizing	Continuous process improvement on all levels	Process change management, technology change management, defect prevention
4 Quantitatively managed	Predictable product and process quality	Quality management, quantitative process management
3 Defined	Standardized and tailored engineering and management process	Organization process focus and definition, product engineering, integrated product management, intergroup coordination, training program, peer reviews
2 Managed	Project management and commitment process but still highly people-driven	Requirements management, project planning, project tracking and oversight, subcontract management, quality assurance, configuration management, measurement
1 Initial	Heroes and massive efforts save projects from failure – often with chaotic results	

The CMMI® has a strong relationship to the three ISO/IEC standards: 12207 (Software Life Cycle Processes), 15504 (Information Technology – Software Process Assessment), and 15939 (Software Measurement Framework already mentioned).

The current model of CMMI® is the CMMI® for Development (CMMI®-DEV), V1.2 model, which was released on August 25, 2006. This model continues to support the five levels of process maturity and has combined the staged and continuous representations of the CMMI® from the earlier release V1.1.

Level 2 of the CMMI® is in the author's opinion, the most difficult to reach with respect to cultural changes in organizations. It calls for documented plans for software projects including size estimates and requirements change management. Estimates of effort, duration, and costs must be done in relation to size, and critical resources must be planned and tracked. Requirements creep must also be tracked and the resulting changes managed. Estimates are typically made by teams of developers.

Level 3 demands that the organization adopts a standardized process framework, e.g., project estimates must be done on the basis of the organizational project history.

Level 4 shows profound process knowledge that is visibly consistent across all staffing levels, functions, and roles in the organization. The title of the level – quantitatively managed – gives a clue to the fact that it demands measurement-based quantitative management.

Level 5 finally asks for organizational continuous process improvement and demands additional quantitative benchmarks.

Overall, the CMMI® provides both a guideline for identifying strengths and weaknesses of the software development processes, and also a roadmap for improvement actions. An extensive set of practical experiences with CMMI® (and other related improvement initiatives) can be found in the book by Ebert et al. (2004): *Best Practices in Software Measurement – How to Use Metrics to Improve Project and Process Performance*. Figure 10.3 shows a possible roadmap for implementation of the CMMI®.

The CMMI® helps to define what to do to reach higher levels of organizational process maturity, but does not say how to do it. The CMMI® maturity level is becoming an increasingly important indicator or gauge for organizational software process quality.

Obviously many organizations fail to reach CMMI® level 2 since they are not capable of measuring software size (including Functional Size Measurement). Moreover, obviously all Key Performance Indicators (KPI) are based on

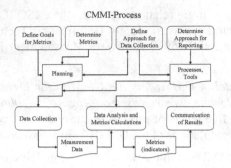

Fig. 10.3. A roadmap for implementation of the CMMI

measurement, and the basic original measure is the size of the software. The fact that organizations like the SEI assume the usage of such simple measures gives an indication of the quality of actual application development in organizations, as well as reflects the culture of the USA, which demands that organizations be given *a choice* rather than a dictate of how to measure. For further information about the current version of the CMMI® and other process maturity models maintained by the SEI refer to their website at http://www.sei.cmu.edu/cmmi/.

10.3. The Goal Question Metric Method

To evaluate the software development process(es) according to the CMMI®, the GQM method has gained widespread acceptance. It is widely used since its goals are easy for beginners, and the structured process enables early successes with measurements. The GQM approach is mostly suitable for a tailored implementation of a measurement initiative. It was originally developed in 1994 by Victor Basili (now retired from the University of Maryland) and Dieter Rombach (Fraunhofer Institute) for performing measurement effectively and efficiently.

The GQM method defines in its first step (G-Goal) at least one measurement *goal*. This goal then leads to a set of measurement *questions* whose answers tell whether or not the goal is being achieved. Questions can center around quality attributes, which are often a prerequisite for reaching the goals. In the third step: *metrics*, measures are defined, which deliver information to answer the questions and to evaluate the degree of goal fulfillment. GQM is a top–down approach to measurement (G→Q→M) but it should also be interpreted bottom–up to ensure that every measure or metric is traceable to at least one goal. The questions should cover the main components of the goal.

GQM in practice is often used after the CMMI® evaluates the maturity level of the organization. After selecting particular process areas (PAs) to be improved, the GQM method is then employed to define the goals, questions, and ultimately the measurement of the current (actual) state and its comparison with the plan (the goals).

The GQM is performed in four phases:

1. Planning: Selection of a project and development of a roadmap
2. Definition: Definition and documentation of goals, questions, metrics (GQM), mostly done in form of assessments
3. Data collection
4. Interpretation.

GQM allows evaluation of the quality of products or processes (Note: this is unsuitable to evaluate the quality of people) in software development. As far as tool support for GQM, there are several supporting models including BOOTSTRAP, FAME, PROFES, Spearmint, SPICE (Software Process Improvement and Capability dEtermination), etc.

Thomas Gantner and Kurt Schneider reported on their practical experiences with GQM at DaimlerChrysler. They found that GQM implementation needs a concentrated effort in the preparation phase. They also reported that the lack of tool support hampered their implementation.

Bill Curtis, one of the original authors of the CMM® for software, relates the story of a man who does not find his house key when he arrives at his home at night. He searches around a lantern, and a passerby asks him if he had lost his keys close to the lantern. "No," answers the man, "but it is impossible to see anything over there in the dark." There is analogy here to GQM and common software measurement initiatives: typically, there is lot of data collected – especially so for that data which are easy to get. After several months of *measuring*, it is still unclear as to what or how to use the data. Goals of measurement cannot be found in this way; they must be articulated and explored in quite an opposite way.

The correct approach is to work with GQM to document the goals for measurement, then ask questions to find out whether corrective action brings you closer or further away from those goals, and then (and only then) to identify only those metrics that directly answer the questions about reaching the goals. Most often, collection of data leads to the discovery of the interpretation and corrective actions lead to achieve the goals.

The following overview from the American author (see Table 10.2) describes a practical example of how to formulate the goals and questions of an organization, and then what metrics can support those questions.

Table 10.2. Goal/question/metric example

Goals, questions (below)	Basic measures (to build appropriate metrics)				
	Project attributes	Function Points	Effort	Defects	Customer contentment measurement
Improve estimating	X	x	x		
Improve productivity	X	x	x		
Improve quality	X	x		X	X
Measure impact of tool support		x	x	X	
Support make-or-buy decisions	X	x	x		
Improve testing		x	x	X	X

Rini van Solingen and Egon Berghout published a book titled *The Goal Question Metric Method* in 2000 (McGraw Hill, Europe), complete with a CD of templates for use when implementing goal-driven measurement. For further information, refer to http://www.iteva.rug.nl/gqm/indexframe.html.

Goal-driven measurement is an SEI-specific adaptation of the GQM method. It is used as the basis for the measurement process framework in both ISO/IEC 15939 and the PSM approach on which ISO/IEC 15939 was based.

10.4 The Balanced Scorecard

The Harvard Business School Professor Robert S. Kaplan and the consultant David P. Norton developed in 1992 *a concept for solving the problem of managers to decide between financial and operative measurement scales.* In cooperation with several organizations which were, at the time, considered to be the best at measuring efficiency, they elaborated a measurement system called the Balanced Scorecard. *It uses four different perspectives for measuring and evaluating the efficiency of an organization:*

1. The financial perspective (e.g., costs, budget)
2. The internal process-related perspective (e.g., productivity, effort, duration, plan vs. actual, enhancement, quality, defects, maintenance, processes – here is the area of IT metrics: costs per new or changed functionality, maturity level)
3. The customer-related perspective (e.g., service levels, customer contentment, market share, customer relations)
4. The innovation- and learning-related perspective (e.g., staff training and education).

These four aspects must be chosen and adapted to fit an organization's specific requirements. The goal of the Balanced Scorecard is the optimization of the financial metrics. Hence, the optimization of the other three aspects is only desired in relation to and dependency on this main aspect. Figure 10.4 shows the general model of the Balanced Scorecard.

It is possible to implement a Balanced Scorecard as a strategic metrics- and management-system for the IT department of an organization. In this way, the development of an IT strategy can be monitored on a long-term scale. Furthermore, the measurements support strategic learning and continual refinement of the strategy. The use of the Balanced Scorecard can shift the focus from one-sided financial or budget discussions in the direction of more qualitative questions, such as the following:

1. Which benefits does IT elaborate?
2. What does IT deliver for our internal and external customers?
3. How innovative is IT?
4. Where do we have an advantage with IT compared with our competitors?

The Balanced Scorecard is primarily a strategic management concept enabling one to coordinate the goals of various parts of an organization transparently, and on all levels from a holistic point of view. IT measurement fits well

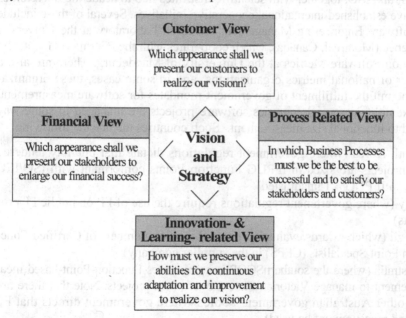

Fig. 10.4. General model of the Balanced Scorecard as used from the German author in his lectures

within the model and supports the strategic goals of the organization. It is recommended that the following four steps be done prior to implementing a Balanced Scorecard:

1. Define accepted and achievable strategic goals (i.e., they will not disappear with a change in management).
2. Identify IT critical success factors.
3. Define the corresponding metrics.
4. Present the results in a Kiviat chart.

The metrics will be mostly derived from the organizational goals following a method similar to the GQM. Balanced Scorecards are often used as part of internal benchmarking in an organization.

10.5 Important Software and Systems Measurement Organizations

There are varieties of software and systems measurement organizations around the world. Famous are the truly international organizations such as IFPUG, ISBSG, and ISO, together with scientific institutes tied to academic universities that have established international cooperative initiatives. Several of these include the Software Engineering Management Research Laboratory at the University of Quebec (Montreal, Canada), which cooperates with the (German) GI Interest Group on Software Metrics at the University of Magdeburg. There are also a number of national metrics organizations, and in some cases, these organizations permit the fulfillment of government mandates for software measurement. For example, in several countries software projects are managed in some way related to functional size measurement. Such countries include the following:

- South Korea (where government regulations dictate that publicly tendered IT projects are sized in IFPUG Function Points conformant with ISO/IEC 20926:IFPUG 4.1 unadjusted)
- Italy (where government regulations require the use of FP on public IT projects)
- Brazil (which awards evaluation points based on numbers of Certified Function Point Specialists (CFPS) in the supplier company)
- Australia (where the southernSCOPE method uses Function-Point-based measurement to manage Victorian State Government projects. Note that there are no other Australian government bodies where government directs that FP based measurement be used)
- Finland (where the northernSCOPE method based on functional size measurement is creating IT project success and is gaining a foothold particularly in the larger state government programs).

10.5.1 Computer Measurement Group (CMG)

The CMG is a nonprofit worldwide organization of data processing profes-
sionals committed to the measurement and management of computer systems
(hardware and software). CMG members are primarily concerned with performance evaluation of existing systems to maximize performance (e.g., response time, throughput, etc.). Another focus of CMG is capacity management,
where planned enhancements to existing systems or the design of new systems
are evaluated to estimate the necessary resources required that would provide
adequate performance at a reasonable cost. The CMG home page is http://
www.cmg.org/. National groups of the CMG are active in Australia, Austria,
Canada, Germany (as CECMG), Italy, South Africa, the United Kingdom (as
UKCMG), and the USA.

10.5.2 COSMIC Consortium

The Common Software Measurement International Consortium (COSMIC) was
founded in late 1998 by a group of experienced software metrics practitioners
from industry and academia with the aim of promoting a new functional size
measurement method known as COSMIC Full Function Points (COSMIC-FFP).
Since the earlier days, the resultant method has undergone dramatic change,
was standardized through the ISO/IEC working group on functional size measurement as an ISO/IEC standard, and is now known as simply the COSMIC
Method.

Approximately 40 professionals from 8 countries combined their efforts voluntarily and proposed some principles for a software Functional Size Measurement method. At the end of 1999, they published the COSMIC Full Function
Point Version 2.0 Measurement Practices Manual (COSMIC:MPM), and made
it available for download from http://www.cosmicon.com. A short overview of
the COSMIC Method is included in the chapter "Functional Size Measurement
Methods" (FSMM). In November 2007, the COSMIC Version 3 was released,
and all documents inclusive of ISO/IEC 19761 will be changed from COSMIC-
FFP to COSMIC.

According to proponents of the method, COSMIC is based on the strengths
of the IFPUG, Mark II, and the NESMA Function Point Methods. It uses four
base functional components: Entry, Exit, Read, and Write. In developing the
method, there was a 14-month field trial period starting in March 1999 in order
to verify in industry the practicability of this new measurement method. This
lead to the advantage of this method, namely the benefit that it started from
beginning on with a measured and approved database of case studies delivering profound metrics for estimation.

Following organizations participated in the field test:

- An Australian and a European space and aircraft organization
- A British bank with MIS applications
- Two European telecommunication organizations
- An Australian and a Canadian software provider operating in military defense environment
- An Australian real-time software consultancy
- A Canadian software consultancy

Following field tests were made:

- Test of the general repeatable interpretation of the Measurement Practices Manual (MPM) Version 2.0
- Development of detailed measurement procedures
- Test for verification that the measurements represent functionality
- Tests for verification that measured data correlate with effort
- Tests for verification that the method was portable to different development environments.

The tests were performed with 18 development projects from 5 organizations (16 new development and 2 enhancement projects) on multiple platforms and with 21 maintenance requests of small functional enhancements in a single organization. There was consistent positive feedback about the test requirements, with the additional benefit of a database of historical data.

The COSMIC Method was developed as follows:

- Designed by an international group of experts on an academic basis
- Drawn on the practical experience of all the main existing FP methods
- Designed specifically to conform to ISO/IEC 14143 Part 1
- Designed to work across MIS and real-time domains, for software in any layer or peer item
- Tested in a variety of field trials before being finalized.

The Measurement Practices Manual (MPM) is available in English, French, Japanese, and Spanish. At the time of this writing, translation into German, Italian, and Turkish is also in progress. There are also three case studies available. Furthermore, the COSMIC Method was approved as an ISO standard in March 2003: ISO/IEC 19761. The COSMIC consortium published the COSMIC Guide to the Implementation of ISO/IEC 19761, which is also available for download http://www.lrgl.uqam.ca/ cosmic-ffp.

The International Software Benchmarking Standards Group (ISBSG) has also approved COSMIC as a data collection standard. The ISBSG Benchmarking Database release 8 (January 2004) contained 66 COSMIC-FFP Version 2.0 projects, and 6 from Versions 1.1 and 1.0. Seventy-five percent were new developments, 25% enhancements, with 65% of projects on PC platforms, 15% in the environment of embedded software, process control, message switching, network management, etc. There are several worldwide research activities under way for further improvement and dissemination of the COSMIC Method (ISO/IEC 19761).

The COSMIC home page is http://www.cosmicon.com, while the standard and publications are hosted at http://www.lrgl.uqam.ca/cosmic-ffp.

10.5.3 Finnish Software Measurement Association (FiSMA)

The FiSMA is an independent registered association focusing on better management through improving the quality and measurability of software and systems engineering. FiSMA's membership is intended for all companies, research units, universities, and other institutes interested in software measurement. At the moment, there are about 40 active member organizations and local software process improvement networks (SPINs).

FiSMA was established in 1992 with the name LATURI user group. In 1998, it changed its name to FiSMA and expanded its operation to the current level. FiSMA is a member organization of the Metrics Associations International Network (MAIN). It has also close cooperation with Australian ISBSG and French Datamax. Also, FiSMA cooperates with similar associations and networks in EU (EuroSPI), Baltia (BaSMA), and Russia areas and maintains a consolidated website (www.fisma.fi).

The first version of the FiSMA FSM method was published in 1991 under the original name Laturi, and funded through a cooperative industry project of the same name. Since then, there has been continuous use and maintenance of the method through the companies of the FiSMA, which were incorporated in 1996. More than 2000 project managers and software practitioners have been trained to use FiSMA FSM method through standardized 2- and 3-day training courses, with several thousand more participating globally in shorter introductory events.

The rules and details about the FiSMA FSM method have been publicly available since the early 1990s and today can be downloaded (in English and Finnish) from www.fisma.fi. FiSMA 1.1 is the fifth functional size measurement method to become an ISO/IEC standard: ISO/IEC 29881.

FiSMA formalized its scope management concept: northernSCOPE in early 2007, and 4SUM Partners (CEO: Pekka Forselius) worked with FiSMA to also create and standardize a new certification for software and systems professionals: Certified SCOPE Manager (CSM) with the European Certificates Association (ECA). 4SUM Partners was incorporated through as a management buyout from STTF, and it retains both the official training materials for the CSM curriculum as well as the professional scope management software: Experience® Pro.

northernSCOPE is a 12-step approach to professional scope management whereby an independent and knowledgeable Scope Manager works on behalf of a systems acquisition customer (often contracting for software and systems development services) as the customer's advocate to facilitate and manage supplier work bid by unit pricing (Euros or US$ or other currency per Function Point) for systems development programs. (Note that a *program* is typically composed of multiple software development projects – most of which can be sized based on functional size measurement.) As such, rather than the ineffective practice of a customer demanding a fixed price estimate from a supplier *before requirements* – which ultimately results in a lose/lose situation for both the customer and supplier – the work is managed and progress is monitored through unit pricing of the work to be done. This permits the customer and supplier to achieve success – the customer can make changes that will be paid for based on the unit pricing, and the supplier is paid for the work that the customer directs the supplier to do.

For further information about northernSCOPE, visit www.fisma.fi/in-english, and for training and certification worldwide in Scope Management based on northernSCOPE, visit www.4sumpartners.com.

FiSMA's Experience database, which is also at the core of the Experience® Pro software, accumulates user project data in conjunction with the ISBSG database (www.isbsg.org). Many internationally renowned researchers have analyzed the FiSMA Experience repository and published their findings in books, articles, or proceedings. The following is a partial list of such researchers:

- Joseph Blackburn (Vanderbilt University, USA)
- Soumitra Dutta (INSEAD, France)
- Khaled El Emam (University of Ottawa, Canada)
- Pekka Forselius (University of Jyväskylä, Finland)
- Cigdem Gencel (Middle East Technical University, Turkey)
- Ross Jeffery (University of New South Wales, Australia)
- Barbara Kitchenham (Keele University, UK)
- Carolyn Mair (Bournemouth University and Brunel University, UK)
- Katrina D. Maxwell (INSEAD, France)
- Risto Nevalainen (Helsinki University of Technology, Finland)
- Rahul Premraj (Bournemouth University, UK and Saarland University, Germany)
- Martin Shepperd (Bournemouth University and Brunel University, UK)
- Luk Van Wassenhove (INSEAD, France)
- Isabella Wieczorek (Fraunhofer Institute, Germany).

For further information about the high-quality Finnish Experience project database, contact Pekka Forselius at pekka.forselius@4sumpartners.com.

10.5.4 German Metrics Organization: DASMA

The nonprofit German software metrics organization: *Deutschsprachige Anwendergruppe für Softwaremetrik und Aufwandschätzung e.V. (DASMA) fosters the development of software measurement standards.* DASMA's mission is concerned with the validation of software in order to improve its usage in economy and administration. DASMA was founded in Darmstadt, Germany in 1993 and as of this writing has in excess of 70 members throughout Austria, Switzerland, and Germany. The DASMA describes itself as a network and professional organization of the German-speaking users of software metrics and estimation, and is in turn a member of the most important international IT measurement organizations.

DASMA alternates hosting the International Workshop on Software Metrics (IWSM) every other year at a location in Germany, and then supports the hosting by Canada alternate years. IWSM in Germany features an English conference track and is held jointly with DASMA's annual MetriKon (*Metrik Konferenz*) and the assembly of the German GI Interest Group on Software Metrics. Since 2003 (DASMA's tenth anniversary) DASMA also presents annual awards at MetriKon for up to three student theses in Software Measurement and Metrics. The participating theses are all downloadable for DASMA members from the DASMA homepage restricted member area at http://www.dasma.org, and MetriKon proceedings may be ordered by contacting the DASMA secretary.

10.5.5 German GI Interest Group on Software Metrics

The German GI Fachgruppe 2.1.10 Software-Messung und -Bewertung is part of the Institute for Distributed Systems of the Faculty of Informatics of the Otto-von-Guericke-Universität in Magdeburg, Germany. The GI Interest Group on Software Metrics was founded in 1992 and offers courses on software techniques. Its president is Professor Reiner Dumke. *The GI Interest Group on Software Metrics is concerned with theoretical foundations of software measurement and evaluation as well as with the practical implementation and the problems arising with the integration in the software development process*, as e.g., certifications, metrics databases, or experience factories.

The GI Interest Group on Software Metrics is active in research, especially in the area of software metrics. There is international cooperation with organizations in industry (e.g., the continuing International Workshops on Software Measurement, IWSM) and with academia, in particular with the École de technologie supérieure at the Université du Québec (Montreal, Canada, Professor Alain Abran) and the CIM (Center d'Interet sur les Metriques, a Canadian metrics association). Furthermore, the GI Interest Group on Software Metrics cooperates with the Fraunhofer IESE (Institute for Experimental Software Engineering) in

Karlsruhe, Germany (under the direction of Professor Dieter Rombach), and also with the European MAIN network.

The GI Interest Group on Software Metrics maintains the Software Measurement Laboratory (SMLab), which is an internet prototype of a software measurement database. It allows Java-based entry of measurement data from the CAME tools: Logiscope, Datrix, and OOM, and delivers reports.

Since 1993, this group has published the biannual *Metrics News* featuring information and papers pertaining to software metrics. The Metrics News changed its name in 2008 to Software Measurement News. Historical editions are available for free download by visiting the GI Interest Group homepage at http://ivs.cs.uni-magdeburg.de/sw-eng/us/, where you will also find plenty information about software metrics, experiments and literature.

10.5.6 International Function Point Users Group (IFPUG)

The IFPUG, headquartered in the USA and founded in Toronto in 1986 has developed the standardized IFPUG Function Point Method to count the functional size of a piece of software. The functional size measurement of software using the IFPUG standard should be done in accordance with the current version as outlined on the IFPUG website at www.ifpug.org. This recommendation facilitates comparability of FP counts between different organizations.

The IFPUG Function Point counting method was published by ISO/IEC as standard 20926 for Functional Size Measurement. Note that in order for the IFPUG functional size measurement method to be conformant with the ISO/IEC 14143-1 Functional Size Measurement – Definition of Concepts, it, as well as the Mark II and NESMA methods, had to be published without mandating any adjustment factor for software complexity (i.e., the General Systems Characteristics – GSCs – present in the IFPUG and other methods had to be made to be an optional step to conform with the ISO/IEC definitional standard).

IFPUG offers four types of certifications:

- Certified Function Point Specialist, CFPS, for Function Point practitioners/ counters
- Certified Software Measurement Specialist, CSMS, for software measurement practitioners
- Certification of software for counting Function Points, and
- Certification of training materials.

IFPUG boasts a membership of corporations and individuals residing in more than 40 countries with the number increasing every year. IFPUG's home page http://www.ifpug.org, delivers plenty of information about software metrics and estimation as well as links to other IT metrics organizations and IFPUG member services.

In 2001, more than 350 people were CFPS and today the number continues to increase – especially in emerging areas of the world where software measurement outsourcing is prevalent such as Korea, China, Brazil, and India. The CFPS certification is valid for a period of 3 years, at which time the CFPS holder has the choice to either rewrite the CFPS examination or compile a documentation set for recertification (see recertification requirements on the website). Certification examinations are offered in many countries, typically in connection with national conferences. As of this writing, the CFPS exam is being automated for delivery through ProMetric centers worldwide in a number of languages. Further information about IFPUG certifications can be found at the IFPUG home page, http://www.ifpug.org.

Several resources are available to assist candidates to prepare for the CFPS exam:

- The book *Measuring the Software Process* (Garmus and Herron, 1995) contains a simulated CFPS examination featuring two sets of multiple-choice questions, and a case study that is a little bit smaller than in the official examination. The answer solutions are also documented. Preparation for the CFPS examination by practicing this prototype examination at least five to six times has proven to be sufficient for some candidates to pass the actual exam, since there are typical questions in this example. Candidates who have counted more than 15,000–20,000 Function Points in practice have a good chance to pass the examination – as long as they have also memorized where to locate the fundamental rules and how to apply them from the IFPUG Counting Practices Manual.
- Quality Plus Technologies, Inc., sells a set of CFPS study guides and Function Point workbooks (volumes 1–3) to assist practitioners to prepare for the CFPS exam. The study guides/workbooks each feature abundant sample test questions and a variety of case studies (together with the solutions), in a manner that simulates the style and questions on the CFPS exam. Visit www.qualityplustech.com to order these CFPS certification support tools.

The actual examination fees, procedures to register, and the locations of regional exams worldwide can be found at the IFPUG website http://www.ifpug.org under the topic "Certifications."

IFPUG also organizes annual conferences to facilitate knowledge transfer, and has approximately ten volunteer committees who work to promote the further development of the IFPUG method.

IFPUG publishes several detailed case studies to illustrate how to apply FP counting to a variety of user requirements for software developed using several approaches (e.g., object-oriented). Additionally, white papers are published by and for members including FP counting of data warehouse applications, client/server software, etc. These and the case studies are available from the IFPUG website (www.ifpug.org) and are updated whenever a new counting practices manual (i.e., a new method release) is published so that all IFPUG publications reflect the current IFPUG standard.

Immediately before the CFPS examination the official registration must be signed as well as the code of ethics of the IFPUG. The examination lasts 3 h and is currently available in English, Italian, Portuguese (Brazilian), Spanish, Korean, and could soon be available in other languages as well. It must be noted that the time pressure during the examination is often considered by examines to be tremendous and is typically underestimated by first-time candidates. The results of the examination are sent to the candidates by post about 4–6 weeks after the examination.

Hints for passing the exam are available at the Yahoo! Group:

www.groups.yahoo.com/group/quality_plus_measurement_forum.

Where group members can look in the message archives and files section of the site.

One copy of the IFPUG *Counting Practices Manual* (CPM) must be brought with each candidate to the CFPS exam, as well as up to two separate quick reference cards (from any organization). The questions refer to many details from the CPM, but time is not sufficient to look up everything so it is essential that exam candidates be familiar with the content and structure of the CPM. The "Hints" of the CPM are also valid for reference; however, the core rules of the CPM take precedence over any hints provided by other documentation. Candidates can bring their own notes with them as long as they are annotated in their copy of the CPM. Our recommendation is the use of a CPM with the important rules and sections marked and the pages tagged with Post-it® notes, so that the relevant sections can be easily located during the exam. (Note: that if one does not know where to find a topic or specific rule wording in the CPM, there is hardly a chance to pass the examination in the time allotted.)

Electronic tools are not allowed in the examination, except for simple pocket calculators. (*Note*: Until recently, the examination was held only in conjunction with IFPUG events or as regional exams; however, automated exams are in the works for this year.) The CFPS examination itself is 3-h long (with some extra time granted on request for nonnative English speakers who take the exam in English) and consists of three parts with a total score of 150:

- Part 1: 50 multiple-choice questions related to IFPUG rules (definitions and concepts from the main Counting Practices Manual and the Glossary).
- Part 2: 50 multiple-choice questions concerning the use and application of IFPUG rules (applying the formulas and interpreting the complexity matrices), but more involved than Part 1.

- Part 3: One or two case studies for which the examinee must demonstrate a complete Function Point count. Usually the case study on the examination features ~15 functions and their associated data entities. The case study section is formulated with text and sometimes screen and report layouts.
- For Parts 1 and 2 of the examination, it is advisable to allocate no more than the first 2 h (about 1 min per question) in order to have enough time to understand and finish counting the Function Points of the case study section.

At least 90% of the answers must be correct in each of the three parts in order to pass the examination. Approximately 65% of the candidates normally pass the examination. In the case of failure, the examination can be repeated within 6 months for a nominal fee. Subsequent examinations currently incur the same fee as the initial examination.

The questions in Parts 1 and 2 are strongly correlated to exact wording in the CPM; in some cases they are actually cited word by word. Subtle changes in question wording can be very superficial (missing, changed, or inserted words!), so candidates must be careful to read questions accurately before answering them. In the case of contradictions between rules and examples in the CPM, the rules take precedence! It is recommended to document the rule with the page number, together with the answer, in case the answer was looked up in the manual (there is not enough time to do this for every question).

All 100 questions of Parts 1 and 2 are of multiple-choice type. There is always only one *best* or most correct answer! There are typical combinations of answers such as (a) abc, (b) xyz, (c) a and b, (d) neither a nor b, etc. It is recommended to document any uncertainties in your answers by annotating them with commentary on the answer sheet itself. (Note that nonnative English speakers are granted an additional 30 min to complete the examination.)

10.5.7 International Software Benchmarking Standards Group (ISBSG)

The ISBSG started in 1994 as an informal consortium of national and international measurement organizations, and has since grown into the most significant not-for-profit benchmarking organization in the world. Members are metrics organizations, with participation from technical advisors (individual functional size measurement experts) and industry.

From http://www.isbsg.org, the ISBSG is a not-for-profit organization that has established, grows, maintains, and exploits three repositories of IT history data to help improve the management of IT globally.

While there are several ISBSG data repositories, the largest is the application development and enhancement repository boasting close to 5,000 projects with its release 10 of the database. In addition, there is a maintenance and support repository, and a package implementation and acquisition repository, with others being planned (including a testing repository).

The ISBSG-preferred unit of size in its repositories is Function Points, and the five ISO/IEC-conformant FSMM are all represented to various degrees. In particular, IFPUG Function Points and FiSMA Function Points dominate the data, followed by NESMA FP, Mark II FP, and COSMIC FP.

ISBSG collects data about software development, enhancement, and maintenance projects with the goal to achieve improvements in software development. Today representatives from Australia, China, Germany, Finland, India, Italy, Japan, the Netherlands, South Korea, Switzerland, the UK, USA, and several other countries actively participate in the ISBSG consortium and meet annually during September or October to formulate the work for the coming year.

The current release 10 of the ISBSG database contains project history on more than 4,000 completed software development projects. The ISBSG also regularly publishes books and special reports based on analysis of its data. Two of the most notable publications include the following:

- The *Software Metrics Compendium* (June 2002), which summarized the analysis of close to 1,300 projects
- *Practical Project Estimation, 2nd edition* (2005) – an essential estimating book presenting ISBSG compatible approaches to software estimating, functional size measurement shortcuts, and a variety of practical project estimating techniques gleaned from analysis of the ISBSG repository.

ISBSG believes that its databases represent data collected from the top 25% of software organizations, because it is the higher level maturity companies (companies at least at level 2 of the CMMI® or SPICE models) that capture and consistently report project completion data.

At the time of this printing, the CD release 10 is available featuring an excel spreadsheet database complete with data on more than 4,000 actual completed software projects. The CD for release 1 of the Maintenance and Support database is also available featuring ~150 projects. Planning is underway for a Project Manager Handbook and an updated release of *The Benchmark* book complete with analysis of the most recent ISBSG database. (See www.isbsg.org for the current product offerings available from ISBSG including the quarterly special reports.)

ISBSG is registered as a not-for-profit organization headquartered in Melbourne, Australia and managed by a member-run volunteer board of directors.

The mission of the ISBSG is to help improve the management of IT resources by both business and government through the provision and exploitation of public repositories of software engineering knowledge, which is standardized, verified, recent, and representative of current technologies.

ISBSG goals include the following:

- Enable the comparison of software development on an international basis
- Find the world-best processes for the improvement and simplification of software development
- Master and improve the global understanding of software engineering techniques
- Enable translation and dissemination of actual techniques for software development
- Extension of available data
- Enhancement of software measurement through the development of a common vocabulary and a unique understanding of technical terminology
- Deliver better information for international business decisions
- Support an international network of practitioners.

The current members of the ISBSG include the following:

- ASMA/SQA (Australian Software Metrics Association)
- IFPUG (International Function Point Users Group)
- NASSCOM (National Association of Software and Service Companies, which serves as the Indian National Metrics Association)
- AEMES (Association Espanola de Metricas del Software)
- DASMA (Deutschsprachige Anwendergruppe for Softwaremetrik and Aufwandschätzung e.V.)
- FiSMA (Finnish Software Measurement Association).

The FiSMA 1.1 FSM Method developed and maintained by the Finnish Software Measurement Association is the fifth FSM Method to be standardized by ISO/IEC.

- GUFPI-ISMA (Italian Software Metrics Association – Gruppo Utenti Function Point Italia)
- JFPUG (Japanese Function Point Users Group)
- NESMA (Netherlands Software Metrieken Gebruikers Associatie)
- SwiSMA (Swiss Software & Service Metrics Association)
- UKSMA (United Kingdom Software Metrics Association)
- CSPIU (China Software Process Improvement Union)
- KOSMA (Korean Software Measurement Association).

The ISBSG offers the following services:

- IT project benchmarking service to allow the members of a national metrics organization or ISBSG to deliver their project data free of charge and with a minimal effort to the ISBSG database. The projects are quality-approved and compared with similar projects in the database. A report with graphical results is provided free of charge to any person or group who submits completed project data to ISBSG.
- Best practice network: everyone who contributes to the database and who is registered in the ISBSG can participate in the network.
- *The Benchmark*: a general benchmarking report. The report has a high benefit for software developers, project leaders, consultants, and organizations as well as academics. ISBSG members and organizations that contribute to the ISBSG database can order the report at a reduced charge.
- Customer-specific analysis and reports: on special demand of a participating organization, the standardized report as well as a customized report according to the organization's data can be delivered. The repository data can also be purchased (CD) for private comparison and analysis.
- Research requests: interested parties (e.g., academic institutes) can get the repository data for research projects by special arrangement free of charge.
- The ISBSG data repository: the number of projects in the ISBSG database increases monthly, and a new release (on CD) is produced on a biannual basis. The following list shows how the ISBSG application development (and enhancement) project database has grown:
  - Release 10 (2007) contains data on over 4,000 projects
  - Release 9 (2005) contained data on 3,034 projects
  - Release 8 (2003) contained 2,048 projects
  - Prior releases were as follows: 2002 with 1,238 projects, 1999 with 789, 1998 with 451, and 1997 with 397.

The data is submitted from over 20 countries with new countries joining annually. A detailed demographic report of project origins is published in *The Benchmark and is available on the website.*

The process of benchmarking of a project with the ISBSG benchmarking database is shown in Fig. 10.5. The home page of the ISBSG, http://www. isbsg.org, provides information about its services.

10.5.8 International Organization for Standardization

The ISO was founded in 1947 and has developed and published more than 11,000 international standards in all economic domains. The Name ISO was chosen from the Greek and means *equal*. The connection of *equal* and *standard* led to the choice of the name ISO. The ISO is independent of any government and does not belong to the United Nations Organization (UNO), although it cooperates closely with many commissions of the UNO. The work of the nearly 30,000 experts from more than 120 countries in the nearly 2,850 working groups of the ISO is voluntary. The groups are managed from the Secretary General in Geneva (Switzerland), which also publishes the standards.

All ISO standards are used voluntarily. The ISO has no legal jurisdiction to prescribe edicts. Since the ISO standards are developed on demand and by the consensus of the teamwork of the international experts involved, its usage is widespread. In the domain of quality management (including software management), the key standards are ISO 9000 *for quality management and quality assurance* and ISO 14000 *on environmental management.*

"ISO (the International Organization for Standardization) and IEC (the International Electrotechnical Commission) form the specialized system for worldwide standardization. National bodies that are members of ISO or IEC participate in the development of International Standards through technical committees technical activity. ISO and IEC technical committees collaborate in fields of mutual interest. Other international organizations, governmental and nongovernmental, in liaison with ISO and IEC, also take part in the work.

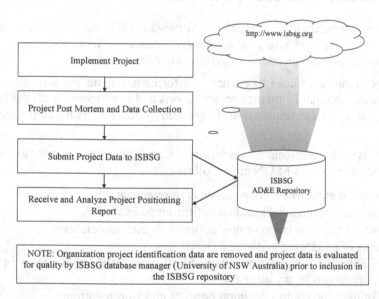

Fig. 10.5. Process of data submission to the ISBSG application development and enhancement (AD&E) benchmarking repository

In the field of information technology, ISO and IEC have established a joint technical committee, ISO/IEC JTC 1 Information Engineering. Draft International Standards adopted by the Joint Technical Committee are circulated to national bodies for voting. Publication as an International Standard requires approval by at least 75% of the national bodies casting a vote." (Taken from the Foreword in ISO/IEC 14143-1:2007).

Subcommittee 7 (SC7) administers and directs the standardization work for Software and Systems Engineering, under which there are a number of Working Groups (WG).

The ISO/IEC JTC SC7 Working Group 12 developed the suite of standards for Functional Size Measurement, ISO/IEC 14143 Parts 1–6 in order to standardize the definitions and concepts for Functional Size Measurements publicly available.

Information about the ISO/IEC software engineering can be found at its home page http://www.iso.org/iso/search.htm. Look for ISO/IEC JTC1 SC7 Systems and Software Engineering standards.

10.5.9 Metrics Association's International Network (MAIN)

The Metrics Association's International Network (MAIN) was founded in 2002 in Brussels, Belgium with the goal to promote, coordinate, and exchange experiences among software metrics user groups worldwide.

MAIN organizers aimed to exchange information about the activities and results of the national IT metrics organizations and to cooperate with the ISO, ISBSG, and other international software and systems measurement organizations.

MAIN is an international network of autonomous software metrics associations. The objectives of MAIN are as follows:

- Exchange of experience among associated organizations
- Influence in international standard definition processes
- Support for the foundation of new national metrics associations
- The aims of MAIN are to do the following:
  - Contribute to the organization of software metrics conferences in co-operation with any other entity
  - Initiate and control common projects and working groups
  - Develop a common knowledge base of documents such as metrics papers, case studies, training materials, measurement guidelines, research initiatives database, benchmark database

Furthermore, the MAIN network supports and fosters the development of IT metrics organizations in countries that do not have national metrics organizations. The MAIN URL is http://www.mai-net.org.

The MAIN network cooperates with other IT metrics organizations such as IFPUG and ASMA (Australia). The JFPUG (Japan) is an associate member, as is the COSMIC consortium. The MAIN Network cooperates with the ISO standardization process. The following national metrics organizations are (as of 2003) MAIN members:

- AEMES (Association Espanola de Metricas del Software)
- DANMET (Danish Software Metrics Association)
- DASMA (Deutschsprachige Anwendergruppe für Softwaremetrik und Aufwandschätzung)
- FiSMA (Finnish Software Measurement Association)
- FPUGA (Function Point User Group Austria)
- GUFPI-ISMA (Gruppo Utenti Funzioni Punti Italiana)
- IT/KVIV (Genootschap Software Metrics Belgium)
- NESMA (Netherlands Software Metrieken Gebruikers Associatie)
- SwiSMA (Swiss Software & Service Metrics Association)
- UKSMA (United Kingdom Software Metrics Association)
- JFPUG (Japanese Function Point User Group).

10.5.10 Software Engineering Institute at Carnegie Mellon University in Pittsburgh, PA, USA

"The SEI is a federally funded research and development center conducting software engineering research in acquisition, architecture and product lines, process improvement and performance measurement, security, and system interoperability and dependability." (from www.sei.cmu.edu)

The SEI manages, coordinates, and develops the CMMI® models used worldwide, as well as many other software acquisition papers, books, and initiatives, including the following:

- The latest CMMI®, Team Software Process (TSP), Personal Software Process (PSP), Six Sigma, and many other models (www.sei.cmu.edu).
- The software engineering information repository: SEIR, a free database, but you must be a registered member of the extranet site in order to access the information (https://seir.sei.cmu.edu/seir/). Of particular interest to reader is the content on Software and systems Measurement where one can download papers, articles, analysis, presentations, tutorials, etc. about measurement.

- Software Engineering Measurement and Analysis (SEMA) website. "The *Software Engineering Measurement and Analysis (SEMA)* Website presents the latest publications, presentations, and training offered by the SEMA initiative. Several online resources for exchanging best practices in software engineering are also available through this site. SEMA helps organizations develop and evolve useful measurement and analysis practices. Organizations that have developed measurement capabilities can leverage that investment by learning to better analyze the data they collect and make more informed business decisions." (from the SEMA website: http://www.sei.cmu.edu/sema/).

10.5.11 Standard Performance Evaluation Corporation (SPEC)

The SPEC is a nonprofit corporation formed to establish, maintain, and endorse a standardized set of relevant benchmarks that can be applied to the newest generation of high-performance computers. SPEC develops suites of benchmarks and also reviews and publishes submitted results from our member organizations and other benchmark licensees. The SPEC organization is well known for processor benchmarks, but nowadays provides benchmarks for graphical systems, application servers, Web servers, mail servers, or different Java implementations. Information about the SPEC can be found at its home page http: // www.spec.org/.

10.5.12 Transaction Processing Performance Council (TPC)

The TPC is a nonprofit corporation founded to define transaction processing and database benchmarks and to disseminate objective, verifiable TPC performance data to the industry. Currently it provides the following benchmarks:

- TPC-C simulates a complete computing environment where a population of users executes transactions against a database
- The TPC Benchmark H (TPC-H) is a decision-support benchmark. It consists of a suite of business-oriented ad hoc queries and concurrent data modifications
- The TPC Benchmark R (TPC-R) is a decision-support benchmark similar to TPC-H, but that allows additional optimizations based on advanced knowledge of the queries
- TPC Benchmark W (TPC-W) is a transactional Web benchmark. The workload is performed in a controlled Internet commerce environment that simulates the activities of a business-oriented transactional Web server.

Information about the TPC can be found at its home page http://www.tpc.org/.

10.6 Internet Links to Measurement Communities

Many other organizations may be available using links from the websites listed here. Typically, IT metrics organizations (Table 10.3) provide information and links to further metrics-relevant URLs. *Note*: As of this printing, all links were active and valid.

Table 10.3. Internet links to measurement communities

Organization	URL
4SUM Partners	http://www.4sumpartners.com
AEMES, Spanish metrics organization	http://www.aemes.fi.upm.es
ASMA/SQA (Australian Software Metrics Association and Software Quality Association of New South Wales) – a SIG of the Australian Computer Society	http://www.asma-sqa-nsw. org.au/index.htm
ASQF (Arbeitskreis Software-Qualität Franken/ISQI), Germany	http:www.isqi.org
BFPUG (Brazilian Function Point Users Group)	http://www.bfpug.com.br
CMG (Computer Measurement Group)	http://www.cmg.org
Center for Systems and Software Engineering (COCOMO II and Barry Boehm at the University of Southern California)	http://csse.usc.edu/csse/
COSMIC – The Common Software Metrics International Consortium (Full Function Points)	www.cosmicon.com
DACS (Data and Analysis Center for Software)	https://www.dacs.dtic.mil/
DASMA (Deutschsprachiger Anwenderverband für Softwaremetriken und Aufwandschätzung e.V.), Germany	http://www.dasma.org
ESI (The European Software Institute), Spain	http://www.esi.es
FiSMA (Finnish Software Measurement Association)	http://www.fisma.fi
GI Fachgruppe 2.1.10 Software-Measurement und -Bewertung, University Magdeburg	http://ivs.cs.uni-magdeburg.de/sw-eng/us/
GUFPI-ISMA, Italian metrics organization	http://www.gufpi.org
Fraunhofer Institut (IESE) in Kaiserslautern	http://www.iese.fhg.de
IFPUG (International Function Point Users Group)	http://www.ifpug.org
ISBSG (International Software Benchmarking Standards Group)	http://www.isbsg.org
ISO/IEC JTC1 SC7 home page	http://www.jtc1-sc7.org/

Table 10.3. *(Cont.)*

IT/KVIV, Genootschap Software Metrics Belgium, Belgian metrics organization	http://www.ti.kviv.be
Longstreet Consulting (President: David Longstreet,)	http://www.softwaremetrics.com
MAIN (Metrics Associations International Network), European metrics organization	http://www.mai-net.org
NESMA (Netherlands Software Metrics Users Association)	http://www.nesma.nl; http://www.nesma.org
PSM (The Practical Software and Systems Measurement Support Center), DoD – Goal-driven measurement framework	http://www.psmsc.com
Quality Plus Technologies, Inc. (President: Carol Dekkers)	http://www.qualityplustech.com who also host a Yahoo!Group on software metrics: www.groups.yahoo.com/Quality_Plus_ Measurement_Forum
QSM (Quantitative Software Management)	http://www.qsm.com
SEI (Software Engineering Institute), CMM® and CMMI®	http://www.sei.cmu.edu
SPEC (Standard Performance Evaluation Corporation)	http://www.spec.org/
SwiSMA (Swiss Software & Service Metrics Association)	http://www.swisma.ch
TPC (Transaction Processing Performance Council)	http://www.tpc.org
Technical University of Berlin (Thomas Fetcke)	http://user.cs.tu-berlin. de/~fetcke/metrics-sites.html
The IT Metrics and Productivity Institute	http://www.itmpi.org/
UKSMA, British metrics organization	http://uksma.co.uk
UQAM/GELOG: Software Engineering Research Laboratory of the Université du Québec at Montreal, Canada	http://www.lrgl.uqam.ca
Dr. Horst Zuse	http://www.cs.tu-berlin.de/~zuse

10.7 Management Summary

Measurement of the functional size of software is an essential part of the measurement of *user* requirements, but it only measures the size of the functional user requirements (*what* the software must do in terms of business processes and tasks).

Software measurements are of such importance that the US Department of Defense (DoD) demands explicit planning and tracking of metrics on every project.

Besides the CMMI®, we direct the reader to the Recommended Approach of the NASA on measurement.

The CMMI® helps to define what to do to reach higher levels of organizational process maturity, but does not say how to do it.

The CMMI® maturity level is becoming an increasingly important indicator or gauge for organizational software process quality.

GQM allows evaluation of the quality of products or processes (*note*: this is unsuitable to evaluate the quality of people) in software development.

The Balanced Scorecard is primarily a strategic management concept enabling one to coordinate the goals of various parts of an organization transparently, and on all levels from a holistic point of view. IT measurement fits well within the model and supports the strategic goals of the organization.

11 Benchmarking of IT Projects

Metrics are ideally suited for comparing IT projects and learning by comparison. This should be the goal of benchmarking: locating one's organizational situation and defining purposeful measures for its optimization on IT projects and finding opportunities for the organization to learn and move ahead in its project management capability. The connections between benchmarking, estimation, planning, and controlling are shown in Fig. 11.1.

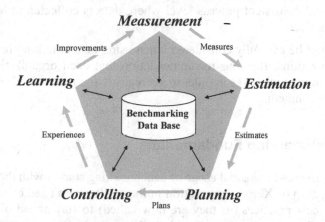

Fig. 11.1. Benchmarking of IT projects

The main question of benchmarking is how we can learn from other organizations in order to improve our own organization. In this chapter, we present concepts for benchmarking and introduce some of the publications available from the International Software Benchmarking Standards Group, ISBSG, (www.isbsg.org) and other IT benchmarking resources. Note: The ISO/IEC JTC1 SC7 standards group (see chapter on measurement organizations) approved at their Berlin plenary meeting in May 2008 a new work item (NWI) to standardize IT Project Performance Benchmarking: ISO/IEC 29155, to create an IT project benchmarking framework. This project will likely include several sub-projects and will include some form of the draft standard for a benchmarking process developed by ISBSG in 2007. Pekka Forselius of Finland is the editor of this project, with Carol Dekkers of the USA and Jacky Takahashi of Japan as project co-editors. ISBSG will participate as an active category C liaison to ISO/IEC JTC1 SC7 and the working group responsible for the project as it moves forward.

Besides ISBSG, there are a number of organizations with information and resources about performance benchmarking including, but not limited to. At the end of this chapter the reader can find a list with valuable links to benchmarking organizations.

According to ISBSG, the projects registered in its application development and enhancement project database represent the top 25% of the software development industry. This is not surprising to note because when one considers that according to Professor Alain Abran at the University of Quebec at Montreal (speaking at the 2005 Software Measurement European Forum): *"only about 1% of the world's software developers do any form of measurement at all."* And it is our experience that those who do measure, typically only have project completion data as required by the ISBSG input questionnaire if they are at a repeatable and consistent process level where data is collected at least at the end of the project.

This should be carefully considered when using benchmarking results from other organizations. It is our recommendation that each organization should perform its own benchmarks in order to get realistic figures for one's own development environment.

11.1 Benchmarking Fundamentals

The first widespread industrial usage of benchmarking started with the efforts of Robert C. Camp of Xerox Corporation in the 1980s, who used benchmarking to discover best practices (as they are now called) to stay ahead of corporate competitors. The processes developed by Camp have been adapted by U.S. companies, and later worldwide in order to survive the strong competition in global markets. Xerox former CEO, David T. Kearns, stated (as quoted by Beth Enslow, American Programmer, 1992), *"Benchmarking is the continuous process of measuring products, services, and practices against the toughest competitors or those companies recognized as industry leaders."*

Camp recommended the following steps in the benchmarking process:

- Identify what should be benchmarked
- Identify candidate comparable organizations
- Define the method(s) of data collection
- Collect data
- Search for a deficit in performance
- Define the future performance goal(s)
- Communication of the results, marketing to gain acceptance

- Posting of goals for the benchmarking processes
- Development of action plans
- Target-oriented actions and control of progress
- Perform necessary adjustments.

There are a variety of definitions for benchmarking in general practice and in theory. The American Productivity and Quality Center (APQC) define benchmarking as follows:

Benchmarking is the process of identifying, sharing, and using knowledge and best practices. It focuses on how to improve any given business process by utilizing top-notch approaches rather than merely measuring the best performance. Finding, studying, and implementing best practices provide the greatest opportunity for gaining a strategic, operational, and financial advantage.

Benchmarking is always differentiated into internal and external benchmarking (see Fig. 11.2). *Internal benchmarking deals with comparing organizations or projects belonging to one's own enterprise.* External benchmarking deals with market-related comparisons to competitors in order to identify best practice processes.

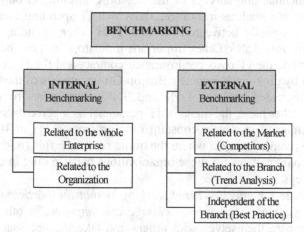

Fig. 11.2. Internal and external benchmarking

The most important consideration is that benchmarking can be seen as a continuous process (see Fig. 11.3) and not as a standalone, one-time only one action. When benchmarking is initiated for an organization, it should be performed on a continual basis so that organizational learning can be achieved through incremental successes.

Benchmarking is used by leading organizations to improve their corporate knowledge through systematic data analysis and an open discussion of project experiences.

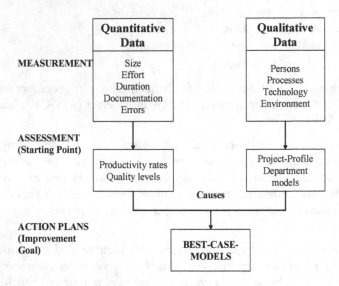

Fig. 11.3. Benchmarking model development

Annual benchmarking surveys of the Boston Consulting Group for specific industry segments, such as insurance, show that IT spending increases numbered 8–10% annually between 1996 and 2001 when spending dropped to an increase of only 3.2%. Other important indicators in these benchmarking "surveys" include the IT costs per insurance contract and the IT cost quota (IT costs divided by gross cash income). Boston Group surveys of the IT cost quotas showed increases between 1.6% and 3.4% every year from 1996 until 2001. On the other hand, the quota of IT personnel as a percentage of the total workforce remained relatively constant ranging from 6.3% to 10.8%. There was only one runaway project where the quota reached a full 16.9%. These are critical dashboard metrics for those organizations participating in these benchmarking surveys.

A prerequisite for effective benchmarking is that the participants (in particular, management) are eager to change and improve; in other words, to truthfully compare themselves with others and take the necessary actions to improve how they do business. As with all initiatives that cause change in the organization, the implementation of benchmarking needs support from senior management. *To succeed, benchmarking relies on the honest and fair play of all concerned, and this simply is not possible in all organizations.*

Benchmarking can provide the backdrop for setting ambitious, but realistic, improvement goals. And as our experience and that of others bears, when the staff involved in benchmarking actually participates in the goal definition, their overall motivation and efficiency increases. On this basis, the organization must focus on developing a learning organization whereby the ability to assimilate new ideas becomes an important concept. Naturally this precludes that the organization is open and receptive to change how it does business based on benchmarking data analysis.

The entire premise of benchmarking for organizational learning is undermined if there are hidden agendas that prevent the real data (i.e., truthful information) from coming forward. Data that are obscured for political or other reasons willderail even the best planned internal benchmarking initiatives and result in an exercise in futility and corporate "espionage" so to speak. Recall the saying "don't shoot the messenger"; this is especially true in measurement and bench-marking. It is critical to impress upon management that data simply reflects the status quo of the organization at a past point in time. It is like "crying over spilt milk"; the only suitable response to data that are not as good as anticipated is simply to ask "what does this mean?" and "what can we do about this to improve our performance in the future?"

Note: Carol Dekkers wrote a light-hearted back page article called "Tackling Software Measurement? Try Proverbs," in May 2005 issue of CrossTalk – the U.S. Department of Defense's Journal of Software Engineering. Visit http:// www.stsc.hill.af.mil/crosstalk/2005/05/0505backtalk.html to read the article.

The process of internal benchmarking can assist organizations to the following:

- Define more concrete goals
- Identify improvement opportunities
- Measure the efficiency of improvements
- Foster the continual improvement process (by tracking progress)
- Answer questions such as the following:

   1. How productive were our last (critical) projects?
   2. Which differences exist between measured departments or projects?
   3. What effect (if any) did a particular tool/action/strategy have on the productivity of our IT development, and quantitatively what was the impact (percent improvement or decrease)?
   4. Is our time to market getting shorter?
   5. Are effort and costs decreasing?
   6. How do we compare to other organizations? (this presents a glance towards external bench-marking).

11.2 Practical Benchmarking Experiences

Be cautious of two "trip-wires" (hidden hazards) when benchmarking:

   1. Presentation of data: When drawing conclusions from the data analysis, be sensitive to the damage hasty comparisons or evaluations can bring to an

organization just learning to digest criticism or highlighting its problems. As such, have someone else review your planned speeches or articles before you communicate your findings.

2. Do not lie with statistics – even if two numbers appear to be correlated, make sure that someone with statistical knowledge does the data analysis: Forget the game of trying to conjure up some brilliant presentation by fiddling with figures and metrics that are simply not related. From experience and Fred Brooks' *Mythical Man Month,* we know that 20 persons cannot finish in 5 months what 10 persons finished in 10 months. Perhaps the 20 person team can finish the work in 8 months (thus shortening the time to market by 20%), 60% more effort (20 persons × 8 months= 160 person months vs. 10 persons × 10 months = 100 person months). This is a simplified view; however, it is important to note that doubling the number of people (from 10 to 20) increases the error rate by sixfold. Other trip-wires regarding benchmarking are shown in Fig. 11.4.

Be Cautious with Benchmarking Data

✍ **Quality of the Metrics data?**
e. g. size of ERP-Systems like SAP
often only estimated roughly?

☞ **Function Point counts and units comparable?**
e.g., IFPUG 3.0...4.2, COSMIC, Mark II,
FiSMA, NESMA?

✍ **Time Accounting?** Calculation of Effort:
-hours, -days, -(person)months and -years comparable?

✍ **Effort?** including overtime? End user effort?

☞ **Duration?** Including stabilization (30 days postimplementation) phase?

✍ **Costs?** How are internal resource costs calculated? Does this
include all external staff? Consultants?

Fig. 11.4. "Trip-wires" when analyzing with benchmarking data

Experience gained from comparisons of benchmarking surveys from different providers shows that the quality of the metrics data used in the studies varied markedly. Before one can compare the results provided by different benchmarking providers, you must consider, for example, whether ERP (enterprise resource planning) systems (normally standard packaged software) are included in the comparison. If an ERP system is included by one provider and not another, your results will be different. In addition, the size of ERP systems is often estimated rather than measured.

There can also be questions about the units of measure or method(s) used by the various providers to arrive at the size of the software. In one situation, the benchmarking provider could not answer the question with which Function Point standard the size of the software was measured. They knew only that Function Points had been measured for the sample. Some benchmarking providers estimate only the size of software in principle or calculate it with backfiring. In a practical case, this lead to an application that was hand counted as 800 IFPUG 4.0 Function Points, being taken into the benchmarking survey with 90 Function Points since the provider principally calculated the function points with their own formula backfired from KSLOC (kilo (thousand) source lines of code).

Benchmarking with the Japanese organization of an international enterprise led to the recognition that the effort hours recorded in the benchmarking database had been entered based on the assumption of 8-person hour days, regardless of the common practice of entering more than 10 working hours per day. This difference in the core effort data made comparisons not possible in an exacting manner, but rather only by rough calculation with additional assumptions.

A common error in effort collection and recording (as mentioned in prior chapters) is when overtime is not measured or included in the project effort. While overtime may not be paid, those hours are still expended to produce the product and will skew estimates (which would not take into account necessary overtime) in the future. An opposite situation occurs when end user effort is included in the project postmortem analysis (which will skew future estimates when you want to estimate only the IT project team effort!).

An important question should always emerge when discussing work effort collection and recording: Was the staff encouraged to measure and report all actually worked hours? Some companies unconsciously "coerce" project teams to "hide" extra hours because they want all reported projects to appear on time and on budget, even if they were not. This is pure organizational schizophrenia: encouraging process improvement by way of measurement, then punishing the messenger when true hours are reported. This is the problem of honesty of person hours.

Also important is the point at which hours and costs are taken. It is critical to be consistent: is, for example, the stabilization phase after installation and release (e.g., a 30 day warranty period) included in the calculations or not?

Costs are often calculated based on internal charges per (development) person hour. They often vary widely in different organizations, besides which there are different cost structures for consultants. Sometimes we can only capture the effort of one's own personnel in support of the consultants in the calculations, and the costs for the consultancy itself are left out. Such exclusions are critical to be noted alongside any cost or effort figures for the project.

In one benchmarking survey, the provider had only a comparison sample size containing data of some organizations whose projects were all only one tenth of the size of the projects of the organization to be compared. Hence it was clear from the beginning that the benchmarking provider's data was of higher productivity (based on so much smaller projects). The downside in this whole situation was that the benchmarking provider did not tell the buyer of the benchmarking study the results about that difference.

Since such differences in data lead to comparison of apples to oranges, the used data must be questioned painstakingly. These examples also show that the choice of the benchmarking provider should also be performed with the same level of conscientiousness. Some benchmarking providers do not even tell the buyers which organizations belong to the comparison group for the benchmark. Remember the famous saying that has saved a thousand lawsuits: *"Trust, but verify!"*

For effective external benchmarking, only those organizations with similar processes can be used: the so called peer organizations. Regrettably, it is not easy to find peer organizations because either organizations are bound by legalities related to data distribution outside the corporation, or they are too scared to release data that could fall into the hands of competitors. Additionally, especially in the case of insurance companies, there is a culture of not wanting to admit that they even have data or that they would participate in benchmarking activities. In fact, some organizations are so paranoid about the marketplace judgment that they disallow their consultants from disclosing that they were ever contracted to provide expertise to the organization.

One of the tasks of an estimation competence center is to support the project leaders for efficient development of their IT projects. This includes delivery of knowledge about a variety of project metrics such as those found in the ISBSG research reports and products.

An international insurance company in Germany received the following results from an international request for information (RFI) about productivity measurement and benchmarking from 17 organizations:

Two organizations used internal benchmarking, five used external benchmarking, and three used a combination of internal and external benchmarking. Of the five organizations using external benchmarking, two relied on the ISBSG database and the resources of Compass Analysis, and one organization self-assessed themselves using the PEP method (performance enhancement program by Quantimetrics). Seven organizations did not use benchmarking at all.

11.3 Benchmarking Databases

A prerequisite for benchmarking is the availability of historic data. This need was recognized early in governmental and military companies in the USA. Valuable data collections were initiated by the US Space System Analysis Group (SSCAG) of the NASA (NASA Ames, end of 1970s; NASA/ SEL Dataset, 1997) and Department of Defense in the U.S. (Architecture Research Facility Dataset, 1979) as well as the Data and Analysis Center for Software (DACS, the Department of Defense (DoD) Software Information Clearinghouse, 1989).

11.3.1 Academic Comparison of Measurement Databases

At the 15th IWSM in Montreal, 2005, René Braungarten (a DASMA students' thesis award winner from 2004) et al. presented a study of a number of software metrics databases, including ISBSG and other important sources of data. His presentation summarizes the relevant literature and delivers a comparison of these databases, including the following:

- ESA/INSEAD Software Development Database
- FiSMA Experience Database (also called Laturi)
- NASA MDP Data Repository
- QSM Project Database
- T-Systems Nova MetricsDB System
- SPR Knowledge Database
- PSM Insight Database
- Ericsson Research Canada MMR.

Some of these databases are not available for public use. For the ESA/INSEAD, a European industrial database, some information could be gathered and presented with the following data as an example. Additionally we present some of the ISBSG published results.

11.3.2 The ESA/INSEAD Database

In 1988, the cost engineering department of the ESA (European Space Agency) started a software metric database to collect and measure effort and productivity data with the support of European military and industrial organizations. By the end of 1993, it was decided that INSEAD (Institut Européen d'Administration des Affaires in Fontainebleau, France, a renowned European Institute for Business Management) should take over the administration of the European database because of their status as a neutral third party. Since 1996, the data collection and dissemination of the results of this military and industrial projects has been performed by INSEAD. Both databases (ESA/INSEAD and SSCAG) were compared on a regular basis.

Up until the survey ceased in 2004, the data were collected by INSEAD with a three part, web-based questionnaire that solicited mandatory information about the deliverer, the project, and the values of the COCOMO cost drivers. For information about the final results of the research, contact Professor Kishore Sengupta (kishore.sengupta@insead.edu).

From 1995 to 2004, the ESA/INSEAD database collected project data from over 100 projects spanning more than 35 organizations across eight European countries. In 2003, there were 108 projects comprising 5.51 Million SLOCs (in the range from two until 413 KSLOCs with an average of 51,010 SLOCs) as well as 22 programming languages and 30,125 person months' effort (in the range of 7.8 until 4,361 with an average of 284).

- Each 39%, 30%, and 23% of the projects are from military environment, space administrations, or industry, respectively.
- 35% of the projects were developed with Ada, 11% in C, 8% in Fortran, 7% in Pascal, 7% in COBOL, and 5% in Assembler.
- 35% are from the UK, 28% from France, 15% from Italy, 7% from Germany, 6% from The Netherlands.

Person months are defined as 144 person hours, the effort is measured with person months, and the productivity is reported as SLOCs per person month.

The most interesting and reasonable approach to using the INSEAD data is to calculate and verify one's own productivity levels on several historical projects before comparing with the average of similar projects in the database. *It is critical to know the basic assumptions used in whatever database where you may want to compare your own projects*: for example, if you do not currently size your projects, it is folly to think that your data can be compared with the database at all.

Results of an investigation of the ESA/INSEAD database reveals that *the dominant reasons for differences and deviations in productivity across database projects are due to organizational variants*. The most reliable and consistent comparisons are based on the application system, the category (on board, message switching, real-time, ground support equipment, simulators, ground control, tool, other), and the programming language.

When using the data to do estimating, it was recognized that accurate estimates depend on the quality of the collected data and how similar they are to the project in question. Estimating in this way can be made with a modest number of historic data but only internally in an organization. When using external databases, ensure that the data are comparable and applicable to your type of development before publishing your estimates.

11.4 ISBSG and Its Products

While the International Software Benchmarking Standards Group (ISBSG) was already introduced as one of the important measurement organizations in the chapter about the Measurement Communities and Resources, its relevance in software benchmarking and estimating justifies further exposure here. As mentioned in this chapter, ISBSG started in 1994 as an informal consortium of national and international measurement organizations, and has since grown into the most significant not-for-profit benchmarking organizations in the world. The ISBSG is a not-for-profit organization that has established, grows, maintains, and exploits three repositories of IT history data to help improve the management of IT globally. Note: unless otherwise stated, when we refer generically to the ISBSG database or "ISBSG CD R(number)" we mean the ISBSG Application Development and Enhancement repository; the largest and most mature of the ISBSG data repositories.

11.4.1 Demographics of ISBSG Repositories

ISBSG supports and delivers a series of products, including guidance documents about benchmarking and project estimating, special analysis reports, benchmarking data, training materials, individual analysis of corporate projects, and, of course, the three project databases: application development and enhancement repository (at the time of this printing is in release 10 or r10), maintenance and support repository, and the package implementation and acquisition repository. There are also additional data repositories being planned, including a testing database.

The following figures from ISBSG demonstrate the worldwide demographic breakdown of the projects included in the r10 of the application development and enhancement database (ISBSG 2007). The other two current data repositories are still in their growth period; in the coming years products based on those repositories will likely be produced. Figure 11.5 displays a breakdown by the country of origin.

Figure 11.6 depicts the breakdown by business type included in the r10 of the application development and enhancement database (ISBSG 2007).

Figure 11.7 shows the type of projects included in the r10 of the application development and enhancement database (ISBSG 2007).

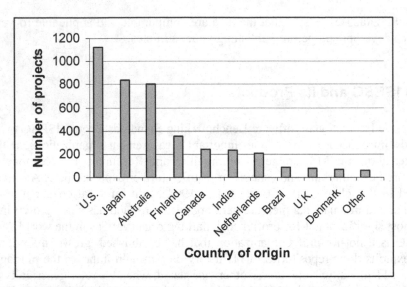

Fig. 11.5. ISBSG CD r10 demographics: projects by country of origin

If benchmarking or estimating are among the reasons for which you want to use ISBSG data, it is important to remember that the ISBSG believes that its projects represent higher productivity levels than the industry norms (ISBSG 2007).

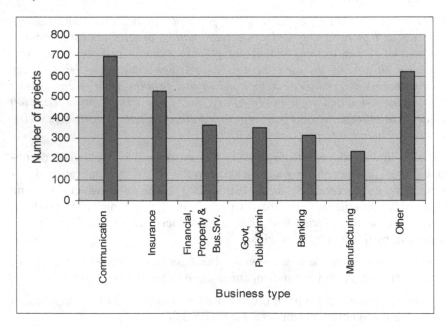

Fig. 11.6. ISBSG CD r10 projects by business type

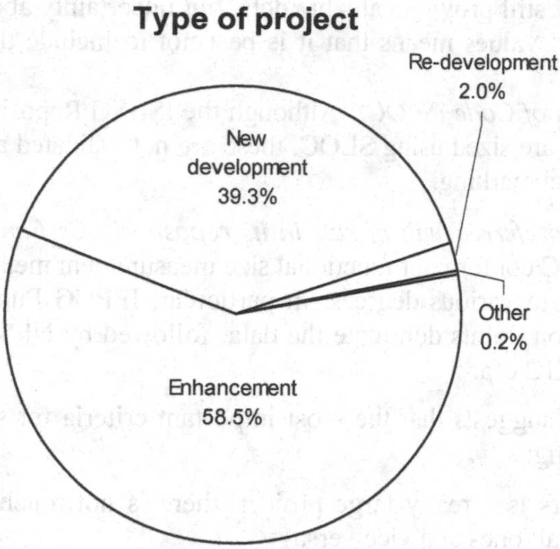

Type of project

Fig. 11.7. ISBSG CD r10 projects by project type

The reasons for this include the following: ISBSG data comes from the domains where FP are used fairly widely, but other industry sectors are severely under-represented; the data are a "convenience sample," (i.e., they are not a sample deliberately chosen to represent the IT industry); the projects are self-selected by their contributors, there is no knowledge of even how representative they are of the organizations that contributed them. ISBSG stresses that these considerations do not lessen the value of the data in the application development and enhancement repository. *Research conducted on the ISBSG sample confirms that the data are self-contained, internally consistent, and contain no apparent anomalies.*

Because of the diversity of the ISBSG projects, the following guidance is useful:

- *Functional sizing methods:* Do not mix pre-IFPUG V4 Function Point projects with V4 and post V4 (the sizing method changed with Version 4.0). New development projects sized using the NESMA standard can be included with IFPUG V4+ projects.
- *Normalized work effort figures:* Consideration should be given to the risks and gains involved in using normalized effort.
- *Work effort breakdown:* Projects with different effort levels should not be analyzed together. Effort level 1 means effort for the development team only; other effort levels include effort from other groups of people (such as support staff, customers, etc).
- *Project Rating:* The ISBSG considers that its projects with a data quality rating of "A" or "B" are suitable for statistical analysis. "C" and "D" rated

projects may still provide valuable data, but uncertainty about some of their size or effort values means that it is best not to include them in statistical analysis.

- *Source Lines of Code (SLOC):* Although the ISBSG Repository does include projects that are sized using SLOC, these are not validated and should not be used for benchmarking.

The ISBSG preferred unit of size in its repositories is Function Points, and the five ISO/IEC conformant functional size measurement methods (FSMM) are all represented to various degrees. In particular, IFPUG Function Points and FiSMA Function Points dominate the data, followed by NESMA FP, Mark II FP, and COSMIC cfp.

The ISBSG suggests that the most important criteria for selecting projects are the following:

- *Size* (if yours is a really large project, there is not much value to you in studying small ones and vice versa)
- *Primary programming language* or *Language type* (e.g., 3GL, 4GL)
- *Development platform* (mainframe, midrange, or PC)
- *Development type* (new development, enhancement or redevelopment)
- Organization type (e.g., Aerospace, Banking, Communications, Construction, Energy, Insurance, Manufacturing, Public Administration, etc.)
- Other criteria that may be important are *Business area type, Application type, User base,* and *Development techniques.*

42 ISBSG Prodcts

The following products are currently available from the ISBSG (www.isbsg.org) or any ISBSG member:

- Corporate and individual subscriptions
- Special analysis reports (see www.isbsg.org for up-to-date listing)
- Project benchmarking service
- Organizational benchmarking service
- "The benchmark" publications: current release, The Benchmark r10 (2008)
- The Data CD for the application development and enhancement repository (currently in release 10 with a new release approximately every 18 months). The CD also contains an additional tool: *the early estimate checker (version 5.0).*
- *Practical Project Estimation, 2nd edition,* 2005 (book)
- *The Software Metrics Compendium,* 2002 (book)
- Estimation course material (available to members)
- Data available for research.

The actual data disc with the repository data with 4,106 projects (release 10 issued in 2007) together with publications and membership can be ordered from the ISBSG homepage at www.isbsg.org. The ISBSG Maintenance and Support database comprises 110 projects (2006).

Table 11.1. The growth of the ISBSG application development and enhancement repository

Data CD release number	Date available	Number of projects
Release 4	April 1997	396
Release 5	March 1998	451
Release 6	April 2000	789
The Software Metrics Compendium (there was no release 7)	June 2002	1,238
Release 8	February 2003	2,040
Release 9	November 2004	3,082
Release 10	2007	4,106

Table 11.1 shows the development of the ISBSG database since release 4 in 1997. It also shows the growth of repository since the volume of more than 2,000 projects from 16 countries increased by more than 50%; as of release 10, there are 4,106 projects in the ISBSG database.

Organizations that want to participate in the benchmarks can submit completed projects using the data collection form from Useful Documentation on the homepage of the ISBSG (http://www.isbsg.org). In exchange for submitting a project to the ISBSG, the participating organization receives a report with the comparison of their project(s) to equal projects from the database, as well as a note regarding the quality of their data submission.

The following results from *The Benchmark* are presented in order to show the benefits of the participation in such an international benchmarking. Some further results are presented in the chapter *Software Metrics –Process Metrics*.

The aim of the benchmarking research (see Fig. 11.7) is to aid organizations to adopt more efficient software development practices. Thus, the data collection is organized in sections, showing the IT projects from different points of view. These include, for example, the following:

- Research about project size and effort
- Research about development productivity
- Research about productivity on different development platforms (mainframe, midrange and PC)
- Comparison of development platforms
- Others.

In the following sections, the results of the ISBSG analyses are presented.

4 Project Characteristics

The ISBSG application development and enhancement repository has changed over the years based on the composition of included projects. This subsection provides tables to show how the database composition has changed to the current release.

Programming Language

COBOL remains the most common of the programming languages (see Table 11.2).

Table 11.2. Programming language

Programming language	Release 4 (%)	Release 5 (%)	Release 6 (%)	The SW metrics compendium (%)	Release 8 (%)	Release 10 (%)
COBOL or COBOL II	44	29	27	24	27	17
Visual basic	5	2	6	7	7	9
JAVA						8
PL/I	14	9	6	5	5	6
C++		1	4	5	17	6
SQL	8	6	6	7	6	3
Natural	15	15	9	7	5	2
Oracle	3	2	5	6	7	4

Programming Language Generations

The large number of programming languages made it more difficult to compare the different projects. Hence, Table 11.3 tries to categorize the programming languages into third and fourth generation as well as generators.

Table 11.3. Programming language generations

Generation	Release 4 (%)	Release 5 (%)	Release 6 (%)	The SW metrics compendium (%)	Release 8 (%)	Release 10 (%)
3GL	46	44	45	51	64	61
4GL	38	47	46	33	30	35
Generator	16	9	9	5	5	4

Development Platform

Most of the projects were developed on mainframes according to the following Table 11.4, with decrease, whereas the percentage of development on PCs increased.

Table 11.4. Development platforms

Platform	Release 4 (%)	Release 5 (%)	Release 6 (%)	The SW metrics compendium (%)	Release 8 (%)	Release 10 (%)
Mainframe	68	69	62	43	60	43
Midrange	19	16	22	19	17	13
PC	7	15	16	17	23	20
Multi						24

Methods

More than half of the projects were developed with in-house methods. In The Software Metrics Compendium report, 21% used a bought (and maybe adapted) method for system development. Release 10 reports that 30% of projects that say anything about techniques report using a waterfall model, but give no further details of techniques used. Of those projects that do describe particular techniques being used, traditional system modeling techniques are used in 57% of them. They are the only techniques listed in 30% of projects; 27% use a combination of traditional modeling and other techniques. The most frequently used development techniques are displayed in Table 11.5.

Table 11.5. Development techniques

Development technique	Release 6 (%)	The SW metrics compendium (%)	Release 8 (%)	Release 10 (%)
Data modeling	64	59	42	36
Event modeling	11	12	8	6
Process modeling	40	38	28	28
Joint application development (JAD)	20	18	12	13
Business area modeling	16	17	10	8
Prototyping	30	29	17	18
Joint application development (JAD)	20	18	12	13
Rapid application development (RAD)	11	14	9	8
Regression tests	20	21	16	22
Multifunctional teams	23	19	12	9
Time boxing	5	3	4	5
OOA	8	10	10	15
OOD	11	13	8	11

Project Size

Project size in the ISBSG databases is predominantly measured in units of functional size, with a negligible number recorded using SLOC. As of the latest release of the repository, the four main Function Point counting approaches represented are IFPUG, COSMIC, FiSMA, and NESMA. Mark II and Feature Points are also featured; however, there are so few such projects (with no new ones contributed for a number of years).

IFPUG projects dominate; however, the numbers of COSMIC, FiSMA, and NESMA projects are steadily increasing.

Conversion factors based on comparisons of the United Kingdom Software Measurement Association (UKSMA) for their projects delivered to the ISBSG database are (no R^2 given) as follows:

$$IFPUG_{3.0\ FP} = 41.4 + 0.77 \times Mark\ II\ FP,$$

$$Mark\ II\ FP = 20.3 + 1.25 \times IFPUG_{3.0\ FP}.$$

Since comparable figures must be adequate (remember to ensure that you are comparing apples to apples), be careful not to use IFPUG 3.0 conversion rates when you are using IFPUG FP 4 or higher standard.

Most of the projects in the ISBSG database have a size of less than 2,000 Function Points. The project size varies and ranges up to 5,000 Function Points for new developments. Some of the projects appear to be very small indeed but there is no common opinion in the IT industry telling at which size a project is too small to be measured in Function Points. It is our experience that projects that are less than 100 FP in size can be unreliable due to the following:

1. Lack of data rigor: projects that are smaller than 100 FP are generally less than 6 person months of effort, and may over represent the amount of project management, learning, and hybrid mixtures of work effort
2. When one views the scatter plots of speed of delivery (FP per person month) and project size (in FP), projects under 100 FP are more volatile and less within the statistical process control of other projects (i.e., those less than 100 FP appear to be very over- or under-productive regardless of the technology used).

John Moses and Malcolm Farrow report from a statistical analysis that Function Points do influence the development effort, together with maximum team size, up to 60% and adding programming language up to 62%. But opposite to other investigations they cannot find any relevant influence of the development platform that they can definitively quantify.

Functional Mix for New Development Projects

Practical Project Estimation, 2nd edition, one of the major contributors of which was the American author of this book, was published in 2005 based on the ISBSG application development and enhancement CD release 9. For IFPUG 4.0 projects that were new development in the database, the following functional

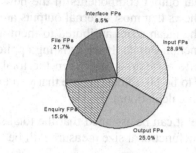

Source: Estimating, Benchmarking & Research Suite Release 9
[209 projects - FPA METHOD: IFPUG 4]

Fig. 11.8. Functional mix for new development projects

mix diagram was presented (see Fig. 11.8, Source: Estimating, Benchmarking & Research Suite release 9 [209 projects – FPA METHOD: IFPUG 4])

If one has to estimate the functional size of a software development project, the relationships of Fig. 11.8 can be used as a rough guideline.

The following examples are taken from Practical Project Estimation, 2nd edition (page 33):

Example 1: If the customer has identified a need and, on developing a logical data model to reflect that need, there are found to be 40 "logical entities," it may be reasonably assumed that these relate to approximately 40 Internal Logical Files (ILFs).

Analysis of the ISBSG Repository also shows that most ILFs in applications are rated as being "low" to "medium" in complexity. The mean score attributed to them across all projects is 8.6 Function Points.

Based upon the above, it can be assumed that the total score for the ILFs component of the Function Point count will be

40 (ILFs) × 8.6 (mean score for ILFs) = 344 FPs.

From the above pie chart (Fig. 11.8) it can be seen that the ILFs component of the Function Point count is typically around 21.7%. On this basis the total functional size of the required application is predicted to be around

FP size = 296 FPs × 100/21.7 = 1,585 FPs.

If the development project is to replace an existing application or deliver similar user functionality to another application, then you may use some of the measures of components from these other applications as a guide.

Example 2: The number of unique reports and extract files output from the existing application which the project is to replace can be assumed to be equivalent to the external output components in the new project. Analysis of the ISBSG Repository shows that most external outputs are rated as being "medium" in complexity. The mean score attributed to them across all projects in the repository is 5.4 Function Points. If the existing application has 47 different reports and three different extract files then the total number of external outputs can be assumed to be 50. (Note: ensure that you exclude any obsolete, unused reports from your calculations).

Based upon the above, it can be assumed that the total score for the external outputs component of the functional size measure will be

50 (EOs) × 5.4 (mean score for external outputs) = 270 FPs.

From Fig. 11.8, it can be seen that the external output component of the functional size measure is typically around 25%. On this basis, the total functional size for the required application is predicted to be around

FP size = 270 FPs × 100/25 = 1,080 FPs.

Warning: Whether the above quick predictive technique is used or a detailed Function Point count is performed to establish size to be used for an early cost indicator for the project, a contingency of 20–30% should be added to allow for functionality not apparent early in the life cycle. Historical data indicates that this scope creep typically occurs as a result of additional functionality being identified as user requirements evolve in subsequent development phases.

Note: The techniques discussed above are valid only if your application or development project is loosely coupled from other applications and fits the profile of projects currently in the ISBSG Repository. Early research indicates that the above relationships may not hold for the domains of real-time, control, scientific, or embedded software.

The technique above can be used ONLY for very rough estimation or extremely quick benchmarking. However, when one has enough similar functional mix data from own, different types of projects, the accuracy improves radically. The next chapters will introduce results from two older researches discussing about geographical differences in functional mix.

Regional Distribution

Table 11.6 shows the regional distribution as of release 5 for average Function Point components of new developments. The software metrics compendium and all further releases of the Benchmark do not contain this analysis, although it could be done using the raw data. The analysis of release 5 (for

Table 11.6. Regional distribution of average Function Point components of new developments

Function Point component	ASEAN	Europe	North America	Total
External inputs (EI)	4.0	4.2	4.9	4.3
External outputs (EO)	5.6	4.9	5.2	5.4
External inquiries (EQ)	3.9	3.8	3.8	3.8
Internal logical files (ILF)	7.4	7.2	7.6	7.4
External logical files (EIF)	5.6	5.3	5.5	5.5
Number of projects	116	32	90	238

which results are shown in Table 11.6) proved that geographic region was not a differentiator for software composition (by function point component) and thus, the analysis was discontinued.

The most important concept to remember from Table 11.6 is that the distribution of functional components has no significant difference regardless of the geographic locale. This reinforces that functional size measurement can work equally well and provide necessary support for software and systems development *worldwide, regardless of where the development or measurement takes place!*

In the IT department of an international insurance company in Germany, the same research was conducted based on internal Function Point project counts in order to improve the precision of functional size estimates for IT projects. The results of these investigations resemble the ISBSG breakdown as shown in Fig. 11.8.

The second topic for analysis is the ratio of the FP attributed to transactions compared to the FP attributed to ILFs. Normally one would expect the "one file model" profile. The one file model presumes that for each ILF of average complexity (10 uFP), there will be an AUDIO set of transactional functions associated with maintenance of the entity:

A = add (assume an average EI = 4 uFP)
U = update (assume an average EI = 4 uFP)
D = delete (assume an average EI = 4 uFP)
I = inquiry (assume an average EQ = 4 uFP)
O = output (assume an average EO = 5 uFP).

This one file model assumes that for each ILF (persistent maintained entity), there would typically be three EI (add, change, delete), one report EO, and 1 browsing EQ.

While this model is a much simplified shortcut, it allows a plausibility check of the Function Point counts. Based on the analysis of the prior version of the ISBSG database (release 5; see Table 11.7), we see a rough analysis of the geographic breakdown of projects. (This was the most recent geographic breakdown of this type).

Table 11.7. Ratios of Function Point components by geographic location

Ratio	ASEAN	Europe	North America	Total
EI/file	2.6	3.8	0.9	2.9
EO/file	1.1	2.6	1.9	1.5
EQ/file	0.9	1.9	1.3	1.1
Number of projects	116	32	90	238

Furthermore, this research assists the practical application of Function Points. It is sometimes difficult to determine all of the functional transactions, especially where there is an absence of up-to-date user documentation or a legacy application involved. It is much easier to find the logical files (persistent data stores), which are used by an application. Once found, the number of FP in the application can be estimated using the functional mix profiles (percentages of each type) or from one file models. An estimate of application software size is thus possible at an early phase of the project, with less effort (and also less precision) long before a proper Function Point count can be performed.

Effort by Level

Work effort hours are reported in ISBSG in units of person hours (PH). Effort figures are categorized into four levels as presented in Table 11.8.

Note that projects recorded in the ISBSG database are predominantly containing data from Level 1: IT project development team work effort.

Table 11.8. ISBSG levels for measured effort

Level	Who is included in Effort
Level 1: IT development team (core team)	Project team + project management + project administration
Level 2: Core team and supporting team	Level 1 + database administration + data administration + quality assurance + data security
Level 3: Stage 2 and computing center support	Level 2 + software support + hardware support + helpdesk support
Level 4: Stage 3 and end user support	Level 3 + end user support

Number of projects and effort for each of the levels of Table 11.8 are given in Table 11.9.

Table 11.9. Number and proportion of projects by level of measured effort

ISBSG database Projects	The SW metrics compendium Number of projects	Proportion (%)
Level 1	688	56
Level 2	240	19
Level 3	19	1
Level 4	291	24
Summary (total)	1,238	100

How do you use these tables in benchmarking? It is probably important to decide the level of effort data that your organization collects before commencing data collection. Also, it is recommended that your organization collect work effort data at a detailed enough level that you can split it to any lower level at a future point in time. That is, if you have the data collected separately for each level, it is advisable to store the data in that form rather than simply recording it at the summary or total level.

Alain Abran et al. (Estimation Models based on Functional Profiles) presented on the IWSM/MetriKon 2004 a study of size/effort relations by programming languages from 236 projects from the ISBSG database (release 8) having high quality data. Their regression analyses results are presented in Table 11.10.

Table 11.10. Effort and size relationships for COBOL, NATURAL, and C

Language	N	Effort (hours), FP = IFPUG 4.1	R^2
COBOL	136	Effort = 9.6 × FP + 2,110.1	0.52
Natural	67	Effort = 11.4 × FP − 922.8	0.84
C	33	Effort = 8.9 × FP + 1,388.1	0.58

Note: The reader should be aware of the poor (i.e., too low) R^2 coefficients for COBOL and C. In other industries such as medicine, tests showing $R^2 > 0.75$ are considered to be reliable, whereas $R^2 < 0.5$ is almost regarded as being contraindicated. The authors do not endorse, but rather simply present these findings for the information of the reader.

Detailed research showed that for the three samples of Table 11.10, the relationship is very strong only for both external input functions (EI, $R^2 > 0.72$) and external output functions (EO, $R^2 > 0.77$).

Effort per Project Phase

The work effort breakdown for development team effort (only) for new development projects is different from enhancement projects. The following figures are from the ISBSG Special Report: Planning projects – project phase ratios: new development (see Fig. 11.8) and enhancements (see Fig. 11.9).

Phase Ratios - New Developments

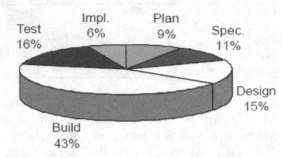

Fig. 11.9. Project team effort ratios for new development projects with six phases recorded (ISBSG 2007)

In earlier versions of the database (pre-2007), there were five phases used in the ISBSG products: planning, specification, programming, test, and installation. With the newest release CD r10 in 2007, the specification phase has now been broken out into its own phase to permit researchers and professionals with a more granular level of data analysis.

Organizations participating (submitting data) to ISBSG typically follow the submission guidelines (submit effort data by phase); however, many organizations may have only collected their data at a higher (summary) level and cannot break it down into its component phases after the fact. Note that the overall effort across five or six phases of software development makes no difference, but you need to ensure that your organization compares itself to a similar organization and the phase breakdowns if you want to achieve good benchmark comparisons.

The following charts are taken from the ISBSG Special Analysis Report: Planning projects – project phase ratios (March 2007. www.isbsg.org), based on a subset of ISBSG projects (see Figs. 11.9 and 11.10). All these project phase ratios can be used as percentage methods.

Even though the measurement methods and work effort stages of individual organizations differ, the results for new development or for enhancement are nearly identical across organizations. *For example, for new development projects:*

- the effort for planning/specification is about 30% (almost 1/3),
- the effort for programming and test is about 60% (nearly 2/3), and
- the effort for installation of the completed software product about 10% of the overall project effort.

Phase Ratios - Enhancements

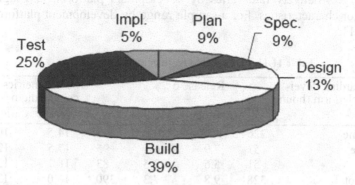

Fig. 11.10. Project team effort ratios for enhancement projects with six phases recorded (ISBSG 2007)

Research involving the different stages of the measured effort was published in the ISBSG compendium, revealing that the effort of the core project team (stage 1) accounted for 75% of the total project effort (including across all stages).

The ISBSG analysis results provide hints for the proportions (effort ratios) of phases in the percentage method for estimation, especially in the absence of one's own organizational data. In any regard, remember that figures obtained from one's own history and one's own organizational environment are always more reliable and more predictable of future performance than theoretical models.

Project Delivery Rate (PDR)

The project delivery rate (PDR) is measured in hours per Function Point (h/FP). The PDR is the main metric for speed of delivery that emerges from analysis of the ISBSG repository. The PDR tells us how many hours are necessary to elaborate one Function Point. That is, *the higher the PDR, the less is the productivity.* The productivity in *Function Points per person month* can easily be calculated from the PDR by dividing 120 (net hours per person month) by the PDR:

$$\text{Productivity} = 120/\text{PDR}.$$

The PDR is also a measure for the efficiency of the IT development, since the less hours are necessary for elaborating a Function Point, the more efficient is the IT development environment.

The project delivery rate varies by development platform, language, and other major characteristics. For a sample range by development platform, see Table 11.11.

Table 11.11. PDRs regarding development platforms

PDR regarding development platform (hours per FP)	Release 6			The SW metrics compendium		
	N	Average	Median	N	Average	Median
Mainframe	226	11.2	9.0	212	14.5	10.7
Midrange	51	7.9	6.1	95	17.5	12.1
PC	51	5.6	3.5	83	18.1	12.8
Overall total	328	9.8	7.3	390	16.0	12.0

N number of projects

Newer repository analysis reports that the mainframe projects have a 1.2 months longer duration on average, whereas midrange projects have 0.8 months average less duration and PC projects 2 months less.

The "Benchmark" releases 6 and 7 (analysis of the databases) deliver figures for PDR related to programming language by development platform. Table 11.12 shows an excerpt of some of the findings.

The PDR average overall for all projects contained in the Repository release 6 is 8 h per Function Point, and considers only the effort of the IT core team (stage 1). When end user effort (and other IT related effort) is added in stage 4, the PDR average increases to 9.5 h per Function Point.

When we harmonize (throw all projects of all organizations, all platforms and all programming languages together) and average the PDR across the release 6 overall repository, the result is a PDR of 9–10 h per FP. In The Software Metrics Compendium, it is reported to be more likely 15–16 h per Function Points.

One question that your organization should be asking before using the ISBSG database and research reports is how do you use the tables above (and those similar to it) for benchmarking? Perhaps you may wish to compare your own figures against them? What kind of decisions can you make? Remember that sustainable measurement relies on a Goal/Question/Metric approach as examined elsewhere in this book.

Table 11.12. PDRs by programming language and platform

Programming Language	Release 6 (mainframe only)			The SW metrics compendium (all platforms)		
	N	Average	Median	N	Average	Median
ABAP				5	15.5	13.8
Access (R. 6 only PC)	21	1.7	1.8	28	3.3	2.0
C (R. 6 only mid-range and PC)	12	15.0	10.3	27	15.6	14.9
COBOL	70	13.3	11.8	64	20.1	16.0
COBOL II	18	16.1	16.7	32	17.0	13.8
EASYTRIEVE	9	11.5	10.8	8	12.9	13.0
IDEAL	4	7.3	6.8			
JAVA				10	26.8	19.6
NATURAL	41	7.3	6.6	21	12.7	9.6
Oracle (R. 6 only midrange and PC)	11	4.2	3.3	49	13.4	10.3
PL/I	22	7.1	5.5	8	15.9	13.6
SQL (R. 6 only mid-range and PC)	13	6.1	6.5	56	16.9	13.6
TELON	11	11.7	8.6	7	14.6	10.9
VISUAL BASIC	4	8.1	7.3	54	13.3	7.5
Other 4GL	20	12.6	10.0	10	12.1	8.4
Program Generators	8	13.7	5.3			
All (R. 6 only mainframe)	207	10.9	8.9	379	15.0	11.9

N number of projects

Project Duration

The PDR is not the only measure of development efficiency. Project duration (in months) is a measure for the elapsed time between the start and the end of a project. Duration is often called the "time to market" and its significance can be major for many organizations, especially those in innovative competitive industries (e.g., cell phone communication software). ISBSG reported in 2002: *Only 10 of 267 projects lasted longer than 30 months. Project duration was mostly 3, 6, or 12 months.*

Another accumulation of projects was found with 4, 7, or 8 months duration. The Software Metrics Compendium delivered the following results from 412 projects: m*ost projects lasted 2 or 8 months (with equal frequency). Only 15% of the repository project took longer than 12 months.*

Two years later in 2004 (release 8), the average project duration decreased by 30% from 11 to 8 months for projects completed since 1996.

The Software Metrics Compendium gives further results for duration of the 412 projects regarding size and effort as displayed in following two Tables 11.13 and 11.14.

Table 11.13. Project duration and its relationship to functional Size (ISBSG 2002)

Size (function points)	Project duration
Less than 300 FPs	1–6 months with productivity of 40–60 FPs per month (very high productivity)
Between 300 and 800 FPs	Range from 5 to 11 months, average = 8 months
Between 800 and 1,400 FPs	Range from 10 to 18 months, average = 12–14 months
Greater than 1,400 FPs	Typically took a minimum of 12 months, on average 18 months (note that this represents a sample size of only 7% of the projects)

Table 11.14. Project duration dependent on effort (ISBSG 2002)

Work effort (Level 1, project team effort)	Project duration
Less than 800 h •	Duration increases with effort. Average is 1 month per 100–200 h effort.
800–2,000 h	3–7 months, on average 5 months
2,000–3,200 h	4–9 months, on average 7 months
3,200–20,000 h	8–12 months, on average 10 months
Greater than 20,000 h	Typically minimum of 14 months, on average 24 months

The chapter *Product- and Process Metrics* contains further regression formulae from The Software Metrics Compendium as compared with formulae from other investigations.

Team Size

The effects of team size have been investigated with eagerness in the ISBSG analyses. When only the development platform was considered, the result was predictable: the larger the project team, the lower the productivity. This is understandable because the need for communication increases directly with increases in team size. During the project, the need for effective communication is continuous between groups and departments, and this results in a lowering of productivity when more persons are involved. The following results were reported in the Software Metrics Compendium (518 projects):

Dividing the project size by team size produces a metric of Function Points per person. Up until a team size of three people, the average responsibility ranges from 115 to 190 FPs per person in a project, with the median being 80–120 FPs per person. *Teams with more than two persons on average up to three persons are responsible for the highest ratios of FPs per person.* The Software Metrics Compendium averages are displayed in Table 11.15.

Table 11.15. Function Point responsibility per person in relation to team size

Maximum team size	Function point responsibility per person
4	60–100
5 to 9	35–70
More than 10	20–50

The Software Metrics Compendium shows that for projects with a size of more than 3,000 FPs, team size is typically between 30 and 50 persons, with PDRs of 20–40 h per FP. This translates into a productivity of 3–4 FP per person month.

Furthermore, The Software Metrics Compendium delivers the following regression formulae for the PDR (project delivery rate), with maximum team size (mTS):

- All platforms (375 projects): PDR = $2.96 \times mTS^{0.636}$, with $R^2 = 0.297$
- Mainframe (105 projects): PDR = $4.40 \times mTS^{0.382}$, with $R^2 = 0.109$
- Midrange (79 projects): PDR = $2.66 \times mTS^{0.655}$, with $R^2 = 0.292$
- PC (65 projects): PDR = $1.57 \times mTS^{0.853}$, with $R^2 = 0.324$

The reader should carefully regard the poor (i.e., too low) regression coefficients for the formulae. As noted previously, in other industries such as medicine, tests that show an $R^2 > 0.75$ are supposed to be reliable, whereas $R^2 < 0.5$ is almost regarded as being contraindicated. We do not endorse, but rather simply present these findings for the information of the reader.

44 Further Results of the ISBSG Research

The main result of ISBSG research is that the programming language is the most influential factor for the PDR (The Benchmark r6, p. 52). After platform and language, only team size and organization type are significant (The Benchmark r6, p. 61).

In summary, the ISBSG research, and in particular, the Compendium and other comprehensive repository analyses, delivers a rich treasure of metrics about system development for the practitioner and researcher alike.

Internet Links to Benchmarking Organiations

Many other organizations may be available using links from the websites listed below (Table 11.16). Typically, Benchmarking organizations provide information and links to further benchmarking-relevant URLs. Note. as of this

Table 11.16. Internet links to benchmarking organizations

Organization	Url
The APQC (The American Productivity & Quality Center	http://www.apqc.org/portal/apqc/site?path=root
Benchmarking Center Middle East (BCME)	http://www.ameinfo.com/news/Company_News/B/BCME/index.html
The Benchmarking Center	http://www.benchmarking.co.uk/content.html
Cutter Benchmarking Review (Journal available by subscription)	http://www.cutter.com/content-and-analysis/journals-and-reports/cutter-benchmark-review.html
The Finnish Software Measurement Association (FiSMA) online databases (for members)	http://www.fisma.fi/in-english/methods/
Gartner Worldwide IT Benchmark Data Exchange	http://www.gartner.com/surveys
Germany: Deutsches Benchmarking Zentrum	http://www.benchmarkingforum.de
Greek Benchmarking Centre	http://www.urenio.org/benchmark/center.html
The Hong Kong Benchmarking Clearinghouse	http://www.hbc.hk/
Integrated Software Industry Benchmarking Association™	http://www.isiba.com/
The IT Metrics and Productivity Institute (ITMPI)	http://www.itmpi.org/
The NASA Benchmarking Clearinghouse at Kennedy Space Center	http://benchmarking.ksc.nasa.gov/KBC/kscbnchmrk.htm
Slovak Benchmarking Information Centre (SBIC)	http://www.sbic.sk/en/
The Software Engineering Institute (SEI) software engineering measurement and analysis (SEMA) and Software Engineering Information Repository (SEIR)	https://seir.sei.cmu.edu/seir/

printing, all links were active and valid. *Note: all websites were operational at the time of this printing.*

Management Summary

Metrics are ideally suited for comparing IT projects and learning by comparison.

The main question of benchmarking is how we can learn from other organizations in order to improve our own organization.

Only about 1% of the world's software developers do any form of measurement at all.

Benchmarking is the process of identifying, sharing, and using knowledge and best practices. It focuses on how to improve any given business process by utilizing top-notch approaches rather than merely measuring the best performance. Finding, studying, and implementing best practices provide the greatest opportunity for gaining a strategic, operational and financial advantage.

The most important consideration is that benchmarking be seen as a continuous process and not as a standalone, one-time only one action. When benchmarking is initiated for an organization, it should be performed on a continual basis so that organizational learning can be achieved through incremental successes.

Benchmarking is used by leading organizations to improve their corporate knowledge through systematic data analysis and an open discussion of project experiences.

A prerequisite for effective benchmarking is that the participants (in particular, management) are eager to change and improve; in other words, to truthfully compare themselves with others and take the necessary actions to improve how they do business. As with all initiatives that cause change in the organization, the implementation of benchmarking needs support from senior management. To succeed, benchmarking relies on the honest and fair play of all concerned, and this simply is not possible in all organizations

When drawing conclusions from the data analysis, be sensitive to the damage hasty comparisons or evaluations can bring to an organization just learning to digest criticism or highlighting of its problems.

Do not lie with statistics – even if two numbers appear to be correlated, make sure that someone with statistical knowledge does the data analysis. Forget the game of trying to conjure up some brilliant presentation by fiddling with figures and metrics that are simply not related.

For effective external benchmarking, only those organizations with similar processes can be used: the so called peer organizations.

One of the tasks of an estimation competence center is to support the project leaders for efficient development of their IT projects. This includes delivery of knowledge about a variety of project metrics such as those found in the ISBSG research reports and products.

A prerequisite for benchmarking is the availability of historic data.

The most interesting and reasonable approach to using the INSEAD data is to calculate and verify one's own productivity levels on several historical projects before comparing with the average of similar projects in the database.

When using external databases, ensure that the data are comparable and applicable to your type of development before publishing your estimates.

ISBSG supports and delivers a series of products, including guidance documents about benchmarking and project estimating, special analysis reports, benchmarking data, training materials, individual analysis of corporate projects.

Research conducted on the ISBSG sample confirms that the data are self-contained, internally consistent, and contain no apparent anomalies.

The ISBSG preferred unit of size in is repositories is Function Points, and the five ISO/IEC conformant functional size measurement methods (FSMM) are all represented to various degrees.

The aim of the benchmarking research is to aid organizations to adopt more efficient software development practices.

Project size in the ISBSG databases is predominantly measured in units of functional size, with a negligible number recorded using SLOC.

Most of the projects in the ISBSG database have a size of less than 2,000 Function Points.

Functional size measurement can work equally well and provide necessary support for software and systems development worldwide, regardless of where the development or measurement takes place!

It is recommended that your organization collect work effort data at a detailed enough level that you can split it to any lower level at a future point in time.

The work effort breakdown for development team effort (only) for new development projects is different from enhancement projects.

For example, for new development projects, the effort for planning/ specification is about 30% (almost 1/3), the effort for programming and test is about 60% (nearly 2/3), and the effort for installation of the completed software product about 10% of the overall project effort.

Research involving the different stages of the measured effort was published in the ISBSG compendium, revealing that the effort of the core project team (stage 1) accounted for 75% of the total project effort (including across all stages).

The PDR is measured in hours per Function Point (h/FP). The PDR as the main measure for speed of delivery is one of the main metrics that emerges from analysis of the ISBSG repository.

The PDR tells us how many hours are necessary to elaborate one Function Point. That is, the higher the PDR, the less is the productivity.

The PDR average overall for all projects contained in the Repository release 6 is 8 h per Function Point and considers only the effort of the IT core team (stage 1).

When we harmonize (throw all projects of all organizations, all platforms, and all programming languages together) and average the PDR across the release 6 overall repository, the result is a PDR of 9–10 h per FP.

Project duration (in months) is a measure for the elapsed time between the start and the end of a project. Duration is often called the time to market.

The effects of team size have been investigated with eagerness in the ISBSG analyses. When only the development platform was considered, the result was predictable: the larger the project team, the lower the productivity.

Teams with more than two persons on average up to three persons are responsible for the highest ratios of FPs per person.

The Software Metrics Compendium shows that for projects with a size of more than 3,000, FPs team size is typically between 30 and 50 persons with PDRs of 20–40 h per FP. This translates into a productivity of 3–4 FP per person month.

The main result of ISBSG research is that the programming language is the most influential factor for the PDR. After platform and language, only team size and organization type are significant.

In summary, the ISBSG research, and in particular, the Compendium and other comprehensive repository analyses, delivers a rich treasure of metrics about system development for the practitioner and researcher alike.

12 The IFPUG Function Point Counting Method

The IFPUG (International Function Point Users Group) Function Point Method (FPM) is a method to measure the (functional) size of software from the user perspective (depicted in Fig. 12.1).

Functional size is defined (according to ISO/IEC 14143-1:2007 Software and Systems Engineering – Software measurement – Functional size measurement – Definitions of concepts) as: "a size of the software derived by quantifying the Functional User Requirements," where the *Functional user requirements* (FUR) are in turn defined as a subset of the User Requirements. Requirements that describe what the software shall do in terms of tasks and services.

As an ISO/IEC conformant Functional Size Measurement (FSM) method, the IFPUG FPM measures the functionality in software delivered to the user as required by the user, and quantified by following the IFPUG Counting Practices Manual (CPM) set of counting rules. Note that functional size is purely the unadjusted function point size as outlined in the following paragraphs.

The term *user* is not defined strictly as a person or end-user, but rather as any person, thing, other application, hardware, or software that needs to interact (send to or receive data from) with a piece of software. This is consistent with the term *actor* in object-oriented or use case technology.

The functional size measure is independent of the nonfunctional requirements, including the technology used for implementation, since the technological aspects of the software development are not part of the functional size.

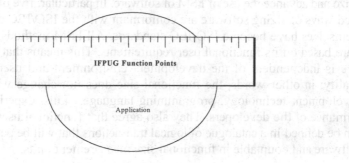

Fig. 12.1. Counting a software application

Function Points are derived from the logical (or functional) user require-ments concept, and the person counting the Function Points will learn a lot about the functional requirements of the software during the process of evalu-ating the functional size.

The following goals are often cited for using the IFPUG FPM:

- Standardized and integrated software measurement
- Improvement of estimation accuracy and project management
- Improvement of quality of the development process
- Knowledge transfer of estimation experiences and lessons learned
- Reduction of complexity and uncertainty in the estimation process (because the object of estimation has been quantified as part of the sizing process)
- Basis for indicators and metrics.

An extract of the exact rules for counting according to IFPUG are provided in a further chapter of this book. There exists a wide variety of information sources about the IFPUG FPM on the Internet; however, the actual IFPUG web-site is http://www.ifpug.org. Note that IFPUG is a not-for-profit users group headquartered in Princeton, NJ, and it is owned and operated by and for the members. IFPUG is not associated or managed by any vendor or consulting organization.

Additional sources of IFPUG methodology information (not all of it in ac-cordance with the official IFPUG function point counting practices) include the following:

- Carol Dekkers, Quality Plus Technologies, Inc.: http://www.qualityplustech.com,
- David Garmus: http://www.davidconsultinggroup.com,
- The IT Metrics and Productivity Institute: http://www.itmpi.org/
- The University of Quebec at Montreal, Canada: http://www.lrgl.uqam.ca,
- Capers Jones and Software Productivity Research: http://www.spr.com.

During the last decade, many advances have been made worldwide to popu-larize and advance the use of FSM of software. In particular, five of the frequently used ways of sizing software are conformant with the ISO/IEC definitions and themselves have become ISO/IEC standards. All FSM methods evaluate soft-ware based on its functional user requirements. This means that the functional size is independent of the development environment and user demands for quality; in other words, the functional size does not change with changes in development technology, programming language, skills, experiences, or per-formance of the developers. They also agree that functional user requirements can be defined in a catalogue of logical transactions that will be performed by the software and countable in functional size measurement units.

The current ISO/IEC conformant FSM methods are:

- ISO/IEC 19761:2002 Information technology, Software and systems engineering – COSMIC-FFP: A functional size measurement method
- ISO/IEC 20926:2002 Information technology, Software and systems engineering – IFPUG 4.1 Unadjusted functional size measurement method: CPM
- ISO/IEC 20968:2002 Information technology, Software and systems engineering – Mark II Function Point Analysis: CPM
- ISO/IEC 24570:2004 Information technology, Software and systems engineering – NESMA functional size measurement method version 2.1: Definitions and counting guidelines for the application of Function Point Analysis
- ISO/IEC 29881:2008 Information technology, Software and systems engineering – FISMA 1.1 functional size measurement method.

12.1 Functional Size Measurement Methods History

The first method that described function point analysis was originally developed in 1979 by A. J. Albrecht from IBM, and first presented publicly at a GUIDE/Share conference. Interest in the method and its application as a basis for objective estimating grew quickly around the world, and by 1986, the IFPUG was formed in Toronto, Canada. The first IFPUG CPM version 1.0 was released in 1988 by the IFPUG. IFPUG 1.0 (as it is abbreviated in general usage) formalized Albrecht's 1984 standard set of function point rules. Since its inception, IFPUG has remained a volunteer, not-for-profit membership organization based in the United States, with members residing in many of the countries where software process improvement and measurement are important. Membership benefits of the IFPUG include the CPM in its current release as well as reduced conference attendance and discounts on publications (see http://www.ifpug.org). The CPM describes the counting rules in a standardized form. Since the first CPM appeared nearly 20 years ago, the IFPUG FPM has been translated into German (IFPUG 4.0), French, Italian, Japanese, Korean, Portuguese, and Spanish. The IFPUG publishes biannually the M*etric Views* – not to be mistaken for the biannual Germany journal: *Metrics News* (also in English, older editions downloadable free of charge) of the German GI Metrics group (http://ivs.cs.uni-magdeburg.de/sw-eng/us/ - the German Metrics News actually changed its name in 2008 to Software Measurement News).

The IFPUG Standard 4.1 is acknowledged as an ISO/IEC Standard 20926, and to conform to ISO/IEC definitions, it had to be published with the 14 GSCs (General System Characteristics for calculation of adjusted Function Points) being *OPTIONAL only*. (ISO/IEC defines "functional size" as describing only the tasks and business processes supported by the software, and the 14GSCs and resultant VAF go beyond mere functional size). The formal release of IFPUG CPM Release 4.2 (2004) included the 14 GSCs as a mandatory step in

IFPUG function point counting; however, the next version of the IFPUG standard when it is submitted to ISO/IEC to replace the ISO/IEC 20926:2002 standard will again reference the Value Adjustment Factor (VAF) as an optional step to conform with the ISO/IEC definitions.

Figure 12.2 shows the evolution of the functional size measurement Methods from IFPUG, COSMIC-FFP, NESMA, FiSMA and Mark II during the last 30 years.

The software functionality measured by the IFPUG counting practices manual rules is clearly based on an elementary process-oriented, stimulus-response-model. This implies that the composite counting items inputs, outputs, and inquiries are each transactional types that interact (receive or send data) in relation to a "user" (as previously defined). This was not so clearly stated in earlier IFPUG CPM releases, and the lack of clarity hindered the usability (and potential applicability) in the past.

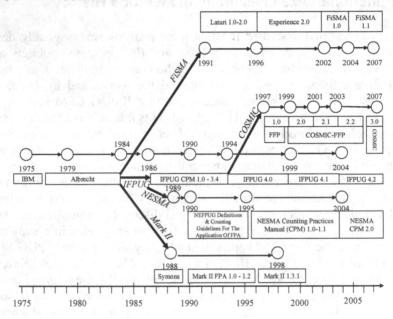

Fig. 12.2. History of Functional Size Measurement (FSM) methods

12.2 The Benefits of the IFPUG FPM

The IFPUG FPM can easily be learned and understood and applied to a variety of software. This becomes important particularly when counts may have to be audited or formally released as part of the quality assurance process. Function Points define objectively the functional size of software applications from the user view, and are typically expressed in the user's language. This is consistent with the understanding about the functionality of their application. The fact that a function point count must be done based on the functional user requirements has the added bonus that it forces the project team to see the software from the perspective of the user and to respond accordingly. The functional elementary processes should identically match the specified functional user requirements. A by-product of function point counting is a better design and improved control during the project.

Authors' note: It has been observed through first hand experience that when the Function Point Analysis is done with the involvement of the end users, they are motivated to better teamwork and more committed engagement. In addition, we have observed that the overall user satisfaction with the project increases. This is a key project success factor according to the Standish Group's annual CHAOS Report.

12.2.1 Leveraging the Use of Function Points (and the Analytical Approach) in Software Development

Figure 12.3 shows how measured Function Points can profitably be leveraged for the software engineering process and project management groups.

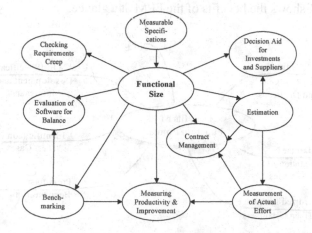

Fig. 12.3. Leveraging Function Points to benefit software development

The following list includes ways that Function Points (FP) can be used in the short term.

- FP size as input for estimation and project management.
- FP list of included functions as the basis for project planning and architectural design.

- FPs allocated to parts of the software as the basis for structuring projects and planning of releases.
- FPs size as a basic metric for quality-planning and management-reviews (common denominator for defect density).
- FP methodology as implicit inspection of requirements for completeness and misunderstandings, and quality improvement of user-specified requirements.
- FP methodology for design of test cases and for estimation of test effort.
- FP size contributes to metrics for stability and reliability (Mean time to failure as a function of size).
- FP size as the basis for software benchmarking and risk analysis.
- List of functional user requirements (on which the count is based) delivers user-oriented documentation of the application.
- FP size at various points in the development life cycle is used for measurement of requirements creep (scope management).
- FP size as one of the input variables for calculation of various productivity and quality metrics.
- FP methodology supports reuse in IT development by early and standardized quantification of business cases in the requirements definition phase, for contracting, for project-estimation, for test case identification, for enhancements, and for documentation.

Figure 12.4 shows the benefits of the FPM at a glance.

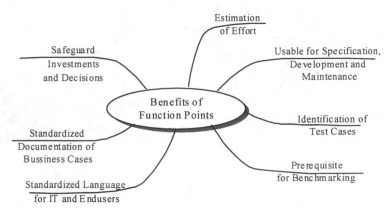

Fig. 12.4. Mind map of benefits of the Function Point Method (FPM)

The principal benefits of the *FPM* include the following:

- The methodology is independent of the development environment as well as the skills or attributes of developers.
- By consequent use of Function Points according to the IFPUG standard and careful documentation of the counting results, the organization gets valuable

interproject consistent data about the size of elaborated and to be developed applications. This information is *the basis for solid effort estimates* for software development.
- Through internationally agreed standardizations based on functional size, *interorganizational benchmarks can be enabled.*

The FPM facilitates estimation in an manner easier and more precise than other assessments of size (such as the use of unqualified judgements of small, medium, or large software size). Function Points can be used during specification, development, enhancement, and maintenance of software, as well as for safeguarding investment decisions. Beneficial side effects are quantified quality (when FP are correlated with defects), risk awareness, easy to be derived test cases, measurable productivity (when correlated to effort hours), and standardized business requirements (for users as well as for developers).

Figure 12.5 shows the areas for application of the FPM.

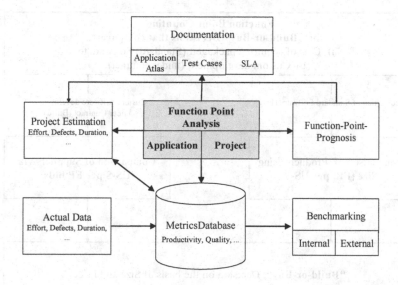

Fig. 12.5. Areas of application of the FPM and/or functional size

12.2.2 Function Points as Part of a Pricing Evaluation Process

Function Points can facilitate comparison of prices from suppliers and to evaluate cost ratios for software under contract (e.g., price per FP or FPs per US-$ or per Euro). This metric (cost per FP) can also be discussed with the software suppliers. Capers Jones reports in *IT Measurement – Practical Advice from the Experts* (IFPUG 2002) that "standard" software such as spreadsheets can be bought for about 0.25 US-$ per FP. Specialized niche products may then cost about 10 to more than 300 US-$ per FP. Development costs of applications may vary widely from a low of 200 US-$ per FP for small systems to more than 5,000 US-$ per FP for large military or defense systems. These prices can be compared with development costs of about 1,500 US-$ per FP in Western Europe and about 350 US-$ in Eastern Europe.

Howard Rubin also contributed a chapter about pricing comparisons in the above mentioned book.

ISBSG publications also discuss how function points can be used as part of price comparisons (see http://www.isbsg.org). The metric "price per FP" can contribute to decisions about whether to "build-or-buy." Note: Build-or-buy is an English expression meaning a decision about "Building" customized software, typically under contract with a supplier; or "Buying" standard packaged software. Figure 12.6 shows how Function Points fits into the decision making process associated with Build-or-Buy decisions.

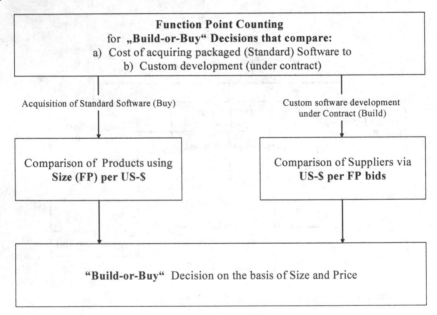

Fig. 12.6. "Make-or-Buy" decision based on using FP size as part of the pricing equation

12.2.3 Function Points as the Basis for Contract Metrics

Another interesting use of Function Points is to directly measure and manage software development performed under contract. Because FP are independent of the tools, techniques, people, and the technical implementation of software, different perspectives between a purchaser and supplier can be discussed objectively on the basis of Function Points. Capers Jones reports in *IT Measurement – Practical Advice from the Experts* that between 1995 and 2001 FPs and LOC metrics were in direct conflict in at least a dozen U.S. Internal Revenue Service (IRS) cases, with the LOC metric being on the losing side of the judicial decision in virtually every case. In one tax case in 1996, both IRS and the defendant used FPs to prove their case. High profile precedents like this helps to resolve any anxiety practitioners may have about the unreliability of software measurement and estimation.

A few examples of contract metrics include the following:

- Contracted price per delivered FP for new development or enhancement.
- Fixed price for a certain number of FPs (new development or enhancement), which can then be normalized to a cost per FP.
- Fixed or FP based pricing for the maintenance of a portfolio with a certain size as measured in FPs (typically done on the basis of cost per 1,000 FP).
- Variation from fixed price (at preagreed cost per FP) if the software size is larger or smaller than negotiated.
- For improvement of team or departmental performance (setting goals, bonus systems) the evaluation may be based on the following:
  - Delivery rate expressed as number of FPs per hour for new development or enhancement
  - Cost per FP for new development or enhancement
  - Maintenance load expressed as number of FPs maintained per person in 1 year (person is often referred to as "Full-Time-Equivalent" or FTE in North America)
  - Defect density expressed as a number of defects per FP
  - % improvement in delivery rate based on comparison between a current and previous delivery rate.

Using function points as part of performance measurement in contractual arrangements, the following measures are generally collected:

- Number of FPs for each project or application (depending on what performance metric is desired: project FP are needed for productivity metrics; application FP are needed to determine support ratios)
- Price points for delivery of different types of development or for different levels of FPs (price per FP)
- Estimated costs, effort hours, duration, anticipate team size (by job role and availability)
- Actual costs, effort hours, duration, actual team size (all at project postmortem)
- Tracking of project progress and measures in the case of delay (together with mitigating factors for delay)
- Approved changes (sized in FP).

In summary:

The effort for planning, performing, and documentation of Function Point counts can be justified as long as FP are used appropriately together with other measures. Function points in and of themselves tell only the functional size of software in a manner similar to the square foot (or square meter) size of a building tells only the area of a floor plan. When used appropriately in performance measurement, function points provide an objective denominator (as in a "per square foot") that normalizes metrics for comparison across software projects. The benefits in such cases far outweigh the costs of the learning curve and organizational resistance, and additionally the structured analytical approach to counting FP provides intangible gains to the requirements process. Capers Jones estimates the effort to implement a fully-functioning measurement and analysis program to be maximally 3% of the cost of a project – not much when you consider the savings that better requirements and accurate estimates can provide.

12.3 Application Areas for Function Points

The primary application areas of the IFPUG FPM are in estimation of new software development and enhancement. The following is a partial list of the most common application areas for FP-based metrics:

1. Estimation of software development costs and/or effort (based on FP and other project attributes)
2. Estimation of maintenance costs and/or effort of implemented systems (based on FP supported per person figures)
3. The Earned-Value method has been applied to some projects based on Function Points for evaluation and delivery. More research is needed in this area. Capers Jones addresses this topic in *IT Measurement – Practical Advice from the Experts*
4. Comparison of functionality of an old system vs. its replacement during reengineering (rebuild)
5. Projection of productivity trends in software development based on historical rates (FP per hour for particular types of development)
6. Cost estimation based on cost per FP or FP per hour (speed of delivery) as a basis for planning of resources and milestones
7. When parts of a project have to be delivered in releases, the functionality can be allocated to and accounted for using FPs
8. Defect density metrics (defects per FP) can be used for better planning of the test phase in the project

9. *FPs can be used for risk assessment.* Capers Jones published in Assessment and Control of Software Risks that projects with less than 500 FPs fail only in 20% of all cases, whereas the failure rate of projects with more than 5,000 FPs is about 40%

10. Pam Morris (in *IT Measurement – Practical Advice from the Experts*) found with regression analyses a correlation ($R^2 = 0.8638$) between the size of an application measured in FPs and the number of persons (P) necessary for maintenance:

$$P = 0.0012 \times FP.$$

Thus, for the maintenance of an application with a size of 1,000 FPs there are 1.2 persons necessary or 1 person per 833 FPs.

It has been suggested that the applicability of the IFPUG FPM is restricted to *commercial applications* (Management Information Systems, MIS) for the reason that the development costs for engineering or other types of more complex applications depends from other factors. (Commercial applications mainly manipulate large data volumes and use many inputs and outputs.)

Technical or scientific applications (e.g., in R&D or production) focus mainly in processing of data, and often involve complex calculations and combinatory problems to be solved. While the IFPUG methodology does not regard these aspects explicitly, it should be noted the factors influencing work effort and cost are explicitly external to any functional size measurement method as defined in ISO/IEC 14143-1:2007 Functional Size Measurement – Definition of Concepts.

For more technical IT projects there is a stronger orientation on processing criteria. In this area input and output functions are often trivial, whereas processing features have an important role. The *COSMIC Method*, presented in the chapter about *variants of the FPM,* claims to address internal processing more concretely, and the reader is directed to select the most appropriate functional size measurement method (amongst the five ISO/IEC conformant methods) to meet their specific needs. The one caveat is that it is usually best to select one method for all of your functional sizing needs so that the functional size of various projects can be effectively and easily compared.

Chris Kemerer from the Massachusetts Institute of Technology (MIT) showed in a research study comparing 15 software projects that the FPM could be used for various types of software beyond management information systems or commercial applications. Furthermore, Kemerer found that estimation based on functional size measurement produced the most consistent and accurate results compared to source-lines-of-code (SLOC) based estimating methods (SLIM, COCOMO, and Estimacs).

12.4 The Evaluation of Function Point-Based Estimation Methods

Noth and Kretzschmar (in their book in 1984) tested 20 different methods of estimating software development effort, and found that those based on sizing with Function Points belong to the few methods that they could recommend for use. This can be seen from their test protocol of the FPM shown in Table 12.1.

According to Noth and Kretzschmar, using function points (functional size measurement) as the input variable for size in effort estimating has the following advantages:

- The size measurement focuses on the functional size, which was regarded as the best option.
- By using a specific organizational experience curve, many different influences can be combined in a single formula and then the particular individual influences do not have to be separately examined in detail.
- The estimating method can easily be adapted according to organizational requirements.

Table 12.1. Test protocol from Noth and Kretzschmar (1984) of estimating models based on size measurement using Function points

Test criteria	Evaluation	1	2	3	4	5
Ease of use	Usability			x		
	Ease of learning				x	
	Effort to develop estimates from the measure				x	
	Tool support		x			
	Transparency	x				
Contribution to project control	Applicable early in the development life cycle	x				
	Structuredness				x	
	Ease to apply iteratively	x				
	Sensitivity analysis				x	
Quality of results	Precision	x				
	Understandability	x				
	Ease of evaluation		x			
	Degree of influence	x				
	Number of parameters			x		
	Objectivity				x	
	Stability		x			
	Defect localization		x			
	Adaptability	x				
	Adaptivity	x				

1, excellent; 5, poor

Noth and Kretzschmar say that the biggest disadvantage of function-point-based estimating methods is that a detailed estimation on an individual module-by-module basis is not possible. *As such, the method is only applicable for gross planning.*

Another evaluation of function point-based estimating was published by Ruede who used the catalogue of criteria from Herrmann:

- *Precision:*
  A high degree of precision can be achieved by the transfer of experiences between the project postmortems and subsequent new development projects. Functional size measurement-based estimating delivers more precise results over the course of usage.
- *Standardization:*
  Functional size (also known as a function point count) can be easily understood by an end user with respect to its content and basic calculations.
- *Early Applicability:*
  Functional size measurement can be used very early since the requirements are the basis for the counts. See also the chapter about Function Point Prognosis in this book.
- *Data Collection:*
  The necessary information for estimation and functional sizing can easily be gathered.
- *Objectivity:*
  Functional size is not influenced by demands from management or individuals.
- *Transparency:*
  Functional size measurement can be done together with the end user. The resultant estimates based on this size can be explained and controlled easily.
- *Degree of Details:*
  The effort for single activities or tasks and to develop specific programs and modules cannot be evaluated using FP-based estimating methods, rather the effort for the lifecycle development of software applications and projects. A detailed view is possible from the user side.
- *Stability:*
  Functional size results are stable even when development techniques or methods change.
- *Flexibility:*
  Functional size deviations can easily be seen during the iterative process and comparisons made between the planned functionality vs. what was actually delivered. Evaluations can be corrected.
- *Ease of Use:*
  Functional size measurement can easily be learned, the number of parameters on which it is based is acceptable, and the sizing process is not time-consuming.

Hence, estimating methods based on the FPM for sizing software fulfill the major prerequisite requirements of a method for estimation of effort.

Besides the test criteria, Ruede published two other essential advantages of using functional size-based estimation:

1. Software development evolves in the direction of IT organizations and neglects the areas of programming replaced by tools. FPMs are the correct way to assess software functional size since the user requirements are the basis for calculations.
2. The productivity of application development can be demonstrated and improvements can be planned based on per FP calculations where the common denominator is functional size.

The above-mentioned study by Kemerer shows also that Function Point counts performed using the same functional size measurement method and release (e.g., IFPUG release 4.2) can be compared between different organizations (benchmarking).

Many users choose to employ size measurement using IFPUG or other Functional Size Measurement Method because of its early applicability in the software life cycle, and also because it delivers objective and consistent estimates of functional size even when requirements are not concrete. Through using FP as the common denominator (similar to using per square foot or per square meter ratios in building construction), function point based estimating also delivers the chance to gain experiences and rules of thumb.

The goals of the IFPUG function point analysis method are to measure small units in order to support flexible comparisons and early deviations from plan. A basis for planning can be elaborated and the controlling of IT projects can be improved. More precise estimates of size (and effort using a FP-based estimating model) for follow-up projects are possible, and effects of changes in the development environment become transparent.

It is important to note that there are obstacles to the universal application of FP-based estimation and functional size measurement, including wide spread prejudices (and ignorance due to misunderstanding or lack of "informed" opinions), leading to the conclusion in some circles that they are not feasible or even that they should be avoided. Figure 12.7 provides some counter-arguments for the types of statements that are often levied against functional size measurement.

12.5 The Optimum Time to Count FPs

The optimum time for a first Function Point count is the end of the requirements analysis. This phase delivers the following:

- Description of the user requirements
- Description of the data structures.

This contains all necessary information for a Function Point count.

The chapter *Estimation Fundamentals: The Right Time for Estimation* at the beginning of this book is also valid for Function Point counting. Note that before this point in the development life cycle, function points can only be *estimated* but not counted.

It does not make sense that a Function Point count is only performed once during project progress, because throughout the project there evolves new information such as scope changes, clarifications to requirements, (as well as requirements creep).

We recommend (consistent with the practices at IBM) to revisit the original Function Point count for any updated information (and changes) at the end of each phase of the software project. This practice also supports the tracking of requirements scope creep and scope management principles.

The counting of Function Points is ideally considered to be a part of the project documentation, reviews, project controlling, and releases at the end of each project phase.

Revisiting the Function Point count at different times as the project progresses enables early adjustments (and corrections) to the resultant effort estimates, and thus it increases the precision and approximation of the actual effort.

Points and counter-points about function points...

PREJUDICE (POINT)	COUNTER-POINT
☛... they are developed by theoreticians or academicians and they are not practical for use.	☺ Originally developed by A. Albrecht as a in-practice project for the development of system software at IBM.
☛... They produce administrative overhead.	☺ The effort to perform FP counts compared to their benefit, and the overall project effort is negligibly low (less than 3%).
☛... They are not usable for object-oriented or other types of application development.	☺ FP's are a Meta-Model that allows a mapping of the functional requirements, no matter in which description or technical implementation is used.

Fig. 12.7. Counter points to prejudices against Function Points

When an effort estimate is required at an earlier stage than at the end of the requirements phase, we recommend the development of one or more Function Point prognosis methods. See the chapter titled *Application of the FPM: Function Point Prognosis* in this book. This requires counting of historical, completed software projects and requires one to perform regression analyses. Experiences from a sample size of 16–20 completed projects can form a reliable basis for such methods. Another approach is to use the SPR-Function Points (see chapter *Variants of the FPM: SPR Function Points*) when you need a FP estimate before completing the requirements phase.

12.6 The Process of Function Point Counting

Before starting a Function Point count using the IFPUG method, the following information must be available to the counter:

- The outputs produced by the *application*
- The inputs entering the *application* across its boundary
- The internal logical files that are maintained by the *application*
- Entities and Relationships between internal logical data
- Inquiries for data retrieval that can be asked of the *application*
- Interfaces between the *application* and other *application*s
- Interfaces between the *application* and its *users*
- Key *logical* processes of the *application*.

Note again that the word *user* in function point terminology means *anything (i.e., human users, other applications, hardware, software, etc.) that interacts with the software.* This is similar to the word "actor" in use case terminology.

The process of Function Point counting is described by IFPUG as follows (see Fig. 12.8):

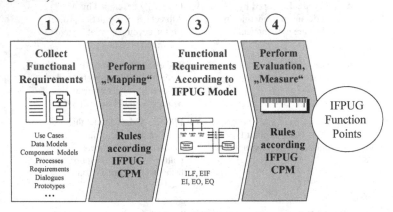

Fig. 12.8. The process of IFPUG Function Point Counting

- Define the type of count
- Define the scope of the count and the system boundary
- Count the unadjusted FPs.

Note that this is now the functional size of the software according to ISO/IEC where functional size is defined as the size of the functional user requirements. Therefore, the functional size of a piece of software equals the UNADJUSTED Function Point count. However, the next two steps, which have been part of the IFPUG method since the beginning, adjust the functional size by considering the effects of some nonfunctional requirements.

It is anticipated that all future releases of the counting practices manual (IFPUG CPM) will include the VAF (steps 5 and 6) as optional to be consistent with the ISO/IEC version of the IFPUG standard.

Optional steps (in the ISO/IEC version of the IFPUG standard, currently still part of the IFPUG CPM 4.2):

- Calculate the VAF after determining the 14 GSCs
- Calculate the adjusted FPs.

We recommend two further steps (regardless of whether steps 4 and 5 are done) that go beyond the IFPUG rules:

6. Document the details of the count.

Function Point counts as well as FP estimates should be performed by project leaders or project team members knowledgeable about the functionality together with support of the competence center. The release of counts and estimates will be more consistent when there is a final quality check done by the competence center. Thus, our recommended final step is:

7. Quality assurance of the FP count by the competence center.

12.6.1 Step 1: Define the Type of Count

There are three types of Function Point counts, the first two specific to IT projects:

1. New development
2. Enhancement
3. Application.

The relationships between these count types are shown in Fig. 12.9.

A *new development* project is the first build of an application. Thus, all delivered functionality is considered to be added. Thus, Function Points counted are the added (= delivered) plus any FP for user required "conversion" functions.

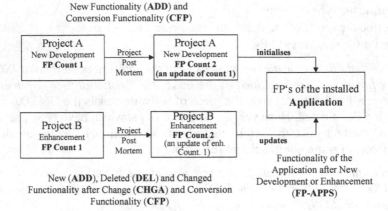

Fig. 12.9. Types of Function Point counts according to IFPUG

An *enhancement* project can add functionality, as well as change or delete functionality. Accordingly, the FP is the summation of the added, changed, and deleted FP, plus any FP for the user required "conversion" functions.

Figure 12.9 demonstrates that the IFPUG methodology regards requirements scope creep based on at least two Function Point counts. The first count will be at project start to measure the planned functionality, while the second will be at project postmortem to measure the actual delivered functionality.

At project postmortem of an enhancement project, the Function Points of the enhanced *application* must also be updated based on what has been added, changed, and deleted.

In the IT department of an international insurance company in Germany, the following standards (see Fig. 12.10) were introduced for definition of an application software (AS):

- Has at least 1 user
- Has at least 1 EI and 1 EO/EQ
- Has a sovereign data-storage, -administration, and -derivation, that is, it has at least 1 ILF (usually, although not necessarily)
- Interfaces must exist to satisfy the logical (functional) user requirements
- Processes business cases completely. Note: the exception is if there are central interfaces or comparable follow up processes involved in the final handling of a process
- Is maintained and administered by one organizational unit (this was a specific internal company standard)
- Different products do not necessarily lead to separate boundaries between ASs
- Inventory or insurance administration will normally be considered as different ASs (specific internal company standard)

> **Attributes for Definition of Applications (AS)**
>
> ✓ There exists at least one user.
> ✓ Maintained entities and data administration (at least one 1 ILF) and
>   Processes for administration (at least 1 EI and 1 EO/EQ).
> ✓ Business cases of the AS are processed until the case is finally
>   elaborated (if final handling is not done by central interfaces or
>   follow up processes).
>
> **Additional Hints for Determination of AS:**
> ✓ AS are mostly administered by different
>   organizational units.
> ✓ The borders of the AS should be defined from
>   user view and not from technical view.
> ✓ Define the AS borders alike as you want to measure
>   and compute your metrics.

Fig. 12.10. Example of an internal corporate standard for the definition of application software

- Statistical reporting of an administered internal file alone is no reason for definition of an AS
- Batch- or interface-processing vs. online processing should not determine the placement of the application boundary
- Different ASs have unique and different functionalities
- Different users may provide a hint of different ASs, except in the case of interface systems.

Business processes of different mandatory authorities are typically administered in different databases. Exception are if there exist also common processes besides the separate processes in the same database. In these cases they are not defined as separate ASs (this is an internal corporate standard as an example for the readers).

12.6.2 Step 2: Define the Scope of the Count and the Application Boundary

The IFPUG FPM distinguishes between the size of a software project (Counting scope) and an application. The size of a project can include several applications each having different functionality from user view (not from technical view) and, thus having different application boundaries. As such, there may be several Function Point counts within a single "business" project.

The definition of the application boundary determines which functionality is counted for the project and which functionality would be counted for external applications.

Some estimators guess that the Function Points have been counted world-wide for about 30,000 applications, but the actual number of discrete software applications is not known other than it is a minority of the actual number of total software applications in existence. As functional size measurement increases in usage, hopefully more than 1% (according to statements by Prof. Alain Abran at the Software Measurement European Forum in 2005) of software organizations will be involved in software measurement.

Principally, the application boundary must be defined from the user view. As depicted in Fig. 12.11, the user is outside the system. After determining the boundary, data files maintained within the application and the associated maintenance functions (create, add change, delete) are counted as internal logical files, with external data files counted for those entities administered and maintained outside the application boundary. In enhancement projects, it has to be regarded that the new application boundary is consistent with the boundary of the base system.

Since the application boundary is critical to the determination of the application functionality, it is important for it to be documented clearly. This includes the description of assumptions used to locate the boundary.

Practically, this documentation (typically including system diagrams) can easily be reused in (or as) architecture diagrams in the application atlas of the organization.

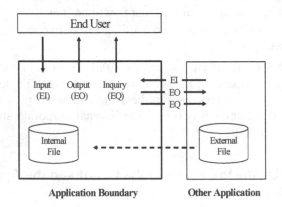

Fig. 12.11. Defining the application boundary

12.6.3 Step 3: Count Unadjusted FPs

The IFPUG Function Point Methodology distinguishes five function types as shown in Table 12.2.

Table 12.2. IFPUG function types

Data function types	*ILF (Internal Logical Files):* Internal logical files with their records and data elements; data that are maintained within the system boundary by the software under consideration. Persistent logical entities
	EIF (External Logical Files): External interface files with their records and data elements; data that are maintained outside the system boundary (by other applications). Persistent logical entities maintained by another application, but referenced by this one
Transaction function types	*EI (External Inputs):* External input functions with their logical data groups and data elements. External inputs are elementary processes
	EO (External Outputs): External output functions data with their logical data groups and data elements. External outputs are elementary processes
	EQ (External Inquiries): External inquiry functions with their logical data groups and data elements. External inquiries are elementary processes

Function Points are counted according to specific IFPUG formulae according to the type of count (see step 5):

- *For enhancement projects:* added plus deleted plus changed plus user required conversion functionality must be counted.
- *Added functionality* enlarges the functional size of the project and the functional size of the base application.
- *Deleted functionality* enlarges the functional size of the project (since it is worked on it), but reduces the functional size of the base application.
- *Changed functionality* enlarges the functional size of the project and can enlarge, reduce, or leave unchanged the functional size of the base application.
- *User required conversion functionality* is counted as part of the functional size of the project, but does not affect the functional size of the base application.

The Function Points are then classified according to a *complexity matrix* into low, average, or high. The result is documented in a Table 12.3.

The sum of the Function Points are called the *unadjusted Function Point count*. This is the functional size according to ISO/IEC. The steps 4 and 5 of the IFPUG method as defined earlier modify (adjust) this unadjusted Function Point count based on the influence of fourteen nonfunctional user requirements.

Note that in the future IFPUG releases (after IFPUG 4.2) it is anticipated that these steps will be deemed to be "optional" steps for consistency with the ISO/IEC version of the IFPUG method.

Table 12.3. Summary of a Function Point Count

Functional type	Complexity	FPs	Number of unique functions	Sum FPs
ILF	Low	7		
	Average	10		
	High	15		
EIF	Low	5		
	Average	7		
	High	10		
EI	Low	3		
	Average	4		
	High	6		
EO	Low	4		
	Average	5		
	High	7		
EQ	Low	3		
	Average	4		
	High	6		
Sum of unadjusted FPs				

The next step involves determining the influence of the 14 GSCs. The sum of the values for the 14 characteristics is called the TDI (Total Degree of Influence). The TDI is then multiplied by 0.01 and added to the constant 0.65 to calculate the VAF:

$$VAF = (TDI \times 0.01) + 0.65.$$

The final but also optional step in the current IFPUG FP method is to calculate the *adjusted FPs*. To do so, the adjusted FP is then calculated by multiplying the unadjusted FPs with the VAF:

$$Adjusted\ FP = unadjusted\ FP \times VAF.$$

Since the 14 GSCs are estimation parameters based on the nonfunctional user requirements, and not part of functional size measurement, only the unadjusted FPs can be considered ISO/IEC-conformant as a functional size measure. *The two steps from the unadjusted FPs to the adjusted FPs take the functional size measurement (unadjusted FP) in the direction of software estimation by considering influences of the nonfunctional requirements in system development.*

In the following sections, each of the IFPUG five function types is described.

Classification of Logical Files

Internal Logical Files (ILF) and External Logical Files (EIF) must be distinguished and counted. The main difference between an ILF and an EIF is that an ILF is maintained by the application being counted, whereas the EIF is maintained by an external application. The technical term "maintain" is defined as an elementary process that changes the data in the entity (including processes whereby data on the file is modified through processes that create data, update or inserting data, change or otherwise modify data, or delete data). Theoretically, all five manipulations must be possible.

The most important consideration is that the entities (logical files) are regarded from the *user view*. Counting FPs after the design phase or later in the project (e.g., after implementation) can leave the Function Point counting practitioner with difficulties to view everything from the user perspective. The only advice is to remember this restriction as often as possible. A technical perspective (as opposed to the user perspective) can obscure the proper viewpoint and result in an over or under count. For example, an application may physically store data about customers across multiple database files, whereas from the user perspective it is one logical file (entity). This should be counted as one ILF.

A prerequisite to accurate Function Point counting is a *logical data model*, not a physical one. The entities of the logical data model are used for counting and as such the Function Point count will disregard supraentities, IT-technical data elements or implementation specific files, group elements, and filler fields.

The EIFs are external interface files (persistent logical entities) as identified from the requirements. These are logical files (entities) maintained by other *application*s and only referenced by the application being counted. Thus, an EIF is an ILF of another application that is simply read or referenced by this application or one can say it is a logical reuse file.

The complexity of internal and external logical files depends on two dimensions:

- The number of data element types (DET)
- The number of record element types (RET).

IFPUG defines these as follows:

DET: A DET is a unique user recognizable, nonrecursive field (in an ILF or EIF).

RET: A RET is a user recognizable logical subgroup of data elements within an ILF or EIF.

Standalone entities are counted (with the exception of hard-coded/non-maintained data and code tables. See the current IFPUG CPM available from http://www.IFPUG.org for full counting rules and exclusions to what is counted) and the number of fields. When a logical entity contains at least one field, then a RET is counted. Key fields are counted only once no matter on how many RETs they are contained.

After determination of the RETs and DETs on a persistent logical entity ("file"), the complexity (low, average, or high) is determined using a complexity matrix (see Table 12.4).

The relative complexity is then translated into unadjusted function points according to the following table (Table 12.5).

The example in Fig. 12.12 shows a logical data model of a salary system.

The example in Fig. 12.2 shows 2 RET (since the indicator is functionally required by different restrictions from law in Germany) and 7 DET. Thus, the file is evaluated as low complexity (Table 12.4) and would be equal to seven unadjusted FP if it is an ILF or five unadjusted FP if it is an EIF (Table 12.5). The higher Function Point count for ILFs as compared to EIFs considers that the file is maintained by the application being counted. Note that this means that there will also be at least one data maintenance EI for that ILF present in the application.

New users of the IFPUG method often have difficulties to distinguish between ILFs and EIFs. A rule of thumb is to count an ILF if data are stored and maintained (and are not part of the exclusions as outlined above), and an EIF when data are only retrieved or extracted or referenced from an entity maintained within another application boundary.

One additional piece of advice to determine if the requirement for the file is a physical (i.e., specific to the technical development language or implementation used) or a logical requirement is to consider whether the requirement would disappear if it was implemented differently. For example, if there is a file that contains a copy of information that is maintained by another application, is extracted from that application, imported to the application being

Table 12.4. Complexity of IFPUG data functions: ILF and EIF

RETs/DETs	1–19 DETs	20–50 DETs	>50 DETs
1 RET	Low	Low	Average
2–5 RETs	Low	Average	High
>5 RETs	Average	High	High

Table 12.5. Unadjusted Function Points based on logical file complexity

Complexity	ILF	EIF
	Number of Unadjusted FP	Number of Unadjusted FP
Low	7	5
Average	10	7
High	15	10

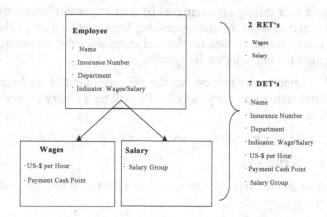

Fig. 12.12. Internal Logical File complexity example

counted, and named with an application specific name, then the question would be "If we had perfect technology (i.e., considering only the user requirements) would we still need to make a copy of the data within our application?" If the answer is "no, we could simply read it from the other application," then we know that the file is an implementation-specific requirement, and the file is simply the physical implementation to read the EIF from the other application. However, if the answer is "Yes, the owner application changes the data all the time, and our application needs a snapshot point in time view of the other application's data", then we know that the requirement is a functional, logical user requirement and the file would be counted as an ILF.

Classification of Transactions

Transactional functions are External Input (EI), External Output (EO) and External Inquiry (EQ), and are defined by IFPUG as follows:

EI: An EI is an elementary process that processes data or control information that comes from outside the application's boundary. The *primary intent* of an EI is to maintain one or more ILFs and/or to alter the behavior of the system. Counted are all elementary input processes having unique processing logic.

EO: An EO is an elementary process that sends data or control information outside the application's boundary. The *primary intent* of an EO is to present information to a user through processing logic other than, or in addition to, the retrieval of data or control information. The processing logic must contain at least one mathematical formula (calculation), create derived data, maintain one or more ILFs, or alter the behavior of the system.

EQ: An EQ is an elementary process that sends data or control information outside the application's boundary. The *primary intent* of an EQ is to present information to a user through the retrieval of data or control information from an ILF or EIF, and in addition, the processing logic contains no mathematical formulae or calculations, creates no derived data, does not maintain an ILF, and does not alter the behavior of the system.

As such, if an elementary process has the primary intent of sending data external to the application boundary, it typically will be a binary choice between an EO or EQ.

Typical examples for transactions are, for example, the following:

EI: Add a new employee

EO: Online or printed reports with calculated data (can also be contained in an export file)

EQ: Online data is input to retrieve and display employee data without any other processing

The example in Fig. 12.13 shows a dialogue for maintenance of an electronic address book with 3 EIs and 1 EQ.

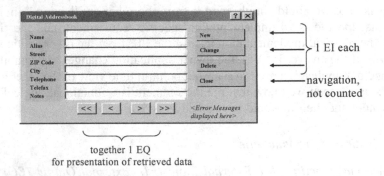

Fig. 12.13. Transactions example

Before counting the unadjusted Function Points, the complexity of each of the transactional functions has to be determined. The complexity of a transaction depends on two dimensions:

- The number of data elements (DET, Data Element Types)
- The number of referenced files (FTR, File Type Referenced).

The number of DETs is determined as the number of data element types that cross the application boundary (in plus out minus duplicate fields that cross both in and out). Counted are the fields used by the transaction plus 1 DET for the ability to specify the function to be performed (e.g., "New" command) plus 1 DET for any error and/or confirmation messages and/or confirm that processing should continue, which are provided as part of the function (regardless of how many are present, it is 1 DET for the total error/confirmation/continuation messages or functionality there may be).

The number of FTRs is simply the number of external and internal logical files required to process the transaction.

The EI "New" in Fig. 12.13 for adding a new address has, for example, 10 DETs (8 for the data fields shown on the dialog from Name through to Notes, plus 1 DET for the function initiator button New plus 1 DET for the display of error message(s)) and 1 FTR (only a single Internal Logical File is needed to create a new entry). The *complexity matrix for EIs* (see Table 12.6) classifies this EI as low.

Table 12.6. Complexity of EIs

FTRs/DETs	1–4 DETs	5–15 DETs	>15 DETs
0–1 FTR	Low	Low	Average
2–3 FTRs	Low	Average	High
>3 FTRs	Average	High	High

Regarding the complexity of EQs, and EOs, one has to consider that either function may consist of an input part as well as an output part. If a DET is included on both the input (question) and output (response) side, it is counted only once. Therefore, the DETs of both parts are added together, but only the ones that are distinct. The same concept holds for FTRs, where if a FTR is accessed both on the input and output sides of an EQ function, it is counted only once.

The applicable *complexity matrix for EOs and EQs* is presented in Table 12.7.

Table 12.7. Complexity of EOs and EQs

FTRs/DETs	1–5 DETs	6–19 DETs	>19 DETs
0–1 FTR	Low	Low	Average
2–3 FTRs	Low	Average	High
>3 FTRs	Average	High	High

The example data retrieval (at the bottom of Fig. 12.13) function has a primary intent to display information to a user. It retrieves data from a logical file, and the elementary process does NOT involve calculations, derive data, update any ILFs, or alter the behavior of the system. It therefore is an EQ.

The EQ has 3 DETs on the input side (the data field "Name" plus 1 DET for the selection button that identifies the function as a query plus 1 DET for any error messages that can occur) and 1 FTR. The output part has 8 DETs (the data field Name plus the other 7 displayed DETs) and 1 FTR. To determine the complexity of the EQ, use 10 DETs (the 3 DET on the input side + 8 DET on the output side – 1 DET, because the Name field is on both sides), and 1 FTR (the same logical file is used on both sides). The resultant complexity is low according to Table 12.7.

The Function Points to be counted for the transactions can be derived again using the appropriate column as shown in Table 12.8. The EQ we just counted from Fig. 12.13 is worth three unadjusted FP.

Table 12.8 Unadjusted Function Points of transactions

Complexity	EI	EO	EQ
Low	3	4	3
Average	4	5	4
High	6	7	6

12.6.4 Step 4: Calculate the VAF after Determining the 14 GSCs

After counting unadjusted Function Points, the *VAF* has to be determined. It is calculated in a formula using the sum of *the values 14 GSCs:*

1. Data Communications
2. Distributed Data Processing
3. Performance
4. Heavily Used Configuration
5. Transaction Rate
6. Online Data Entry
7. End-User Efficiency
8. Online Update
9. Complex Processing
10. Reusability
11. Installation Ease
12. Operational Ease
13. Multiple Sites
14. Facilitate Change.

The *Degree of Influence (DI)* of each of these characteristics is rated on a scale from 0 (no influence) to 5 (strong influence). There exists a set of exacting definitions in the IFPUG CPM for determining the DI for each of the 14 GSCs (see Chap. 15, *IFPUG Function Point Counting Rules*). The DI's of the 14 GSCs are added together, and the sum is *called Total Degree of Influence (TDI)*. From this the VAF is calculated with the formula

$$VAF = (TDI \times 0.01) + 0.65.$$

This leads to the result that the VAF ranges from 0.65 to 1.35; thus adjusts the unadjusted Function Point count by up to ±35%. A typical VAF (e.g., in the IT department of an international insurance company in Germany) is for host applications to range from about 1.0–1.1. Experiences of other organizations confirm that VAFs between 0.95 and 1.1 are typical in Europe and elsewhere in the world.

The 14 GSCs correlate strongly with the six categories outlined in ISO/IEC 9126 *Quality Attributes* that play an important part in a quality assurance plan (see also chapter *Estimation Fundamentals: ISO 9126 Quality Attributes and IFPUG GSCs* in this book).

Note that the ISO/IEC 9126 standard is slowly being replaced by the SQUARE series of ISO/IEC standards that expand and further define "Quality Metrics" for software and systems.

12.6.5 Step 5: Calculate the Adjusted FPs

As can be seen from Fig. 12.9 (see *step 1: Define the Type of Count*) the following *three types of count are distinguished:*

1. New development
2. Enhancement
3. Application.

According to the type of count, the Function Points are calculated using specific (and different) formulae as described below.

Function Points for new development projects: A new development project adds functionality to the software application. Further functionality can evolve if existing data must be converted and integrated in the new system (migrations). The adjusted Function Points of a new development project are calculated using the VAF:

$$DFP = (UFP + CFP)VAF,$$

where DFP is the development Function Points, adjusted; UFP is the unadjusted Function Points; CFP is the Function Points from conversions (migrations), which are functions specifically required by users (e.g., user requested conversion reports comparing the results of the existing vs. the new cutover payroll system being installed). These are user-specified and requested reports that are of essence during the development project, but are never put into the production software for ongoing use. (For this reason, the conversion functionality is NOT counted in the base or installed application Function Point count.); and VAF is the Value Adjustment Factor of the application.

Function Points for enhancement projects: An enhancement project changes the functionality of an existing application. The following cases can occur (often all four together):

• New functionality is added
• Existing functionality is changed

- Existing functionality is deleted
- Conversion (migration) functionality is required.

Since the GSCs always pertain to the entire application, they must be evaluated both before and after an enhancement project. Two VAFs are distinguished when calculating the FP for enhancement projects: VAFA and VAFB. The Function Points of an enhancement project are calculated with the following formula:

$$EFP = [(ADD + CHGA + CFP)VAFA] + (DEL \times VAFB),$$

where EFP is the enhancement Function points, adjusted; ADD is the added functionality, new; CHGA is the unadjusted FPs for change of functionality after enhancement; CFP is the unadjusted Function Points for conversion functionality; VAFA is the VAF of application after enhancement project; DEL is the unadjusted FPs for functionality deleted; and VAFB is the VAF of application before enhancement project.

Examples for enhancement of functionality may be as follows:

- A batch transfer for exchange of data with another application is obsolete (deletion of functionality)
- The user demands additional reports from the application (addition of new functionality)
- An already existing report should show additional data elements (change of existing functionality).

Function points of an application: In this case it has to be determined if the application is delivered the first time (initialization of new development) or if an existing application is enhanced (the enhancement project updates the application size). In both cases, when the count is for a project, there may occur conversion (migrations) functionality. Conversion functionality does not change the size of the applications. Hence, the FPs of an application after the completion of a new development project are calculated as follows:

$$AFP = ADD \times VAF,$$

with AFP the application FPs after new development (adjusted), ADD the added functionality of the new development (unadjusted), and VAF the Value Adjustment Factor.

In the situation of the update of an existing application by an enhancement project, the Function Points are calculated according to the following formula:

$$AFP = [(UFPB + ADD + CHGA) - (CHGB + DEL)]VAFA,$$

with AFP the application FPs after new development (adjusted), UFPB the unadjusted FPs before enhancement, ADD the added functionality of the new development (unadjusted), CHGA the unadjusted FPs for change of functionality after changing it, CHGB the unadjusted FPs for change of functionality before changing it, DEL the unadjusted FPs for deletion of existing functionality, and VAFA the VAF of application after enhancement.

Maintenance projects: Here it has explicitly to be stated that a pure maintenance project does not alter the functionality of an application (i.e., Maintenance projects typically are equal to zero function points). However, if the maintenance project DOES alter the functionality, then it is really an enhancement project according to IFPUG terminology, regardless of what the business might use to classify the project.

Note that this also occurs in the opposite manner: if the business classifies a project as an enhancement, but there is no alteration of any logical functionality in the project, then the project, according to IFPUG FP terminology, is actually a maintenance project and would warrant a Function Point count.

12.6.6 Step 6: Document the Count

This step is not part of the IFPUG method, however it is one of two final steps recommended by the authors - even if the optional adjustment factor steps 4 and 5 are not done. The first Function Point count of a new development project succeeds or fails along with the planning of the measurement. Hence, the right people often have to meet and allocate enough time to review the necessary (requirements) documentation. The final Function Point count of a new development project after delivery occurs at the project postmortem to measure the actual delivered functionality. *This means revisiting and often updating the first Function Point count.*

If the final documentation is complete and structured according to the requirements, then it becomes a trivial matter to update the final delivery Function Point count, and the effort to perform it is minimized.

Persons who neglect to adequately document their Function Point counts could be considered by some to diminish the value (and auditability) of the counting and measurement process itself.

The documentation of a Function Point count should at a minimum comprise the following information:

- The type of count
- Name of the project or application (as applicable)
- Date of the count and name of the counter and participants
- Indication of whether it is a first or final (delivered) count (if the count is for a project)

- Counting practice release used to count (e.g., IFPUG 4.2)
- List of the documentation used for the count (e.g., requirements document version n.n dated dd/mm/yy, object diagram dated dd/mm/yy)
- The system boundary (description and/or diagrams)
- The logical files and transactions
- The elementary processes counted
- A description of any processes or functions excluded from the count (e.g., duplicate functions, menus, or files required for implementation reasons)
- The VAF and the values of the 14 GSCc
- The unadjusted and adjusted FPs
- Assumptions and decisions that had an influence on the count
- Project description and identifying attributes (e.g., platform, development language(s), team size, and any situations that occurred during the project such as changes in direction, delays, changes of management, canceled functionality, etc.).

The process should be at least formal enough that there are usable documents available for subsequent reporting. Thus, at least some forms should be used that enable structured documentation of the aforementioned items. Furthermore, it must be communicated ("publicly stated within the organization") which forms are to be completed to document the FP counts and who is responsible for their completion. In Appendix A of this book there is an example checklist that can be used as a general form to document IFPUG Function Point counts. The form can be tailored for use with other functional size measurement methods.

Furthermore, the same rigor and discipline should be used with these FP measurement activities as is used in accounting, bookkeeping, and controlling departments. When quality assurance of a Function Point count is done by a competence center or by a Certified Function Point Specialist (CFPS), the documentation should be structured in such a manner that any other experienced Function Point counter could understand and get an overview of the Function Point count in the shortest time possible.

Many organizations use an automated tool to document their counts, for example, the FP repository tool: Function Point Workbench™ (FPW) – see the chapter *Tools for Estimation* in this book for details. Tools such as these deliver reports in a structured way (hierarchy diagrams and hierarchy trees) that can easily be prepared for web presentation as well as in other formats. Practical experience of the authors attests that the effort to count enhancement projects and to update the application baseline is minimized when historic counts are available in a structured form as provided by a tool such as FPW™.

The graphical documentation of the application boundary can often be done with graphical software as, for example, MS PowerPoint or Visio, and in the absence of automated diagrams or tools, even a manual diagram with the boundary depicted can be scanned and attached to the Function Point count automated files (e.g., MS Excel spreadsheet).

Besides it can be recommended to document for each project a log-book (alike a ship's log) with following additional (to the before mentioned) information of the count:

Who did what at which time?
At which time in the project was the count done?
Which special aspects are valid for the project and how is it characterized in the project portfolio?
Which suggestions and decisions were used and for which reasons?
How was the process of the count/estimation performed?
What are the next measures and when are they to be done and by whom?
Which documentation was used for counting?
A cross-reference between physical fields and logical functions.

This logbook is a standard text software document and can be added (as well as the system boundary diagram) to the count documentation in the FPW™ or other FP repository software. In Appendix A of this book we have included an example of such a logbook.

Using the processes described here and tools (checklists and forms as well as software), the organization gains clear, well-structured, and standardized documentation of all Function Point counts. *Enhancement projects* can thus proceed from precise knowledge of the existing application, and can reuse many of the documents as a basis for subsequent enhancement count(s). In addition, it becomes an easy task to verify Function Point counts going forward.

12.6.7 Step 7: Quality Assurance of the Count by the Competence Center

A Function Point count should be reviewed before its final release by a third person or a competence center. In this way, a quality report can show formal or content-related contradictions or weaknesses in the process or in the Function Point counts. For this quality assurance (QA) step, the following three topics can be examined with a QA checklist:

1. Prerequisites
2. Process
3. Documentation.

The first topic checks if the prerequisites for the count were adequate. This requires that the Function Point counters were trained and whether they were provided with adequate information to gain enough knowledge about the logical functionality of the application and/or project.

The second topic examines the formal process of the Function Point count and, by using random checks ensures that the graphical diagrams and other documentation is consistent with the resultant FP lists of transaction and files (maybe documented in a tool).

The final topic is a check that all necessary information about the Function Point count has been adequately documented.

The results of the checklist can be documented in a short report. Together, the checklist and the report become the quality report. In Appendix A of this book is a sample checklist that can be used to perform the quality assurance of a Function Point count.

12.7 The Process to Implement the IFPUG Function Point Counting Method

The process to implement IFPUG Function Point Counting in an organization is similar to that of introducing estimation as outlined in the chapter *The Implementation of Estimation*. Similar tasks and prerequisite steps must be considered and dealt with before the measurement process becomes an organizational habit and becomes part of the way of doing business. In addition, some of the effort for the implementation of a formal estimation can be transferred to the implementation of the Function Point counting processes.

Günter Büren reports on a project sponsored by the European Community whereby 113 person days of effort were required to implement Function Point counting and an estimating process in a small consultancy.

As a rule of thumb, one can say that an experienced Function Point counter is able to count between 300 and 1,000 Function Points a day. The higher rate of counting can surely be reached if all relevant (and up-to-date) documentation is at hand, and if the count is done with automated tool support. The Function Point counting effort could actually end up to be as much as triple to this if project documentation is not at hand, is incomplete, differs from the implemented application, is not available at all, and if there is no tool support.

On the other hand, the effort for Function Point counts for large IT projects can be in the range of several person days. Professor Dumke states that the software development work of 10 person years can rarely be Function Point counted in a single day.

Note that the minimum time needed to perform a well-documented and detailed Function Point count rarely is less than half a day for the following reasons:

1. It takes time to understand what is involved in the project or application functionality (no matter how big it may be).
2. It takes time to explain the process of Function Point counting to project participants.
3. It takes time to assemble and gain even a high-level appreciation for the needed count documentation and what has been assembled for the count.
4. It takes time to perform the count (even if it is small).
5. It takes time to document and record the information for the Function Point count.

All together, it typically takes at least half a day to be able to do all of these tasks.

Critical success factors for the implementation of IFPUG Function Point Counting in an organization include the following:

- Proper planning of the process to introduce and embed the prerequisite tasks needed to perform Function Point counts in the organization (information gathering, training and participation of management, counters, project team members, and a competency center staff knowing about what Function Point counting can and cannot do; and development and documentation of a Function Point counting process manual and organization specific counting conventions).
- A comparable (stable) development environment where Function Point counting is intended to be applied.
- Realistic expectations about FP based measurement and estimation.
- Committed (and visible) management support.
- An understanding that measurement is a necessary prerequisite for estimation, planning, management, controlling, and improvement of the software development tasks.
- Automated support for measurement and recording of project effort.
- The planning and resource allocation of the necessary effort to learn and become proficient in Function Point counting.
- The readiness to give insight (and feedback) to the processes needed and into the development of necessary documentation.
- Acceptance of the need for control of the processes of measurement and estimation.
- Training of the staff and gaining of experiences in a competence center.

12.8 The Limitations of the IFPUG Function Point Counting Method

The FPM is naturally criticized by users of the SLOC-based metrics, but also by proponents and inventors of alternative methods (such as Mark II, COSMIC). Some of the arguments are politically motivated; however, there remain weaknesses in the IFPUG method (and in other functional size measurement methods).

No matter what methodology is used, the most important consideration is consistency in the application of the method, adequate training of the involved staff, and appropriate usage of an applicable (and calibrated) estimation method.

All investigations so far have led to the result that functional size measurement is the most effective and reliable means of measuring software size that can be used effectively in the early phases of the software development life cycle.

Practically, the question is often raised about the *precision of estimation methods* based on functional size measurement. Shigeru Nishiyama of Japan performed a study of five new development projects in 1999, which were counted by two Function Point Counters (called fpA and fpB) and the results were analyzed thoroughly. His regression analysis resulted in

$$\text{Count by fpB} = 0.97\text{fpA} + 4.01, \quad \text{with } R^2 = 0.999.$$

The negligible difference of 3% between the two counters resulted from different interpretations of vague descriptions in the requirements documents, and from intersections in the declaration of EIs, EOs, and EQs in the IFPUG CPM. See the table *Not defined cases* in the chapter *IFPUG Function Point Counting Rules* in this book.

By design, Function Points do not correlate with every aspect of software development, but they were never intended to do so. FP cannot measure the customer contentedness nor can they be used to measure individual productivity. Pam Morris of Australia documented a list of situations for which FP are not applicable:

- In the area of software maintenance:
  - o Defect correction
  - o Table changes
  - o Perfective and corrective maintenance
  - o Production systems support and control
  - o Response behavior of the system
  - o Security and access control
- Consultancy and ad-hoc support
- Project progress and implementation.

It has been often quoted that if all one has is a hammer, then everything looks like a nail (the analogy to FP measurement is that if you only have FP as a measurement, then everything appears to be Function Point countable). Conversely, a good toolkit contains a combination of tools each suitable to perform particular tasks, such as a screwdriver for screws, a hammer for nails, and a level to hang pictures evenly. Similarly, FP must be balanced by other measures to adequately manage the software development environment.

12.9 Management Summary

The IFPUG FPM is a method to measure the (functional) size of an application (piece of software) from the user view.

As an ISO/IEC conformant Functional Size Measurement method, the IFPUG FPM measures the functionality in software delivered to the user as required by the user, and quantified by following the IFPUG CPM set of counting rules.

The functional size measure is independent of the nonfunctional requirements, including the technology used for implementation, since the technological aspects of the software development are not part of the functional size.

Function Points are derived from the logical (or functional) user requirements concept, and the person counting the Function Points will learn a lot about the functional requirements of the software during the process of evaluating the functional size.

At this point it may be worthwhile to note that there are at least five ISO/IEC conformant functional size measurement methods.

The IFPUG FPM can easily be learned and understood and applied to a variety of software.

It has been observed through first hand experience that when the Function Point Analysis is done with the involvement of the end users, they are motivated to better teamwork and more committed engagement. In addition, we have observed that the overall user satisfaction with the project increases. This is a key project success factor according to the Standish Group's annual CHAOS Report.

FP size at various points in the development life cycle is used for measurement of requirements creep (scope management).

FP methodology supports reuse in IT development by early and standardized quantification of business cases in the requirements definition phase, for contracting, for project-estimation, for test case identification, for enhancements, and for documentation.

The FPM methodology is independent of the development environment as well as the skills or attributes of developers.

Function Points can facilitate comparison of prices from suppliers and to evaluate cost ratios for software under contract.

ISBSG publications also discuss how function points can be used as part of price comparisons (see http://www.isbsg.org). The metric price per FP can contribute to decisions about whether to build-or-buy.

Another interesting use of Function Points is to directly measure and manage software development performed under contract.

The effort for planning, performing, and documentation of Function Point counts can be justified as long as FP are used appropriately together with other measures.

Capers Jones estimates the effort to implement a fully-functioning measurement and analysis program to be maximally 3% of the cost of a project – not much when you consider the savings that better requirements and accurate estimates can provide.

The primary application areas of the IFPUG FPM are in estimation of new software development and enhancement.

FPs can be used for risk assessment.

The COSMIC Method, presented in the chapter about variants of the FPM, claims to address internal processing more concretely, and the reader is directed to select the most appropriate functional size measurement method (amongst the five ISO/IEC conformant methods) to meet their specific needs.

Chris Kemerer from the Massachusetts Institute of Technology (MIT) showed in a research study comparing 15 software projects that the FPM could be used for various types of software beyond management information systems or commercial applications.

Estimating methods based on the FPM for sizing software fulfills the major prerequisite requirements of a method for estimation of effort.

The goals of the IFPUG function point analysis method are to measure small units in order to support flexible comparisons and early deviations from plan.

The optimum time for a first Function Point count is the end of the requirements analysis.

It does not make sense that a Function Point count is performed only once during project progress because throughout the project there evolves new information such as scope changes, clarifications to requirements (as well as requirements creep).

We recommend (consistent with the practices at IBM) to revisit the original Function Point count for any updated information (and changes) at the end of each phase of the software project. This practice also supports the tracking of requirements scope creep and scope management principles.

The counting of Function Points is ideally considered to be a part of the project documentation, reviews, project controlling, and releases at the end of each project phase.

Revisiting the Function Point count at different times as the project progresses enables early adjustments (and corrections) to the resultant effort estimates, and thus it increases the precision and approximation of the actual effort.

When an effort estimate is required at an earlier stage than at the end of the requirements phase, we recommend the development of one or more Function Point prognosis methods.

Function Point counts as well as FP estimates should be performed by project leaders' or project team members' knowledgeable about the functionality together with support of the competence center.

There are three types of Function Point counts, the first two specific to IT projects: New development, Enhancement, Application.

A new development project is the first build of an application. Thus, all delivered functionality is considered to be added.

An enhancement project can add functionality, as well as change or delete functionality.

At project postmortem of an enhancement project, the Function Points of the enhanced application must also be updated based on what has been added, changed, and deleted.

The IFPUG FPM distinguishes between the size of a software project (Counting scope) and an application.

Principally, the application boundary must be defined from the user view.

Since the application boundary is critical to the determination of the application functionality, it is important for it to be documented clearly. This includes the description of assumptions used to locate the boundary.

Since the application boundary is critical to the determination of the application functionality, it is important for it to be documented clearly. This includes the description of assumptions used to locate the boundary.

Practically, this documentation (typically including system diagrams) can easily be reused in (or as) architecture diagrams in the application atlas of the organization.

The two steps from the unadjusted FPs to the adjusted FPs take the functional size measurement (unadjusted FP) in the direction of software estimation by considering influences of the nonfunctional requirements in system development.

ILF and EIF must be distinguished and counted.

The EIFs are external interface files (persistent logical entities) as identified from the requirements.

The complexity of internal and external logical files depends on two dimensions: the number of DET and the number of RET.

New users of the IFPUG method often have difficulties to distinguish between ILFs and EIFs. A rule of thumb is to count an ILF if data are stored and maintained (and are not part of the exclusions as outlined above), and an EIF when data are only retrieved or extracted or referenced.

Transactional functions are EI, EO, and EQ.

The complexity of a transaction depends on two dimensions: the number of data elements (DET) and the number of referenced files (FTR).

After counting unadjusted Function Points, the VAF has to be determined. It is calculated in a formula using the sum of the values 14 GSCs.

The 14 GSCs correlate strongly with the 12 ISO/IEC 9126 Quality Attributes that are an important part of a quality assurance plan.

The first Function Point count of a new development project succeeds or fails along with the planning of the measurement. Hence, the right people often have to meet and allocate enough time to review the necessary (requirements) documentation.

The final Function Point count of a new development project after delivery occurs at the project postmortem to measure the actual delivered functionality. This means revisiting and often updating the first Function Point count.

Persons who neglect to adequately document their Function Point counts could be considered by some to diminish the value (and auditability) of the counting and measurement process itself.

The process should be at least formal enough that there are usable documents available for subsequent reporting.

Furthermore, the same rigor and discipline should be used with these FP measurement activities as is used in accounting, bookkeeping, and controlling departments.

Besides that it can be recommended to document for each project a logbook (alike a ship's log).

A Function Point count should be reviewed before its final release by a third person or a competence center.

As a rule of thumb, one can say that an experienced Function Point counter is able to count between 300 and 1,000 Function Points a day.

The Function Point counting effort could actually end up to be as much as triple to this if project documentation is not at hand, is incomplete, differs from the implemented application, not available at all, and if there is no tool support.

On the other hand, the effort for Function Point counts for large IT projects can be in the range of several person days.

No matter what methodology is used, the most important consideration is consistency in the application of the method, adequate training of the involved staff, and appropriate usage of an applicable (and calibrated) estimation method.

All investigations so far have led to the result that functional size measurement is the most effective and reliable means of measuring software size that can be used effectively in the early phases of the software development life cycle.

By design, Function Points do not correlate with every aspect of software development, but they were never intended to do so. FP cannot measure the customer contentedness nor can they be used to measure individual productivity.

13 Functional Size Measurement Methods (FSMMs)

There are currently five different ISO/IEC Functional Size Measurement Method standards, four of which are outlined in this chapter, plus the IFPUG method (unadjusted), which was described in an earlier chapter. Additionally, there are variants of the IFPUG method and also of other methods that purport to measure the size of software. For convenience of the reader, the ISO/IEC standards are included here, and the other sizing measures are included in the chapter "Variants of the IFPUG Function Point Counting Method."

Functional Size Measurement is a term coined by the International Organization for Standardization/International Electrotechnical Commission (ISO/ IEC) in its suite of standards numbered 14143-1 through 14143-6. The definition and framework standard of the series is ISO/IEC 14143-1 Software and Systems Engineering – Software Measurement – Functional Size Measurement – Definition of concepts. This standard was most recently updated and published in 2007, replacing the first published version in 1998. Note that ISO/IEC standards have a lifespan of 5 years from the date of publication, after which they must be reviewed by ISO/IEC to ensure ongoing relevance. ISO/ IEC working groups can then reaffirm a standard as it is, withdraw it, or update it (and a new work item proposal is launched to revise it). The 14143-1: 2007 standard reaffirmed the standard and then republished it via an ISO-specific process called a technical corrigendum to correct minor technical defects and editorial defects.

See the chapter "Measurement Communities and Resources" in this book for more details about the ISO/IEC standards related to functional size measurement.

The most important definitions from ISO/IEC 14143-1:2007 include the following:

- *Functional Size Measurement* (*FSM*): the process of measuring Functional Size
- *Functional Size*: a size of the software derived by quantifying the Functional User Requirements
- *Functional User Requirements* (*FUR*): a subset of the User Requirements. Requirements that describe what the software shall do, in terms of tasks and services

- *FSM Method* (*FSMM*): a specific implementation of FSM defined by a set of rules, which conforms to the mandatory features of this part of ISO/IEC 14143.

The Finnish Software Measurement Association (FiSMA) states that the typical user viewpoint for Functional Size Measurement is to estimate the effort for a software project. Other important industry uses of FSM are presented in Fig. 13.1.

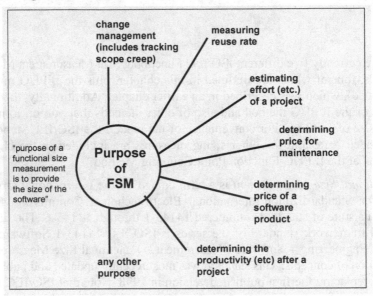

Fig. 13.1. Common purposes of functional size measurement (FiSMA 1.1)

13.1 Short Characterizations of ISO/IEC-Conformant FSMMs

There are five ISO/IEC-conformant FSMMs currently published. All of them use a different approach to measure the size of software to be developed.

As stated many times throughout this book, the functional size of a piece of software is *one of* the main drivers in effort estimation. As mentioned in the chapter about Variants of the IFPUG Function Point Counting Method, Ton Dekkers reported at MetriKon 2003 that *a minimum size in Function Points is necessary for reliable estimations*: about 200 FP (IFPUG) or about 100 Cfsu (Cosmic Functional Size Units – soon to be referred to as simply *COSMIC Function Points* – CFP). This threshold is similar for maintenance projects. Dekkers states that a minimum size of 100 MFP (NESMA Maintenance Function Points) or 60 MCFP (Maintenance CFP, COSMIC) is a prerequisite for reliable estimating.

At the time of this printing the five (see Table 13.1) ISO/IEC Functional Size Measurement Method standards that conform to the mandatory provisions of ISO/IEC 14143-1 Definitions of concepts include the following:

Table 13.1. ISO/IEC Functional Size Measurement Method standards

Functional Size Measurement Method (FSMM)	ISO/IEC standard number
IFPUG 4.1 Unadjusted Function Point Counting Method	ISO/IEC 20926
COSMIC-FFP (Vs. 2.1) – A Functional Size Measurement Method	ISO/IEC 19761
FiSMA 1.1 Functional Size Measurement Method	ISO/IEC 29881
Mark II Function Point Analysis – Counting Practices Manual	ISO/IEC 20968
NESMA Functional Size Measurement Method version 2.1 – Definitions and counting guidelines for the application of Function Point Analysis	ISO/IEC 24570

This book addresses the IFPUG Function Point Counting Method as a separate chapter not only because it is the first and longest standing method, but also because it is the basis for the demonstrated experiences of the authors.

Nonetheless, the remaining four ISO/IEC Functional Size Measurement Methods warrant a closer look. Each one is further outlined in this chapter.

The ISBSG *Practical Project Estimation, 2nd edition (2005)* devotes a number of chapters to the various FSMMs and also to shortcut methods to arrive at an estimated functional size. It should be noted that one of the most important critical success factors for software measurement and estimation is a consistent unit and methodology for measuring the software's functional size.

The following Fig. 13.2 explains the relationship between the various ISO standards and the functional size measurement methods presented in this chapter.

13.2 COSMIC

The Common Software Measurement Consortium (COSMIC) first developed the COSMIC-Full Function Point (FFP) method in an effort to provide a Functional Size Measurement Method specifically designed to meet the mandatory provisions of ISO/IEC 14141-1 and to address what COSMIC perceived as a gap in the ability of any method to measure the size of real-time applications. COSMIC-FFP was published as ISO/IEC 19761 COSMIC-FFP – A Functional Size Measurement Method.

Note: the COSMIC consortium in 2007 changed the name of the method to COSMIC (dropping the FFP) and changed the Cfsu (COSMIC functional sizing unit) designation of the measurement unit to CFP (COSMIC Function Points). We have updated all references from this point on in this chapter to reference simply COSMIC when we refer to the method, and used CFP to refer to the units – for currency and consistency.

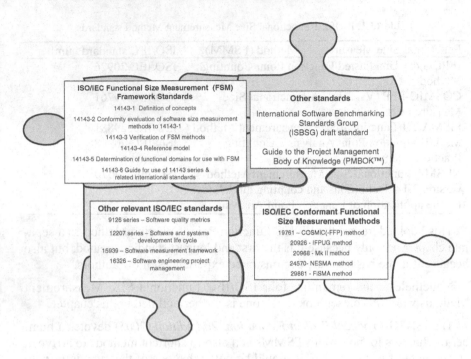

Fig. 13.2. Relationship between the various ISO standards and the functional size measure ment methods presented in this chapter

The COSMIC consortium was founded in 1998 as a volunteer organization of experts of software measurement from Australia, Canada, Finland, Germany, Ireland, Italy, and Japan.The COSMIC group consists of about 40 people from 8 countries who combined their effort voluntarily and proposed principles for a software Functional Size Measurement method. At the end of 1999, they published *the COSMIC-FFP Version 2.0 Measurement Practices Manual (MPM)*, and made it publicly available on the Web. Since then, the basic rules have not changed and, version 2.2 was standardized within ISO/ IEC and published as an international standard (*ISO/IEC 19761:2003 COSMIC-FFP – A Functional Size Measurement Method*).

The COSMIC website (http://www.cosmicon.com) released the COSMIC Method v3.0 in 2007 and stated: "Version 3.0 represents the first major update of the COSMIC method for four years (the previous version was 2.2) and as the designation implies, the new documents contain important advances and clarifications of the method. *Note, however, the basic model used to measure a functional size of software via the COSMIC method has not changed since it was first published in 1999.*"

Various COSMIC documents (e.g., the Measurement Practices Manual) are currently available in a number of languages including Arabic, English, French,

Japanese, and Spanish with additional translations either underway or planned. Also available is the COSMIC Guide to the Implementation of ISO/IEC 19761.

This guide, as well as a number of other documents can be downloaded from http://www.gelog.etsmtl.ca/cosmic-ffp or from http://www.cosmicon. com.

The main goal of the COSMIC project was the development, delivery, and market acceptance of a new method of software measurement:

- Suited for as many as possible application areas (priority for business and real-time software)
- As a component for estimation applicable early in the software life cycle
- Suitable for performance measurement.

Thus, the COSMIC Method is the first functional sizing method with the following characteristics:

- Designed by an international group of experts on an academic and theoretical basis
- Drawn on the practical experience of all the main existing FP methods
- Designed specifically to conform to ISO/IEC 14143 Part 1
- Designed to work across MIS and real-time domains, for software in any layer or peer item
- Tested and revised through field tests before being finalized.

The COSMIC Method has an emerging number of users worldwide and is now considered to be an acceptable sizing measure in various estimating software packages (including KnowledgePlan™ and Experience® Pro software, and also within the ISBSG database).

13.2.1 The COSMIC Counting Process

For measuring with COSMIC the purpose, scope, and boundaries of the measurement have to be defined. Then the Functional User Requirements (FUR) are collected in the so-called Mapping Phase, expressed in the form of the COSMIC generic software model. In the last step, the identified components are classified according to their size, and the measurement results are aggregated (see Fig. 13.3).

At times, software is bounded by hardware. In the so-called *front end*, software used by a human user is bounded by I/O hardware or by engineered devices such as sensors or relays. In the so-called *back end*, software is bounded by persistent storage hardware.

COSMIC measures the size of a piece of software from four distinct types of data movement characterizing the functional flow of data attributes (see Fig. 13.4).

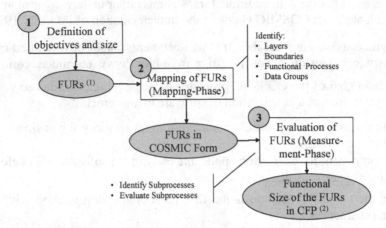

(1) Functional User Requirements in any suitable form (Functional User Requirements)
(2) COSMIC -unit of measure (COSMIC function points) – formerly called Cfsu (COSMIC
    Functional Size Unit). Changed to CFP in 2007.

Fig. 13.3. The process of counting COSMIC Function Points

COSMIC Principles for the software to be measured:

- The software gets input from a user and produces output required by a user.
- The software manipulates units of information, which are shown as data groups with attributes.
- The functional size is directly proportional to the number of data movements necessary to perform the functional processes.

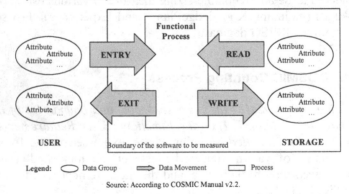

Source: According to COSMIC Manual v2.2.

Fig. 13.4. COSMIC model for measurement

For the front end, two *types of data movement* (ENTRIES and EXITS) allow the exchange of data with users across a *boundary*. In the back end, two types of movement (READS and WRITES) allow the exchange of data attributes with the persistent storage hardware. There are four base functional components (BFC) counted in the COSMIC method:

- *ENTRY*: this BFC moves attributes of a data group from a user across the application boundary to the functional process that needs the data. The data are updated, and data manipulations such as validation are included.
- *EXIT*: this BFC moves attributes of a data group from the functional process across the application boundary to a user. The data will not be read but data manipulations such as formatting are included.
- *READ*: this BFC moves attributes of a data group from a persistent storage to the functional process that needs the data.
- *WRITE*: this BFC moves attributes of a data group from a functional process back to the persistent storage.

Note: It is important to remember that a data movement relates to exactly one data group. If a functional process, for example, uses information from three different persistent data groups (e.g., person, department, relation between person and department), then the method would count three distinct Reads. The COSMIC manual explicitly states that data groups are mainly entities of an ER model in the third normal form.

The functional size in COSMIC depends only on data movements. A data movement is defined as one CFP = one COSMIC Function Point.

Luca Santillo presented at IWSM 2005 in Montréal a COSMIC list for data manipulation and movement classifications (see Table 13.2).

An advantage of this concept is that various interpretations of the elementary process do not affect the measurement result in COSMIC.

In COSMIC, there is no discussion of what constitutes elementary processes since the functional size is derived – one level deeper – from the number of data movements. More critical to COSMIC is the determination of data groups since the data movements are derived from them.

13.2.2 Software Layers in COSMIC

An important difference to the IFPUG method is the concept of software layers such as tiers, service structures, or component deployments for the architectural reasoning of boundaries.

The COSMIC methodology delivers the possibility to use the same user view (single end-user perspective) as traditional IFPUG, as well as other views such as the developer view.

Figure 13.5 shows the classical end-user view that ignores the other layers of the system architecture and has its focus purely on the application.

In another example, the developer wants to determine the size of the user requirements that influence a three-tier architecture with the following components:

Table 13.2. Data manipulation and movement classification per COSMIC (Santillo, 2005)

Action	Measured as COSMIC movement	Include it as manipulation
Validations are performed		Yes (Validation) → Read
Mathematical formulae and calculations are performed		Yes (Creation)→ Write
Equivalent values are converted		Yes (Validation) →Read
Data is filtered and selected by using specified criteria to compare multiple sets of data		Yes (Validation)→ Read
Conditions are analyzed to determine which are applicable		Yes (Validation)→Read
One or more data groups are updated	Yes (Write)	
One or more data groups are referenced	Yes (Read)	
Data or control information is retrieved	Yes (Read)	
Derived data is created by transforming existing data to create additional data		Yes (Creation)→ Write
Behavior of the system is altered		Yes (Creation)→ Write
Prepare and present information outside the boundary	Yes (Exit)	
Capability exists to accept data or control information that enters the application boundary	Yes (Entry)	
Data is resorted or rearranged		Yes (Creation)→ Write

- Graphical user interface
- Business rules
- Data services.

The components are shown in Fig. 13.5. These three layers each have a unique set of users.

Different abstractions are typically used for different measurement purposes. For business application software, the abstraction commonly assumes that the users are one or more humans who interact directly with the business application software across the boundary; the I/O hardware is ignored. In contrast, for real-time software the users are typically the engineered devices that interact directly with the software, that is, the users *are* the I/O hardware.

Thus, for example, the layers of the graphical user interface, business rules, and data services in Fig. 13.6 are all separately considered by the COSMIC approach.

Figure 13.7 shows a second example from developer view where the user requirements influence all four layers of the application.

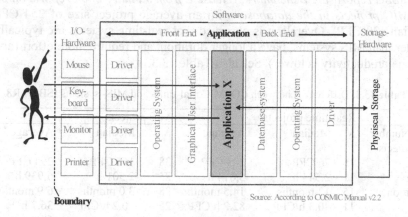

Fig. 13.5. COSMIC software layers for business applications from end-user view

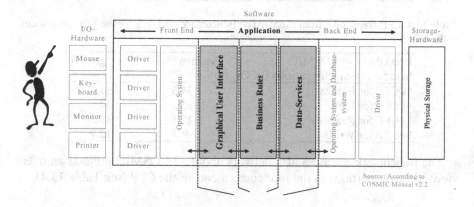

Fig. 13.6. COSMIC software layers for three-tier architecture from developer view – example 1

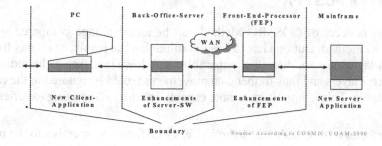

Fig. 13.7. COSMIC software layers for four-tier architecture from developer view – example 2

13.2.3 ISBSG Data with Respect to COSMIC

The ISBSG report: the Benchmark, release 8 from January 2004 reports on 66 COSMIC projects in the database, with an average project size of 254 CFP (median 120 CFP). Overall, it is observed that real-time systems are typically smaller than MIS systems, have a longer duration, and require more effort (and thus the productivity is lower). See also Table 13.3.

Table 13.3. Differences between COSMIC real-time- and MIS- systems ISBSG R8

	Real-time projects			MIS projects		
N = Number of projects	N	Median	Average	N	Median	Average
Size	15	76 CFP	203 CFP	38	165 CFP	293 CFP
Effort	11	2,544 h	5,614 h	25	2,501 h	6,939 h
Duration	15	13 months	14.5 months	38	3.0 months	6.9 months
PDR	11	40.3 h/CFP	82.2 h/CFP	25	10.2 h/CFP	36.7 h/CFP
Productivity	15	9.0 CFP/ month	11.5 CFP/ month	38	45.9 CFP/ month	74 CFP/ month

Table 13.4. CFP breakdown from *ISBSG*: The Benchmark release 8 for the four components of the COSMIC

Breakdown of COSMIC base functional components (BFC)	Median (%)	Average (%)
% CFP for Entries	36.3	33.4
% CFP for Exits	35.2	34.6
% CFP for Reads	17.1	19.3
% CFP for Writes	9.7	12.7

The Benchmark release 8 also delivers about 52 COSMIC projects an overview of the proportions of the four components of the CFP (see Table 13.4).

13.2.4 Comparison Between Counts Done Using COSMIC and IFPUG FPA

The layer concept of COSMIC Method can be an advantage compared with the IFPUG method. But one has to keep in mind that the results of counts from different layers are not directly comparable. It follows that further boundaries for different layers and thus further data movements would be ignored in the case of less layers. This is important to note especially when elaborating experience curves.

Nevertheless, the COSMIC Method offers a different perspective to the previously established and known methods for Functional Size Measurement such as IFPUG, FiSMA, Mark II, and NESMA. Its acceptance, use, and thus the number of available case studies increase step by step.

Table 13.5. Comparison of the concepts of IFPUG FP counting method and COSMIC concepts

IFPUG release 4.2	COSMIC version 2.2

Measures processes and data:
  Three functional types for processes
    External Input (EI)
    External Output (EO)
    External Inquiry (EQ)
  Two functional types for logical data files
    Internal Logical Files (ILF)
    External Logical Files (EIF)
	Measures explicitly (sub)processes based on data movements according to the following:
	  Four functional types for (sub) processes
	    Input of data (ENTRY)
	    Reading of data (READ)
	    Writing of data (WRITE)
	    Output of data (EXIT)

Minimum: 3 FP	Minimum: 2 CFP
Maximum: 7 FP	Maximum: no limitations (continuous scale)
Considers the access to logical persistent data files – once per process (FTR)	Considers the unique accesses to logical persistent data files (data files are not explicitly counted) on the level of reading and/or writing (READ, WRITE)
Considers unique data element types (DETs) to determine the complexity of the transactional functions	Considers groups of data fields in relation to the subprocesses ENTRY and EXIT
Processes can have a complexity of low, average, or high depending on the number of used data element types (DET) and data files (FTR)	Each unique subprocess (READ, WRITE, ENTRY, EXIT) counts as a CFP. This implies that all subprocesses have equal complexity
No explicit rules for multitier architectural concepts in software development	Explicit rules for multitier architectural concepts (Layer concept)
Explicit focus on external user view without regarding aspects of implementation	The rules are defined in order to enable different views (e.g., end user, developer) and architectural concepts (e.g., Client/Server) for counting
There exists exactly one unique logical boundary per application (Application Boundary)	A boundary exists between two different layers. Since applications to be counted can have several layers, there could exist many boundaries The IFPUG concept (end-user view, no differentiation of layers) appears to be a subset of the counting possibilities of the COSMIC Method
All counts are principally comparable if the standards are applied	All counts with equal view and equal layer concept are comparable.

A comparison of five applications counted with the IFPUG FP method and COSMIC, respectively, showed nearly no differences in the MIS environment, but a 76% difference in real-time environment.

This is not a major surprise because the two methods measure a functional size of the software in a different manner.

Table 13.5 shows a comparison of the major characteristics of both methods.

In *the Fetcke study* in 1999, four software applications of a data storage system were measured. These were business applications with few data entities; all four applications handled three entities or fewer, and the entities were all referred to by the elementary processes (according to IFPUG FPA). In this study, all details of the measurement process were reported for both IFPUG 4.1 and for COSMIC version 2.0. It should be noted that, while the Fetcke study used COSMIC version 2.0, the results reported are considered valid also for the current version.

The sizes of the four projects in *unadjusted IFPUG FP* (*uFP*) and *COSMIC* (*CFP*) are as follows:

- Data Warehouse: 77 uFP, 81 CFP
- Large Warehouse Customer Business: 56 uFP, 52 CFP
- Customer Management: 49 uFP, 51 CFP
- Manufacturer's Warehouse: 40 uFP, 38 CFP.

A correlation analysis provided the following relation with $R^2 = 0.97$:

$$CFP = 1.1uFP - 7.6$$

Using the conversion formula, a deviation of 4% in average (range from 0% to 8%) could be found.

Alain Abran et al. presented at IWSM 2005 in Montréal the so-called *Desharnais study* of six projects from a governmental organization measured both with IFPUG 4.1 FPA and with COSMIC 2.2. Regression analysis delivered the following conversion formula:

$$CFP = 1.35uFP(IFPUG) + 5.5, R^2 = 0.98$$

The project size ranged between 87 and 936 CFP/uFP.

13.3 FiSMA 1.1 Functional Size Measurement Method

The first version of the FiSMA FSM Method was published in 1991 under the original name Laturi and funded through a cooperative industry project of the same name. Since then, there has been continuous use and maintenance of the method through the establishment of the Finnish Software Measurement Association (FiSMA), incorporated in 1996 (http://www.fisma.fi). The early versions of FiSMA 1.1 were known by other names (Laturi Function Points and Experience Function Points). The current name: FiSMA 1.1 FSM Method is consistent with the name of the maintenance organization, and better reflects that FiSMA 1.1 is the result of 15 years of cooperative Finnish industry involvement in its development and evolution. The FiSMA 1.1 Functional Size Measurement Method is the newest member of the ISO/IEC FSMM standards and is known under the name ISO/IEC 29881:2008 FiSMA 1.1 Functional Size Measurement Method.

The user community of the FiSMA FSM Method was organized in 1990, and over 2000 project managers and software practitioners have been trained to use FiSMA FSM.

The documentation for the FiSMA FSM Method is publicly available (http://www.fisma.fi) in English and Finnish. Tool support for FiSMA FSM has facilitated rigorous application of the method and made the measurement results readily verifiable. The FiSMA Experience® repository currently contains data from more than 850 completed software projects including FiSMA functional size and effort details. This database continues to grow as more completed projects are submitted.

From the specification (FiSMA): FiSMA 1.1 is based purely on Functional User Requirements. User requirements can be thought of as functional – what the software does, and nonfunctional – how the software must perform (including quality requirements). For FiSMA 1.1, the Functional User Requirements are the object of measurement. While some FSM methods are process oriented, FiSMA 1.1 is service oriented. Process-oriented methods require the identification of all functional processes supported by the piece of software. In contrast, service-oriented methods, such as FiSMA 1.1, require identification of all different *services* provided by the piece of software.

The FiSMA 1.1 relationship chain between users and the developed piece of software involves user needs and services as presented in Fig. 13.8.

FiSMA 1.1 identifies seven distinct base functional component (BFC) classes:

- Interactive end-user navigation and query services (q)
- Interactive end-user input services (i)
- Noninteractive end-user output services (o)
- Interface services to other application (t)
- Interface services from other applications (f)
- Data storage services (d)
- Algorithmic and manipulation services (a).

Each BFC class of FiSMA 1.1 further decomposes into several BFC types. All together, there are 28 BFC types. Figure 13.8 depicts the relationships between the BFC classes and their component BFC types. Each BFC class is explained in the clauses that follow.

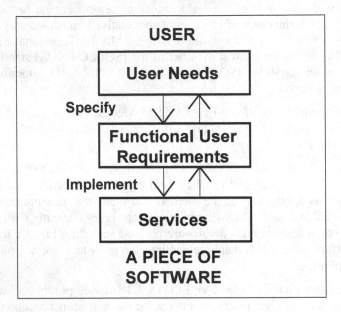

Fig. 13.8. FiSMA 1.1 links between users and a piece of software

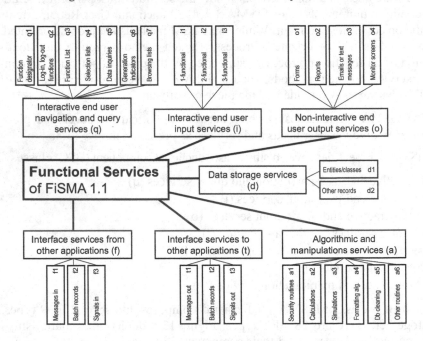

Fig. 13.9. FiSMA 1.1 BFC classes and BFC types

Note: For ease of presentation, Fig. 13.9 uses the following short form conventions: (a) Each of the seven BFC classes is denoted by a single alphabetic character and (b) Each BFC type is prefixed by its class alphabetic character and a sequential integer number that has been assigned to it.

13.3.1 The FiSMA 1.1 Measurement Process

The FiSMA 1.1 measurement process consists of the following steps:

1. *Gather documentation* and software development artifacts to describe the functional user requirements for the software (to be or already) developed. These include any items such as use cases, preliminary user requirements, use manuals, entity relationship diagrams, screen, report, or database mockups, data flow diagrams, etc. – anything that describes what the software will do in terms of tasks or services, independently of any quality or technical requirements.
2. *Determine the Scope* of the FSM: The Scope of FiSMA 1.1 is determined by the purpose for doing the FSM and includes the FUR to be developed or enhanced in the project or application to be counted.
3. *Determine which are the Functional User Requirements* to be measured by FiSMA 1.1 by determining the Scope as outlined in step 1 and include only those user requirements that describe what the software is to do in terms of tasks and services.
4. *Identify the BFCs* within the Functional User Requirements from step 2 in two main parts: (1) measuring the end-user interface services, and (2) measuring indirect services. If one of these two parts does not exist for the piece of software, then the process consists only of measuring the services that are present.
5. *Classify the BFCs* into the appropriate BFC type by mapping each BFC identified to the descriptions of the BFC types that follow. Be cautious to identify duplicate logical functionality so that it is counted only once per instance of the FSM. Two BFC types are considered to be duplicate if they have the same characteristics (i.e., identical BFC types with the same values for each of the component parts for the BFC type, i.e., identical data elements, reading references, and/or writing references as appropriate for the BFC type.).
6. *Assign the appropriate numeric value to each BFC* using the calculations outlined for each BFC type.
7. *Calculate the Functional Size* by adding together the size for each component part. The unit of measure for FiSMA 1.1 is the FiSMA Function Point or Ffp.

Note: Each equation that follows includes one or more constants whose value was derived through research in the FiSMA 1.1 development. The value for each constant represents the number of a particular item (e.g., data fields) equal to 1 Ffp for the type. We have denoted the value of each constant in the equations that follow using the notation "–>" followed by the value.

13.3.2 FiSMA 1.1 Components

The listing of components presented here is abridged for brevity. For detailed descriptions of FiSMA 1.1 components and examples, see the FiSMA 1.1 manual downloadable from http://www.fisma.fi.

Interactive End-User Navigation and Query Services (q)

This class of BFC involves data and/or services crossing the boundary into or out of the software. Interactive end-user navigation and query services specify all parts of the interactive user interface where there is no maintenance of persistent data stored in the system. Maintenance refers to any service where data is changed as a result of the service and includes, for example, creating, updating, or deleting. The number of functional size units for each navigation and query service depends on the number of data elements of the BFC and the number of unique entities that need to be referenced. (There is an indirect relationship between the entities identified in this step as being referenced and the BFC types identified within the BFC Class called data storage services. Each independent entity identified as a reference in this BFC type must also be explicitly counted once in the software application's stored data).

In FiSMA 1.1, the BFC class *Navigation and query services* are divided into seven BFC types:

1. *Function designator* (q1) is a service that provides a uniquely identifiable visual way for a user to indicate the specific service(s) to be performed.
2. *Log-in and log-out functions* (q2) usually does not update persistent data. They control user access and prevent illegal use.
3. *Function list* (q3) is a service to provide a set of pre-defined alternatives to enable a user to indicate the specific service(s) to be performed.
4. *Selection lists* (q4) show a list of acceptable parameter values to the end user. Often they are very simple, showing values of one single data item, but they may be more complicated.
5. *Data inquiries* (q5) show the specific contents of data store(s) to the end user.
6. *Generation indicators* (q6) help the user to prepare the data and/or control information for a subsequent service. Very often they are connected to some other type of functional services, such as a report or manipulation routine.

7. *Browsing lists* (q7) show a list of similar data elements, typically the most important details to help filter the entities for further operations.

The size for each service within this BFC class is given by the following equation:

$$S_q = a_q + n/d_q + r_r/c_q,$$

where

S_q = size of query (dialog, menu, etc.)
n = number of data elements, fields
r_r = number of reading references to entities
d_q = BFC class specific number of data elements = 1 Ffp → 7.00
c_q = BFC class specific number of reading references = 1 Ffp → 2.00
a_q = establishment cost = 0.2 Ffp.

Interactive End-User Input Services (i)

This class of BFC involves data and/or services crossing the boundary into the software. Interactive end-user input services specify all parts of the interactive user interface where there is maintenance of data store(s) of the software. Data storage consists of logical entities (data records). Maintenance refers to any service where data is changed as a result of the service, and includes, for example, creating, updating, and deleting. From a user's point of view, interactive end-user services perform those business tasks that change the data contents of the software. From the information system point of view, end users manipulate system data using interactive end-user services.

The number of functional size units of input functions depends on the number of different data elements of the BFC measured, and the number of needed reading and writing references to unique entities. (There is a direct relationship between the entities identified in this step as writing references and the BFC types identified within the BFC Class: data storage services. Each independent entity identified as a writing reference in this BFC type must also be explicitly counted once as stored data.)

In FiSMA 1.1, end-user input services are divided into three BFC types:

- *One-functional input dialogs* (i1) support only one of the three maintenance types: create, update, or delete.
- *Two-functional input dialogs* (i2) support two of the three maintenance types: create, update, and/or delete.
- *Three-functional input dialogs* (i3) support all three maintenance types: create, update, and delete.

The size for each service within this BFC class is given by the following equation:

$$S_i = m\,(a_i + n/d_i + r_w/c_i + r_r/b_i),$$

where

S_i = size of input

m = functionality multiplier; value 1, 2, or 3, depending on how many functions create, update, and delete the BFC incorporates

n = number of data elements, fields

r_w = number of writing references to entities

r_r = number of only reading references to entities

d_i = BFC class specific number of data elements = 1 Ffp →5.00

c_i = BFC class specific number of writing references =1 Ffp →1.50

b_i = BFC class specific number of reading references = 1 Ffp →2.00

a_i = establishment cost, 0.2 Ffp.

Noninteractive End-User Output Services (o)

This class of BFC involves data and/or services crossing the boundary out of the software. Noninteractive end-user output services specify all parts of the user interface that are noninteractive and do not maintain data store(s) of the software. The number of functional size units of output functions depends on the number of different data elements of the BFC and the number of needed reading references to entities. There is an indirect relationship between the unique entities identified in this step as being referenced and the BFC types identified within the BFC Class: data storage services. Each independent entity identified as a reference in this BFC type must also be explicitly counted once as stored data.

FiSMA 1.1 output services are divided into four BFC types:

- *Output forms* (o1) are services resulting in printed or displayed documents, which always present the same layout (e.g., a receipt).
- *Reports* (o2) are services resulting in printed or displayed documents, whose layout may vary within the specified framework according to the presented data (e.g., product list or sales report).
- *E-mails and text messages* (o3) are services resulting in electronically transmitted output documents, which have a standardized structure. The structure often contains title fields, data fields, and optional attachments.
- *Monitor screen output* (o4) service involves continuously displayed documents, which are updated regularly in consequence of data changes (e.g., measurement display of a process).

The size for each service within this BFC class is given by the following equation:

$$S_o = a_o + n/d_o + r_r/c_o,$$

where

S_o = size of output
n = number of data elements, fields
r_r = number of reading references to entities
d_o = BFC class specific number of data elements = 1 Ffp →5.00
c_o = BFC class specific number of reading references = 1 Ffp →2.00
a_o = establishment cost, 1.0 Ffp.

Interface Services to Other Applications (t)

This class of BFC involves data and/or services crossing the boundary out of the software. Interface services to other applications specify all automatic data transfers that move data from the measured piece of software to another application or any device. The number of functional size units of outbound interface functions depends on the number of different data elements of the BFC measured (i.e., the number of attributes) and the number of needed reading references to entities.

There is an indirect relationship between the entities identified in this step as being referenced and the BFC types identified within the BFC Class: data storage services. Each independent entity identified as a reference in this BFC type must also be explicitly counted once as stored data.

FiSMA 1.1 outbound interface functions are divided into three BFC types:

- *Messages to other applications* (t1) are services where data groups are sent on-line, usually in real-time, to any other application.
- *Batch records to other applications* (t2) are services where data groups are written to a temporary file for transfer to another application.
- *Signals to devices or other applications* (t3) are services where data strings or single pieces of information are sent to any other application or device (e.g., a LED).

The size for each service within this BFC class is given by the following equation:

$$S_t = a_t + n/d_t + r_r/c_t,$$

where

S_t = size of interface to other application
n = number of data elements (attributes)
r_r = number of reading references to entities
d_t = BFC class specific number of data elements = 1 Ffp →7.00
c_t = BFC class specific number of reading references = 1 Ffp →2.00
a_t = establishment cost, 0.5 Ffp.

Interface Services from Other Applications (f)

This class of BFC involves data and/or services crossing the boundary into the software. Interface services from other applications specify all automatic data transfers that receive data groups that are provided and sent by another application or any device.

The number of functional size units of inbound interface services from other applications depends on the number of different data elements of the BFC measured, and the number of reading and writing references to entities.

There is an indirect relationship between the entities identified in this step as being referenced and the BFC types identified within the BFC Class: data storage services. Each independent entity identified as a writing reference in this BFC type must also be explicitly counted once as stored data.

FiSMA 1.1 divides this BFC class into three BFC types:

- *Messages from other applications* (f1) are services where data are received on-line, usually in real-time from any other application
- *Batch records from other applications* (f2) are services where data are received in groups or *batches* from any other application
- *Signals from devices or other applications* (f3) are services where data strings or single pieces of information are received from any other application or device (e.g., a sensor).

The size for each service within this BFC class is given by the following equation:

$$S_f = a_f + n/d_f + r_w/c_f + r_r/b_f,$$

where

S_f = size of interface from other application
n = number of data elements, fields
r_w = number of writing references to entities
r_r = number of only reading references to entities
d_f = BFC class specific number of data elements = 1 Ffp →5.00
c_f = BFC class specific number of writing references = 1 Ffp →1.50
b_f = BFC class specific number of reading references = 1 Ffp →2.00
a_f = establishment cost, 0.2 Ffp.

Data Storage Services (d)

This class of BFC involves data storage associated with data crossing the boundary by means of another BFC class into the software. Data storage services specify a group or collection of related and self-contained data in the real world, about which the user requires the software to provide one or more data stores. Data storage services are functional services provided by the piece of software to satisfy these data storage requirements. These *groups or collections of related and self-contained data* are often called entities, data groups, data classes, or objects of interest, depending on the terminology used in the development environment.

Data storage services result in data stores and make data available for maintenance, inquiry, or output. *Note*: Data storage services are typically implemented as tables in relational databases, or as records in data files in general.

The number of functional size units of data storage services depends on the number of different data elements (i.e., the number of attributes related together) in the self-contained group or collection.

In this FSM method, data storage services are divided into two BFC types:

- *Entities or classes* (d1) are data storage services resulting in one or more unique data stores representing fundamental things of relevance to the user, and about which persistent information is stored.
- *Other record types* (d2) are the other types of data storage services and result in one or more unique data stores besides that which are counted as entities or classes.

The size for each service within this BFC class is given by the following equation:

$$S_d = a_d + n/d_d,$$

where

S_d = size of entity or record
n = number of data elements (attributes)
d_d = BFC class specific number of data elements = 1 Ffp $\rightarrow$ 4.00
a_d = establishment cost, 1.5 Ffp.

Algorithmic and Manipulation Services (a)

This class of BFC involves data and/or services performed by the software to independently transform data that may or may not cross the boundary. Algorithmic and manipulation services are user-defined, independent data manipulation functions usually associated with another type of BFC. However, independence means that the functionality of the service is extra to the service provided by any other BFC type. Algorithmic manipulation may consist of arithmetic and/or logical operations.

The number of functional size units of algorithmic and manipulation services depends on the number of different operations performed and the number of different variables needed to perform the service.

In this FSM method algorithmic and manipulation services are divided into six BFC types:

- *Security routines* (a1) are manipulating services providing security features such as encryption, decryption, advanced authorization, etc.

- *Calculation routines* (a2) are manipulating services providing arithmetic or logical counting services.
- *Simulation routines* (a3) are manipulating services providing simulative calculating services.
- *Formatting routines* (a4) are manipulating services providing special format conversion services (i.e., beyond typical, simple editing). *Note:* An example of a formatting routine could be changing table rows into graphics.
- *Database cleaning routines* (a5) are manipulating services supporting data storage maintenance, such as removing unnecessary records and combining or cumulating data elements based on user-defined rules. *Note*: These routines are often scheduled and performed in batch mode.
- *Other manipulation routines* (a6) include all independent user-defined data manipulation services, which are not counted as any other algorithmic and manipulation BFC-type functions.

The size for each service within this BFC class is given by the following equation:

$$S_a = a_a + n/d_a + r_c/c_a,$$

where

S_a = size of algorithm
n = number of data elements (variables, operands)
r_c = number of rules, operations
d_a = BFC class specific number of data elements = 1 Ffp →5.00
c_a = BFC class specific number of calculation rules = 1 Ffp →3.00
a_a = establishment cost, 0.1 Ffp.

The functional size (S) of a piece of software is the sum of the sizes (S_x) of BFCs by class as outlined earlier:

$$S = S_q + S_i + S_o + S_f + S_t + S_d + S_a.$$

13.3.3 Research Related to FiSMA 1.1 FSMM

A number of researchers around the world have performed rigorous data analysis on the FiSMA Experience project repository to validate the relationship of software size measured using the FiSMA FSM Method to development effort. The FiSMA functional size has been validated through formal published research reports and has always been found to have a positive R^2 correlation to development effort. In fact, the FiSMA FSM Method is one of the few existing FSM Methods (either ISO recognized or not) that has been subject to such extensive academic research.

Any of the research reports alone could be considered as important evidence of the usefulness of the FiSMA FSM Method, but taken in combination, they prove unequivocally that the FiSMA FSM Method is sound, valid, and verifiable as an FSMM. A few of the researchers involved in analyzing the FiSMA Experience repository have published either books or articles about their findings and include the following:

- Katrina D. Maxwell (INSEAD, France)
- Barbara Kitchenham (Keele University, UK)
- Risto Nevalainen (Helsinki University of Technology, Finland)
- Khaled El Emam (University of Ottawa, Canada)
- Isabella Wieczorek (Fraunhofer Institute, Germany)
- Martin Shepperd (Bournemouth University and Brunel University, UK)
- Ross Jeffery (University of New South Wales, Australia)
- Rahul Premraj (Bournemouth University, UK and Saarland University, Germany)
- Joseph Blackburn (Vanderbilt University, USA)
- Soumitra Dutta (INSEAD, France)
- Luk Van Wassenhove (INSEAD, France)
- Pekka Forselius (University of Jyväskylä, Finland)
- Cigdem Gencel (Middle East Technical University, Turkey)
- Carolyn Mair (Bournemouth University and Brunel University, UK).

13.4   Mark II Function Point Method

The Mark II Method is primarily used in the UK, and it was originally developed by Charles R. Symons in 1988. It includes the counting of entities and relationships in the data model. *The Mark II Counting Practices Manual* is available free of charge from the UKSMA homepage (United Kingdom Software Measurement Association), http://www.uksma.co.uk. It is also acknowledged (without the GSCs) as an FSMM by ISO/IEC: *ISO/IEC 20968:2002 Mk II Function Point Analysis — Counting Practices Manual*.

According to Charles Symons, Mark II was developed to do the following:

- Reduce subjectivity by measuring entities and their performance instead of files
- Get equal Function Point figures when counting a whole system or adding the counts of all parts of a system independent of the boundaries of the partial systems
- Mainly measure the effort instead of the functionality delivered to the end user
- Add 5 complexity factors to the 14 GSCs in the IFPUG Function Point Method.

Mark II improves the measurement of very simple and very complex trans-actions and is a mapping of modern system analysis methods that are easy to be calibrated (only four variables). It is unknown how widespread the MK II method usage is at the current time – especially since its originator, Charles Symons, is deeply involved in the COSMIC consortium.

Mark II gives more weight to the inputs and less to the outputs than the IFPUG method. For small projects, there are slight differences in measurement of size.

Mark II and COSMIC start from the point that files are implied by the requirement of an output response stimulated by an input. This is counted with the input, the process, and the output. Hence, Mark II and COSMIC do not count the files in order to avoid multiple counting.

Comparisons with an earlier IFPUG release (version 3.0) were done for projects registered by UKSMA in the ISBSG database, which showed following correlations (no R^2 given):

$$1 \text{ IFPUG } 3.0 \text{ FP} = 41.4 + 0.77 \times \text{Mark II FP}$$

$$1 \text{ Mark II FP} = 20.3 + 1.25 \times \text{IFPUG } 3.0 \text{ FP}$$

The following factors influenced these equations:

- The relation of transactions to data elements
- The relation of entities to data elements
- The relation of files to data elements
- The relation of transactions, outputs, and inquiries.

Mark II optionally can use the 14 IFPUG GSCs plus the following five additional characteristics:

- Requirements from other software systems
- Security, check ability, data security
- User training
- Direct use by third parties
- Documentation.

Should a user choose to make use of these 19 GSC's, they can be modified and additional ones can also be added to the group.

Mark II appears to be more data oriented than the IFPUG method and may be easier to learn since it has less rules and functional components to count. Mark II and COSMIC deliver a more linear measure of functional size than does the IFPUG method.

13.5 NESMA FPA

In 1989, the NESMA (Netherlands Software Metrics Association) published their first standard for FPA, based on the principles of the Albrecht FPA method. The NESMA method version 2.1 is also acknowledged as an ISO/IEC Standard: *ISO/IEC 24570:2004 NESMA Functional Size Measurement Method, version 2.1 — Definitions and counting guidelines for the application of Function Point Analysis.* The method is available in Dutch and English, and can be downloaded from the NESMA website at http://www.nesma.nl.

Earlier versions of the NESMA standard led to sizing results that were significantly smaller than sizing results obtained with the IFPUG Function Point counting method due to a variation in the IFPUG and NESMA rules and rule interpretations. However, through close collaboration, the current versions of both standards are now highly comparable, and according to NESMA members who also serve on the IFPUG Counting Practices Committee, the methods are 95–99% the same.

As part of the standard the NESMA has also developed an early usable Function Point prognosis method, *Indicative Function Point Counting.* This method counts the ILFs and estimates for each ILF: 3 EI, 2 EO, and 1 EQ, all classified as average complexity. For each read-only file there is counted 1 EO and 1 EQ with average complexity. All EIs, EOs, and EQs are counted with average complexity. Summation delivers the Indicative Function Points with an error range of +/− 50%.

13.5.1 Similarities and Differences Between NESMA and IFPUG Function Point Standards

The following information is from the NESMA website (http://www.NESMA.nl, document V2.0 from June 8, 2004).

NESMA and IFPUG have worked closely to avoid divergence between their respective counting standards since 1990. To facilitate this cooperation, NESMA counting practices committee members have also served as members of the IFPUG counting practices committee. In fact, one of these NESMA experts has even chaired the IFPUG counting practices committee (to the present day).

While there have been areas of difference in the past, the work done by NESMA's own committees has proven valuable to effect similar rule clarifications in the IFPUG Function Point counting standard, creating even greater convergence between the IFPUG and NESMA counting practices.

Because there are regular updates made to both organizations' counting practices manual and associated documents, we recommend that the reader refers to the NESMA website (http://www.NESMA.nl) for up-to-date progress between the two standards and their convergence and areas of commonality.

The following text is directly from the NESMA website:

The NESMA counting guidelines have been stable since version 1.0 of the manual was published in 1989. In Appendix C of the second version of the *NESMA Counting Practices Manual* (1996), the differences between the two standards were first described. That description is no longer valid. The newest version (2.2) of the *NESMA Counting Practices Manual* (2004) no longer cottains an explanation of the differences. The new document is available at http://www. nesma.nl.

In the *NESMA Counting Practices Manual*, version 2.0, a percentual difference was stated for the lower number of Function Points usually obtained by IFPUG. Unfortunately, this percentage, although merely meant to be an indicative value, was taken as a matter-of-fact. Because the remaining differences have been further reduced, this percentage is no longer valid. Actual versions of the NESMA and IFPUG Counting Practices Manuals: IFPUG NESMA Handboek Telrichtlijnen FPA, versie 2.2 [2004] and IFPUG *Counting Practices Manual* (CPM), release 4.2 [IFPUG, 2004] – are practically the same guidelines.

NESMA and IFPUG both use the same terminology, albeit in a different language. The NESMA maintains a list of English words related to FPA. This can be downloaded from the NESMA site.

Both NESMA and IFPUG differentiate the same five types of user functions: ILGV (ILF), KGV (EIF), IF (EI), UF (EO), OF (EQ). The rules for determining the type and complexity of a function are the same, with a few exceptions:

- External Inquiry vs. External Output
- Complexity of an External Inquiry
- Implicit Inquiry
- Code data (Code tables)
- Physical media
- Queries with multiple selections (*and/or* situations).

In the following, each of the four topics is described in more detail.

External Inquiry vs. External Output: For IFPUG, an External Inquiry is defined as a function that presents data to a user from a logical file (ILF or EIF) without undergoing additional processing (such as calculations, updates to an ILF, etc.). In all other cases, it is considered an External Output. For NESMA, the same rules apply, but in addition, a unique selection key must have been entered and the output must be fixed in scope. In some cases, therefore, IFPUG will count an External Inquiry while NESMA counts the same function as an External Output (e.g., *Show all customers*). The impact of this difference *is marginal* for the number of Function Points for a system or project because only the type of function (External Inquiry or External Output) is affected; not the number of counted functions.

Complexity of an External Inquiry: For NESMA, the functional complexity of the input part of an External Inquiry is based on the complexity rules for an External Input function; the complexity of the output part is based on the rules for an External Output function. The more complex of the two will be used as the complexity of the External Inquiry. For IFPUG, the functional complexity is determined in the same way as all other transactions, by counting the number of data element types crossing the application boundary and identified in the data functions. In practice, the impact of this difference is marginal for the number of Function Points for a system or project.

Implicit Inquiry: When modifying or deleting data, the data is often first presented to the user for viewing. This is known as an *implicit inquiry*. For NESMA, the underlying goal of a function is always the primary objective. NESMA therefore does not consider the implicit inquiry as a separate transactional function, but as an integral part of the modify function or delete function. The data element types presented to the user by the implicit inquiry are therefore added to those counted in the modify function or delete function. NESMA will only count the External Inquiry if it is specifically identified by the user for the purpose of querying data; IFPUG does not have specific rules for this situation in CPM 4.2. Some IFPUG counters will therefore count this as a separate External Inquiry function (if counted nowhere else). The impact of this difference is *marginal* for the number of Function Points in a system or project. Usually the user will have defined this function as an (explicit) inquiry (and it will thus be counted). The implicit inquiry will then not be counted (again) because the same function can not be counted twice.

Code tables: In general, entities can be seen as being composed of primary data (business objects) or composed of secondary data (supportive data). In the case of primary data, both NESMA and IFPUG follow the same counting guidelines as of CPM 4.2 (2004). Secondary data usually consist of code tables, also called "FPA-tables" by NESMA. As an example, consider the "translation table": article code _ article description. During data function counting, NESMA will classify all code tables as one ILF and/or one EIF. The number of record types will be set equal to the number of identified code tables. Altogether, the FPA table-ILF will also count for one External Input, one External Inquiry, and one External Output. For the FPA table-EIF no transactional functions are counted, even though External Inputs or External inquiries may be present. Since CPM 4.2 (2004), IFPUG considers code tables to be an implementation of technical or quality requirements for the user, and not part of the functional requirements. In accordance with the ISO FSM standard, IFPUG has therefore decided that code tables and the transactional functions associated with them are not to be counted using Function Points. Once again, the impact of this difference is *marginal* for the number of Function Points for a system or project. The difference will be *at most* 25 Function Points for an FPA table ILF, and 20 Function Points for an FPA table EIF.

Note: The *IFPUG Counting Practices* Committee periodically issues updates, called CPM (counting practices manual) releases and normally it takes some time before major changes are adopted by all IFPUG counters. The effects on benchmarking data become apparent even later.

Physical media: Physical media is ignored in NESMA counting practices. NESMA looks at the underlying functionality. If the number of data element types and the logical processing are the same, input entered through different media will be counted as one External Input by NESMA. The same holds true for External Outputs. Reports that can be presented on different media (print, screen, etc.) are counted as one External Output function (when the number of data element types and the logical processing remain the same). In CPM 4.2, no specific counting guidelines are given by IFPUG for this situation, however, IFPUG is resolving whether to conform to the NESMA counting guideline in this matter. It is anticipated that a definitive decision will be made in 2008 concerning counting multimedia using the IFPUG method.

Inquiries containing multiple selection criteria (*and/or* situations). In the NESMA counting guidelines only mutually exclusive selections are to be counted. IFPUG has no specific guidelines for this situation. Some IFPUG counters therefore, count every conceivable combination of selection criteria as separate functions, which may result in large differences in Function Points among IFPUG counters.

It is anticipated that the IFPUG will, at some time in the future, adopt the NESMA counting guideline.

13.5.2 NESMA Function Points for Enhancements

The NESMA published in 2001 *A Guide for Function Point Counting of Enhancement Projects* based on the NESMA FPA standard. This guide defines a way to count maintenance and enhancement.

This NESMA Standard was presented during the IFPUG Fall conference in 2000 in San Diego. This publication is also available from the NESMA homepage http://www.nesma.nl/english/download.htm.

Enhancements are all changes of the functionality of an application system. This results in a change, addition, or deletion of functions. Enhancement that only adds functions is new development.

Maintenance is divided in three categories: *corrective, perfective, and adaptive maintenance*. For Estimation purposes, the functionality that is tested is added to the changed, added, and deleted functionality.

The NESMA method calculates Enhanced Function Points (EFP) by weighting the Function points with an *impact factor*. The impact factor has a range of 0.25–1.5 depending on how much the functionality of the application is impacted by the enhancement.

13.6 Outlook for Functional Size Measurement Methods

The ISBSG database release 10 includes 4,106 total complete projects, and the five ISO/IEC Functional Size Measurement Methods (FSMMs) are featured prominently. Table 13.6 shows the numbers of projects by the software sizing method used. The ISO/IEC Functional Size Measurement Methods are highlighted.

Table 13.6. ISBSG CD release 10 breakdown by sizing method

Software sizing method	Number of Projects
IFPUG 4.0	988
IFPUG addendum to existing standards	841
IFPUG not specified	732
FiSMA 1.1	340
IFPUG 4.1	308
IFPUG 4.2	231
IFPUG 3	154
COSMIC-FFP	117
NESMA	152
Mark II	35
LOC	146
IFPUG 2	15
IFPUG 3.4	12
Dreger	10
Backfired	8
Automated	4
Unknown	3
Albrecht	2
Feature Points	2
Retrofitted	2
In-house	1
Other	1
System Components	1

Note: Highlighted cells depict ISO/IEC FSMMs

For the users of measurements it is most desirable that there will be only few methods (to be comparable, e.g,. for benchmarking) but applicable ones. Here is a recommendation that is still valid: Less is more!

13.7 Management Summary

There are five ISO/IEC-conformant FSMMs currently published. All of them use a different approach to measure a size of software to be developed.

As stated many times throughout this book, the functional size of a piece of software is *one of* the main drivers in effort estimation.

The Common Software Measurement Consortium (COSMIC) first developed the COSMIC-Full Function Point (FFP) method in an effort to provide a Functional Size Measurement Method specifically designed to meet the mandatory provisions of ISO/IEC 14141-1 and to address what COSMIC perceived as a gap in the ability of any method to measure the size of real-time applications.

For measuring with COSMIC, the purpose, scope, and boundaries of the measurement have to be defined. Then, the Functional User Requirements (FUR) are collected in the so-called *Mapping Phase*, expressed in the form of the COSMIC generic software model.

The functional size in COSMIC depends only on data movements. A data movement is defined as one CFP = COSMIC Function Point.

An advantage of this concept is that various interpretations of the elementary process do not affect the measurement result in COSMIC.

An important difference to the IFPUG method is the concept of software layers such as tiers, service structures, or component deployments for the architectural reasoning of boundaries.

The ISBSG report: *The Benchmark*, release 8 from January 2004 reports on 66 COSMIC projects in the database, with an average project size of 254 CFP (median 120 CFP). Overall, it is observed that real-time systems are typically smaller than MIS systems, have a longer duration, and require more effort (and thus the productivity is lower).

The layer concept of COSMIC Method can be an advantage compared with the IFPUG method. But one has to keep in mind that the results of counts from different layers are not directly comparable. It follows that further boundaries for different layers and thus further data movements would be ignored in the case of less layers. This is important to note especially when elaborating experience curves.

Nevertheless, the COSMIC Method offers a different perspective to the previously established and known methods for Functional Size Measurement such as IFPUG, FiSMA, Mark II, and NESMA.

The FiSMA 1.1 Functional Size Measurement Method is the newest member of the ISO/IEC FSMM standards and is known under the name ISO/IEC 29881:2008 FiSMA 1.1 Functional Size Measurement Method.

From the specification (FiSMA): FiSMA 1.1 is based purely on Functional User Requirements.

FiSMA 1.1 identifies seven distinct base functional component (BFC) classes: Interactive end-user navigation and query services (q), Interactive end-user input services (i), Noninteractive end-user output services (o), Interface services to other application (t), Interface services from other applications (f), Data storage services (d), Algorithmic and manipulation services (a).

A number of researchers around the world have performed rigorous data analysis on the FiSMA Experience project repository to validate the relationship of software size measured using the FiSMA FSM Method to development effort.

The Mark II Method is primarily used in the UK and was developed by Charles R. Symons in 1988. It includes the counting of entities and relationships in the data model.

Mark II improves the measurement of very simple and very complex transactions and is a mapping of modern system analysis methods that are easily to be calibrated (only four variables).

Mark II gives more weight to the inputs and less to the outputs than the IFPUG method. For small projects, there are slight differences in measurement of size.

Mark II appears to be more data oriented than the IFPUG method and may be easier to learn since it has less rules and functional components to count. Mark II and COSMIC deliver a more linear measure of functional size than the IFPUG method.

In 1989, the NESMA (Netherlands Software Metrics Association) published their first standard for FPA, based on the principles of the Albrecht FPA method. The NESMA method version 2.1 (without the GSCs) is also acknowledged as an ISO/IEC Standard.

As part of the standard, the NESMA has also developed an early usable Function Point prognosis method – Indicative Function Point Counting.

The NESMA published in 2001 *A Guide for Function Point Counting of Enhancement Projects* based on the NESMA FPA standard. This guide defines a way to count maintenance and enhancement.

For the users of measurements, it is most desirable that there will be only few methods (to be comparable, e.g., for benchmarking) but applicable ones. Here is a recommendation that is still valid: Less is more!

14 Variants of the IFPUG Function Point Counting Method

There are a number of variants of the IFPUG Function Point method in different countries. This chapter provides an overview of some of these variants.

The IFPUG FP method is an ISO/IEC standard (the ISO standard currently at the time of printing is ISO/IEC 20926 IFPUG 4.1 unadjusted Function Point Counting Method). In addition, there are four additional functional size measurement methods (FSMMs) recognized by ISO/IEC, each of which uses its own approach to measure a piece of software's functional size. These FSMMs are identified and described in further detail in the previous Chapter Functional Size Measurement Methods.

Capers Jones published a list of 35 variants of the IFPUG Function Point Method, which includes a *motley crew* of different sizing methods. Among those listed were:

- Prior versions of the IFPUG method from 1.0 (1986) through to 4.2 (2004)
- Well-known and publicized variants such as Feature Points
- Unknown or obsolete variants such as the Australian Software Metrics Association (ASMA) method (of which ASMA board members were unaware)
- Obsolete variants such as 3D Function Points
- Standalone Prior versions of the FSMMs described above
- Other measures of software size not necessarily based on the IFPUG method such as Object Points.

The following methods are characterized as IFPUG variants and are *only mentioned for historical reasons* as information to the reader:

- SPR Function Points
- Feature Points
- 3D Function Points.

These IFPUG Function Point variants consist of the following steps:

- Classification and counting of specific model parameters (data, objects, functions, etc.), evaluation of the application's nonfunctional requirements or

characteristics (similar to the GSCs in the IFPUG methodology), and calculation of the software *size*
- The size is then used to estimate the development effort by computing the effort with an experience curve. The elaboration of an experience curve must be done before the introduction of the method.

In addition, we present a number of other sizing methods in this chapter including the following:

- Object points and size measures intended to address the size of software developed using O-O (object-oriented) development
- Data points
- Use Case Points (UCP).

These variants are also methods to quantify the size of the software to be developed. Size is a well-documented and accepted influencing factor in software development effort estimation. Ton Dekkers reported at the MetriKon 2003 conference that the lower level threshold (minimum size) for reliable estimates is ~200 IFPUG FP for development, or a minimum size of 100 MFP (NESMA Maintenance Function Points) is needed for maintenance.

14.1 The Data Point Method

The Data Point Method is a little-known variant of the IFPUG Function Point Method that was developed by Harry Sneed to size software based on data objects. Size is derived by examining the data objects, the user interface, information objects and their data elements, attributes, and relations. The user interface consists of screens, reports, and system messages.

Data Points result from the number of:

- Information objects
- Attributes
- Communication objects
- Input data and output data
- Views.

Instead of the 14 GSCs approach to non-functional requirements used in the IFPUG method, the Data Point Method relies on eight quality factors and ten project conditions. Tool support is also available from Harry Sneed of Case Consult GmbH in Germany (PC-CALC, see chapter "Tools," which contains a subsection "Internet Addresses for Estimation Tools").

14.2 Feature Points

Feature Points is mentioned only for information because its inventor, Capers Jones, officially discontinued formal support of the method several years ago. Even so, there are practitioners who continue to adhere to the Feature Point approach for sizing their software applications and projects.

Feature Points was developed and introduced by Capers Jones in 1984 to address the needs of the engineering and scientific community and its software. Feature points was built on the IFPUG foundation of five functional components and introduced *algorithms* as the sixth component to be counted. Feature points also reduced the number of General Systems Characteristics down to 2.

A couple of drawback to Feature Points becoming a standard included:

1. Algorithms were not precisely defined.
2. There was a lack of correlations to other FP variants.

While still there are estimating models that recognize Feature Points, Capers Jones discontinued his support (per online discussions on the now defunct CRIM listserv), in favor of fully endorsing the IFPUG Function Point counting method. In the posting, Capers asserted that part of the original rationale behind Feature Points was to overcome the psychological barrier held by engineers who could not embrace the fact that the productivity on complex engineering projects could be lower than on others.

14.3 Object Point Methods

In 1990, Luiz Laranjeira was working at the University of Texas in Austin and researching the size estimation of object-oriented systems. Soon after, Mark Lorenz of IBM wrote in his book *Object Oriented Software Development – Practical Guide* about object-oriented measurement and measures. Then in 1994, Chidamber and Kemerer from MIT (Massachusetts Institute of Technology) published an important publication on object-oriented measurement.

Since then, there has been a score of publications about object-oriented measurement and object-oriented methods, including those by Henderson-Sellers, Hateras Software, Lorenz, Minkiewicz, and others (See also the chapter on Object-Oriented Metrics). Associated with this, Jensen reported on *Effort Points.*

There are also many articles and surveys reporting on the use of IFPUG FP in object-oriented environments, such as those by Fetcke, Catherwood, and others. IFPUG published their Case Study 3, specifically to demonstrate how to apply the IFPUG Function Point Counting in OOA (Object-Oriented Analysis) and OOD (Object-Oriented Design) software development.

In 1996, Harry Sneed of Germany also published his *Object-Point* method (not to be confused with his other aforementioned Data Point method). Sneed differentiates between an object model (classes), communication model (messages or interfaces), and process model (processes or transactions). Accordingly, he aggregates Class Points, Message Points, and Process Points that are weighted with quality attributes and project factors. Sneed's publication has incomplete details and shows some inconsistencies that hindered the dissemination and adoption of his method.

The future will tell whether there will emerge a special Object Point method that will gain widespread adoption, or whether the established IFPUG method (or other functional size measurement method) will prevail in the object-oriented environment.

14.4 SPR Function Points

SPR Function Points are mentioned here for informational purposes because they are referenced in published literature. The experience of the authors suggests that the use of SPR Function Points is not common.

SPR Function Points were a simplified variant of IFPUG function points in the early 1980s. They were developed by Capers Jones of SPR (Software Productivity Research) who also developed Feature Points. SPR Function Points-simplified FP counting by eliminating the low/average/high classification for IFPUG Functional Components and counted all files (ILF, EIF) and transactions (EI, EO, EQ) as *average. Additionally*, the 14 *GSCs were distilled down to two*: *problem complexity and data complexity.*

SPR Function Points also introduced the functional mix concept used today in publications of the International Software Benchmarking Standards Group (ISBSG). The functional mix concept states that the unadjusted FP of an entire project or application could be approximated if the contribution of only one of the five functional components is known. This was also supported by SPR's Checkpoint for Windows tool (now known as KnowledgePlan™).

When approximating using a functional mix, caution is urged because the degree of error ranges in this process is higher than with other approximation methods. A calculation in an international insurance company in Germany came to the conclusion that the error range was significantly higher by using the SPR Function Point approximation method than with the use of the self-calculated proportions of the components of the Function Point Method.

14.5 3D Function Points

3D (three-dimensional) Function Points are also mentioned here for historical purposes because they too can be found in literature. It is unknown whether there is any continued usage of the 3D FP method and whether they were ever used outside of the Boeing Company where they were first introduced. 3D Function Points were published by Scott A. Whitmire in 1992 of Boeing Computer Services after 2 years of development. The method makes assumptions similar to the Feature Point method that software development depends not only on its data and functions, but also on control flows. 3D Function Points took the approach that software size depends on three dimensions:

- Data-rich dimension (measured using IFPUG FP)
- Control-rich dimension (measured by evaluating the transitions and states)
- Process-rich dimension (measured by evaluating the data transformations)

In the original 3D Function Point Method, the results of each dimension were added together to get the 3D FP size.

Note that in the late 1990s, the American author spoke at an international measurement conference in the USA where Scott Whitmire also spoke. In his presentation, Scott stated that he had revised his original 3D FP approach and now advocated working with the results of each dimension separately and no longer supported adding them together.

14.6 Use Case Points (UCP)

UCP were developed in 1993 by Gustav Karner not as a size measure in and of itself, but only as part of as an estimating method. In the UCP method, the size in units of UCP is multiplied by a productivity factor originally set to 20 h per UCP. Schneider and Winter further recommend a more realistic range from 20 to 28 h per Use Case Point to take into consideration the contingency of working in teams. Information about the details of the Use Case Points Method (UCPM) can be found at http://www.uea.ac.uk/~a168955/effort_estimation/use_case_points.html

The adjusted UCP are derived by multiplying the UUCP (unadjusted UCP) by the Technical Complexity Factor and by the Environmental Complexity Factor. The UCP *sizing* method is depicted in Fig. 14.1.

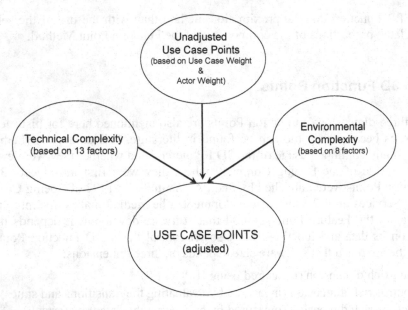

Fig. 14.1. UCP software sizing method (*note*: the productivity factor converts UCP into an effort estimate).

The unadjusted UCP (UCP) are determined by a three-step process:

1. The *Unadjusted Use Case Weight* (UUCW). This value is determined by the total number of activities contained in all the use case scenarios.
2. The *Unadjusted Actor Weight* (UAW). This value is determined by the combined complexity of all the use case actors.
3. UUCP = UUCW + UAW.

14.6.1 Unadjusted Use Case Weight (UUCW)

The UUCW is calculated by counting the number of use cases in each category (simple, average, complex according to Table 14.1), then multiplying each category of use case with its weight, and then adding the results.

Table 14.1. Computing UUCW.

Use case type	Definition	Factor
Simple	3 or fewer transactions or <5 analysis classes	5
Average	4–7 transactions or 5–10 analysis classes	10
Complex	More than 7 transactions or >10 analysis classes	15

UUCW = (Number of simple use cases × 5) + (Number of average use cases × 10) + (Number of complex use cases × 15)

14.6.2 Unadjusted Actor Weight (UAW)

To calculate the UAW, actors must be classified as Simple, Average, or Complex based on their interactions (see Table 14.2).

Table 14.2. Computing UAW.

Actor type	Definition	Factor
Simple	Program interface	5
Average	Interactive, or protocol-driven interface	10
Complex	Graphical interface (human)	15

The UAW is calculated by counting the number of actors in each category, multiplying each total by its specified weighting factor, and then adding the products.

14.6.3 Unadjusted Use Case Points (UUCP)

The UUCP are calculated by adding the UUCW and the UAW:

$$UUCP = UUCW + UAW$$

14.6.4 Technical Complexity Factor

This is the first of two complexity factors that modify the UUCP based on project factors.

The *technical* complexity factor examines aspects of the project and implementation-specific details (some are similar to the GSCs in the IFPUG FP Counting method).

To get the technical complexity factor, go through the list of possible technical factors and rate each one on a scale of 0–5. (A "0" rating means the factor is irrelevant to the project, a "5" rating means it is essential).

For each of the 18 factors, multiply its score from 0 to 5 by its weight (a constant value) and then sum the results. The final result is then substituted into a Technical Complexity Factor calculation. Table 14.3 depicts the technical factors.

14.6.5 Environmental Complexity Factor

This is the second of the two complexity factors, and it considers the impact of the experience (or lack thereof) of the project team. For each of the eight factors, rate it on a scale from 0–5. ("0" means the factor is irrelevant to the project, "5" means it is essential). Each factor is calculated by multiplying its score by its weight and producing a sum of the results. The final result becomes the Environmental Complexity Factor. See Table 14.4 for details.

Table 14.3. Technical complexity factor.

Technical factor number	Technical factor description	Weight	Value (0–5)	Weight × value
T1	System will be distributed (released)	2		
T2	Performance objectives	1		
T3	End-user efficiency	1		
T4	Complex internal processing	1		
T5	Code must by reused	1		
T6	Easy to install	0.5		
T7	Easy to use	0.5		
T8	Portable	2		
T9	Easy to change	1		
T10	Concurrent	1		
T11	Includes special security features	1		
T12	Provides direct access for third parties	1		
T13	Special user training facilities are required	1		
	Total technical complexity factor			

Table 14.4. Environmental complexity factors.

Environmental factor number	Environmental factor description	Weight	Value	Weight × value
EF1	Familiar with RUP	1.5		
EF2	Application experience	0.5		
EF3	Object-oriented experience	1		
EF4	Lead analyst capability	0.5		
EF5	Motivation	1		
EF6	Stable requirements	2		
EF7	Part-time workers	−1		
EF8	Difficult programming language	−2		
	Total environmental complexity factor			

14.6.6 Calculate Adjusted Use Case Points

Finally, UCP (adjusted) are calculated using this formula:

$$UCP = UUCP \times TCF \times ECF$$

where

    UUCP = unadjusted Use Case Points
     TCF = total technical complexity factor
    ECFC = total environmental complexity factor

14.7 Outlook

Considering all of the variants of the IFPUG Function Point counting method, one can summarize that the measurement of inputs, outputs, algorithms, logical files, entities, relationships, and data elements delivers a sound basis for measurement.

Since there are also now five ISO/IEC internationally recognized standards for Functional Size Measurement, the market will decide which method(s) gain preference based on the measurement needs of practitioners.

Mathias Lother, Reiner Dumke, and Alain Abran presented at the IWSM 2001 a comparison of variants of the IFPUG Function Point counting method in three tables that are combined here as Table 14.5.

Table 14.5. Variants of the Function Point Method in comparison.

Method	Application area			Support	
	Algorithmic/ Scientific	Management information systems	Real-time, embedded	Tool support	Data in ISBSG database
DeMarco's Big Bang	Yes			Yes. At least: • PC-CALC • SoftCalc	No
Feature Points	Yes			Yes. At least: • SoftCalc • KnowledgePlan™	No
Boeing 3D			Yes	Checkpoint/ KnowledgePLAN™	No
IFPUG		Yes		Checkpoint/ KnowledgePLAN™, PC-CALC, Function Point Workbench™, FPC Analyzer, Experience® Pro	Yes

For the users of measurement, it is most desirable that there be only a few methods to choose from (to be comparable, e.g., for benchmarking) but amongst them highly applicable ones. Here is a recommendation that is still valid: Less is more! And, measure consistently!

The American author attended an European International Project Management Association (IPMA) and International Cost Estimation Council (ICEC) joint conference in 2005 and discovered that the building construction industry is as divided about how to size a floor plan as the FP industry is divided about the best way to decide about determining the functional size of a piece of software.

Construction engineers argued whether the floor plan should be sized on the basis of taking measurements from the outside walls, inside walls, half way into the framed wall, as well as how to count the square foot size (or square meter size) of a staircase – as half the area on each of two floors, as full area on both floors, or not at all. It is reassuring (while not altogether comforting) to know that the construction industry with all its wisdom and best practices can still argue about something as mundane as how to consistently measure the area of a floor plan. Again the consistency of measurement methods is a pre-requisite to creating comparability!

14.8 Management Summary

The variants of the Function Point Method deliver a method to quantify the size of the software to be developed.

The Data Point Method is a little-known variant of the IFPUG Function Point Method that was developed by Harry Sneed for estimating based on use of data objects.

Feature Points are mentioned here only as information because its inventor, Capers Jones, officially discontinued formal support of the method several years ago.

Feature Points was developed and introduced by Capers Jones in 1984 to address the needs of the engineering and scientific community and its software.

Feature points was built on the IFPUG foundation of five functional components by introducing algorithms as the sixth component to be counted.

There has been a plethora of publications about object-oriented measurement and other object-oriented methods.

In 1996, Harry Sneed of Germany published his *Object-Point* method (not to be confused with his other aforementioned Data Point method).

SPR Function Points are mentioned here for informational purposes because they are mentioned in published literature.

SPR Function Points simplified FP counting by eliminating the low/average/ high classification for IFPUG Functional Components and counting all files (ILF, EIF) and transactions (EI, EO, EQ) as *average*.

3D (three-dimensional) Function Points are also mentioned here for historical purposes because they too can be found in literature. It is unknown whether there is any continued usage of the 3D FP method – and whether they were ever used outside of the Boeing Company where they were first introduced.

UCP were developed in 1993 by Gustav Karner as an estimating method whereby the size in UCP is multiplied by a productivity factor originally set to 20 h per UCP.

For the users of measurement, it is most desirable that there be only a few methods to choose from (to be comparable, e.g., for benchmarking) but amongst them highly applicable ones.

Here is a recommendation that is still valid: Less is more! And, *measure consistently!*

15 Using Functional Size Measurement Methods

This chapter presents different approaches and experiences in the practical use of Functional Size Measurement. We begin with a report about experiences of an organization that was able to develop a Function Point Prognosis and present related information from other organizations about early Function Points, also called Function Point estimation or FP proposals.

One of the biggest challenges is that estimates are required as early as possible from both the customer (acquirer) and supplier (contractor) point of view. Early estimation requires good documentation of both the assumptions supporting the FP estimation, and subsequently the estimates of work effort. *Ultimately, the counting and estimation data should serve as a treasure for measurement programs. Experiences show that valuable information can be gained from appropriate analysis of collected data.*

An additional benefit of the FP documentation (FP count or FP estimate details) for an international insurance company in Germany was that it found value in its Function Point Prognosis via regression analysis. Since FP size is an important measure to estimate project work effort, the organization thus gained the synergistic benefit to do reliable estimates early in its IT project life cycle. Of course, a complete FP count at the end of the requirements analysis is obligatory, as well as an improved estimate of work effort at this time.

This is only one example presented here since other organizations did similar research. There is strong evidence that different environments lead to different results. This means that each organization should develop its own heuristic solution(s). Nevertheless, comparisons with other organizations are valuable for the enterprise.

15.1 Function Point Prognosis

Since Function Point counts use the requirements documents as a prerequisite, the so-called Function Point Prognosis or resultant estimates are valuable.

Because of the increasing demand for estimates of work effort even before requirements are written, a number of early FP prediction models have been developed. This is similar to estimating the square feet for a building for which there is only a sketchy floor plan. Estimating the FP to be developed from an idea of what the customer needs but cannot easily articulate is the first step – and an uncertain one – which then leads to the second step, that is, use of the FP size estimate as the input size variable in a work effort estimating software model.

Because of the importance of these early FP size estimations, Meli and Santillo (1999) published a comparative review of early Function Point estimation methods that illustrates the valuable collection of worldwide efforts in this direction.

Experiences in the IT department of an international insurance company show that the necessary high-level information required to even do a FP estimate can be established early in discussions with the project leader. *Early* means that the customer or acquirer organization is in the initial or *forming* stage of launching a software and systems development project in an organization. Early means the beginning of a project, or in stable environments it may mean even a year prior to project launch, when portfolio planning is done for the upcoming year. Of course, planning based on relatively undocumented user requirements is prone to high risk and margins of error due to the uncertainty of preliminary estimates. During this process and in cooperation with a competence center, the interfaces and tasks of the project can be collected, and a rudimentary boundary diagram for the envisaged application can be documented. A valuable support for this Function Point Prognosis was that all of the existing software applications had already been FP-counted. This means that all of the interfaces were well known and could be taken into account early.

From the initial launch of the insurance company's measurement program in 1996, it was a long journey to arrive at the desired results of being able to benefit from knowing the size of one's application in conjunction with any new development or enhancement project. The success achieved to date has been the culmination of sufficient and committed management support. The year 2002 was devoted to the introduction of project FP counting, estimation (based on a Function Point Prognosis), and productivity ratios.

This chapter focuses on the follow-up investigation (expanded to 78 applications from the 20 original applications) in the IT department of an international insurance company. Research papers were originally published by the German author, Bundeschuh (1997–2002) in the *Metrics News* of the German GI Interest Group on Software Metrics with the title *Function Point Prognosis* (http://ivs.cs.uni-magdeburg.de/sw-eng/us/giak/MN-98-2.HTM) in 1997, 1998, 2001, and 2002. The 2002 publication in *Metrics News was* titled: *2002: Function Point Prognosis Approved* (http://ivs.cs.uni-magdeburg.de/sw-eng/us/giak/MN-02-1.HTM). This final article clearly showed the validity of the prognosis formulae in this organization.

This prognosis method was developed using regression analysis. *The Function Points are in this case calculated from the numbers of EIs and EOs that were known and counted without being classified as low, average, or high.* An error range of 12% could be determined for these early counts compared with later Function Point counts at the end of the requirements analysis (regression coefficient $R^2 > 0,948$, see Table 15.1, IO = number of EIs and EOs).

Table 15.1. Function Point Prognosis formulae of the IT department of an international insurance company (Bundschuh, 1997–2002)

	Number of applications	R^2	Error (%)	Prognosis formula
2001				
Total	78	0.9483	13	FP = 7.8 × IO + 43
Host	69	0.9498	12	FP = 7.9 × IO + 40
PC	9	0.9503	21	FP = 6.4 × IO + 172
1998				
Total	39	0.9589	20	FP = 7.6 × IO + 50
Host	28	0.9580		FP = 7.9 × IO + 11
PC	11	0.9760		FP = 6.5 × IO + 134
1997				
Total	20	0.9525	13 (median 11)	FP = 7.3 × IO + 56

The use of these prognosis formulae was recommended to the project leaders as rules of thumb with +15% added on as an error range (also called contingency).

The correlations were not as reliable for the other components (EQ, ILF, and EIF) or for subsets of small, medium, and large applications. Figure 15.1 shows, as an example, the results of such a regression analysis:

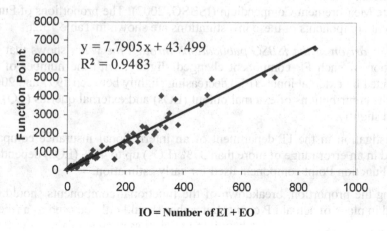

FP Prognosis based on IO's

$$y = 7.7905x + 43.499$$
$$R^2 = 0.9483$$

IO = Number of EI + EO

Fig. 15.1. Regression analysis for development of the Function Point Prognosis

The 1998 data were analyzed independently by Noel in a joint research with the Software Engineering Management Research Laboratory, Université du Québec à Montréal (UQAM), Canada, which obtained similar results. Noel applied the same method to seven projects with COSMIC to find a similar correlation for COSMIC Function Points, but the sample was too small for reliable results. Noel reported in his thesis an error range of 20%.

Nishiyama (1998) of Japan reports his findings regarding a Function Point Prognosis for which regression analysis led to the following prognosis formula based on the number of reports (lists, reports), screens, and files (with a regression coefficient $R^2 = 0.99$ and an error range of less than 20%).

$$PFP = 12.31 \times R + 6.01 \times S + 8.05 \times F,$$

where PFP = Prognosis Function Points, R = number of reports, S = number of screens, and F = number of files.

Meli and Santillo (1999) presented another Function Point Prognosis, e.g.:

32–40 Function Points per ILF (35–38 for GUI – Graphical User Interfaces) or from NESMA (metrics organization of The Netherlands):

$$IS = 35 \times (number\ of\ ILF) + 15 \times (number\ of\ EIF),$$

where IS = Indicative Size in FP, and the number of ILFs and EIFs are counted separately.

15.1.1 Function Point Proportions

Another approach is to estimate the Function Points from the proportions of the EIs, EOs, EQs, ILFs, and EIFs. There are results from the IT department of an international insurance company, as well as actual data from the ISBSG in its Software Measurement Compendium (ISBSG, 2002). The proportions of Function Point components of these investigations are shown in Table 15.2.

A comparison of the ISBSG publications through the years shows that the proportion of each FP component changed slightly, with the number of FP contributed by external inputs (EIs) decreasing slightly between 1997 and 2002, while the contributions of external output (EOs) and external queries (EQ) increased slightly.

Investigation in the IT department of an international insurance company resulted in an error range of more than 37% (EOs) up to 48% (EQs) depending on the Function Point component used for early estimation.

Using the proportion, breakdown of the functional components should not be used in place of actual FP counts but rather should only be used as a rule of thumb for plausibility checks when doing quality assurance of Function Point counts.

Table 15.2. Proportions of the Function Point components from the IT department of an international insurance company

Source: IT department of an international insurance company (2001)	Number of application systems	Percentage of FP contributed by functional component				
Platform		EI	EO	EQ	ILF	EIF
Total	78	22	39	8	16	14
Host	69	21	40	8	16	15
PC	9	28	31	12	19	10
ISBSG Report (June 2002)	311 New development	29	24	15	24	8
Metric views (IFPUG)		26–39	22–24	12–14	24	4–12
IT department of an international insurance company:						
1998 Total	39	25	39	14	17	6
1996/1997 Total	20	27	39	11	18	5
1997 Total	12	18	43	12	18	9
1996 Total	8	34	35	11	18	2

Further *rules of thumb* used in practice (literature sources unknown) include the following:

- The number of IT staff members in a project (ITM):
  ITM = FP/150,
  where FP = size of the application to be developed.
- The number of IT staff members necessary for the maintenance of an application (MAM):
  MAM = FP/3,500
- The estimated costs in Euro for software development in Western Europe (C):
  C = FP × (1,500 €) per FP
- The annual growth (G) percentage of software size after the first release:
  G = FP × 7%
- The requirements creep per month of project duration (RC) in units of Function Points:
  RC = FP × 2%
- The number of calendar months from requirements concept until delivery (M):
  $M = \text{FP}^{0.4}$
- The error potential (E):
  $E = \text{FP}^{1.2}$
- The number of required test cases (T):
  $T = \text{FP}^{1.25}$

- The number of pages of documentation (*P*):
   $$P = FP^{1.15}$$

This demonstrates how valuable it can be to collect Function Point count data centrally so that organizational learning can occur and to be able to improve the quality of estimates. Furthermore, the data demonstrate that that the Function Point Prognoses are specifically related to the development environment. They are only to be used as rules of thumb for quality assurance of their practitioners' own counts and estimates. There is always a considerable demand for reliable information to use for early estimates.

15.1.2 Other Early Function Point Proposals

As interesting as this is the comparison of average Function Points, that is, the answer to the question: "how many Function Points have an EI, EO, EQ, ILF, or EIF typically?"

The average complexity for each functional component as outlined in the IFPUG counting practices manual (IFPUG, 2004) gives the following number of unadjusted Function Points (uFP):

   EI = 4 uFP; EO = 5 uFP; EQ = 4 uFP; ILF = 10 uFP; EIF = 7uFP.

The ISBSG database (r5 was most recent to publish this particular breakdown) exhibits different figures, as does the IT department of an international insurance company (see Table 15.3).

Table 15.3 shows that the average Function Points in the IT department of an international insurance company increased over the years. This could hint at growing complexity in this environment; however, this assumption must consider that there is no comparability given since the number of counted applications also increased.

The average Function Points are said to be stable ratios in similar environments, and thus are appreciated as a rule of thumb for quick Function Point Prognosis. This rule of thumb saves time because the additional effort for classification of the components as low, average, and high can be saved – especially, since at the early phases of development (i.e., before requirements are finished) these are typically unknown.

For the administration of one ILF, it can be assumed that there would typically be the one file model *profile: at least three external inputs (EI) – one for each of the add, change, and delete maintenance functions, one output (EO), and one inquiry (EQ) typically manifested as a browse function. Research from the ISBSG database and the IT department of an international insurance company delivered the following figures (see Table 15.4.).*

Table 15.3. Number of average Function Points by IFPUG functional component

Number of applications by data source:	Average Function Points				
	EI	EO	EQ	ILF	EIF
IT department of an international insurance company (2001)					
Total – 78	4.7	5.9	4.4	8.6	6.5
Host – 69	4.7	5.9	4.6	8.7	6.5
PC – 9	4.3	5.7	3.8	7.6	6.5
IFPUG unadjusted FPs for average complexity	4	5	4	10	7
ISBSG R5	4.3	5.4	3.8	7.4	5.5
ISBSG R5 Europe	4.2	4.9	3.8	7.2	5.3
IT department of an international insurance company (1998)					
Total – 39	4.6	5.7	4.3	8.2	6.1
Host – 28	4.8	5.7	4.5	8.5	6.2
PC – 11	4.0	5.7	3.9	7.3	5.4
IT department of an international insurance company (1997)					
Total – 20	4.6	5.5	4.3	8.1	5.7

Table 15.4. Maintained entities (ILF) proportion compared with other IFPUG Functional Components

	IT department of an international insurance company			ISBSG r5	
Applications	2001	1998	1997	Europe	Total
N	78	39	20	32	238
Number of EI per ILF	2.6	2.7	2.7	3.8	2.9
Number of EO per ILF	3.6	3.3	3.7	2.6	1.5
Number of EQ per ILF	0.9	1.4	1.2	1.9	1.1
Number of EIF per ILF	0.6	0.5	0.4	–	–

Note: ISBSG r5 was the most recent with this type of breakdown

Accordingly, the IT department of an international insurance company calculated the proportions of the other components in comparison to inputs and outputs (see Table 15.5).

Table 15.5. Input (EI) and output (EO) proportions compared with other IFPUG Functional Components

Input		Output	
78 Applications	2001	78 Applications	2001
Number of EO per EI	1.3	Number of EI per EO	0.7
Number of EQ per EI	0.3	Number of EQ per EO	0.3
Number of ILF per EI	0.4	Number of ILF per EO	0.3
Number of EIF per EI	0.2	Number of EIF per EO	0.2

15.1.3 IFPUG General Systems Characteristics (GSC)

Another result of the internal insurance company research was that the *VAF* (*Value Adjustment Factor*) in the IT department of the company was typically in the range of a low of 0.73 (characteristic of migrations or conversion projects) up to a high of 1.22, with the average VAF = 0.95. (For host/mainframe, applications, the average VAF was 0.94, and for PC-based applications, the average VAF was 0.96.) These values were also used as a rule of thumb when plausibility checks for quality assurance of Function Point counts were performed.

Accordingly, the range of typical scores for each of the 14 GSCs can be compared. Figure 15.2 shows such a comparison where the gray bars are bounded by the statistical high and low values, and the median value is depicted as a dash in the center area of each bar.

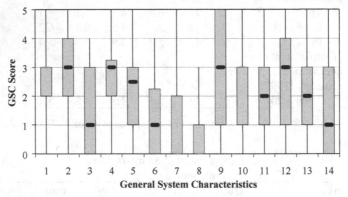

Comparison of the 14 GSC Scores (Host)
Source: IT department of an international insurance company

Fig. 15.2. Comparison of the values of 14 GSCs (IT department of an international insurance company – 2001)

15.1.4 Benefits of Early Function Point Estimates

In this chapter, some of the aforementioned results of the exploration of measured data are summarized, with a focus on the early Function Point estimates.

Early collection of the information about interfaces, component parts of the project, and formal documentation of the same, along with a diagram of the application boundary (later used for the organizational architecture atlas) are all prerequisites to establish early Function Point Prognosis. When accompanied by a counting log (simple Word document with notes about special FP counting decisions), the project gains a valuable overview about the application portfolio and projects within. In general, these also might include reference numbers (key figures) for quality assurance (percentages, rules of thumb).

Another well-known consequence of careful measurement and documentation of the Function Point counts is a higher level quality of the requirements documents, since they are used, checked, and typically revised. Often they are not available or not yet developed at the start of Function Point counting, and therefore must be developed/revised after the count. The result of multiple *eyes* examining the same requirements documentation multiple times leads also to a overall better requirements, and accompanying increased efficiency in software development. These are all secondary effects of Function Point counting, and some clients even attest that these benefits may be worth far more at times than the actual number of Function Points, at least at the beginning of a measurement initiative.

With the available details, one can calculate with an Excel *problem solver*, the average FP component complexity across the five functional components (i.e., how many FPs does a *typical* EI, EO, EQ, ILF, or EIF have in the actual, in-practice environment). It is widely agreed that this measure is stable and can be used as a rule of thumb for quick estimation of counts, since the components need not be classified as low, average, or high.

Note that it is always better to use your own organization's functional component average Function Point value rather than the IFPUG averages, because of the demonstrated difference (see previous tables). Another learning experience was that the average Function Point size increased over time, which may be caused by growing complexity in the application development environment. Such results can only be gained by continuous recording and examination of the measured data over an elapsed time period.

These findings, compared with those from other organizations, show that such data collection can be used to find heuristic solutions for FP Prognosis, by using either Function Point proportions (*typical FP*), function ratios, regression formulae, or rules of thumb. *There is evidence that different environments demand tailored solutions; this leads to our recommendation that* each organization develops its own knowledge base (experience database) of heuristic solutions, and should distinguish between different development platforms, etc., when doing so.

15.2 Estimation of Person Months of Work Effort Based on Function Points

Function Points can provide valuable input for work effort estimates. For this purpose, the regression formulae from the chapter "Product- and Process-Metrics," productivity, cost, and duration can be used. In addition, information from the various ISBSG products can provide information on which to double-check estimates for effort, development productivity, project duration, and team size.

The Volkswagen AG in Europe collected early experiences using early Albrecht FP (pre-dates the IFPUG standards) and published their own, now outdated formulae for effort (see also the chapter "Estimating Maintenance Effort, Estimation of Maintenance Effort after Delivery" for details). In addition, the team observed the *bathtub curve* for maintenance effort. (The curve is called a bathtub curve because of its shape (see fig. 6.1) – it begins with an initial high of 1.4 h per FP in the first year of development, decreases to ~0.6 h/FP (better) by the sixth year, and then rises again to an average of 1 h/FP from the 13th year on).

Formulae are always only valid in the corresponding environment. Thus, they cannot be used reliably as a 1:1 relationship in other organizations. It would be purely coincidental if one of the mentioned formulas would fit adequately in another organization, without needing calibration. And the quality of the data must always be checked. For regression formulas, always ensure that the regression coefficient is given as well as the sample size on which the formula is based. This means that every organization must elaborate its own regression analyses to get the most valuable results and leverage the value of their own data. These analyses must be performed on a regular basis since the environment changes over time.

The VW curve is very old (early Albrecht Function Points) – the publication by R. Großjohann is from 1994. It is mentioned here only as an example to show what is possible with well-documented Function Point counts.

In multivariate analyses it is always found that more than one parameter (such as functional size) influences the effort for system development. The use of estimation tools therefore makes sense, since they allow for control of many influential parameters. When initiating the start of a metrics program, it can be useful to perform a regression analysis with three small, three medium, and three large projects at their postmortem reviews, by collecting functional size and effort (Function Points and effort hours) to get started with an estimation formula.

15.3 Productivity Analysis

The Function Point Method is well suited to be a part of calculating project productivity. However, it must be stressed that productivity is not a personnel metric, but rather a process metric influenced by tools, techniques, skills, programming language, etc. As such, it should never be used to attempt to compare persons or their productivity. Organizations that make the mistake of ignoring this in advance and attempting to measure people find themselves in a position of having to backtrack and perform major damage control. Just do not do it! The result of misusing productivity results in skepticism and mistrust of the entire measurement initiative. Such a malpractice can destroy years of successful nurturing of a metrics program in record time.

When comparing the productivity of projects and organizations, one always has to regard that no two IT projects or organizations are exactly equal or comparable in the many parameters relevant to estimating and work effort. Thus, productivity comparisons can only provide hints for process improvement opportunities and the drivers that cause differences in productivity.

This approach is a prerequisite for the intelligent use of productivity data. Caution must be used when dealing with productivity, in a manner similar to the caution required when using most rules of thumb as plausibility check. A rule of thumb is a generic guideline and unsuitable for financial decisions or objective go/no-go project decisions. These recommendations are supported by the observation that measures show a large variance. For example, large organizations with high communication distribution needs and strict requirements for high-quality software exhibit substantially lower productivity levels (FP per person month) than small organizations with significantly less communication and quality constraints, using the same technology.

Using the ISBSG Repository Data Disc r10 (ISBSG, 2007) with its research tool "Early Estimate Checker V5.0," it is possible to perform customized data analysis with any subset of the more than 4,000 projects in the database.

According to ISBSG: "*The ISBSG Early Estimate Checker* V5.0 is a software tool that utilizes the data in the ISBSG Repository Data CD release 10 with regression analysis to quickly generate estimates of the work effort and elapsed time, *(duration),* required to carry out and complete a software development project, plus project delivery rate and speed of delivery. Use it to do the following:

- Generate initial *rough* estimates in the early stages of software development projects.
- Validate existing project estimates (*e.g., bottom–up estimates generated from a project's work breakdown*).
- Assess the reasonableness and likely risk associated with a quoted estimate (*where on the range from most conservative to most optimistic is the estimate positioned?*)."

The following screen illustrates the reality checker functionality available (see Fig. 15.3).

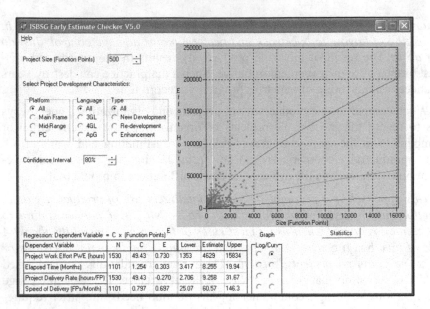

Fig. 15.3. ISBSG: The early estimate checker (version 5.0)

15.4 Typical Function Point Counting Experiences

The Function Point counting rules contained in the IFPUG Counting Practices Manual can be challenging for the uninitiated personnel. Beginners can do themselves a favor by taking an IFPUG-certified FP workshop (typically 2 days and available on CD, as an online workshop, or in person. For further details contact the American author.).

Most organizations that implement Function Points as a core measurement competence develop their own internal collection of FAQs (Frequently Asked Questions) to assist with daily counting and provide some handy examples. These hints and tips – especially for beginning practitioners – are a valuable aid from the experiences of a large organization.

The examples in this chapter are not meant as a new standard but as guidance to mentor and coach new counters. The examples were all discussed with consultants and certified Function Point specialists (CFPS), and thus the examples are intended to work with the IFPUG standard. This chapter contains the FAQs from a large international insurance company.

Note: The examples identified herein were collected/gathered during the start-up phase of a metrics implementation program in the IT department of an international insurance company.

15.4.1 Business Functions Overview

Figure 15.4 shows the potential logical functions for counting Function Points.

Since different but unique cases arise fairly often in practice, we present some hints for interpreting the functional user requirements in the next sections.

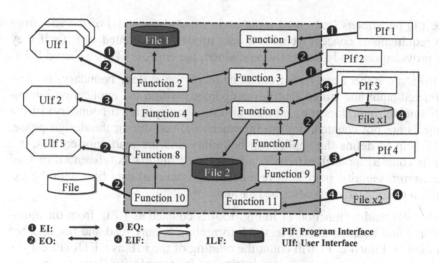

Fig. 15.4. Typical counting situations

15.4.2 Internal Logical Files (ILF)

The standalone, persistent, maintained entities of the relational data model are counted, as well as other user-mandated data stores (e.g., legislated sequential files). Combined or linked entities that have their own attributes need to be taken into account and analyzed. Questions such as the following emerge: "Are person and task separately administered? Does a many-to-many relationship exist between these entities?" If so, then both the entities are counted each as its own ILF, as long as there are attributes on each entity.

Backup files are only counted if explicitly mandated by the user due to legal or regulatory requirements. If the only reason for them to exist is to satisfy IT technical or security reasons, then the data store is not counted. Note that *code* tables (i.e., with code, description, and other space-saving attributes) are not counted as ILF, nor is their maintenance (i.e., cannot count EI, EO, or EQ for their maintenance or retrieval) or retrieval counted (i.e., cannot be counted as FTR on any elementary process). (Note that this is a difference in the "almost identical" NESMA method, whereby NESMA counts a single ILF and its maintenance to account for "code" tables no matter how many. The three other ISO/IEC FSM methods: FiSMA, COSMIC and Mark II recognize and count a single systems entity. See the chapter on FSMMs or consult specific FSMM websites for further details.)

15.4.3 External Interface Files (EIF)

The I/O parameters (only used input and output data fields) of the EIF from the requirements concept (relational data model) are counted as EIFs if they are provided read-only access (if maintained, the entity is likely a shared ILF).

EIFs are either data read from outside of the system boundary, or data extracted/input and stored (but never updated) within the application boundary. Internal interfaces (i.e., no data crosses the application boundary) of the projects are not counted, nor are interfaces defined during the design phase. EIFs help to define the application boundary and are read-only entities. An EIF is counted for each externally administered file that is referenced or read (e.g., error, security, help, edit, reference, transactional data file) with the exception of code tables as described earlier.

The file read by function 11 in Fig. 15.4 is counted as 1 EIF from the application being counted as long as the information is only read and not updated on the file. Function 11 will count the reading of the EIF as a FTR (File Type Referenced) as part of the determination of its complexity (low, average, or high).

15.4.4 External Input (EI)

Error processing messages, confirmation messages, and messages that ask whether processing should continue together count as a total of 1 DET for the according external input.

Dialogue Start, Dialogue Integration

Starting a dialogue from outside the system boundary via an interface is counted as 1 EI, e.g., if the first process is started via a standard dialogue-concept start screen. Strict navigation or menu functions (that do not launch data retrieval for display on a follow-up screen) are not counted.

Interfaces Between Client/Server Platform and Host Mainframe

Migration of data by the application to be counted (e.g., PC application) from an external application (e.g., host): 1 EI for the application to be counted, 1 EO for the host application. (Note that strictly speaking, IFPUG rules necessitate evaluating whether the output is an EO or EQ depending on the particular processing, but based on the fact that there is only 1 FP difference between an EO and EQ, this corporation chose to simplify the FP process by stating all outputs of this type will be counted as EO's.)

If the functionality additionally presents data to the host application screen (retrieved from the application to be counted), then 1 EO is also counted for the sending application (the application to be counted) and 1 EI is counted for the host application if the retrieved data is stored. (Authors' note: again these are simplified rule conventions for the insurance corporation. Strict IFPUG rule adherence would involve ascertaining the output to be an EO or EQ, and determining whether data into the host application was stored simply displayed. These site-specific rule conventions eased the counting burden while maintaining consistency and repeatability of counts.)

Log-On

A log-on function that invokes security control (validating the log-on ID/password combination) is usually counted as 1 EQ, unless the system behavior is changed and/or if ILFs are changed by it, at which time it would instead be counted as an EI.

Update

An update function that causes a data update of one of more ILF in batch or interactive dialogue is counted as 1 EI. The files that are updated are in turn counted as appropriate ILFs if they have not already been counted.

If the user can invoke identical functionality from multiple screens, then such functionality counts only once. For example, if a customer addition can be done from three separate screens with identical processing, it is counted as an EI only once.

Multiple ways to initiate or launch the same function (e.g., Alt_+key, Add +key, Key+enter) do not affect the fact that the function is counted only once.

Batch

1 EI is counted for each elementary process transaction that causes an update to a data file and needs separate processing.

Migrations

Migrations are counted as 1 EI for each RET that it updates (internal rule). *Question for the counters*: Are other outputs produced additionally, for example, migration reports? If yes, Then they are each counted as 1 EO, too. (Strict

IFPUG rules again would require determination of EO versus EQ for each report. This counting convention simplified things be counting all migration reports as EO.)

Screens

- *Radio buttons*
Radio buttons typically represent data elements (DETs) as part of EI functions or the input (selection) side of EO or EQ functions. Radio buttons in a data group are counted as 1 DET since there can be only one field chosen. Both option fields in Fig. 15.5 are thus only counted (together) as 1 DET.

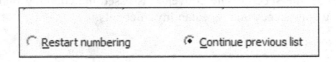

Fig. 15.5. Radio buttons

- *Check boxes*
Contrary to radio buttons, check boxes allow for multiple values to be checked at the same time. Thus, each check box (as long as each is a unique, nonrecursive, nonrepeating field) is counted as 1 DET. For example, the two check boxes in Fig. 15.6 are counted as 2 DETs.

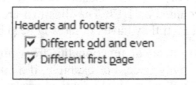

Fig. 15.6. Check boxes

- *Input and Output Fields*
Input and output fields that cross into or out of the application boundary are regarded (and counted) as data elements with the elementary process to which they apply. The input and output fields for customer, street, postal ZIP code, city, and date of last order in Fig. 15.7 are thus counted as 1 DET each as applicable with one of more associated EI, EO, or EQ to which they are a part.

The input and output fields on screens are counted as DETs, ignoring literals, and counting only once any field that is both an input and an output field.

If there is error handling (messages), confirmation messages, and/or messages asking if processing should continue in relation to an EI, EO, or EQ, then that functionality is counted as 1 DET whether one or more of the message types occur.

For noncode tables (i.e., reference tables, rules tables, master files, etc.), the unique, nonrepeated, nonrecursive columns are each counted as a separate DET, without literals.

Enter or OK button(s) or PF keys (the total for all command/initiator buttons or keys) are counted as 1 DET together for the applicable function to which they apply (trigger).

- 1 EO or 1 EQ is, e.g., counted for each of the following coherent processes (as long as it meets the definition of IFPUG's "elementary process"):
  - Retrieval of data displayed on a called screen or report (see the chapter on IFPUG Function Points for details of how to discern an EO from an EQ function)
  - When an elementary function is separated into several follow-up screens, the function(s) must be counted as elementary functions (self-contained) including the data elements from all follow-on screens together
  - If the same screen is used for the three elementary functions add, change, and delete, then it is counted as 3 EI.

15.4.5 External Output (EO)

Are data transferred in batch transactions from the application to be counted to an external application or user? If so, then this transaction is counted as 1 EO or EQ in the sending application, and potentially as one or more EIs in the receiving application.

- EOs are also counted for elementary processes that create derived data or involve calculations if the primary intent of the process is to present data to a user (or another application). A process whose primary intent is to present data outside the application boundary is either counted as an EO or an EQ – but not both. (It is a binary choice between EO and EQ – see the chapter on IFPUG rules.)
- An elementary process designed to produce output, which purely retrieves data from one or more ILF/EIF for display or presentation to a user is counted as an EQ (not as an EO)
- With EOs and EQs, all logical files (ILF/EIF) that are read or changed during processing of the EO are counted as FTRs
- With a delete, the implicit EQ (for showing the data to be deleted) is not counted. (Note: Under IFPUG rules, an implicit query that displays data for the user prior to a change or delete is counted once as an EQ as long as it is unique functionality not counted elsewhere. NESMA rules differ in this area and do not count any implicit EQ associated with change or delete functionality).

Online Reports

Typical external outputs of applications with GUI are often online reports with text and/or graphics. The same information can often be shown as follows:

- Text
- Pie chart
- Bar chart, etc.

Each of these presentations is counted as 1 EO. The same holds if the reports are printed on different media (online, paper, microfiche, etc.).

Author's note: The question of how to *officially* count multimedia functionality according to strict IFPUG rules is currently under debate by a task force within IFPUG. At the time of printing, there has been no definitive guidance published. This corporation chose to again simplify things by counting all as EO rather than having counters go through the process of determining whether they were strictly an EO or an EQ.

Two reports with identical formatting, one on a detailed level, and one as summary are each counted as separate functionality. The summary report (due to calculations) is 1 EO, and the detailed report (depending on its processing and whether it derives new data or contains calculations of its own) will be an EO or an EQ.

A statement or parameter (unique) in a report generator required by the user for flexible reporting is counted as 1 DET per parameter in the according report.

In graphic output there is only 1 DET counted for a text field and its numerical equivalent (note that to count 2 DET would incorrectly reflect the IT technical view rather than the user view).

An export file is counted as 1 EO or 1 EQ depending on the processing involved.

Interfaces Client/Server ↔ Host

Export of data by the application to be counted (e.g., PC application) to an external application (e.g., host): typically 1 EO for the application to be counted, 1 EI for the host application. Are there any selection parameters delivered from the host to request specific data as part of the transaction? If yes, then those parameters (if unique from the output fields) will increase the DET count for the EO or EQ that is output.

One EI is counted for each function and also for add, change, and delete functions sent to the PC from the other host application.

15.4.6 External Inquiries (EQ)

Requests for data retrieval that come from outside the system boundary that require delivery of data from the application to be counted, with the prerequisite that no processing (other than data retrieval) is done with the data in the application being counted, are counted as EQ. This includes branching in the dialogue of the other application (but the interface is not typically counted as an EIF in this case).

EQs may be pairs of information flows that only read stored data, or may be one-way data that goes out of the application where only data retrieval (and no other processing) is performed (e.g., monthly data listing).

- One update and one inquiry are counted as 1 EI and 1 EQ.
- A screen with, e.g., 23 fields in the output part and 1 field in the input part would be counted as an EQ – do not count the screen more than once!
- For input parts of EQs or EOs, count as FTR only the file types that are used in the transaction (normally zero), or more if they are additionally required. Make sure you count the input part together with the output (display, file, report) part that goes with it. (Note: NESMA also differs in this particular area. See the chapter on FSMM's for more details.)
- Help is 1 EQ per level of help, not per screen and not counted as EO. Thus for help functionality there is counted 1 EQ for each kind of help (system help, dialogue help, field help) to a maximum of 3 EQs per application if all three levels are present.
- For output parts of EQs or EOs, count as FTR only files that are used in the transaction (normally many).
- Log on with security (password demand) counts maximally 2 FTR and 4 DET (user name, password, error, trigger).
- An EQ with printed answer is counted as 1 EQ, not as EO.
- List boxes or tables for choice are counted as EQ if they dynamically deliver data back from EIFs or ILFs. (i.e., lists of static values such as *yes or no* do not count).
- No EQ is counted for derived data (i.e., retrieval of data that are used for calculation) – count an EO in that case.
- Identical EQs shall not be counted multiple times (e.g., the same browse/data retrieval before update and change would count as an EQ only once. Identical queries invoked from different screens with identical processing would count as an EQ only once).

Conversion

If there are no calculations for conversions, then 1 EQ is counted for inquiries. Loading of data from an old application master file to update (convert) into the new file counts as 1 EI.

Branching

Branching into the dialogue of another application is counted as 1 EQ as long as data is passed out to the other application (e.g., when branching into a central customer dialogue for retrieval of a customer, the originating application sends the customer identifier) and returned to the application to be counted.

Drop-Down Lists

Dropdown lists are typical for GUI interfaces. One has to distinguish between dynamic and static list fields. Dynamic lists deliver the content retrieved from an ILF/EIF at the moment when the user opens the list, which is counted as an EQ. The static list fields deliver the content of the list field already at the initialization of the according dialogue or screen. Only the dynamic dropdown lists are counted as EQ; the static ones are not counted at all.

Note that *code tables* create a unique sort of situation: even if code tables are maintained by a user, they are not to be counted according to strict IFPUG 4.2 rules – this means not as ILF or EIF, not for maintenance (i.e., not as EI, EO, EQ), not when its data is displayed in a list box (i.e., not as a drop-down EQ).

Often there can be found several follow-up inquiries combined with dropdown list fields. As an example: A dialogue for showing customer information contains a dynamic drop-down list for different customers along with display fields of different customer information. When the user chooses a customer from the list field, the display fields are filled with the additional customer information of the according customer (see Figs. 15.7 and 15.8). In this case, we have two follow-up inquiries (2 EQs). The first is the choice of the customer and the second is the display of the additional customer information.

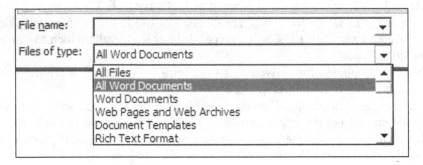

Fig. 15.7. Drop-down list fields

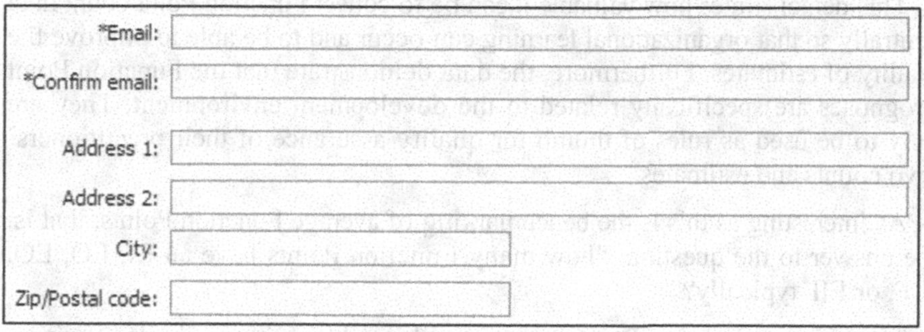

*Email:	
*Confirm email:	
Address 1:	
Address 2:	
City:	
Zip/Postal code:	

Fig. 15.8. Example of dialogue customer data

15.5 Management Summary

One of the most challenging tasks is that estimates are required as early as possible from both the customer (acquirer) and supplier (contractor) point of view.

Early estimation requires good documentation of both the assumptions supporting the FP estimating, and subsequently the estimates of work effort.

Ultimately, the counting and estimation data should serve as a treasure for measurement programs.

Experiences show that valuable information can be gained from appropriate analysis of collected data.

There is strong evidence that different environments lead to different results. This means that each organization should develop its own heuristic solution(s). Nevertheless, comparisons with other organizations are valuable for the enterprise.

Since Function Point counts use the requirements documents as a prerequisite, the so-called Function Point Prognosis or resultant estimates are valuable.

Experiences in the IT department of an international insurance company show that the necessary high-level information required to even do a FP estimate can be established early in discussions with the project leader.

Of course, planning based on relatively undocumented user requirements is prone to high risk and margins of error due to the uncertainty of preliminary estimates.

Another approach is to estimate the Function Points from the proportions of the EIs, EOs, EQs, ILFs, EIFs.

This demonstrates how valuable it can be to collect Function Point count data centrally so that organizational learning can occur and to be able to improve the quality of estimates. Furthermore, the data demonstrate that the Function Point Prognoses are specifically related to the development environment. They are only to be used as rules of thumb for quality assurance of their practitioners' own counts and estimates.

As interesting as this is the benchmarking of average Function Points, that is, the answer to the question: "how many Function Points have an EI, EO, EQ, ILF, or EIF typically?"

The average Function Points are said to be stable ratios in similar environments, and thus are appreciated as a rule of thumb for quick Function Point Prognosis.

Early collection of the information about interfaces, component parts of the project, and formal documentation of the same, along with a diagram of the application boundary (later used for the organizational architecture atlas) are all prerequisites to establish early Function Point Prognosis. When accompanied by a counting log (simple Word document with notes about special FP counting decisions), the project gains a valuable overview about the application portfolio and projects within. In general, these also might include reference numbers (key figures) for quality assurance (percentages, rules of thumb).

Another well-known consequence of careful measurement and documentation of the Function Point counts is a higher level quality of the requirements documents, since they are used, checked, and typically revised.

Note that it is always better to use your own organization's functional component average Function Point values rather than the IFPUG averages.

These findings, compared with those from other organizations, show that such data collection can be used to find heuristic solutions for FP prognosis, by using either Function Point proportions (*typical FP*), function ratios, regression formulae, or rules of thumb.

There is evidence that different environments demand tailored solutions; this leads to our recommendation that each organization develops its own knowledge base (experience database) of heuristic solutions, and should distinguish between different development platforms, etc., when doing so.

Function Points can provide valuable an input for work effort estimates.

Formulae are always only valid in the corresponding environment. Thus, they cannot be used reliably as a 1:1 relationship with other organizations.

In multivariate analyses it is always found that more than one parameter (such as functional size) influences the effort for system development.

The Function Point Method is well suited to be a part of calculating project productivity. However, it must be stressed that productivity is not a personnel metric, but rather a process metric influenced by tools, techniques, skills, programming language, etc. As such, it should never be used to attempt to compare persons or their productivity.

Organizations that make the mistake of ignoring this advance and attempting to measure people find themselves in a position of having to backtrack and perform major damage control. Just do not do it!

The result of misusing productivity results in skepticism and mistrust of the entire measurement initiative. Such a malpractice can destroy years of successful nurturing of a metrics program in record time.

When comparing the productivity of projects and organizations, one always has to regard that no two IT projects or organizations are exactly equal or comparable in the many parameters relevant to estimation and work effort.

Using the ISBSG Repository Data Disc R10 (ISBSG, 2007) with its research tool "Early Estimate Checker V5.0," it is possible to perform customized data analysis with any subset of the more than 4,000 projects in the database.

16 Estimation of Data Warehouses, Web-Based Applications: Software Reuse and Redevelopment

Data Warehouse and Web-based application development are an increasing part of modern software development, but are different from conventional software development in that they typically involve considerations of software reuse and redevelopment.

These topics give rise to questions of how to measure the software size on data warehouse developments and how to estimate effort when reuse and redevelopment is involved. That is why this chapter deals with the special aspects of sizing Data Warehouses and Web-based application development, as well as work effort estimating with special consideration to software reuse and redevelopment.

16.1 Function Point Counts of Data Warehouse Projects

Luca Santillo, a certified Function Point specialist (CFPS) in Rome, Italy, presented in 2001 in the international FESMA conference in Heidelberg, Germany, his experiences with effort estimation of Data Warehouse projects. The following is excerpted from his report.

The requirements of Data Warehouse projects are significantly different from requirements of transaction oriented systems (see Table 16.1).

A Data Warehouse System consists of three parts: data collection, system administration, and data retrieval (OLAP: Online Analytical Processing).

The system processes:

- Should be consistent with the organizational structure (e.g., each organizational unit has its own Data Warehouse).
- Should preserve the autonomy.
    - o Of the Data Warehouse regarding each data mart.
    - o Of each data mart regarding other data mart(s).

Table 16.1. Comparison of transaction oriented systems vs. data warehouse systems (Santillo 2001)

	Transaction oriented systems	Data warehouse systems
Task	Perform daily operations	Retrieval and analysis of Information
Structure	RDBMS optimized for transaction processing	RDBMS optimized for queries
Data model	Normalized	Multidimensional
Retrieval	SQL	SQL plus advanced analysis Tools
Data type	Operational data	Data for analysis of business
Data characteristic	Detailed	Summarized and detailed
Data indexes	Few	Many
Data joins	Many	Some
Duplicated data	Normalized DBMS	Denormalized DBMS
Aggregates and derived data	Rare	Often

There are many users of a Data Warehouse System:

- Data Warehouse administrator
- Database administrator
- Data retrieval (OLAP) Administrator
- End-user
- Each interface system.

Peter Hill, the executive director of ISBSG reports in the *ISBSG Software Project Estimation Workbook* (1999) on page 19 the following information about Data Warehouse Systems: "Many information systems are characterized by code and reference-tables for checking the validity, consistency, and integrity of other data, and for data selection. In Data Warehouse Systems the proportion of code and reference-tables compared to functional size is about 60% where "normal" MIS often have a proportion of 30–40%."

For the measurement of the functional size of Data Warehouse projects, many special aspects have to be taken into account for Function Point counting. In particular, *the definition of the system boundary is of importance* since it strongly influences the measurement results. If misplaced, the system boundary may give rise to improbable estimates.

16.1.1 Experiences of Star Schema Design Function Point Counts

Using a Star Schema design (see Fig. 16.1), Luca Santillo reported his findings in function point counting.

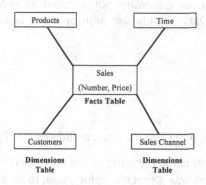

Fig. 16.1. Star schema for a data warehouse system

Classification of Files

There is a special case of data collection when the Data Warehouse System delivers the extracted information to the Data Warehouse (or the independent data mart) by its own procedures (extraction, transformation, and filling). The extracted information is not counted as EIFs because the system of origin (the operational application) formats and sends the extracted information out of its application boundary as an EO (if there are calculations or derived data as part of the process) or an EQ (if there is not). The target system does not collect this data and read it, instead it process into its boundary the extracted data – this would count as one or more EIs in the receiving (target) application.

The data in a Data Warehouse System are organized in a new design, the so-called Star Schema or multidimensional file model (which may be a snowflake schema). Each star point of the schema would be counted as an ILF of the Data Warehouse System.

Each existing and dimensional table is a RET of this ILF. Analogous to this is each logical cube (an ILF) with $N + 1$ RETs, where N is the number of dimensions (axes of the cube).

In case of the snowflake schema where the hierarchical dimensions are split into their levels (e.g., month, quarter, year), the tables of the second order do not count as additional RETs, because the already counted RET is valid for the whole dimension ("time" in this example).

Each hierarchy consists of two DETs: the dimensions level and the value (e.g., time scale: month, quarter, year; and the time value: Jan, Feb,...QI, QII, 2007, 2008,...).

Other attributes in the tables (except attributes that implement an additional hierarchy) are counted as additional DETs for the ILF (logical data).

Technical metadata are generally not counted as independent ILFs. Exceptions (where the Data Warehouse administrator is the user) include the following:

- User profiles
- Privileges
- Processing rules
- User statistics.

Some organizational metadata may be candidates for ILFs, for example:

- Data dictionary (what is the meaning of the attributes?)
- Historical data (when was a specific value given to an attribute?)
- Data about persons responsible for data (who delivered a value to an attribute?).

Classification of Transactions

Since reading the external data is from the Data Warehouse perspective, only one logically completed process, there is only one EI counted for each identified goal. Data administration of the Data Warehouse include the standard maintenance processes to update/change, delete, and view (browse) the metadata.

Use of the data warehouse data by end users is counted as an EO or an EQ depending on the kind of usage. Thus, there is at least one EO or one EQ counted per logical star of the Data Warehouse.

Drill down or pull up functions read the same logical files at different hierarchy levels. These are all DETs of the same logical star. The different levels of views are counted only once since they belong to the same EO or EQ.

The drill down trigger is usually delivered from OLAP tools in the form of a list box for each drillable attribute. These functions are counted as 1 L EQ (drop down) for each different attribute of each individual star.

16.1.2 Recommendations for Function Point Counting of OLAP Cube Design

The competence center and its data warehouse developers at an international insurance company in Germany built on Santillo's approach and documented the following ideas for counting OLAP Design Data Warehouses according to the IFPUG Method. These are presented after a short description of some OLAP specific concepts. The application in question has 3,173 unadjusted Function Points with the following functional mix: 36% of uFP are ILF, 55% EI, 9% EO, and 1% EIF and EQ (together). The IFPUG Value Adjustment Factor (VAF) for the application was 1.07.

OLAP-Specific Concepts

OLAP (Online Analytical Processing) enables multidimensional representation and evaluation of data, for use in controlling, accountancy, sales, etc. These data are stored in an OLAP Cube where there are hierarchy and attribute dimensions. Figure 16.2 depicts OLAP specific technical terms.

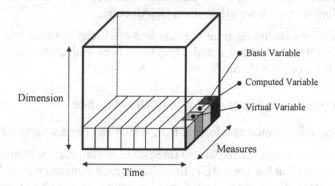

Fig. 16.2. OLAP specific concepts

Dimensions are structural components of multidimensional data cubes. Each dimension consists of elements that can be aggregated to a certain type or concept. The names of subsidiary organizations can be, for example, elements of a dimension subsidiary (in case of an insurance these subsidiaries can include life, health, auto, etc.). Dimensions represent an index to identify values in a data cube.

Hierarchy is defined as the representation of levels in a dimension, which may be composed of multiple hierarchy levels. In the insurance example above, the dimension organization could have two hierarchy levels: the upper level with the insurance holding, the lower with the subsidiaries.

Attribute dimensions are additional one- or multilevel hierarchies that describe or group elements (input-elements) of an existing (base-) dimension.

For navigation in the *multidimensional hierarchic structures, drill downs* are used. This is done to decompose aggregated values. Within one dimension, the aggregated value of a higher hierarchy can be decomposed into its components (at a lower hierarchy level) by drilling down into the data.

The opposite situation is called *roll up, where data are aggregated into higher hierarchy level.*

Aggregation or Consolidation is the aggregation of "deeper" values (i.e., from a lower level) to a higher hierarchy value, for example, by summing up.

Measures or variables are the coefficients that exist in an OLAP cube. Normally there are a number of different types of variables, for example, base variables, computed, and virtual variables. Virtual variables are computed on-line at runtime.

All coefficients (measures or variables) are filled from a central fact file. This fact file contains the content of the dimensions as well as the according values per coefficient that are stored then in an OLAP cube.

All dimensions including time periods and coefficients (measures or variables) of an OLAP cube are listed as System files and count files, and are counted as ILFs or parts thereof.

Classification of Data Function Types of OLAP Cubes

An OLAP cube is counted as a logical ILF, which can have several RETs.

Each base and computed coefficient (measures or variables) within an OLAP cube is an ILF with at least one RET. In addition, each dimension is an ILF with at least one RET. Computed coefficients (measures or variables) are, in this context, variables that are computed based on existing base variables and are physically stored in the cube.

Each user dimension coefficient (measure or variable) is counted as an ILF with several DETs, which in this case are the number of dimensions and the value. Virtual variables that are computed online are only counted as DETs in reports or queries. The dimension "time" is also counted as an ILF, with its values (e.g., month and year) each counted as a DET.

In each hierarchy level of a dimension there are two DETs: the hierarchy level and the value.

The attribute dimensions and the time variable are additional RETs of the according dimension. Each attribute dimension is, in this case, counted as one RET.

Classification of Transactions of OLAP Cubes

The retrieval (read) of external data for batch processing from an OLAP cube perspective represents a unique, logically self-contained, process. Each dimension file and each file per variable are counted as one EI. The use of the data (sent outside the application boundary) by the end user is counted as either an EO or an EQ, depending on whether the elementary process meets the requirements for an EO (calculation, derived data, updating ILF, or changing system behavior) or an EQ. When counting a report it will be either an EO or an EQ multiplied by the number of dimensions and multiplied by the number of logical media required by the user.

Note: At the time of this printing, the International Function Point Users Group (IFPUG) was still debating how to resolve the issue of Function Point counting of multiple output media. The international insurance corporation made the independent decision to count each logical output media as a separate EO or EQ as the user requested. For example, if a report was required online and on paper according to the user requirements, the EO or EQ would be counted twice. The FTR (file types referenced) to be counted in this case are the number of dimensions and the number of computed variables. DETs are counted in the same way as reports in any other type of application and include all the user-required, unique, nonrepetitive, and nonrecursive fields on the report and all computed variables.

Drill down and drill up are two opposite ways to read the same data at different hierarchy levels. Thus, different levels of user-views are counted only once since they belong to the same logical function.

The drill down trigger is, in OLAP tools, usually a list box for every drillable attribute. This mechanism is counted only as a low complexity EQ for each attribute of each different logical dimension. For example, these are counted in the same manner as drop down list boxes – low EQ – as they are in traditional applications.

Virtual variables, which are computed online, are Eos.

The aforementioned approach clearly demonstrates that the Function Point Method can be used for Data Warehouse counting, using the star schema, snowflake schema, and OLAP Design. The American author instructs a one day Function Points for Data Warehouses workshop with ample case studies and practice. The workshop is taught as an onsite workshop, a public class, or in conjunction with IFPUG events. See www.qualityplustech.com for further details.

16.2 Estimating Web Development

Web development is different from conventional software development because of its use of n-tier component-based architectures (often four or five tiers). Often, existing applications are integrated. The implementation of component based software is encapsulated. This functional orientation and independence of implementation does not change the counting of Function Points, but supports the usage of the Function Point Method as part of the estimation approach for web development.

According to Magiera, *the architecture and topology of web developments is a challenge and hierarchically complex.* These observations were reported at the 2004 SMEF conference in Rome, and included an experience report in using the COSMIC method for a web development.

Web development can be categorized as follows:

- Enhancement of existing applications by adding with "web front-ends" or portals to the application
- New development of complete web-based applications
- Static web pages.

To perform the functional size measurement of new development or enhancements, any of the five ISO/IEC conformant functional size measurement methods (IFPUG, FiSMA, NESMA, COSMIC, or Mark II) can be used. Nevertheless, web-based development will typically result in counting "peculiarities" or challenges. The IFPUG New Environments Committee published a white paper in the IFPUG homepage http://www.ifpug.org, with hints for counting an E-commerce application with *n*-tier component based architecture. (In addition, Quality Plus Technologies conducts a targeted one day knowledge transfer workshop titled Function Point Analysis for Web-based Development. See www.qualityplustech.com for further details.)

C. Jones wrote in the *IFPUG IT Measurement: Practical Advice from the Experts* that there is a lack of empirical data for web development. He theorizes that most of these applications are so small (less than 500 Function Points) that organizations do not bother to function point count them. Albeit, there was measured high productivity for web development (more than 25 Function Points per person month). The quality in these cases is not worse than a typical mainframe application; however, it is observed that defects are found much earlier because they are more visible if a website does not function correctly.

According to the peculiarities of the new environment there is one paragraph in this chapter devoted to each of the following:

- Estimation of web developments
- Function Point counting of web developments
- Software reuse and redevelopment.

In *Practical Project Estimation, 2nd edition (ISBSG, 2005)*, Chap. 15 is dedicated to estimating Web-based software development projects.

16.2.1 Enhancement of Existing Applications with Web Front-Ends

The rationale behind enhancing existing applications with web front-ends is often the desire to present functionality of existing applications to a higher volume and greater variety of users. Since web browsers are readily available to most users in an organization, front-ends present themselves as cost-efficient and quick-to-market solutions. The goal is often to save time and effort formerly dedicated to software distribution and installation. Web-based applications (especially portals or simple web-front end panels) can be much simpler in structure and quicker to market with small teams than traditional application development.

Front-ends are usually implemented using HTML-based forms, embedded scripts, and dynamically generated HTML pages that communicate with existing applications or databases.

Estimates can, in this case, be done in the same way using expert estimation as when estimating software development using other technologies. In addition, performing an estimate based on Functional Size Measurement can also be efficient and expedient. This demonstrates again that the independence of functional size measurement from the technology is a huge benefit.

The enhancement of an existing application with an inquiry dialogue implemented using web technology is, for example, counted with Function Points as an enhancement. In IFPUG terminology, the inquiries coded in the web front-end are counted as EQs or EOs, and updated or otherwise altered master files are counted as ILF or EIF according to the Function Point rules. Other peculiarities of the Function Point counts of web applications are dealt with at the end of this chapter.

After the functional size of an enhancement is done, the effort can be estimated using productivity ratios from experience data.

Important: Since the productivity of web applications varies greatly from developments built with other technologies, it is critical to develop special experience databases.

The rapid time-to-market demanded for web-based development (rapid prototyping, agile programming) mostly imply unstable, poor, or evolving requirement concepts. This can challenge functional size measurement, especially when the project team does not yet know what the requirements will be. *The rapid adoption of new technologies in an organization can lead to the result that collected measures, and measurement processes can quickly become outdated at the time of implementation.*

16.2.2 New Development of Complete Web-Based Applications

Web-based applications are principally classic client/server applications with front-end web technology. *Usually the user logic is represented in an application server and the data in a database server.* Together with the client this constitutes the so-called classical three-tier architecture (see Fig. 16.3). For functional size measurement the same rules hold as for regular applications.

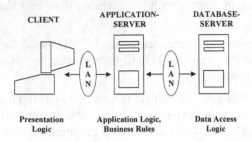

Fig. 16.3. Three-tier architecture for a web-based application

Frallicciardi proposed four *usability measures* for web-based applications:

- End-user efficiency to be measured on the basis of the following:
  - o Highlighting of mandatory fields
  - o Drop-down lists
  - o Navigational help
  - o Online help files
- Completeness:
  - o Number of user accesses to online help functions
  - o Number of quickly exited web pages
  - o Number of error messages occurring during a session
  - o Required time to navigate to another web page
- Effectiveness based on the following:
  - o Daily number of transactions cancelled by the end-user
  - o Daily number of sessions cancelled without completing a transaction
- Efficiency based on the following:
  - o Necessary time to successfully complete a transaction
  - o Number of transactions successfully completed during a certain time period (e.g., 1 h).

16.2.3 Static Web Pages

Static web pages present different challenges to the estimation of effort for the development of static web pages. Static web pages are different hard-coded, HTML pages linked to each other. Web pages can contain both textual and multimedia objects (movies, sounds, etc.). The layout and linking of the pages is done with special development tools (HTML editors), code generators such as MS Frontpage, or directly with an integrated text editor.

Effort to complete this kind of web-based development is not contained in the implementation of user functionality, but rather in programming and linking the content elements. Because of the interpretations of the IFPUG rules (see www. ifpug.org), there are typically zero FP associated with software developed for static web pages. As such, the IFPUG method is not well suited to count static web pages or menu linked pages.

The ISO/IEC conformant FSM method: FiSMA 1.1, identifies and counts function lists and function designators as logical user functionality. These two types of functions are required by the users and FiSMA 1.1 can be applied to provide counts for the functions, some of which may physically manifest themselves as menus or icons in the final implementation. Refer to the chapter on FSMMs for further details.

This leaves the estimator to do an expert estimate on the basis of the number and size of pages, complexity of links, etc.

16.2.4 Function Point Counts of Web Applications

Since web applications are a relatively new application area for Function Point counting, a collection of FAQs (Frequently Asked Questions) from daily counting and some handy examples have been collected. These hints for handling daily questions should be an aid from the experiences of other organizations and should not be misunderstood as a new standard.

It can be difficult to define the system boundary since web applications are often embedded in *n*-tier architecture and often combined with ERP (Enterprise Resource Planning, e.g., SAP or People soft) systems. The ERP systems must be customized and reconfigured in these cases. The ERP programmable business objects and remote function calls (RFCs) of these systems are usually counted as EIs along with associated ILFs that they maintain. There may also be EIFs. Often MIS software are combined with web applications. The interactions with other applications can be a challenge for identification of EIFs and ILFs, as well for the definition of the boundary.

Often the number of end-users cannot be estimated and potentially can be extremely large. There are also a number of new kinds of end-users: webmasters and application administrators.

Besides this, the determination of the elementary process transactions (EI, EO, EQ) can be sometimes troublesome as there can be many more transactions as compared to traditional development.

It is important to recognize the elementary processes beyond a single web page, since logical business functions often require many physical web screens with embedded navigation and end-user efficient (technical) GUI oriented implementations.

Beyer and Tolomei described their experiences with measuring the functional size of a B2B (Business-to-Business) E-Commerce project. The system comprised a web-based marketplace processing real-time transactions. *The authors present the problem that web-GUIs were built dynamically.* Hence DETs and FTRs from EIs, EOs, and EQs change during runtime. There exist also more drill downs and combo boxes with more complex and dynamic queries than are found in common, non-web based environments. Thus, the proportions of EQs to EIs and EOs are typically higher than in host or Client/Server applications.

J. Jones reported in the *IFPUG IT Measurement – Practical Advice from the Experts* an example of *the Function Point count of the Java Pet Store (JPS)*. This example can be recommended to readers who want a first exposure to web-based application functional sizing.

An international insurance company made the following experiences with Function Point counting during the development of a B2C (Business-to-Customer) web application.

Classification of Data Function Types of Web Applications

ILF: ILF are counted for Resource Property Files with user relevant entries. If there is the functionality to define text paragraphs (user maintained) for use in automatic letter assembly or generation, then an ILF should be counted for those standard paragraphs (also the maintenance functions of add, change, delete, and a query function would be counted as appropriate if they are used with this ILF).

For all *XSL-scripts,* one ILF in total is counted, where each recognizable different script is a DET. Content pages are also counted as ILF with each content page representing a RET. An event log file is also counted as an ILF.

EIF: The PDF documents are counted as one EIF for all content together, with one RET for each functional requirement and as many DETs as there are pages.

Classification of Transactions in Web-Based Applications

EI: Login is typically an EI because of the event *login writing* that updates an ILF, with one DET for each event. The business functions *password forgotten* and *change password* are counted as 1 EQ (retrieval of password for display) and 1 EI (update password), respectively.

EO: Letter writing is one or more EO or EQ.

EQ: Links to other systems are counted as 1 EQ low each as long as data is passed (e.g., userid, product description, sending system, etc). Links to navigation functions only are not counted.

Each business function that uses a *content page* is counted as 1 EQ. *Static pages* (HTML or JSP – Java Server Pages) are counted as 1 EQ if they represent a business function. The input part is 1 DET for the trigger. The output part has 0 FTR and 1 DET for the content of the page. Each function referencing an *XSL-script* is counted as an additional FTR. If a JSP contains static content as well as input and output fields then it is not counted. Each call to a PDF form is counted as 1 EQ with the number of pages equal to the number of DETs.

Important: Other organizations often use the following standard for counting *PDF documents:* if it is a system that creates PDF documents from operative data then the stored document data are counted as an ILF, and creation and storage of the PDF document are counted as EI functions (create and store is a single elementary EI together). If the document is not stored it is 1 EQ or EO instead. Viewing a stored PDF (if counted as an ILF or EIF) is then 1 EQ.

DET: Comments and error messages created by Java Script or JSP (Java Server Pages) are only counted as 1 DET for each business function. Each entry of events in the user-requested events log file is counted as 1 DET.

IFPUG General System Characteristic (GSC) Values for Web Applications

There is an essential difference from classical host applications for the adjusted function points of web-based applications. Web applications are similar to Client/Server applications in that they typically score high on half of the characteristics. GSCs are part of the IFPUG Function Point Method that attempt to evaluate nonfunctional requirements, for example,

1. Data communication:
   TP systems with multiple protocols, classified as 5
2. Distributed processing:
   Online and in both directions, classified 4 or 5
3. Performance:
   No particular score, but if 24×7 access is required and sub-second response time is essential in the application, then this is typically 3 or 4 or 5
4. Heavily used configuration:
   May or may not be applicable
5. Transaction rate:
   If application is similar to high volume site such as Amazon.com with constantly high transaction volume, then this is typically going to be 3 or higher
6. Online data entry:
   More than 30% of EIs are interactive data entries, classified 5
7. End-user efficiency:
   Prototyping with many user efficient functions, classified 4 or 5

8. Online update:
   Maybe applicable, depends on what the functionality of the application includes
9. Complex processing:
   Password control (security), complex logic, multimedia, classified as a minimum of 3
10. Reusability:
    Reuse of code on multiple levels can typically score as high as 4 or 5
11. Installation easy:
    May or may not be applicable
12. Operational ease:
    May or may not be applicable
13. Multiple sites:
    Implementation across many different unknown sites or browser softwares, often scores 2 or higher
14. Facilitate change:
    May or may not be applicable.

Thus the VAF of web applications sums up to 0.98 for only a subset of the GSCs and is higher in total.

For the example count of the Java Pet Store (JPS), the VAF was 1.22; and the IIC for a B2C application scored a VAF of 1.07.

The IFPUG Practices Committee has studied the relevance of the 14 GSCs for new development. With the exclusion of the GSCs from the ISO/IEC standard (IFPUG Vs. 4.1), the GSCs have waned in overall industry adoption – even among IFPUG users. The current IFPUG Counting Practices Manual (CPM) release 4.2 includes the GSCs (and new textual guidance words). However, to be an ISO/IEC standard, the GSCs must not be part of the functional sizing process. This does not mean that an organization must abandon the GSCs, quite the contrary. It means that the VAF is outside the ISO definition of what constitutes functional size measurement.

16.2.5 Estimating Web Development with the CoBRA Method

The CoBRA method (Cost, Benchmarking, and Risk Assessment) was developed at the end of the nineties by the Fraunhofer Institute for Experimental Software Engineering (IESE). It was used in 1998 by a large German software development organization in a pilot project (using SLOC as size measure) for a small Australian software development organization developing web applications. Melanie Ruhe (winner of the DASMA students' thesis award 2003) reported in her thesis about this project and the applicability of the CoBRA method.

Using the CoBRA method, a causal model is developed with expert knowledge and factors influencing effort. For this reason, the size of completed projects, together with the size of the new software (the project), are measured. The influencing factors are evaluated, and then the effort and cost drivers of the completed projects are taken into account. With this data, Monte Carlo Simulations are performed leading to a "likelihood distribution" of effort. In this way, the effort can be estimated followed by the discussion of risks.

The following *cost drivers* (similar to those used in COCOMO II and in the ISBSG reports) were identified by the experts in Ruhe's research:

1. Degree of innovation of the requirements (rank 1.3)
2. Speed of change in requirements (rank 1.8)
3. Quality of project management (rank 2.6)
4. Participation of end users (rank 2.6)
5. Quality of specification methods (rank 2.9)
6. Project team communication skills (rank 3.4)
7. Software reliability (rank 4.5)
8. Technical skills of the developers (rank 4.7)
9. Technological experience of the project team (rank 4.7)
10. Degree of innovation of the technology (rank 4.8)
11. Maintainability (rank 5.1).

Sensitivity analysis showed that the cost drivers 2 and 3 had the most influence on work effort. Ruhe investigated 12 projects in her thesis, and sized them using the WEBMO method (see following chapter) and the COSMIC method as suitable. Measurement improvements were reported in the range of a 20% on average to estimating accuracy.

16.2.6 The WEBMO Estimation Method

The WEBMO estimation method was developed in 2000 by Donald J. Reifer (USC) on the basis of 64 software projects. It is an enhancement of the COCOMO II Early Design Model. It measures software size using Web Objects, and is a modification of Function Point counting tailored for Intranet and Internet environments. The Web Objects are then used to estimate KSLOCs and, from these, the effort. The Web Objects measure the five Function Point components, plus the following four components (see also Fig. 16.4):

1. Multimedia files
2. Web components
3. Scripts
4. Links (XML, HTML, and code lines of query languages).

Operands and operators must be distinguished and the classification is done with tables similar to those used in the IFPUG Function Point Method. There is a table for SLOC per Web Object depending on the programming language. Together with nine cost drivers (similar to the COCOMO II Early Design Model) the project effort and duration can then be estimated using the formulae provided.

Similar to Sneed's Object Points, the WEBMO method documentation leaves the reader with outstanding questions (especially for recognition of Web Objects).

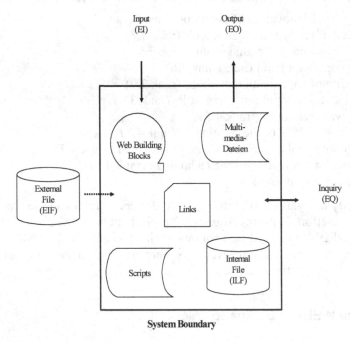

Fig. 16.4. Counting components for the web objects method (Refer, 2000)

16.3 Software Reuse and Redevelopment

Many IT projects today use existing (legacy) software and then add new functionality. This can be more cost effective than total replacement or redevelopment. Adding new functionality to existing software seems to generate less effort than new development, and the budget is often lower and easier to approve. Software project effort, however, depends on many factors and this idea has still to be verified.

One of the most important factors of software development is the development of new components for reuse. This has the advantage that existing functionnality (and often the associated function point count of the component functions) can be reused. The result should be an increase in the productivity of the IT department, and also in the efficiency of Function Point counts. Thus the proverb holds:

Reuse can be a key success strategy. Reuse is especially utilized for horizontal services such as support and connection of components and platforms with functionalities, like, for example, security, transaction management, view into directories, data management, and others.

Reusability saves development costs and therefore can influence the ROI of the project. Thus, the effort dedicated to the implementation of reused components should be measured separately in order that the correct ROI can be calculated. This means that effective reuse depends on the existence of a data dictionary and richly documented components.

The decision about which components should be developed as reusable is one of the most important decision to be made at the beginning of a project. Therefore, we recommend that a special workshop be organized with the project team. Of course this does not preclude the need for the regular estimation conference as outlined previously.

Functionality that is reused should not be function point counted more than once if it was already counted in the application. Design for reuse is often becomes an issue when measurement and estimating using functional size measurement are initiated. Reuse can have a positive effect on work effort (design, coding, and testing of components is already done) or a negative effect on work effort (if additional project teams and stakeholders must be interviewed and involved in the project). As such, the Finnish Software Measurement Association (FiSMA) has developed a reuse multiplier that is used together with Functional Size, Situation Analysis, and an appropriate delivery rate from ISBSG or based on a reliable Experience database, to estimate work effort. Their FiSMA Reuse Analysis is outlined in a paper available for download in English from www.fisma.fi/in-english/methods and it is also included in Experience® Pro software from 4SUM Partners (www.4SUMPartners.com).

Santillo recommends the following activities when sizing a project where reuse of existing software packages is involved:

- *Re-design* can evolve if adaptations for the new objective cannot be integrated in the existing design. This requires adding an adaptation of already developed functionality (reword) to this project.
- *Re-implementation* is necessary in the form of new code.

- *Re-test* is required when neither redesign nor reimplementation occur. This is a necessary prerequisite to guarantee the usability of the software functionality in the new environment.

Besides the reuse of existing software, *redevelopment* of existing software may be done instead of new development. For such projects, there is often only a technical design necessary and only minor and few changes, if any, to hardware and software. For this type of project, automatic tools for code generation can be used.

The ISBSG benchmarking database (release 8) contains 55 redevelopment projects (3%) out of a total of 2,027 projects (56% of the total are enhancements and 41% new development). Out of the 55 redevelopment projects, there are two with a size of more than 2,300 Function Points, six larger than 2,000 FP, eleven larger than 1,000 FP, and the remaining thirty projects are less than 500 FP. The median for the size of the redevelopment projects is close to 1,000 FP. Of the total number of 2,027 projects, 99 had a goal to customize standard software (3 were redevelopment projects, 36 were new developments, and 59 were enhancement projects).

Seventeen of the redevelopment projects delivered detailed information about the Function Point components (see Table 16.2).

Table 16.2. Proportions of FP components in redevelopment projects

Percentage	EI	EO	EQ	ILF	EIF
Median	32.7	24.9	9.2	24.1	9.1
Average	32.5	23.8	9.2	25.0	9.5

The FP proportions for redevelopment projects are similar to new development projects, with slightly higher percentage of EIs and EIFs and slightly lower EQs.

Phase proportions of the redevelopment projects compared to new developments and enhancements are shown in Table 16.3 (reference ISBSG, CD r8).

Table 16.3. Phase proportions for the various types of software development

Phase	All projects		New development		Redevelopment		Enhancement	
	N	%	N	%	N	%	N	%
Planning		4		6		7		3
Specification		23		20		9		27
Programming		41		48		29		37
Test		22		17		14		26
Installation		10		9		41		7
Sum	363		151		22		190	

Furthermore, ISBSG also published the defect density (see Table 16.4) and Project Delivery Rate (PDR, see Table 16.5) for the same data.

Table 16.4. Defect density expressed as defects per FP

Defect density	N	Median (defects/FP)	ISBSG release 8
New development	165 (52%)	0.0179	1 defect per 56 FP
Redevelopment	8 (3%)	0.0203	1 defect per 49 FP
Enhancement	142 (45%)	0.0182	1 defect per 55 FP
Total number of projects	315		

Table 16.5. Project Delivery Rate (PDR) in hours per FP for various types of software development

PDR (hours/FP)	N	Median (hr/FP)	Average (hr/FP)
New development	173	8.8	12.9
Redevelopment	8	23.6	19.6
Enhancement	303	13.3	17.0
Total or average	484	11.4	15.5

Note: in Table 16.5 - a higher PDR indicates a lower productivity.

16.4 Management Summary

The requirements of Data Warehouse projects are significantly different from requirements of transaction oriented systems.

In Data Warehouse Systems the proportion of code and reference-tables compared to functional size is about 60%, where "normal" MIS often have a proportion of 30–40%.

The data in a Data Warehouse System are organized in a new design, the so-called Star Schema or multidimensional file model (which may be a snowflake schema).

OLAP (Online Analytical Processing) enables multidimensional representation and evaluation of data for use in controlling, accountancy, sales, etc. These data are stored in an OLAP Cube where there are hierarchy and attribute dimensions.

The aforementioned approach clearly demonstrates that the Function Point Method can be used for Data Warehouse counting, using the star schema, snowflake schema, and OLAP Design.

Web development is different from conventional software development because of its use of n-tier component-based architectures (often four or five tiers). Often, existing applications are integrated. The implementation of component based software is encapsulated.

The rationale behind enhancing existing applications with web front-ends is often the desire to present functionality of existing applications to a higher volume and greater variety of users.

The rapid time-to-market demanded for web-based development (rapid prototyping, agile programming) mostly imply unstable, poor, or evolving requirement concepts.

The rapid adoption of new technologies in an organization can lead to the result that collected measures and measurement processes can quickly become outdated at the time of implementation.

Web-based applications are principally classic client/server applications with front-end web technology. Usually the user logic is represented in an application server and the data in a database server.

There is an essential difference from classical host applications for the adjusted function points of web-based applications. Web applications are similar to Client/Server applications in that they typically score high on half of the characteristics.

Reuse can be a key success strategy.

Reusability saves development costs and therefore can influence the ROI of the project.

Functionality that is reused should not be function point counted more than once if it was already counted in the application.

Besides the reuse of existing software, redevelopment of existing software may be done instead of new development.

17 IFPUG Function Point Counting Rules

This chapter comprises the most important definitions and rules (without the hints, examples and further explanations) of the Counting Practices Manual (CPM) of the IFPUG Release 4.2, for example, the definitions for type of count and system boundary, the counting rules for the files (ILF, EIF) and transactions (EI, EO, EQ), as well as for the 14 GSCs. There is intentionally some redundancy with the chapter about "The IFPUG Function Point Counting Method" in order to increase readability. This chapter focuses more on the technical rule details, while Chap. 11 is aimed to provide an overview.

Note that while IFPUG infrequently produces updated releases to its CPM, the core rules have not changed since release 4.0 in 1994. In addition, the complexity matrices for each counted function (i.e., what constitutes Low, Average, or High for each function) and the FP values of each have not changed since their introduction in 1984. It is not anticipated that IFPUG will modify any of the core rules in the counting practices manual for many years to come, however, guidance on how to apply the rules in emerging technologies will continue to be published. Readers who are using IFPUG as their FSM standard are recommended to stay current with the guidance documents by visiting www.ifpug.org.

As of 2009, IFPUG plans to publish its core manual of counting rules in conjunction with ISO/IECs routine 5 year maintenance cycle for all ISO/IEC international standards, and publish a separate document that includes the rule interpretations and examples of how to apply them in practice. IFPUG 4.2 and earlier releases of the CPM were published as an all-inclusive document (sometimes supplemented by interim white papers) and the size was an unwieldy 300+ pages of rules, rule interpretations, examples, exceptions, etc., all interspersed in a single tome. The new strategy of publishing the Function Point Counting rules as an independent and standalone document (which will also be the ISO/IEC standard) of less than 50 pages will streamline the understanding and, hopefully, the dissemination and widespread use of the IFPUG method.

17.1 Overview of IFPUG CPM Release 4.2 (Also known as *IFPUG 4.2*)

The following Table 17.1 summarizes the major process steps involved in performing an IFPUG FP count.

Table 17.1. IFPUG FP counting steps overview

---

1. Determine the type of count
2. Determine the purpose and scope of the count, and the application boundary
3. Identify and classify the files (data function types) and logical transactions (transactional function types):

(3a) Data Function Types		*ILF (Internal Logical Files)*: Internal logical files with their logical record types and data elements; data that are maintained within the application boundary. These are persistent logical entities maintained within the application boundary.
		EIF (External Logical Files): External interface files with their logical record types and data elements; data that are maintained by users in another application outside the application boundary (i.e., from other applications). These are persistent logical entities referenced (only) but not maintained by the application being counted.
(3b) Transaction function types		*EI (External Inputs)*: External input functions with their logical data groups and data elements.
		EO (External Outputs): External output functions with their logical data groups and data elements.
		EQ (External Inquiries): External inquiry functions with their logical data groups and data elements.
4. Determine the value adjustment factor[a]	Determine the value adjustment factor (VAF) by scoring 14 general system characteristics (GSCs) according to their degree of influence [DI, on a scale from 0 (no influence) to 5 (strong influence)]	1. Data communications 2. Distributed data processing 3. Performance 4. Heavily used configuration 5. Transaction rate 6. Online data entry 7. End-user efficiency 8. Online update 9. Complex processing 10. Reusability 11. Installation ease 12. Operational ease 13. Multiple sites 14. Facilitate change
5. Calculate the adjusted FP count[a]	Multiply the unadjusted FP from 3 by the VAF in 4	Result is adjusted FP

---

[a]*Note that steps 4 and 5 go beyond the ISO/IEC definition of "Functional Size Measurement"* because it considers the impact of nonfunctional factors (the GSCs). As such, these steps are *optional* and not mandatory in the ISO/IEC 20926 IFPUG 4.1 unadjusted FP method. The authors recommend that 2 additional steps be done for implementation of any FSM Method: 6. Document the count; and 7. Perform Quality Assurance on the count. Further details are included in previous chapters.

17.2 Determine the Type of Count

The IFPUG Function Point Method distinguishes three types of counts, two of them for IT projects:

Note that the word "project" in the context of Function Point (FP) counting refers to the new development or enhancement of a single software application. As such, if the business or user defines a project and groups several FP "projects" together for accounting or other purposes, there must be several FP counts done - one for each of the applications involved. Further details follow.

1. New development (project)
2. Enhancement (project)
3. Application (baseline).

The relationships between these types of counts are shown in Fig. 17.1.

A new development project is the first build of an application. This means that all of the functionality is new (added) and we count the added (=delivered) and conversion Function Points as applicable. Consider this similar to a new construction project.

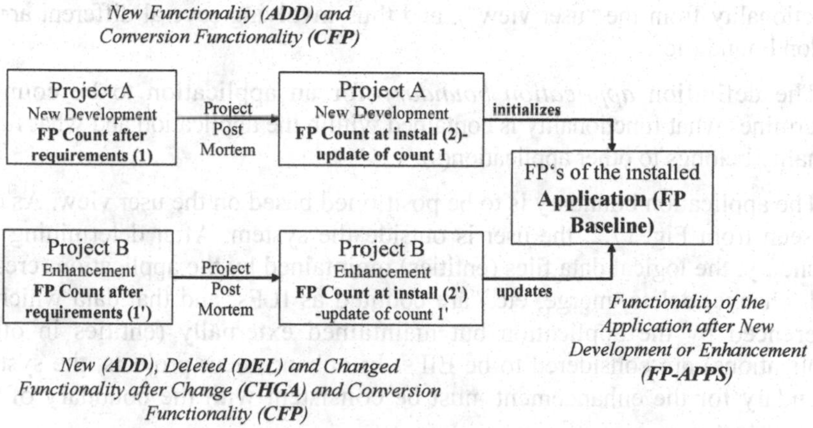

Fig. 17.1. Types of IFPUG FP counts and their relationships to each other

An enhancement project can add functionality to an existing application, as well as change or delete it. Accordingly for the enhancement project count, only the added, changed, deleted, and conversion (as applicable) Function Points are counted. Consider this similar to a renovation project.

At the completion of an enhancement project, the application baseline Function Points (after the enhancements have been applied) must be evaluated. This is similar to updating the square foot size of a building after a renovation is complete.

17.3 Determine the Purpose and Scope of the Count and the Application (System) Boundary

Note: In the following text, the word *application* is often used interchangeably with the word *system* to mean a piece of software.

The Function Point Method according to IFPUG 4.2 (IFPUG 2004) distinguishes between the size of a piece of software under development (Counting scope) and the size of an installed application. To quote Frank Mazzucco, past-president of IFPUG, project FP (development or enhancement projects) are FP "in motion" (i.e., being worked on), while application FP are FP "at rest" (i.e., the base size of the installed application).

Another way of looking at the project vs. application FP is to consider that the project size is the size of the floor plan being worked on (new construction or renovation area), while the application size is the size of the floor plan as it exists after the new construction is done, or at the end of a renovation (i.e., application count is a point-in-time functional size).

The FP count of an enhancement or development project can involve new development and changes to several applications (each having its own set of functionality from the "user view"), and thus involving several different application boundaries.

The definition *application boundary* for an application to be counted determines what functionality is contained within the application and what functionality belongs to other application(s).

The application boundary is to be positioned based on the user view. As can be seen from Fig. 17.2, the user is outside the system. After determining the boundary, the logical data files (entities) maintained by the application (create, add, change, delete, merge, etc.) are counted as ILFs, and that data which is referenced by the application but maintained externally (entities in other applications) are considered to be EIFs. In enhancement projects, the system boundary for the enhancement must be consistent with the boundary of the base system.

Because the application boundary significantly affects the application functionality (i.e., what functions are performed by the software vs. what functions are outside the scope of the software), it is important for it to be documented clearly. This includes the description of assumptions that were used to position the application boundary.

Practically this system diagram can easily be reused in, or as, architecture diagrams in the applications atlas of the organization.

Figure 17.3 presents one company's standard to define an application.

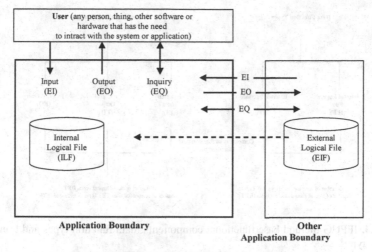

Fig. 17.2. Defining the application boundary

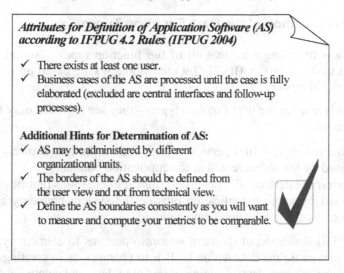

Fig. 17.3. Example of a company standard for definition of application system (AS)

17.4 Count Unadjusted FPs

To count the unadjusted FPs, the data function types and transaction function types must be identified and classified according to their complexity (see Fig. 17.4).

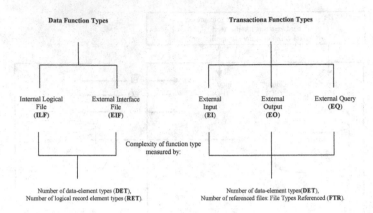

Fig. 17.4. IFPUG method base functional components: data function types and transaction function types

17.4.1 Classification of the Data Function Types

It has always to be regarded that all of the function types (also called Base Functional Components or BFC in ISO terminology) are based on the logical perspective of the *user*.

This holds true for the data function types – they are regarded only from the user viewpoint.

- *ILF*: (internal logical file) persistent logical data groups (entities) that are maintained by the software within the application boundary
- *EIF*: (external interface file) persistent logical data groups (entities) that are maintained by another application outside the system boundary and only referenced by the application being counted.

The IFPUG definition of the term *maintain* pertains to elementary, logical processes that cause the data within an ILF to change – as in creating the file, adding or inserting new data, changing or updating data, and deleting data. For a logical data grouping to be considered as an ILF, at least one variation of these four types of data manipulation must be identified as a function of the software. If the logical data grouping is maintained by another application and referenced or read (but not maintained) by the system being counted, then the data grouping is considered to be an EIF.

The complexity of internal and external files depends from two factors:

- The number of data elements (DET, Data Element Types)
- The number of logical subgroups or record element types (RET).

IFPUG defines these terms as follows:

DET: A Data Element Type is a unique, user recognizable, nonrecursive field (in an ILF or EIF).

RET: A Record Element Type is a user recognizable subgroup of data elements within an ILF or EIF.

Note: All of the text that follows in the Sects. 17.4 and 17.5, unless otherwise noted, were taken from the IFPUG CPM release 4.2 (2004). To obtain a copy of the current CPM, refer to the IFPUG website at http://www.ifpug.org.

Rules for Determination of RETs

A RET is a user recognizable subgroup of data elements within an ILF or EIF.

There are two types of subgroups:

Optional subgroups are those that the user has the option of using one or none of the subgroups during an elementary process that adds or creates an instance of the data

Mandatory subgroups are subgroups where the user must use at least one.

One of the following two rules applies when counting RETs:

- Count a RET for each optional or mandatory subgroup of the ILF or EIF
- If there are no subgroups, count the ILF or EIF as one RET.

Rules for Determination of DETs

A DET is a unique user recognizable, nonrepeated field.

1. Count a DET for each unique user recognizable, nonrepeated field maintained in or retrieved from the ILF or EIF through the execution of an elementary process. For example, an insurance number separated and stored in several physical fields is counted as 1 DET
2. When two applications maintain and/or reference the same ILF/EIF, but each maintains/references separate DETs, count only the DETs being used by each application to size that ILF/EIF
3. Count a DET for each piece of data required by the user to establish a relationship with another ILF or EIF.

ILF Identification Rules

An ILF is a user identifiable group of logically related data or control information maintained within the boundary of the application. The primary intent of an ILF is to hold data maintained through one or more elementary processes of the application being counted.

All of the following counting rules must apply for the information to be counted as an ILF:

1. The group of data or control information is logical and user identifiable
2. The group of data is maintained through an elementary process within the application boundary being counted.

EIF Identification Rules

An EIF is a user identifiable group of logically related data or control information referenced by the application, but maintained within the boundary of another application. The primary intent of an EIF is to hold data referenced through one or more elementary processes within the boundary of the application counted. This means an EIF counted for an application must be an ILF in another application.

All the following counting rules must apply for the information to be counted as an EIF:

1. The group of data or control information is logical and user identifiable
2. The group of data is referenced by, and external to, the application being counted
3. The group of data *is not maintained by* the application being counted
4. The group of data is maintained in an ILF of another application.

Tables 17.2 and 17.3 show the complexity and unadjusted Function Point definitions of the data function types.

ILF and EIF Classification Rules

Table 17.2. Complexity of data (IFPUG CPM)

RETs	DETs		
	1–19 DETs	20–50 DETs	>50 DETs
1 RET	Low	Low	Average
2–5 RETs	Low	Average	High
>5 RETs	Average	High	High

Table 17.3. Unadjusted Function Points for files (IFPUG CPM)

Complexity	ILF	EIF
Low	7	5
Average	10	7
High	15	10

17.4.2 Classification of the Transaction Function Types

External Input (EI)

An EI is an elementary process that processes data or control information that comes from outside the application boundary. The primary intent of an EI is to maintain one or more ILFs and/or to alter the behavior of the system.

Counted are all inputs with different processing logic. Figure 17.5 shows a company standard with rules of thumb to distinguish EIF and EI.

Counting of Interfaces:
Rule of thumb for distinguishing EIF and EI

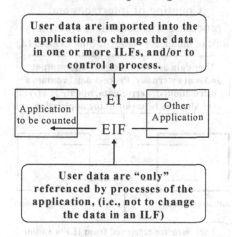

Fig. 17.5. Rules of thumb to distinguish EIF and EI

External Output (EO)

An EO is an elementary process that sends data or control information outside the application boundary. The primary intent of an EO is to present information to a user through processing logic other than, or in addition to, the retrieval of data or control information. The processing logic must contain at least one mathematical formula or calculation, create derived data, maintain one or more ILFs, or alter the behavior of the system.

External Inquiry (EQ)

An EQ is an elementary process that sends data or control information outside the application boundary. The primary intent of an EQ is to present information to a user through the retrieval of data or control information from an

ILF or EIF. The processing logic contains no mathematical formulae or calculations, and creates no derived data. No ILF is maintained during the processing, nor is the behavior of the system altered.

This comprises online inputs that generate outputs and do not change ILFs. Figure 17.6 shows a company standard with rules of thumb to distinguish EO and EQ.

The Primary Intent of a Transaction

The main difference between the transactional function types is their primary intent (see Table 17.4).

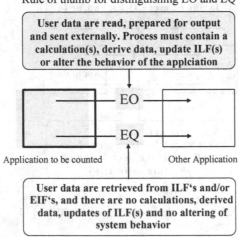

Counting of Interfaces and
processes that send data externally
Rule of thumb for distinguishing EO and EQ

User data are read, prepared for output and sent externally. Process must contain a calculation(s), derive data, update ILF(s) or alter the behavior of the applciation

EO

EQ

Application to be counted   Other Application

User data are retrieved from ILF's and/or EIF's, and there are no calculations, derived data, updates of ILF(s) and no altering of system behavior

Fig. 17.6. Rules of thumb to distinguish EO and EQ

Table 17.4. The primary intent of a transaction (IFPUG CPM)

Function	Transactional function type		
	EI	EO	EQ
Alter the behavior of the system	PI	F	N/A
Maintain one or more ILFs	PI	F	N/A
Present information to a user	F	PI	PI

Abbreviations: PI = the primary intent of the transactional function type, *F* = a function of the transactional function type, but is not the primary intent and is sometimes present, *N/A* = the function is not allowed by the transactional function type

Processing Logic

The processing logic is defined as requirements specifically requested by the user to complete an elementary process.

The following Table 17.5 summarizes which forms of processing logic may be performed by the transactions.

Beyond Pure IFPUG Defined Situations

Table 17.5 covers most but not all possible counting situations that can occur. Thus several organizations tried to standardize the counting decisions for these situations with a decision table. Since beginners with the Function Point Method sometimes have problems when they happen to encounter one of these situations, a company standard was defined in the IT department of an international insurance company in Germany (abbreviated here neutralized as IIC) as shown in decision Table 17.6.

Table 17.5. Forms of processing logic (IFPUG CPM)

Form of processing logic	Transaction type		
	EI	EO	EQ
1. Validations are performed	C	C	C
2. Mathematical formulae and calculations are performed	C	M*	N
3. Equivalent values are converted	C	C	C
4. Data are filtered and selected by using specified criteria to compare multiple sets of data	C	C	C
5. Conditions are analyzed to determine which are applicable	C	C	C
6. At least one ILF is updated	M*	M*	N
7. At least one ILF or EIF is referenced	C	C	M
8. Data or control information is retrieved	C	C	M
9. Derived data is created	C	M*	N
10. Behavior of the system is altered	M*	M*	N
11. Prepare und present information outside the boundary	C	M	M
12. Capability to accept data or control information that enters the application boundary	M	C	C
13. Resorting or rearranging a set of data	C	C	C

M = it is mandatory that the function type perform the form of processing logic, $M*$ = it is mandatory that the function type perform at least one of these (M*) forms of logic, C = the function type can perform the form of processing logic, but it is not mandatory, N = function type cannot perform the form of processing logic

Table 17.6. Decision table for undefined cases with IIC internal company standard

	Counting situation																				
IFPUG rule	1	2	3	4	5	6	7	8	9	10	11	12	13	14	15	16	17	18	19	20	21
Primary intent: input	Y	Y	Y	Y	Y	Y	N	N	N	N	N	N	N	N	N	N	N	N	N	N	N

(Continued)

Table 17.6. *(Cont.)*

Primary intent: output	Y	N	N	N	N	Y	Y	Y	Y	Y	Y	Y	Y	Y	Y	Y	Y	Y	Y	N
Data received from outside boundary	–	Y	Y	Y	Y	N	–	–	–	–	–	–	–	–	–	–	Y	N	–	–
ILF is updated	–	Y	N	N	N	–	–	–	Y	N	N	Y	N	N	Y	N	N	–	–	–
Change system behavior	–	–	Y	N	N	–	–	–	–	Y	N	–	J	N	–	Y	N	–	–	–
Present data outside boundary	–	–	–	Y	N	–	Y	Y	Y	Y	Y	Y	Y	Y	Y	Y	Y	Y	Y	N
Derived data produced as part of function	–	–	–	–	–	–	Y	N	N	N	N	N	N	N	N	N	N	N	–	–
Calculation(s) part of function (e.g., Use math. Formula)	–	–	–	–	–	–	–	Y	N	N	N	N	N	N	N	N	N	N	–	–
Retrieval of data from ILF/EIF	–	–	–	–	–	–	–	–	Y	Y	Y	–	–	–	–	–	N	N	–	–
Reference to an ILF	–	–	–	–	–	–	–	–	–	–	–	Y	Y	Y	–	–	N	N	–	–
Reference to an EIF	–	–	–	–	–	–	–	–	–	–	–	–	–	Y	Y	Y	N	N	–	–
EI	X	X																		
EO						X	X													
EQ									X				X			X				
Undefined: IIC internal decision: count as EO			X					X	X			X	X			X	X	X		
IIC internal decision: count as EO								X	X			X	X			X	X			
IIC internal decision: Count as EQ			X																X	

(Continued)

Impossible (or not countable)	X X		X X X
EI, EO, EQ as Table 17.5	X		

EI Identification Rules per IFPUG. 4.2

For an EI, the primary intent of an elementary process is to maintain an ILF or alter the behavior of the system.

All the following rules must apply for the elementary process to be counted as a unique occurrence of an EI:

- The data or control information is received from outside the application boundary
- At least one ILF is maintained if the data entering the boundary is not control information that alters the behavior of the system
- For the identified process, one of the following three statements must apply:
  - Processing logic is unique from the processing logic performed by other EIs for the application
  - The set of data elements identified is different from the sets identified for other EIs for the application
  - The ILFs or EIFs referenced are different from the files referenced by other EIs in the application.

FTR Identification Rules for EIs per IFPUG 4.2

A FTR is

- *An ILF read or maintained by a transactional function or*
- *An EIF read by a transactional function.*

The following rules apply when counting FTRs:

- Count an FTR for each ILF maintained
- Count an FTR for each ILF or EIF read during the processing of the EI
- Count only one FTR for each ILF that is both maintained and read.

DET Identification Rules for EIs per IFPUG 4.2

A DET is a unique user recognizable, nonrepeated field.

The following rules apply when counting DETs:

1. Count a DET for each unique user recognizable, nonrepeated field that enters or exits the application boundary and is required to complete the EI

2. Do not count fields that are retrieved or derived by the system and stored on an ILF during the elementary process if the fields did not cross the application boundary
3. Count a DET for the capability to send a system response message outside the application boundary to indicate an error occurred during processing, confirm the processing is complete, or verify that processing should continue
4. Count one DET for the ability to specify an action to be taken even if there are multiple methods for invoking the same logical process.

EO and EQ Shared Identification Rules per IFPUG 4.2

For an EO or EQ, the primary intent of the elementary process is to present information to a user.

All the following rules must apply for the elementary process to be counted as a unique occurrence of an EO or EQ:

- The function sends data or control information external to the application boundary
- For the identified process, one of the following three statements must apply:
  - Processing logic is unique from the processing logic performed by other EOs or EQs for the application
  - The set of data elements identified is different from the sets identified for other EOs or EQs in the application
  - The ILFs or EIFs referenced are different from the files referenced by other EOs or EQs in the application.

Additional EO Identification Rules per IFPUG 4.2

In addition to adhering to all shared EO and EQ rules, *at least one* of the following rules must apply for the elementary process to be counted as a unique EO:

- The processing logic of the elementary process contains at least one mathematical formula or calculation
- The processing logic of the elementary process creates derived data
- The processing logic of the elementary process maintains at least one ILF
- The processing logic of the elementary process alters the behavior of the system.

Additional EQ Identification Rules per IFPUG 4.2

In addition to adhering to all shared EO and EQ rules, *all* the following rules must apply for the elementary process to be counted as a unique EQ:

- The processing logic of the elementary process retrieves data or control information from an ILF or EIF
- The processing logic of the elementary process does not contain a mathematical formula or calculation
- The processing logic of the elementary process does not create derived data.
- The processing logic of the elementary process does not maintain an ILF
- The processing logic of the elementary process does not alter the behavior of the system.

Shared FTR Identification Rules for EOs and EQs per IFPUG 4.2

A FTR is

- *An ILF read or maintained by a transactional function or*
- *An EIF read by a transactional function.*

The following rule applies when counting FTRs for both EOs and EQs:

- Count an FTR for each ILF or EIF read during the processing of the elementary process.

Additional FTR Identification Rules for EOs per IFPUG 4.2

The following additional rules apply when counting FTRs for EOs:

- Count an FTR for each ILF maintained during the processing of the elementary process
- Count only one FTR for each ILF that is both maintained and read during the elementary process.

Shared DET Identification Rules for EOs and EQs per IFPUG 4.2

The following rules apply when counting DETs for both EOs and EQs:

- Count a DET for each unique user recognizable, nonrepeated field that enters the application boundary and is required to specify when, what, and/or how the data is to be retrieved or generated by the elementary process
- Count a DET for each unique user recognizable, nonrepeated field that enters or exits the boundary
- If a DET both enters and exits the boundary, count it only once for the elementary process
- Count one DET for the capability to send a system response message outside the application boundary to indicate an error occurred during processing, confirm the processing is complete, or verify that processing should continue

- Count one DET for the ability to specify an action to be taken even if there are multiple methods for invoking the same logical process
- Do not count fields that are retrieved or derived by the system and stored on an ILF during the elementary process if the fields did not cross the application boundary
- Do not count literals as DETs
- Do not count paging variables or system-generated stamps.

Classification Rules for Transactional Functions per IFPUG 4.2

Tables 17.7–17.9 show the complexity and unadjusted Function Point definitions of the transactional function types.

Table 17.7. Complexity of EIs (IFPUG CPM)

FTRs	DETs		
	1–4 DETs	5–15 DETs	>15 DETs
0–1 FTR	Low	Low	Average
2 FTRs	Low	Average	High
>2 FTRs	Average	High	High

Table 17.8. Complexity of EOs and EQs (IFPUG CPM)

FTRs	DETs		
	1–5 DETs	6–19 DETs	>20 DETs
0–1 FTR	Low	Low	Average
2–3 FTRs	Low	Average	High
>3 FTRs	Average	High	High

Note that the case FTR = 0 in Table 17.8 is only relevant for EOs.

Table 17.9. Unadjusted function points of EI, EO, or EQ (IFPUG CPM)

Complexity	EI	EO	EQ
Low	3	4	3
Average	4	5	4
High	6	7	6

17.5 Calculate the Adjusted FPs

For calculation of the adjusted FPs the *Value Adjustment Factor (VAF)* has to be determined. This is done by adding the *Degrees of Influence (DI)* of the *14 General System Characteristics (GSC)* to the so-called *Total Degree of Influence (TDI)*.

It must always be regarded that this step does not belong to ISO/IEC conformant Functional Size Measurement, but is a step to include nonfunctional (quality) requirements for the purposes of estimation. The functional size by the VAF is based on the values of the 14 GSCs according to application requirements and the environmental influences. Note that also the NESMA and Mark II Function Point Methods maintain similar GSCs and in their ISO conformant versions, these GSCs were dropped from the methods in order to be ISO compliant.

17.5.1 Determining the VAF

The formula for calculation of the VAF is

$$VAF = (TDI \times 0.01) + 0.65,$$

where TDI (as outlined above) is the total of values of evaluating the 14 GSCs.

Hence, the VAF is maximally 1.35 and minimally 0.65, and therefore can adjust the unadjusted Function Points by as much as +/– 35%.

17.5.2 The 14 GSCs

The 14 GSCs are a set of 14 "characteristics" that evaluate aspects of the complexity of the application. Always evaluate the overall application on the basis of these characteristics – never just a project:

1. Data communications
2. Distributed data processing
3. Performance
4. Heavily used configuration
5. Transaction rate
6. Online data entry
7. End-user efficiency
8. Online update
9. Complex processing
10. Reusability
11. Installation ease
12. Operational ease
13. Multiple sites
14. Facilitate change.

Degrees of Influence

Based on the stated user requirements, each GSC must be evaluated in terms of its DI on a scale from zero to five as simplified in Table 17.10. IFPUG has provided further guidance for each of the GSCs, which are presented individually in the subsections that follow.

Table 17.10. Degrees of Influence (DI) (IFPUG CPM)

Score as	Influence of the particular GSC
0	Not present or no influence
1	Incidental influence
2	Moderate influence
3	Average influence
4	Significant influence
5	Strong influence throughout

Data Communications

Data Communications (see Table 17.11) describes the degree to which the application communicates directly with the processor.

Table 17.11. Data communications

Score as	Descriptions to determine the DI
0	Application is pure batch processing or standalone application
1	Application is batch but has remote data entry *or* remote printing
2	Application is batch but has remote data entry *and* remote printing
3	Application includes online data collection or TP (teleprocessing) front end to a batch process or query system
4	Application is more than a front-end, but supports *only one* type of TP communications
5	Application is more than a front-end and supports *more than one* type of TP communications

The data and control information used in the application are sent or received over communication facilities. Devices connected locally to the control unit are considered to use communication facilities. Protocol is a set of conventions that permit the transfer of or exchange of information between two systems or devices. All data communication links require some type of protocol.

Distributed Data Processing

Distributed Data Processing describes the degree to which the application transfers data among physical components of the application.

Distributed Data Processing (see Table 17.12) functions are a characteristic of the application within the application boundary.

Performance

Performance (see Table 17.13) describes the degree to which the response time and throughput performance considerations influenced the application development.

Application performance objectives, stated or approved (or implied) by the user, *in either* response or throughput, influence (or will influence) the design, development, installation, and support of the system.

Table 17.12. Distributed data processing

Score as	Descriptions to determine the DI
0	Data is not transferred or processed on another component of the system
1	Data is prepared for transfer, then is transferred and processed on another component of the system, for user processing
2	Data is prepared for transfer, then is transferred and processed on another component of the system, *not* for user processing
3	Distributed processing and data transfer are online and in *one* direction only
4	Distributed processing and data transfer are online and in *both* directions
5	Distributed processing and data transfer are online and are dynamically performed on the most appropriate component of the system

Table 17.13. Performance

Score as	Descriptions to determine the DI
0	No special performance requirements were stated by the user
1	Performance and design requirements were stated and reviewed but no special actions were required
2	Response time or throughput is critical during *peak* hours. No special design for CPU utilization was required. Processing deadline is for the next business cycle
3	Response time or throughput is critical during *all business* hours. No special design for CPU utilization was required. Processing deadline requirements with interfacing systems are constraining
4	In addition, stated user performance requirements are stringent enough to require performance analysis tasks in the design phase
5	In addition, performance analysis tools were used in the design, development, and/or implementation phase to meet the stated user performance requirements

Heavily Used Configuration

Heavily Used Configuration is the degree to which computer resource restrictions influenced the development of the application.

A heavily used operational configuration (see Table 17.14) may require special considerations when designing the application. For example, the user wants to run the application on existing or committed equipment that will be heavily used.

Table 17.14. Heavily used configuration

Score as	Descriptions to determine the DI
0	No explicit or implicit operational restrictions are included
1	Operational restrictions do exist, but are less restrictive than a typical application. No special effort is needed to meet the restrictions
2	Operational restrictions do exist, but are typical for an application. Special effort through controllers or control programs is needed to meet the restrictions
3	Stated operational restrictions require special constraints on *one* piece of the application in the central processor or a dedicated processor
4	Stated operational restrictions require special constraints on the *entire* application in the central processor or a dedicated processor
5	In addition, there are special constraints on the application in the distributed components of the system

Transaction Rate

Transaction Rate describes the degree to which the rate of business transactions influenced the development of the application.

The transaction rate (see Table 17.15) is high, and it influences the design, development, installation, and support of the application. Users may require what they regard as normal response time even during times of peak volume.

Table 17.15. Transaction rate

Score as	Descriptions to determine the DI
0	No peak transaction period is anticipated
1	Low transaction rates have minimal effect on the design, development, and installation phases
2	Average transaction rates have some effect on the design, development, and installation phases
3	High transaction rates affect the design, development, and/or installation phases
4	High transaction rate(s) stated by the user min the application requirements or in the service level agreements are high enough to require performance analysis tasks in the design, development, and/or installation phases
5	High transaction rate(s) stated by the user min the application requirements or in the service level agreements are high enough to require performance analysis tasks and, in addition, require the use of performance analysis tools in the design, development, and/or installation phases

Online Data Entry

Online Data Entry describes the degree to which data is entered or retrieved through interactive transactions.

Table 17.16. Online data entry

Score as	Descriptions to determine the DI
0	All transactions are processed in batch mode
1	1–7% of transactions are interactive
2	8–15% of transactions are interactive
3	16–23% of transactions are interactive
4	24–30% of transactions are interactive
5	More than 30% of transactions are interactive

Online data entry (see Table 17.16) for data entry, control functions, reports, and queries are provided in the application.

End-User Efficiency

User Efficiency (see Table 17.17) describes the degree of consideration for human factors and ease of use for the user of the application measured.

Table 17.17. End-user efficiency

Score as	Descriptions to determine the DI
0	None of the above
1	One to three of the above
2	Four to five of the above
3	Six or more of the above, but there are no specific user requirements related to efficiency
4	Six or more of the above, and stated requirements for user efficiency are strong enough to require *design tasks* for human factors to be included
5	Six or more of the above, and stated requirements for user efficiency are strong enough to require the *use of special tools and processes* in order to demonstrate that the objectives have been achieved

The online functions provided emphasize of a design for user efficiency (human factor/user friendliness). The design includes the following:

- Navigational aids (e.g., function keys, jumps, dynamically generated menus, hyperlinks)
- Menus
- Online help and documents
- Automated cursor movement
- Scrolling
- Remote printing (via online transmission)
- Preassigned function keys (e.g., clear screen, request help, clone screen)
- Batch jobs submitted from online transactions

- Drop down list box
- Heavy use of reverse video, highlighting, colors, underlining, and other indi-
  cators
- Hardcopy documentation of online transactions (e.g., screen print)
- Mouse interface
- Pop-up windows
- Templates and/or defaults
- Bilingual support (supports two languages: count as four items)
- Multilingual support (supports more than two languages: count as six items).

Online Update

Online Update describes the degree to which ILFs are updated online.

The application provides online update (see Table 17.18) for the ILFs.

Table 17.18. Online update

Score as	Descriptions to determine the DI
0	None
1	Online update for one to control files is included. Volume of updating is low and recovery is easy
2	Online update for four ore more control files is included. Volume of updating is low and recovery is easy
3	Online of major ILFs is included
4	In addition, protection against data loss is essential and has been specially designed and programmed in the system
5	In addition, high volumes bring cost considerations into the recovery process. Highly automated recovery procedures with minimum human intervention are included

Complex Processing

Complex Processing describes the degree to which processing logic influenced the development of the application.

The following components are present:

- Sensitive control and/or application-specific security processing
- Extensive logical processing
- Extensive mathematical processing
- Much exception processing, resulting in incomplete transactions that must be processed again
- Complex processing (see Table 17.19) to handle multiple input/output possi-
  bilities.

Table 17.19. Complex processing

Score as	Descriptions to determine the DI
0	None of the above
1	Any one of the above
2	Any two of the above
3	Any three of the above
4	Any four of the above
5	All five of the above

Reusability

Reusability (see Table 17.20) describes the degree to which the application and the code in the application have been specifically designed, developed, and supported to be usable in other applications.

Installation Ease

Installation Ease describes the degree to which conversion from previous environments influenced the development of the application.

Table 17.20. Reusability

Score as	Descriptions to determine the DI
0	No reusable code
1	Reusable code is used within the application
2	Less of 10% of the application code developed is intended for use in more than one application
3	10% or more of the application code developed is intended for use in more than one application
4	The application was specifically packaged and/or documented to ease reuse, and the application is customized at the source code level
5	The application was specifically packaged and/or documented to ease reuse, and the application is customized for use by means of user parameter maintenance

Conversion and installation ease (see Table 17.21) are characteristics of the application. A conversion and installation plan and/or conversion tools were provided and tested during the system test phase.

Operational Ease

Operational Ease describes the degree to which the application attends to operational aspects, such as start-up, back-up, and recovery processes.

Table 17.21. Installation ease

Score as	Descriptions to determine the DI
0	No special considerations were stated by the user, *and no* special setup is required for installation
1	No special considerations were stated by the user, *but* special setup is required for installation
2	Conversion and installation requirements were stated by the user, and conversion and installation guides were provided and tested. The impact of conversion on the project *is not* considered to be important
3	Conversion and installation requirements were stated by the user, and conversion and installation guides were provided and tested. The impact of conversion on the project *is* considered to be important
4	In addition, to 2 above, automated conversion and installation tools were provided and tested
5	In addition, to 3 above, automated conversion and installation tools were provided and tested

Table 17.22. Operational ease

Score as	Descriptions to determine the DI
0	No special operational considerations other than the normal back-up procedures were stated by the user
1–4	One, some, or all of the following items apply to the application. Select all that apply. Each item has a point value of one, except as noted otherwise. Start-up, back-up, and recovery processes were provided, but human intervention is required Start-up, back-up, and recovery processes were provided, but *no* human intervention is required (count as two items) The application minimizes the need for tape mounts and/or remote data access requiring human intervention The application minimizes the need for paper handling
5	The application is designed for unattended operation. Unattended operation means *no human intervention* is required to operate the system other than to start up or shut down the application. Automatic error recovery is a feature of the application

Operational Ease (see Table 17.22) is a characteristic of the application. Then application minimizes the need for manual activities, such as tape mounts, paper handling, and direct on-location manual intervention.

Multiple Sites

Multiple Sites (see Table 17.23) describes the degree to which the application has been developed for different hardware and software environments.

Table 17.23. Multiple sites

Score as	Descriptions to determine the DI
0	The needs of *only one* installation site were considered in the design
1	The needs of *more than one* installation site were considered in the design, and the application is designed to operate only under *identical* hardware and/or software environments
2	The needs of *more than one* installation site were considered in the design, and the application is designed to operate only under *similar* hardware and/or software environments
3	The needs of *more than one* installation site were considered in the design, and the application is designed to operate only under *different* hardware and/or software environments
4	Documentation and support plan are provided and tested to support the application at multiple installation sites and the application is as described by 2
5	Documentation and support plan are provided and tested to support the application at multiple installation sites and the application is as described by 3

Facilitate Change

Facilitate change (see Table 17.24) describes the degree to which the application has been developed for easy modification of processing logic or data structure.

Note: this characteristic is evaluated in 3 steps, 1. evaluate the Flexible Query (A below) using the guidelines for 0, 1, 2, or 3; then 2. evaluate the business control data (B) as 0, 1, or 2 using the guidelines; and finally 3. Add the values from A) and B) together to get the score and use table 17.24 to determine the 'degree of influence'.

Table 17.24. Facilitate change

Score as	Descriptions to determine the DI
0	Non of the above
1	A total of one item from above
2	A total of two items from above
3	A total of three items from above
4	A total of four items from above
5	A total of five items from above

The following characteristics can apply for the application:

A. Flexible Query

1. Flexible Query and report facility is provided that can handle *simple* requests (count as one item)
2. Flexible Query and report facility is provided that can handle requests of *average* complexity (count as two items)
3. Flexible Query and report facility is provided that can handle *complex* requests (count as three items).

B. Business Control Data

1. Business control data is kept in tables that are maintained by the user with online interactive processes, but changes take effect only on the *next* business cycle (count as one item)
2. Business control data is kept in tables that are maintained by the user with online interactive processes, but changes take effect *immediately* (count as two items).

17.5.3 Calculation of the Adjusted Function Points

Adjusted FPs for New Development Projects

A new development project adds functionality. Further functionality can evolve by conversion (migration) of historic data that have to be integrated into the new system. Figure 17.7 shows the effect on the FP count.

From both parts (UFP + CFP), the adjusted FPs of a new development project are calculated according the formula

$$DFP = (UFP + CFP) \times VAF, \text{ with}$$

DFP: Development FP = New Functionality (ADD)
UFP: Unadjusted FPs
CFP: Conversion FPs
VAF: Value Adjustment Factor

Note that Fig. 17.7 shows that the FPs for conversion functionality do not become part of the base application count.

Adjusted FPs for Enhancement Projects

An enhancement changes the functionality of an application. This comprises the following:

Addition of new functionality (ADD)
Change of existing functionality (CHG)
Deletion of existing functionality (DEL)
Conversion functionality (CFP)

Figure 17.8 visualizes the FP counting of an enhancement project.

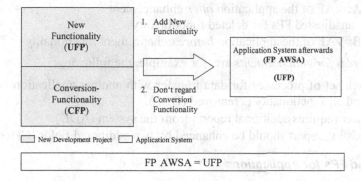

Fig. 17.7. Function Points for new development projects

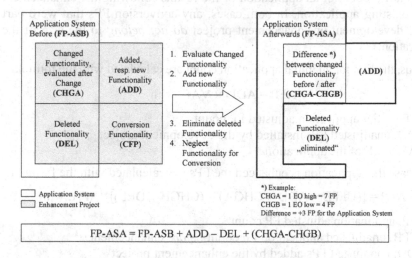

Fig. 17.8. Function Points of enhancement projects

For an adjusted FP count the VAF of the base application must be evaluated on a before and after basis. Since the VAF of the enhanced application differs from the application beforehand, there have to be distinguished two VAFs (VAFB, VAFA). The adjusted FPs of an enhancement are thus calculated by following formula:

$$EFP = [(ADD + CHGA + CFP)VAFA] + (DEL \times VAFB), \text{ with}$$

EFP: FPs of the enhancement project
ADD: unadjusted FPs of the added functionality
CHGA: FPs for changed existing functionality, *after* the change
CFP: FPs of the conversion

VAFA: VAF of the application *after* enhancement
DEL: unadjusted FPs for deleted functionality
VAFB: VAF of the application *before* enhancement functionality

Examples for enhancements are, for example, the following:

- A batch set of processes for data transfer with another application is obsolete and all functionality is removed (DEL).
- The user requires additional reports from the system (ADD).
- An existing report should be enhanced by two additional fields (CHG).

Adjusted FPs for Applications

The first step for FP counting an application base size is to determine if it is an initial FP count of an application or the results following the enhancement of an existing application. In both cases, any conversion FPs that were part of the development or enhancement project *do not belong* to the size of the application.

Thus, the FPs for an initial application count are calculated with the formula

$$AFP = ADD \times VAF, \text{ with}$$

AFP: initial application adjusted FP count
ADD: unadjusted FPs installed by the development project
VAF: VAF of the application

In case the application is enhanced the FPs are calculated with the formula

$$AFP = [(UFPB + ADD + CHGA) - (CHGB + DEL)]VAFA, \text{ with}$$

AFP: application adjusted FP count
UFPB: unadjusted application FP count *before* enhancement
ADD: unadjusted FPs added by the enhancement project
CHGA: unadjusted FP count of changed functionality *after* enhancement
CHGB: unadjusted FP count of changed functionality *before* enhancement
DEL: unadjusted FP count of deleted functionality
VAFA: VAF of the application *after* enhancement

Maintenance projects:

Maintenance effort is a necessary part of an application life cycle. *It has to be regarded that a pure maintenance project does not change the functionality of an application. If a so-called maintenance project does cause changes to application functionality, then in FP terminology, it is an enhancement and not maintenance!* (And vice versa, if a so-called *enhancement* project does not add/change/delete the functionality of an application, then in FP terminology it is considered to be a maintenance project not an enhancement project no matter what others may label it to be!)

17.6 Management Summary

The IFPUG 4.2 Function Point Method distinguishes three types of counts, two of them for IT projects: New development (project), Enhancement (project), Application (baseline).

A new development project is the first build of an application. This means that all the functionality is new (added) and we count the added (=delivered) and conversion Function Points as applicable. Consider this similar to a new construction project.

An enhancement project can add functionality to an existing application, as well as change or delete it. Accordingly for the enhancement project count, only the added, changed, deleted, and conversion (as applicable) Function Points are counted.

At the completion of an enhancement project, the application baseline Function Points (after the enhancements have been applied) must be evaluated.

The Function Point Method according to IFPUG 4.2 (IFPUG 2004) distinguishes between the size of a piece of software under development (Counting scope) and the size of an installed application.

The FP count of an enhancement project can involve changes to several applications (each having its own set of functionality from the "user view," but not from the technical or physical view), and thus involving several different system boundaries.

The definition *application boundary* for an application to be counted determines what functionality is contained within the application and what functionality belongs to other application(s).

The application boundary is to be positioned based on the user view.

Because the application boundary significantly affects the application functionality (i.e., what functions are performed by the software vs. what functions are outside the scope of the software), it is important for it to be documented clearly. This includes the description of assumptions that were used to position the application boundary.

Practically this system diagram can easily be reused in, or as, architecture diagrams in the applications atlas of the organization.

To count the unadjusted FPs, the data function types and transaction function types must be identified and classified according to their complexity.

It has always to be regarded that all of the function types (also called Base Functional Components or BFC in ISO terminology) are based on the logical perspective of the *user*.

The IFPUG definition of the term *maintain* pertains to elementary, logical processes that cause the data within an ILF to change – as in creating the file, adding or inserting new data, changing or updating data, and deleting data in the file.

The complexity of internal and external files depends from two factors: the number of DET and the number of logical subgroups or RET.

A RET is a user recognizable subgroup of data elements within an ILF or EIF.

A DET is a unique user recognizable, nonrepeated field.

An EI is an elementary process that processes data or control information that comes from outside the application boundary.

Counted are all inputs with different processing logic.

An EO is an elementary process that processes data or control information that comes from outside the application boundary.

An EQ is an elementary process that sends data or control information outside the application boundary.

The main difference between the transactional function types is their primary intent.

The processing logic is defined as requirements specifically requested by the user to complete an elementary process.

For an EI, the primary intent of an elementary process is to maintain an ILF or alter the behavior of the system.

For an EO or EQ, the primary intent of the elementary process is to present information to a user.

A new development project adds functionality. Further functionality can evolve by conversion (migration) of historic data that have to be integrated into the new system.

For calculation of the adjusted Function Points the VAF has to be determined.

The 14 GSCs are a set of 14 *characteristics* that evaluate aspects of the complexity of the application. Always evaluate the overall application on the basis of these characteristics – never just a project.

Maintenance effort is a necessary part of an application life cycle. It has to be regarded that a pure maintenance project does not change the functionality of an application. If a so-called maintenance project does cause changes to application functionality, then in FP terminology, it is an enhancement and not maintenance!

18 Functional Size Measurement Case Studies

This chapter presents a set of functional user requirements, together with the results of applying the five ISO/IEC-conformant Functional Size Measurement Methods (FSMMs) to determine the functional size of the software.

The following case study was adapted from the Course Registration case study available from the Common Software Metrics International Consortium (COSMIC) website (www.cosmicon.com), where you can find the link for COSMIC publications.

This chapter starts with the presentation of the functional requirements of the Course Registration case study and the according use case diagram in the first two sections, followed by functional size measurement of the requirements in the following order: COSMIC, FiSMA, IFPUG, Mark II, NESMA, and a concluding comparison.

18.1 Case Study Description: Course Registration System

The functional requirements given later describe a project to develop software to replace the front end of the existing Course Registration System with a new system. The new Course Registration System will allow students and professors to access the system through personal computers (PCs). The current registration system, used since 1985, lacks the capacity to handle the current and future student and course load projections. In addition, the current system is an outdated mainframe technology, and only supports access through Registration Office clerks. The new system will enable all professors and students to access the system through PCs connected to the college computer network and through any personal computer connected to the Internet. The new system will bring the college to the leading edge in course registration systems and improve the image of the college, attract more students, and streamline administrative functions.

Table 18.1 identifies the main use cases for the functions required by the user stakeholders for the Course Registration System. The use case descriptions follow in the next section.

Table 18.1. Use case requirements for the new Course Registration System

Use case number	Use case for Course Registration System
1	Logon (by all users)
2	Maintain professor information (by the registrar)
3	Select courses to teach (by professors)
4	Maintain student information (by the registrar)
5	Register for courses (by students)
6	Monitor for course full (by the application)
7	Close registration (by the registrar)
8	Submit grades (by professors)
9	View report card (by students)

18.1.1 Logon

Brief Description:

This use case describes how a user logs into the Course Registration System. The actors starting this use case are Student, Professor, and Registrar.

Flow of Events:

The use case begins when the actor types his/her name and password on the Logon form.

Basic Flow – Logon:

The system validates the actor's password and logs him/her into the system. The system displays the Main Form and the use case ends.

Alternate Flows – An Invalid Name/Password:

If in the basic flow the system cannot find the name or the password is invalid, an error message is displayed. The actor can type in a new name or password or choose to cancel the operation, at which point the use case ends.

18.1.2 Maintain Professor Information

Brief Description:

This use case allows the Registrar to maintain professor information in the registration system. This includes adding, modifying, and deleting professors from the system. The actor of this use case is the Registrar.

Flow of Events:

The use case begins when the Registrar selects the *maintain professor* activity from the Main Form.

Basic Flow – Add a Professor:

1. The Registrar selects *add a professor*.
2. The system displays a blank professor form.
3. The Registrar enters the following information for the professor: name, date of birth, social security number, status, and department. The system validates the data to insure the proper data format and searches for an existing professor with the specified name. If the data is valid the system creates a new professor and assigns a unique system-generated id number.
4. This number is displayed, so that it can be used for subsequent uses of the system.

Steps 2–4 are repeated for each professor added to the system. When the Registrar has finished adding professors to the system the use case ends.

Alternate Flows – a. Modify a Professor:

1. The Registrar selects *Modify a professor*.
2. The system displays a blank professor form.
3. The Registrar types in the professor id number he/she wishes to modify.
4. The system retrieves the professor information and displays it in the form.
5. The Registrar modifies one or more of the professor information fields: name, date of birth, social security number, status, and department.
6. When changes are complete, the Registrar selects *save*.
7. The system updates the professor information.

Steps 2–7 are repeated for each professor the Registrar wants to modify. When edits are complete, the use case ends.

Alternate Flows – b. Delete a Professor:

1. The Registrar selects *delete a Professor*.
2. The system displays a blank professor form.
3. The Registrar types in the id number of the professor whose information is to be deleted.
4. The system retrieves the professor information and displays it in the form.
5. The Registrar selects *delete*.
6. The system displays a delete verification dialog confirming the deletion.
7. The Registrar selects *yes*.
8. The professor is deleted from the system.

Steps 2–8 are repeated for each professor the Registrar wants to modify. When the Registrar has finished deleting professors from the system, the use case ends.

Alternate Flows – c. Professor Already Exists:

If in the *Add a Professor* basic flow, a professor already exists with the specified name, an error message, *Professor Already Exists* is displayed. The Registrar can either change the name, choose to create another professor with the same name, or cancel the operation at which point the use case ends.

Alternate Flows – d. Professor Not Found:

If in the *Modify a Professor* subflow or *Delete a Professor* subflow, a professor with the specified id number does not exist, the system displays an error message, *Professor not found*. Then the Registrar can type in a different id number or cancel the operation at which point the use case ends

18.1.3. Select/Deselect Courses to Teach

Brief Description:

This use case allows a professor to select the course offerings (date- and time-specific courses will be given) from the course catalog for the courses that he/she is eligible for and wishes to teach in the upcoming semester. The actor starting this use case is the Professor. The Course Catalog System is an actor within the use case.

Flow of Events:

The use case begins when the professor selects the *select courses to teach* activity from the Main Form.

Basic Flow – Select Courses to Teach:

1. The system retrieves and displays the list of course offerings the professor is eligible to teach for the current (upcoming) semester.
2. The system also retrieves and displays the list of courses the professor has previously selected to teach.
3. The professor selects and/or deselects the course offerings that he/she wishes to teach for the upcoming semester.
4. The system removes the professor from teaching the deselected course offerings.
5. The system verifies that the selected offerings do not conflict (i.e., have the same dates and times) with each other or any offerings the professor has previously signed up to teach.
6. If there is no conflict, the system updates the course offering information for each offering the professor selects.

Alternate Flows – a. No Courses Available:

1. If in the basic flow the professor is not eligible to teach any courses in the upcoming semester the system will display an error message.
2. The professor acknowledges the message and the use case ends.

Alternate Flows – b. Schedule Conflict:

1. If the system finds a schedule conflict when trying to establish the course offerings the Professor should take, the system will display an error message indicating that a schedule conflict has occurred. The system will also indicate which the conflicting courses are.

2. The professor can either resolve the schedule conflict (i.e., by cancelling his selection to teach one of the course offerings) or cancel the operation, in which case any selections will be lost and the use case ends.

Alternate Flows – c. Course Registration Closed:

1. If, when the Professor selects *select courses to teach*, registration for the current semester has been closed, a message is displayed to the Professor and the use case terminates.
2. Professors cannot change the course offerings they teach after registration for the current semester has been closed. If a professor change is needed after registration has been closed, it is handled outside the scope of this system.

18.1.4 Maintain Student Information

Brief Description:

This use case allows the Registrar to maintain student information in the registration system. This includes adding, modifying, and deleting students from the system. The actor for this use case is the Registrar.

Flow of Events:

The use case begins when the Registrar selects the *maintain student* activity from the Main Form.

Basic Flow – Add Student:

1. The Registrar selects *add student*.
2. The system displays a blank student form.
3. The Registrar enters the following information for the student: name, date of birth, social security number, status, and graduation date.
4. The system validates the data to insure the proper format and searches for an existing student with the specified name.
5. If the data is valid the system creates a new student and assigns a unique system-generated id number.

Steps 2–5 are repeated for each student added to the system. When the Registrar has finished adding students to the system the use case ends.

Alternative Flows – a. Modify a Student:

1. The Registrar selects *modify student*.
2. The system displays a blank student form.
3. The Registrar types in the student id number he/she wishes to modify.
4. The system retrieves the student information and displays it on the screen.

5. The Registrar modifies one or more of the student information fields: name, date of birth, social security number, student id number, status, and graduation date.
6. When changes are complete, the Registrar selects *save*.
7. The system updates the student information.

Steps 2–7 are repeated for each student the Registrar wants to modify. When edits are complete, the use case ends.

Alternate Flows – b. Delete a Student:

1. The Registrar selects *delete student*.
2. The system displays a blank student form.
3. The Registrar types in the student id number for the student information that is to be deleted.
4. The system retrieves the student information and displays it in the form.
5. The Registrar selects *delete*.
6. The system displays a delete verification dialog confirming the deletion.
7. The Registrar selects *yes*.
8. The student is deleted from the system.

Steps 2–8 are repeated for each student deleted from the system. When the Registrar has finished deleting students to the system the use case ends.

Alternate Flow – c. Student Already Exists:

1. If in the *Add a Student* subflow the system finds an existing student with the same name, an error message is displayed *Student Already Exists*.

2. The Registrar can change the name, create a new student with the same name, or cancel the operation at which point the use case ends.

Alternate Flow – d. Student Not Found:

If in the *Modify a Student* or *Delete a Student* subflows the student name is not located, the system displays an error message, *Student Not Found*. The Registrar can then type in a different id number or cancel the operation at which point the use case ends.

18.1.5. Register for Courses

Brief Description:

This use case allows a Student to register for course offerings in the current semester. The Student can also modify or delete course selections if changes are made within the add/drop period at the beginning of the semester. The Course Catalog System provides a list of all the course offerings for the current semester. The main actor of this use case is the Student. The Course Catalog System is an actor within the use case.

Flow of Events: The use case begins when the Student selects the *maintain schedule* activity from the Main Form.

Basic Flow – Create a Schedule:

1. The Student selects *create schedule*.
2. The system displays a blank schedule form.
3. The system retrieves a list of available course offerings from the Course Catalog System.
4. The Student selects four primary course offerings and two alternate course offerings from the list of available offerings.
5. Once the selections are complete the Student selects *submit*.
6. The *Add Course Offering* subflow is performed at this step for each selected course offering.
7. The system saves the schedule.

Alternate Flows – a. Modify a Schedule:

1. The Student selects *modify schedule*.
2. The system retrieves and displays the Student's current schedule (e.g., the schedule for the current semester).
3. The system retrieves a list of all the course offerings available for the current semester from the Course Catalog System.
4. The system displays the list to the Student.
5. The Student can then modify the course selections by deleting and adding new courses.
6. The Student selects the courses to add from the list of available courses. The Student also selects any course offerings to delete from the existing schedule.
7. Once the edits are complete the Student selects *submit*.
8. The *Add Course Offering* subflow is performed at this step for each selected course offering.
9. The system saves the schedule.

Alternate Flows – b. Delete a Schedule:

1. The Student selects the *delete schedule* activity.
2. The system retrieves and displays the Student current schedule.
3. The Student selects *delete*.
4. The system prompts the Student to verify the deletion.
5. The Student verifies the deletion.
6. The system deletes the schedule.

Alternate Flows – c. Save a Schedule:

At any point, the Student may choose to save a schedule without submitting it by selecting *save*. The current schedule is saved, but the student is not added to any of the selected course offerings. The course offerings are marked as selected in the schedule.

Alternate Flows – d. Add Course Offering:

1. The system verifies that the Student has the necessary prerequisites and that the course offering is open.
2. The course offering is marked as *enrolled in* in the schedule.

Alternate Flows – e. Unfulfilled Prerequisites or Course Full:

If in the *Add Course* subflow the system determines that the Student has not satisfied the necessary prerequisites or that the selected course offering is full, an error message is displayed. The Student can either select a different course offering or cancel the operation, at which point the use case is restarted.

Alternate Flows – f. No Schedule Found:

If in the *Modify a Schedule* or *Delete a Schedule* subflows the system is unable to retrieve the Student's schedule, an error message is displayed. The Student acknowledges the error, and the use case is restarted.

Alternate Flows – g. Course Catalog System Unavailable:

If the system is unable to communicate with the Course Catalog System after a specified number of tries, the system will display an error message to the Student. The Student acknowledges the error message and the use case terminates.

Alternate Flows – h. Course Registration Closed:

If when the student selects *maintain schedule*, registration for the current semester has been closed, a message is displayed to the Student and the use case terminates. Students cannot register for courses after registration for the current semester has been closed.

18.1.6. Monitor for Course Full

The system shall ensure that no course is filled beyond the limit of 10 students.

18.1.7 Close Registration

Brief Description:

This use case allows a Registrar to close the registration process. Course offerings that do not have enough students are cancelled. Course offerings must have a minimum of three students in them. The billing system is notified for each student in each course offering that is not cancelled, so that the student can be billed for the course offering. The main actor of this use case is the Registrar. The Billing System is an actor involved within this use case.

Flow of Events:

The use case begins when the Registrar selects the *close registration* activity from the Main Form.

Basic Flow – Successful Close Registration:

1. The system checks to see if a Registration is in progress. If it is, then a message is displayed to the Registrar and the use case terminates.
2. The Close Registration processing cannot be performed if registration is in progress.
3. For each open course offering, the system checks to make sure that at least three students have registered, and that a Professor has signed up to teach the course offering. If so, the system closes the course offering and sends a transaction to the billing system for each student enrolled in the course offering.

Alternate Flows – a. Less than Three Students in the Course Offering:

If in the basic flow less than three students signed up for the course offering, the system will cancel the course offering. The Cancel Course Offering subflow is executed at this point.

Alternate Flows – b. Cancel Course Offering:

1. The system cancels the course offering.
2. For each student enrolled in the cancelled course offering, the system will modify the student's schedule.
3. The first available alternate course selection will be substituted for the cancelled course offering. If no alternates are available, then no substitution will be made.
4. Control returns to the Main flow to process the next course offering for the semester.
5. Once all schedules have been processed for the current semester, the system will notify all students, by mail, of any changes to their schedule (e.g., cancellation or substitution).

Alternate Flows – c. No Professor for the Course Offering:

If in the basic flow there is no professor signed up to teach the course offering, the system will cancel the course offering. The Cancel Course Offering subflow is executed at this point.

Alternate Flows – d. Billing System Unavailable:

If the system is unable to communicate with the Billing System, the system will attempt to resend the request after a specified period. The system will continue to attempt to resend until the Billing System becomes available.

18.1.8 Submit Grades

Brief Description:

This use case allows a Professor to submit student grades for one or more classes completed in the previous semester. The actor in this use case is the Professor.

Flow of Events:

The use case begins when the Professor selects the *submit grades* activity from the Main Form.

Basic Flow – Submit Grades:

1. The system displays a list of course offerings the Professor taught in the previous semester.
2. The Professor selects a course offering.
3. The system retrieves a list of all students who were registered for the course offering.
4. The system also retrieves the grade information for each student in the offering. The system displays each student's information and any grade that was previously assigned for the offering. For each student on the list, the Professor enters a grade: A, B, C, D, F, or I.
5. The system records the student's grade for the course offering. If the Professor wishes to skip a particular student, the grade information can be left blank and filled in at a later time. The Professor may also change the grade for a student by entering a new grade.

Alternative Flows – a. No Courses Taught:

If in the basic flow, the Professor did not teach any course offerings in the previous semester the system displays an error message and the use case ends.

Alternate Flows – b. Course Cancelled:

If too many students withdrew from the course during the add/drop period and the course was cancelled after the beginning of the semester, the system displays an error message. If the Professor chooses to cancel the operation the use case terminates, otherwise is restarted at step 2 of the basic flow.

18.1.9 View Report Card

Brief Description:

This use case allows a Student to view his/her report card for the previously completed semester. The Student is the actor of this use case.

Flow of Events:

The use case begins when the Student selects the *view report card* activity from the Main Form.

Basic Flow – View Report Card:

1. The system retrieves the grade information for each of the courses the Student completed during the previous semester.
2. The system prepares, formats, and displays the grade information.
3. When the Student has finished viewing the grade information the Student selects *close*.

Alternative Flows – a. No Grade Information Available:

If in the basic flow the system cannot find any grade information from the previous semester for the Student, a message is displayed. Once the Student acknowledges the message the use case terminates.

18.2 Use Case Diagram

See Fig. 18.1 for the use case diagram.

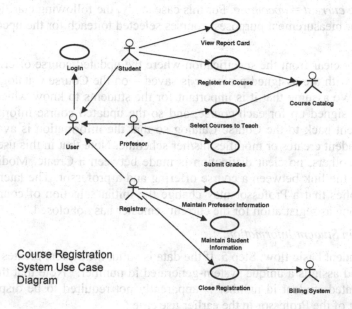

Course Registration
System Use Case
Diagram

Fig. 18.1. Use case diagram for the Count Registration System

18.2.1 Assumptions regarding the Use Cases

The following notes were made by the COSMIC core team as part of the evaluation of this case study. Because these notes pertain to the *functionality* of the use cases and not to any particular functional size measurement method, we have applied them equally to all of the FSMM's in this chapter:

Maintain Professor:

"We assume that the result of selecting *maintain professor* is that the suboptions to *add professor*, *modify a professor*, and *delete a professor* are displayed for selection. Similarly, we assume that selecting any of the other options on the Main Form, as described later, results in displaying corresponding suboptions for selection."

Modify professor alternate use case: "Note that this step of *Save* is mentioned only in this *Modify a Professor* use case, except for the use case 5 *Save a Schedule*, which has a specific effect."

Select Courses to Teach.

Basic flow: "This sentence could be interpreted as either the courses selected over all semesters, or courses selected within the current semester, where we assume *current = upcoming*. For this case study, the following clarification is made for measurement purposes: courses selected to teach for the upcoming semester."

"It is not clear from the specification where the updated course offering information with the assigned professor is saved – on the Course Catalog or on the CRS. We assume that it is important for the students to know which professor has signed up for each course, and so the updated course information must be sent back to the Course Catalog so that the information is available when a student creates or modifies his/her schedule. Note that in this use case, unlike the others, no clear distinction is made between a Create, Modify, or Delete for the link between a course offering and a professor. The later paragraph implies that a Professor may change the initial selection of courses to teach as long as registration for the current semester has not closed."

Maintain Student Information:

Add student basic flow: Step 5. If the data is valid, the system creates a new student and assigns a unique system-generated id number. "Note that the system-generated student id number is apparently not required to be displayed, unlike that of the Professor in the earlier use case."

Alternate flow – b. Delete student: "Apparently a student can be deleted without any checks on whether he/she has a Student/Course Registration and without deleting any associated Schedule(s) or Report Card(s)."

Maintain Schedules – c. Save a Schedule:

At any point, the Student may choose to save a schedule without submitting it by selecting *Save*. The current schedule is saved, but the student is not added to any of the selected course offerings. The course offerings are marked as *selected* in the schedule. "*We assume* that *at any point* means that this Save action can occur while performing a Create or Modify functional process. A Save cannot be performed unless a Schedule already exists and is displayed to the Student. So a Save is not a separate functional process, but an optional step in a Create or Modify functional process. It makes no sense for a Save to be needed during a Delete functional process. Note that this Save action by a Student is not the same action as the Save of a Schedule by the System."

Alternate Flows – d. Add Course Offering 1:

The system verifies that the Student has the necessary prerequisites and that the course offering is open. "The detailed rules, and corresponding data groups for checking that the student has the necessary prerequisites, are not described in the specifications; for this measurement scope, it is taken as a given that the rule is simple and involves reading a single data group; we have called this a 'Schedule history record' and assumed that it is held in the Course Registration system. The system then adds the Student to the selected course offering (assuming both tests are passed successfully). The course offering is marked as *enrolled in* in the schedule. Note also that the distinction between when a course is *available* and when it is *open* is not clear in the Specification. We have assumed for simplicity that these are synonyms."

Monitor for Course Full:

The system shall ensure that no course is filled beyond the limit of 10 students. "In the specifications it is not clear whether the requirement is to do this once at the closure of registration, or that this is done every time a student adds a course to his schedule. For this case study, we have assumed that the requirement is to verify this condition every time a student adds/modifies a course to his schedule. Otherwise, many students could sign up for courses that were already overbooked, which would not be the best way to proceed. For this to be possible, the Course Registration System must communicate back to the Course Catalogue every time a student adds, modifies, or deletes a course offering on his schedule, so that the Course Catalog record for each course offering always contains the latest data on the number of students enrolled. We have assumed this requirement. With these assumptions, this monitoring occurs as part of the create, modify, and delete Schedule functional processes and is not itself a separate functional process."

Close Registration:

The Close Registration processing cannot be performed if registration is in progress. "It is not clear how the check on whether a registration is in progress can be carried out. If it is performed by the Course Registration application, then there must be communication between the *Register for Courses* use cases and this *Close Registration* use case. But this functionality is not described, so we have ignored it in this analysis."

"As with previous use cases, we assume that the count of the number of students signed up for each course is maintained on the Course Catalog system."

Alternate Flows – b. Cancel Course Offering:

"The way in which the system deals with students' alternative course selections is unclear in this specification. The specification appears to state that courses with less than three students enrolled are cancelled and only then are alternatives examined – which might reveal that many students have chosen the course as an alternative but, too late, it has already been cancelled. Fortunately for the functional sizing the sequence of the logic is immaterial."

Alternate Flows – d. Billing System Unavailable:

If the system is unable to communicate with the Billing System, the system will attempt to resend the request after a specified period. The system will continue to attempt to resend until the Billing System becomes available. "There is another functional process implied <here>, which has been ignored. Logically, the functionality of *sending a transaction to the billing system for each student enrolled in the course offering* as described earlier cannot take place until the processing of all selections of all students for all courses has been completed. So the *Close Registration* process must create a file of billing data, and a separate functional process must send the data to the Billing System, triggered either by the end of the *Close Registration* process or, if previous attempts to transit have failed because the Billing System is unavailable, by a *try again* time signal in the Course Registration system."

Submit Grades, Brief Description:

This use case allows a Professor to submit student grades for one or more classes completed in the previous semester. "*We assume* this means *the semester just ended.*"

Basic Flow – Submit Grades: 4.

The system also retrieves the grade information for each student in the offering "i.e., that was previously assigned for the offering. Note that the specification for this use case does not distinguish clearly the *Add* and *Modify* cases."

18.3. COSMIC (Cfp) Count of Course Registration system

18.3.1 Identification of Layers

There is a single software layer for this set of requirements.

18.3.2 Identification of Users

The users who interact with this software are as follows:

- a. Users who send information to the software:
    - College Users: Students, Professors, Course Registrar
- b. Users who receive information from the software:
    - College Users: Students, Professors, Course Registrar
    - Course Catalog System
    - Billing System
    - Mail subsystem.

18.3.3 Application Boundary

The application boundary for the Course Registration System is shown in Fig. 18.2.

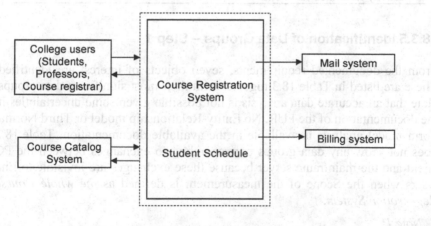

Application Boundary

Fig. 18.2. The Application Boundary for the Course Registration System

18.3.4 Identification of Triggering Events – Step 1

From the textual descriptions of the requirements, 14 candidate triggering event(s) are identified as listed in Table 18.2.

Table 18.2. List of candidate triggering events – step 1

No.	Main Form menu selection	14 Triggering events
1	Actor accesses the Logon form	1. Actor types his/her name and password on the Logon form
2	Registrar selects the *maintain professor* activity from the Main Form	2. Add a Professor 3. Modify a Professor 4. Delete a Professor
3	Professor selects the *select courses to teach* activity from the Main Form	5. Professor selects his/her courses to teach
4	Registrar selects the *maintain student* activity from the Main Form	6. Add a Student 7. Modify a Student 8. Delete a Student
5	Register for course: Student selects the *maintain schedule* activity from the Main Form	9. Create a Schedule 10. Modify a Schedule 11. Delete a Schedule
6	Registrar selects the activity *close registration* from the Main Form	12. Registrar starts the Close Registration functional process
7	The Professor selects the *submit grades* activity from the Main Form	13. Professor submits grades
8	The Student selects the *view report card* activity from the Main Form	14. Student Views Report Card

18.3.5 Identification of Data Groups – Step 1

From the documented requirements, seven objects of interest are identified. These are listed in Table 18.3 together with their most significant data groups. Note that an accurate data analysis is not possible given some uncertainties in the documentation of the FUR. No Entity-Relationship model or Third Normal Form model analysis is available in the available documentation. Table 18.3 does not show any data groups corresponding to exchanges between the PC client and the mainframe server because these exchanges are invisible to End Users when the Scope of the measurement is defined as *the whole Course Registration System*.

   Note 1:

It might be that the Course Catalog System distinguishes data held about each *Course* from data held about each *Course offered in the current seminar*, i.e., there are two objects of interest. The former would have time-independent

Table 18.3. List of objects of interest and data groups – step 1

Source/ destination of data	Object of interest	Data groups	Data attributes	Comments
Users	User	User data	User ID, User name, password	
Registrar	Professor*	Professor data	Prof. ID, name, date of birth, social security number, status, department	
Registrar	Student*	Student data	Student's ID, name, date of birth, social security number, status, graduation date	
Course Catalog System	Course	Course data	All information relevant to a course registered in the Course Catalog	See note 1 later
Course Catalog System	Course offering	Course offering data	Course offering ID, no. of students signed up, professor ID signed up	This data relates to the current semester
Student	Schedule item*	Schedule item data	Student ID, course offering ID, primary/alternate course preference indicator, selected/enrolled status	
Professor	Schedule item*	Student grade	Student ID, course offering ID, grade	Note that *Student grade* is another data group of the object of interest *Schedule item*
Previous cycles of the Registration System	Schedule history item*	Schedule history record	Student ID, course offering ID, date of course grade (for previous courses)	
Mail System	Schedule item*	Student schedule changes message	Student's schedule; not all data attributes are specified in the documentation	
Billing System	Schedule item*	Invoice item	Student ID, course offering ID, fee payable (for each course offering that the student has been accepted for)	Not all data attributes are specified in the documentation
Registry System	System	Error message		See note 4

*From the requirements, we conclude that data about the asterisked objects of interest are stored persistently on the Course Registration System. Data about the *Course* and *Course offering* objects of interest are stored persistently on the Course Catalog System. [User is assumed to be maintained elsewhere.]

data about the course, e.g., course description, prerequisites, etc. The latter would have, for example, attributes such as the ID of the professor signed up to teach the course this semester, the total number of students signed up so far, etc. We have no information in the specification on whether the Course Catalog System makes this distinction, but it seems more logical that it does than that it does not.

So we have assumed that two objects of interest exist, namely the *Course* and the *Course offering*, where the latter has data about the course for the current semester. But an assumption that there is only one object of interest (*course offering*) would also be valid. This assumption affects the measured size because we have assumed that some functional processes need only *Course-offering* data (e.g., when a student creates a *Schedule*) whereas other functional processes need *Course* attributes as well (e.g., to check the prerequisites for a particular course). But these assumptions might be wrong. For example, it might be that a student needs to see the *Course* data as well as *Course-offering* data when creating a Schedule.

Note 2:

The *Student Schedule* is not a separate object of interest. There is no data held about a Student Schedule. It is a collection of up to six occurrences of a data group for each student showing the course offerings that he/she has signed up for as *primary or alternate* and as *selected or enrolled*. We have named each of these data groups *schedule item data*, to distinguish it from the name of the object of interest (*schedule item*) of the group. The complete Student Schedule appears, for example, when a student displays the collection of up to six courses that he/she has signed up for.

Note 3:

The 'List of professors' is not a separate object of interest of data group. See note 2: No data are held about the list.

Note 4:

The *System* is not really an object of interest. All we know is that the software produces error messages. There is no need to identify an object of interest, just as there is no value in identifying the object of interest of a pure command data movement.

Definitions of the seven objects of interest (in alphabetic order)

- *Course*: A standard series of lectures, etc., on a specific subject from the College Course Catalogue
  - *Key*: Course ID. Other attributes (assumed): Course name, description, Prerequisite Course ID. Note: Registration by a Student for a particular Course offering may depend on successful attendance at (i.e., passing) a *prerequisite* course.

- *Course Offering*: A Course that is available for students to enrol during a particular Semester
  - *Key*: Course ID, Semester ID. Other attributes: dates, times, locations of the lectures, etc., availability indicator (open/closed/canceled), assigned Professor, number of students enrolled
- *Professor*: A person who may register to deliver a Course offering in the current Semester, for a Course that he is eligible to teach.
  - *Key*: Professor ID. Other attributes: name, address, date of birth, SSN, status, Department, phone, fax, e-mail
- *Student*: A person who can register to attend a Course offering
  - *Key*: Student ID. Other attributes: name, DOB, status, graduation date
- *Schedule item*: One of the maximum of six entries in a Student Schedule when a Student selects or enrols in a Course offering
  - *Key*: Student ID, Course-offering ID. Other attributes: Student preference status (primary, alternate), registration status (selected, enrolled in), grade awarded, fee payable, etc.
- *Schedule history item*: An instance of a specific student having attended a specific Course offering during a previous semester
  - *Key*: Student ID, Course-offering ID, Semester date. Other attributes: Grade awarded
- *User*: Any person (Registrar, Professor, or Student) who is authorized to use the Course Registration system
  - *Key*: User ID. Other attributes: User name, password.

18.3.6 Identification of Functional Processes – Step 1

From the documented requirements with each triggering event, there are 14 candidate functional processes.

1. User Logon
2. Add a Professor
3. Modify a Professor
4. Delete a Professor
5. Professor selects/deselects his/her courses to teach
6. Add a Student
7. Modify a Student
8. Delete a Student
9. Create a Schedule
10. Modify a Schedule
11. Delete a Schedule
12. Registrar starts the Close Registration functional process
13. Professor submits grades
14. Student Views Report Card.

18.3.7 Identify Data Movements – Candidate Functional Processes – Step 1

For all functional processes in the previous steps, all data movements of a data group must be identified. Important: the reader is reminded of <the previous> paragraph where it is stated that in this step 1, the requirements are interpreted literally and analyzed assuming that each explicitly identified event triggers only one functional process.

The detailed analysis in step 2 identifies, however, that in some cases there should almost certainly be more than one functional process from what would have initially appeared to be a single triggering event. When this happens, this will be noted in Table 18.4 by using a dashed line to indicate where one functional process might end and the next start. These dashed lines are only relevant to the discussion in step 2. In Table 18.4, the numbers in the ID Process column refer to the numbers in the Requirements section of this document.

Table 18.4. COSMIC count summary for Course Registration System project (COSMIC, 2007)

Subprocess description	Data group	Type of data movement	Cfp	Sum Cfp
Use case 1: Logon				
Process 1: Logon				
Triggering event: Actor types name and password on the logon form				
Actor enters name and password	System	E	1	
Read name and password	User data	R	1	
Display error message	Messages	X	1	
				3
Use case 2: Maintain professor information				
Process 2: Add a professor				
Triggering event: Registrar selects the *add a professor* activity				
Registrar enters information for the Professor	Professor data	E	1	
The system validates the entered data and checks if a professor of the same name exists already	Professor data	R	1	
The system creates a new Professor	Professor data	W	1	
Display the system generated Professor ID number	Professor data	X	1	
Display error message	Messages	X	1	
				5

(Continued)

Subprocess description	Data group	Type of data movement	Cfp	Sum Cfp
Process 3: Modify a professor				
Triggering event: Registrar selects the *modify a Professor* activity				
Registrar enters Professor ID	Professor ID	E	1	
The system retrieves the Professor information	Professor data	R	1	
The system displays the Professor information	Professor data	X	1	
The Registrar enters the modified Professor data	Professor data	E	1	
When changes are complete, the Registrar selects *Save*	This is not a distinct data movement. It only indicates that the Entry of the data (see earlier) is completed	*This will be omitted from now on in all other use cases*	0	
The system updates the Professor information	Professor data	W	1	
Display error message	Messages	X	1	
				6
Process 4: Delete a professor				
Triggering event: Registrar selects the *delete a Professor* activity				
Registrar enters Professor ID	Professor ID	E	1	
The system retrieves the Professor information	Professor data	R	1	
The system displays the Professor information	Professor data	X	1	
Registrar enters the delete command for the selected Professor	Professor ID	E	1	
The system prompts the Registrar to confirm the deletion	System prompt command	N/A not a data group movement	0	
The Registrar confirms the deletion	Professor ID	N/A repetition of earlier Delete Entry	0	
Professor is deleted from the system	Professor data	W	1	
Display error message	Message	X	1	
				6

Use case 3: *Select/deselect courses to teach*

Process 5: Select/deselect Courses to teach

Triggering event: Professor selects/deselects the *select courses to teach* activity from the Main Form

(Continued)

Table 18.4. *(Cont.)*

Subprocess description	Data group	Type of data movement	Cfp	Sum Cfp
Start the *select courses to teach* process	Select courses to teach command	E	1	
The system requests (from the Course Catalog database) the list of courses the professor has previously selected to teach and others that he is eligible to teach	Course-offering data	X	1	
The system receives the requested data	Course-offering data	E	1	
The system displays the requested data	Course-offering data	X	1	
The Professor selects and/or de-selects the course offerings that he/she wishes to teach for the upcoming semester	Course-offering data	E	1	
The system sends the Professor's selected or deselected course offerings to the Course Catalog system	Course-offering data	X	1	
The Course Catalog system verifies that the selected offerings do not conflict and returns any conflicting pairs	Course-offering data	E	1	
Conflicting pairs of courses are displayed	Course-offering data	X	1	
Display error message	Messages	X	1	
				9

Use case 4: *Maintain student information*

Process 6: Add a student
Triggering event: Registrar selects *add student*

Registrar enters student data	Student data	E	1	
The system validates the data and checks if a student of the same name already exists	Student data	R	1	
The system creates a new student	Student data	W	1	
Display error message	Messages	X	1	
				4

Process 7: Modify a student
Triggering event: Registrar selects *modify student*

Registrar enters student ID	Student ID	E	1	
The system retrieves the student information	Student data	R	1	
The system displays student information	Student data	X	1	

(Continued)

Subprocess description	Data group	Type of data movement	Cfp	Sum Cfp
Registrar modifies one or more of the student information fields	Student data	E	1	
The system stores the modified data	Student data	W	1	
Display error message	Messages	X	1	
				6

Process 8: Delete a student
Triggering event: Registrar selects *delete student*

Subprocess description	Data group	Type of data movement	Cfp	Sum Cfp
Registrar enters student ID	Student ID	E	1	
The system retrieves the student information	Student data	R	1	
The system displays student information	Student data	X	1	
Registrar enters *delete* command	Student id	E	1	
The system prompts the Registrar to confirm the deletion	System prompt command	N/A not a data group movement	0	
The Registrar confirms the deletion	Confirmation message	N/A repetition of earlier Delete Entry)	0	
Student is deleted from the system	Student data	W	1	
Display error message	Messages	X	1	
				6

Use case 5: *Register for courses*
Process 9: Create a schedule
Triggering event: Student selects *create a schedule*

Subprocess description	Data group	Type of data movement	Cfp	Sum Cfp
Student enters *create schedule*	Start create schedule command	E	1	
Request the course offerings from the Course Catalog System	Course-offering data	X	1	
Receive the available course offerings from the Course Catalog System for the current semester	Course-offering data	E	1	
The system displays the list of available course offerings	Course-offering data	X	1	
The student selects 4 primary courses and 2 alternate courses and submits them to this application	Schedule item data	E	1	
The system verifies with the Course Catalog system what prerequisites are needed	Course data	$1 \times X$ $1 \times E$	1 1	
The system verifies whether the Student has satisfied the necessary prerequisites	Schedule history record	R	1	

(Continued)

Table 18.4. *(Cont.)*

Subprocess description	Data group	Type of data movement	Cfp	Sum Cfp
Validated Schedule items are returned to the Course Catalog system so that it can maintain the student count for each course	Schedule item data	X	1	
The Course Catalog system verifies that the course offering is still open and that less than 10 students are enrolled		N/A not part of the Course Registration System	0	
Schedule items are marked as *enrolled in* and are made persistent in the Student's schedule on the Course Registration System	Schedule item data	W	1	
The system saves the schedule (this happens when the Schedule items are made persistent by the earlier Write)		N/A	0	
Student may choose to save a schedule without submitting it by selecting *save*	Schedule item data	E	1	
The course offerings are marked as *selected* in the schedule and are saved	Schedule item data	W	1	
Display error message	Messages	X	1	
				13

Process 10: Modify a schedule

Triggering event: Student selects the *modify schedule* activity from the Main Form

Student enters a *modify a schedule* command	Modify a schedule command	E	1	
The system retrieves the Student's current schedule	Schedule item data	R	1	
The system displays the Student's current schedule	Schedule item data	X	1	
The system retrieves all the course offerings available for the current semester from the Course Catalog System	Course-offering data	1 × X 1 × E	2	
The system displays the list of available course offerings	Course-offering data	X	1	
The student enters the modifications to his Schedule item(s)	Schedule item data	E	1	
The system verifies with the Course Catalog system what prerequisites are needed	Course data	1 × X 1 × E	1 1	
The system verifies whether the Student has the necessary prerequisites	Schedule history record	1 × R	1	

(Continued)

Subprocess description	Data group	Type of data movement	Cfp	Sum Cfp
Validated Schedule items are returned to the Course Catalog so that it can maintain the student count for each course	Schedule item data	X	1	
The Course Catalog system verifies that there are less than 10 students enrolled and that the course offering is still open		N/A	0	
Schedule items are marked as *enrolled in* and are made persistent in the Student's schedule on the Course Registration System when saved by the system	Schedule item data	W	1	
Student may choose to save a schedule without submitting it by selecting *save*	Schedule item data	E	1	
The course offerings are marked as *selected* in the schedule and are saved	Schedule item data	W	1	
Display error message	Messages	X	1	
				15

Process 11: Delete a schedule

Triggering event: Student selects the *delete schedule* activity from the Main Form

Student enters *delete schedule* command	Delete Schedule command	E	1	
The system retrieves the student's current schedule	Schedule item data	R	1	
The system displays the student's current schedule	Schedule item data	X	1	
The student enters the deletion command for the schedule	Delete Schedule command	E	1	
The system prompts the Student to verify the deletion	System Prompt command	N/A	0	
The student confirms the deletion	Schedule item data	N/A repeat of Entry data	0	
The system updates the student's schedule	Schedule item data	W	1	
The system sends the deleted schedule items to the Course Catalog system so that the latter can update the number of students enrolled for each course	Schedule item data	X	1	
Display error message	Messages	X	1	
				7

Use case 6: *Monitor for course full*

Use case 7: *Close registration*

Process 12: Close Registration

Triggering event: Registrar selects the *close registration* activity from the Main Form

(Continued)

Table 18.4. *(Cont.)*

Subprocess description	Data group	Type of data movement	Cfp	Sum Cfp
Registrar enters *Close Registration*	Close registration command	E	1	
Read if a Registration is in progress	System	N/A; see Sect. 2: Not enough details for measurement purposes	0	
Display error message	Messages	X	1	
Obtain Course offering data (with no. of students enrolled, etc.) from the Course Catalog	Course-offering data	$1 \times X$ $1 \times E$	2	
Read Schedule items to obtain the *enrolled* and *alternate* course selection	Schedule item data	R	1	
Check that at least three students are signed up: if not, cancel course and examine student's alternatives	Data manipulation	N/A		
Send info for a billing transaction for each student accepted for the course	Invoice item	X	1	
Update the course offerings on the course catalog	Course-offering data	X	1	
Update each student's schedule	Schedule item data	W	1	
Send info on any schedule changes to students through mail subsystem	Student schedule changes message	X	1	

9

Use case 8: *Submit grades*

Process 13: Submit grades
Triggering event: The Professor selects the *submit grades* activity from the Main Form

The Professor decides to submit grades	Start process *submit grades*	E	1	
The system retrieves the courses the Professor taught from the Course Catalog	Course-offering data	$1 \times X$ $1 \times E$	2	
Course offerings are displayed	Course-offering data	X	1	
The Professor selects a course offering	Course-offering selection	E	1	
For each course offering, selected in turn, the system retrieves the schedule items for all students who were registered for each course offering	Schedule item data	R	1	

(Continued)

Subprocess description	Data group	Type of data movement	Cfp	Sum Cfp
The system also retrieves the grade information for each student in the course offering that had been entered previously (if any)	Grade is the second data group within the Schedule item data Object of interest	R	1	
The system displays each schedule item for each student including any grade that was previously assigned for the offering	Schedule item data and Grade	2X	2	
The professor enters or changes the student's grade for the course offering	Schedule item data	E	1	
The system records the student's grade for the course offering	Schedule item data	W	1	
Display error message	Messages	X	1	
				12

Use case 9: *View report card*

Process 14: View Report Card

Triggering event: The student selects the *view report card* activity from the Main Form

The Student selects the *view report card* activity from the Main Form	Start *view report card* process	E	1	
The system retrieves the grade information for each of the courses the Student completed during the previous semester	Schedule item data Grade	2R	2	
The system prepares, formats, and displays the grade information	Schedule item data and Grade	2X	2	
When Student has finished viewing the grade information the Student selects *close*	Student's Grades	A control command, not a separate data movement	0	
Display error message	Messages	X	1	
				6
	Total Functional Size in Cfp:			107

There are additional notes for interested readers who wish to formally apply the COSMIC method and would like additional guidance (and justification for the earlier counting details) from the COSMIC core team at http://www.lrgl.uqam.ca/cosmic-ffp/casestudies_with_ISO_19761_2003.html.

18.4 FiSMA (Ffp) Count of Course Registration System

The following is taken from the FiSMA (Finnish Software Measurement Association) 1.1 functional size measurement method (FiSMA, 2008):

The FiSMA 1.1 measurement process consists of the following steps:

Gather documentation and software development artifacts to describe the functional user requirements for the software (to be or already) developed. These include any items such as use cases, preliminary user requirements, use manuals, entity relationship diagrams, screen, report or database mock-ups, data flow diagrams, etc. – anything that describe what the software will do in terms of tasks or services, independently of any quality or technical requirements.

Determine the Scope of the FSM: The Scope of FiSMA 1.1 is determined by the purpose for doing the FSM and includes the FUR to be developed or enhanced in the project or application to be counted.

Determine which are the Functional User Requirements to be measured by FiSMA 1.1 by determining the Scope as outlined in 1 and include only those user requirements that describe what the software is to do in terms of tasks and services.

1. Identify the BFCs within the Functional User Requirements from earlier 2 in two main parts: (1) measuring the end-user interface services, and (2) measuring indirect services. If one of these two parts does not exist for the piece of software, then the process consists only of measuring the services that are present.
2. Classify the BFCs into the appropriate BFC type by mapping each BFC identified to the descriptions of the BFC types in clause 4. Be cautious to identify duplicate logical functionality so that it is counted only once per instance of the FSM. Two BFC types are considered to be duplicate if they have the same characteristics (i.e., identical BFC types with the same values for each of the component parts for the BFC type, i.e., identical data elements, reading references, and/or writing references as appropriate for the BFC type).
3. Assign the appropriate numeric value to each BFC using the calculations outlined for each BFC type <see the chapter on Functional Size Measurement Methods that contains the specific FiSMA rules>.
4. Calculate the Functional Size as outlined at the end of this section.

18.4.1 Step 1 and Step 2

Collect documentation and determine the scope of the measurement: Using the Fig. 18.2, the scope is the Course Registration system and its functional user requirements.

18.4.2 Step 3

Determine which are the Functional User Requirements to be measured by FiSMA 1.1: The functional user requirements are as described in the use cases of Sect. 18.1 for the Course Registration System.

18.4.3 Step 4

Identify the BFC's within the Functional User Requirements: This step identifies the BFC's within the Functional User Requirements from earlier 2 in two main parts:

1. Measuring the end-user interface services
2. Measuring indirect services as outlined in Fig. 18.3

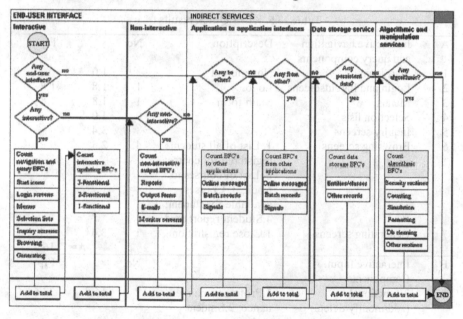

Fig. 18.3. FiSMA 1.1 process (FiSMA, 2008)

18.4.4 Steps 5–7

FiSMA provides for two levels of measurement to assess FiSMA function points (Ffp):

1. KISS (keep it simple stupid) Quick
2. FiSMA 1.1 detailed measurement

The first approach called KISS Quick assigns an average number of function points (Ffp) to each identified function. This level is especially useful when the number of data elements and reading or writing references is unknown.

The second level is called FiSMA 1.1, which is used to evaluate the functional user requirements at a detailed level, and is appropriate for use once the number of data elements and data entities are known.

The following sections present the Course Registration case study results counted both using KISS Quick and FiSMA 1.1.

18.4.5 KISS Quick

The results of the KISS Quick method as applied to the Functional User Requirements of the Course Registration System are shown in Table 18.5.

Table 18.5. KISS Quick results

A	Interactive navigation and query components	Description	No.	×	Ffp
1	Start icons	None found		1.0	
2	Login and logoutscreens	Logon	1	1.8	1.8
3	Menus	Main form	1	1.8	1.8
4	Selection lists		0	1.0	
5	Inquiry screens			3.4	
6	Browsing screens	1. List of all students registered for course; 2. List of courses to teach; 3. Courses available for student; 4.Student report card	4	2.3	9.2
7	Generating screens	1.Close registration	1	3.4	3.4
				A=	16.2
B	Interactive Input Components		No.	×	Ffp
8	3-functional (add/modify/delete) screens	1.Professor maintenance; 2.Student maintenance	2	16.8	33.6
9	2-functional input screens			11.2	
10	1-functional input screens	1.Select/deselect courses to teach; 2. Student schedule; 3. Student grades	3	5.6	16.8
				B=	50.4
C	Noninteractive Output Components		No.	×	Ffp
11	Output forms			4.9	

(Continued)

12	Reports			6.5	
13	E-mails and text messages	1. Mail to student (via mail system)	1	3.0	3.0
14	Output monitor screens			6.5	
				C=	3.0
D	Interfaces from other applications (or hw)		No. ×		Ffp
15	Online message types in	1. Course and course offerings retrieved; 2. Userid/password validation result; 3. Courses and number of students registered;	3	5.5	16.5
16	Signals from devices			2.0	
17	Batch record types in			5.5	
				D=	16.5
E	Interfaces to other applications (or hw)		No. ×		Ffp
18	Online message types out	1. Cancel/close offering due to <3 students; 2. Billing system data; 3. Grades are updated; 4. User data (validate); 5. Selection data for courses	5	3.6	18
19	Signals to devices			1.4	
20	Batch record types out			3.6	
				E=	14.4
F	Data storage services		No. ×		Ffp
21	Entities or classes (oo)	1. Student, 2. Professor, 3. User	2	3.9	7.8
22	Other persistent records			3.9	
				F=	7.8
G	Independent algorithmic and manipulation services		No. ×		Ffp
23	Security routines			5.1	
24	Counting routines	1. Calculate/control attendees	1	5.1	5.1
25	Simulation routines			5.1	
26	Formatting routines			5.1	
27	Database cleaning routines			5.1	
28	Other algorithmic routines	1. Automatic schedule modify, 2. Add/drop period control	2	5.1	10.2
				G=	15.3
KISS Quick early Size = A + B + C + D + E + F + G = (units = Ffp)					127.2

18.4.6 FiSMA 1.1 Detailed Measurement

The results of applying the FiSMA 1.1 method to the functional user requirements of the Course Registration System are shown in Table 18.6.

Table 18.6. FiSMA 1.1 results

BFC Type	Name of FUR	No. of data items	No. of reading refs.	No. of writing refs.	No. of operations	Size (Ffp)
Logon	Logon form	5	1			1.4
Menu	Main form	7	1			1.7
Browsing screens	Report card	10	2			2.6
Browsing screens	List of all students registered for course	3	1			1.1
Browsing screens	List of courses to teach	3	2			1.6
Browsing screens	Courses available for student	3	1			1.6
Generating Screens	Close registration	4	2			1.8
3-functional screens	Maintain Professor information	16	1	1		13.7
3-functional screens	Maintain Student information	16	1	1		13.7
1- functional screen	Select/deselect courses to teach	11	1	1		3.6
1- functional screen	Student schedule update	7	1	1		2.8
1- functional screen	Student grade update	8	2	1		3.6
E-mails and text messages	Mail to student (via mail system)	8	2			3.6
Online message types in	1. Validate userid /password combination	2	1	1		1.8
Online message types in	2. Course offering data	5	1			2.4
Online message types in	3. Courses and number of students	4	1	1		2.2

(Continued)

Online message types out	1. Cancel/close offering due to <3 students (and any registration data)	5	1	1.7
Online message types out	2. Data to Billing system	5	3	2.7
Online message types out	3. Grade update info	8	2	2.6
Online message types out	4. Course selection data	5	1	1.7
Online message types out	5. User information (validate user)	2	1	1.3
Entities or classes	Professor	10		3.5
Entities or classes	Student	15		4.5
Counting routines	Calculate/ control attendees	3	3	1.7
Other algorithmic routines	Automatic schedule modify	15	10	6.4
Other algorithmic routines	Add/drop period control	6	5	3.0
TOTAL Ffp				**88.3**

Notes:

1. FiSMA: Use case No. 1: Logon includes: 1 logon, 1 menu (Main Form)
2. FiSMA: Use case no. 3: Select/deselect courses to teach includes the following: 1 of the 1-input, 1 Browse screen, 1 Message out, 1 Message in
3. FiSMA: Use case no. 5: Maintain Schedule includes the following: 1 of the 1-input, 1 Browse, 1 Other Algorithm (add/drop), 1 Message out (duplicate message out is not counted), 1 Message in (duplicate message in is not counted)
4. FiSMA: Use case no. 7: Close registration includes the following: 1 Generation dialog, 2 Messages out (message to billing system; course cancel message to course catalog system), 1 Other Algorithm (automatic schedule modify)
5. FiSMA: Use case no. 8: Submit Grades includes the following: 1 of the 1-input, 1 Browse (course offerings duplicate is not counted), 1 Browse (students registered in course), 1 Message Out (Update grades).

18.5 IFPUG (FP) Count of Course Registration System

Table 18.7 summarizes the IFPUG function point counting process. Note that for purposes of illustration and comparison, this chapter is intended to illustrate how to count Functional Size using the ISO-conformant methods – which means that the process of functional size ends with the completion of step 4 in the table.

Note: In simple terms, this means that for functional size measurement, IFPUG function points would be reported as unadjusted FP.

18.5.1 IFPUG Step 1: Determine the Type of Function Point Count

This function point count is for the new development project to replace the original Course Registration System.

Table 18.7. IFPUG FP counting approach

IFPUG Counting Step	Procedure
1	Determine the type of function point count
2	Identify the counting scope and application boundary
3	Count the data functions to determine their contribution to the unadjusted function point count
4	Count the transactional functions to determine their contribution to the unadjusted function point count
5	Determine the value adjustment factor
6	Calculate the adjusted function point count

Note that steps 5 and 6 go beyond ISO/IEC definition of functional size, and therefore we perform only steps 1–4 for this case study

18.5.2 IFPUG Step 2: Identify the Counting Scope and Application Boundary

The counting scope includes functional user requirements of the new Course Registration as outlined in the use cases in Sect. 18.1. The application boundary is shown in Fig. 18.4.

18.5.3 IFPUG Step 3: Count the Data Functions to Determine Their Contribution to the Unadjusted Function Point Count

According to the IFPUG standard, the following definitions apply (IFPUG, 2004):

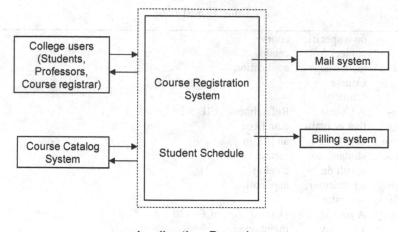

Application Boundary

Fig. 18.4. Application boundary for IFPUG counting of Course Registration System

Internal Logical Files:

An internal logical file (ILF) is a user identifiable group of logically related data or control information maintained within the boundary of the application. The *primary intent of an ILF* is to hold data maintained through one or more elementary processes of the application being counted.

External Interface Files:

An external interface file (EIF) is a user identifiable group of logically related data or control information referenced by the application, but maintained within the boundary of another application. The *primary intent of an EIF* is to hold data referenced through one or more elementary processes within the boundary of the application counted. This means an EIF counted for an application must be in an ILF in another application.

There is no entity-relationship diagram, data model, or object model from which to be sure of the data relationships and entities. However, the data analysis used in the COSMIC determination of stand-alone data stores follows sound analysis principles, and the data groupings are, therefore, also used here.

Table 18.8 shows the results of step 3: Count the data functions.

Table 18.8. Data function results for IFPUG FP count of Course Registration System

Entity/ data group	Description	Primary intent	Type	DET	RET	Complexity	Unadjusted FP
Course	A standard series of lectures, etc.	Reference data from an ILF in	EIF	<19	1	Low	5

(Continued)

Table 18.8. *(Cont.)*

	on a specific subject from the College Course Catalog	course catalog application					
Course-offering (see note 1 immediately following Table 18.3)	A Course that is available for students to enroll during a particular semester	Reference data from an ILF in course catalog application	EIF	<19	1	Low	5
Professor	A person who may register to deliver a Course offering in the current semester, for a Course that he is eligible to teach	Data maintained by Course Registration System	ILF	<20	1	Low	7
Student + schedule item(s) + schedule item history (see note 2 in Sect. 18.3)	A person who can register to attend a Course offering	Data maintained by Course Registration System	ILF	Based on assessment in 18.3, assumed <20	3 (Student, schedule item, schedule item history – different DET from Schedule Item)	Low	7
User	Any person (Registrar, Professor, or Student) who is authorized to use the Course Registration System	Data Maintained external to Course Reg. System – assumed that it is maintained in another application boundary	EIF	2 (user id, password)	1	Low	5
		Total	EIF			3 Low	15
		Total	ILF			2 Low	14

18.5.4 IFPUG Step 4: Count the Transactional Functions to Determine Their Contribution to the Unadjusted Function Point Count

According to the IFPUG standard, the following definitions apply (IFPUG, 2004):

External Input:

An external input (EI) is an elementary process that processes data or control information that comes from outside the application boundary. The *primary intent of an EI* is to maintain one or more ILFs and/or to alter the behavior of the system.

External Output:

An external output (EO) is an elementary process that sends data or control information outside the application boundary. *The primary intent of an EO* is to present information to a user through processing logic other than, or in addition to, the retrieval of data or control information. The processing logic must contain at least one mathematical formula or calculation, create derived data, maintain one or more ILFs, or alter the behavior of the system.

External Inquiry:

An external inquiry (EQ) is an elementary process that sends data or control information outside the application boundary. *The primary intent of an EQ* is to present information to a user through the retrieval of data or control information from an ILF of EIF. The processing logic contains no mathematical formulas or calculations, and creates no derived data. No ILF is maintained during the processing, nor is the behavior of the system altered.

Table 18.9 summarizes the list of use cases as originally presented in Sect. 18.1. The results of applying IFPUG functional size measurement to the Course Registration's functional user requirements is shown in Table 18.10.

Table 18.9. Course Registration use cases

Use case	Use case name for Course Registration System
1	Logon (by all users)
2	Maintain professor information (by the registrar)
3	Select courses to teach (by professors)
4	Maintain student information (by the registrar)
5	Register for courses (by students)
6	Monitor for course full (by the application)
7	Close registration (by the registrar)
8	Submit grades (by professors)
9	View report card (by students)

Table 18.10. IFPUG FP transactional function type summary for Course Registration System Project

Description	Primary intent	Type	DET	FTR/RET	Complexity	Unadjusted FP
Use case 1: Logon						
Logon (validate user id and password)	Present data retrieved to users	EQ	<19	1 (User)	Low	3
Use case 2: *Maintain Professor information*						
Registrar: add professor	Maintain ILF	EI	<16	1 (Professor)	Low	3
Registrar: retrieve and display professor infor-mation (implied query)	Present data retrieved to registrar	EQ	<19	1 (Professor)	Low	3
Registrar: modify professor (includes save)	Maintain ILF	EI	<16	1 (Professor)	Low	3
Registrar: delete professor (includes confirming delete)	Maintain ILF	EI	<16	1 (Professor)	Low	3
Use case 3: *Select/Deselect courses to teach*						
Professor: Display course offerings available for this professor for this semester, plus those already selected	Present retrieved data to professor	EQ	6–19	3 assumed (professor, course offerings, course)	Average	4
Professor: Select/ deselect courses and save (update) course offerings. *Note*: conflicting pairs display is part of this function, not a standalone process → selections sent to other system to up-date course offering	Maintain ILF	EI	5–15	2 assumed (course offering, professor)	Average	4
Use case 4: *Maintain student information*						
Registrar: add student	Maintain ILF	EI	<15	1 (Student)	Low	3
Registrar: display student information (implied query)	Present retrieved data to registrar	EQ	<19	1 (Student)	Low	3

(Continued)

Registrar: update student	Maintain ILF	EI	<15	1 (Student)	Low	3
Registrar: delete student	Maintain ILF	EI	<5	1 (Student)	Low	3
Use case 5: Register for Courses						
Student: display available course offerings (different logic from professor display of course offerings)	Present retrieved data to Student	EQ	6–19	2 (course of-fering, course, student for courses already selected)	Average	4
Student: Maintain schedule (4 courses + 2 alternates) if pre-requisites are met) → selections sent to other system to maintain student count for each course -- update student schedule records	Maintain ILF	EI	5–15	3 assumed (course offering, student, course catalog (w/prerequisit e info))	High	6
Student: display schedule (implied query)	Present retrieved data to student	EQ	6–19	2 (student, course offering)	Average	4
Use case 6: Monitor for Course Full						
System sets busi-ness rule for max. attendees per course offering = 10 (checks course offerings to verify level). No explicit trigger (time or anything else) and no data crosses boundary (either in or out) to any user	Assumed to be done as part of other functional processes (Internal process)	N/A				
Use case 7: Close Registration						
Registrar: close Registration (includes cancella-tion and student schedule update) → update sent to other system to update course offering	Send updates to other application to close/cancel course offer-ing, update student ILF	EO	6–19	3 assumed (student, course offer-ing, course)	Average	5

(Continued)

Table 18.10. *(Cont.)*

System: send billing system notice of courses closed but not cancelled (with student info for billing)	Present retrieved data to user (assumed no calc.)	EQ	6–19	2 assumed (course offering, student)	Average	4
System: notify all students by mail of any changes to their schedule	Present retrieved data to user	EQ	6–19	2 assumed (course offering, student)	Average	4
Use case 8: Submit Grades						
Professor: List of course offerings taught in previous semester	Present retrieved data to user	EQ	6–19	1 assumed (Course offering)	Low	3
Professor: List of all students registered for selected course offering and grades for each	Present retrieved data to user	EQ	6–19	2 assumed (student, course offering)	Average	4
Professor: enter/update student grades (one process that updates record that already exists)	Maintain ILF	EI	5–15	1 assumed (student)	Low	3
Use case 9: View Report Card						
Student: view report card for previous semester	Present retrieved data to user	EQ	6–19	2 assumed (Course offering, student)	Average	4

18.5.5 IFPUG Summary Unadjusted FP Count for Course Registration System

Table 18.11 shows the result of the unadjusted FP count for the Course Registration System.

Table 18.11. IFPUG FSM results

Function type	Functional Complexity		Complexity Totals		Function Type Totals (unadjusted FP)
ILF	2	Low	× 7 =	14	
	0	Average	× 10 =	0	
	0	High	× 15 =	0	
					14
EIF	3	Low	× 5 =	15	
	0	Average	× 7 =	0	

(Continued)

	0	High	× 10 =	0	
					15
EI	7	Low	× 3 =	21	
	1	Average	× 4 =	4	
	1	High	× 6 =	6	
					31
EO	0	Low	× 4 =	0	
	1	Average	× 5 =	5	
	0	High	× 7 =	0	
					5
EQ	4	Low	× 3 =	12	
	7	Average	× 4 =	28	
	0	High	× 6 =	0	
					40
IFPUG Function Point Count (uFP)					105

18.6 Mark II Function Point Count of Course Registration System

This functional size measurement is based on the Mark II method from the U.K. Software Measurement Association, UKSMA. Note that the details of Mark II are outlined in the chapter on functional size measurement methods. The steps in Mark II for determining the size of the Course Registration System are depicted in Fig. 18.5 later.

Every logical transaction consists of the three elements of input, process, and output. MkII FPA makes the following basic assumptions regarding the functional size of these three elements:

- The size of the input element is proportional to the number of uniquely processed Data Element Types (DETs) composing the input side of the transaction
- The size of the processing element is proportional to the number of Data Entity Types (or *entities*) referenced during the course of the logical transaction
- The size of the output element is proportional to the number of uniquely processed DETs composing the output side of the transaction The Functional Size (Function Point Index) is the weighted sum over all Logical Transactions, of the Input Data Element Types (Ni), the Data Entity Types Referenced (Ne), and the Output Data Element Types (No).

So the Function Point Index (FPI) for an application is as follows:

$$FPI = Wi \times SNi + We \times SNe + Wo \times SNo,$$

where *SN* means the sum over all Logical Transactions, and the industry average weights per Input Data Element Type (Input DET), Data Entity Type Reference (ER), and Output Data Element Type (Output DET) are, respectively, Wi = 0.58; We = 1.66; Wo = 0.26.

Measure Functional Size

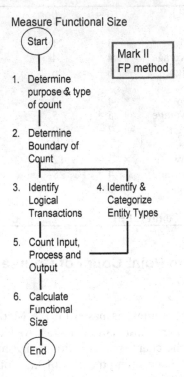

Fig. 18.5. Mark II steps for size measurement of the Course Registration System

Table 18.12 presents the Mark II results.

Table 18.12. Mark II FSM results

Transaction name	Event or query	No. of input DET	Entity types referred to	No. of ER	Response	No. of output DET	Mark II FP
Use case 1: Logon							
Logon	Query	2	User	1	Main Form/error	1	3.08
Use case 2: Maintain professor information							
Create	Event	5: DOB, name, SSN, status, dept.	Professor	1	Ok/error	2: error msg, Professor no.	5.08
Update	Event	5	Professor	1	Ok/error	2	5.08
Delete	Event	1	Professor	1	Ok/error	2	2.76
Implied query	Query	1	Professor	1	Professor information	5	3.54

(Continued)

Transaction name	Event or query	No. of input DET	Entity types referred to	No. of ER	Response	No. of output DET	Mark II FP
Use case 3: Select/Deselect courses to teach							
Select courses to teach (by professors)	Query	1	Course catalog, course offering	2	Course list	4: date, name, course time, already selected flag	4.94
Select courses to teach (by professors)	Event	4: course name, date, time, professor	Professor, Course catalog, course offering	3	Ok/error	1	7.56
Use case 4: Maintain student information							
Create	Event	5: name, DOB, SSN, status, dept.	Professor	1	Ok/error	2 (error msg, professor no.)	5.08
Update	Event	5	Professor	1	Ok/error	2	5.08
Delete	Event		Professor	1	Ok/error	2	2.76
Implied query?	Query	1	Professor	1	Professor information	5	3.54
Use case 5: Register for Courses							
Display available courses?	Query	1	Course, Course offering	2	Course offering information	3 name, date, time	4.68
Register for courses (by students)	Event	4: student, course name, date, time	Student, Course offering	2	Ok/error	2	6.16
Display schedule	Query	1	Student	1	Student schedule information	4 (Course no. (1–6), name, date, time)	3.28
Use case 6: Monitor for Course Full							
Courses available	Query	1: Trigger	Course offering	1	Course no., name, date, time, full message	5	3.54
Use case 7: Close Registration							
Close registration (by the registrar)	Event	3	Student, Course offering	2	Ok/error	8	7.14

Table 18.12. *(Cont.)*

Transaction name	Event or query	No. of input DET	Entity types referred to	No. of ER	Response	No. of output DET	Mark II FP
Use case 8: Submit grades							
View students and grades	Query	1	Student, Course offering	2	Student information	5 (Student, grade, course, date, time)	5.2
Submit grades (by professors)	Event	3: student, course, grade	Student, Course offering	2	Ok/error	2	5.58
Use case 9: View Report Card							
View report card	Query	2: Student, semester	Student	1	Report card info	3 Student, course grade	3.6
					Total MK II unadjusted FP		87.68

18.7 NESMA Count of Course Registration System

NESMA is a FSMM that is the most similar to the IFPUG method, but there are still several differences between them. The NESMA website offers the paper: FPA according to NESMA and IFPUG, the present situation (version 2.0, 8 June 2004) downloadable from www.nesma.nl. This paper outlines the remaining differences between NESMA and IFPUG. The following excerpt provides a summary:

"Practically the same guidelines" as IFPUG (4.2): NESMA and IFPUG both use the same terminology, albeit in a different language. The NESMA maintains a list of English words related to FPA. This can be downloaded from the NESMA site.

Both NESMA and IFPUG differentiate the same five types of user functions: ILGV (ILF), KGV (EIF), IF (EI), UF (EO), OF (EQ).

The rules for determining the type and complexity of a function are the same, with a few exceptions:

- External Inquiry vs. External Output
  multiple rows/occurrences within an output, -even without calculations- constitutes an EO for NESMA. External queries must have a fixed size of the output, e.g., number of records returned.
- Complexity of an External Inquiry
  the complexity is determined by evaluating the input side complexity (low, average, high) using the EI matrix; then evaluating the output side complexity (low, average, high) using the EO matrics; then the complexity of the query is the side which has the highest complexity (input or

output) and scoring it using the EQ values for low, average, or high. (IFPUG uses the sum of DETs and FTRs found on the input and output sides – eliminating duplicates – and evaluated the result against the EO/EQ matrix to determine the complexity of the EQ)

- Implicit Inquiry
  counted as part of the originating EI for NESMA. (IFPUG counts implied queries as standalone EQ)
- Code data (Code tables)
  are counted together as a single FPA-Table ILF or EIF (IFPUG does not count these at all)
- Physical media
- Queries with multiple selections (*and/or* situations)
  For further details, refer to the NESMA website (www.nesma.nl) for the full paper.

18.7.1 NESMA FP Count of Data Functions

Based on the paper outlined earlier and a review of the IFPUG count of the case study, the data entities and their functional size appear to be the same as for the IFPUG count. Table 8.13 shows this summary.

Note that ILGV is the same as an ILF (internal logical file) in IFPUG terminology, and KGV is the same as EIF (external interface file).

Table 18.13. Data functions for NESMA count of Course Registration System

Entity/data Group	Description	Type	DET	RET	Complexity	NESMA FP
Course	A standard series of lectures, etc. on a specific subject from the College Course Catalog	EIF (KGV)	<19	1	Low	5
Course offering (see note 1 immediately following Table 18.3)	A Course that is available for students to enroll during a particular Semester	EIF (KGV)	<19	1	Low	5
Professor	A person who may register to deliver a Course offering	ILF (ILGV)	<20	1	Low	7

(Continued)

Table 18.13. *(Cont.)*

	in the current Semester, for a Course that he is eligible to teach					
Student+ schedule item(s) + schedule item history (see note 2 in Sect. 18.3)	A person who can register to attend a Course offering	ILF (ILGV)	Based on assessment in 18.3, assumed <20	3 (Student, schedule item, schedule item history – different DET from Schedule item)	Low	7
User	Any person (Registrar, Professor, or Student) who is authorized to use the Course Registration System	FPA-Table EIF (KGV)	2 (user id, password)	1	Low	5
		ILF (ILGV)			*2 Low*	*14*
		EIF (KGV)			*3 Low*	*15*

18.7.2 NESMA FP Count of Transactional Functions

The following table outlines the NESMA count for the use cases (Table 18.14). Note that IF is an EI (external input) in IFPUG terminology, UF is an EO (external output), and OF is an EQ (external query).

Table 18.14. NESMA FSM transactional function type summary for Course Registration System Project

Description	Type	DET	FTR/ RET	Complexity	NESMA FP
1 Logon					
Logon (validate userid and password) with standard trigger and output	Not counted--				
2 Maintain Professor					
Registrar: add professor	EI (IF)	<16	1	Low	3

(Conintued)

Registrar: modify professor (includes save and inquiry DET display)	EI (IF)	<16	1	Low	3
Registrar: delete professor (includes confirming delete and inquiry DET display)	EI (IF)	<16	1	Low	3
3 Deselect/Select courses to teach					
Professor: Display course offerings available for this professor for this semester, plus those already selected	Part of EI (IF) - implied query not counted	0			
Professor: Select/de-select courses and save (update) course offerings. Note: conflicting pairs display is part of this function, not a standalone process	EI (IF)	5–15	3 assumed (course offering, professor, course)	High	6
4 Maintain student information					
Registrar: add student	EI (IF)	<15	1	Low	3
Registrar: update student (includes inquiry display DET)	EI (IF)	<15	1	Low	3
Registrar: delete student (includes inquiry display DET)	EI (IF)	<15	1	Low	3
5 Maintain schedule					
Student: Display available course offerings (different logic from professor display of course offerings)	EO (UF) due to multiple record output	· 6–19	2 (course offering, course, student for courses already selected)	Average	5
Student: Maintain schedule (4 courses + 2 alternates) if prerequisites are met) all update student records (includes inquiry DETs)	EI (IF)	5–15	3 assumed (course offering, student, course w/pre-requisite info)	High	6
Student: Save schedule in progress → not considered a standalone elementary process					

(Conintued)

Table 18.14. *(Cont.)*

6 Monitor course <10 attendees					
System sets business rule for max. attendees per course offering = 10. (Checks course offerings to verify level). No explicit trigger (time or anything else) and no data crosses boundary (either in or out) to any user	N/A				
7 Close course					
Registrar: Close Registration (includes cancelation and student schedule update) → primary purpose: send update to other system to update (close) course offering	EO (UF) Multiple line output	6–19	3 assumed (student, course offering, course)	Average	5
System: Send billing system notice of courses closed but not canceled (with student info for billing)	EQ (UF) Multiple line output	6–19	2 assumed (course offering, student)	Average	5
System: Notify all students by mail of any changes to their schedule	EQ (UF) Multiple line output	6-19	2 assumed (course offering, student)	Average	5
8 Maintain grades					
Professor: Enter/update student grades (one process that updates record that already exists) includes querying of courses and students	EI (IF)	16+	2 assumed (student, course offering)	High	6
9 View report card					
Student: View Report Card: for previous semester	EO (UF) Multiple line output	6–19	2 assumed (Course offering, Student)	Avg	5

Table 18.15 shows the result of the unadjusted NESMA FP count for the Course Registration System.

18.8 Comparison of Results of FSM Methods

Table 18.16 shows the results of the various ISO-conformant FSM Methods to the Course Registration System's functional user requirements. All results are in unadjusted units of measure.

Table 18.15. NESMA FSM count of Course Registration System

Function Type	Functional Complexity		Complexity Totals		NESMA Function Type Totals (unadjusted NESMA FP)
ILF	2	Low	× 7 =	14	
	0	Average	× 10 =	0	
	0	High	× 15 =	0	
					14
EIF	3	Low	× 5 =	15	
	0	Average	× 7 =	0	
	0	High	× 10 =	0	
					15
EI	6	Low	× 3 =	18	
		Average	× 4 =	0	
	3	High	× 6 =	18	
					36
EO	0	Low	× 4 =	0	
	2	Average	× 5 =	10	
	0	High	× 7 =	0	
					10
EQ	0	Low	× 3 =	0	
	3	Average	× 4 =	12	
	0	High	× 6 =	0	
					12
NESMA Function Point Count (NESMA FP)					87

Table 18.16. Summary of FSM sizes of the Course Registration System using the 5 ISO/IEC-conformant FSMMs

Use Case No.	FSM → Data entity	COSMIC Cfp	FiSMA Ffp	IFPUG uFP	Mark II FP unadjusted	NESMA FP
1	Internal entity: professor	0	3.5	7	0	7
2	Internal entity: student	0	4.5	7	0	7
3	Internal entity: user	0	2.5	7	0	7
4	External entity: course catalog	0	Counted w/messages	5	0	5
5	External entity: course offering	0	Counted w/messages	5	0	5

(Continued)

Table 18.16. *(Cont.)*

Use Case No.	FSM → Use case	COSMIC Cfp	FiSMA Ffp	IFPUG uFP	Mark II FP unadjusted	NESMA uFP
1	Logon	3	6.2	3	3.08	0
2	Maintain professor	17	13.7	12	16.46	9
3	Deselect/ select courses to teach	9	9.3[1]	8	12.5	6
4	Maintain student information	16	13.7	15	16.46	9
5	Maintain schedule	35	7.4[2]	17	18.62	11
6	Monitor course < 10 attendees	0	1.7	0	3.54	0
7	Close course	9	18.4[2]	13	7.14	13
8	Maintain grades	12	7.3[2]	10	10.78	6
9	View report card	6	2.6	4	3.6	4
	Total count (units specific to FSMM)		88 Ffp	105 uFP	87 Mk II FP unadj.	87 NESMA FP

FiSMA Notes:

1. Select/deselect courses to teach includes message out to request course list from Course Catalog system, and message in containing the retrieved data.
2. The size of use case does not include the messages to/from Course Catalog system because they are duplicated from use case 3 (Select/deselect courses to teach).

19 Functional Size Measurement: Additional Case Studies

This chapter provides three additional examples of Functional Size Measurement applied to functional user requirements COSMIC (one case study: Valve Control System); and IFPUG (two case studies: Function Point Calculator, Training Administration Application).

19.1 COSMIC Case Study

The following case study (the real-time *Valve Control System*) is an excerpt (*only requirements and count result, no remarks*) of one of the publicly available COSMIC Case Studies. For further information visit http://www. gelog.etsmtl.ca/cosmic-ffp/index.html.

19.1.1 Valve Control System

The Valve Control System used in this case study corresponds to the set of Reference User Requirements (RUR) from annex B.9 of the ISO technical report: ISO/IEC TR 14143-4.

19.1.2 Measurement Viewpoint, Purpose, and Scope

For the purposes of the case study, the following is given.

Measurement viewpoint:

The measurement viewpoint in this case study is that of the software developer who is interested in quantifying the functionality of the software he has to develop.

Measurement purpose:

The measurement purpose is to measure all of the Functional User Requirements (FUR) of the software requirements as documented in the set of Reference User Requirements (RUR) and as selected for this case study using the COSMIC functional sizing method. FUR are a subset of the RUR and pertain only to *what* the application software will do.

Measurement scope:

The measurement scope is all of the Functional User Requirements within the set RUR B.9 – and only these. The measurement scope is therefore a subset of the reference user requirements documented in this ISO/IEC case study, that is, only those related to software and not those related to the hardware or technology.

19.1.3 Requirements

Context:

The requirements given here describe what functions are included in the behavior of the control valve that controls a mechanical device to change gears on an automatic transmission installed in a land vehicle.

The valve can be open or closed: it is open by default and closed to engage the gear change mechanism. The process controls the amount of time the valve is closed during an operating cycle of several thousand microseconds. A clock supplying the operating cycle reference triggers the process.

INPUT – The process uses the following as input:

- A sensor signal (Gc) indicating whether gear change is in progress (value 1) or not (value 0)
- A sensor signal (Su) indicating, during gear change, whether shifting to upper gear (value 1) or lower gear (value 0)
- A sensor signal (Idl) indicating whether the transmission is under stress (value 0) or idling (value 1)
- A binary flag *A* whose value is stored in the processor ROM memory or
- A binary flag *B* whose value is stored in the processor ROM memory
- Binary flags *A* and *B* describe some general configuration characteristics of the automatic transmission.

OUTPUT – The process produces the following as output:

Time (*T*), during one operating cycle, during which the control valve must be closed.

Requirements:

PART A – Determine general operating condition
Determine whether operating slowly or quickly from the closed state of the hydraulic valve.

IF (Gc = 1
    AND Idl = 1
    AND A = 0
    AND B = 0)
THEN, operating under normal condition, perform PART B
IF (Gc = 1
    AND Idl = 0
    AND Su = 1
    AND A = 0
    AND B = 0)
THEN, operating during gear change, perform PART C.

PART B – Control to open hydraulic valve slowly from its closed state

Reset T to the smaller value of either INIT or the value of T during the last process cycle, where INIT is a constant stored in the computer ROM memory,

$$\text{Compute the new value of } T: T = T - (\text{Cst\_X} \times \text{ET}),$$

where Cst_X is a constant stored in the processor ROM memory and ET is the elapsed time since an action that opens the hydraulic valve slowly from its closed state has been activated.

Condition for completion:

If the following conditions are met then valve control is passed to another process:

T is smaller or equal to LT
or
Slp is greater or equal to Uslp,

where LT is a lower threshold of time and Uslp is an upper threshold of the amount of slip stored in the processor ROM memory. Slp is the current amount of slip, which denotes the difference of number of revolutions between the engine output shaft and the power train shaft. The value is computed and updated according to the following formula and stored in the processor RAM memory.

$$\text{Slp} = |E_{\text{rev}} - \text{PS}_{\text{rev}}|,$$

where E_{rev} is the engine's output shaft revolutions and PS_{rev} is the power train shaft revolutions. Both variables' values are supplied by concurrent processes using input from separate sensors and placing the calculated result in the processor RAM memory.

PART C – Control to open the hydraulic valve quickly from its closed state

Reset T to the smaller value of either INITS(Vs) or the value of T during the last processing cycle, where INITS is a table of initial values stored in the processor ROM memory and Vs is the vehicle speed, which is computed and updated by another process and stored in the computer RAM memory.

Compute the new value of T: $T = T - (INCR(Vs)) \times ET$,

where INCR is a table of increments, which depend on the speed of the vehicle stored in the processor ROM memory, and ET is the elapsed time since an action to close the hydraulic valve quickly from its closed state has been activated.

Condition for completion: if the following conditions are met then valve control is passed to another process.

T is smaller or equal to LT where LT is a lower time threshold stored in the processor ROM memory.

Note: From a functional size measurement perspective, the data attributes and data structures preserved in the processor ROM and RAM memory are considered to reside within the software boundary.

19.1.4 COSMIC Measurement Procedure

Identification of layers

There is a single software layer for this set of requirements.

Identification of users
The users that interact with this software are the following mechanical devices:
   <L1>Send information to the software:
        <sublist>Clock
        <sublist>Sensors: GC, Su, and IDL
   <L1>Receives information from the software:
        <sublist>A control valve

From the requirements, as written, there are no human users, nor are there other software applications interacting with this software.

Boundary
Based on the written requirements, we can identify the software boundary as shown in Fig. 19.1. The data groups are listed in Table 19.1.

Identification of triggering events:
From the documented requirements, a single triggering event is identified:
A Clock supplying the operating cycle reference, which triggers the process.

Identification of data groups:
From the documented requirements, the following data groups are identified:

Note 1: Much data needed by the process must be obtained from ROM. We assume that all these data are attributes of one Object of interest, namely the *fixed parameter set for the valve control process*; this parameter set may be unique to this valve-type and even to this automatic transmission, perhaps even to this vehicle. This assumption is justified as follows.

Physically, it is likely that the data needed for any one cycle is obtained at one time from the ROM and not as a succession of Reads.

The COSMIC *deduplication* rule assumes that all data needed for any one Object of interest is obtained in only one data movement.

N.B. This assumption may be incorrect. The ROM(s) may store other data for other functional processes. If we had this wider knowledge, we might find that the data is organized into groups for more than one Object of interest. But we do not have this wider knowledge and so we make this simple assumption (based on the RUR as documented).

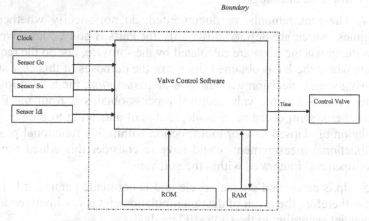

Fig. 19.1. Valve control (case study) software boundary

Table 19.1. Valve control (case study) data groups

Data sources/ destinations	Objects of interest	Data groups	Data attributes
Clock	Op. cycle trigger event	Clock signal	Clock signal
Sensors	Gear-change status	Gc	Gc
	Shift direction	Su	Su
	Stress/idle status	Idl	Idl
ROM	Valve-type X	Valve-type X's fixed parameter set for the valve control process	Flag A or Flag B, INIT, Cst_X, LT, Uslp, INITS 1, 2, 3, etc., INCR 1, 2, 3, etc.
RAM	Engine	E_{rev}	E_{rev}
	Power train	PS_{rev}	PS_{rev}
	Vehicle	Vs	Vs
	Period since last action	ET	ET
Control valve	Period valve-to-be-closed	T	T
Total of data groups		10	

Note 2: It might be argued that by definition a ROM, whose contents cannot be maintained by software, should be regarded as a User of the software being measured, and hence it should be shown as outside the software Boundary, rather than as memory within the Boundary.

We have adopted the view that the ROM is within the Boundary, as its contents must have been written by some other process during the ROM manufacture, perhaps involving software. Hence, the functional process being measured obtains the data it needs from the ROM by a Read data movement.

If the alternative view had been adopted that the ROM is a User, then the data required by the functional process being measured would be obtained by an Entry, rather than by a Read. The size of the functional process in Cfp given later would be unchanged.

Note 4: The requirements, as documented, do not specify whether the Elapsed times (which are defined differently for Parts B and C) are given by the hardware, or whether they are calculated by the software, nor do the requirements state where the ET is obtained from. For the purposes of this case study, the following system decision was taken as an *assumption*: the ET is provided by another process and the valve control process obtains it from the RAM. Should another system decision be made, that is of allocating to the hardware the calculation of elapsed time or to a function within this functional process, another functional measurement would have to consider this added function to be developed and integrated within the software.

Note 5: Slp is calculated on each cycle and is not made persistent between cycles. It is therefore the result of data manipulation and is not involved in any data movement according to the COSMIC method.

Identification of functional processes:

From the documented requirements with a single triggering event, there is one *candidate* functional process, which is as follows:

The control of time during the operating cycle of the control valve.

The measurement procedure must assess whether a candidate functional process is a COSMIC one or not.

Each candidate process must satisfy the following questions in order to be validated as a COSMIC functional process:

- Does it operate on a unique cohesive and independently executable set of data movements performing a set of FURs?
- Is it triggered by an event (triggering event)?
- Does the triggering event occur outside the boundary of the software?
- Does the process execute all that is required to be done in response to the triggering event?

These questions are investigated in Table 19.2: *Time-based control of the valve.*

The time-based control of the valve process is therefore a COSMIC functional process.

Table 19.2. Valve control (case study): time-based control.

Question	Answer	Comments
Does it operate on a unique cohesive and independently executable set of data movements performing a set of FURs?	Yes	
Is it triggered by an event?	Yes	Clock signal event
Does the triggering event occur outside the boundary of the software?	Yes	The clock is outside of the software – see Fig. 19.1
Does the process execute all that is required to be done in response to the triggering event?	Yes	According to the given requirements

Identify data movements:

For the single functional process in the previous steps, all data movements of a data group must be identified.

In this case study, the Message Sequence Diagram (Fig. 19.2) has been prepared to facilitate the identification of the data movements, and to ensure that all data movements have been identified.

Message sequence diagram

List of data movements:

The detailed list of the data movements identified is presented in Table 19.3.

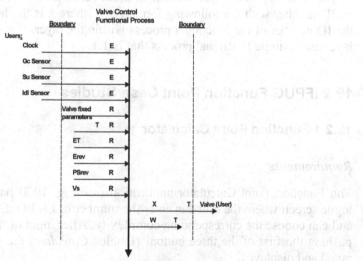

Fig. 19.2. Valve control (case study) message sequence diagram.

Table 19.3. Valve control (case study) data movements.

Functional process name	Triggering event	Data movements identification	Data group	Data movement type	Cfp
Time-based control of the valve	Clock cycle signal	Receive clock cycle signal	Clock	E	1
		Receive signal of Gc Sensor	Gc	E	1
		Receive signal of Su gear change	Su	E	1
		Receive signal of Idl Sensor	Idl	E	1
		Read valve fixed parameters	Valve fixed parameters	R	1
		Read of T from RAM	T	R	1
		Read ET from RAM	ET	R	1
		Read Erev from RAM	E_{rev}	R	1
		Read PSrev from RAM	PS_{rev}	R	1
		Read Vs from RAM	Vs	R	1
		Send T to the control valve	T	X	1
		Write T to RAM	T	W	1
Total functional size in Cfp				ΣCfp	12

The following labeling convention is used: the functional process is assigned an ID number with the following format: x.y where x is the layer ID and y is the ID number of the functional process within the layer. Here, this is a single layer and a single functional process that is 1.1.

19.2 IFPUG Function Point Case Studies

19.2.1 Function Point Calculator

Requirements

The Function Point Calculator application (see Fig. 19.3) has only one dialogue screen where the user can enter the number of EI, EO, EQ, ILF, and EIF and can choose the corresponding complexity. After input of the 14 GSCs and pushing the first of the three buttons (labeled *Calculate*) the results are computed and displayed.

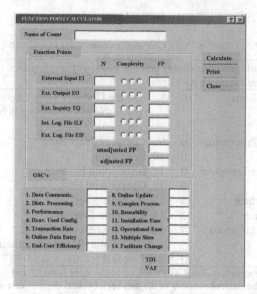

Fig. 19.3. Function Point Calculator (case study) requirements

Pushing the second button (labeled *Print*) delivers a printout of the actual count including the date of calculations, a descriptive text for EI (External Input), EO (External Output), EQ (External Query), ILF (Internal Logical File), EIF (External Interface File) together with a count (from internal memory) of how many counts have been done to date, and message text at the bottom stating that a FP count is the functional size of an application, and other input parameters are necessary to produce reliable effort estimates. The entered data is not stored, nor is there any error handling.

The third button (labeled *Close*) is to exit the calculator.

The Function Point Calculator (case study) count details are displayed in Tables 19.4 and 19.5.

Results According to IFPUG

Table 19.4. Function Point Calculator (case study) result.

Description	Type	DET	FTR/RET	Complexity	N	Unadjusted FPs
Calculations	EO	19	0	Low	1	4
Print output	EO	20+	0	Average	1	5
Sum of unadjusted FPs						9
VAF						0.72
Adjusted FPs						6 adjusted FPs

Notes: Calculation output display: 19 DET: Name, #ILF, ILF FP, #EIF, EIF FP, #EI, EI FP, #EO, EO FP, # EQ, EQ FP total unadjusted, total adjusted, GSC#, value (this is a multiple occurring group with 14 occurrences), TDI, VAF, command key (calculate), error/confirmation message. In addition, the printed output includes the count, message, and date of calculations

The VAF and GSCs are shown in Table 19.5.

Table 19.5. Function Point Calculator (case study) GSCs and VAF.

Function Point Calculator (case study) general system characteristics (GSCs) and Value adjustment factor (VAF)			
1. Data Communications	0	8. Online Update (Note: There are NO ILFs; therefore, nothing is being updated)	0
2. Distributed Data Processing	0	9. Complex Processing	0
3. Performance	0	10. Reusability	0
4. Heavily Used Configuration	0	11. Installation Ease	0
5. Transaction Rate	0	12. Operational Ease	0
6. Online User Interface	5	13. Multiple Sites	0
7. End-User Efficiency	2	14 Facilitate Change	0
Subtotal degrees of influence	7	Subtotal degrees of influence	0
		Total degrees of influence (TDI)	7

$$VAF = 0.65 + (TDI \times 0.01) = 0.65 + (7 \times 0.01) = 0.72$$

Note: Adjusted FPs are always rounded. For this case study, there is no EI and no ILF, since data are not stored. (Note that the internal memory of the number of counts done to date is not included as an ILF because it is stored in flash memory and is not populated through an elementary process of the application.)

19.2.2 Training Administration Application

Source: Example study adapted and translated from H. Balzert, Lehrbuch der Softwaretechnik (originally in German).

Requirements

- *Goals*: The organization Teachware Inc. shall get support from the product for administration of their training courses.

- *Application areas*: The product is used for customer and course administration. Several inquiries should be answered by the users who are the staff of Teachware Inc.

Product data:

LD10   Relevant data about the customers are to be stored.

LD20   If a customer belongs to an organization then relevant data about the organization must also be stored.

LD30   Relevant data about courses, course types, and trainers are to be stored.

LD40   If a customer books a course then the according booking data are to be stored.

Product functions:

LF10   Create, change, and delete of customers (may or may not include organization). Customers who are currently booked for a course cannot be deleted (reference checking required).

LF20   Report summary information for the customer: booking confirmation summary, withdrawal summary information trend report, customer registration history.

LF30   Create, change, and delete of courses and course types.

LF40   Create, change, and delete of trainers, as well as maintaining relationship with courses and course types.

LF50   Create, change, and delete of bookings.

LF60   Invoice production.

LF70   Summary Reports production: participants, turnover, participants' certificates (each of which is a separate user requirement).

Product restrictions:

IL10   Function L10 must not need more than 5-s response time. All other response times must be less than 0.9 s.

IL20   Requirements for processor performance are constrained.

For quality restrictions: see Table 19.6.

Table 19.6. Training Administration (case study) quality restrictions.

Product quality	Very good	Good	Average	Mediocre	Irrelevant
Functionality		X			
Reusability				X (GSC no. 10 = 1)	
User interface	X (GSC no. 7 = 3)				
Installation ease				X (GSC no. 12 = 1)	
Facilitate change				X (GSC no. 14 = 1)	

For result see Table 19.7.

Table 19.7. Training Administration (case study) result using IFPUG FSM

Description	Type	DET	FTR/RET	Complexity	Number of functions	Unadjusted FPs
LD10 – customer data (including organization)	ILF	20–50	2	Average	1	10
LD20 – no unique ILF; these data are the second RET of LD10	–	–	–	–	–	–
LD30 – 3 logical files (course, course type – not a code table, trainer)	ILF	<50	1	Low	3	21
LD40 – booking data (independent entity used for invoicing and scheduling)	ILF	<50	1	Low	1	7
LF10 – create	EI	>15	1	Average	1	4
LF10 – change (with implicit browse display)	EI	>15	1	Average	1	4
	EQ	<20	1	Low	1	3
LF10 – delete	EI	<5	2	Low	1	3
LF 20 – 4 different EO (all with calculations), suggest average	EO	–	–	Average	4	20
LF30 – like LF10: Add, change course (5–15,2), query course (<20,1), delete course (<15,1); add, change course type (5–15,2), query course type (<20,1), delete course type (<15,1)	EI	5–15	2	Average	4	16
	EQ	<20	1	Low	2	6
	EI	<15	1	Low	2	6
LF40 – add, change trainer (5–15,2), query trainer (<20,1), delete trainer (<15,1), link/unlink trainer and course (5–15,2), link/unlink trainer and course type (5–15,2), query trainer with course and type relationships (6–19,3)	EI	5–15	2	Average	4	16
	EQ	<20	1	Low	1	3
	EI	<15	1	Low	1	3
	EQ	6–19	3	Average	1	4
LF50 – relate customer and course: create, view, delete (*low*)	EI	<16	3	High	2	12
	EQ	<19	1	Low	1	3
	EI	<16	1	Low	1	3
LF60 – invoice (data	EO	15	3	Average	1	5

(Continued)

from customer, booking
and course)

LF 70 – like LF60	EO	15	3	Average	3	15
				Sum unadjusted FP		164 unadjusted FP
				VAF (see later)		0.91
				Adjusted FP		149 adjusted FP

Training Administration (case study) general system characteristics (GSCs)
and value adjustment factor (VAF)

1. Data communications	4	8. Online update (major ILF)	3
2. Distributed data processing	0	9. Complex processing	0
3. Performance (constrained)	4	10. Reusability (Table 19.6)	1
4. Heavily used configuration	0	11. Installation ease (Table 19.6)	1
5. Transaction rate (high stated)	4	12. Operational ease	0
6. Online data entry (all online)	5	13. Multiple sites	0
7. End-user efficiency	3	14. Facilitate change (Table 19.6)	1
Subtotal degrees of influence	20	Subtotal degrees of influence	6
		Total degrees of influence (TDI)	26

$$VAF = 0.65 + (TDI \times 0.01) = 0.65 + (26 \times 0.01) = 0.91$$

20 Tools for Estimation

A science is as mature as its measurement tools. (Louis Pasteur)

A method without tool support has little chance for survival, and will encounter extra resistance for widespread use. The investment in the right tool suited for estimation for your organization can bring benefit for the organization without any doubt, even if the benefit cannot be measured exactly. But, first a warning:

"A fool with a tool is still a fool!"

This proverb teaches us that information and training in estimation are a necessary prerequisite for the success of a metrics initiative. *The first lesson to be imparted in training for the project leaders is that the tool does not do their job of estimation.* The same premise holds true with estimation tools as it is with project management tools: estimating tools must be "fed" with good estimating parameters in order to generate realistic estimates; project management tools do not replace the planning process (which has to be done in the head of a project leader) – it only supports the outcome once the planning parameters have been entered. In the same manner as school children must learn their times tables before they can make effective use of a calculator (especially to be able to detect a wrong answer), project leaders must understand the concepts of software estimation before using a tool for its support.

The next important lesson concerns the honesty of estimation, which can be stated as the question to the trainer: "How can I administer three separate estimates: one for the steering committee, one for my boss, and for my best guess (correct) one?". This is a matter of estimation culture in an organization, but this lesson must be learned if the maturity levels of estimating are to be taken seriously. Here the remarks about estimation and bargaining apply as further outlined in the chapter "The Estimation Challenges."

Tools used without the necessary expertise or knowledge cannot deliver solid results. It is especially critical when using estimation tools that the customizing and the estimation parameters be properly adjusted. This is too arduous a task if done with the support of a metrics specialist who knows the tool in question very well. And the process of calibration can be done better if historical data are available from the beginning to boost the precision of estimates for your particular environment.

One must also keep in mind that estimation has to do with uncertainty per se. *Estimation results involving significant digits after the decimal point deludes one into believing in a nonexistent accuracy and lulls even the most experienced professional into deceptive safety.* The results of any tool is only ever as good as the information provided as input. It is a good and prudent practice to reinforce estimates done with tools by performing estimates using different methods in order to compare and improve the estimation process.

In the case of deviation between estimates, a number of learning can emerge about the object of estimation, the evaluation of the estimation parameters, the prerequisites of the estimation, the estimation environment, and the assumptions made. *This can provide valuable hints for project risk assessment, too.* The importance of performing multiple estimates cannot be overemphasized, especially when one considers the consequences of an unrealistically low estimate in a fixed-price bid, which could render a project team insolvent with only one project! Applying a variety of models to the object of estimation is similar to getting multiple expert opinions on an important decision – it is better to make an informed decision based on a variety of perspectives than on a single one, especially if the one happens to be based on assumptions that turn out to be wrong.

The experiences of the German author are based on the personal, corporate experience at a large international insurance corporation using a specific set of software tools. Nevertheless, this experience can easily be transferred to the use of any other appropriate estimation tool that meets your organizational needs. Figure 20.1 demonstrates the process of tool-based estimation.

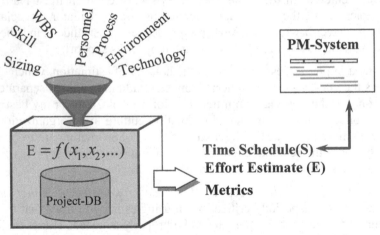

Source: Marketing materials for SPR's KnowledgePLAN™

Fig. 20.1. Tool-based effort estimation

20.1 The Benefits of Estimation Tools

Tools for estimation can deliver many benefits: they can help the project leader to do work more efficiently, and as well, can offer strategic benefits to the organization:

- Earlier documentation about the parameters used in the estimation (tool-based)
- Transparency and consistency of input parameters
- Standardization (and removal of subjectivity)
- Management of complexity.

This fosters the common use of estimation methods – a major key success factor for their acceptance. Furthermore, estimation tools assist in project oversight by organizing the many parameters for estimation.

Estimation tools provide operational benefits for the project leader by supporting the planning in terms of the following:

- Software size to be delivered
- Development life cycle (tasks, phases)
- Project complexity (hierarchy, classification, Work Breakdown Structure)
- Resource management
- Time schedules and milestones
- Simulation of alternatives.

Some of the tools have interfaces to project management tools (e.g., KnowledgePLAN interfaces with MS Project, and Experience® Pro provides export files). Thus estimation tools can help to reduce planning time and to improve planning results including the following:

- Reduced time for planning and time to market
- Improved results from planning
- Improved user satisfaction through automation
- Reduced maintenance effort.

Thus the estimation tools help the project leader to do his estimations in an efficient and professional way and support the acceptance of estimation methods.

The major benefits (time saving, quality, and efficiency improvement) are harvested on a project by project basis over time. Tools foster additional positive side effects, including an improvement of acceptance and transparency, standardization, and establishing an estimation culture.

To gain the maximum benefits, one must be trained in the use of and strictly adhere to the method on which the tool is based. To make the tool indispensable, the organization must also supplement the tool dataset with enough historical data (especially about project sizes and effort) from actual, completed projects.

20.2 Effort Estimation Tools

There are many software tools available for the estimation of project work effort and out of the top 60 commercial tools, more than half of these are Function Point based. Since 1992, nearly every month a new software estimation tool has appeared on the market. By 2000, there were 50 tools in the USA and 25 available in Europe. Many of these tools are "black boxes," with their mode of estimation kept hidden as intellectual property of the vendor. Sometimes, the tool supports a special estimation method, and we present a few examples here especially to show some experiences made with them.

The Measurement Laboratory of the University of Magdeburg in Germany (http://ivs.cs.uni-magdeburg.de/sw-eng/agruppe/forschung) presents in its homepage already more than 30 CAME-tools (CAME: Computer Assisted Software Measurement and Evaluation), together with an accompanying book and a tool overview categorized by application area.

Another resource for estimating tools can be found at the Data & Analysis Center for Software (DACS): http://www.dacs.dtic.mil. From this URL one has to proceed to cost estimation http://www.dacs.dtic.mil/databases/url/key. hts?keycode=4 and further on to cost estimating software tools: http://www. dacs.dtic.mil/databases/url/key.hts?keycode =4:152&islowerlevel=1.

Some smaller tools, mostly for cost estimation, are offered either for free (download from the internet) or on a commercial basis and include tools such as COSTAR (based on COCOMO II), CostXpert, SoftCalc, Softest, and REVIC. See also the corresponding list with URLs of tools in the last paragraph of this chapter. While the following list is incomplete, we provide it to give an impression of some known tools with estimation features:

- Agile COCOMO II 2.0 (USA) – http://sunset.usc.edu/cse/pub/research/ AgileCOCOMO/AgileCOCOMOII/Main.html;
- AMI tool (Application of Metrics in Industry, GQM and CMMI, France)
- Artemis Views (project management tool with estimation component)
- Bachmann (tool for automatic Function Point counting based on requirements)
- CA Clarity™ (formerly known as ABT Project Workbench)
- Checkpoint for Windows (SPR), predecessor of KnowledgePLAN, Experience data from about 7,000 projects, Business area related database available, for example, telecommunication, insurances, etc. Note that we include Checkpoint for windows in this book because it was the toolset used by the International Insurance Corporation, where measurement and estimation was successfully implemented. While Checkpoint is no longer commercially available (replaced by KnowledgePLAN(TM)), it is the concepts that we wish to emphasize.

- COMET (CORBA Measurement Tool, University of Magdeburg, Germany)
- COSAM (Customer Satisfaction Measurement, University of Magdeburg, Germany)
- COSMOS (Cost Management with Software Metrics of Specification Tools, The Netherlands)
- COSTAR (by Softstar Systems Inc., USA), based on COCOMO II and experience data from about 8,000 projects
- DATRIX (code measurement for C, C++, Canada)
- DOCTOR HTML (Evaluation of Websites, USA)
- DOORS (IBM/Rational) and Rational ROSE
- ESTIMACS, Planmacs, Superproject (Computer Associates)
- Experience® Pro (4SUM Partners) – for estimating and scope management of software and systems projects based on functional size measurement (supports sizing in FiSMA FP, IFPUG FP, Mark II FP, and COSMIC Cfp, and backfiring)
- Function Point Modeler (Germany)
- Function Point Workbench (Charismatek) – for administration of Function Point counts (no estimation tool) Administration of organization wide FP database, Interface to Checkpoint for Windows (CKWIN) and Knowledge PLAN
- LDRA Testbed (United Kingdom)
- LOGISCOPE (Verilog, France)
- Measurement Aglets (University of Magdeburg, Germany)
- METKIT (Metrics Tool Kit, United Kingdom)
- Metrics One (Rational, USA)
- MJAVA (incl. Chidamber/Kemerer-metrics, University of Magdeburg, Germany)
- MOOD (Metrics for OOD, Portugal)
- PRICE S (Price Systems)
- Project Bridge and Project Management Workbench (Hoskyns)
- QUALMS (Quality Analysis and Measurement Tool, United Kingdom)
- R2ESTIMATOR™ (by r2estimating, USA)
- RMS (Reading Measuring System, Germany)
- SCOPE (function point repository tool by Total Metrics, Australia)
- SLIM, (Quantitative Software Management) and Estimate Express (the scaled down SLIM), SLIM Metrics and SLIM Control
- SLIM Palm Tool (SLIM for the Palm handheld Computer, University of Magdeburg, Germany)
- SmallCritic (Smalltalk Measurement and Evaluation, Germany)
- Smalltalk Measure (University of Magdeburg, Germany)
- S.M.A.R.T. Predictor (DDB Software Inc.)
- SoftCalc (Harry Sneed, Case Consult, Germany)

- SOFT-ORG (Germany)
- STW-METRIC (Software Test Workbench, USA)
- Synquest (Bootstrap, Switzerland)
- SystemStar (by Softstar Systems) based on the COSYSMO model
- Understand for C++ (SciTools)
- ZD-MIS (Zuse Drabe Measurement Information System, Germany).

20.3 The Use of Estimation Tools

An international organization uses, for example, the tools shown in Fig. 20.2 in an integrated project management environment from size measurement via estimation and project management until effort management and controlling.

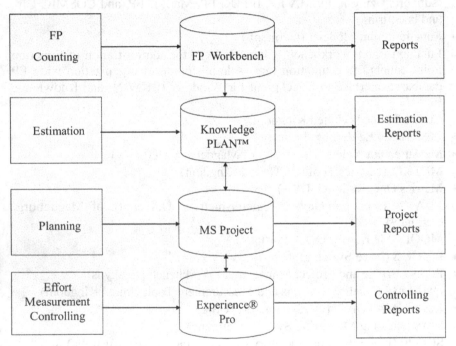

Fig. 20.2. Example of an integrated tool environment

Capers Jones published following information about the functional size of tool software (IFPUG book *IT Measurement – Practical Advice from the Experts*):

- Software development teams need tools with a total size of about 50,000 Function Points
- Project leaders need tools with more than 30,000 Function Points
- Quality assurance teams with tool support of a size of more than 10,000 Function Points delivered better quality than team with smaller sized tools
- Project leaders with tool support in excess of 25,000 Function Points estimate, plan, and control their projects better than those with less tool support
- Artemis Views and KnowledgePLAN, for example, have each a functional size of about 3,500 Function Points.

20.3.1 A Survey About the Usage of Productivity Measurement Tools

An international insurance company in Germany performed a survey about the experiences of productivity measurement tools or databases and got following feedback from 17 organizations from all continents, except Africa:

- Eleven organizations use experience databases, 6 do not
- Three of the 11 use MS Access, one uses MS Excel, and two others used their own development or historical data collection
- Three did not deliver an answer to this question
- The following data were reported to be collected in the databases:
    - Metrics of projects
    - Project start date and end date
    - Project duration in months
    - Actual measured effort
    - Function Points
    - Information about projects
    - Project leader and team
    - Type of project
    - Target environment
    - Programming language
    - Complexity of the application system
    - Team experience
    - Tool set.

20.3.2 The Process of Estimating with Tool Support

Generally the usage of estimation tools follows a process similar to the following:

1. Measurement of software size (to be developed or enhanced)
2. Selection of project tasks (Work Breakdown Structure, WBS)
3. Estimation of effort
4. Planning of resources
5. Cost estimation
6. Planning of milestones.

The estimation tools use two strategies to accomplish this:

- Microestimation (bottom up)
- Macroestimation (top down).

Micro estimation starts from the project activities and aggregates all partial estimations to a total. Hence this kind of estimation is more complex than macroestimation. The advantage is that estimation errors are typically restricted to (contained within) the affected task. Since estimates can comprise any detail of projects the microestimation is the more precise of the two approaches.

Macroestimation aims at the estimation of whole projects. After estimation of effort and duration the decomposition to the project phases is done. Macroestimation can be done more easily but has the disadvantage that estimation errors can affect several (up to all) phases. To summarize: *macroestimation is well suited for quick and early estimations.*

Estimation tools use, according to Capers Jones (How Software Estimation Tools work), three fundamental relations:

1. *Assignment scope:* This is the size of work for which a person is responsible
2. *Production rate:* This is the size of work that a person can finish in a certain time
3. *Duration:* This is the effort for a task divided by the number of persons available to do it.

These three relations are normally used in estimation tools in the following order:

1. Size divided by assignment scope delivers the number of required persons (resources).
2. Size divided by production rate delivers the effort.
3. Effort divided by the number of persons delivers the duration.

These equations appear to be relatively simple, but can be complicated to handle in practice since assignment scope and production rate are often not known precisely enough to estimate acceptable results. The benefit of an estimation tool thus depends on how flexible it is with respect to the input of different estimation parameters.

Simulations with an estimation tool deliver the advantage of being able to calculate the influence of single estimation parameters (productivity metrics, quality metrics, duration, effort) regarding different goals. Thus the critical success factors of a project can be determined quickly and easily. The expert system KnowledgePLAN from SPR, for example, delivers a *sensitivity analysis* – a "hit list" of 16 criteria, which are candidates for improvement measures. The experience of the German author is that project leaders generally don't use their tools for simulations thus giving away chances for risk prevention and project success.

Interesting to read is a comparison of estimation tools published from C.F. Kemerer, 1993, at the Massachusetts Institute of Technology (MT). In this comparison, ESTIMACS (Function Point based) delivered an average error of 85%, COCOMO (SLOC based) of 601%, and SLIM (SLOC based) of 701% in estimations early in the software life cycle. In an insurance company in Philadelphia, estimations with KnowledgePLAN and S.M.A.R.T. Predictor were compared and showed a variance of less than 7% regarding the estimated costs and effort. Both estimates were also close to the actual values at project postmortem.

The organizations Bachmann and Texas Instruments developed tools several years ago, which they stated were capable of automatic counting of Function Points from requirements artifacts. Such tools are seen critically since it cannot be guaranteed that the counts are performed from user view. Also IFPUG has to-date not certified any software capable of performing Function Point counts according to the CPM (Counting Practices Manual). Capers Jones will be releasing a tool in the coming months which may provide functionality of this type.

There are tools capable to check the code and deriving Function Point "counts" from it. Such tools clearly follow a technical view and not the user view demanded for the Function Point method. When the code is already available, preferably SLOC should be counted as the quick and easy measure of software size – this would then make more sense!

20.4 Checkpoint for Windows (CKWIN)

Note: this section on CKWIN is based on the German author's experience at the international insurance corporation where he used the tool extensively. Capers Jones developed Checkpoint for windows – CKWIN in the late 1980s. Since then it has evolved into KnowledgePLAN, which is a knowledge-based expert system by SPR (Software Productivity Research). SPR was founded in 1985 by Capers Jones, who is best known for his many books on Software Measurement, cost estimation, and observations on the software industry.

The difference between KnowledgePLAN and CKWIN can roughly be outlined as follows:

KnowledgePLAN has less estimation parameters compared to its predecessor, CKWIN. Thus the estimates can be performed quicker. It is compatible with MS Project. Hence, project plans from MS Project can be imported into KnowledgePLAN and vice versa estimations from KnowledgePlan can be imported in MS Project as Work Breakdown Structures. Estimations in KnowledgePLAN follow the same steps as in Checkpoint for Windows. Since the author had direct experiences with CKWIN, it is anticipated that the KnowledgePLAN tool would arrive at similar results.

Checkpoint for windows administrated more estimation parameters than KnowledgePLAN and had, additionally, a comfortable benchmarking menu. While this feature enabled a quick comparison of projects with each other, the toolset no longer supports this in the KnowledgePLAN product.

Note: While Checkpoint for windows is no longer commercially available, we feature it in this book because it was the tool of choice and available during the successful measurement and estimating process implementation at the international insurance organization based in Germany.

Table 20.1 provides an overview regarding the project type and classification in the original knowledge base of CKWIN (now KnowledgePLAN). The current product can be enhanced by one's own organizational projects.

Table 20.1. Number of projects in the CKWIN project database

Project type	MIS	Out-sourcing	Commercial	Systems	Military	Other	Total	Percent
New	470	51	150	848	61	372	2,063	60.54
Enhancement	1,128	85	278	1,554	147	419	3,632	53.78
Maintenance	282	34	128	424	37	140	1,058	15.67
Total	1,880	170	555	2.825	245	930	6,753	100

Over the past 18 months, the knowledge base has been enhanced by the inclusion of the International Software Benchmarking Standards Group (ISBSG) projects into the KnowledgePLAN product.

20.4.1 Early Estimates

Checkpoint for Windows allowed early estimation in a quick estimation mode based on the more than 6,000 projects in its database using only a few of the estimation parameters. The parameters also cover some of the above mentioned application areas. As a prerequisite, a preliminary (estimated) software size input figure is needed as well as *soft and hard data (see Fig. 20.3).*

The first step to determining the size of a piece of software is to decide what functional size measurement method to use (e.g., IFPUG, FiSMA, COSMIC, NESMA, Mark II) or whether to use thousand lines of code (KSLOC) should be used. See also the chapter "Variants of the IFPUG Function Point Counting Method." An early estimate is only as good as the input of estimated size of the functional requirements (as far as they are known or can be derived from similar IT projects whose size in Function Points is known). The product then computes from this a delivery rate metric in units of Function Points per hour (FP/h). Using this ratio, the duration of the project can then be estimated.

The *hard data* needed to do any estimating (quick or detailed) includes information about project classification, project goal(s), programming language(s), and activities (tasks) of the Work Breakdown Structure.

The *soft data* comprise information about personnel, technology, process of software development, and project environment. The estimating tool also uses simplified McCabe complexity factors as input parameters.

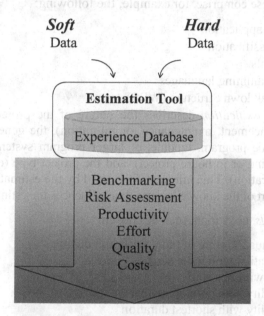

Fig. 20.3. Estimation with an expert system

Given these inputs of hard factors, soft factors, and the estimated software size, calculations are performed based on the database, for example, effort (total, for the IT core project, for end user involvement, and each of this for all phases). Metrics for productivity and quality, schedules and costs are also delivered as output.

In the detailed estimating mode, there are approximately 200 parameters on which the resultant estimate is based. According to Capers Jones, these 200+ parameters are of central importance (drivers) for the quality and productivity of software development. Capers stated that he believes that hard data alone cannot answer the question why one IT project performed better than another –it is only the combination of soft and hard data that makes sense.

In practical usage it was found that estimates must be done early in the software development process if the goal of increasing the precision of estimates and defect management is to be better controlled and improved.

20.4.2 Input: Hard Data

Hard data parameters are those input figures that are truly measurable and determinable. These comprise, for example, the following:

- The size of the application
- The project classification
- The project goals
- The used programming languages
- The Work Breakdown Structure (WBS)
- The *project classification* describes the nature of the project (new development, enhancement, maintenance, or migration), the general dependencies (stand alone program, module, or larger program system), the project class (outsourcing or in house project), and the project type (e.g., interactive database application). This information is used by the estimating tool to determine that part of the knowledgebase that influences the estimation at most.

As *project goals,* six variants can be chosen:

1. Standard: equal mixture of time, staff, and quality
2. Shortest duration with more staff
3. Least effort with less staff
4. Highest quality with normal number of staff
5. Highest quality with shortest duration
6. Highest quality with least effort.

Changing of only a single parameter "project goals" and analyzing the productivity and quality, the relationship between the primary goals, known as *the devils square of project management*, can be simulated easily and can lead to an impressive learning effect.

To evaluate the relative impact of a particular *programming language*, a conversion table known as the "language levels" or backfiring table is used.

A language level is, according to IBM, the number of Assembler statements which are on average necessary to write, for example, a COBOL statement (Assembler equivalent). CKWIN/KnowledgePLAN (and the SPR website at www.spr.com) contains a table with more than 600 programming languages and their Assembler equivalents. A part of this table is shown in chapter on Estimation Methods. The user can choose different programming languages from the table and estimate their percentage proportions, from which the estimating tool calculates the resulting assembler equivalent for the chosen mixture of languages.

In addition, the tasks/activities of the *Work Breakdown Structure (WBS)* can be chosen from a list by checkboxes and according to four different levels of the WBS: Project, phase, activity, and task. Project is the largest and task is the smallest level. The names of the tasks, activities, and phases can be customized with an included configuration tool, but not the relation, for example, to which activity a task belongs.

20.4.3 Input: Soft Data

Soft data are ordinal in terms of their relative evaluation, for example, like school grades:

1. Excellent
2. Good
3. Average
4. Mediocre
5. Poor.

The value from 1–5 delivers the most difficulties since *ordinal measures can be very subjective.* For example, one can ask if the difference between 2 and 3 is the same as between 4 and 5. It can be most problematic to explain to a project leader the difference between, for example, 3.7 and 3.8 simply and plausibly.

To secure interproject consistency in this regard, it is recommended to do the evaluation with more than one person, for example, with a member of the competence center who can also transfer the experiences to other estimations.

Capers Jones distinguishes four categories of soft data critical to the evaluation of software productivity and quality (see Fig. 20.4).

The input for *personnel* characterizes skill, the experience, and abilities of the staff in project management, the developers, end users, and maintenance personnel.

Technology characterizes the used software tools and platforms for development.

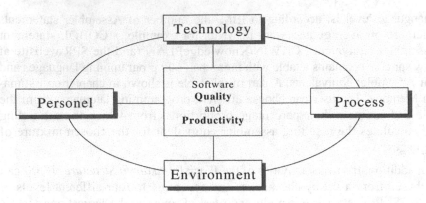

Fig. 20.4. Estimation parameters for quality and productivity of software

The factors of *process* cover the development methods, the effectiveness of defect removal, and the quality assurance process.

The parameters for *environment* ask for external factors that influence the IT project. This comprises geographic factors, office size, and maintenance equipment.

Table 20.2 gives an impression of how to evaluate soft data, showing one parameter from each of the four categories with its evaluation criteria.

Table 20.2. Evaluation of soft data

Evaluation	Description
Personnel: Motivation of the project team	
1	The project team is highly motivated
2	The largest part of the project team is motivated
3	Normal engagement and motivation
4	Motivational problems
5	Very poor morale
Technology: Stability of the development hardware	
1	Stabile, highly compatible platforms of one provider
2	Standardized platform with adapted compatibility
3	Hardware from different providers with high mutual compatibility
4	Hardware from different providers with acceptable mutual compatibility
5	Instable, changing, incompatible platforms.
Process: Test procedures	
1	Separate test department and developer and user test
2	Separate test department and developer test
3	Formalized test with comparison of results vs. known criteria
4	Test without test goals or test criteria
5	Occasional quick test under time pressure

(Continued)

Environment: Office noise and interruption	
1	Low office noise and few interruptions
2	Low office noise and frequent interruptions
3	Some office noise and few interruptions
4	Some office noise and frequent interruptions
5	Essential office noise and frequent interruptions

Another feature of many software estimating tools is a *risk/value analysis* of the project to be estimated. The evaluation of the parameters is according to the four aforementioned parameters. The result of these so-called *special factors* is not essentially relevant for the estimation itself, but answering the questions provides a good insight into the risk potential of the IT project compared to its benefits. The result is a portfolio diagram as shown in Fig. 20.5 for an average project.

If the dot for the project is in the left low quadrant of the square, it is to be considered a star since its risks are low and its benefit is high. In the right upper square are the dogs with low benefit and high risk. Projects in the other two quadrants should be thoroughly analyzed for their risks and value.

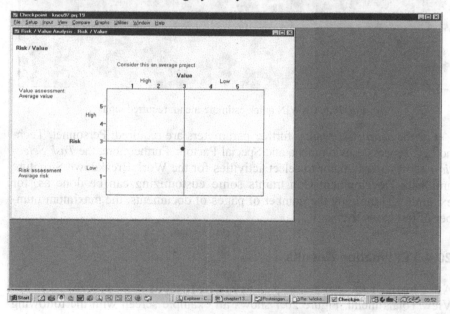

Fig. 20.5. Risk/value analysis example

20.4.4 Estimation Modes

CKWIN/KnowledgePLAN has two usable estimation modes:

1. Quick estimate for rough estimations
2. Detailed estimate.

The *quick estimate* is for a first estimation at project start when there are only a few facts known. The input comprises only some of the parameters, the so called *Required Input*: Project Description, Project Classification, Project Goals, Project Complexity, Function Sizing, Source Code, and Project Costs. Figure 20.6 shows the according menu.

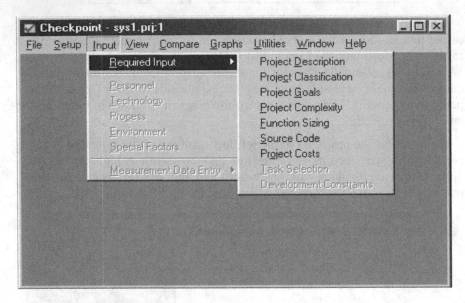

Fig. 20.6. CKWIN quick estimate menu: required input

For the *detailed estimate,* further parameters are required: Personnel, Technology, Process, Environment, and Special Factors. Furthermore, the *Task Selection* allows an estimator to select activities for the Work Breakdown Structure and with Development Constraints some customizing can be done as, for example, determining the number of pages of documents, the maximum number of test cases, etc.

20.4.5 Estimation Results

After input of the estimation parameters, the results can be analyzed in the View/Totals menu. Figure 20.7 shows an example screen with the following details:

Information about some relevant input data, *Project Profile* lists the chosen evaluations for, e.g., Project nature and scope, Project class and type, and goals.

Development and user shows estimations for the following:

- Project duration: Schedule Months
- Project effort: Person Months
- Staff Headcount
- Costs
- Delivered Function Points
- Base Function Points
- Document pages

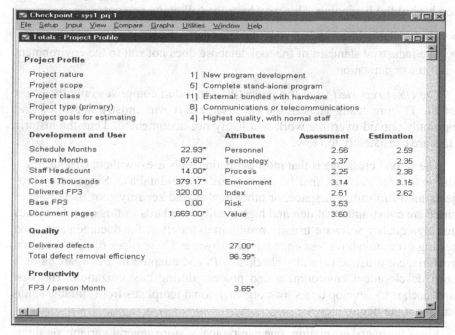

Fig. 20.7. CKWIN estimation results: view totals

Quality shows estimated

- Delivered defects
- Total defect removal efficiency
  Productivity is shown in Function Points per person month.
  Further information can be seen by scrolling down.

This screen is a summary of the estimation results. Further estimation results can be seen in the submenus of the View screen, for example, about the distribution of persons in the project phases or dates, costs and effort for many details of the project life cycle. The unit for project effort can be chosen from person hours, -days, -months, or -years. For benchmarking it should be set to person hours in order to be comparable (see the chapter about "Estimation Fundamentals," "Time Accounting").

20.4.6 Customizing and Calibrating the Software Tool

A prerequisite for tool acceptance is its calibration to company standards (customizing). The first step for customizing is to check the precision of the estimation results from your estimating tool and comparing it with historic data from project postmortems. The historic data have to be used to determine the necessary input for the tool and have to be compared with the estimation results. This procedure has to be done several times, until the data deliver comparable results. In the first iteration the results differ a lot. Mostly the estimations are too high at the beginning. This may have the following reasons:

- The available historic data were not complete.
- The industrial standard of the tool database does not suit to the environment of the organization.

The effort reported from the project leaders often comprises only the effort of the IT core team. Hence, the end user effort was mostly neglected and normally unpaid overtime work was likely not documented. Thus the historic data are consistently too low.

The second challenge is that most estimating tools use – without customizing – the *industrial average*, that is, the average of the database. Since many projects are from military, space, or other quality and security sensitive projects, there are constraints that demand high quality standards in this data. Demands for high quality software usually results in extra effort for documentation and testing over and above less constrained software. These types of nonfunctional requirement must be carefully checked with and adapted to the organization's own development environment and process during customization. The best approach is to develop one's own organizational templates from suitable simulations at the beginning.

Since for every estimation, one can typically store several variants or simulations of the estimates, the last one with the actual data at project postmortem should be stored for comparison with earlier variants. From this comparison much can be learned and this last estimation should be used to create future portfolios and templates. This enables *continuous process and estimation precision improvement*.

The most important challenge is the *establishment of a consistent time accounting process*. Large organizations normally calculate a productivity of about 75% for effective project work of the personnel. Twenty-five percent are for vacation, training, sickness, and other not directly project-oriented work in the organization. Estimating tools such as CKWIN/KnowledgePlan allows the adjustment of these fundamental parameters in the Setup menu as standards in the beginning. *The best situation for facilitating comparisons is a time accounting process based on person hours,* since this avoids the incompatibility of person months or person years between different organizations.

Other standards to be customized may include the work breakdown structure (with a specific set of deliverables and tasks) as well as documentation and quality requirements. Some tools support the customization of this standard.

Once the historic data give precise results, it can be started to estimate future projects. Projects (with historic data) of about the same size and nature can be gathered in a portfolio and this can be used as the basis for future estimations, too. With more new projects, the organizational database and experience increases and the estimations will be more precise. Then the portfolios can be enlarged and differentiated and templates can be derived from "good" portfolios.

20.4.7 Simulations of Estimates with an Automated Tool

A very useful application of CKWIN (or any other estimation tool that has this feature) is simulations in order to answer questions for process improvement and study the influence of single estimation parameters (estimation metrics, quality metrics, duration, effort). Questions such as how project durations can be reduced by reduction of requirements creep and project complexity can then be investigated. The criteria for these influential factors for project duration will be shown. But these criteria will only lead to shorter project duration, if adequate measures for the improvement of these criteria can be performed. CKWIN supported simulations with a sensitivity analysis computing a hit list of 16 criteria that mostly influence the effort of the actual estimation.

CKWIN also supported simulations by variation of its input parameters by supporting the administration of variants of project estimations. Once senior management asked to perform simulations with the concrete goal to find the most effective parameters affecting project duration using the historical estimation of a typical IT project. This simulation of a project with the goal to determine factors for shorter project duration is described in the following. The simulation team proceeded in following steps:

The project simulation started with the sensitivity analysis in order to see from the automated tool the parameters that had the greatest influence on project duration. With the sensitivity analysis the tool showed the 16 strongest parameters for the project goals: duration, effort, productivity, and quality. The result was a hit list of parameters mostly influencing the matching goal, independent of the actual parameter value. For the demanded investigations only the goal project duration was of relevance.

Next these parameters were improved successively by about one unit at a time, documented in tables and reset afterwards. For the evaluation of the parameters CKWIN used a scale ranging from 1 to 5. On this scale a value between

1.00 and 2.99 gave a positive result, and between 3.00 and 5.00 a negative influence for the estimation results. The default was N/A (Not Applicable), and the value 3.00 was considered to be the industry (database) average. The values could be set in hundreds. But this precision makes no sense since one cannot explain, for example, the difference between 2.75 and 2.76, and the difference in the results would also be marginal. In some cases there were used halves, for example, 3.5 in cases when it could not be decide between, for example, 2.00 and 3.00.

When modifying the parameters, according to the hit list of the sensitivity analysis, it was found that 3 of the 16 parameters could not be used for shorter durations since they had the best values (=1.00) from the start on.

The hit list of parameters is sorted in decreasing order. The first parameter has the most effect for shorter duration. The last parameter delivered astonishingly a three-day longer duration. The next step was the summation of the parameters, followed by step-by-step improvement to the best evaluation 1. All simulations were documented in analogous tables, which are not shown here.

The software tool also provided an alternative for the improvement of an IT project with the report on weaknesses. In this case the weaknesses are the parameters with values between 3.50 and 5.00. Again, these parameters were modified step-by-step and in sum.

Figure 20.8 gives an overview regarding the results of the simulations by stepwise improvement of the parameters.

The most important for the demanded goal is the column "Time Reduction" that relates to the line 1 (Basic Value) of column "Duration," with a duration of 914 days. This was estimated with the standard goals: equal mixture of time, staff, and quality. Alternatively, there were simulations with the goal: shortest duration with more staff. The values computed are shown both in absolute days and proportional percentages. Figure 20.8 thus shows that already with the change of the goal, the duration could have been reduced by 32.6% with equal quality and more staff (138 persons instead of 86) without changing any other parameters.

For better evaluation of potential side effects and determination of runaways also the target parameters effort, team size, and quality were documented. Also the quality in delivered defect and the defect removal rate were recorded. A low number of delivered defects is an appreciated goal. For calculation of person months the person days were divided by 20. This was necessary since CKWIN delivered effort and duration either in days or months

The according Parameters enlarged by 1 each (PARAMETER)	Duration Hours (Days)	Duration Time (Days)	Time Reduction Hours (Days)	Time Reduction Time (%)	Time Reduction Hours (Days)	Time Reduction Time (%)	Effort Hours (PM)	Effort Time (PM)	Team Size Hours (#)	Team Size Time (#)	Quality – Delivered Defects Hours (#)	Quality – Delivered Defects Time (#)	Quality – Defect Removal Rate Hours (%)	Quality – Defect Removal Rate Time (%)
1 Basic Value	914	616			298	32.60	852.7	835.1	86	138	1255	1235	78.75	78.55
Individual Office Environment	843	577	71	7.77	337	36.87	807.7	791.4	86	141	1255	1335	78.75	78.55
2 Development Personnel Experience	864	591	50	5.47	323	35.34	773.4	756.0	86	132	1188	1263	78.58	78.29
3 Office Noise and Interruption Environment	880	597	34	3.72	317	34.68	828.8	811.6	86	141	1255	1335	78.75	78.55
4 Project Organization Structure	886	594	28	3.06	320	35.01	845.3	828.2	86	138	1255	1335	78.75	78.55
5 Product Memory Utilization Restrictions	890	604	24	2.63	310	33.92	836.5	819.7	86	138	1255	1335	78.75	78.55
6 Product Performance/Execution Speed Restrictions	890	604	24	2.63	310	33.92	836.5	819.7	86	138	1255	1335	78.75	78.55
7 Development Personnel Tool and Method Experience	890	604	24	2.63	310	33.92	837.4	820.3	86	138	1255	1335	78.75	78.55
8 Tool, Equipment and Supplies	891	604	23	2.52	310	33.92	838.4	821.2	86	138	1255	1335	78.75	78.55
9 Functional Novelty	895	606	19	2.08	308	33.70	825.8	808.0	86	145	1186	1260	78.54	78.26
10 New Data Complexity	898	596	16	1.75	318	34.79	774.2	759.0	84	138	1161	1240	77.83	77.56
11 New Code Complexity	903	596	11	1.20	318	34.79	731.7	714.4	79	130	1051	1127	76.49	76.27
12 New Problem Complexity	903	596	11	1.20	318	34.79	731.7	714.4	79	130	1051	1127	76.49	76.27
13 Design Automation Environment	917	611	-3	-0.33	303	33.15	815.5	795.3	86	135	1119	1178	77.51	76.98

Fig. 20.8. Simulation results overview example

The simulations clearly demonstrated that there were a large number of ways to finish projects earlier. But not all parameters can be influenced by senior managers, project mangers, or the project team, as, for example, the involvement of the users.

The lesson learned is that tools should be used more frequently for simulations. This rule also proved to be valid for project planning tools. Experiences in daily project life showed that this rule is almost neglected by project leaders, leaving them without an essential aid for project survival.

20.4.8 Estimation Portfolios and Templates

One of the most important tasks for preservation of the organizational estimation know how is the customizing of the estimation tool by the development of own estimated project portfolios and templates in addition to the delivered basis of projects inherent in the tool. The tool vendors normally are proud to publish the number of the inherent projects used for the deliverance of the results, but they never deliver the details, as, for example, the ISBSG does, selling the database together with analysis tools. The ISBSG (since 2006) includes the Reality Checker as part of its database release (http://www. isbsg. org).

It is of vivid importance for an organization to group *equal* projects into a portfolio. This is done based on the idea that projects of similar kind will also show similar behavior and thus can be estimated in the same manner (with similar estimation parameters). Automated software tools such as CKWIN deliver the functionality to group projects into a portfolio in order to compare other projects with this portfolio (the average of the projects in that portfolio). A next step is to extract an estimation template from such a portfolio in order to use this template for the estimation of further projects. Such a template is like an own database of the estimation tool.

Now, what are similar projects or, asked in another manner, which projects should be put together in a portfolio? Looking into the literature you will find a lot of project characteristics that can be candidates for categorizations, for example, the following:

- Kind of development
  - New program development
  - Enhancement
  - Migrations
  - Project post mortems
- Platform
  - Batch systems
  - PC systems
  - Client/server systems
  - Data warehouse applications
  - OO systems
  - web applications.

The kind of development and the platform were used as categorizations and the projects were grouped according to size (small, medium, large). A prerequisite was to find out all the projects of a common category. The tool was not of much help in finding out which projects fit together in one portfolio, since it just showed each single project. It displayed the projects according to the categories and thus allowed to evaluate which projects should be taken into a portfolio. This was an important enhancement to the estimation tool, since from then on own templates for estimation could be created easily.

Figures 20.9–20.13 give an overview of some of the categories from the estimating add-on tool CKWIN Reader/Writer, showing estimation parameters of, for example, kind of development and platform with productivity, quality, and staff. All figures show in the first four columns the project scope (Project-classification: new program development, enhancement, maintenance), the platform (host, PC, C/S, DW), the Project short name, and the start date of the project.

Figure 20.9 shows all ten project postmortems in the German international insurance project database in CKWIN with the estimation figures of the CKWIN assessment estimation:

- Person hours
- Function Points, environment
- Assessment index (Index: refers to all attribute questions in personnel, process, technology, environment sections)
- Personnel
- Process
- Technology
- Benefit
- Risk.

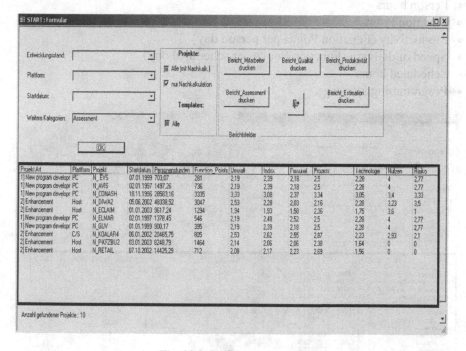

Fig. 20.9. Project postmortems

The CKWIN figures ranged from 1 to 5 with the database average of 3.0. Thus figures above 3.0 are better than the average and the larger ones show worse results.

There are five PC new development projects and four host enhancement project postmortems; the PC projects having sizes of 281, 736, 3,335, and 546,395 Function Points. The host projects have a size of 3,047 and 1,249 and 1,464 and 712 Function Points, respectively.

Figure 20.10 shows all templates (the estimation figures of CKWIN are 0 since this are templates to be used for start of an estimation).

There are six new program development and five enhancement templates: nine for host (four new program developments) and each two for PC and C/S environment.

Figure 20.11 shows all 13 new program development projects on PC platform with the estimation figures of the CKWIN productivity estimation parameters:

- Person hours
- Function Points
- Productivity (Function Points per person day)
- Speed of delivery (Function Points per scheduled day)
- Scheduled hours
- Programming language.

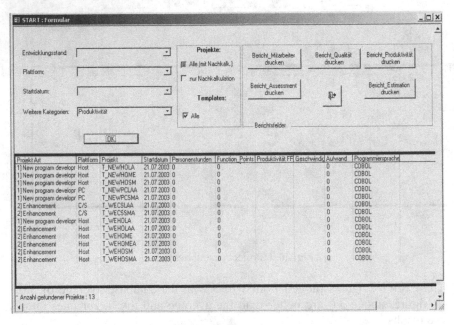

Fig. 20.10. Templates

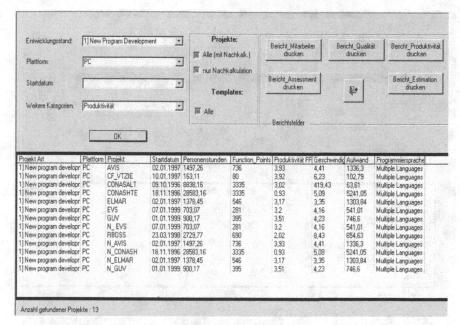

Fig. 20.11. New program development PC – productivity parameters

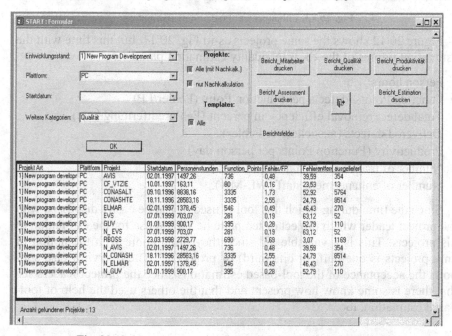

Fig. 20.12. New program development PC – quality parameters

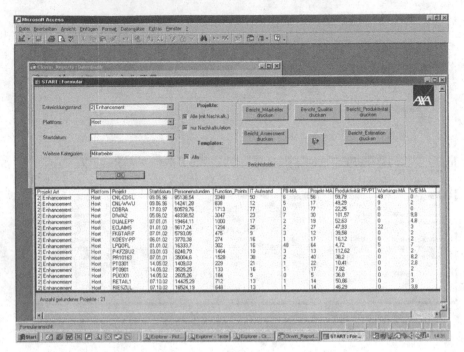

Fig. 20.13. Enhancement host – staff parameters

Figure 20.12 shows the same projects as in Fig. 20.11, but this time with the estimation figures of the CKWIN quality estimation parameters:

- Person hours
- Function Points, defects per Function Point (Fehler/FP)
- Total defect removal efficiency in percent (Fehlerentfernungsrate)
- Delivered defects (ausgelieferte Fehler).
- Productivity (Function Points per person day)
- Number of maintenance staff (Wartungs-MA)
- Number of enhancement staff (WE-MA).

Since the time during which this tool is used, it can be easily discussed with the project leader which project or template he should use for the estimation of his projects. This is a valuable aid since they often come with the notion of "my projects is one half (or one third) of project x". The overview also supports the acceptance of the tool-based estimations since the project leaders see that there is some know how present and that the others used the help of tool-based estimation, too.

20.5 Experience® Pro Project Sizing, Estimating, and Scope Management Software

Experience® Pro is a software tool that supports the functional size measurement, estimating, progress reporting, closing, and organizational learning (learning from completed projects) for software development and enhancement projects. The tool supports a variety of ISO/IEC conformant functional size measurement methods, as well as a backfiring model, and has three estimating modes:

- First estimate (this can be initiated before requirements and updated until the first baseline requirements are measured)
- Improved estimate (based on version 1 of the estimate which is the output of the First estimate step above. Each subsequent estimate is done based on receipt of progress reported by the project team or accepted changes to the baseline. Each estimate becomes an incremental version of the prior one)
- Final review (for closing a completed project and entering project actual data)
- Additionally, Experience® Pro provides a project portfolio management mode that facilitates portfolio project reporting.

Experience® Pro software is owned by 4SUM Partners based in Finland with offices in the USA and emerging locations globally (www.4sumpartners. com). The estimating modes are supported by a high quality database of over 800 completed projects (validated by approximately a dozen university researches over the past decade), as well as a version of the ISBSG database. Figure 20.14 shows the concepts behind estimation used in Experience® Pro.

20.5.1 Experience® Pro First Estimate

This mode creates an initial estimate of work effort based on more than a dozen input parameters including project classifiers, development language, functional size parameters (early), business area, project type, situational analysis (ND21, new development 21 factors), etc. Only one initial estimate per project (version 1.0) can be created for a project.

Fig. 20.15 depicts the Project Initiating Screen where the basic project classification and other elements are selected to perform the first estimate as depicted in the model of Fig. 20.14. This screen is the first screen to appear when the user selects "First Estimate" from the Experience® Pro starting menu.

The output of the first estimate process will be a version 1 estimate screen similar to the one shown in Fig. 20.16 (but the version number will be 1) and the progress will show 0%.

20.5.2 Experience® Pro Improved Estimate

The first estimate is used as the basis for the improved estimate mode (for which multiple subsequent versions can be created as the project progresses). In this estimating mode, additional and more detailed parameters (such as situation analysis) are input into the software tool, and analogies such as ISBSG and the Experience® database can be used as a comparator to gauge the reality of the estimate. This mode creates a second to nth estimate and the user can enter the progress (in %) for each function that is worked on since the lastestimate. Reports will provide an analysis of the partial (to date) delivery of the user functionality (base functional components) that is complete when the data is entered. When functionality is canceled part-way through the project (i.e., partial completion of the function), Experience® Pro keeps track of the incremental changes and partial delivery (based on functional size measurement). Approved changes are also entered by their functional type, and their delivery is then tracked over the rest of the project through to completion.

Fig. 20.16 summarizes the functionality of the Improved Estimate mode.

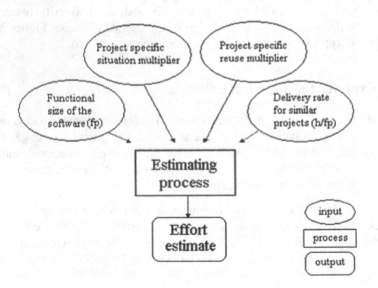

Fig. 20.14. Experience®Pro estimating model

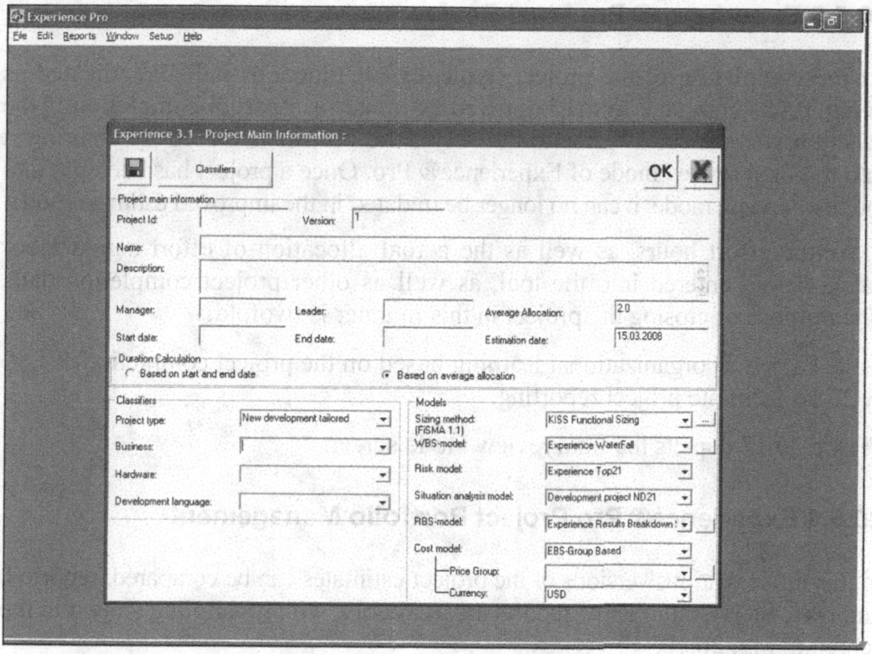

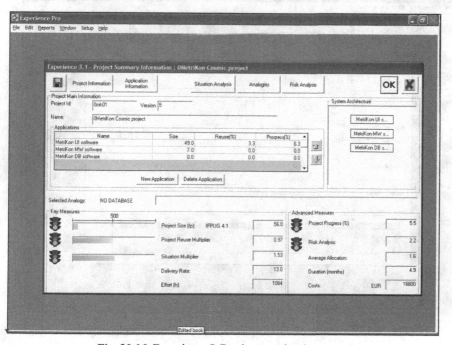

Fig. 20.15. Project initiating screen (before the First estimate is performed) in Experience® Pro

Fig. 20.16. Experience® Pro improved estimate mode

20.5.3 Experience® Pro Final Review

At the completion of the project (typically all functions will be indicated as being 100% complete in the improved estimate or a partial completion if the function was cancelled prior to delivery), the project is closed by entering it into the final review mode of Experience® Pro. Once a project has been put into the final review mode, it can no longer be updated in the improved estimate mode.

Actual effort hours, as well as the actual allocation of effort across labor categories is entered into the tool, as well as other project completion data. The purpose of closing the project in this manner is twofold:

1. To permit organizational learning based on the project completion
2. To facilitate project reporting.

Figure 20.17 depicts the final review mode screen.

20.5.4 Experience® Pro Project Portfolio Management

In this mode, various versions of the project estimates can be compared, reported, and reviewed. A number of reports are available, with a sampling shown in the screen in Fig. 20.18.

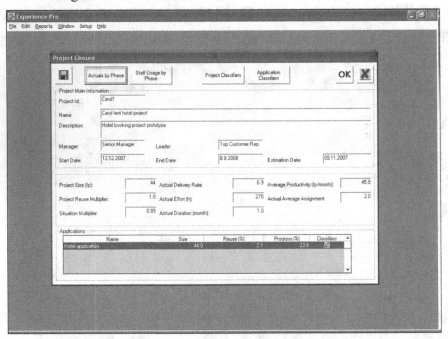

Fig. 20.17. Experience® Pro final review (closed and completed project)

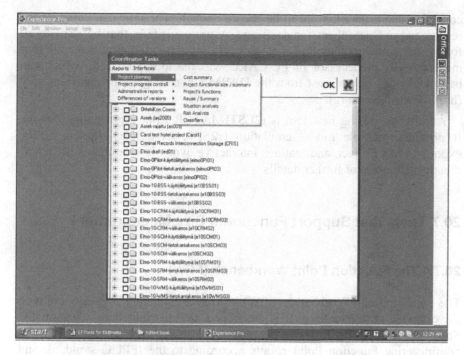

Fig. 20.18. Experience® Pro project portfolio management

20.5.5 Experience® Pro Application Maintenance Estimating

Experience® Pro also supports application maintenance estimating. For further
information and details about this mode and the use of the MT22 maintenance
situation analysis see the Appendix and the chapter on Estimating Maintenance.
For further product information visit www.4sumpartners.com.

20.6 Other Estimation Tools

There were already early table calculation sheets developed for ordered documentation of Functional Size Measurements and estimations. They can easily
be enhanced with macro programming or VBA (Visual Basic for Applications)
to become small applications.

Interesting is the tool PC-CALC from Harry Sneed, Case Consult Gmbh
(former SES: Software Engineering Service GmbH). It supports four estimation methods: Data Point method, Function Point method, COCOMO, and Component Analysis. It thus delivers four different estimations since Harry Sneed

considers one estimation not to be secure enough. The user can compare the results and evaluate them for decisions. A prerequisite is that he is fit in all four estimation methods and that he performs the estimation with all four methods. The predecessor of PC-CALC was the tool Soft-Calc, which can be downloaded free of cost from the DASMA homepage – for members only (http://www.dasma.org).

Another promising new tool is r2ESTIMATOR from r2estimating (USA). It provides multiple model emulation (r2SEF, COCOMO Jensen, NPR), exports to MS Project, and features interactive dynamic graphics. Visit www.r2estimating.com for further details.

20.7 Tools that Support Functional Size Measurement

20.7.1 The Function Point Workbench (FPW)

The Function Point Workbench (FPW) is an award winning software tool with a worldwide customer base. It is developed and distributed by Charismatek Software Metrics Pty Ltd. of Australia (www.charismatek.com). It aims at administering Function Point counts according to the IFPUG standard, and since 1998 it has been certified as type 1 software by IFPUG.

The documentation of the counts can be visualized by reports, lists and graphics, and exports in different formats. The main advantage is that it enables a centralized administration and thus an overview of the functional know how of an organization about its processes and applications, and provides an easy-to-use graphical interface. Figure 20.19 shows the Function Point Counting approach used in FPW.

The FPW is used for support of Function Point Counting and for structured documentation of the user requirements on application-, project-, and phase-level. The Function Point counter usually visits the end user with the FPW on his Laptop and documents the business cases directly with tool support. He thus can discuss the diagrams and documentation online with the end user and transfer the count to a central database afterwards. That is most effective requirements documentation delivering automatic overview on organizational level.

The FPW uses an imbedded method for guided counting of Function Points and thus enables reuse of existing functions in other projects. With in FPW's functionality, import or export function data can be exchanged in different formats, for example, .csv. CKWIN and KnowledgePlan tools both have an import feature for FPW counts.

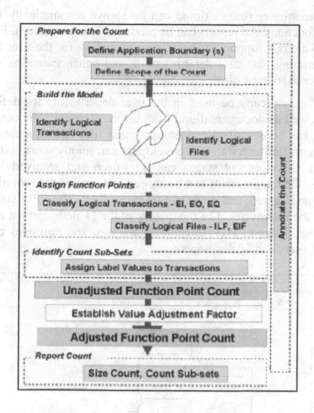

Fig. 20.19. Function Point Workbench approach to IFPUG function point counting

Figures 20.20 and 20.21 show FPW screen samples of a hierarchy diagram and the classification of a transaction. The software application is entered in the FPW in a tree structure by drag and drop. The root of the tree is the whole application system and its leaves are the transactions. Thus the business case is documented on the lower level of the structural tree (right hand side of Fig. 20.20). A very convenient feature is that the counts for any part of the tree can be seen at once.

This supports immediate overview over the whole or parts of the functionality when the system structure is entered. That is especially an advantage when the functional size of a changed (modified or new or deleted) function has to be determined during an enhancement project. Practical use showed that also the functional size of very small changes could be found within a few mouse clicks. A prerequisite is the proper use and documentation along the menus and user view of the applications.

The business cases (transactions) can be shown automatically in a list or grouped by functions. All reports can be produced in paper, screen, Excel tables or HTML. This is a support for basic documentation for the user for estimation, programming, test case determination, and enhancement as well as for training material for new hires.

The FPW can already be used in the user departments for definition and modeling as well as documentation of the business cases. They can be related to a project, can be described and grouped, and files and data can be associated with them. End users and IT developers can jointly work with this centralized data. Development stages can be frozen and archived in different phases. Thus, the requirements can be agreed and documented jointly, changes can be seen and agreed, and goals can be committed. The FPW supports with this abilities the improvement of the quality of the IT development and enables early warnings, helps to avoid misunderstandings, and improves cooperation between end users and IT developers.

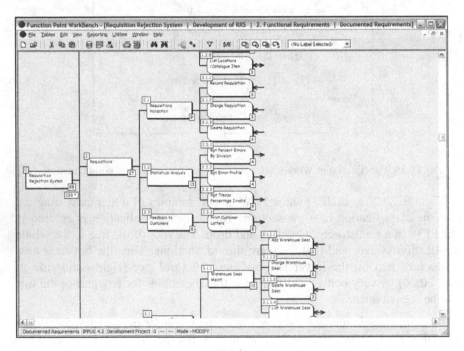

Fig. 20.20. FPW hierarchy diagram

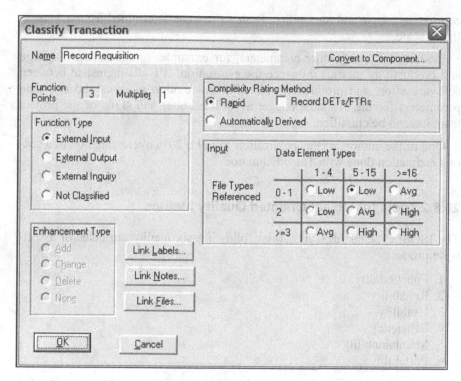

Fig. 20.21. FPW classification of a transaction

20.8 Tools for Object Oriented Metrics and Estimation

20.8.1 A Tool for Cost and Effort Estimation of OO Software Projects

K. Jantzen presented in the Informatik Spektrum of the German GI in February 2003 the estimation tool Tassc:Estimator (http://www.tassc-solutions.com) for cost and effort estimation of object-oriented, web-based, or component-based software projects. Project risks can also be evaluated with it. The tool can be used as standalone or as add-in, for example, in the Rational Rose tool or in the Together tool. Their system models can be imported into Tassc: Estimator, which can also produce input data for MS Project. As with all tools, a customizing before its use is a necessary prerequisite.

The basis of the Tassc:Estimator estimations are Use Cases, classes, subsystems, interfaces, components scripts, web pages that are all classified with different qualificators. A Use Case, for example, has the qualifiers: functional size, complexity, reuse and reusability. Their values are determined from a 4- or 5-figure scale.

Besides that many other parameters, for example, programming language and productivity metrics influence the estimation. It is distinguished between software effort and production tasks. For calculation of costs and end date parameters for the available budget as well number and skills of the project team have to be classified.

One of the authors of this publication found a 20% overestimation in a second estimation done with Tassc:Estimator.

20.8.2 Tools for Object Oriented Quality Metrics

The ISO/IEC standard 9126 defines following six quality attributes of a software product:

1. Functionality
2. Reliability
3. Usability
4. Efficiency
5. Maintainability
6. Portability.

Abran et al., studied Java and C++ source code tools for measuring the quality of object-oriented software and found four candidates for closer investigation:

- CodeCheck
- Datrix
- Insure++
- Logiscope.

Insure++ visualizes the program flow and works as compiler and thus is no static analysis tool. It aims to defect in storage, storage loss, and storage addressing. The other three can be used for static analyses and rule checking.

Logiscope consists basically of three components, an audit module for the analysis of quality and structure, a rule checker for controlling the usage of programming standards, and a test checker for measurement of the test coverage.

Besides other programming languages, ADA, C, C++, and Java are supported. It supports static and dynamic analyses and provides criticality predictions for source code.

Table 20.3. Tools and object oriented quality attributes

Tool	Metric	ISO/IEC 9126 quality attribute			
		Reliability	Efficiency	Maintainability	Portability
Insure++	I/O-errors	Yes			
	Storage defects	Yes			
	Storage loss	Yes			
	Storage addressing		Yes		
	Program optimization		Yes		
Logiscope	Direct recursion		Yes	Yes	
	Indirect recursion		Yes	Yes	
	Average coupling between objects			Yes	
	Coupling between classes			Yes	
	Coupling between objects			Yes	
Datrix	Class attributes			Yes	
	Class methods			Yes	
	Class inheritance coupling			Yes	
	Class documentation			Yes	
	Data coupling			Yes	
	Coupling between routines			Yes	
	Dimension and complexity of routines			Yes	
	Programming standards of routines			Yes	
	Testability of routines			Yes	
Co-deCheck	Initialization of array, structure, and union				Yes
	Bit fields-standards				Yes
	Commentaries in macro definitions				Yes
	Leading blanks in enclosed field names				Yes
	Lex_nonstandard				Yes
	Lex_trigraph				Yes
	Nested name tags				Yes
	System variable				Yes
	Blanks in preprocessor commands				Yes

The *static analysis* performs a syntactic and semantic analysis of the source code, is programming language-dependent, and delivers the input for complexity measurements, call graphs, control graphs, quality reports, etc.

During the *dynamic analysis* during execution of the measured program, there are permanently written data into a log file that are used later to calculate test coverage and support test data generation as well as measurement of the test status.

The quality model of Logiscope delivers regarding C++ reports on program-, class-, and function level.

Both authors report that there was no metric found during their research, which measured the quality attribute usability (partial characteristics: understandability, learn-ability, applicability, attractivity). Table 20.3 shows the four tools and their relation to four of the six quality attributes.

This source code analyses deliver a large number of metrics that can directly be used for documentation, structuring, and improvement of software.

As examples, two relations between the above metrics and quality attributes are commented here:

A strong coupling, especially between routines and global variables, always indicates that components are not independent from each other. This directly influences maintainability.

Inheritance coupling indicates directly how good the object-oriented concept of inheritance is used. The same holds for the usage of recursions.

20.9 Website URLs for Estimation Tools

> This overview cannot be complete and actual after date of publication. Thus, the authors deny any responsibility for risks and side effects from broken links!

Table 20.4. Website URLs for estimation tools

Tool	Organization	URL
CAME	Universität of Magdeburg, Software Measurement Laboratory	http:/ivs.cs.uni-magdeburg.de/ sw-eng/agruppe/forschung
Cicero.Test, Cicero.Tracker	Cicero Consulting Gmbh, Klagenfurt	http://w4.cicero-consulting.com/
Construx Cost Estimation Software	Construx Software Builders Inc.	http://www.construx.com
CostXpert	Cost Xpert Group, Inc., San Diego, CA	http://www.costxpert.com
Estimacs	Computer Associates	http://www.cai.com
Experience® Pro	4SUM Partners	http://www.4sumpartners.com
Function Point Workbench (FPW)	Charismatek Software Metrics Pty Ltd. (Australia)	http://www.charismatek.com.
KnowledgePlan (formerly Checkpoint for Windows)	Software Productivity Research (SPR), Hendersonville, NC	http://www.spr.com
Logiscope	Verilog	http://www.verilogusa.com/home.htm
McCabe	McCabe & Associates	http:/www.mccabe.com
PC CALC	Case Consult GmbH, Flachstr. 13, 65197 Wiesbaden	E-Mail: harry.sneed@caseconsult.com
PQMPlus	Q/P Management Group	http://www.qpmg.com
PriceS (Price Estimating Suite)	Price, Mount Laurel, NJ	http://www.pricesystems.com
R2ESTIMATOR	r2Estimating, Scottsdale, AZ	http://www.r2estimating.com
SCOPE	Total Metrics	http://www.totalmetrics.com
SEER	Galorath Inc.	http://www.galorath.com
SLIM	QSM, McLean, Virginia	http://www.qsm.com
Tassc:Estimator	Tassc Software Solutions, East Kilbride, Scotland	http://www.tassc-solutions.com

20.10 Management Summary

A science is as mature as its measurement tools. (Louis Pasteur)

A method without tool support has only a little chance for survival and cannot find the necessary acceptance for widespread use.

A fool with a tool still remains a fool!

The first lesson learned in trainings is for the project leaders that the tool does not do their job of estimation.

Tools used without expertise cannot deliver solid results.

Estimation results with decimal points delude a not existing accuracy and lull the user in deceptive safety.

The major benefits (time saving, quality, and efficiency improvement) are harvested project per project over time and thus summon up accordingly in an organization. Besides this there emerge positive side effects as, for example, improvement of acceptance and transparency, standardization, and an estimation culture.

Microestimation starts from the project activities and aggregates all partial estimations to a total.

Macroestimation aims at the estimation of whole projects. After estimation of effort and duration, the decomposition to the project phases is done.

Macroestimation is well suited for quick and early estimations.

Simulations with an estimation tool deliver the advantage to calculate the influence of single estimation parameters (productivity metrics, quality metrics, duration, effort) regarding different goals. Thus the critical success factors of a project can be determined.

In practical usage it was found that estimations must be done early in the software development process if precision of estimation and defect management shall be better controlled and improved.

A prerequisite for tool acceptance is its calibration to company standards (customizing).

The lesson learned is that tools should be used more frequently for simulations. This rule is also valid for project planning tools. Experience in daily project life showed that this rule is almost neglected by project leaders, leaving them without an essential aid for project survival.

One of the most important tasks for preservation of the organizational estimation know how is the customizing of the estimation tool by the development of own estimated project portfolios and templates in addition to the delivered basis of projects inherent in the tool.

Appendix

A.1 A Logbook for Function Point Counts

Note: the following logbook example is an adapted version from the IT department of an international insurance company.

A.1.1 Organizational Information

Table A.1. Header for inclusion in the corporate logbook

Application System	ZAR
Date:	May 2006
Reason for Count:	Enhancements per Release April 2006
Counter:	Mrs. Carolus
	Mr. Alarus
Application Specialist:	Mrs. Miller
	Mr. Stones

A.1.2 Documentation (Input) for the Function Point count

Documentation for the FP count included the following documents:

- From the Function Point Workbench™ the version »1st count 05.2001« was taken as the basis. Following the quality assurance check and final project delivery, the version »Correction of count 05.2001« was elaborated and stored.
- In the Visio-file ZAR.vsd, the boundary of the system ZAR was illustrated.
- This logbook was used as a basis and was stored for future reporting.
- In the document ZAR-Applications.doc were listed all ZAR-applications with production cycles and jobs (e.g., each PMS-list produced represents an EO from the user perspective).
- The data model in version 3.4 according to the Case Tool xyz was consulted to determine the appropriate data groupings for the ILFs and EIFs.

A.1.3 Architecture, Boundary

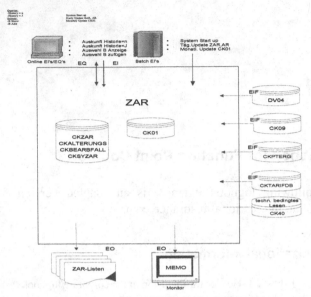

Fig. A.1. Example application boundary of ZAR for inclusion in the corporate logbook

A.1.4 Comments Relevant to the Function Point Count

The following text is provided for illustration purposes:

- The log-file from the online portion of the application was counted as an EI. In the batch portion of the application, some listings were crossed out to symbolize that they were counted only once (they were duplicates). See also FP LINK NOTES for the listings.

- The OPC-application CK72B#SPLIT implemented in the fall of 2003 had no new functions from the user perspective. Therefore, this OPC-application was not documented together with the Function Point Application ZAR. It is recommended that the Function Point Applications ZAR and AR be integrated.

- Both systems maintain the same databases that were accordingly counted as ILFs in both applications. Typically, however, a database is only primarily owned and maintained by one application. It was determined that these two applications, while they appeared to be separate from a physical standpoint, actually supported a single set of user functionality and therefore should be counted as one.

- Applications with less than 200 adjusted Function Points deliver outliers in benchmarking, according to our metrics competence center. We know that the rules of thumb can only be used with much care (actually ZAR has 129 adjusted FPs and AR also has 129 adjusted FPs).

A.1.5 Results

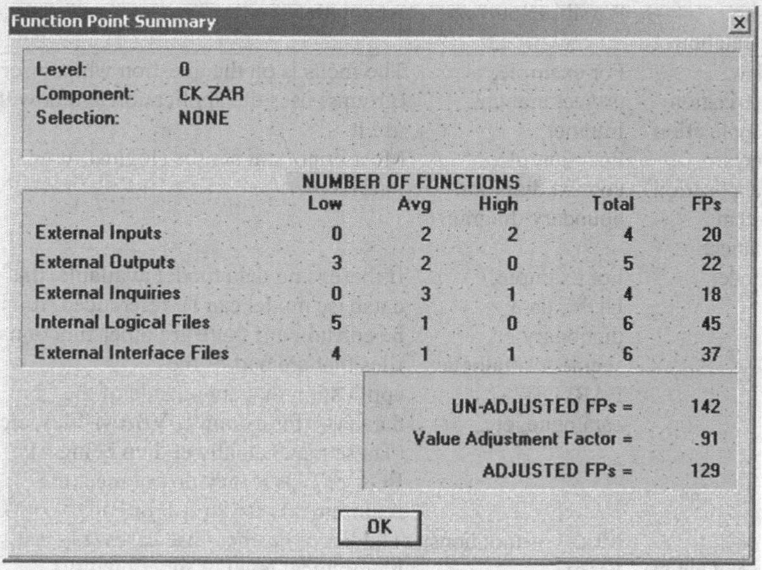

Function Point Summary   ×

Level:	0
Component:	CK ZAR
Selection:	NONE

NUMBER OF FUNCTIONS					
	Low	Avg	High	Total	FPs
External Inputs	0	2	2	4	20
External Outputs	3	2	0	5	22
External Inquiries	0	3	1	4	18
Internal Logical Files	5	1	0	6	45
External Interface Files	4	1	1	6	37

UN-ADJUSTED FPs =	142
Value Adjustment Factor =	.91
ADJUSTED FPs =	129

OK

Fig. A.2. Example count result of application ZAR for inclusion in the corporate logbook

A.2 Checklists

Note: the following checklist examples are adapted and enhanced versions based on existing checklists from the IT department of an international insurance company.

A.2.1 Checklist for Function Point Count Kickoff

Experiences show that to perform a project FP count an average of 1.5–2 days effort should be planned (based on an "average" size project of 500–1,000 FP). A prerequisite to counting is the gathering and assembling of the documentation to support the count (e.g., project documents that describe the functionality from the user perspective). We have found that the most efficient way to do the count is with two persons and a laptop.

Additional people are not necessarily more efficient or productive to the counting process, and can actually detract from the effort if there is wide disagreement about what constitutes the functionality (sometimes it is a status issue to be involved in all meetings on all topics. Do not allow yourself to be drawn into this unproductive situation).

Table A.2. FP count kickoff checklist

Necessary Documentation	Possible Sources	Annotations
Overview, characterization of the application	For example, project manual, Intranet	The focus is on the question which user (groups) uses the application and how they use it.
Architecture of the application and system environment	For example, context diagram, boundary diagram	Most important are the (logical) user interfaces.
Data model	For example, UDM, data dictionary, segment catalogue, EAR; DB2-catalogue, etc.	If there is no data model available, the database model can be referenced. It must be consulted if there are other functional files that are part of the application that are outside of the database, for example, VSAM-files, etc. (These may actually end up being EIs, EOs, or EQs if they do not meet the requirements for an ILF or EIF).
Functionality (online and batch)	Model of functions, list of business use cases	The list of business use cases (highest hierarchical level of functionality) often delivers hints for definition of project structuring.
Online functionality	Direct viewing of the screens, report layouts, user manual	The granularity of the Function Point count aims at »user related elementary processes« (e.g., create, change, etc.); which are often implemented in practice as menus or initiated via PF-keys.
Batch parts	Model of functions, user manual	The batch parts of the application must be regarded from user view. Often it is helpful to examine the batch portion of the application by results, e.g.: –Output processing, printed output (lists, reports, letters, output files, or datasets) –Letters for advertisement campaigns –Data stores (e.g. administrations, partner organizations), forwarding letters –Annual reports or other actualizations –Maintenance of central data, consolidations of data Additionally, a view on the changing counting scope during project progress) can help to secure the functional completeness of the batch part for the Function Point count: which batch functions run daily, monthly, annually, etc.

The application specialist should have detailed knowledge about the application as viewed by the user(s). Note that knowledge of the physical and architectural (programming) details are not conducive to the FP count but knowledge of the data model definitely is.

The main criterion for preparation of the count is the availability and currency of the necessary documentation that describes the user requirements for functionality.

A.2.2 Checklist for Function Point Count Assessment

Table A.3. FP count assessment checklist

Allocated resource responsible for the FP count (expertise and process):
Application system-number, Application name, department:
Project-number, -name/department:
Phase completed when this FP count is to be done (Study, requirements, actualization, project postmortem):
Type of count (Project: new development, enhancement, migration; application system: base count, postenhancement base):
Date of the FP count:
Date of assessment:

	Prerequisites for the FP count *Quality criteria*	o.k.	not o.k.
1.1	Has the FP counter attended a FP course? Or	☐	☐
1.2	Does the person performing the count consulted with and secured the availability of a member of the competence center? Reason (only when not o.k. or if the question is not applicable):	☐	☐
2.1	Is the FP counter a project team member (for the project or application being counted)? Reason (only when not o.k. or the question is not applicable):	☐	☐
2.2	Did the project team participate in the FP count? Reason (only when not o.k. or the question is not applicable):	☐	☐
3.1	Has the FP counter more than one year's worth of participation or knowledge about the basic application system?	☐	☐
3.2	Was the task of »Function Point Counting« included in the project plan? Reason (only when not o.k. or the question is not applicable):	☐	☐
4.1	Is a FP count of the basic application system documented in the Function Point Workbench™? Where: Or	☐	☐

(Continued)

Table A. 3. *(Cont.)*

		o.k.	not o.k.
4.2	There was adequate written documentation about the basic system? Where:	☐	☐
	–Screen documentation	☐	☐
	–Transaction documentation	☐	☐
	–Interface documentation	☐	☐
	–Database documentation	☐	☐
	–Output documentation (e.g. Print documentation)	☐	☐
	Or		
4.3	Was the basic system knowledge obtained through documented interviews?	☐	☐
	Reason (only when not o.k. or the question is not applicable):		
5.1	Is the logbook of the FP count up to date? Where:	☐	☐
	Reason (only when not o.k. or the question is not applicable):		
5.2	Are the assumptions, suggestions, restrictions, and unanswered questions about the project/application documented?	☐	☐
	Reason (only when not o.k. or the question is not applicable):		
6.1	Is the migration (if there is one) counted and separately documented?	☐	☐
	Reason (only when not o.k. or the question is not applicable):		
6.2	Are outsourced parts (if there are) counted and separately documented?	☐	☐
	Reason (only when not o.k. or the question is not applicable):		

Process during FP count			
Quality Criteria		*o.k.*	*not o.k.*
1.	Was the FP count done according to the current IFPUG release (n.n)?	☐	☐
	Reason (only when not o.k. or the question is not applicable):		
2.	Was there a system diagram with the system boundary and data flows? Where:	☐	☐
	Reason (only when not o.k. or the question is not applicable):		
3.	Are the EIs, EOs, and EQs determined by the system boundary and data flows?	☐	☐
	Reason (only when not o.k. or the question is not applicable):		
4.	Is there an overview about the data files (entities)?	☐	☐
	Reason (only when not o.k. or the question is not applicable):		
5.	Are the ILFs and EIFs determined by the data files?	☐	☐
	Reason (only when not o.k. or the question is not applicable):		
6.	Are the Function Points of the EIs, EOs, EQs, ILFs, and EIFs correctly counted (e.g., in case of an enhancement count)	☐	☐
	Reason (only when not o.k. or the question is not applicable):		
7.	Are the 14 GSCs classified according to the organizational standard?	☐	☐
	Reason (only when not o.k. or the question is not applicable):		
8.	Did the VAF change?	☐	☐
	Reason (only when not o.k. or the question is not applicable):		

(Continued)

		o.k.	Not o.k.
9.	Were the 14 GSCs compared to the quality attributes?	☐	☐
	Reason (only when not o.k. or the question is not applicable):		
10.	Are the 14 GSCs consistent with each other?	☐	☐
	Reason (only when not o.k. or the question is not applicable):		
11.	Did the requirements change compared to the last FP count?	☐	☐
	Reason (only when not o.k. or the question is not applicable):		
12.	Are the results consistent with other comparable projects in terms of size or with other sizing methods (e.g., SPR-method, number of dialogues × 10, rules of thumb, FP-Prognosis), if available?	☐	☐
	Reason (only when not o.k. or the question is not applicable):		
13.	Did the requirements change (for a delivered project) since the first FP count?	☐	☐
	Reason (only when not o.k. or the question is not applicable):		

	Documentation of the FP count *Quality criteria*	*o.k.*	*Not o.k.*
1.1	Is the FP Count documented in the Function Point Workbench™ and can it be clearly understood? Where is it stored?	☐	☐
	Reason (only when not o.k. or the question is not applicable):		
1.2	Is the description in the Function Point Workbench™ completely answered (per the company standard)?	☐	☐
	Reason (only when not o.k. or the question is not applicable):		
2.	Is the number of EIs, EOs, EQs, ILFs, and EIFs from the system diagram identical to what the counter has recorded in the Function Point Workbench™?	☐	☐
	Reason (only when not o.k. or the question is not applicable):		
3.	Are the annotations from the FP count documented? Where:	☐	☐
	Reason (only when not o.k. or the question is not applicable):		
4.	Are the assumptions and counting decisions for the FP count documented in the logbook? Where?	☐	☐
	Reason (only when not o.k. or the question is not applicable):		
5.	Are the figures/results comparable to other projects of similar type?	☐	☐
	Reason (only when not o.k. or the question is not applicable):		
6.	Are the percentages of the EIs, EOs, EQs, ILFs, and EIFs consistent with the rules of thumb?	☐	☐
	Reason (only when not o.k. or the question is not applicable):		

Are there any open questions that have to be answered:			
Nr.	Question	Who	With whom?

	Name	Signature
Done by:		
Checked by:		
Released by:		

A.2.3 Checklist for Project Postmortem of IT-Projects

Table A.4. Project postmortem checklist

Name or person responsible for the project
postmortem (for functionality and for the
process):
Project number, -name/department:
Type of project (new development, en-
hancement, migration):
Development platform (Host, PC, C/S,
Data Warehouse, Web):
Date of project postmortem:
Date of quality assurance:

Documentation of the FP Count		
Quality Criteria	*Yes*	*No*
1. Is there an actual/final FP count documented in the Function Point Workbench™? Where?	☐	☐
Reason (only in case of No):		
2. Is there a first FP count from specification phase or earlier besides the project postmortem (delivered) FP count?	☐	☐
Reason (only in case of No):		
3. Was the size of the project tracked during the project progress (requirements creep), i.e., was the delivered FP count compared to the first FP count?	☐	☐
Reason (only in case of No):		

Comparison of Estimate to Actual Effort		
Quality Criteria	*Yes*	*No*
1. Was the original estimate compared with the actual project effort at delivery?	☐	☐
Reason (only in case of No):	☐	☐
2. Were the differences from the original estimate and the actual effort measured and analyzed together with the competence center?	☐	☐
Reason (only in case of No):		
3. Is the Checkpoint/KnowledgePLAN™ file completed for the project delivery (in particular, the classification of the soft factors, and the project classification completed at the end of the project)?. Was the file delivered to the competence center?	☐	☐
Reason (only in case of No):		

Analysis of the Actual Project Effort		
Quality Criteria	*Yes*	*No*
1. Are the records in the time accounting system consolidated and complete?	☐	☐
Reason (only in case of No):		

(Continued)

2.	Was the actual effort analyzed for IT core team, interfaces, support, and end user participation? What are the percentages of effort for each group?	☐	☐
	Reason (only in case of No):		
3.	Was the actual effort analyzed by phase (study, specification, etc.)? What are the percentages of effort for each phase?	☐	☐
	Reason (only in case of No):		

Quality Assurance, Reuse

Quality Criteria		*Yes*	*No*
1.	Is there a list of all detected defects and are they all documented? Where?	☐	☐
	Reason (only in case of No):		
2.	Was there any analysis done to project how many defects may occur during maintenance? Where is it documented?	☐	☐
	Reason (only in case of No):		
3.	Were checklists and procedures developed during the project? If yes, were they presented to the competence center so that they can be reused on future projects?	☐	☐
	Reason (only in case of No):		
4.	Were programs and concepts developed in the project? If yes, were they presented to the competence center so that they can be reused on future projects?	☐	☐
	Reason (only in case of No):		
5.	Were checklists, processes, procedures, programs, etc. developed for reuse presented to the staff for communication to the rest of the IT department (e.g., via Intranet, project presentation, organizational newspaper, etc.)?	☐	☐
	Reason (only in case of No):		

Metrics of the Project

Quality Criteria		*Yes*	*No*
1.	Was the productivity of the total project calculated in FP per person month? What was it?	☐	☐
	Note for users who prefer the speed of delivery (PDR) instead: Was the speed of Delivery (PDR) calculated with FP per person month? What was it?		
	Reason (only in case of No):		
2.	Was the delivery rate for the project calculated per calendar day (FP per calendar day)? What was it?	☐	☐
	Reason (only in case of No):		
3.	Was the cost ratio of the project measured in US-$ per FP?	☐	☐
	Reason (only in case of No):		

(Continued)

Table A. 4. *(Cont.)*

4.	Were the costs analyzed by the following criteria? Costs of internal staff Costs of external staff Costs of central resources (computing center, administration, etc.) Costs of purchased tools, software-packages, etc. Reason (only in case of No):	☐	☐
5.	Was there an analysis done related to "on-time" delivery as [abs(actual days – planned days)]? What was the deviation? Reason (only in case of No):	☐	☐
6.	Was the actual defect density calculated (number of defects detected to date post-delivery per FP)? What is it? Reason (only in case of No):	☐	☐

Project post-mortem
This section pertains to the analysis of the most important problems and crises of the project (3–7 topics) are reviewed in order to deliver preventive and improvement recommendations.

Problem, description of crisis or
situation:
Actions taken to mitigate crisis:
Effectiveness of these actions:
Post-project evaluation of the
situation and recommendations
of future actions:

Are there any open questions that have to be answered:

Nr.	Question	Who (with whom)	Date

	Name	Signature
Done by:		
Checked by:		
Released by:		

A.2.4 Checklist for Assessment of Estimation

Table A.5. Estimation assessment checklist

Name of person responsible for the
estimation (for functionality and for
the process):
Project number, -name/department:
Phase (Study, requirements, actualization, project postmortem):

(Continued)

Type of project (new development,
enhancement, migration):
Development platform (Host, PC,
C/S, Data Warehouse, Web):
Date of project postmortem:
Date of quality assurance:

Prerequisites for the estimation Quality Criteria	o.k.	Not o.k.
1.1 Did the estimator have a Checkpoint/KnowledgePLAN™-training? Or	☐	☐
1.2 Did the estimator have the counsel and availability of a member of the competence center? Reason (only when not o.k. or the question is not applicable):	☐	☐
2. Was the estimator a member of the project team? Reason (only when not o.k. or the question is not applicable):	☐	☐
3. Is there a quality-assured first FP count from the end of the requirements phase? Reason (only when not o.k. or the question is not applicable):	☐	☐

Process of Estimation Quality criteria	o.k.	Not o.k.
1. Is the logbook of the estimation completed? Where? Reason (only when not o.k. or the question is not applicable):	☐	☐
2. Did the estimate include a description of the phases it included? Reason (only when not o.k. or the question is not applicable):	☐	☐
3. Are the assumptions, decisions, and open questions documented? Reason (only when not o.k. or the question is not applicable):	☐	☐
4. Was the appropriate template for the project estimate been chosen? Which one? Reason (only when not o.k. or the question is not applicable):	☐	☐
5. Was the appropriate estimation mode chosen (Quick, Detailed Estimate)? Which one? Reason (only when not o.k. or the question is not applicable):	☐	☐
6. Is the Setup correct (according to the organizational Time Accounting)? Reason (only when not o.k. or the question is not applicable):	☐	☐
7. Are the hard factors classified and are they plausible? Reason (only when not o.k. or the question is not applicable):	☐	☐
8. Are the soft factors classified and are they plausible? Reason (only when not o.k. or the question is not applicable):	☐	☐
9. Have changes to the restrictions of the hard factors as compared to the last estimate been considered? Reason (only when not o.k. or the question is not applicable):	☐	☐

(Continued)

Table A. 5. *(Cont.)*

		o.k.	Not o.k.
10.	Have changes to the restrictions for personnel compared to the last estimate been considered?	☐	☐
	Reason (only when not o.k. or the question is not applicable):		
11.	Have changes to the restrictions for technology compared to the last estimate been considered?	☐	☐
	Reason (only when not o.k. or the question is not applicable):		
12.	Have changes to the restrictions for the process compared to the last estimate been considered?	☐	☐
	Reason (only when not o.k. or the question is not applicable):		
13.	Have changes to the restrictions for environment compared to the last estimate been considered?	☐	☐
	Reason (only when not o.k. or the question is not applicable):		
14.	Have changes of the restrictions for risks compared to the last estimate been considered?	☐	☐
	Reason (only when not o.k. or the question is not applicable):		
15.	Was a sensitivity analysis performed?	☐	☐
	Reason (only when not o.k. or the question is not applicable):		
16.	Was a comparison made between versions of the estimate?	☐	☐
	Reason (only when not o.k. or the question is not applicable):		
17.	Is the actual project effort documented? Where?	☐	☐
	Reason (only when not o.k. or the question is not applicable):		

	Documentation of the Estimation *Quality Criteria*	o.k.	Not o.k.
1.	Was the estimate done using KnowledgePLAN™ or another estimating tool (specify which one)?	☐	☐
	Reason (only when not o.k. or the question is not applicable):		
2.	Can the actual relevant estimate be identified from the version description in Checkpoint/KnowledgePLAN™?	☐	☐
	Reason (only when not o.k. or the question is not applicable):		
3.	Is the documentation of the distribution of effort with the Excel-sheet available (total effort, project duration)?	☐	☐
	Reason (only when not o.k. or the question is not applicable):		
4.	Are the results compared to similar projects plausible?	☐	☐
	Reason (only when not o.k. or the question is not applicable):		

Are there any open questions that have to be answered:

Nr.	Question	Who	With whom

	Name	Signature
Done by:		
Checked by:		
Released by:		

A.3 FiSMA Situation Analysis Model MT22

The purpose of the Experience situation analysis method MT22 is to help to estimate annual maintenance and modification projects. The model consists of 22 standard productivity factors. They are classified into four categories: Organization (6 factors), Process (5 factors), Product (6 factors) and People (5 factors). Each factor in each category has five alternative values. The basic idea in rating is that "the better the circumstances for the maintenance are, the more positive rating the factor gets."

"++"   = Excellent situation, circumstances much better than in average case

"+"   = Good situation, circumstances better than in average case

"+/–" = Normal situation in the productivity point of view

"–"   = Bad situation, circumstances worse than in average case

"––" = Very bad situation, circumstances much worse than in average case.

Rating of each factor is weighted based on experience data. The ideal or target weights should be 1.10, 1.05, 1.00, 0.95, and 0,90 (from –– to ++) and they should be distributed normally, 5–20–50–20–5%.

Table A.6. Categories and names of MT22 productivity factors

Organization	Release and version policy
Organization	Resource availability for future needs
Organization	Contracting procedure
Organization	Number of stakeholders
Organization	Priority setting and control of changes
Organization	Organizational culture
Process	*Source code edition methods and tools*
Process	*Testing methods and tools*
Process	*Documentation methods and tools*
Process	*Communication methods and tools*
Process	*Roll-out methods and tools*
Product	Functionality requirements
Product	Reliability requirements
Product	Usability requirements
Product	Efficiency requirements
Product	Maintainability requirements
Product	Portability requirements
People	*Development environment skills of staff*
People	*Application knowledge of staff*
People	*Networking skills of staff*
People	*Motivation and responsibility of staff*
People	*Team atmosphere*

Note that FiSMA also supports the ND21 (New Development) situation analysis for gauging the productivity factors on new development projects. See www.fisma.fi/in-english/methods to download this and the MT22 situation analysis presented below.

A.3.1 Organization Factors

Release and Version Policy

The clarity, formality, internal integrity, and long-term planning of future releases and versions.

Table A.7. Release and version policy factors

—	Many different customer specific versions and delivery packages, which are built case by case after required modifications.
–	Many customer specific versions and release packages, and their installation and deployment is allocated to end-users.
+/–	Some customer-specific versions and releases of the same delivery.
+	All customers get the same standard delivery. New versions are released according to future needs.
++	All customers get the same standard delivery. Future releases are planned and agreed for the foreseen future.

Resource Availability for Future Needs

Adequacy of resources and systematic allocation of staff, hardware, software, work space, and required skills for the planned maintenance period.

Table A.8. Resource and availability for future needs factors

—	Organization has no defined rules and practices in resource management. Applications have no responsible person. Continuous lack of resources.
–	Organization has mechanism for workload management, and it is at least partially in use. Each application has responsible person, but he/she has many other responsibilities. Availability of resources is uncertain.
+/–	Organization has defined mechanism to manage critical resources. Each application has responsible person(s). Some delays to get other resources.
+	Organization has well-defined mechanism to manage all resources, and it is followed largely. Responsibilities are fully allocated to suitable person(s) and also required back up resources are nominated. Other resources are available on request with short notice.
++	Organization has well-defined mechanism to manage all resources, and it is followed fully. All required responsibilities and back up resources are nominated and their availability is well ensured. Also other resources are available on request.

Contracting Procedure

Consistency, completeness, and granularity of maintenance contract to define each service type and/or service transaction, mutual responsibilities, level of services, acceptance criteria of deliveries, and other required contract conditions.

Table A.9. Contracting procedure

—	Maintenance service is not based on any contract or other documented practice.
–	Maintenance service is performed according to continuous framework agreement, but separate services and deliveries are not identified.
+/–	Maintenance service is based on continuous framework agreement, and each service transaction is recorded by supplier and accepted at least orally by customer/end user.
+	Maintenance service is based on separate service agreements and each service delivery is based on mutually accepted documents.
++	Each service type is based on documented mutual agreement, and is an element of continuous framework agreement. Each delivery is based on mutually approved specification document.

Number of Stakeholders

Number of people and/or organizations involved in management and decision making of maintenance service and deliveries

Table A.10. Number of stakeholders

—	Number of people and organizations involved in implementation and decision making of change requests is high (both more than 5).
–	Either the number of people or organizations involved in implementation and decision making of change requests is high (either number of people or organizations more than 5).
+/–	Number of people and organizations involved in implementation and decision making of change requests is typical/average (both 2–4).
+	Either the number of people or organizations involved in implementation and decision making of change requests is low (1–2) and the other is not high (not more than 5).
++	Number of people and organizations involved in implementation and decision making of change requests is low (both 2 or less).

Priority Setting and Control of Changes

Classification and analysis of change requests by defined criteria (for example, criticality, urgency, and cost) to prioritize change requests and decide on required actions of both parties.

Table A.11. Priority setting and control of changes

—	No agreed classification for errors, failures, and change requests.
–	Only application specific error classification is in use.
+/–	Organization wide error and failure recording and classification is in use and it is used to prioritize fixing actions
+	Organization has classified each application by business criticality and classifies also each error and failure, respectively. Each change request is analyzed by benefit/cost method.

(Continued)

Table A. 11. (Cont.)

++	All applications and error and failure types have widely known criticality classification and consistent benefit/cost analysis method. All responsible persons (operators etc.) are fully aware of all problem situations and required actions.

Organizational Culture

Common attitudes among staff and appreciation of maintenance at company level, appropriate awarding mechanism, and other cultural factors.

Table A.12. Organizational culture

—	Organization and people are enthusiastic of new technologies and projects only. New development projects are highly appreciated, maintenance "just must." No visibility for maintenance work, no awarding mechanism for maintenance projects and services.
–	Importance of maintenance is known, but not shown. No communication and awarding mechanism for maintenance.
+/–	Organization values maintenance but does not motivate people in maintenance work in any means. Maintenance is mentioned in top management presentations and is part of company-wide measurement program.
+	Maintenance has good image in company as a key long-term success factor and profit maker. Maintenance is a profession, and is part of recruiting campaigns
++	Maintenance has good image in company and has strong motivation and commitment among top management and staff. People want maintenance responsibilities and activities. Maintenance is measured at organizational delivery and individual levels and is part of awarding mechanism.

A.3.2 Process Factors

Source Code Edition Methods and Tools

The level and impact of code editors, translation tools, code libraries, and code integrity tools and procedures.

Table A.13. Source code edition methods and tools

——	Development environment and tools are not in proper use and widely known. Several hardware platforms
–	Development environment and tools are in moderate use, but are immature and new versions are needed frequently. Some guidelines and standards are in partial use.
+/–	Development environment and tools are in common use. Guidelines, procedures, and standards are created, but only in partial use.
+	Development environment and tools are well known and in common use. Guidelines, procedures, and standards are in use and easily accessible.

(Continued)

++	Environments and tools are an integrated set, and automate major parts of manual tasks. Simple, well-known development environment and only one hardware platform.

Testing Methods and Tools

Level and impact of tools and procedures to manage test cases and materials, test activities, regression tests, and test results.

Table A.14. Testing methods and tools

—	No testing practices and standards. Test materials are derived separately each time when required.
–	Testing activities and standards exist, but test case derivation and reuse is difficult. All data is file-based, only manual handling of files and data.
+/–	Testing is well performed and largely supported by standards. Test data is managed with appropriate tools and/or scripts.
+	One test material package, which can be modified for different test situations. Testing process and appropriate tools are well documented and in proper use.
++	Each application/software component has well-defined test suite (scripts and materials) for all defined testing phases. Regression testing is tool-supported, where appropriate.

Documentation Methods and Tools

Level and impact of tools and procedures to create, manage, and distribute required application documents for maintenance staff and end users.

Table A.15. Documentation methods and tools

—	No common procedure and widely used professional practices for documentation.
–	No common guidelines and procedures for any documentation, only some version and change control in use.
+/–	Good documentation of each application, change request, and error/failure. Follow-up of documented changes, errors, and failures is in use.
+	Application documents are well managed, controlled, and maintained. Mostly manual documentation.
++	Well-defined process for documentation of each application. Documentation is tool-based and in wide, firms use.

Communication Mechanisms

Level and impact of methods, tools, and procedures to record, communicate, and handle change requests, errors, and failures.

Table A.16. Communication mechanisms

—	No defined approach for communicating. Required information is distributed for all potential parties to avoid "communication gap." Many kinds of media are in use.
–	Communication mechanism is defined, but only in partial use. Some guidelines are available.
+/–	Communication mechanism is documented, and in proper use. It is not integral part of maintenance process.
+	Communication is well integrated with maintenance activities and process. No tools, but some templates and distribution lists are in use.
++	Multiple tools for communication are in proper use and well aligned with actual work processes. Templates support major part of communication.

Roll-Out Methods and Tools

Level and impact of tools and procedures to roll-out modified programs/applications and related data to operation environment.

Table A.17. Roll-out methods and tools

—	No defined approach for rollouts. Deployment is work intensive and depends on key staff.
–	Some documents about rollouts are made and in use. Some separate tools in use.
+/–	Roll-out is a well-defined process and it is followed largely. One dominant tool to perform roll-out and record roll-out status. No easy traceability and version status of rollouts.
+	Well-established work process for roll-out. Good version control and traceability.
++	Roll-out and version control has already long history in organization and is fully automated.

A.3.3 Product Factors

Functionality Requirements

Variety and complexity of the requirements and business rules, level of interfaces.

Table A.18. Functionality requirements

—	Virginal and complex application area, security critical big (thousands of FPs) multitier system for various, multicultural users. Many authorization levels for users. Some complex, algorithmic functions.
–	Various user groups and access levels to applications and data. Many interfaces with other systems. Some business rules require special application knowledge from developers and testers.

(Continued)

+/–	Some user groups with slightly different access control. Mostly simple business rules.
+	Only a couple of user groups, only some interfaces with other systems. All business rules are relatively simple.
++	Only one user group, all have same access control. No interfaces with other systems. Functionality is simple data movement to and from user (screens, reports).

Reliability Requirements

Severity of failures and impact of failures to users and operation.

Table A.19. Reliability requirements

—	Operation faults may endanger human lives or cause great economic or environmental losses, the application must recover without losing any data in any case.
–	Failures can cause major economic loss and image suffering, can lead to negative news in mass media.
+/–	Faulty operation can cause harm for some hundred users, can reflect negatively in operation of 2–3 other applications.
+	Failures can cause harm for some tens of users, but they can tolerate short operation breaks even daily. Some impacts in max one other application.
++	Failure has impacts only in some users. Maximally weekly or monthly operation period, error can be fixed without operational losses. No impacts on any other applications

Usability Requirements

Number of users, support for various skill levels of users, continuous operation, special requirements to attract users.

Table A.20. Usability requirements

—	A very big number of different types of end-users all over the world, with different levels of experience at software usage, a high-level customization and help facilities required. 24 h/day, 7 days/week operation requirement.
–	2–3 different types of users with various skills and languages, requiring automated multilevel help function, the use of software during interactive customer service. 24 h/day operation requirement.
+/–	Limited number of regular users, who can be trained in advance. Mostly in back-office use, sometimes in direct customer service. Max 20 h/day operation.
+	Application for small number of users. Only in back-office functions. Operation in working hours is required.
++	Only few expert users or one team, all located at one site, not very frequent use.

Efficiency Requirements

Requirements for response and transaction processing time, differences in operational and computer load, transaction and data volumes.

Table A.21. Efficiency requirements

—	Very big volume of real-time transactions, big differences in operation load, need for simultaneous online and batch processing. Millions of records in database, many kinds of nonpredictable inquiry needs.
–	Hundreds of simultaneous end-users in multiple sites, most of response time requirements critical, queuing in transaction processing causes operational loss for services.
+/–	Max one hundred simultaneous end-users. Response time requirements are flexible but critical for work efficiency, mostly only predefined inquiry needs.
+	Simple database, straightforward, and predictable data requests from few simultaneous end-users.
++	Simple and small database, no simultaneous end-users or complex data requests, total number of transactions not more than tens per day.

Maintainability Requirements

Stability of the environment, standardized code and component structures, clarity of architecture, pressure for changes.

Table A.22. Maintainability requirements

—	Very large strategic (target lifetime more than 20 years) software at a volatile business area with frequent changes of laws and standards and business rules. Also the maintenance speed is essential, logging and the defect messages must be clear, exact, and instructive for developers
–	Large software (target lifetime from 10 to 20 years), frequent changes of laws or standards or business rules. Time to analyze defect messages, change the programs and test them is always some hours but not more.
+/–	Average size tactical (target lifetime from 5 to 10 years) software, monthly changes of laws, standards and business rules. Maintenance timing is reasonably flexible, a couple of days rather than hours, an application specific error log needed.
+	Rather small rarely changing software (target lifetime from 2 to 5 years), no application specific diagnostics needed.
++	Temporary software (target lifetime less than 2 years) with no intention to enhance for new requirements.

Portability Requirements

Adaptability and installability to different environments, openness of architecture and structural components, volatility of platforms and environments.

Table A.23. Portability requirements

— Users of the software are located in many kind of organizations, with various platforms (hardware, browsers, operating systems, middleware, data communication protocols, etc), various versions, and various upgrading frequencies.

– The software must operate on many different platforms (hardware, browsers, operating systems, middleware, data communication protocols, etc) and on several versions of them.

+/– Every version of the software must run on several versions of a certain platform (hardware, browser, operating system, middleware, data communication protocol, etc), the upgrading frequencies of the users are rather predictable.

+ The software must run on a certain platform (hardware, browser, operating system, middleware, data communication protocol, etc), for which the software is tested. Only one "latest version" of software is required. Some customers or user groups may use older versions, but they do not need to be interoperable with new version.

++ The software must run only on a certain platform (hardware, browser, operating system, middleware, data communication protocol, etc) in which upgrading process is completely manageable (for example, most of the mainframe environments). Several tens of similar applications are running on the same platform.

A.3.4 People Factors

Development Environment Skills of Staff

Experience and knowledge of maintenance staff in development environment, tools, and platforms (design, implementation, testing, version control, operation, documentation, communication)

Table A.24. Development environment skills of staffskills of staff

---
— Development environment and tools are new for the whole maintenance staff. The average experience time is less than 3 months. Special expertise is difficult to get. Training needs are not satisfied.

– At least one responsible person has reasonable knowledge of environments (3 months to 2 years). Special knowledge is difficult to get. Training is partially available.

+/– At least one of some responsible persons has good knowledge of environments (several years). Average experience is 1–3 years. Special knowledge is largely available on request. Training is available on essential tools.

+ All responsible persons know well the environments and tools (2–5 years). Some persons can give hands-on support in tools. Training is available on all tools.

++ The software must run only on a certain platform (hardware, browser, operating system, middleware, data communication protocol, etc), which upgrade process. The whole maintenance staff knows all the tools very well (>5 years experience). Support available for the specific needs of the project. No need for training.

Application Knowledge of Staff

Knowledge of the maintenance staff in the applications and interfacing systems (both the supplier and the customer).

Table A.25. Application knowledge of staff

—	The business area knowledge of maintenance staff is very small, less than 12 months. No expertise on interfacing systems.
–	The application experience is small on vendor side, and software knowledge is small on customer side. Maintenance staff has no special knowledge on interfacing systems.
+/–	Maintenance staff has quite good experience of the business area and application domain, 1–3 years in average. At least some people have good overall understanding of the application portfolio.
+	The business area and application domain experience is good both on the supplier and the customer sides. The experience is 3–6 years in average, some have >5 years experience.
++	Both the supplier and the customer representatives know the business area and application domain very well (in average >5 years), including the understanding of the business as total. Good understanding of application portfolio among the whole maintenance staff.

Networking Skills of Staff

Level of team building and networking among maintenance staff, ability to cooperate with partners.

Table A.26. Networking skills of staff

—	Maintenance staff consists of new people, no mutual working history and experiences. Responsible persons have no common language. No connection with external stakeholders.
–	Part of maintenance staff has common working history, max 2 years. Management and experts have mutual communication and understanding problems. Ad hoc connections with stakeholders.
+/–	Maintenance staff has some year's common working history (2–5 years). Mutual communication is open and works quite well. Cooperation with stakeholders is done when required.
+	Maintenance staff has long common working history (>5 years). No mutual communication problems between management and experts. Regular cooperation with stakeholders.
++	Maintenance staff has very long common working history (>10 years). No communication problems between management and experts. Stable and continuous cooperation with stakeholders, even when responsibilities are allocated to new staff.

Motivation and Responsibility of Staff

Personal motivation to develop application and customer business

Table A.27. Motivation and responsibility of staff

——	Maintenance staff has no interest to develop application. Maintenance is considered as mandatory extra duty, which should be avoided. Easy to transfer responsibility to other staff members.
–	Maintenance staff members are not interested to develop application, expect some limited responsibilities that are explicitly allocated to them.
+/–	Maintenance staff members are performing maintenance activities according to plan and take the development responsibility.
+	Maintenance staff members are interested to develop application and take personal responsibility over the whole application area, as defined.
++	Maintenance staff is interested to develop customer's business, like introduction of new technology, competitive position of applications, and new changes in interfacing systems. Real responsibilities are far over the minimal requirements defined in maintenance contract.

Team Atmosphere

Influence on working conditions, self-learning, professional career opportunities.

Table A.28. Team atmosphere

——	Maintenance staff feels that their work effort is highly underappreciated. Continuous lack of resources. No influence on daily work and working conditions. Unfair or unknown feedback on work.
–	Maintenance staff feels that their work is underappreciated, and leads to at least temporary resource conflicts and inadequate training. Only some influence on daily work at individual level, weak feedback on work results.
+/–	Maintenance staff feels that their work is moderately appreciated. Resourcing and training are quite adequate. Mostly good influence on daily work, sometimes resource conflict with continuous responsibilities and project duties.
+	Maintenance work and results are well appreciated. Resourcing and training are adequate. Each individual has good influence on daily working arrangements. Good feedback from work, fair awarding.
++	Excellent feelings about maintenance work among the whole staff and management. Resourcing and training are adequate. Good knowledge on all feedback from management and customer, awarding is fair. Full responsibility and self-control at individual level on personal working conditions and satisfaction of new professional requirements.

Literature

Abran, A., Dumke, R., Desharnais, J., Ndyaje, I., Kolbe, C., A Strategy for a Credible & Auditable Estimation Process Using the ISBSG International Data Repository, in Dumke et al. (Ed.): Software Measurement and Estimation, Shaker Verlag, Aachen, 2002, pp. 246–258

Abran, A., Gil, B., Lefebvre, E., Estimation Models based on Functional Profiles, in: Proceedings of the International Workshop on Software Metrics and DASMA Software Metrik Kongress, IWSM/MetriKon 2004, November 2–5, 2004, Königs-Wusterhausen, Germany, Software Measurement – Research and Application, Shaker Verlag, Aachen, 2004, pp. 195–212, ISBN 3-8322-3383-0

Abran, A., Nguyenkim, H., Measurement of the maintenance process from a demand based perspective, in: Journal of Software Maintenance and Evolution: Research and Practice, 1993, 5: pp. 63–90

Abran, A., Robillard, PN., Function point analysis: An empirical study of measurement processes, in: IEEE Transactions on Software Engineering, 1996, 22(12): pp. 895–903

Abran, A., Desharnais, J. -M., Aziz, F., From Function Points to COSMIC-FFP, in: Proceedings of the 15th International Workshop on Software Measurement, Innovations in Software Measurement, September 12–14, 2005, Montréal, Canada, pp. 227–240, Shaker Verlag, Aachen, 2005, ISBN 3-8322-4405-0

Abran, A., Silva, I., Primera, L., Field studies using functional size measurement in building estimation models for software maintenance, in: Journal of Software Maintenance and Evolution: Research and Practice, 2002, 14: pp. 1–34

Al Qutaish, R. E., Abran, A., An Analysis of the Design and Definitions of Halstead's Metrics, in: Proceedings of the 15th International Workshop on Software Measurement, Innovations in Software Measurement, September 12–14, 2005, Montréal, Canada, pp. 337–352, Shaker Verlag, Aachen, 2005, ISBN 3-8322-4405-0

Albrecht, A. J., Measuring Application Development Productivity, Proceedings of Joint SHARE, GUIDE, and IBM Application Development Symposium, White Plains, New York, October 1979, pp. 83–93

Antoniol, G., Calzolari, F., et al., Adapting Function Points to Object Oriented Information Systems, in: Proceedings of CAiSE '98, 1998

April, A. A., Al-Shurougi, D., Software Product Measurement for Supplier Evaluation, in: Proceedings of the FESMA Conference 2000, Madrid

ASMA, Sizing in Object-Oriented Environments, Australian Software Metrics Association, Victoria, Australia, 1994

Ayers, M., Critical Success Factors for Developing and Implementing a Contractual Metrics Program, in: IFPUG, IT Measurement – Practical Advice from the Experts, Addison-Wesley Pearson Education Inc., Indianapolis, 2002, ISBN 0-2017-4158-X, pp. 445–454

Azzouz, S., Abran, A., A PROPOSED Measurement Role in the Rational Unified Process and its Implementation with ISO 19761: COSMIC-FFP, in: Proceedings of the Software Measurement European Forum 2004 (SMEF2004), Rome, Istituto di Ricerca Internationale S.r.l., Milano, 28.–30.1.2004, S. 356–368, ISBN 8-8866-7433-3

Basili, V., Caldiera, G., Rombach, H., Goal question metric paradigm, in: J. J. Marciniak, (Ed.): Encyclopedia of Software Engineering, Wiley, New York, 1994, pp. 528–532

Bayer, S., Tolomei, V., The Role of Functional Metrics in B2B E-Commerce Project Success, in: IFPUG, IT Measurement – Practical Advice from the Experts, Addison-Wesley Pearson Education Inc., Indianapolis, 2002, ISBN 0-2017-4158-X, pp. 655–676

Beckett, D., Llorence, P. C., Metrics in Support of Estimating in a Large Software Services Company, in: IFPUG, IT Measurement – Practical Advice from the Experts, Addison-Wesley Pearson Education Inc., Indianapolis, 2002, ISBN 0-2017-4158-X, pp. 323–336

Beyers, C. P., Estimating Software Development Projects, in: IFPUG, IT Measurement – Practical Advice from the Experts, Addison-Wesley Pearson Education Inc., Indianapolis, 2002, ISBN 0-2017-4158-X, pp. 337–362

Bierfert, H., Verinnerlichung als Start und Ziel von Metriken – SW-Metriken zwischen Akzeptanz und Relevanz, in: Dumke, R. R. (Hrsg.): Software-Metriken in der Praxis, Tagungsband (Proceedings) (Proceedings) des DASMA Software Metrik Kongresses MetriKon 2001, Shaker Verlag, Aachen, 2002, ISBN 3-8322-0470-9

Boehm, B. W., Characteristics of Software Quality, North Holland, Amsterdam, 1978

Boehm, B. W., Software Engineering Economics, Prentice Hall, New York, 1981

Boehm, B. W., Wirtschaftliche Softwareproduktion, Prentice Hall, NewYork, 1986

Boehm, B. W., et al., Software Cost Estimation with COCOMO II, Englewood Cliffs, NJ, Prentice Hall, 2000

Boehm, B. W., Requirement-Led Project Management, Discovering David's Slingshot by Robertson, Suzanne and James, Pearson Education, 2005

Braungarten, R., Kunz, M., Farooq, A., Dumke, R., Towards Meaningful Metrics Data Bases, in: Proceedings of the 15th International Workshop on

Software Measurement, Innovations in Software Measurement, September 12–14, 2005, Montréal, Canada, pp. 1–34, Shaker Verlag, Aachen, 2005, ISBN 3-8322-4405-0

Briand, L. C., El Emam, K., Bomarius, F., COBRA: A Hybrid Method for Software Cost Estimation, Benchmarking, and Risk Assessment, in: Proceedings of the 20th International Conference on Software Engineering, April 1998, pp. 390–399

Brooks, F., The Mythical Man Month 2nd Edition (20th anniversary edition), Addison Wesley, Reading, MA, 1995 ISBN 3-8266-1355-2)

Büren, G., Bundschuh, M., Dumke, R. (Hrsg.), Software-Messung in der Praxis – Tagungsband (Proceedings) des DASMA Software Metrik Kongresses METRIKON 2003, Shaker Verlag, Aachen, 2003, ISBN 3-8322-2146-8

Büren, G., Hopf, H. -G., Softwaremetriken als notwendige Voraus-setzung für Projektcontrolling in der Software-Entwicklung, in: Software-Metriken in der Praxis, Tagungsband (Proceedings) des DASMA Software Metrik Kongresses MetriKon 2001, Shaker Verlag, Aachen 2002, ISBN 3-8322-0470-9

Büren, G., Kroll, I., First Experiences with the Introduction of an Effort Estimation Process. In: CONQUEST'99: Quality Engineering in Software Technology, Conference on Quality Engineering in Software Technology. Nuremberg (1999), pp. 132–144

Buglione, L., Abran, A., The Software Measurement Body of Know-ledge, in: Proceedings of the Software Measurement European Forum 2004 (SMEF2004), Rome, Istituto di Ricerca Internationale S.r.l., Milano, 28.–30.1.2004, S. 84–94, ISBN 8-8866-7433-3

Bundschuh, M., Aufwandschätzung als Voraussetzung für die Projektplanung, in: Bernecker, M., Eckrich, K., Handbuch Projektmanagement, R. Oldenbourg Verlag, München, 2003, ISBN 3-4862-7444-9, S. 239–259

Bundschuh, M., Die Function Point Methode im praktischen Einsatz bei Softwareprojekten, in: Schelle et al., Projekte erfolgreich managen, BDU, 13. Aktualisierungs- und Ergänzungslieferung, November 1999

Bundschuh, M., Estimation of Maintenance Tasks, in: Dumke, R. et al., Software Measurement and Estimation – Proceedings of the 12th International Workshop on Software Measurement, 2002, Shaker Verlag, Aachen, 2002, ISBN 3-8322-0765-1, pp. 125–136

Bundschuh, M., Function Point Prognosis, in: Metrics News, Vol, 3, Nr. 2, December 1998

Bundschuh, M., Function Point Prognosis Approved, in: Metrics News, Vol, 7, Nr. 1, July 2002

Bundschuh, M., Software Measurement and -Metrics in external Enterprises, in: Metrics News, Vol, 7, Nr. 2, December 2002

Bundschuh, M., Peetz, W., Siska, R., Aufwandschätzung mit der Function Point Methode, TüV Rheinland GmbH, Köln, 1991, ISBN 3-8858-5982-3

Card, D., What Makes a Software Measure Successful, in: American Programmer, September 1991

Card, D., The Role of Measurement, in: Software Engineering, July 1998

Cartwright, M., Shepperd, M., Building Predictive Models from Object-Oriented Metrics, in: Proceedings of the 8th ESCOM Conference, Berlin, 1997, pp. 51–55

Catherwood, B., Sood, M., Armour, F., Continued Experiences Measuring Object Oriented System Size, in: Proceedings of the 8th ESCOM Conference, Berlin, 1997, pp. 56–61

Chidamber, S. R., Kemerer, C. F., A Metrics Suite for Object Oriented Design, MIT Sloan School of Management, 1993

Chidamber, S. R., Kemerer, C. F., A Metrics Suite for Object Oriented Design, IEEE Transactions on Software Engineering, Vol. 20, No. 6, June 1994, pp. 476–493

Clark, E., Tracking Software Progress, in: IFPUG, IT Measurement – Practical Advice from the Experts, Addison-Wesley Pearson Education Inc., Indianapolis, 2002, ISBN 0-2017-4158-X, pp. 223–236

Coley, D., Considerations for getting Maximum Benefit from an Enterprise-Wide Metrics Repository, in: IFPUG, IT Measurement – Practical Advice from the Experts, Addison-Wesley Pearson Education Inc., Indianapolis, 2002, ISBN 0-2017-4158-X, pp. 455–462

Combes, H., Peeters, B., van Huysduynen, M. H., Proceedings of the 1998 FESMA Conference, Antwerpen, 6.–8.5.1998, ISBN 9-0760-1903-7 *COSMIC* System:http: Case Studies with ISO 19761 (2003), C(course) Registration *consortium,* //www.lrgl.uqam.ca/cosmic-ffp/casestudies_with_ISO_19761_2003.html, 2008

Cowderoy, A., (Editor), Proceedings of the 1997 ESCOM Conference, Berlin, 26.–28.5.1997

Crosby, P. B., Quality is Free, Mentor Books, New York, NY, 1979

Curtis, B., Krasner, H., Shen, V. Y., Iscoe, N., On Building Software Process Models Under the Lamppost, ICSE 1987, pp. 96–105

Da Silveira, M. L. B., EDS Brazil Metrics Program: Measuring for Improvement, in: IFPUG, IT Measurement – Practical Advice from the Experts, Addison-Wesley Pearson Education Inc., Indianapolis, 2002, ISBN 0-2017-4158-X, pp. 85–96

Dekkers, C. A., Not Your Father's Function Points, in: Proceedings of the ICSSEA 2006, Dec. 5, 2006, Paris, France http://deptinfo.cnam.fr/CMSL/icssea/icssea2006/icssea2006_US/progra-full.html

Dekkers, C. A., Guide to Software Measurement Start-up one-day workshop, Quality Plus Technologies, Inc., www.qualityplustech.com, 2000-current.

Dekkers, C. A., How and When Can Functional Size Fit with a Measurement Program?, in: IFPUG, IT Measurement – Practical Advice from the Experts, Addison-Wesley Pearson Education Inc., Indianapolis, 2002, ISBN 0-2017-4158-X, pp. 161–169

Dekkers, C. A., Secrets of Highly Successful Measurement Programs, Cutter IT Journal, Vol. 12, No. 4, pp. 29–35, 1999

Dekkers, C. A., Tackling software measurement? try proverbs, backtalk column, crosstalk in: the Journal of Defense Software Engineering, May 2005, www.stsc.hill.af.mil/crosstalk

Dekkers, C. A., Forselius, P., Increase ICT Project Success with Concrete Scope Management, in Proceedings of the Project Management Institute 2007 Asia Pacific (Hong Kong) and 2007 North American (Atlanta) congresses, 2007

Dekkers, C. A., Gunter, I., Using "Backfiring" to Accurately Size Software: More Wishful Thinking than Science?, IT Metrics Strategies, Cutter Information Corp., November 2000, Volume VI, No. 11, Cutter Consortium, www.cutter.com/consortium/.

Dekkers, C. A., Lundquist, G., The proof is in the ratios: Turning raw data into meaningful software metrics, in: The Journal of The Quality Insurance Institute, July 1996

Dekkers, C. A., McQuaid, P., The Dangers of using software metrics to (mis)manage, IEEE IT Professional, Mar/April 2002.

Dekkers, T., Funktionalgrößen Meßmethoden sind auch in Verb-esserungsprojekten anwendbar, in: Software-Messung in der Praxis, Tagun-gsband (Proceedings) des DASMA Software Metrik Kongresses MetriKon 2003, 10.–11. November 2003, Neu-Ulm. Shaker Verlag, Aachen, 2003, S. 55–67, ISBN 3-8322-2146-8

Dekkers, T., Benchmarking is an Essential Control Mechanism for Management, in: Proceedings of the International Workshop on Software Measurement, September 12–14, 2005, Montréal, Canada, pp. 107–122, Shaker Verlag, Aachen, 2005, ISBN 3-8322-4405-0

DeMarco, T., Controlling Software Projects, Prentice Hall, Englewood Cliffs, NJ, 1982, ISBN 0-9170-7232-4

DeMarco, T., Warum ist Software so teuer? ... und andere Rätsel des Informationszeitalters, Carl Hanser Verlag, München Wien, 1997, ISBN 3-4461-8902-5

DeMarco, T., Why Does Software Cost So Much? And other puzzles of the information age, Dorset House, New York, NY, 1995, ISBN 0-9326-3334-X

DeMarco, T., Lister, T., Peopleware 2nd Edition, Dorset House, New York, NY, Feb 1999, ISBN 0-9326-3343-9

Dery, D., Abran, A., Investigation of the Effort Data Consistency in the ISBSG Repository, in: Proceedings of the International Workshop on Software Measurement, September 12–14, 2005, Montréal, Canada, pp. 123–136, Shaker Verlag, Aachen, 2005, ISBN 3-8322-4405-0

Doyle, J., Standardizing a SLOC Counting Tool to Support ISO and CMM Requirements, in: IFPUG, IT Measurement – Practical Advice from the Experts, Addison-Wesley Pearson Education Inc., Indianapolis, 2002, ISBN 0-2017-4158-X, pp. 569–576

Dreger, J. B., Function Point Analysis, Prentice Hall, Englewood Cliffs, NJ, 1989

Dueck, G., Ein Indikatorenhoch über Deutschland! Starke Triebwinde, in: Informatik Spektrum, Band 26, Heft 1, February 2003, S. 39–44

Dumke, R., Softwareentwicklung nach Maß – Schätzen – Messen – Bewerten, Vieweg, Wiesbaden, 1992

Dumke, R., Abran, A., Software Measurement – Current Trends in Research and Practice, Deutscher Universitäts Verlag, Wiesbaden, 1999, ISBN 3-8244-6876-X

Dumke, R., Bundschuh, M., (Hrsg.), Software-Metriken in der Praxis – Tagungsband (Proceedings) des DASMA Software Metrik Kongresses MetriKon 2002, Shaker Verlag, Aachen, 2002, ISBN 3-8322-0470-9

Dumke, R., Foltin, E., Koeppe, R., Winkler, A., Softwarequalität durch Meßtools, Vieweg, Wiesbaden, 1996

Dumke, R., Zuse, H., (Hrsg.), Theorie und Praxis der Softwaremessung, Deutscher Universitäts Verlag, Wiesbaden, 1994, ISBN 3-8244-2061-9

Dumke, R., et al., Software Measurement and Estimation in Proceedings of the 12th International Workshop on Software Measurement, 2002, Shaker Verlag, Aachen, 2002, ISBN 3-8322-0765-1

Ebert, C., Dumke, R., Software-Metriken in der Praxis, Springer, Berlin, 1996, ISBN 3-5406-0372-7

Ebert, C., Dumke, R., Bundschuh, M., Schmietendorf, A., Best Practices in Software Measurement – How to Use Metrics to Improve Project and Process Performance, Springer, 2004

End, W., Gotthardt, H., Winkelmann, R., Softwareentwicklung, 4. Auflage, Berlin München, 1984

Estol, C., Measurements Necessary to Support an IT Balanced Scorecard: IT Indicators, in: IFPUG, IT Measurement – Practical Advice from the Experts, Addison-Wesley Pearson Education Inc., Indianapolis, 2002, ISBN 0-2017-4158-X, pp. 473–489

Fenton, N., Software Metric: A rigorous Approach, Chapmann & Hall, London, 1991

Fenton, N., Software Quality Assurance and Measurement, International Thomson Computer Press, Boston, MA, 1997, ISBN 1-8503-2174-4

Fetcke, T., The warehouse software portfolio, a case study in functional size measurement, Technical report no. 1999-20, Département d'Infor-matique, Université du Quebec á Montréal, Canada, 1999

Fetcke, T., Abran, A., Nguyen, T., Function Point Analysis for the OO-Jacobson Method: A Mapping Approach, in: Proceedings of the FESMA Conference 1998, Antwerp, pp. 395–402

Finck, M., Hampp, T., Eine Untersuchung zum Metrikeinsatz in der Industrie, in: Tagungsband (Proceedings) des DASMA Software Metrik Kongresses MetriKon 2005, Shaker Verlag, Aachen, 2005, pp. 33–42, ISBN 3-8322-4615-0

Finnish Software Measurement Association (FiSMA), FiSMA 1.1 Functional Size Measurement Method, Helsinki, Finland, www.fisma.fi, 2008

Foltin, E., Schmietendorf, A., Estimating the Cost of Carrying out Tasks Relating to Performance Engineering, in: Dumke, R., Abran, A. (Eds.): New Approaches in Software Measurement, Proceedings of the 10th International Workshop IWSM 2000, Springer, Berlin Heidelberg New York, 201, pp. 55–72, ISBN 3-5404-1727-3

Forselius, P., Discipline to Software Development – Learn to Distinguish Project Management from Other Management Levels, in: Proceedings of the 19th IPMA Global congress, New Delhi, India, November 2005

Forselius, P., Dekkers, C., Karvinen, M., Kosonen, M., Program Management Toolkit – for software and systems development, Finnish Information Processing Association (FIPA), Talentum, Finland, April 2008, ISBN 978-952-14-1338-4

Frallicciardi, L., Measuring the Usability of E-Commerce Applications, in: IFPUG, IT Measurement – Practical Advice from the Experts, Addison-Wesley Pearson Education Inc., Indianapolis, 2002, ISBN 0-2017-4158-X, pp. 677–687

Galorath, D. G., Effectively Utilizing Software Metrics: Project Metrics, in: IFPUG, IT Measurement – Practical Advice from the Experts, Addison-Wesley Pearson Education Inc., Indianapolis, 2002, ISBN 9-780201-741582, pp. 237–254

Gantner, T., Schneider, K., Zwei Anwendungen von GQM: Ähnlich, aber doch nicht gleich, in: Software-Messung in der Praxis, Tagungsband (Proceedings) des DASMA Software Metrik Kongresses MetriKon 2003, 10.–11. November 2003, Neu-Ulm. Shaker Verlag, Aachen, 2003, S. 19-33, ISBN 3-8322-2146-8

Garmus, D., Enhanced Estimation: On Time, Within Budget, in: IFPUG, IT Measurement – Practical Advice from the Experts, Addison-Wesley Pearson Education Inc., Indianapolis, 2002, ISBN 9-780201-741582, pp. 363–375

Garmus, D., Herron, D., Measuring the Software Process, Yourdon Press, Prentice Hall, Englewood Cliffs, NJ, 1995, ISBN 0-1334-9002-5

Gencel, C., Demirors, O., Yuceer, E., A Case Study Using Functional Size Measurement Methods for Real Time Systems, in: Proceedings of the International Workshop on Software Measurement, September 12-14, 2005, Montréal, Canada, pp. 159–178, Shaker Verlag, Aachen, 2005, ISBN 3-8322-4405-0

Goldensen, D., Jarzombek, J., Rout, T., Measurement and Analysis in Software Process Improvement, in: IFPUG, IT Measurement – Practical Advice from the Experts, Addison-Wesley Pearson Education Inc., Indianapolis, 2002, ISBN 9-780201-741582, pp. 577–604

Goldfarb, S., Introduction to Metrics in Outsourcing, in: IFPUG, IT Measurement – Practical Advice from the Experts, Addison-Wesley Pearson Education Inc., Indianapolis, 2002, ISBN 9-780201-741582, pp. 519–535

Goodman, P., Practical Implementation of Software Metrics, McGraw-Hill, New York, 1993

Grady, R. B., Practical Software Metrics for Project Management and Process Improvement, Prentice Hall, Englewood Cliffs, NJ, 1992, ISBN 0-1372-0384-5

Granja, C., Oller, A., Function Points Analysis Based on Requirement Specification, a Case Study, in: Proceedings of the 14th International Workshop IWSM 2004/Metrikon, Shaker, Aachen, 2004, pp. 473–481 ISBN 3-3822-3383-0

Großjohann, R., Über die Bedeutung des Function-Point-Verfahrens in rezessiven Zeiten, in: Dumke, R., Zuse, H. (Hrsg.), Theorie und Praxis der Softwaremessung, S. 20–34, Deutscher Universitäts Verlag, Wiesbaden, 1994, ISBN 3-8244-2061-9

GUFPI-ISMA, Proposals for Project Collection and Classification from the Analysis of the ISBSG Benchmark 8, in: Proceedings of the 14th International Workshop IWSM 2004/Metrikon, Shaker, Aachen, 2004, pp. 547–573 ISBN 3-3822-3383-0

Gupta, R., Gupta, S. K., Object Point Analysis, in: IFPUG 1996 Fall Conference, Dallas, Texas, 1996

Habela, P., Glowacki, E., Serafinskli, T., Subieta, K., Adapting Use Case Model for COSMIC-FFP Based Measurement, in: Proceedings of the International Workshop on Software Measurement, September 12–14, 2005, Montréal, Canada, pp. 195–207, Shaker Verlag, Aachen, 2005, ISBN 3-8322-4405-0

Hamann, D., Beitz, A., Müller, M., Solingen, R. van, Using FAME Assessments to Define Measurement Goals in: Reiner Dumke, Alain Abran (Eds.): New Approaches in Software Measurement, Proceedings of the 10th International Workshop, IWSM 2000, Berlin, Germany, October 2000, Springer, Berlin Heidelberg New York, 2001, pp. 220–232, ISBN 3-5404-1727-3

Hall, T., Baddoo, N., Wilson, D., Measurement in Software Process Improvement Programmes: An Empirical Study, in: R. Dumke, A. Abran (Eds.): New Approaches in Software Measurement, Proceedings of the 10th International Workshop, IWSM 2000, Berlin, Germany, October 2000, Springer, Berlin Heidelberg New York, 2001, pp.73–82, ISBN 3-5404-1727-3

Halstead, M. H., Elements of Software Science, Elsevier North-Holland, New York, NY, 1977

Heemstra, F. J., Software cost estimation, in: Information Software Technology, 1992, 34(10): pp. 627–639

Henderson-Sellers, B., Object-Oriented Metrics – Measures of Complexity, Prentice Hall, Englewood Cliffs, NJ, 1996, ISBN 0-1323-9872-9

Herrmann, O., Kalkulation von Softwareentwicklungen, München Wien, 1983

Hindel, B., Qualität ist meßbar: Software-Metriken, in: Design & Elektronik, Nr. 24 vom 26.11.1996, S. 50–55

Höglund, M., Project Metrics Using Effort Metrics For Tracking, in: IT Measurement – Practical Advice from the Experts, Addison-Wesley Pearson Education Inc., Indianapolis, 2002, ISBN 9-780201-741582, pp. 255–269

Hongxing, L., What Can Function Point Analysis Do to Support CMM?, in: IFPUG, IT Measurement – Practical Advice from the Experts, Addison-Wesley Pearson Education Inc., Indianapolis, 2002, ISBN 9-780201-741582, pp. 605–611

Hürten, R., Function-Point Analysis – Theorie und Praxis, Expert, Renningen-Malmsheim, 1999, ISBN 3-8169-1676-7

Hufschmidt, B., Software Balanced Scorecards: The Icing on the Cake, in: IFPUG, IT Measurement – Practical Advice from the Experts, Addison-Wesley Pearson Education Inc., Indianapolis, 2002, ISBN 9-780201-741582, pp. 493–502

Humphrey, W. S., Managing the Software Process, Addison-Wesley, Reading, MA, 1989

IEEE Computer Society: Software and Systems Vocabulary (SE VOCAB), http://www.computer.org/sevocab ,2008

IFPUG, Website Certification Page: www.ifpug.org/certification/software. htm, 2008.

IFPUG, Counting Practices Manual, Release 4.2, IFPUG, Princeton Junction, NJ, January 2004, ISBN 0-963-1742-9-0

IFPUG, Counting Practices Manual, Release 4.1, IFPUG, Princeton Junction, NJ, January 1999, ISBN 0-963-1742-9-0

IFPUG, IT Measurement – Practical Advice from the Experts, Addison-Wesley Pearson Education Inc., Indianapolis, 2002, ISBN 9-780201-741582

Iorio, T., IFPUG Function Point analysis in a UML framework, in: Proceedings of the Software Measurement European Forum 2004 (SMEF2004), Rome, Istituto di Ricerca Internationale S.r.l., Milano, 28.–30.1.2004, S. 356-368, ISBN 8-8866-7433-3

ISBSG, Practical Project Estimation 2nd Edition, ISBSG, Warrandyte, Victoria, 2005, ISBN 0-9577-2011-4

ISBSG, Software Project Estimation – A Workbook for Macro-Estimation of Software Development Effort and Duration, ISBSG, Melbourne, Victoria, 1999, ISBN 0-9577-2010-6

ISBSG, The Benchmark, Release 5, ISBSG, Warrandyte, Victoria, 1998

ISBSG, The Benchmark, Release 6, ISBSG, Warrandyte, Victoria, 2000, ISBN 0-9577-2016-5

ISBSG, The Benchmark, Release 8, ISBSG, Warrandyte, Victoria, 2004, ISBN 0-9577-2018-1

ISBSG, The Benchmark, Release 10, ISBSG, Warrandyte, Victoria, March 2008, ISBN 0-9577201-3-0

ISBSG, Application Development and Enhancement Data Repository Release 10, Warrandyte, Victoria, Feb. 2007, www.isbg.org

ISBSG, Report on Release 10 Repository Demographics January 2007: CD R10, ISBSG, Warrandyte, Victoria, www.isbsg.org

ISBSG, The Software Metrics Compendium, ISBSG, Warrandyte, Victoria, 2002, ISBN 0-9577-2012-2

ISBSG, Special Analysis Report: Planning projects – project phase ratios, March 2007, Warrandyte, Victoria, www.isbsg.org

Iorino, T., IFPUG Function Point Analysis in a UML Framework, in: Proceedings of the Software Measurement European Forum 2004 (SMEF2004), Rome, Istituto di Ricerca Internationale S.r.l., Milano, 28.–30.1.2004, S. 150–159, ISBN 8-8866-7433-3

ISO/IEC, ISO/IEC 14143-6: Guide for the use of ISO/IEC 14143 series and related international standards, 2006, ISO Geneva, Switzerland

Jantzen, K., Kosten- und Aufwandsschätzung von Softwareprojekten – Projektschätzung mit Tassc:Estimator, in: Informatik Spektrum, Band 26, Heft 1, Februar 2003, S. 47–52

Jeffery, R., Software Models, Metrics, and Improvement, in: Proceedings of the 8th ESCOM Conference, Berlin, 1997, pp. 6–11

Jones, C., Applied Software Measurement, McGraw-Hill, New York, 1996, ISBN 0-0703-2826-9

Jones, C., Assessment and Control of Software Risks, Prentice Hall, Englewood Cliffs, NJ, 1994, ISBN 0-1374-1406-4

Jones, C., Estimating and Measuring Object-Oriented Software, Technical Report, Software Productivity Research Inc., Burlington, MA

Jones, C., Estimating Software Costs: Bringing Realism to Estimating, 2nd Edition, McGraw-Hill, New York, 2007, ISBN-13: 979-0-07-148300-1

Jones, C., Geriatric Issues of Aging Software, March 17, 2007

Jones, C., How Software Estimation Tools work, Technical Report, Software Productivity Research Inc., Burlington, MA, April 6, 2002

Jones, C., Patterns of Software Systems Failure and Success, International Thomson Computer Press, Boston, MA, 1995, ISBN 1-8503-2804-8

Jones, C., Programming Productivity, McGraw-Hill, New York, 1986, ISBN 0-0700-32811-0

Jones, C., Software Quality, International Thomson Computer Press, Boston, MA, 1997, ISBN 1-8503-2867-6

Jones, C., The Expanding Roles of Function Point Metrics in: IFPUG, IT Measurement – Practical Advice from the Experts, Addison-Wesley Pearson Education Inc., Indianapolis, 2002, ISBN 9-780201-741582, pp. 3–30

Jones, J., Metrics in E-Commerce: Function Point Analysis and Component-Based Software Measurement, in: IFPUG, IT Measurement – Practical Advice from the Experts, Addison-Wesley Pearson Education Inc., Indianapolis, 2002, ISBN 9-780201-741582, pp. 689–714

Kan, S. H., Metrics and Models in Software Quality Engineering, Addison Wesley, Reading, MA, 1995, ISBN 0-2016-3339-6

Kaner, C., Bach, J., Nguyen, H. Q., Falk, J., Testing Computer Software, 3rd Edition, Volume 3 (Manager's Volume), in preparation, 2002. (A similar series of questions was proposed in the talk "Measurement of the Extent of Testing", Proceedings of the Pacific Northwest Software Quality Conference, Portland, Oregon, October 17, 2000.)

Karner, G., Metrics for Objectory. Diploma Thesis, University of Linköping, Sweden, No. LiTHIDA-Ex-9344:21, 1993

Kearns, D. T., as quoted by Beth Enslow, American Programmer, (now Cutter IT Journal), 1992

Kemerer, C. F., Reliability of Function Point Measurement: A Field Experiment, in Communications of the ACM (CACM), 36(2), 1993, S. 85–87

Kindler, A., von Schneyder, W., Aufwandschätzung von Projekten – zwischen Fehlanzeige und Perfektion, in: Software-Messung in der Praxis, Tagungsband (Proceedings) des DASMA Software Metrik Kongresses MetriKon 2003, 10.–11. November 2003, Neu-Ulm. Shaker Verlag, Aachen, 2003, S. 107–119, ISBN 3-8322-2146-8

Kitchenham, B., Software Metrics, Blackwell Publication, Cambridge, MA, 1996

Kitchenham, B., The certainty of uncertainty, in: Proceedings of the European Software Measurement Conference (FESMA) 1998, S. 17 ff., Technologisch Instituut, Antwerp, Belgium, ISBN 9-0760-1903-7

Koch, S., Verwendung der Data Envelopment Analysis im Kontext von ERP Implementierungsprojekten: Vergleich und Aufwandschätzung, in: Tagungsband (Proceedings) des DASMA Software Metrik Kongresses MetriKon 2005, Shaker Verlag, Aachen, 2005, pp. 19–32, ISBN 3-8322-4615-0

Landmesser, J. A., Enhanced Estimation, in: IFPUG, IT Measurement – Practical Advice from the Experts, Addison-Wesley Pearson Education Inc., Indianapolis, 2002, ISBN 9-780201-741582, p. 379

Lederer, A. L., Prasad, J., Information systems software cost estimating: A current assessment, in: Journal of Information Technology, 1993,(8): pp. 22–33

Löper, S., Zehle, M., ESMIT-Evaluation of Software Metrics in the Design Phase and their Implication on Case Tools, Master Thesis, Blenkinge Institute of Technology, Sweden, 2003

Lorenz, M., Object Oriented Software Development – Practical Guide, Prentice Hall, Englewood Cliffs, NJ, 1993

Low, G. C., Jefferey, J. R., Function Points in the Estimation and Evaluation of the Software Process, in: IEEE Transactions on Software Engineering, 1990, 16(1): pp. 64–71

Lubashevsky, A., An Early Estimation of Software Reliability Based on the Size Estimation and the Software Process Assessment of Large Telecom Systems, in: IFPUG, IT Measurement – Practical Advice from the Experts, Addison-Wesley Pearson Education Inc., Indianapolis, 2002, ISBN 9-780201-741582, pp. 171–182

Magiera, E., Comparison of Function Point Analysis and COSMIC-FFP for Web-Applications, in: Proceedings of the Software Measurement European Forum 2004 (SMEF2004), Rome, Istituto di Ricerca Internationale S.r.l., Milano, 28.–30.1.2004, S. 369–376, ISBN 8-8866-7433-3

Mah, M., IT Organization, Benchmark Thyself, in: IFPUG, IT Measurement – Practical Advice from the Experts, Addison-Wesley Pearson Education Inc., Indianapolis, 2002, ISBN 9-780201-741582, pp. 31–51

Marthaler, V., Keim, S., Establishing Central Support for Software Sizing Activities in a Large Organization, in: IFPUG, IT Measurement – Practical Advice from the Experts, Addison-Wesley Pearson Education Inc., Indianapolis, 2002, ISBN 9-780201-741582, pp. 183–196

Maxwell, K. D., Software Development Productivity, in: Advances in Computers, Vol. 58, Elsevier Science, ISBN 0-1201-2158-1

Maxwell, K. D., Applied Statistics for Software Managers, Prentice Hall, Upper Saddle River, NJ, 2002

McCabe, T. J., A Complexity Measure, IEEE Transactions on Software Engineering Vol. SE-1, No. 3 (1976), S. 312–327 ff.

McConnell, S., After the Gold Rush, 2004 Software and Systems Technology Conference, Salt Lake City, UT, 19.-22. April 2004

McKinlay, M., The Top Ten (Or So) Reasons For Not Implementing EVM, IPMA/ICEC European Conference April 2006, Ljubljana, Slovenia

Melton, A., (Editor), Software Measurement, Thomson Computer Press, Boston, MA, 1996, ISBN 1-8503-2178-7

Meli, R., Early and Quick Function Point Analysis from Summary User Requirements to Project Management, in: IFPUG, IT Measurement – Practical Advice from the Experts, Addison-Wesley Pearson Education Inc., Indianapolis, 2002, ISBN 9-780201-741582, pp. 417–441

Meli, R., Santillo, L., Function Point Estimation Methods: A Comparative Overview, in: Proceedings of the FESMA Conference 1999, Amsterdam, ISBN 90-76019-07-X, pp. 271–286

Morris, P., Function Points as Part of a Measurement Program, in: IFPUG, IT Measurement – Practical Advice from the Experts, Addison-Wesley Pearson Education Inc., Indianapolis, 2002, ISBN 9-780201-741582, pp. 197–220

Moses, J., Farrow, M., A Consideration of the Variation in Development Effort Consistency Due to Function Points, in: Proceedings of the Software Measurement European Forum 2004 (SMEF2004), Rome, Istituto di Ricerca Internationale S.r.l., Milano, 28.–30.1.2004, S. 247–256, ISBN 8-8866-7433-3

Muller, M., Abran, A., (Editors), Metrics in Software Evolution, R. Oldenbourg, München, 1995, ISBN 3-4862-3589-3

Myerson, B., Email posting on now-defunct CRI List-serv about Unified Modeling Language and IFPUG Function Point, June 16, 1999. Quantimetrics, South Africa.

Nagano, S., Ajisaka, T., Improvement of analysis model by removing improper parts based on functional size measurement, in: Proceedings of the 15th

International Workshop on Software Measurement, Innovations in Software Measurement, September 12-14, 2005, Montréal, Canada, pp.241–254, Shaker Verlag, Aachen, 2005, ISBN 3-8322-4405-0

Natale, D., et al., GUFPI-ISMA, Proposals for Project Collection and Classification from the Analysis of the ISBSG Benchmark 8, in: Proceedings of the 14th International Workshop IWSM 2004/Metrikon, Shaker, Aachen, 2004, pp. 547–573 ISBN 3-3822-3383-0

NASA: NASA Cost Estimating Handbook, April 2002, http://eclipse99. ksc.nasa.gov/shuttle/nexgen/Nexgen_Downloads/NASA_CEH_Final_Product ion_Copy_April_2002.pdf, 183 pages.

Nelson, M. M., Clark, J., Spurlock, M. A., Curing the Software Requirements and Cost Estimating Blues: The Answer is Easier than you Think, PM, November–December 1999, pp. 54–60.

NESMA, Function Point Analysis for Software Enhancement, Guidelines Version 1.0, 2002, http://www.nesma.org

Nevalainen, R., Peeters, B., Poels, G. van Huysduynen, M.H., Proceedings of the 1999 FESMA Conference, Amsterdam, 4.–8.10.1999

Nishiyama, S., On More Effective Uses of Function Point Analysis, in: Proceedings of the FESMA Conference 1998, Antwerp, Belgium, pp. 525–532

Noth, T., Kretzschmar, M., Aufwandschätzung von DV-Projekten, Springer, Berlin Heidelberg New York,1984, ISBN 3-5401-2904-9

Pace, D., Calavaro, G., Cantone, G., Function Point and UML: State of the Art and Evaluation Model, in: Proceedings of the Software Measurement European Forum 2004 (SMEF2004), Rome, Istituto di Ricerca Internationale S.r.l., Milano, 28.–30.1.2004, S. 138–149, ISBN 8-8866-7433-3

Pastor, O., Abrahao, S. M., Molina, J. C., Torres, I., A FPA-like Measure for Object-Oriented Systems from Conceptual Models, in: Reiner *Dumke and Alain Abran* (Eds.): Current Trends in Software Measurement, Proceedings of the IWSM 2001, Shaker Verlag, Aachen, 2001

PMI – Project Management Institute, A Guide to the Project Management Body of Knowledge, 3rd Edition. (PMBOK Guides), PMI, Newton Square, PA, USA, 2004

Punter, T., Software Messen und Bewerten mit GQM Light, in: Software-Messung in der Praxis, Tagungsband (Proceedings) des DASMA Software Metrik Kongresses MetriKon 2003, 10.–11. November 2003, Neu-Ulm. Shaker Verlag, Aachen, 2003, S. 35–44, ISBN 3-8322-2146-8

Putnam, L. H., Myers, W., Measures for Excellence – Reliable Software On Time, Within Budget, Yourdon Press – Prentice Hall, Englewood Cliffs, NJ, 1992, ISBN 0-1356-7694-0

Putnam, L. H., Myers, W., The Core of Software Planning, in: IFPUG, IT Measurement – Practical Advice from the Experts, Addison-Wesley Pearson Education Inc., Indianapolis, 2002, ISBN 9-780201-741582, pp. 53–65

Reifer, D .J. Web Development: Estimating Quick-to-Market Software, in: IEEE Software, November/December 2000, pp. 54–67

Rösler, P., Warum prüfen oft 50 mal länger dauert als Lesen und andere Überraschungen aus der Welt der Software-Reviews, in: Tagungsband (Proceedings) des DASMA Software Metrik Kongresses MetriKon 2005, Shaker Verlag, Aachen, 2005, pp. 251–261, ISBN 3-8322-4615-0

Rosner, P., Hall, T., Mayer, T., Measuring object-orientedness: The invocation profile, in Dumke, R., Abran, A. (Eds.): New Approaches in Software Measurement, Proceedings of the 10th International Workshop IWSM 2000, pp. 18–28, Springer, Berlin Heidelberg New York, ISBN 3-5404-1727-3

Rubin, H., Software Benchmark Studies For 1995, Howard Rubin Associates, Pound Ridge, NY, 1995

Rubin, H., Work Output Measurement: IT Work Units, in: IFPUG, IT Measurement – Practical Advice from the Experts, Addison-Wesley Pearson Education Inc., Indianapolis, 2002, ISBN 9-780201-741582, pp. 67–82

Ruede, P., Theorie und Praxis der Function-Point-Methode, BIFOA Fachseminar "Schätzung der Software-Kosten und Verbesserung der Produktivität der Softwareentwicklung", BIFOA, Köln 1985

Ruhe, M., The Accuracy and Early Effort Estimation of Web Applications, Diplomarbeit (Thesis), Universität Kaiserslautern, Fachbereich Informatik, August 2002

Rule, G., "Small project', 'medium-size project' and 'large project': what do these terms mean? PowerPoint presentation. Software Measurement Services Ltd. (SMS), copyright 2004-2005, 124 High Street, Edenbridge, Kent, United Kingdom, TN8 5AY.

Russac, J., Cheaper, Better, Faster: A Measurement Program That Works, in: IFPUG, IT Measurement – Practical Advice from the Experts, Addison-Wesley Pearson Education Inc., Indianapolis, 2002, ISBN 9-780201-741582, pp. 147–158

Salvador, R. J., Litigation, The Product of Not Practicing Function Point Metrics, in: IFPUG, IT Measurement – Practical Advice from the Experts, Addison-Wesley Pearson Education Inc., Indianapolis, 2002, ISBN 9-780201-741582, pp. 537–551

Santillo, L., ESE: Enhanced Software Estimation, in: IFPUG, IT Measurement – Practical Advice from the Experts, Addison-Wesley Pearson Education Inc., Indianapolis, 2002, ISBN 9-780201-741582, pp. 391–406

Santillo, L., Functional details visualization and classification in the COSMIC FSM framework, in: Proceedings of the 15th International Workshop on Software Measurement, Innovations in Software Measurement, September 12-14, 2005, Montréal, Canada, pp. 255–266, Shaker Verlag, Aachen, 2005, ISBN 3-8322-4405-0

Santillo, L., Size & Estimation of Data Warehouse Systems, in: Proceedings of the FESMA Conference 2001, Heidelberg, pp. 315–326

Schmietendorf, A., Dumke, R., Kostenverteilung im IT-Life Cycle, in: Software-Messung in der Praxis, Tagungsband (Proceedings) des DASMA

Software Metrik Kongresses MetriKon 2003, 10.–11. November 2003, Neu-Ulm. Shaker Verlag, Aachen, 2003, S. 121–134, ISBN 3-8322-2146-8

Schneider, G., Winters, J., Applying Use Cases – A Practical Guide, Addison-Wesley Longman, Inc. 1998

Sengupta, K., The Experience Trap, Harvard Business Review, February 2008, hbr.org, pp. 94–101

Shackelton, S. K., Keeping a Well-Balanced Scorecard, in: IFPUG, IT Measurement – Practical Advice from the Experts, Addison-Wesley Pearson Education Inc., Indianapolis, 2002, ISBN 9-780201-741582, pp. 503–516

Shepperd, M., Mair, C., Forselius, P., An Empirical Analysis of Software Productivity, in: Proceedings of the Software Measurement European Forum (SMEF) 2006, Rome, Italy

Simon, D., Simon, F., Das wundersame Verhalten von Entwicklern beim Einsatz von Quellcode-Metriken, in: Tagungsband (Proceedings) in DASMA Software Metrik Kongress: MetriKon 2005, Shaker Verlag, Aachen, 2005, pp. 263 –272, ISBN 3-8322-4615-0

Sirma, E., Ist-Analyse des Benchmarking im IT-Ressort eines Versicherungsunternehmens, Diplomarbeit (Thesis), Fachhochschule Köln, Fachbereich Informatik, Campus Gummersbach, Juli 2003, DASMA student thesis award November 2003, http://www.dasma.org

Sneed, H. M., Aufwandschätzung für Web-basierte Informationssysteme und die Struktur der Softwareindustrie, in: Wirtschaftsinformatik, Nr. 3, 2002, S. 202–205

Sneed, H. M., Schätzung der Entwicklungskosten von objektorientierter Software, in: Informatik Spektrum 19, S. 133–140, Springer, 1996

Sneed, H. M., Software-Qualitätssicherung für kommerzielle Anwendungssysteme, R. Müller, 1983

Software Engineering Institute (SEI), The Capability Maturity Model Integration (CMMI®) for development version 1.2, Carnegie Mellon University, Pittsburgh, PA, www.sei.cmu.edu/cmmi, August 2006

Software Productivity Consortium, The Software Measurement Guidebook, Thomson Computer Press, Boston, MA, 1996, ISBN 1-8503-2195-7

Standish Group, The CHAOS Report, 25.3.2003,http://www.standishgroup .com

Stutzke, R., Estimating Software-Intensive Systems: Project, Products, and Processes, Addison-Wesley, copyright 2005 by Pearson Education, Inc. Upper Saddle River, NJ, ISBN 0-201-70312-2

Symons, C. R., Software Sizing and Estimating, Mark II Function Point Analysis, Wiley, Chichester, 1991, ISBN 0-4719-2985-9

Thaller, G. E., Software Metriken, Heinz Heise, Hannover, 1994, ISBN 3-8822-9038-2

Theden, P., Kennzahlen für Qualitätstechniken, 11.6.2003, http://www.symposion.de/qw/qw_09.htm

Tran-Cao, D. Lèvesque, G., Meinier, J.G., A Field Study of Software Functional Complexity Measurement, in: Proceedings of the 14th International Workshop IWSM/MetriKon 2004, Shaker, Aachen, 2004, pp. 175–193, ISBN 3-3822-3383-0

Uemura, T., Kusumoto, S., Inoue, K., Function Point Measurement Tool for UML Design Specification, in: Proceedings of the METRICS '99, Florida, USA, 1999, pp. 62–69

UKSMA, Measuring Software Maintenance and Support, Version 0.5, Draft, July 1st, 2001, http://www.uksma.co.uk

UKSMA, MK II Function Point Analysis Counting Practices Manual, Version 1.3.1, http://www.uksma.co.uk, 1998

UKSMA and ISBSG, Quality Standards: Defect Measurement Manual, V1.a, http://www.uksma.co.uk/public/defstan1a.pdf, October 2000

UQAM, Full Function Points Measurement Manual, Version 2.0, http://saturne.info.uqam.ca/recherche/index.html, 1999

van Solingen, R., Berghout, E., The Goal Question Metric Method, McGraw Hill, New York, 2000

Vergilio, S. R., Chaves, L. B., Object Oriented Software Metrics and the Testing Activity: Some Empirical Results, in: Proceedings of the FESMA Conference 2000, Madrid

Vogelezang, F., Dekkers, T., One year experience with COSMIC-FFP, in: Proceedings of the Software Measurement European Forum 2004 (SMEF2004), Rome, Istituto di Ricerca Internationale S.r.l., Milano, 28.–30.1.2004, S. 346–355, ISBN 8-8866-7433-3

Vogelezang, F., Lesterhuis, A., Applicability of COSMIC-FFP in administrative environment Experiences of an early adopter, Sogeti Netherlands B.V., 2003

Vollmann, S., Aufwandschätzung im Software Engineering, IWT, Vaterstetten bei München, 1990, ISBN 3-8832-2277-1

Weinberg, Dr. G., Quality Software Management, Dorset House, New York, NY, 1992, ISBN 0-9326-3322-6

Weller, E. F., Applying Statistical Process Control to Software, in: IFPUG, IT Measurement – Practical Advice from the Experts, Addison-Wesley Pearson Education Inc., Indianapolis, 2002, ISBN 9-780201-741582, pp. 629–651

Whitmire, S. A., Applying Function Points to Object-Oriented Software Models, in: Keynes, J., (Ed.): Software Engineering Productivity Handbook, McGraw-Hill, New York, 1992, pp. 229–244

Wittmann, W., Unternehmung und unvollkommene Information, Köln, Opladen, 1959

Wolle, B., Analyse von ABAP- und JAVA-Anwendungen im Hinblick auf die Software-Wartung, in: Software-Messung in der Praxis, Tagungsband (Proceedings) des DASMA Software Metrik Kongresses MetriKon 2003, 10.–11. November 2003, Neu-Ulm. Shaker Verlag, Aachen, 2003, S. 45–54, ISBN 3-8322-2146-8

Wolverton, R. W., The Cost of Developing Large-Scale Software, IEEE Transactions on Computers Vol. C-23, No. 6, June 1974, pp. 615–636

Woodward, S. M., Using Project Metrics to More Efficiently Manage Projects, in: IFPUG, IT Measurement – Practical Advice from the Experts, Addison-Wesley Pearson Education Inc., Indianapolis, 2002, ISBN 9-780201-741582, pp. 271–292

Xenos, M., Stavrinoudis, D., Zikouli, K., Christodoulakis, D., Object-Oriented Metrics – A Survey, in: Proceedings of the FESMA Conference 2000, Madrid, Spain.

Zuse, H., Software Complexity – Measures and Methods, DeGruyter, Berlin, New York, 1991

Zuse, H., A Framework for Software Measurement, DeGruyter, Berlin, New York, 1997, ISBN 3-1101-5587-7

Zuse, H., Resolving the Mysteries of the Halstead Measures, in: MetriKon 2005 Praxis der Softwaremessung, pp.107 – 122, Shaker Verlag, Aachen 2005, ISBN 3-8322-4615-0

Index